The Official CompTIA® Network+® Student Guide (Exam N10-007): 2019 Update

The Official CompTIA® Network+® Student Guide (Exam N10-007): 2019 Update

COURSE EDITION: 1.0

Acknowledgements

James Pengelly, Author

Pamela J. Taylor, Content Developer

Peter Bauer, Content Editor

Michelle Farney, Content Editor

Thomas Reilly, Vice President Learning

Katie Hoenicke, Director of Product Management

Evan Burns, Senior Manager, Learning Technology Operations and Implementation

James Chesterfield, Manager, Learning Content and Design

Becky Mann, Senior Manager, Product Development

Katherine Keyes, Content Specialist

Notices

Table of Contents

About This Course

CompTIA is a not-for-profit trade association with the purpose of advancing the interests of IT professionals and IT channel organizations and its industry-leading IT certifications are an important part of that mission. CompTIA's Network+ certification is a foundation-level certification designed for IT professionals with around one year of experience, whose job role is focused on network administration.

The CompTIA Network+ exam will certify the successful candidate has the knowledge and skills required to troubleshoot, configure, and manage common network devices; establish basic network connectivity; understand and maintain network documentation; identify network limitations and weaknesses; and implement network security, standards, and protocols. The candidate will have a basic understanding of enterprise technologies, including cloud and virtualization technologies.

The Official CompTIA® Network+® (Exam N10-007): 2019 Update will teach you the fundamental principles of installing, configuring, and troubleshooting network technologies and help you to progress a career in network administration. In this course, you will build on your existing user-level knowledge and experience with personal computer operating systems and networks to master the fundamental skills and concepts that you will need to use on the job in any type of networking career.

This course can benefit you in two ways. If you intend to pass the CompTIA Network+ (Exam N10-007) certification examination, this course can be a significant part of your preparation. But certification is not the only key to professional success in the field of computer security. Today's job market demands individuals with demonstrable skills, and the information and activities in this course can help you build your computer security skill set so that you can confidently perform your duties in any network-related role.

Course Description

Target Student

This course is intended for entry-level computer support professionals with a basic knowledge of computer hardware, software, and operating systems who wish to increase their knowledge and understanding of networking concepts and acquire the required skills to prepare for a career in network support or administration, or who wish to prepare for the CompTIA Network+ certification. CompTIA Network+ is the first certification IT professionals specializing in network administration and support should earn. Network+ is aimed at IT professionals with job roles such as network administrator, network technician, network installer, help desk technician, and IT cable installer.

This course is also designed for students who are seeking the CompTIA Network+ certification and who want to prepare for the CompTIA Network+ N10-007 Certification Exam.

Prerequisites

A typical student taking the CompTIA Network+ course should have a minimum of nine months of professional computer support experience as a PC or help desk technician. To ensure your success in this course, you should possess basic Windows® and Linux® user skills and a fundamental understanding of computer and networking concepts. You can obtain this level of skills and knowledge by taking the following official CompTIA courses:

- *The Official CompTIA® A+® Core 1 (Exam 220-1001)*
- *The Official CompTIA® A+® Core 2 (Exam 220-1002)*

Note: The prerequisites for this course might differ significantly from the prerequisites for the CompTIA certification exams. For the most up-to-date information about the exam prerequisites, complete the form on this page: *certification.comptia.org/training/exam-objectives*.

Course Objectives

In this course, you will describe the major networking technologies and systems of modern networks and configure, manage, and troubleshoot modern networks.

You will:

- Explain the OSI and TCP/IP Models.
- Explain properties of network traffic.
- Install and configure switched networks.
- Configure IP networks.
- Install and configure routed networks.
- Configure and monitor ports and protocols.
- Explain network application and storage issues.
- Monitor and troubleshoot networks.
- Explain network attacks and mitigations.
- Install and configure security devices.
- Explain authentication and access controls.
- Deploy and troubleshoot cabling solutions.
- Implement and troubleshoot wireless technologies.
- Compare and contrast WAN technologies.
- Use remote access methods.
- Identify site policies and best practices.

How to Use This Book

As You Learn

To obtain CompTIA certification, you must master the content found in the CompTIA exam objectives document. This exam blueprint is divided into numbered domains and objectives. Each objective contains unnumbered content examples. While this course provides complete coverage of those domains, objectives, and content examples, it does not do so in the same order as the exam blueprint. This course is divided into lessons, and each lesson contains several topics, covering a subject or a set of related subjects. Lessons are arranged in a logical sequence to cover topics that are fundamental first and help you to develop your mastery of the exam content progressively. The results-oriented topics provide the information you need to accomplish the objectives. Each topic has various types of activities designed to enable you to solidify your understanding of the informational material presented in the course. Information is provided for reference and reflection to facilitate understanding and practice.

At the back of the book, you will find a glossary of the definitions of the terms and concepts used throughout the course. You will also find an index to assist in locating information within the instructional components of the book. As the course does not follow the CompTIA exam domain and objectives order, there is a mapping table that shows the lesson and topic where each objective and content example is discussed. In many electronic versions of the book, you can select links on key words in the content to move to the associated glossary definition, and on page references in the index to move to that term in the content. To return to the previous location in the document after selecting a link, use the appropriate functionality in your PDF viewing software.

As You Review

Any method of instruction is only as effective as the time and effort you, the student, are willing to invest in it. In addition, some of the information that you learn in class may not be important to you immediately, but it may become important later. For this reason, we encourage you to spend some time reviewing the content of the course after your time in the classroom.

As a Reference

The organization and layout of this book make it an easy-to-use resource for future reference. Taking advantage of the glossary, index, and table of contents, you can use this book as a first source of definitions, background information, and summaries.

Course Icons

Watch throughout the material for the following visual cues.

Student Icon	Student Icon Descriptive Text
	A **Note** provides additional information, guidance, or hints about a topic or task.
	A **Caution** note makes you aware of places where you need to be particularly careful with your actions, settings, or decisions, so that you can be sure to get the desired results of an activity or task.
	Video notes show you where an associated video is particularly relevant to the content. These videos can be accessed through the course website.
	Additional **Practice Questions** are available in the Assessment section on the course website.

Using the Activities

To complete most of the hands-on activities in this course, you will configure one or more virtual machines (VMs) running on your Hyper-V-enabled HOST computer. The following conventions are used in the steps in each hands-on activity:

- Numbered lists—tasks or challenges for you to complete as you progress through an activity.
- Alphabetized lists—detailed steps for you to follow in the course of completing each task.
- Using the mouse—when instructed to click or select, use the main mouse button; when instructed to right-click, use the secondary button (that is, the button on the right-hand side of the mouse, assuming right-handed use).
- File and command selection—files, applets, dialog tabs, and buttons or menus that you need to select as part of a step are shown in bold. For example: Select **OK**, Select **Control Panel**, and so on.
- Sequences of commands—a sequence of steps to follow to open a file or activate a command are shown in bold with arrows. For example, if you need to access the system properties in Windows, this would be shown in the text by: **Start→Control Panel→System**.
- Using the key combos—key combinations where you must press multiple keys simultaneously are shown in bold with a plus sign. For example: Press **Ctrl+C** to copy the file. Sometimes you need to use both the keyboard and the mouse. For example: **Ctrl+click** means hold down the **Ctrl** key and click the main mouse button.
- Commands and typing—Any information that you must enter using the keyboard—other than command-line commands—is shown in bold italic. For example: Type ***webadmin@somewhere.com***. Italic text can also represent some sort of variable, such as your student number, as in Your computer has been configured with the IP address 192.168.10.*x*. Command-line commands are shown in Cutive Mono. For example: Enter `ping 10.0.0.5`, or even `ping 10.0.0.x`.

Lesson 1
Explaining the OSI and TCP/IP Models

LESSON INTRODUCTION

The CompTIA® Network+® certification covers a wide range of knowledge and skills that apply to different networking job roles. A networking job role requires a fundamental knowledge of network terminology, components, standards, types, and configurations. In this lesson, you will identify the basic concepts of networking theory.

With a background in CompTIA Network+ information and skills, your networking career can move in many directions. Whether you are a network support technician, installer, or administrator, knowledge of basic networking theory provides the necessary foundation needed for learning more advanced networking concepts. A good grasp of fundamental networking theory will help you succeed in any network-related job role.

LESSON OBJECTIVES

In this lesson, you will:

- Describe the functions of the layers of the OSI model.
- Describe the functions of the layers of the TCP/IP model.

Topic A
Explain OSI Model Layers

EXAM OBJECTIVES COVERED
1.2 Explain devices, applications, protocols, and services at their appropriate OSI layers.
1.3 Explain the concepts and characteristics of routing and switching.

Network implementations are built on common network standards and models of networking that describe how devices and protocols interconnect. In this topic, you will identify how the implementation and support of these systems refer to an important common reference model: the Open Systems Interconnection (OSI) model. The OSI model breaks the data communication process into discrete layers. Being able to identify the OSI layers and the functions of devices and protocols working at each layer will enable you to implement and troubleshoot networks.

NETWORK BOUNDARIES

A **network** is two or more computer systems linked together by some form of transmission medium that enables them to share information. It does not matter whether the network contains two or thousands of machines; the concept is essentially the same. You can think of any network in terms of **nodes** and **links**. The nodes are devices that communicate on the network and the links are the communications pathways between them.

A network will provide services to its users. Historically, these services have included access to shared files, folders, and printers, plus email and database applications. Modern networks provide more diverse services, including web applications, Voice over IP (VoIP), and multimedia conferencing.

Networks of different sizes are classified in different ways. A network in a single location is often described as a **local area network (LAN)**. This definition encompasses many different sizes of networks with widely varying functions and capabilities. It can include both residential networks with a couple of computers, and enterprise networks with hundreds of servers and thousands of workstations. Networks in different geographic locations but with shared links are called **wide area networks (WANs)**.

OPEN SYSTEMS INTERCONNECTION (OSI) MODEL

The **International Organization for Standardization (ISO)** developed the **Open Systems Interconnection (OSI) reference model** in 1977. It was designed to aid understanding of how a network system works in terms of both the hardware and software components by separating the function of such components to discrete layers. The model was published in 1983 as ISO 7498, but the most current version of the document is located at *iso.org/standard/20269.html*.

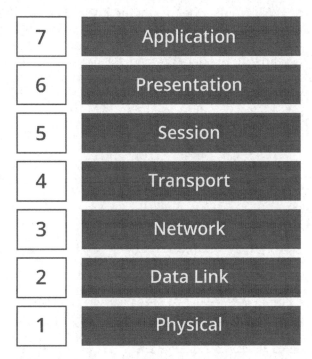

7	Application
6	Presentation
5	Session
4	Transport
3	Network
2	Data Link
1	Physical

The OSI model.

Note: *To remember the seven layers, use the following mnemonic: All People Seem To Need Data Processing.*

As the complexity of computer hardware and software increases, the problem of successfully communicating between these systems becomes more difficult. Dividing these difficult problems into "sub-tasks" allows them to be readily understood and solved more easily. Using this layered approach means that a vendor can work on the design and debugging for one layer without affecting any of the others.

Each layer performs a different group of tasks required for network communication. Although not all network systems implement layers using this structure, they all implement each task in some way. The OSI model is not a standard or a specification; it serves as a functional guideline for designing network protocols, software, and appliances and for **troubleshooting** networks.

PROTOCOL DATA UNITS (PDUs)

A **protocol** is a set of rules enabling systems to communicate by exchanging data in a structured format. Two of the most important functions of a protocol are to provide **addressing** (describing where data should go) and **encapsulation** (describing how data should be packaged for transmission). The basic process of encapsulation is for the protocol to add fields in a **header** to whatever data (**payload**) it receives from an application or other protocol. A network will involve the use of many different protocols. For example, the concept of local addressing and **network addressing** for switching and routing within and between networks is usually performed by different protocols.

At each layer, for two nodes to communicate they must be running the same protocol. The protocol running at each layer communicates with its equivalent (or **peer**) layer on the other node. This communication between nodes at the same layer is described as a **same layer interaction**. To transmit or receive a communication, on each node, each layer provides services for the layer above and uses the services of the layer below. This is referred to as **adjacent layer interaction**.

When a message is sent from one node to another, it travels down the stack of layers on the sending node, reaches the receiving node using the transmission media, and then passes up the stack on that node. At each level (except the Physical layer), the sending node adds a header to the data payload, forming a "chunk" of data called a **protocol data unit (PDU)**. This process is known as **encapsulation**.

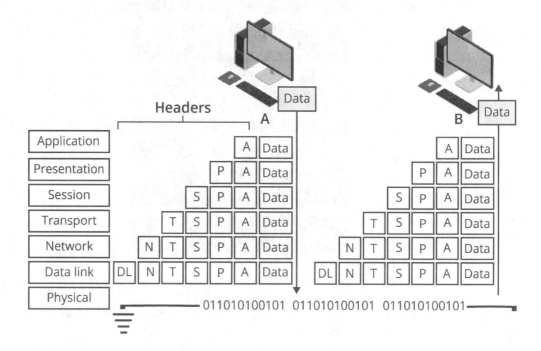

Encapsulation and de-encapsulation. (Image © 123RF.com.)

For example, on a typical local network, on the sending node, data is generated by an application such as HTTP, which will include its own application header. At the Transport layer, a TCP header is added to this application data. At the Network layer, the TCP segment is wrapped in an IP header. The IP packet is put into an Ethernet frame at the Data Link layer, then the stream of bits making up the frame is transmitted over the network at the Physical layer.

The receiving node performs the reverse process (**de-encapsulation** or **decapsulation**). For example, it receives the stream of bits arriving at the Physical layer and decodes an **Ethernet** frame. It extracts the IP packet from this frame and resolves the information in the IP header, then does the same for the TCP and application headers, eventually extracting the application data for processing by a software program.

 Note: *You might notice that this example seems to omit some layers. This is because "real world" protocols do not conform exactly to the OSI model.*

LAYER 1 (PHYSICAL)

A **node** is any device that can communicate on the network via one or more network **interfaces**. This term can be used to describe endpoint devices, such as computers, laptops, servers, IP phones, **smartphones**, or printers, and connecting or forwarding devices, such as switches and routers. A node on a wireless network is often called a **station**. The term **host** is often used in TCP/IP networking to mean an end system device, such as a computer.

A **link** between network nodes is created using some form of **transmission** or **physical media**. Typically, this takes the form of a cable, but **wireless** media that uses technologies such as radio transmissions can provide the same function. The **Physical layer** (PHY) of the OSI model (layer 1) is responsible for the transmission and receipt of bits from one node to another node. At the Physical layer, a **segment** is one where all the nodes share access to the same media. A network is typically divided into segments to cope with the physical restrictions of the network media used, to improve performance, or to improve security.

The Physical layer specifies the following:

- Physical topology—The layout of nodes and links as established by the transmission media.
- Physical interface—Mechanical specifications for the network medium, such as cable specifications, the medium connector and pin-out details (the number and functions of the various pins in a network connector), or radio transceiver specifications.
- The process of transmitting and receiving signals over the network medium, including modulation schemes and timing/synchronization.

Devices that operate at the Physical layer include:

- **Transceivers**—The part of a network interface that sends and receives signals over the network media.
- **Repeaters**—A device that amplifies an electronic signal to extend the maximum allowable distance for a media type.
- **Hubs**—A multiport repeater, deployed as the central point of connection for nodes.
- **Media converters**—A device that converts one media signaling type to another.
- **Modems**—A device that converts between digital and analog signal transmissions.

LAYER 2 (DATA LINK)

Relatively few networks are based on directly connecting hosts together. Rather than making hosts establish direct links with one another, each host is connected to a central node, such as a hub, a switch, or a wireless access point. The central node provides a forwarding function, receiving the communication from one node and sending it to another. The addresses of interfaces within the same network are described as **local addresses** or **hardware addresses**.

The **Data Link layer** (layer 2) is responsible for transferring data between nodes on the same logical segment. At the Data Link layer, a **segment** is one where all nodes can send traffic to one another using hardware addresses, regardless of whether they share access to the same media. A layer 2 segment might include multiple physical segments. This is referred to as a **logical topology**.

The Data Link layer organizes the stream of 1s and 0s (bits) arriving from the Physical layer into structured units called **frames**. Each frame contains a network layer packet as its **payload**. The Data Link layer adds control information to the payload in the form of **header** fields. These fields include a source and destination hardware address.

Construction of a frame (simplified).

The last part of the frame usually contains some sort of error checking. Protocols at most layers perform a consistency check to verify that data has been transferred correctly. The Data Link layer is capable of only very basic error checking, such as identifying truncated or corrupt frames. There is no function to acknowledge or retransmit damaged frames. That function is handled at higher layers of the OSI model.

Another important function at the Data Link layer is determining how multiple nodes can share access to the network media. For example, a bus-based topology uses **contention** as a media access method. A **ring-based topology** uses a token-passing access method.

LAYER 2 DEVICES

Connectivity devices found at the Data Link layer include:

- **Network adapters** or **network interface cards (NICs)**—A NIC joins a host to network media (cabling or wireless) and enables it to communicate over the network by assembling and disassembling frames.
- **Bridges**—A bridge joins two network segments while minimizing the performance reduction of having more nodes on the same network. A bridge has multiple ports, each of which functions as a network interface.
- **Switches**—An advanced type of bridge with many ports. A switch creates links between large numbers of nodes more efficiently.
- **Wireless access points (APs)**—An AP allows nodes with wireless network cards to communicate and creates a bridge between wireless networks and wired ones.

The following figure illustrates how layer 1 and layer 2 devices establish different types of network segmentation. The hosts attached to the hubs are in the same physical segment and share access to the network media. Hubs just repeat signals with no sort of layer 2 processing involved. The bridge creates a link between the two physical segments so that hosts in segment A can send and receive messages to hosts in segment B. The bridge does perform layer 2 processing and forwards only appropriate traffic, based on the hardware addresses of nodes in segments A and B.

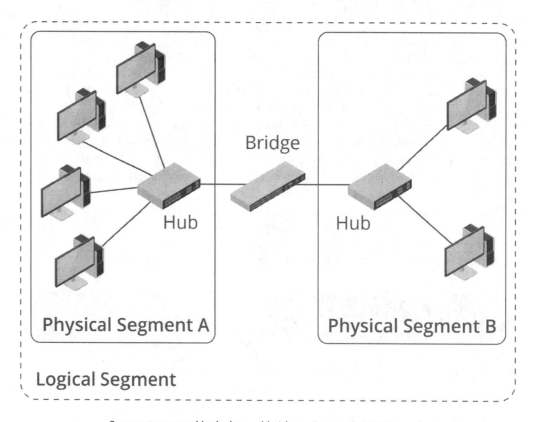

Segments created by hubs and bridges. (Image © 123RF.com.)

IEEE 802 STANDARDS

Over the years, many protocols, standards, and products have been developed to cover technologies working at the Physical and Data Link layers of the OSI model. The most important of these are the IEEE **802 standards**, published by the **LAN/MAN Standards Committee** (*ieee802.org*) of the **Institute of Electrical and Electronics Engineers (IEEE)**. The IEEE is a professional body that oversees the development and registration of electronic standards.

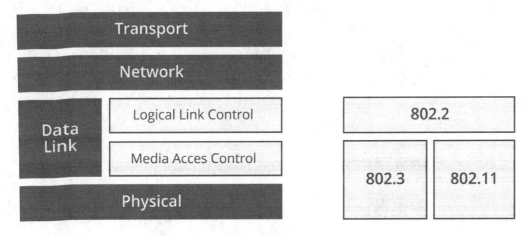

Comparison of IEEE 802 and the OSI model.

The IEEE splits the functions of the Data Link layer into two sublayers: **Media Access Control (MAC)** and **Logical Link Control (LLC)**.

IEEE 802.3 (ETHERNET) AND THE MAC SUBLAYER

The **Media Access Control (MAC) sublayer** defines how multiple network interfaces share a single transmission medium. It covers the following:

- Logical topology—bus or ring.
- Media access method—contention or token passing.
- Addressing—the format for the hardware address of each network interface.
- Frame format.
- Error checking mechanism.

The **IEEE 802.3** standard specifies protocols that implement the functions of the MAC sublayer, plus signaling and media specifications at the Physical layer. IEEE 802.3 is based on the Ethernet networking product, developed by the DIX consortium, consisting of Digital Equipment Corporation (DEC), Intel®, and Xerox®. While the product name is not used in 802.3 standards documentation, it is otherwise universally referred to as **Ethernet**.

Ethernet is now the only widely supported standard for cabled LANs. The IEEE 802.11 series of standards (Wi-Fi) are used to implement wireless local area networks (WLANs).

IEEE 802.2 (LOGICAL LINK CONTROL)

The **IEEE 802.2** standard for the **Logical Link Control (LLC) sublayer** is used with other 802 protocols, such as 802.3 (Ethernet) and 802.11 (**Wi-Fi**). The LLC protocol provides a standard Network-layer service interface, regardless of which MAC sublayer protocol is used.

LAYER 3 (NETWORK)

The **Network layer** (layer 3) is responsible for moving data around a network of networks, known as an internetwork or the Internet. While the Data Link layer is capable of forwarding data by using hardware addresses within a single segment, the Network layer moves information around an internetwork by using logical network and host IDs. The networks are often heterogeneous; that is, they use a variety of Physical layer media and Data Link protocols.

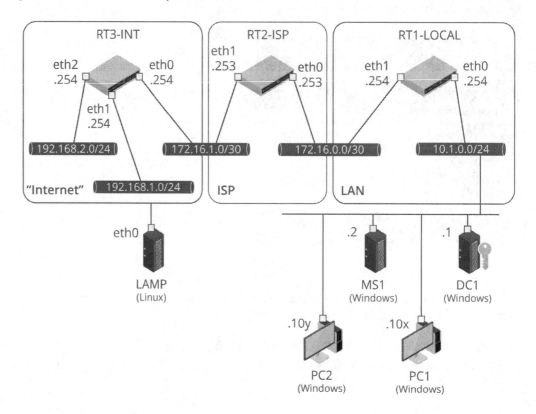

Routing occurs at the Network layer. (Image © 123RF.com.)

The Network layer transfers information between networks by examining the destination Network-layer address or logical network address, and routing the packet through the internetwork by using intermediate systems (**routers**). The packet moves, router by router (or hop by hop), through the internetwork to the target network. Once it has reached the destination network, the hardware address can be used to deliver the packet to the target node.

 Note: The general convention is to describe PDUs packaged at the Network layer as packets or datagrams, and messages packaged at the Data Link layer as frames. Packet is often used to describe PDUs at any layer, however.

The main appliance working at layer 3 is the router. Other devices include layer 3 switches, which combine the function of switches and routers, and basic firewalls.

SWITCHING VS. ROUTING COMPONENTS

The following figure illustrates how both switching and routing components might be used in a typical network. The whole network is connected to the wider Internet via a **WAN router/firewall**. This is a type of router that can communicate using the different layer 2 formats of the link to the Internet and the Ethernet frame format used on the LAN. It also has an important security function, using a firewall to prevent unwanted traffic entering or leaving the LAN. Another router is used to divide the network into three logical **subnetworks**. These subnets are mapped to layer 2 segments. Two segments are served by switches and one by a legacy hub device.

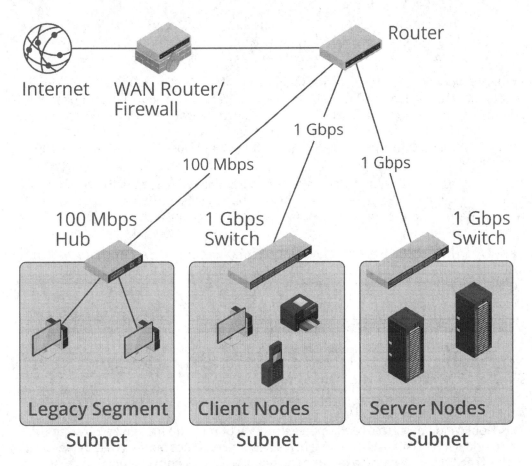

Positioning network components. (Image © 123RF.com.)

Nodes within each subnet can address one another directly, but they can only communicate with nodes in other subnets via the router. The nodes in the switched segments can use the full 1 Gbps link speed. The nodes in the legacy segment share access to the media bandwidth of 100 Mbps.

A **backbone** describes a fast link between other segments of a network. The backbone carries all the communications occurring between nodes in separate segments. High bandwidth **backbone segments** are used between the router and the switches.

LAYER 4 (TRANSPORT)

The first three layers of the OSI model are primarily concerned with moving frames and datagrams between nodes and networks. At the **Transport layer** (also known as the end-to-end or host-to-host layer), the *content* of the packets starts to become significant. Any given host on a network will be communicating with many other hosts using many different types of networking data. One of the critical functions of the Transport layer is to identify each type of network application by assigning it a **port number**. For example, data from the HTTP web browsing application can be identified as port 80, while data from an email server can be identified as port 25.

At the Transport layer, on the sending host, data from the upper layers is packaged as a series of layer 4 PDUs, referred to as **segments**. Each segment is tagged with the application's port number. The segment is then passed to the Network layer for delivery. The host could be transmitting multiple HTTP and email packets at the same time. These are **multiplexed** using the port numbers onto the same network link.

Note: In fact, each host assigns two port numbers. On the client, the destination port number is mapped to the service that the client is requesting (HTTP on port 80, for instance). The client also assigns a random source port number (47,747, for instance). The server uses this client-assigned port number (47,747) as the destination port number for its replies and its application port number (80 for HTTP) as its source port. This allows the hosts to track multiple "conversations" for the same application protocol.

At the Network and Data Link layers, the port number is not significant—it becomes part of the data payload and is invisible to the routers and switches that implement the addressing and forwarding functions of these layers. At the receiving host, each packet is extracted from its frame and then identified by its port number and passed up to the relevant handler at the upper Session and Application layers. Put another way, the traffic stream is de-multiplexed.

The Transport layer is also responsible for ensuring **reliable data delivery**, should the application require it. Reliable delivery means that any lost or damaged packets are resent. The Transport layer can overcome the lack of reliability in the lower level protocols.

Devices working at the Transport layer include multilayer switches—usually working as load balancers—and many types of security appliances, such as more advanced firewalls and intrusion detection systems (IDSs).

SESSION AND PRESENTATION LAYERS

The upper layers of the OSI model are less clearly associated with distinct real-world protocols. These layers collect various functions that provide useful interfaces between software applications and the Transport layer.

LAYER 5 (SESSION)

Most application protocols require the exchange of multiple messages between the **client** and server. This exchange of such a sequence of messages is called a **session** or **dialog**. The **Session layer** (Layer 5) represents the **dialog control** functions that administer the process of establishing the dialog, managing data transfer, and then ending (or tearing down) the session. Sessions can work in three modes:

- One-way/simplex—Only one system is allowed to send messages; the other only receives.
- Two-way alternate (TWA)/half-duplex—The hosts establish some system for taking turns to send messages, such as exchanging a token.
- Two-way simultaneous (TWS)/duplex—Either host can send messages at any time.

LAYER 6 (PRESENTATION)

The **Presentation layer** (Layer 6) transforms data between the format required for the network and the format required for the application. For example, the Presentation layer is used for character set conversion. The communicating computers may use different character coding systems, such as American Standard Code for Information Interchange (ASCII) and Unicode; the peer Presentation layers agree to translate the data into one of the formats, or they will both translate the data into a third format. The Presentation layer can also be conceived as supporting data compression and **encryption**. However, in practical terms, these functions are often implemented by encryption devices and protocols running at lower layers of the stack or simply within a homogenous Application layer.

LAYER 7 (APPLICATION)

The **Application layer** (Layer 7) is at the top of the OSI stack. An Application-layer protocol doesn't encapsulate any other protocols or provide services to any protocol.

Application-layer protocols provide an interface for software programs on network hosts that have established a communications channel through the lower-level protocols to exchange data. For example, one of the most-used services provided by the Application layer is file transfer. Different OSs and file systems may use entirely different file naming conventions and file formats, and the Application layer must overcome these differences. More widely, upper-layer protocols provide most of the services that make a network useful, rather than just functional, including network printing, email and communications, directory lookup, and database services.

 Note: *The OSI model has a stricter definition of the Session, Presentation, and Application layers than is typical of actual protocols used on networks. You won't need to identify specific differences between them on the Network+ certification exam.*

It is important to distinguish between network application **protocols** and the software application **code** (programs and shared programming libraries) that runs on computers. Software programs and operating systems make use of **application programming interfaces (APIs)** to call functions of the relevant part of the network stack. Examples of APIs include:

- Network card drivers could use the Network Driver Interface Specification (NDIS) API to implement functions at the Data Link layer.
- The Sockets/WinSock APIs implement Transport- and Session-layer functions.
- High-level APIs implement functions for Application-layer services such as file transfer, email, web browsing, or name resolution.

OSI MODEL SUMMARY

The following image summarizes the OSI model, listing the PDUs at each layer, along with the types of devices that work at each layer.

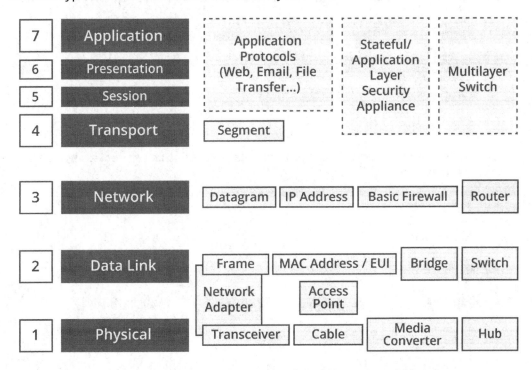

Devices and concepts represented at the relevant OSI model layer.

 Note: *To learn more, watch the related* **Video** *on the course website.*

Activity 1-1
Discussing OSI Model Layers

SCENARIO
Answer the following questions to test your understanding of the content covered in this topic.

1. **What OSI model layer transmits bits from one device to another and modulates the transmission stream over a medium?**

   ○ Physical

   ○ Transport

   ○ Data Link

   ○ Network

2. **At which OSI layer do programs on a network node access network services?**

   ○ Data Link

   ○ Physical

   ○ Application

   ○ Presentation

3. **Which OSI layer is responsible for establishing reliable connections between two devices?**

   ○ Transport

   ○ Presentation

   ○ Application

   ○ Data Link

4. **Which OSI layer packages bits of data from the Physical layer into frames?**

   ○ Presentation

   ○ Transport

   ○ Session

   ○ Data Link

5. **At which sublayer of the OSI model do network adapter cards operate?**

6. **What component is responsible for translating the computer's digital signals into electrical or optical signals that travel on network cable?**

7. **True or False? The Session layer is responsible for passing data to the Network layer at the lower bound and the Presentation layer at the upper bound.**

8. **Which OSI layer handles the concept of logical addressing?**

9. **At which OSI layer is the concept of a port number introduced?**

Topic B

Explain the TCP/IP Suite

EXAM OBJECTIVES COVERED
1.3 Explain the concepts and characteristics of routing and switching.

While the OSI model has its uses for network design and troubleshooting, in practical terms networking is dominated by the TCP/IP suite. In this topic, you will examine the main protocols that make up TCP/IP and view their placement in relation to the OSI model.

TCP/IP PROTOCOL SUITE

Network segments are built from the physical and logical topologies created by products working at the Physical and Data Link layers of the OSI model. On top of the Physical and Data Link infrastructure design are the internetworking and application protocols. **Protocols** are procedures or rules used by networked computers to communicate. For communication to take place, the two computers must have a protocol in common. Often, several protocols used for networking are designed to work together. This collection of protocols is known as a **protocol suite**.

Note: *Another commonly used term is **protocol stack**. This term describes a collection of protocols and the logical order in which they work together.*

Several protocol suites have been used for LAN and WAN communications over the years. However, the overwhelming majority of networks have now converged on the use of the **Transmission Control Protocol/Internet Protocol (TCP/IP)** suite. Most network implementations you will be required to undertake will depend on the use of TCP/IP.

The TCP/IP protocol suite maps to a four-layer conceptual model: Application, Transport, Internet, and Link (or Network Interface). This model is referred to as the **Internet Protocol Suite**, the **Department of Defense (DoD) model**, or the **ARPA model** (*tools.ietf.org/html/rfc791* and *tools.ietf.org/html/rfc793*). Each layer in the Internet Protocol Suite corresponds to one or more layers of the OSI model.

The following figure demonstrates how the OSI model compares with the TCP/IP protocol stack. Some of the OSI layers are performed by a single protocol, some layers are performed by several protocols, and some protocols cover several layers. This reflects the emphasis on performance and efficiency in real-world networking. Each layer of encapsulation consumes processing power and bandwidth, as each header consists of a series of bytes that must be transmitted and decoded in addition to the application data. Consequently, actual protocol stacks tend to be simpler than the OSI model.

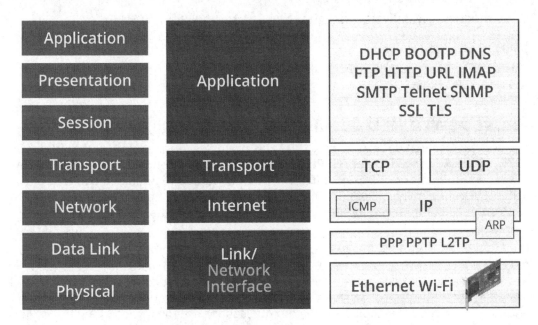

Comparing the OSI and TCP/IP models. (Image © 123RF.com).

 Note: *To learn more, watch the related* **Video** *on the course website.*

TCP/IP MODEL LAYERS

The functions of the layers of the TCP/IP model are described in the following sections.

LINK/NETWORK INTERFACE LAYER

The **Link** (or **Network Interface**) layer is the equivalent of the OSI Physical and Data Link layers. It defines the host's connection to the network media. This layer includes the hardware and software involved in the interchange of frames between hosts. The technologies used can be LAN-based (Ethernet or Wi-Fi) or WAN-based (T-carrier, ISDN, or DSL).

INTERNET LAYER

The **Internet** (or more precisely **Internetwork**) layer provides addressing and routing functions. It also provides the ability to **fragment** large frames from the Network Interface layer into smaller packets. The Internet layer uses several protocols, notably the **Internet Protocol (IP)** and **Address Resolution Protocol (ARP)**, to facilitate the delivery of packets.

 Note: *ARP is sometimes thought of as working at the Data Link layer (layer 2) in OSI terms because it needs to reference hardware (MAC) addresses and is not routable. On the other hand, a layer 2 protocol such as Ethernet does not require ARP to function, while a layer 3 protocol such as IP does (at least, in any practical sense). The best solution is to think of ARP as a layer 2.5 protocol and leave it at that.*

TRANSPORT LAYER

The **Transport** layer—or **Host-to-Host** layer—establishes connections between the different applications that the source and destination hosts are communicating with. It breaks Application-layer information into segments. TCP/IP provides two methods of data delivery:

- **Connection-oriented delivery** using the **Transmission Control Protocol (TCP)**.

- **Connectionless delivery** using the **User Datagram Protocol (UDP)**.

APPLICATION LAYER

This is the layer at which many TCP/IP services (high-level protocols) can be run, such as FTP, HTTP, and SMTP.

PACKET-SWITCHED VS. CIRCUIT-SWITCHED NETWORKS

The original research underpinning TCP/IP was performed in the late 1960s and early 1970s by the **Advanced Research Projects Agency (ARPA)**, which is the research arm of the **US Department of Defense (DoD)**. The DoD wanted to build a network to connect separate military sites. The prototype was a research network called ARPANET. This connected four university sites using a system described as a **packet switching** network.

Prior to this development, any two computers wanting to communicate had to open a direct channel, known as a **circuit**. A circuit is a dedicated path established between two locations, such as two routers or two modems. The circuit could be permanently available, but in the case of a **circuit-switched path**, the routers negotiate a link, then once the connection is established, all communications are forwarded along the same path. At the end of the communication, the connection is broken down and the path becomes available for another connection to use. If this circuit were broken, the computers would stop communicating immediately.

Packet switching introduces the ability for one host to forward information to another using any available path. A packet switching protocol is described as **robust** because it can automatically recover from communications link failures. It re-routes data packets around an internetwork of available paths. If transmission lines are damaged or if a router fails to respond, it can use any available network path that remains. This figure shows an example of an internetwork system. A packet being sent from Network A to Network D may be sent via Network C, the shortest route. If this route becomes unavailable, the packet is routed using an alternate path, such as A-F-E-D.

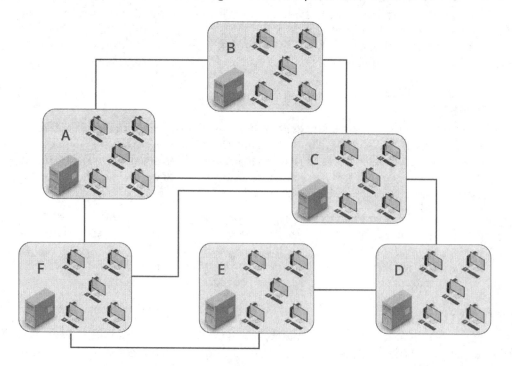

Packet switching networks. (Image © 123RF.com.)

Another feature of packet-switching networks is that data is divided into small chunks. Sending large chunks of information has always presented problems. If a message is lost or damaged, resending the whole message uses a lot of bandwidth and introduces a substantial delay. The **fragmentation** capability of the Internet Protocol to divide large messages into numerous small packets means that a single packet can be resent at relatively little cost if it is lost or damaged during transmission. It also means that the protocol can work with different types of underlying Data Link protocol frame formats and sizes.

TCP/IP AND INTERNET STANDARDS

TCP/IP is supported on nearly every network host and network appliance. It is not the property of any one vendor, however. TCP/IP is an open standard to which anyone can suggest modifications and enhancements. Similarly, TCP/IP and the Internet are inextricably linked. Although no single organization owns the Internet or its technologies, several organizations are responsible for the development of the Internet and consequently TCP/IP.

INTERNET SOCIETY (ISOC)

The purpose of **ISOC** (*isoc.org*) is to encourage the development and availability of the Internet. It provides organizational resources to the Internet Architecture Board (IAB).

INTERNET ARCHITECTURE BOARD (IAB)

The **IAB** (*iab.org*) is the technical committee of ISOC and is responsible for setting Internet standards and publishing these standards as **Requests for Comments (RFCs)**. Among other responsibilities, the IAB governs the following groups:

- **Internet Engineering Task Force (IETF)** (*ietf.org*)—focuses on solutions to Internet problems and the adoption of new standards.
- **Internet Assigned Numbers Authority (IANA)** (*iana.org*)—manages allocation of IP addresses and maintenance of the top-level domain space. IANA is currently run by **Internet Corporation for Assigned Names and Numbers (ICANN)**.

IANA allocates addresses to regional registries who then allocate them to local registries or **Internet service providers (ISPs)**. The regional registries are Asia/Pacific (APNIC), North America and Southern Africa (ARIN), Latin America (LACNIC), and Europe, Northern Africa, Central Asia, and the Middle East (RIPE NCC).

REQUESTS FOR COMMENTS (RFCs)

TCP/IP standards are developed by consensus. The process for adopting Internet standards revolves around the production of documents called **Requests for Comments (RFCs)**. The standards for TCP/IP are published via these RFCs. Some RFCs describe network services or protocols and their implementation, while others summarize policies. An older RFC is never updated. If changes are required, a new RFC is published with a new number. It is always important to verify you have the most recent RFC on a particular topic. Not all RFCs describe standards. Some are designated informational, while others are experimental. The official repository for RFCs is at *rfc-editor.org*, and they are published in HTML format at *tools.ietf.org/html*.

 Note: *References to RFCs in this course are for your information should you want to read more. You do not need to learn them for the certification exam.*

Activity 1-2
Discussing the TCP/IP Suite

SCENARIO

Answer the following questions to test your understanding of the content covered in this topic.

1. **To which layer of the OSI model does the TCP/IP model Internet layer correspond?**

2. **Which TCP/IP model layer might also be described as the Host-to-Host layer?**

3. **What is fragmentation?**

4. **Which organization is responsible for the development of Internet standards?**

Summary

In this lesson, you learned about some basic network terminology and about the use of the OSI model and TCP/IP model to define the functions of network technologies in layers.

- Networks comprise nodes, transmission media, local networking devices, routing devices, and protocols.
- The OSI model is used to analyze network functions in layers (Physical, Data Link, Network, Transport, Session, Presentation, and Application). It is important to be able to relate network hardware and protocols to the appropriate OSI layer.
- The TCP/IP protocol suite is the basis of the Internet and used for many LANs and private WANs. It uses a simpler four-layer model compared to OSI (Link, Internet, Transport, and Application).

How will knowing the OSI model help you perform networking tasks?

What is your experience with network components?

Practice Questions: Additional practice questions are available on the course website.

Lesson 2
Explaining Properties of Network Traffic

LESSON INTRODUCTION

In this lesson, you will explore the properties of the Physical and Data Link layers in more depth. Ethernet is the foundation of most local networks, and it is vital for network technicians and administrators to have a sound understanding of how it operates.

LESSON OBJECTIVES

In this lesson, you will:

- Explain media types and access methods.

- Deploy Ethernet standards.

- Describe the properties of MAC addressing and ARP and configure packet sniffers/protocol analyzers to capture and examine network traffic.

Topic A
Explain Media Types and Access Methods

EXAM OBJECTIVES COVERED
1.3 Explain the concepts and characteristics of routing and switching.

In this topic, you will identify the primary data transmission methods. As a network professional, you will probably be expected to monitor network performance and response time. The manner in which data is transmitted between nodes on a network can significantly affect network traffic and performance. You will need to understand the characteristics and potential effects of the network traffic transmission methods to understand their impact on the network.

SIGNALING AND MODULATION

The **transmission medium** is the physical channel through which **signals** travel to allow nodes to communicate with one another. All network signaling uses electromagnetic radiation of one type or another. Electromagnetic radiation means transmitting signals as electric current, infrared light, or radio waves. Different types of transmission media can be classified as cabled or wireless:

- **Cabled**—A physical signal conductor is provided between two nodes. Examples include cable types such as **copper** or **fiber optic cable**. Cabled media can also be described as **bounded media**.
- **Wireless**—Uses free space between nodes (no signal conductor), such as **microwave radio**. Wireless media can also be described as **unbounded media**.

Computers can process only information in a **digital** format. Digital means that the information is represented using discrete **binary values** (ones and zeroes). Many transmission media and networking products support **digital signaling**. Digital signaling uses a transmission technique called **line coding**, which is essentially a series of discrete pulses. The pulses could be implemented by high and low voltages or by on/off light transmissions to represent the ones and zeroes of binary digital data. This makes the transmission less susceptible to interference, and it makes it easier to regenerate the transmission over longer distances.

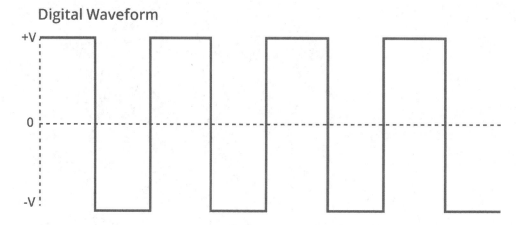

A digital waveform is characterized by a series of discrete pulses.

Some transmission media support only **analog signaling**, requiring a more complex **modulation scheme** to represent the digital information as it is transmitted over the analog channel. An analog signal is characterized by a smooth sine wave, oscillating between maximum and minimum values over time. As the wave can take any value between those limits, it must be **sampled** at intervals to produce discrete binary values.

Sampling is also necessary when an analog input, such as speech, needs to be converted to digital. When sampling like this, you must balance quality with available bandwidth. For example, telecommunications links are based on 64 Kbps channels because that is the bandwidth requirement for carrying digitized voice calls to an acceptable calling standard. This is derived as a result of the following calculation, derived from the Nyquist theorem that the sampling rate must be twice the signal bandwidth.

1. The voice frequency range is (or is assumed to be) 4000 Hz. This must be sampled at twice the rate (8000 Hz or 8 KHz) to ensure an accurate representation of the original analog waveform.
2. The sample size is 1 byte (or 8 bits). Therefore, 8 KHz x 8 bits = 64 Kbps.

BANDWIDTH, BAUD, AND BIT RATE

One important characteristic of a transmission medium is its **bandwidth**. The bandwidth is the range of frequencies available to the communications channel. Digital signaling typically uses **baseband transmission**, meaning that the complete bandwidth of the media is available to a single transmission channel. Some communications technologies divide the available media bandwidth using multiplexing schemes, such as time-based access or division into smaller frequency bands.

When used to discuss **channel capacity** like this, bandwidth is measured in units of time called **hertz (Hz)** representing the number of signaling cycles that can be completed per second. This can be measured in different multiples, from cycles propagating once per second (1 Hz) to those propagating thousands (KHz), millions (MHz), billions (GHz), or trillions of times per second (THz). If the medium supports a range of frequencies from 0 to 100 MHz, it has 100 MHz channel bandwidth. As another example, if a wireless radio transmits in the frequencies between 5040 MHz and 5060 MHz, it has 20 MHz bandwidth.

Having a greater range of frequencies available allows the medium to carry more information per second. Consequently, rather than referring to channel width, the term **bandwidth** is also often used in data communications just to mean the **data rate**, or the amount of information that can be transferred per second. When speaking about the data rate, you need to distinguish **baud** rate from bit rate.

A signal transmitted over a communications channel consists of a series of events referred to as **symbols**. A symbol could be something like a pulse of higher voltage in an electrical current or the transition between the peak and the trough in an electromagnetic wave. The number of symbols that can be transmitted per second is called the **baud rate**. The baud rate is measured in hertz (or MHz or GHz).

The **bit rate** is the amount of information that can be transmitted, measured in **bits per second (bps)**, or some multiple thereof. In order to transmit information more efficiently, a signaling method might be capable of representing more than one bit per symbol. In this case, the bit rate will be higher than the baud rate.

The **data rate** is determined by a combination of signaling speed (baud) and encoding method, but also by distance and noise.

DISTANCE LIMITATIONS, ATTENUATION, AND NOISE

Each type of media can consistently support a given data rate only over a defined **distance**. Some media types support higher data rates over longer distances than others. **Attenuation** and **noise** enforce distance limitations on different media types.

- **Attenuation** is the loss of **signal strength**, expressed in decibels (dB). dB expresses the ratio between two measurements; in this case, signal strength at origin and signal strength at destination.
- **Noise** is anything that gets transmitted within or close to the channel that isn't the intended signal. This serves to make the signal itself difficult to distinguish, causing errors in data and forcing retransmissions. This is expressed as the signal to noise ratio (SNR).

TRANSMISSION MEDIA TYPES

Most data networks use either copper or fiber optic cable media or radio-based wireless media.

COPPER CABLE

Copper cable is used to transmit electrical signals. The cable between two nodes creates a low voltage electrical circuit between the interfaces on the nodes. There are two main types of copper cable: twisted pair and coaxial (coax). Electrical signals are susceptible to interference and dispersion. There is some degree of impedance in the copper conductor; signals can leak easily from the wire, and noise can also leak into the wire. This means that copper cable suffers from high attenuation, meaning that the signal loses strength over long links.

FIBER OPTIC CABLE

Fiber optic cable carries very high frequency radiation in the infrared light part of the electromagnetic spectrum. Even though high frequencies are used, they are very closely contained within the optical media and can propagate more easily. The light signals are also not susceptible to interference or noise from other sources. Consequently, fiber optic cable supports higher bandwidth over longer links than copper cable.

WIRELESS RADIO

Radio frequency (RF) waves can propagate through the air between sending and receiving antennas. This requires much more power than with electrical signals passing over copper conductors, however. The use of the radio part of the electromagnetic spectrum is regulated by national governments and (to some extent) standardized internationally by the **International Telecommunications Union (ITU)**. Use of many frequency bands requires a license from the relevant government agency. Wireless radio networking products operate in the high-frequency (microwave), unregulated Industrial, Scientific, and Medical (ISM) bands (2.4 GHz and 5 GHz). In these bands, there is a limit on power output, and there is also often substantial interference, which means range is limited. Also, each product must work within a narrow frequency range, allowing bandwidths in the MHz ranges only.

MEDIA ACCESS CONTROL AND COLLISION DOMAINS

A multiple access area network must share the available communications capacity between the various nodes that use it. **Media access control (MAC)** refers to the methods a network technology uses to determine when nodes can communicate on the media and to deal with possible problems, such as two devices attempting to communicate simultaneously.

With controlled or **deterministic media access**, a central device or system specifies when and for how long each node can transmit. One example is the Token Ring product, where the ability to transmit on the network is determined by a token, which passes from node to node. Deterministic access methods are beneficial when network access is time critical. For example, in an industrial setting, key control and safety equipment, such as flow-shutoff sensors in chemical storage facilities, must have a guaranteed transmission time. Deterministic systems ensure that a single node cannot saturate the media. All nodes get a chance to transmit data.

In a **contention-based MAC** system, each network node within the same **collision domain** competes with the other connected nodes for use of the transmission media. A collision domain includes all the hosts attached to the same cable segment or connected via the same hub. When two nodes transmit at the same time, the signals are said to collide and neither signal can reach its destination. This means that they must be re-sent, reducing available bandwidth. The **collisions** become more frequent as more nodes are added, and consequently the effective data rate is reduced.

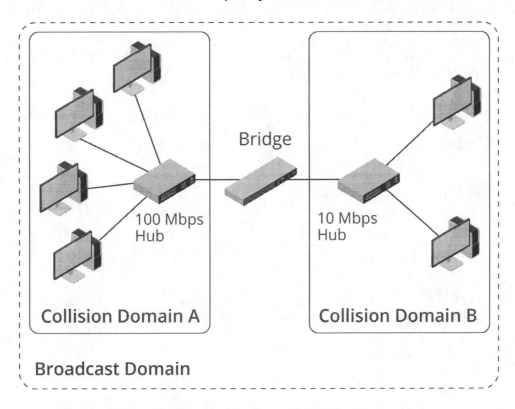

Collision domains. (Image © 123RF.com.)

This figure shows how bridge devices create separate collision domains. Each hub is a shared access media area. The nodes connected to the hubs share the available bandwidth—a 100 Mbps Ethernet for domain A and a 10 Mbps Ethernet for domain B—because only one node within each collision domain can communicate at any one time. The bridge isolates these segments from each other, so nodes in domain B do not slow down or contend with nodes in domain A. The bridge does allow nodes to communicate with the other domain, by forwarding only the appropriate traffic, creating a single **broadcast domain**.

CSMA/CD, CSMA/CA, AND SWITCHING

The Ethernet protocols governing contention and media access are called **Carrier Sense Multiple Access (CSMA)** protocols:

- **Carrier sense**—detect activity on the media.
- **Multiple access**—multiple nodes using the same media.

Use of these protocols enforces limitations on the minimum and maximum lengths of cable that can be used and the size of frames transmitted. Each frame must fill the cable segment before the end of transmission is reached, or a frame could be sent and involved in a collision and lost without the sending node being aware of it. Ethernet shared access using CSMA protocols use **half-duplex** transmissions. This means that a node can transmit or receive but it cannot do both at the same time.

There are two types of CSMA protocols:

- **CSMA/CD** with **Collision Detection**.
- **CSMA/CA** with **Collision Avoidance**.

CSMA WITH COLLISION DETECTION

Ethernet's **Carrier Sense Multiple Access with Collision Detection (CSMA/CD)** protocol defines methods for detecting a collision on different types of media. In most cases, this is when a signal is present on the interface's transmit and receive lines simultaneously. On detecting a collision, the node broadcasts a jam signal. Each node that was attempting to use the media then waits for a random period (**backoff**) before attempting to transmit again.

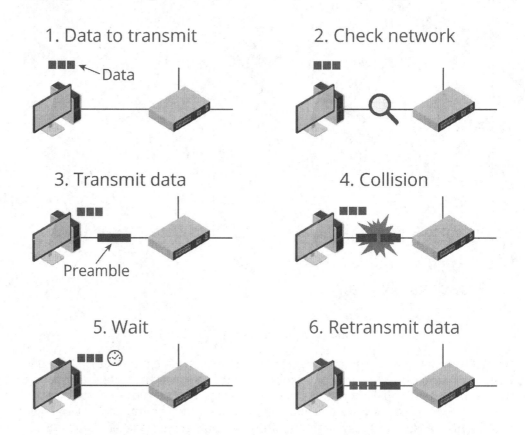

The CSMA/CD media access method. (Image © 123RF.com.)

CSMA WITH COLLISION AVOIDANCE

The **Carrier Sense Multiple Access with Collision Avoidance (CSMA/CA)** protocols use schemes such as "request to send" to gain access to the media. Nodes listen to the media before transmitting and transmit only if the media is clear. A node wanting to transmit but detecting activity must wait and try later. This reduces the number of collisions, but it adds overhead in terms of extra control signaling. The IEEE 802.11 Wi-Fi standard uses CSMA/CA.

SWITCHED NETWORKS

Contention-based access methods do not scale to large numbers of nodes within the same collision domain. This problem is overcome by using **switches**. A switch establishes a temporary circuit between two nodes that are exchanging messages. Using a switch means that each switch port is in a separate collision domain. With switches, collisions occur only if the device attached to a switch port is operating in half-duplex mode. Furthermore, collisions affect only that port.

By eliminating the effect of contention, switches allow for **full-duplex** transmissions, where a node can transmit and receive simultaneously. When a link is configured as full duplex, the CSMA/CD protocol is not used.

BROADCAST DOMAINS

Within a collision domain on a shared medium, any given node will receive all the traffic transmitted within that domain. However, it will choose to process only traffic that is specifically addressed to it. This is referred to as **unicast** traffic, which is traffic that is addressed by the sender to a single recipient.

It is useful to have a mechanism to transmit the same traffic to multiple nodes. This is referred to as **broadcast** traffic. This is accomplished using a special type of destination address. Broadcast traffic is often used when a host needs to discover the address of another host or when it needs to autoconfigure its own address. Broadcasts are also used by routers to communicate updates to one another. Nodes that share the same broadcast address are said to be within the same **broadcast domain**. Broadcast traffic introduces efficiencies in some circumstances but inefficiencies in others. If the broadcast domain is very large, the amount of broadcast traffic will be correspondingly great and consume a disproportionate amount of bandwidth. This becomes an important factor in designing a network that works efficiently.

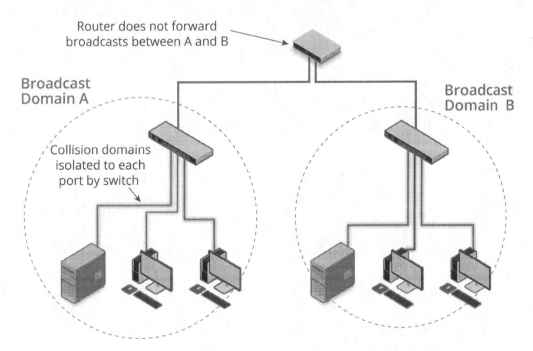

Collision and broadcast domains on a switched network. The switches isolate collision domains to each port, while the router does not forward broadcasts. (Image © 123RF.com.)

Collision domains are isolated from one another at layer 2 of the OSI model by devices such as bridges and switches. All devices attached to a hub are part of the same collision domain; devices on either side of a bridge are in separate collision domains. Using switches effectively eliminates the concept of a collision domain entirely.

Broadcast domains are normally established by routers, operating at layer 3 of the OSI model. A broadcast domain could contain multiple collision domains, but the reverse is not true. A single collision domain can be associated with only one broadcast domain.

When a broadcast domain is defined in terms of logical networks, at layer 3, typically the same boundary has to be established at the Data Link layer (layer 2). In the normal course of operations, any host attached to the same hub, bridge, or unmanaged switch would be in the same broadcast domain. This model is too restrictive for the way modern networks are designed, however. Network designers can take advantage of the **virtual LAN (VLAN)** feature of modern Ethernet switches. A VLAN is a means of creating separate layer 2 broadcast domains on the same switch or configuring separate broadcast domains across a fabric of distributed switches. VLANs are a means of overcoming the physical topology to match the layer 2 logical topology to the layer 3 logical topology.

Activity 2-1

Discussing Media Types and Access Methods

SCENARIO

Answer the following questions to test your understanding of the content covered in this topic.

1. **What is attenuation?**

2. **Why might the baud rate be different from the bit rate?**

3. **True or False? All the nodes shown in the following figure are in the same collision domain.**

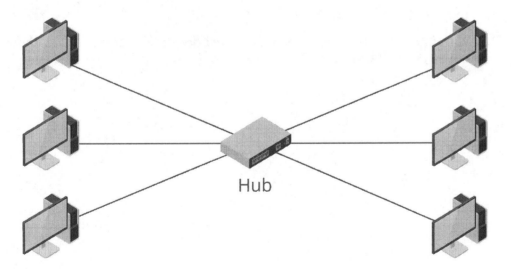

Hub

4. **Identify the transmission method depicted in the following graphic.**

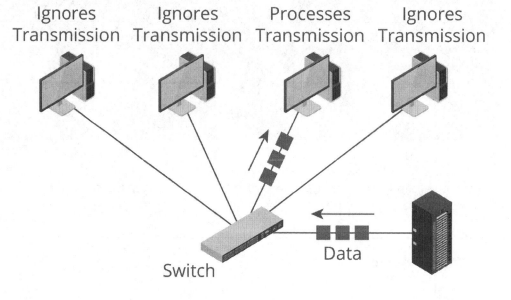

○ Broadcast

○ CSMA/CD

○ CSMA/CA

○ Unicast

○ Switched

5. **With CSMA/CD, what will happen if a host has data to transmit and there is already data on the cable?**

6. **Assuming unmanaged switches, how many broadcast domains are present in the following figure?**

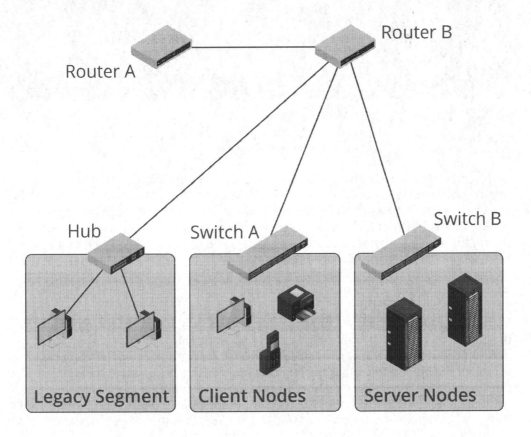

Topic B
Deploy Ethernet Standards

EXAM OBJECTIVES COVERED
1.3 Explain the concepts and characteristics of routing and switching.
2.1 Given a scenario, deploy the appropriate cabling solution.

In this topic, you will identify the components used in an Ethernet network implementation. Ethernet continues to dominate the wired LAN product market. Its popularity is largely based on its ease of installation and upgradability. Large and small networks use Ethernet technology to provide both backbone and end-user services. Due to the wide deployment of Ethernet today, you will undoubtedly be required to manage and troubleshoot Ethernet networks.

ETHERNET FRAME FORMAT

Many technologies have been developed to enable local networks using different media and media access methods and have subsequently fallen by the wayside, leaving Ethernet as the only mainstream cabled LAN product. Ethernet supports a variety of media options and is based upon inexpensive equipment. It was created in the 1960s at the University of Hawaii for the ALOHA network and was first used commercially by **DEC, Intel, and Xerox (DIX)** in the late 1970s. It was standardized by IEEE as 802.3 (*grouper.ieee.org/groups/802/3*) in 1983. Ethernet uses baseband signaling and the CSMA/CD method for media access control.

The basic format of an Ethernet frame is shown in the following figure.

Construction of an Ethernet frame.

PREAMBLE
The preamble and Start Frame Delimiter (SFD) are used for clock synchronization and as part of the CSMA/CD protocol to identify collisions early. The preamble consists of 8 bytes of alternating 1s and 0s with the SFD being two consecutive 1s at the end. This is not technically considered to be part of the frame.

ADDRESSING
The destination and source address fields contain the MAC addresses of the receiving and sending nodes. A **Media Access Control (MAC) address** is a unique identifier for each Ethernet network adapter interface. A MAC address is also referred to as a local or hardware/physical address. A MAC address is 48 bits long (6 bytes).

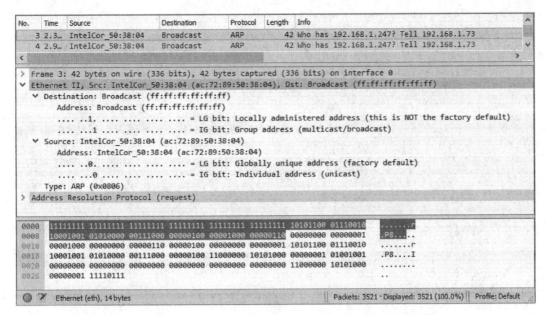

Fields in the Ethernet header shown in the Wireshark packet capture application. This application does not capture the preamble or the Frame Check Sequence. (Screenshot courtesy of Wireshark.)

FRAME LENGTH AND MAXIMUM TRANSMISSION UNIT (MTU)

The official 802.3 standard defines a 2-byte field to specify the size of the data field or **payload**. The payload can normally be between 46 and 1500 bytes. The upper limit of the payload is also referred to as the **maximum transmission unit (MTU)**. However, most Ethernet products follow the original DIX specification, referred to as Type II frames, and use the field to indicate the type of network layer protocol contained in the frame—IPv4 or IPv6, for instance. These Ethertypes are values of 1536 or greater; anything less than that is interpreted as the data length. For example, IPv4 is coded as the hex value 0x0800, or 2048 in decimal, while IPv6 is 0x86DD.

To comply with CSMA/CD, the minimum length of an Ethernet frame is 64 bytes, so the payload must be at least 46 bytes. If this is not the case, it is automatically padded with redundant data. The maximum size of an Ethernet frame is normally 1518 bytes, excluding the preamble. Some Gigabit and 10GbE Ethernet products support **jumbo frames** with much larger MTUs. Such products are not standardized, however, making interoperability between different vendors problematic.

ERROR CHECKING

The error checking field contains a 32-bit (4-byte) checksum called a **Cyclic Redundancy Check (CRC)** or **Frame Check Sequence (FCS)**. The CRC is calculated based on the contents of the frame; the receiving node performs the same calculation and, if it matches, accepts the frame. There is no mechanism for retransmission if damage is detected nor is the CRC completely accurate at detecting damage; these are functions of error checking in protocols operating at higher layers.

*Note: To learn more, watch the related **Video** on the course website.*

ETHERNET DEPLOYMENT STANDARDS

Ethernet deployment standards provide a network designer the assurance that infrastructure will meet the bandwidth requirements of applications. The standards specify the bit rate that should be achieved over different types of media up to the supported distance limitations. These Ethernet media specifications are named using a three-part convention, which is often referred to as **xBASE-y**. This describes:

- The bit rate in megabits per second (Mbps) or gigabits per second (Gbps).
- The signal mode (baseband or **broadband**). All types of Ethernet use baseband transmissions, so you will only see specifications of the form *xBASE-y*.
- A designator for the media type.

For example, 10BASE-T denotes an early implementation that works at 10 Mbps, uses a baseband signal, and uses twisted pair copper cabling. Ethernet can use Unshielded Twisted Pair (UTP) rated to a particular Cat standard or fiber optic cabling. Fiber optic cabling is divided into Single Mode (SMF) and MultiMode (MMF) types, and MMF is categorized by Optical Mode designations (OM1, OM2, OM3, and OM4).

FAST ETHERNET

When it came time to update the original 10BASE-T Ethernet standard, the IEEE 802.3 committee decided on an approach that ensured backward compatibility, and created the **IEEE 802.3u** specification, better known as **Fast Ethernet**. Fast Ethernet uses the same CSMA/CD protocols as the original Ethernet specifications but with higher frequency signaling and improved encoding methods, raising the bit rate from 10 Mbps to 100 Mbps. The 100BASE-TX standard refers to Fast Ethernet working over Cat 5 (or better) Unshielded Twisted Pair (UTP) copper cable with a maximum supported link length of 100 meters (328 feet).

 Note: There are a couple of obsolete standards defining use over Cat 3 cable (100BASE-T4 and 100BASE-T2). The set of copper standards can collectively be referred to as 100BASE-T.

Fast Ethernet allows only one or two hubs, though this does not apply if the hubs are stacked using a proprietary backplane (the stack counts as one device). The standards documentation also defines two classes of hubs: Class I hubs are used to connect different media—twisted pair and fiber optic, for instance—and only one device per network is allowed if this type of hub is used. In most modern networks, however, the restriction is overcome by using switches in place of hubs.

Fast Ethernet also introduced an **autonegotiation** protocol to allow devices to choose the highest supported connection parameters (10 or 100 Mbps and half- or full-duplex). 10BASE-T Ethernet specifies that a node should transmit regular electrical pulses when it is not transmitting data to confirm the viability of the link (**link integrity test**). Fast Ethernet codes a 16-bit data packet into this signal advertising its service capabilities (speed and half- or full-duplex). This is called a **Fast Link Pulse**. Fast Link Pulse is backward-compatible with 10BASE-T but not mandatory, as it is under Gigabit Ethernet and later. A node that does not support autonegotiation can be detected by one that does and sent ordinary link integrity test signals, or **Normal Link Pulses**.

Fast Ethernet would not be deployed on new networks, but you may need to maintain it in legacy installations.

GIGABIT ETHERNET

Gigabit Ethernet builds on the standards defined for Ethernet and Fast Ethernet. The bit rate is 10 times faster than Fast Ethernet. The Gigabit Ethernet standard over fiber is documented in IEEE 802.3z. There are variants for long wavelength optics (LX), required for long distance transmission, and short wavelength optics (SX). The various fiber standards are collectively known as **1000BASE-X**. The IEEE also approved 1000BASE-T, a standard utilizing Cat 5e (or better) copper wiring. This is defined in IEEE 802.3ab.

Specification	Cable	Maximum Distance
1000BASE-T	UTP (Cat 5e/Cat 6/Cat 6A)	100 m (328 feet)
1000BASE-SX (770 to 850nm)	MMF (OM1: 62.5/125)	220 m (721 feet)
	MMF (OM2: 50/125)	550 m (1804 feet)
1000BASE-LX (1270 to 1355nm)	MMF (62.5/125 or 50/125)	550 m (1804 feet)
	SMF (9/125)	5 km (3.1 miles)

 Note: *For 1000BASE-T, Cat 5 is also acceptable (if properly installed), but Cat 5 cable is no longer available commercially. Unlike Ethernet and Fast Ethernet, Gigabit Ethernet uses all four pairs for transmission and is thus more sensitive to crosstalk.*

In terms of network design, Gigabit Ethernet is implemented using switches, so only the restrictions on cable length apply. The maximum distance refers to cabling between the node and a switch port, or between two switch ports.

Gigabit Ethernet is the mainstream choice for new installations of access networks (cabling to allow client workstations network access). The main decision would be whether to use copper or fiber cable. Fiber cable would give better upgrade potential in the future, while copper cable would be cheaper to install.

10 GIGABIT ETHERNET (10GbE)

10 Gigabit Ethernet (10GbE) multiplies the nominal speed of Gigabit Ethernet by a factor of 10. 10GbE is not deployed in many access networks, however, as the cost of 10GbE network adapters and switches is high. The major applications of 10GbE Ethernet are:

- Increasing bandwidth for server interconnections and network backbones, especially in data centers and for storage area networks (SAN).
- Replacing existing switched public data networks based on proprietary technologies with simpler Ethernet switches (Metro Ethernet).

10GbE is less likely to be deployed for client connectivity in general purpose office buildings. It might be used where a company's business requires very high bandwidth data transfers, such as TV and film production.

10GbE Ethernet is standardized under several publications with letter designations, starting with 802.3ae, which are periodically collated. At the time of writing, IEEE 802.3-2018 is current.

Specification	Cable	Maximum Distance
10GBASE-T	UTP (Cat 6)	55 m (180 feet)
	F/UTP (Cat 6A)	100 m (328 feet)
	S/FTP (Cat 7)	100 m (328 feet)
10GBASE-SR (850nm)	MMF (OM3: 50/125)	300 m (984 feet)
	MMF (OM4: 50/125)	400 m (1312 feet)
10GBASE-LR (1310nm)	SMF (9/125)	10 km (6.2 miles)
10GBASE-ER (1550nm)	SMF (9/125)	40 km (25 miles)

10GbE works only with switches in full-duplex mode.

The 10GBASE-R short, long, and extra-long wavelength standards all have WAN specifications (10GBASE-SW, 10GBASE-LW, and 10GBASE-EW) that allow interoperability with SONET infrastructure.

Note: *You should only need to know the distance limitations for 10GBASE-T for the certification exam. Note that there are many more variants and proprietary implementations of both Gigabit Ethernet (https://en.wikipedia.org/wiki/Gigabit_Ethernet) and 10GbE (https://en.wikipedia.org/wiki/10_Gigabit_Ethernet#Standards).*

Activity 2-2
Discussing Ethernet Standards

SCENARIO
Answer the following questions to test your understanding of the content covered in this topic.

---

1. **What is an MTU?**

2. **True or False? The CRC mechanism in Ethernet allows for the retransmission of damaged frames.**

3. **True or False? A computer with a 10BASE-T Ethernet adapter cannot be joined to a 100BASE-T network.**

4. **What maximum distance is defined in standards documentation for 1000BASE-LX running over MMF?**

Topic C

Configure and Monitor Network Interfaces

EXAM OBJECTIVES COVERED
1.3 Explain the concepts and characteristics of routing and switching.
5.2 Given a scenario, use the appropriate tool.

A network interface is the means by which a node is connected to the media and exchanges data with other network hosts. As a network technician, you will frequently be involved with installing, configuring, and troubleshooting network interfaces. You must also be able to capture and analyze network traffic, using a packet sniffer.

NETWORK INTERFACE CARDS (NICs)

The transceiver component responsible for physically connecting the node to the transmission medium is implemented in a **network adapter**, **network adapter card**, or **network interface card/controller (NIC)**. At the Data Link layer, the NIC is also responsible for organizing data into frames and providing each interface with a hardware address. A multiport NIC may have more than one interface. Each Ethernet network interface port has a unique hardware address known as the **Media Access Control (MAC) address**. This may also be referred to as the Ethernet address (EA) or, in IEEE terminology, as the **extended unique identifier (EUI)**.

MEDIA ACCESS CONTROL (MAC) ADDRESS FORMAT

A MAC address consists of 48 binary digits (6 bytes). The format of the number differs depending on the system architecture. It is often displayed as 6 groups of 2 hexadecimal digits with colon or hyphen separators or no separators at all (for example, `00:60:8c:12:3a:bc` or `00608c123abc`) or as 3 groups of 4 hex digits with period separators (`0060.8c12.3abc`, for instance).

Note: *Hexadecimal uses digits 0 through 9 and letters A, B, C, D, E, and F to represent the 16 possible values of each hex digit.*

The IEEE gives each card manufacturer a range of numbers, and the manufacturer hard-codes every interface produced with a unique number from their range. This is called the **burned-in address**. The first six hex digits (3 bytes or octets), also known as the **Organizationally Unique Identifier (OUI)**, identify the manufacturer of the adapter. The last six digits are a serial number.

An organization can decide to use **locally administered** addresses in place of the manufacturers' universal coding systems. This can be used to make MACs meaningful in terms of location on the network, but it adds a significant amount of administrative overhead. A locally administered address is defined by changing the U/L bit from 0 to 1. The rest of the address is configured using the card driver or network management software. It becomes the network administrator's responsibility to ensure that all interfaces are configured with a unique MAC.

The I/G bit of a MAC address determines whether the frame is addressed to an individual node (0) or a group (1). The latter is used for broadcast and multicast transmissions. A MAC address consisting entirely of 1s is the broadcast address (ff:ff:ff:ff:ff:ff) and should be processed by all nodes within the same broadcast domain.

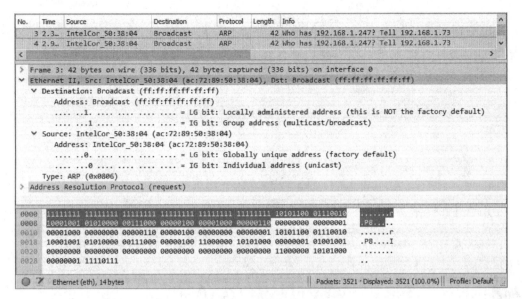

Captured Ethernet frame showing the resolved OUI and I/G and U/L bits in the destination (broadcast) and source addresses. (Screenshot courtesy of Wireshark.)

Note: *An EUI-64 is a 64-bit hardware address. A translation mechanism allows a 48-bit MAC address to be converted to an EUI-64. EUI-64 addresses can be used with IPv6.*

UNICAST AND BROADCAST TRAFFIC

When a sending interface addresses a single receiving interface, this is referred to as a **unicast transmission**. In the following figure, the node with MAC address 0206.0000.6666 sends a frame of data addressed to 0206.0000.1111 (the server). The server recognizes its own MAC address and copies the frame for processing. The nodes are all wired to a hub, which means they are all within the same shared access medium (collision domain). Consequently, the frame is transmitted on all ports. All the other hosts receive the frame but ignore it, as the destination address does not match their own.

If the central device were a switch, only the server would receive the unicast packet. The switch tracks which MAC addresses are associated with each of its ports and only forwards unicast traffic over the correct port.

Under certain circumstances, it is necessary for a host to **broadcast** data to all the other nodes on the network. At layer 2, a broadcast frame is given the hardware address of ff:ff:ff:ff:ff:ff. Both hubs and switches transmit broadcast frames out of all ports except the source port.

Note: *This is the case for unmanaged switches. With managed switches, this behavior can be changed by configuring virtual LANs (VLAN).*

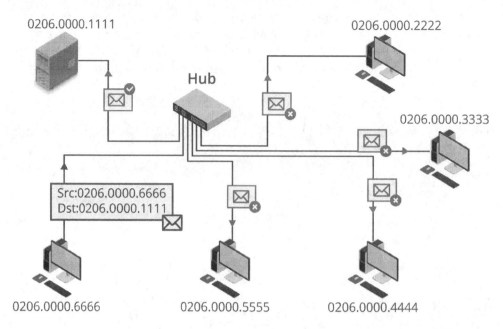

Checking the destination address of a frame in a unicast transmission. (Image © 123RF.com.)

ADDRESS RESOLUTION PROTOCOL (ARP)

When two hosts communicate using TCP/IP, an **Internet Protocol (IP) address** is used at the Network layer to identify each host. However, transmission of data must take place at the Physical and Data Link level using the local or hardware/MAC address of the interface. The TCP/IP suite includes the **Address Resolution Protocol (ARP)** to perform the task of resolving an IP address to a hardware address.

When both sending and receiving hosts are on the same local network (connected to the same hub, for instance), local address resolution takes place as follows:

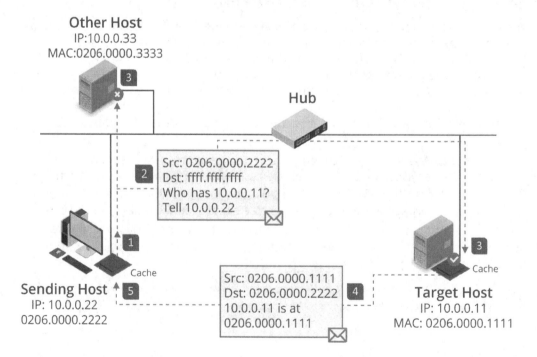

Local address resolution. (Image © 123RF.com.)

1. When the destination IP address has been determined to be a local address, the source host checks its ARP table cache for the required hardware address (MAC address) of the destination host.
2. If the MAC address is not present in cache, ARP builds a request and broadcasts it onto the network.
3. The broadcast is processed by all the hosts on the local segment, but unless the request contains its own IP address, most hosts ignore it.
4. If the target host recognizes its own address, it updates its cache with the MAC address of the source host. It then replies to the source host.
5. The source host receives the reply, updates its cache table, and communication is established.

If the host is on a remote network, then the local host must use a router (its default gateway) to forward the packet. Therefore, it must determine the MAC address of the gateway using ARP.

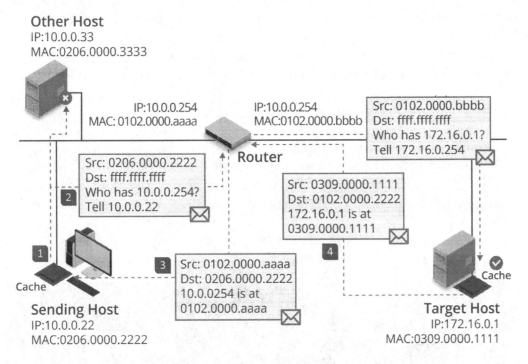

Remote address resolution. (Image © 123RF.com.)

1. When the destination IP address has been determined to be a remote address, the sending host determines the IP address of its default gateway (router). The sending host then examines its ARP table cache for the necessary IP address/MAC address mapping of the **gateway**.
2. If the mapping for the gateway address is not found in the cache, it broadcasts an ARP request for the default gateway's IP address (***not*** the IP address of the remote destination host).
3. Hopefully, the router will respond to the request by returning its hardware address. The sending host then forwards the packet to the default gateway to deliver to the remote network and the destination host.
4. At the router, IP determines whether the destination is local or remote. If local, it uses ARP for the address resolution. If remote, it checks its routing table for an appropriate gateway to the remote network.

ARP CACHE UTILITY

ARP broadcasts can generate considerable traffic on a network, which can reduce performance. To optimize this process, the results of an ARP broadcast are cached in an **ARP table**. If the entry is used within the timeout period, the entry is held in the cache for a few minutes before it is deleted. Entries in the ARP table cache are automatically timed out in case a hardware address changes (for example, if a network card is replaced).

 Note: *The timeout for the ARP cache varies by operating system and version and can often be configured manually.*

The cache is an area reserved in memory that contains the IP/Internet address and the associated hardware/physical address. Before an ARP broadcast is performed, the cache is always checked for the correct MAC address. Broadcasting is reduced further as the host receiving an ARP request extracts the IP address and hardware address of the source host and places this information in its ARP cache before transmitting an ARP reply.

The `arp` utility can be used to perform functions related to the ARP table cache. You would use this to diagnose a suspected problem with local addressing and packet delivery.

- `arp -a` (or `arp -g`) shows the ARP cache contents. You can use this with *IPAddress* to view the ARP cache for the specified interface only. The ARP cache will not necessarily contain the MAC addresses of every host on the local segment. There will be no cache entry if there has not been a recent exchange of frames.
- `arp -s IPAddress MACAddress` adds an entry to the ARP cache. Under Windows, *MACAddress* needs to be entered with hyphens between each hex byte.
- `arp -d *` deletes all entries in the ARP cache; it can also be used with *IPAddress* to delete a single entry.

```
Microsoft Windows [Version 10.0.14393]
(c) 2016 Microsoft Corporation. All rights reserved.

C:\Users\administrator>arp -a

Interface: 10.1.0.100 --- 0x2
  Internet Address        Physical Address      Type
  10.1.0.1                00-15-5d-01-ca-bf     dynamic
  10.1.0.2                00-15-5d-01-ca-c2     dynamic
  10.1.0.101              00-15-5d-01-ca-c1     dynamic
  10.1.0.254              00-15-5d-01-ca-32     dynamic
  10.1.0.255              ff-ff-ff-ff-ff-ff     static
  224.0.0.22              01-00-5e-00-00-16     static
  224.0.0.252             01-00-5e-00-00-fc     static
  239.255.255.250         01-00-5e-7f-ff-fa     static
  255.255.255.255         ff-ff-ff-ff-ff-ff     static

C:\Users\administrator>_
```

Output from the arp command showing network (IP) addresses mapped to physical (MAC) addresses. Host interfaces are learned (dynamic), while broadcast and multicast interfaces are configured statically. (Screenshot used with permission from Microsoft.)

Note: *These are some uses of the command in Windows. Syntax for Linux and UNIX is often different. Check the help for the utility on the system you are using to learn about the switches and arguments available.*

PACKET SNIFFERS

One of the most important tools used for network support is a **protocol analyzer**. This is the tool that allows inspection of traffic received by a host or passing over a network link. A protocol analyzer depends on a **packet sniffer**. A sniffer captures frames moving over the network medium. This might be a cabled or wireless network.

Note: *Often the terms sniffer and protocol analyzer are used interchangeably, but be aware that they might be implemented separately.*

A basic **software-based sniffer** will simply interrogate the frames received by the network adapter by installing a special driver. Examples include `libpcap` (for UNIX® and Linux®) and its Windows® version **winpcap**. These software libraries allow the frames to be read from the network stack and saved to a file on disk. Most also support filters to reduce the amount of data captured.

By default, a network interface processes only the packets that are directed to that card (unicast or multicast traffic) or broadcast messages. Most host-based packet sniffers can make a network adapter work in **promiscuous mode**, so that it processes all unicast traffic within the Ethernet broadcast domain, whether it is intended for the host machine or not. While this approach works for a hub, where all traffic is repeated on every port, on a switched network, the switch makes decisions about which port to forward traffic to, based on the destination address and what it knows about the interfaces connected to each port. This means that to capture unicast traffic intended for other hosts, the sniffer needs to be connected to a suitably configured spanning port (mirrored port).

Note: *Most Ethernet adapters and drivers support the function of a protocol analyzer working in promiscuous mode. When it comes to sniffing wireless traffic and the monitor mode equivalent of promiscuous mode, the situation is more complex. Many wireless adapter chipsets and/or drivers do not allow monitor mode and so prevent the capture of management frames and traffic not addressed to the host.*

A **hardware sniffer** might be capable of tapping the actual network media in some way. Also, a hardware sniffer might be required to capture at wirespeed on 1+ Gbps links. A workstation with basic sniffer software may drop large numbers of frames under heavy loads.

tcpdump

tcpdump is a command-line packet capture utility for Linux, though a port of the program (`windump`) is available for Windows (*winpcap.org/windump*). The basic syntax of the command is:

```
tcpdump -i eth0
```

Where `eth0` is the interface to listen on (you can substitute with the keyword `any` to listen on all interfaces of a multi-homed host). The utility will then display captured packets until halted manually (by pressing **Ctrl+C**). The operation of the basic command can be modified by switches. For example, the `-w` and `-r` switches write output to a file and read the contents of a capture file respectively. The `-v`, `-vv`, and `-vvv` can be used to increase the amount of detail shown about each frame while the `-e` switch shows the Ethernet header.

`tcpdump` is often used with some sort of filter expression:

- Type—filter by `host`, `net`, `port`, or `portrange`.
- Direction—filter by source (`src`) or destination (`dst`) parameters (host, network, or port).
- Protocol—filter by a named protocol rather than port number (for example, `arp`, `icmp`, `ip`, `ip6`, `tcp`, `udp`, and so on).

Filter expressions can be combined by using Boolean operators:

- `and` (&&)
- `or` (||)
- `not` (!)

Filter syntax can be made even more detailed by using parentheses to group expressions. A complex filter expression should be enclosed by quotes. For example, the following command filters frames to those with the source IP 10.1.0.100 and destination port 53 or 80:

```
tcpdump -i eth0 "src host 10.1.0.100 and (dst port 53 or dst port 80)"
```

Note: *Refer to tcpdump.org for the full help and usage examples.* `ngrep` *(https://github.com/jpr5/ngrep) is another useful packet capture and analysis tool. As well as the standard filter syntax, it supports use of regular expressions (https://regexr.com) to search and filter capture output. You can also use the netcat tool (https://nmap.org/ncat/) to copy network traffic from one host to another for analysis.*

Note: *To learn more, watch the related **Video** on the course website.*

Activity 2-3

Discussing Network Interface Configuration and Monitoring

SCENARIO
Answer the following questions to test your understanding of the content covered in this topic.

1. **What is an I/G bit?**

2. **If a mapping for a local destination host is not found in a source host ARP cache, how does the source host send an ARP request?**

3. **If a packet is addressed to a remote network, what destination MAC address will the sending node use?**

4. **True or False? The arp utility allows you to discover another host's MAC address.**

5. **On a switched network, what configuration changes must be made to allow a host to sniff unicast traffic from all hosts connected to a switch?**

6. **Write the command to use tcpdump to capture traffic from the IP address 172.16.16.254 on the interface eth0 and output the results to the file router.pcap.**

Activity 2-4
Exploring the Lab Environment

BEFORE YOU BEGIN
Complete this activity using Hyper-V Manager on your **HOST** PC.

SCENARIO
In this activity, you will familiarize yourself with the systems you will be using in the course activities.

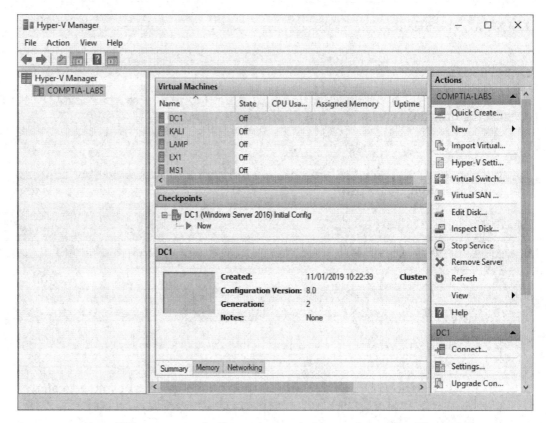

Hyper-V Manager console. (Screenshot used with permission from Microsoft.)

 Note: *Activities may vary slightly if the software vendor has issued digital updates. Your instructor will notify you of any changes.*

1. Access the settings page for the **DC1** VM, and locate options to adjust the system memory and network settings.

    Unless you are instructed to use software installed directly on the **HOST** PC, most activities will use VMs in the Hyper-V environment. For some activities, your instructor may ask you to adjust the resources allocated to each VM. You must do this before booting the VM.

a) Open **Hyper-V Manager** 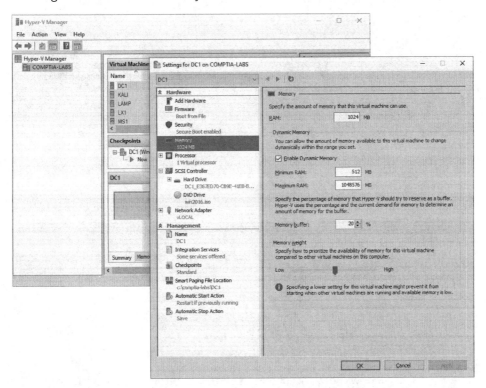 and then right-click the **DC1** VM and select **Settings**.

b) Select **Memory**.
   In some activities, you may increase or decrease the amount of RAM allocated to a VM depending on the **HOST** resources, the number of VMs that the activity requires, and the usage of each VM in the activity.

Adjusting memory allocated to a VM. (Screenshot used with permission from Microsoft.)

c) Select **Network Adapter**.
   In some activities, you will change the virtual switch that an adapter uses. As you can see, this Windows VM is connected to the **vLOCAL** switch. Some VMs are configured with more than one adapter. You will be learning about the topology of the switches during the activities.

d) Expand **Network Adapter** and then select **Advanced Features**.
   This page shows you the adapter MAC address, which you may need to verify for some activities. In some activities, you may need to check the **Enable MAC address spoofing** check box to allow pen testing tools to work properly.

   You may also need to change the **Mirroring mode** setting between **None**, **Source**, and **Destination**. Mirroring mode allows another VM to sniff the unicast packets addressed to a remote interface (like a spanned port on a hardware switch).

e) Select **Add Hardware**.
   If you are asked to add an extra network adapter, this is the menu to use. Most VMs will work with the option **Network Adapter**. In some cases, though, you may be asked to select **Legacy Network Adapter**.

f) Select **Cancel**.

The VM has one or more checkpoints. These are used to reset the VM to its starting conditions. Some activities may prompt you to create a checkpoint. Unless instructed otherwise, apply the **Initial Config** checkpoint when starting an activity.

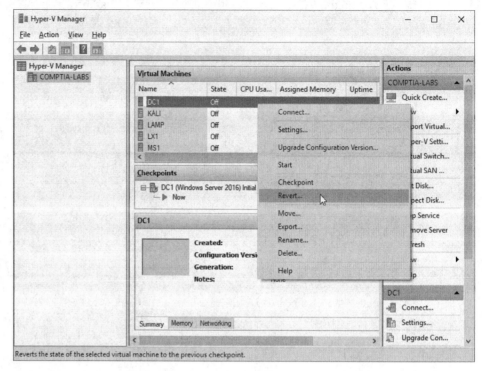

Reverting to a checkpoint. (Screenshot used with permission from Microsoft.)

The Windows network contains a domain controller and member server both running Windows Server 2016.

- **DC1** is configured as the network's domain controller (DC). Normally, the DC role should not be combined with other roles, but to minimize the number of VMs you have to run, this machine is also configured as a DNS server and CA (Certificate Authority) server. This VM is configured with a static IP address (10.1.0.1).

- **MS1** is configured as a member server for running applications. It runs a DHCP service to perform automatic IP addressing for clients connecting to the network. It also has the IIS web server and the email server hMail installed. This VM is also configured with a static IP address (10.1.0.2).

The Windows network also contains two workstation VMs running Windows 10 (**PC1**) and Windows 7 (**PC2**). Both of these VMs use the DHCP server on **MS1** for automatic address configuration (in the range 10.1.0.100 to 10.1.0.110).

 Note: *You will usually use the username **515support\Administrator** or the local account **Admin** to log on to the Windows PCs. Each user account uses the password **Pa$$w0rd** (awful security practice, but it makes the activities simpler for you to complete).*

2. Start the **KALI** VM and navigate the desktop environment.

The **KALI** VM is running the Kali pen testing/forensics Linux distribution, created and maintained by Offensive Security (*kali.org*). You will be using this VM for some security posture assessment and pen testing activities. Kali is based on the Debian Linux distribution with the GNOME desktop environment.

a) Right-click the **KALI** VM and select **Connect**. In the connection window, select the **Start** button. Log on with the username **root** and the password **Pa$$w0rd**

Note: *If you leave Kali, the screen will lock. To restore the screen, you must drag the privacy shader up, rather than just select it.*

b) Take a few moments to familiarize yourself with the desktop. Some key points to note are:

- The icon bar on the left (called the **Dash**) contains shortcuts to some of the applications, notably Terminal, Firefox (web browser), Thunderbird (email client), File Browser, and Wireshark.
- The cable icon in the top panel allows you to change network settings using the Network Manager application.
- The power icon allows you to reboot and shut down the VM.

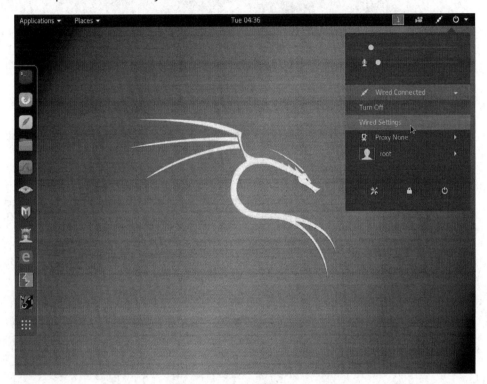

Gnome desktop in the KALI VM (kali.org). Use the Dash on the left to open applications and the menu bar to configure settings such as the network interface. (Screenshot courtesy of Offensive Security.)

c) Right-click the desktop and select **Open Terminal**. Run `ip a` to check the network adapter configuration.

 Note: *Remember that the Linux command-line is case-sensitive.*

eth0 does not have an IPv4 (inet) address. The adapter is configured to use DHCP, but no DHCP server is currently available.

d) Select the **Action** menu in the connection window. Select **Revert** and then confirm with **Revert**.

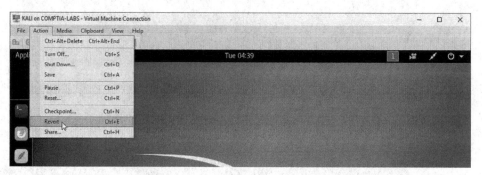

The VM Connection window menu. Some settings can be modified while the VM is running, and you can control the VM's state by using the Action menu. (Screenshot used with permission from Offensive Security.)

In most activities, you will be reverting the VMs using this process.

e) Close the connection window.

3. In the activities, you will use various network appliance VMs to implement routing and security functions. Identify the following VMs in the Hyper-V Manager console:

- **RTx** VMs—These VMs are running the VyOS distribution (*vyos.io*) and are used to route traffic between the different subnets configured on the various virtual switches. You will be discovering more about the network topology in later activities, so nothing further will be explained here.

- **PFSENSE**—This is a security appliance created by Netgate (*pfsense.org*) from the OpenBSD version of UNIX. pfSense is operated using a web GUI (**http://10.1.0.254**). The username is **admin** and the password is **Pa$$w0rd**.

- **SECONION**—Security Onion (*securityonion.net*) is a network security monitoring (NSM) tool. It provides various GUI and web interfaces to its intrusion detection and incident monitoring tools. The username is **administrator** and the password is **Pa$$w0rd**.

VyOS uses a different command prompt, designed to replicate the command-line interface of a router or switch appliance.

a) Right-click the **RT1-LOCAL** VM, and select **Start** to boot the VM. Double-click the **RT1-LOCAL** VM to open its console window.
When the VM has booted, a **vyos login** prompt will be displayed.

b) Type **vyos** and press **Enter**.

 Note: Remember that all commands in VyOS are case-sensitive.

c) Type **Pa$$w0rd** and press **Enter**.

d) After logging on, type **show configuration** and press **Enter**.
The report shows the interfaces that have been configured, as well as the account and interface used for console access.

e) Navigate through the report:

- Use the **Up Arrow** or **Down Arrow** keys to move line-by-line.
- Use **Spacebar** to go one page forward.
- Press **b** to go back one page.
- Press **q** to quit scrolling output.

 *Note: In VyOS and Ubuntu, use **Shift+Page Up** and **Shift+Page Down** to scroll through previous output.*

f) Type **s** then press **Tab**. Type **h** and press **Tab** and then press **Tab** again.

Tab completion will select the appropriate command if what you have typed could only end in the rest of the command, or it displays a list of possible commands or parameters if not.

g) Press **q** to exit the command list. Type **int** then press **Tab** and then press **Enter** to view a status report for the configured interfaces.
If you have clicked in the window, there will be a **To release your mouse pointer press Ctrl+Alt+Left Arrow** message in the status bar. This type of VM lacks the Hyper-V integration components to manage the mouse cursor, so you must use this key combination if you cannot click outside the VM connection window.

h) Type **poweroff** (or use **Tab** completion) and press **Enter**. Type **y** then **Enter** to confirm.

i) Close the VM's connection window.

4. Observe the two Linux servers that can be operated at a Linux command line:
   - **LAMP** is built on the Ubuntu Server distribution (*ubuntu.com*) and runs the familiar Linux, Apache, MySQL, and PHP functions of a web server. **LAMP** is also installed with email and DNS servers. As a server distribution, this VM has no GUI shell. The username is **lamp** and the password is **Pa$$w0rd**.
   - **LX1** is a CentOS Linux distribution that has been installed with intentionally vulnerable web services. The username is **centos** and the password is **Pa$$w0rd**.

   a) Double-click the **LAMP** VM to open its console and select the **Start** button to boot it. When the VM has booted, a **lamp login** prompt will be displayed.

   b) Type **lamp** and press **Enter**.

    Note: Remember that all commands in Linux are case-sensitive.

    *Note: If you start the **LAMP** VM and then only log on to it later, you might find that the logon prompt has disappeared. Just type the username **lamp** then press **Enter** and the password prompt will be shown.*

   c) Type **Pa$$w0rd** and press **Enter**.
   To run system-level commands in this distribution of Linux, you have to precede them with the `sudo` command to obtain elevated (root) privileges. Restarting the network adapter is an example of a system-level command.

   d) Type the following command and then press **Enter**:

   ```
   sudo ifconfig eth0 down && sudo ifconfig eth0 up
   ```

   e) Type **Pa$$w0rd** and press **Enter**.

    Note: You do not have to enter the password every time you use `sudo`. The password gets cached for a few minutes.

   f) Run the following command to shut down the VM:

   ```
   shutdown -h now
   ```

   g) Close the LAMP connection window.
   In the remainder of the activities, you will not be instructed to close the console windows. Keep them open or closed between activities to suit your preference.

5. Discard changes made to the VMs in this activity.
   a) In the **Hyper-V Manager** console, right-click the **DC1** VM icon and select **Revert**. If prompted, select **Revert** again to confirm.
   If you have booted any of the other VMs to inspect them, revert them back to their initial configuration now. In the **Hyper-V Manager** console, each VM should be listed as **Off**.

Note: *If you make a mistake with a revert or shut down operation, you can restore a snapshot by selecting the VM icon, then in the* **Checkpoints** *pane, right-click the* **Initial Config** *checkpoint and select* **Apply.**

Activity 2-5
Configuring Ethernet Networking

BEFORE YOU BEGIN

Start the VMs used in this activity in the following order, adjusting the memory allocation first if necessary, and waiting at the ellipsis for the previous VMs to finish booting before starting the next group. You do not need to connect to a VM until prompted to do so in the activity steps.

1. **DC1** (1024—2048 MB)
2. ...

Start the following VMs only when prompted during the activity steps.

1. **RT1-LOCAL** (256 MB)
2. **MS1** (1024—2048 MB)
3. **PC1** (1024—2048 MB)

 Note: *If you can allocate more than the minimum amounts of RAM, prioritize **DC1**.*

SCENARIO

In this activity, you will investigate the way hosts connect to a network and the address properties of network adapters. You will also use packet capture tools to analyze network traffic. This activity is designed to test your understanding of and ability to apply content examples in the following CompTIA Network+ objectives:

- 1.3 Explain the concepts and characteristics of routing and switching.
- 5.2 Given a scenario, use the appropriate tool.

---

1. Use **Ethernet Properties** and **Device Manager** to discover what properties and configurable settings the virtual network adapter has.

   a) In the **Hyper-V Manager** console on the **HOST**, double-click the **DC1** VM icon to open a console window.

   b) When the **DC1** VM has booted, sign in with the username ***Administrator*** and the password ***Pa$$w0rd***
   At logon, **Server Manager** will start. Wait for this to initialize before proceeding.

   c) In **Server Manager**, select the **Local Server** node from the list on the left-hand side. In the **Properties** pane, select the **10.1.0.1, IPv6 enabled** link next to **Ethernet**. This opens the **Network Connections** applet, listing the connections configured on the local machine. In this case, there is a single connection named **Ethernet**.

   d) Right-click the **Ethernet** connection and select **Properties**.
   This dialog box lists the protocols, services, and clients available to use with this connection. Checked items are bound (or active). These protocols and services run at the Network layer of the OSI model or higher. At the moment, you are more interested in the Physical and Data Link layer properties of the connection.

   e) Select the **Configure** button.
   This displays a properties dialog box for the adapter that makes the connection.

Note: *You can also access this dialog box via* **Device Manager**.

Although the adapter is a virtual one (implemented entirely as software), you can still consider its properties as working at the Physical and Data Link layers, in OSI terms.

f)   Select the **Driver** tab and record the following information. (You will need to use the **Driver Details** button too.)

* Provider: _____
* Date: _____
* Version: _____
* File path: _____

Driver information is often required when you are troubleshooting a faulty adapter.

Driver details for the Hyper-V virtual NIC. (Screenshot used with permission from Microsoft.)

g) Select the **Advanced** tab. Take a few moments to observe the different parameters that can be configured, then select the **Network Address** property.

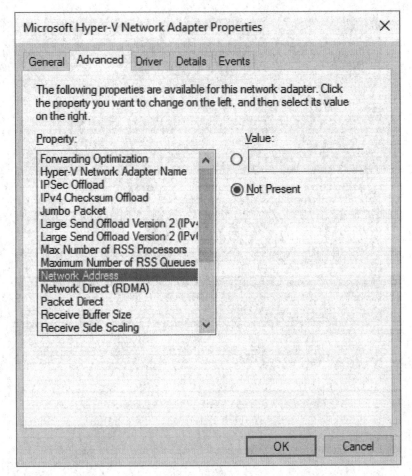

Adapter properties for the Hyper-V virtual NIC. (Screenshot used with permission from Microsoft.)

While it is only rarely used, this parameter allows you to define a locally administered hardware or MAC address, rather than using the MAC address burned into the physical adapter. Again, even though this is a virtual NIC, it follows the same rules for MAC addressing as any other interface. The OUI is Microsoft and the host part is generated by Hyper-V.

h) Optionally, make some notes about the properties you can set here. You will be comparing these to a real network adapter driver later.

i) Select the **Cancel** button.

2. Use command line tools to investigate the adapter properties.

a) On the **DC1** VM's connection window, from the menu, select **File→Settings**. Expand the **Network Adapter** node and select **Advanced Features**.

b) Record the value listed under MAC address: _____

c) Select **Cancel**.

d) Click back in the VM, then select the **Start** button, type *cmd*, and press **Ctrl+Shift +Enter** to load the **Command Prompt** as administrator. Confirm the UAC prompt by selecting **Yes**.

e) Type the following command and press **Enter**.

```
ipconfig /all
```

```
Microsoft Windows [Version 10.0.14393]
(c) 2016 Microsoft Corporation. All rights reserved.

C:\Users\Administrator>ipconfig /all

Windows IP Configuration

   Host Name . . . . . . . . . . . . : DC1
   Primary Dns Suffix  . . . . . . . : corp.515support.com
   Node Type . . . . . . . . . . . . : Hybrid
   IP Routing Enabled. . . . . . . . : No
   WINS Proxy Enabled. . . . . . . . : No
   DNS Suffix Search List. . . . . . : corp.515support.com

Ethernet adapter Ethernet:

   Connection-specific DNS Suffix  . : corp.515support.com
   Description . . . . . . . . . . . : Microsoft Hyper-V Network Adapter
   Physical Address. . . . . . . . . : 00-15-5D-01-CA-75
   DHCP Enabled. . . . . . . . . . . : No
   Autoconfiguration Enabled . . . . : Yes
   IPv6 Address. . . . . . . . . . . : fdab:cdef:0:1::1(Preferred)
   Link-local IPv6 Address . . . . . : fe80::4c5b:e7b2:c568:8ccd%4(Preferred)
   IPv4 Address. . . . . . . . . . . : 10.1.0.1(Preferred)
   Subnet Mask . . . . . . . . . . . : 255.255.255.0
   Default Gateway . . . . . . . . . : fdab:cdef:0:1::ffff
                                       10.1.0.254
   DHCPv6 IAID . . . . . . . . . . . : 50337117
   DHCPv6 Client DUID. . . . . . . . : 00-01-00-01-23-CA-27-9D-00-15-5D-01-CA-75
   DNS Servers . . . . . . . . . . . : fdab:cdef:0:1::1
                                       10.1.0.1
   NetBIOS over Tcpip. . . . . . . . : Enabled
```

Output from the ipconfig command. (Screenshot used with permission from Microsoft.)

f) Check the **Physical Address** assigned to the **Ethernet** adapter.
It should be the same value as you recorded earlier.

g) Leave the command prompt open.

Note: *The MAC address is referred to in many different ways. The use of* **Network Address** *in the adapter properties is the most confusing. With most driver software, this parameter is more typically labeled* **Locally Administered Address***.*

3. Examine the properties of a real network controller.

a) On the **HOST** PC, right-click the **Start** button and select **Device Manager**. Expand **Network Adapters**, then double-click the icon representing your computer's physical adapter or controller.

b) Select the **Advanced** tab. Look for a link speed and duplex configuration option. What is it set to?

This option is not implemented on the Hyper-V virtual adapter. On a modern network, this should almost always be set to **Auto Negotiation**. This would only be set to a lower speed or half-duplex option if using a hub or legacy switch model.

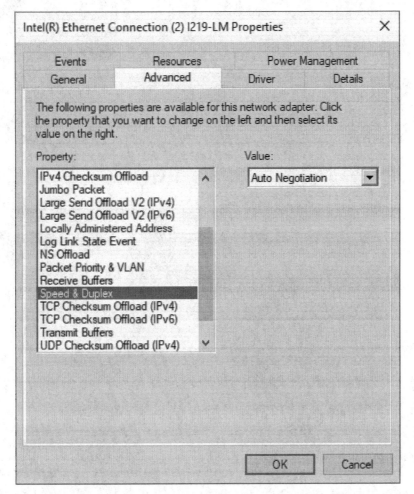

Adapter properties for a hardware NIC (Intel I219-LM). This NIC has no remote wake capability. (Screenshot used with permission from Microsoft.)

c) Does the installed adapter support any Wake On LAN (WoL) features?

Your answer will depend on the physical NIC installed in your **HOST** computer.

d) Select **Cancel** to close the dialog box.

e) Close **Device Manager**.

4. Investigate ARP and the use of the Wireshark protocol analyzer to capture and inspect network traffic. The ARP cache table contains entries for hosts that have been contacted recently (the cache is cleared every few minutes). This reduces the frequency of ARP broadcasts.

The MAC/hardware/physical address is used to identify and communicate with other nodes on the same local network at the Data Link layer. This sort of local addressing is not configured directly, however. The local address is used under the hood in conjunction with IP addressing. The Address Resolution Protocol (ARP) performs the task of mapping between an IPv4 address and an adapter's local (MAC) address.

In the activities, the following VMs are configured to connect to the vLOCAL virtual switch. In Hyper-V, you don't have to do anything to start the switches. They are always running in the background.

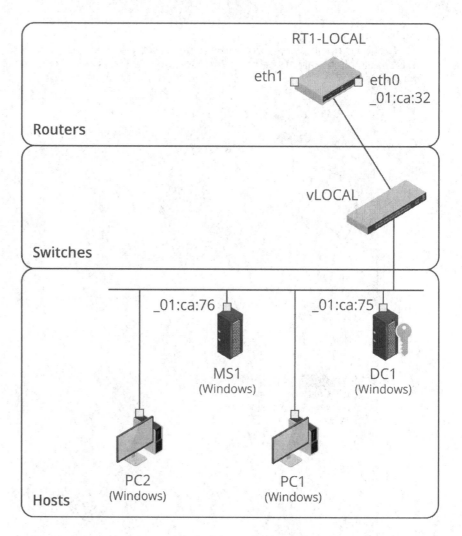

Physical topology of the devices connected to the vLOCAL virtual switch. The square icon in the middle represents the switch, while the round icon at the top is the router.

a) On the **DC1** VM, in the command prompt, run the following command:

```
arp -a
```

```
C:\Users\Administrator>arp -a

Interface: 10.1.0.1 --- 0x4
  Internet Address      Physical Address      Type
  10.1.0.255            ff-ff-ff-ff-ff-ff     static
  224.0.0.22            01-00-5e-00-00-16     static
  224.0.0.252          01-00-5e-00-00-fc     static
  239.255.255.250      01-00-5e-7f-ff-fa     static

C:\Users\Administrator>_
```

Output from the arp command. (Screenshot used with permission from Microsoft.)

This displays the ARP cache table. The only entries should be for the network broadcast address (10.1.0.255) used to address every machine on the local network and multicast addresses (starting 224 and 239) used by Windows' network discovery protocols.

Remember that the virtual switches used by the VMs are isolated from the **HOST**. There are no other VMs on this network yet, so it is not surprising that there are no host addresses.

b) Leave the command prompt open.

c) On the **DC1** VM, double-click the **Wireshark** icon on the desktop.

Wireshark is an example of packet capture (or sniffing) software. It allows you to view the contents of packets being sent to and from the local machine (and, in some circumstances, other machines).

> **Note:** *In fact, Wireshark is the protocol analyzer part. A software library and driver called **winpcap** does the actual packet sniffing. It is common usage to describe Wireshark as a sniffer, though.*

When it is first loaded, Wireshark displays a text box to enter a capture filter and a list of local connections.

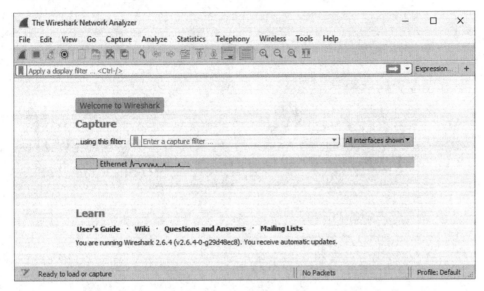

Wireshark capture options. (Screenshot courtesy of Wireshark.)

d) Select the **Enter a capture filter** box and type ***arp or ip***
This filters the capture to ARP and IPv4 traffic.

e) Select the **Start Capture** button.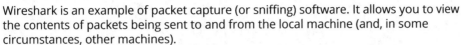
If you observe the window for a minute or two, there should not be much traffic. You may see ARP broadcasts trying to locate the interface with IP address 10.1.0.254. Note that the capture filter is listed in the title bar.

f) Switch to the **Hyper-V Manager** console on the **HOST**, and start the **RT1-LOCAL** VM. (You do not need to open a console window.)

g) Switch back to the **DC1** VM console, and watch the packet capture window while the **RT1-LOCAL** VM boots. Maximize the window and adjust the size of the panes so that you can view the frames clearly.
You will see that this generates some ARP requests, plus one reply from 10.1.0.254 (**RT1-LOCAL**) to 10.1.0.1 (**DC1**) confirming its IP address.

h) Switch to the **Hyper-V Manager** console on the **HOST**, and start the **MS1** VM. (You do not need to open a console window.)

i) Switch back to the **DC1** VM console, and watch the packet capture window while the **MS1** VM boots.
Booting this VM creates considerably more network activity than the **RT1-LOCAL** VM.

j) If necessary, select the **AutoScroll** button to turn off autoscrolling, and then scroll to the top of the capture.
One of the most useful options in packet analysis software is filtering by different criteria. You have already applied a **capture** filter to only record packets that match the filter in the first place. You can also apply a **display** filter to the captured data. You can construct complex filter criteria by building an expression or by right-clicking in the frame analysis pane.

k) Select the first ARP frame in the top pane and in the middle pane, right-click **Address Resolution Protocol**, and select **Apply as Filter→Selected**.

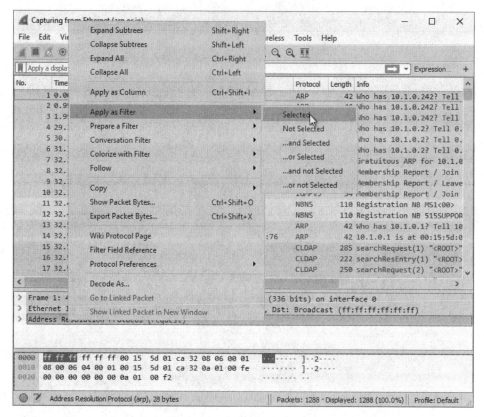

Applying a filter. (Screenshot courtesy of Wireshark.)

The frames panel now shows only ARP traffic. The filter expression **arp** has been added to the filter panel, and the panel is highlighted green to show that a filter is in effect.

5. Examine the results of the ARP packets generated when **MS1** boots.

   a) Observe that **MS1** broadcasts three ARP requests for its own IP address (10.1.0.2); there is no reply to these broadcasts.

    *Note: If another machine did own 10.1.0.2, **MS1** would detect a duplicate IP address, configure an APIPA range address, and prompt the user to change the configuration.*

   b) Observe that **MS1** then broadcasts a gratuitous ARP, which tells other machines on the network that it now owns 10.1.0.2.
   This claim is accepted by the other VMs without any sort of authentication.

   c) Observe that **MS1** broadcasts several requests to locate the MAC addresses of 10.1.0.1 and 10.1.0.254.
   It does this because 10.1.0.1 is configured as its DNS resolver and 10.1.0.254 is its default gateway. If you look through the frames, you should see responses to these requests.

d)   Look at the source and destination MAC addresses used in these frames, and identify which IP owns which MAC address:

- 10.1.0.1: _____
- 10.1.0.2: _____
- 10.1.0.254: _____

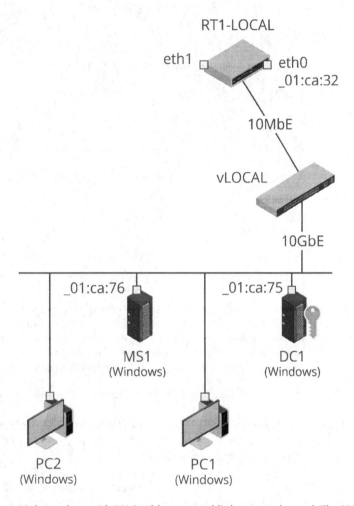

vLOCAL switch Data Link topology with MAC addresses and link type and speed. The MAC addresses you see for the Windows VMs will vary. (Image © 123RF.com.)

The link speed between the Windows VMs and the switch is 10GbE, and between the switch and the VyOS VM it is 10MbE. These are the link speeds that the virtual NICs negotiate with the virtual switch. Remember that in this virtualized environment, no physical network hardware is involved and no frame transfer is occurring. "Network activity" just involves the **HOST** PC moving data from one memory buffer to another, but the same rules and protocols have to be applied and configured.

e)   What is the destination MAC address of broadcast frames?
The ARP requests are broadcast using the destination address
`ff:ff:ff:ff:ff:ff`.

f)   In **Wireshark**, select an ARP frame in the top pane and expand the **Ethernet II** analysis in the second pane.

Observe that the Ethernet frame (Data Link layer) simply contains source and destination MAC addresses and a protocol type field that identifies ARP as the data in the payload. Wireshark decodes the OUI, and you can expand the MAC fields to decode the multicast/broadcast bit and locally administered bit.

g) Select the **Type: ARP (0x0806)** field.

Note the selection in the packet bytes pane at the bottom. If you look before that, you will see the hex representations of the destination and source addresses.

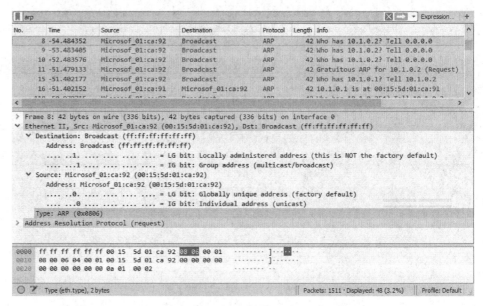

Identifying the location of parts of the frame within the packet bytes pane. (Screenshot courtesy of Wireshark.)

h) Expand the **Address Resolution Protocol** frame analysis.

The ARP header contains sender and target MAC and IP addresses. There is also a field for the ARP type (request or reply) and an indicator from Wireshark that the request **Is Gratuitous** (you need to select the gratuitous ARP frame to see this). ARP is a very simple protocol. IP and higher-level packets often contain many more fields.

i) In the display filter bar, select the **Clear** button.

6. The VMs you have started so far all use static IP addressing. Start another packet capture on **DC1**, then start **PC1** and observe the network traffic generated by the address autoconfiguration process.

a) On **DC1**, in Wireshark, select the **Restart** button to start another packet capture with the current options set. When you are prompted to save the packet capture, select **Continue without Saving**.

b) Switch to the **Hyper-V Manager** console on the **HOST**, and start the **PC1** VM. (You do not need to open a console window.)

c) Switch back to the **DC1** VM console, and watch the packet capture window while the **PC1** VM boots.

d) What do you notice that is different about the packet capture at the start?

PC1 uses DHCP so it broadcasts to discover a server that can allocate it an address. **MS1** (10.1.0.2) responds to this request. This precedes the ARP traffic, which is similar to what you observed before.

e) Stop the packet capture by selecting the **Stop Capture** button.

f) Select the **Close** button in the Wireshark window. At the **Unsaved packets** prompt, select **Quit without Saving**.

g) In the command prompt, run the following command:

```
arp -a
```

The ARP cache table should contain a few more entries now.

```
Internet Address      Physical Address    Type
10.1.0.2              00-15-5d-01-ca-76   dynamic
10.1.0.101            00-15-5d-01-ca-77   dynamic
10.1.0.254            00-15-5d-01-ca-32   dynamic
10.1.0.255            ff-ff-ff-ff-ff-ff   static
224.0.0.22            01-00-5e-00-00-16   static
224.0.0.252           01-00-5e-00-00-fc   static
239.255.255.250       01-00-5e-7f-ff-fa   static

C:\Users\Administrator>
```

As more machines join the network, the ARP cache is updated with more entries. (Screenshot used with permission from Microsoft.)

h) Leave the command prompt open.

7. Run `tcpdump` from the Linux-based **VyOS** VM.

While a graphical tool such as Wireshark is easy to use, sometimes it is necessary to use a command line packet capture utility, such as `tcpdump`.

a) Switch to the **Hyper-V Manager** console on the **HOST** and double-click the **RT1-LOCAL** VM icon to open a connection window.

b) Log on with the username **vyos** and password **Pa$$w0rd**

To run `tcpdump`, you need to use the **root** account.

c) Run the following command and confirm with **Pa$$w0rd** when prompted:

```
su -
```

d) Using the **root** account, run the following command to show the command syntax:

```
tcpdump -h
```

The command output also lists the versions of tcpdump and libpcap.

e) To display more extensive help, run the following command:

```
man tcpdump
```

f) Press **Page Down** to browse the help pages and then press **q** if you want to quit viewing the help file.

g) Run the following command (remember that the Linux command prompt is case-sensitive):

```
tcpdump -D
```

This command lists the interfaces configured on the local host. **eth0** is the one connected to the vLOCAL switch.

h) To start a packet capture, run the following command:

```
tcpdump -i eth0 'ip'
```

i) After seeing some frames (you might need to be patient or initiate some network activity on the Windows VMs), press **Ctrl+C** to halt.

As you can see, the output from tcpdump is not that easy to interpret. You might want to use the tool as part of a script to log network traffic to a file for analysis later, though.

j) To write a packet capture to a file, run the following command:

```
tcpdump -i eth0 -w icmp.pcap 'icmp'
```

k) Press **Ctrl+Alt+Left Arrow** to release the mouse cursor from the **RT1-LOCAL** VM. Switch to the **DC1** VM.

l) Run the following commands:

```
ping 10.1.0.254
```

```
ping 10.1.0.1
```

```
ping 10.1.0.2

ping 10.1.0.10
```

m) Switch back to the **RT1-LOCAL** VM and press **Ctrl+C**.

n) To open the capture file, run the following command:

```
tcpdump -enr icmp.pcap
```

The **-e** switch shows the Ethernet header and the **-n** switch shows IP addresses, rather than trying to resolve host names. If necessary, you can press **Shift+Page Up** and **Shift+Page Down** to scroll.

Only the pings sent to 10.1.0.254 are captured with the replies.

8. If you want to capture all the traffic for a particular link, you have to configure a way to copy all the unicast traffic to the sniffer interface. On a hardware switch, this would be accomplished using a switched port analyzer (SPAN) port. You will simulate this by using a feature of Hyper-V's virtual switch.

a) From the **RT1-LOCAL** VM's connection window menu, select **File→Settings**.

b) Expand the **eth0** node, and select the **Advanced Features** node.

c) From the **Mirroring mode** box, select **Destination**. Select **OK**.

d) From the **DC1** VM connection window menu, select **File→Settings**.

e) Expand the **Network Adapter (vLOCAL)** node, and select its **Advanced Features** node.

f) From the **Mirroring mode** box, select **Source**. Select **OK**.

g) On the **HOST**, in Hyper-V Manager, right-click the **MS1** VM and select **Settings**.

h) Expand the **Network Adapter (vLOCAL)** node, and select its **Advanced Features** node.

i) From the **Mirroring mode** box, select **Source**. Select **OK**.

9. With port mirroring configured, run another packet capture, and test with the same ping commands as before.

a) Switch back to the **RT1-LOCAL** VM and run the following command:

```
tcpdump -i eth0 -w span.pcap
```

b) Switch to the **DC1** VM. Run the following commands:

```
ping 10.1.0.254

ping 10.1.0.1

ping 10.1.0.2

ping 10.1.0.10
```

c) Switch back to the **RT1-LOCAL** VM and press **Ctrl+C**.

d) Run the following command to open the capture file with a display filter:

```
tcpdump -nr span.pcap 'icmp'
```

You should now see the ping requests and replies between **DC1** (10.1.0.1) and **MS1** (10.1.0.2).

e) Run the following command:

```
tcpdump -eni eth0 'arp or icmp'
```

f) Switch to the **DC1** VM. Run the following commands:

```
arp -d

ping 172.16.0.254
```

```
arp -a
```

g) Observe the entries in the ARP cache, and then switch to the **RT1-LOCAL** VM. Press **Ctrl+C** to halt the packet capture. Scroll through the output to follow the sequence of ARP messaging and pings.

```
08:48:04.580264 00:15:5d:01:ca:75 > ff:ff:ff:ff:ff:ff, ethertype ARP (0x0806), l
ength 42: Request who-has 10.1.0.254 tell 10.1.0.1, length 28
08:48:04.580314 00:15:5d:01:ca:32 > 00:15:5d:01:ca:75, ethertype ARP (0x0806), l
ength 42: Reply 10.1.0.254 is-at 00:15:5d:01:ca:32, length 28
08:48:04.580902 00:15:5d:01:ca:75 > 00:15:5d:01:ca:32, ethertype IPv4 (0x0800),
length 74: 10.1.0.1 > 172.16.0.254: ICMP echo request, id 1, seq 65, length 40
08:48:04.580922 00:15:5d:01:ca:32 > 00:15:5d:01:ca:75, ethertype IPv4 (0x0800),
length 74: 172.16.0.254 > 10.1.0.1: ICMP echo reply, id 1, seq 65, length 40
08:48:05.593374 00:15:5d:01:ca:75 > 00:15:5d:01:ca:32, ethertype IPv4 (0x0800),
length 74: 10.1.0.1 > 172.16.0.254: ICMP echo request, id 1, seq 66, length 40
08:48:05.593428 00:15:5d:01:ca:32 > 00:15:5d:01:ca:75, ethertype IPv4 (0x0800),
length 74: 172.16.0.254 > 10.1.0.1: ICMP echo reply, id 1, seq 66, length 40
08:48:06.606409 00:15:5d:01:ca:75 > 00:15:5d:01:ca:32, ethertype IPv4 (0x0800),
length 74: 10.1.0.1 > 172.16.0.254: ICMP echo request, id 1, seq 67, length 40
08:48:06.606447 00:15:5d:01:ca:32 > 00:15:5d:01:ca:75, ethertype IPv4 (0x0800),
length 74: 172.16.0.254 > 10.1.0.1: ICMP echo reply, id 1, seq 67, length 40
08:48:07.617280 00:15:5d:01:ca:75 > 00:15:5d:01:ca:32, ethertype IPv4 (0x0800),
length 74: 10.1.0.1 > 172.16.0.254: ICMP echo request, id 1, seq 68, length 40
08:48:07.617306 00:15:5d:01:ca:32 > 00:15:5d:01:ca:75, ethertype IPv4 (0x0800),
length 74: 172.16.0.254 > 10.1.0.1: ICMP echo reply, id 1, seq 68, length 40
08:48:09.589781 00:15:5d:01:ca:32 > 00:15:5d:01:ca:75, ethertype ARP (0x0806), l
ength 42: Request who-has 10.1.0.1 tell 10.1.0.254, length 28
08:48:09.590377 00:15:5d:01:ca:75 > 00:15:5d:01:ca:32, ethertype ARP (0x0806), l
ength 42: Reply 10.1.0.1 is-at 00:15:5d:01:ca:75, length 28
^C
```

Viewing remote address resolution in a packet capture. The ICMP request directed at 172.16.0.254 is sent to MAC address _01:ca:32 (the eth0 interface of RT1-LOCAL).

The IP address 172.16.0.254 is not local to this network. Consequently, **DC1** does not attempt to use ARP messaging to locate it. Instead, it uses ARP messaging to discover the MAC address of its default gateway (10.1.0.254). There is no mapping in its cache because you cleared the cache with **arp -d**. It then sends the ping request to the **RT1-LOCAL** VM, which performs the necessary forwarding of requests and replies. In this case, it is a simple enough task as 172.16.0.254 is the address configured for its other interface, eth1.

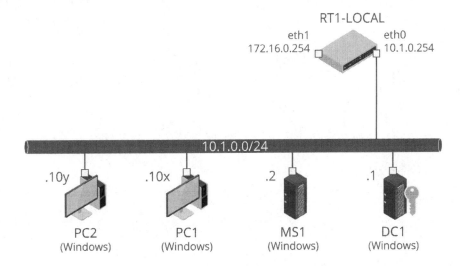

Logical (layer 3/IP) topology of the local network. (Image © 123RF.com.)

10. Discard changes made to the VMs in this activity.

   a) Switch to the **Hyper-V Manager** window.

b)   Select one of the running VMs. From the **Action** menu, select **Revert** then select the **Revert** button (or use the right-click menu in the **Hyper-V Manager** console). Select another VM and revert it, continuing to revert all the VMs to their saved checkpoints.

Summary

In this lesson, you learned about the characteristics of transmission media and Data Link protocols, with a special focus on Ethernet. You also learned about the link-local properties of network interfaces and how to capture network traffic.

- Transmission media and Physical and Data Link layer technologies can be distinguished by several factors, including modulation scheme, bandwidth, media type, and access control method.
- Most LAN products are based on IEEE 802.3 (Ethernet).
- Ethernet includes specifications for a range of speeds (10/100 Mbps and 1/10 Gbps) using different media (principally copper twisted pair and fiber optic).
- Addressing schemes apply at layer 2 (MAC) and layer 3 (Network/IP). Layer 2 MAC addresses (48-bit) are mapped to layer 3 IPv4 addresses (32-bit) by ARP.
- Packet sniffers allow for the capture of frames sent to and received by a network node or over a network link.

Which types of transmission media do you have experience working with?

Which software tools have you found to be useful to capture and analyze network traffic?

 Practice Questions: *Additional practice questions are available on the course website.*

Lesson 3

Installing and Configuring Switched Networks

LESSON INTRODUCTION

Concepts such as network topologies and collision and broadcast domains are realized by network appliances such as hubs, bridges, and switches. Installing, configuring, and troubleshooting these devices will be a regular task for you during your career in network administration.

LESSON OBJECTIVES

In this lesson, you will:

- Install and configure hubs and bridges.
- Install and configure switches.
- Compare and contrast network topologies.
- Compare and contrast network types.

Topic A

Install and Configure Hubs and Bridges

 EXAM OBJECTIVES COVERED
2.2 Given a scenario, determine the appropriate placement of networking devices on a network and install/configure them.

Not all networks use the latest technologies. There are often good reasons for companies to keep old but functional devices in service. Apart from supporting these legacy devices, it is important for you to understand how they work, because this knowledge can inform your use of newer types of devices.

HUBS

Most Ethernet networks are implemented so that each node is wired to a central networking device, such as a hub, bridge, or switch. Hubs and bridges are no longer widely deployed as standalone appliances, as their role has been taken on by more advanced devices, such as Ethernet switches. Nevertheless, it is important to understand the basic functions they perform.

A **hub** is the central point of connection for 10BASE-T Ethernet and 100BASE-TX Fast Ethernet segments. Hubs act like a repeater (they are also known as **multiport repeaters**) so that every port receives transmissions sent from any other port. Every port is part of the same shared media access area, and consequently within the same **collision domain**. All communications are half-duplex, using the CSMA/CD protocol. The bandwidth of the network (10 Mbps or 100 Mbps) is shared between all nodes. Hubs work at the Physical layer of the OSI model only; they have no frame-processing logic.

A hub is internally wired with transmit (Tx) and receive (Rx) pairs for each port.

The hub connects the nodes on the network as follows:

1. The workstation node on the left sends a frame using its Tx pair.
2. The hub receives a weakened and distorted transmission at port 1 on its Tx pair.
3. The hub regenerates the transmission, performs a crossover, and floods the regenerated transmission out of all its other ports on the receive (Rx) pair.
4. The server and other workstation nodes receive the frame on their Rx pairs.

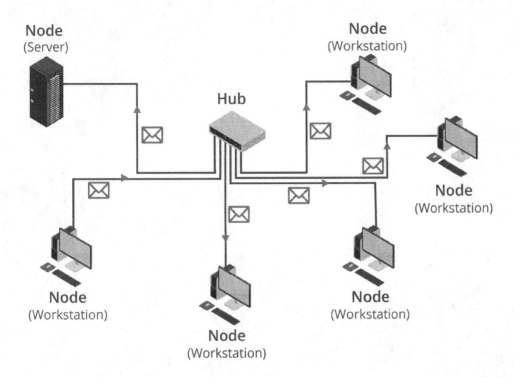

Using a hub to implement a physical star topology. (Image © 123RF.com.)

If a hub does not provide enough ports, two hubs can also be linked together by using a special cable type called a **crossover cable**.

This works as follows:

1. Computer A sends a transmission through its Tx pair.
2. Hub 1 receives a weakened and distorted transmission at port 1 on its Tx pair.
3. The hub regenerates the transmission, performs a crossover, and transmits the regenerated transmission out of all its other ports on the receive (Rx) pair. One of these ports is connected to hub 2 via a crossover cable.
4. Because hub 2 now receives the transmission on its Tx pair via the crossover cable, it regenerates the transmission, performs a crossover, and transmits it over all the other ports on the Rx pair.
5. Computer B receives the transmission from hub 2 on its Rx pair.

When hubs are connected like this, all the nodes remain with the same collision domain.

 Note: *Fast Ethernet is restricted to using two hubs within a single network, but this restriction does not apply to a switched network. Gigabit and 10GbE Ethernet require the use of switches.*

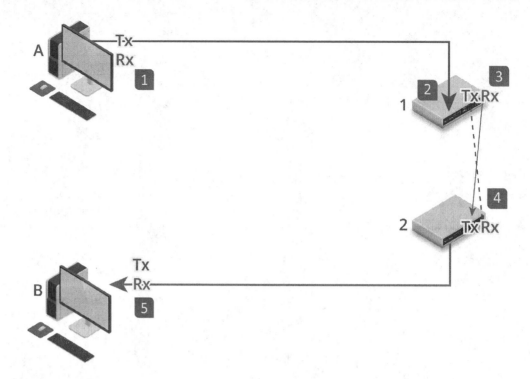

Crossover cable between cascading hubs. (Image © 123RF.com.)

There are no configuration options for a hub. You just connect the device to a power source and then connect the network cables for the hosts that are going to be part of the network segment served by the hub.

> **Note:** *The LAN ports on the SOHO wireless router/modems used for DLS and cable Internet access are quite likely to work as a hub. Some models may work as switches, though. Check the vendor documentation to be sure.*

BRIDGES

An Ethernet **bridge** provides communications between two or more segments. Like a hub or repeater, a bridge can overcome some distance limitations of the network media, but it can also be used to segment the network. A network might be divided into two or more segments to reduce the number of collisions caused by having too many nodes contending for access. Bridges work at the Data Link layer because they need to parse the MAC addresses within frames. Segments on different bridge ports are in separate **collision domains** but the same **broadcast domain**.

A bridge works as follows:

1. Computer A sends a transmission to computer D. The frame contains a source hardware address of M_A and a destination hardware address of M_D.
2. The bridge listens to all traffic on all attached segments and consequently receives the transmission at port 1.
3. The bridge reads the destination address in the frame and, using its MAC address table, determines the port to which the network card with hardware address M_D is attached. In this example, the bridge locates the hardware address M_D in its port:MAC address table and forwards the transmission out of port 2 only.

    An Ethernet bridge builds the MAC address table in memory. When the bridge is initialized, the bridging table is empty, but information is constantly added as the bridge listens to the connected segments. Entries are flushed out of the table after a period to ensure the information remains current.

4. If no record of the hardware address exists or the frame is a broadcast or multicast, then the bridge floods the frame to all segments except for the source segment (acting like a hub).

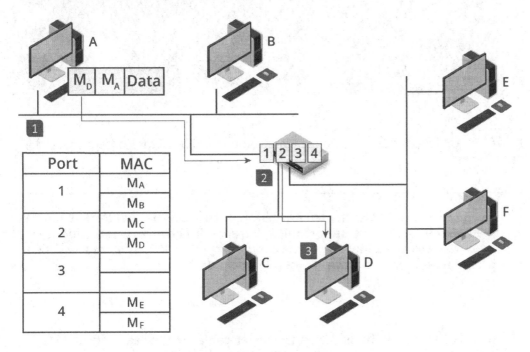

Port	MAC
1	M_A
1	M_B
2	M_C
2	M_D
3	
3	
4	M_E
4	M_F

Bridge operation. (Image © 123RF.com.)

Most bridges are only able to link segments using the same frame type (for example, Ethernet to Ethernet), but they can be used to link different segments with different cable types (such as coax and twisted pair).

Activity 3-1
Discussing Hubs and Bridges

SCENARIO

Answer the following questions to test your understanding of the content covered in this topic.

1. True or False? Devices can only transmit on an Ethernet network when the media is clear, and the opportunity to transmit becomes less frequent as more devices are added. Also, the probability of collisions increases. These problems can be overcome by installing a hub.

2. If you connect two hubs with a crossover cable, are nodes connected to either hub in the same collision domain?

3. True or False? A bridge does not forward broadcast or multicast traffic.

Topic B

Install and Configure Switches

EXAM OBJECTIVES COVERED
1.3 Explain the concepts and characteristics of routing and switching.
2.2 Given a scenario, determine the appropriate placement of networking devices on a network and install/configure them.
4.6 Explain common mitigation techniques and their purposes.

Switches are fundamental network connectivity devices, so you are certain to encounter them in the network environments that you support. There are many types of switches, however. Understanding the range of capabilities of these devices will prepare you to support a wide variety of network environments.

ETHERNET SWITCHES

Ethernet networks implemented with hubs rely on a contention-based technology for accessing the media. Nodes can transmit on the network only when the media is free. These opportunities become less frequent as more devices are added to the network and the probability of collisions increases.

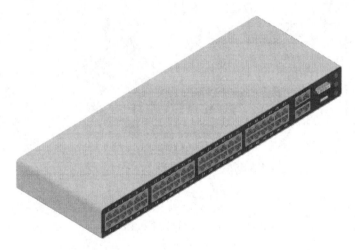

An example of a workgroup switch. (Image © 123RF.com.)

The problems created by contention can be overcome by moving from a *shared Ethernet* system to *switched Ethernet*. This move involves the replacement of hubs and bridges with **switches**. Switches have now almost completely replaced legacy devices such as hubs and bridges. Gigabit Ethernet and Ethernet 10GbE cannot be installed without using switches.

SWITCH FORWARDING DECISIONS

An Ethernet switch performs the same sort of function as a bridge, but in a more granular way and for many more ports than are supported by bridges. Each switch port is a separate collision domain. In effect, the switch establishes a point-to-point link between any two network nodes. This is referred to as **microsegmentation**. This works as follows:

1. Computer A transmits a frame intended for Computer B.
2. The switch receives the frame into a port buffer and reads the destination MAC address from the Ethernet frame. The port buffer holds frames until they can be processed. The switch can also perform error checking on the frame by using the CRC.
3. The switch uses its MAC address table to look up the port connected to the destination MAC address.
4. The switch uses its high-speed backplane to send the frame out on port 3 for computer B to receive (creating a temporary virtual circuit).
5. None of the other connected devices (such as computer C) see any activity on the network while this process takes place. Therefore, these other devices are able to transmit and receive at the same time.

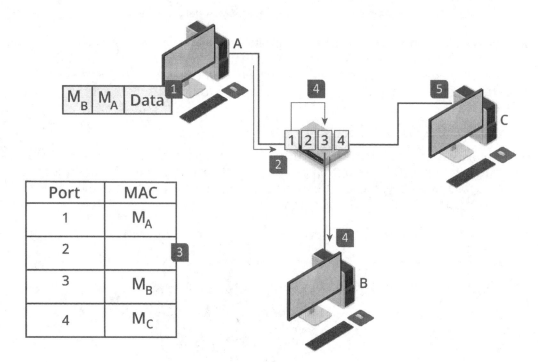

Switch operation. (Image © 123RF.com.)

Because each port is in a separate collision domain, collisions can occur only if the port is operating in half-duplex mode. This would only be the case if a legacy network card or a hub is attached to it. Even then, collisions affect only the microsegment between the port and the connected interface; they do not slow down the whole network. As with a bridge, though, traffic on all switch ports is in the same broadcast domain, unless the switch is configured to use virtual LANs (VLANs).

MAC ADDRESS TABLE

If a MAC address cannot be found in the **MAC address table**, then the switch acts like a hub and transmits the frame out of all the ports, except for the source port. This is referred to as **flooding**. The switch builds the MAC address table by analyzing incoming frames for the source MAC address. It can then add a MAC address entry for the port number. Entries remain in the MAC address table for a period before being flushed. This ensures problems are not encountered when network cards (MAC addresses) are changed. The address table is implemented as **content addressable memory (CAM)**, a special type of memory optimized for searching, rather than random access. Consequently, the MAC address table is often also referred to as the CAM table.

You can query the MAC address table of a switch to find the MAC address or addresses associated with a particular port using a command such as:

```
show mac address-table
```

```
NYACCESS1#show mac address-table dynamic
           Mac Address Table
-------------------------------------------------

Vlan    Mac Address       Type        Ports
----    -----------       --------    -----
   1    000a.8aa2.135e    DYNAMIC     Fa0/23
   1    08cc.683e.fd18    DYNAMIC     Fa0/23
   1    08cc.683e.fd40    DYNAMIC     Fa0/23
   1    18e7.285f.0c28    DYNAMIC     Fa0/24
   1    44ad.d916.2598    DYNAMIC     Fa0/24
   1    5006.04be.159d    DYNAMIC     Fa0/1
Total Mac Addresses for this criterion: 6
```

Displaying dynamic entries in the MAC address table of a Cisco switch. (Image © and Courtesy of Cisco Systems, Inc. Unauthorized use not permitted.)

 *Note: The MAC address table is **not** the same as an ARP table. A MAC address table maps known MAC addresses to interface ports on the switch. An ARP table is maintained by a layer 3 device to cache known MAC address to IP address mappings.*

ETHERNET SWITCH TYPES

Switches from different vendors come in a variety of ranges to support various sizes of networks. While a basic model might feature 12 to 48 ports and little scope for expansion, advanced switches support interconnections via high-speed backplanes and expandable capacity through plug-in modules plus power supply redundancy, management consoles, and interface converters for fiber optic connectivity.

The market is dominated by Cisco's Catalyst series (over 55% of sales), but other notable vendors include HP® Enterprise, Huawei, Juniper®, Arista, Linksys®, D-Link, NETGEAR®, and NEC.

Ethernet switches can be distinguished using the following general categories:

- **Unmanaged** versus **managed**—On a SOHO network, switches are more likely to be unmanaged, standalone units that can be added to the network and run without any configuration. The switch functionality might also be built into an Internet router/modem (though such devices may only have hub functionality for the LAN ports). On a corporate network, switches are most likely to be managed. This means the switch settings can be configured. If a managed switch is left unconfigured, it functions the same as an unmanaged switch does.
- **Stackable**—Switches that can be connected together and operate as a group. The switch stack can be managed as a single unit.
- **Modular** versus **fixed**—A fixed switch comes with a set number of ports that cannot be changed or upgraded. A modular switch can take plug-in cards, meaning they can be configured with different numbers and types of ports.
- **Desktop** versus **rack-mounted**—Simple unmanaged switches with 5 or 8 ports might be supplied as small freestanding units that can be placed on a desktop. Most larger switches are designed to be fitted to the standard-size racks that are used to hold networking equipment.

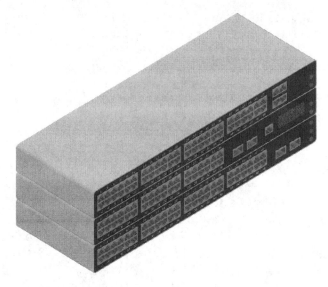

An example of a modular chassis that allows provisioning multiple access switches. (Image © 123RF.com.)

 Note: *There are many types of switches other than Ethernet switches (or "basic switches"). Some are used to implement WANs (ATM and SONET switching, for instance), and some are used to forward traffic at OSI layers 3 and above.*

SWITCH INTERFACE CONFIGURATION

Configuration of a managed switch can be performed either over a web interface or at some sort of command line. Once you have established a connection to the switch's management interface, you can configure settings for each of the switch port interfaces. These settings control the network link configured for each client device attaching to the switch.

```
FastEthernet1/0/1 is up, line protocol is up (connected)
  Hardware is Fast Ethernet, address is f41f.c253.7103 (bia f41f.c253.7103)
  MTU 1500 bytes, BW 100000 Kbit/sec, DLY 100 usec,
     reliability 255/255, txload 1/255, rxload 1/255
  Encapsulation ARPA, loopback not set
  Keepalive set (10 sec)
  Full-duplex, 100Mb/s, media type is 10/100BaseTX
  input flow-control is off, output flow-control is unsupported
  ARP type: ARPA, ARP Timeout 04:00:00
  Last input 00:00:51, output 00:00:00, output hang never
  Last clearing of "show interface" counters never
  Input queue: 0/75/0/0 (size/max/drops/flushes); Total output drops: 0
  Queueing strategy: fifo
  Output queue: 0/40 (size/max)
  5 minute input rate 0 bits/sec, 0 packets/sec
  5 minute output rate 0 bits/sec, 0 packets/sec
     18 packets input, 1758 bytes, 0 no buffer
     Received 4 broadcasts (2 multicasts)
     0 runts, 0 giants, 0 throttles
     0 input errors, 0 CRC, 0 frame, 0 overrun, 0 ignored
     0 watchdog, 2 multicast, 0 pause input
     0 input packets with dribble condition detected
     111 packets output, 13828 bytes, 0 underruns
     0 output errors, 0 collisions, 1 interface resets
     0 unknown protocol drops
```

Viewing interface configuration on a Cisco switch. (Image © and Courtesy of Cisco Systems, Inc. Unauthorized use not permitted.)

Switches normally support a range of Ethernet standards so that older and newer network adapters can all be connected to the same network. In most cases, the port on the switch is set to **autonegotiate** speed (10/100/1000) and full- or half-duplex operation. A static configuration can be applied manually if necessary.

 Note: Problems can occur if the interface on the switch is set to autonegotiate but the connected interface is set manually (or vice versa). The main scenario requiring a static configuration is when attaching a legacy hub to a switch. If autonegotiation fails, the interface will be configured according to a default logic. That will typically resolve to 10 Mbps half-duplex transmission.

PORT MIRRORING

Unlike a hub, a switch forwards unicast traffic only to the specific port connected to the intended destination interface. This prevents sniffing of unicast traffic by hosts attached to the same switch. There are circumstances in which capturing and analyzing network traffic is a legitimate activity, however, and **port mirroring** provides the facility to do this. Port mirroring copies all packets sent to one or more source ports to a mirror (or destination) port. On a Cisco switch, this is referred to as a **switched port analyzer (SPAN)**.

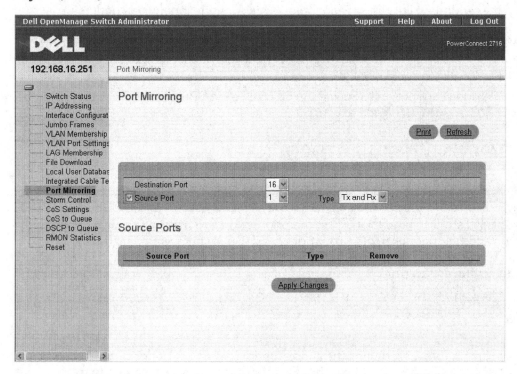

Configuring port mirroring on a Dell switch. (Screenshot courtesy of Dell.)

The mirror port would be used by management or monitoring software, such as a packet sniffer, network analyzer, or intrusion detection system (IDS) sensor. Either ingress or egress traffic, or both, can be captured. Optionally, in order to avoid overloading the monitoring system, packets may be filtered based on criteria such as protocol ID or TCP/UDP port number.

This describes local port mirroring where the source and destination ports are on the same switch. On advanced switches, it is possible to perform remote port mirroring by making the destination port a port on another switch.

Note: Port mirroring demands a lot of processing and can lead to the switch hardware becoming overloaded and consequently crashing. If possible, test any security solution that requires port mirroring under typical loads before deploying it on a production network.

SWITCHING LOOPS AND BROADCAST STORMS

In a network with multiple bridges, implemented these days as switches, there may be more than one path for a frame to take to its intended destination. Multiple paths are part of good network design as they increase **resilience**; if one link fails, then the network can remain operational by forwarding frames over a different path. As a layer 2 protocol, Ethernet has no concept of "time to live," so layer 2 broadcast traffic could continue to loop through a network with multiple paths indefinitely.

Switching loops cause flooded frames to circulate the network perpetually, causing what is often called a **broadcast storm**. A broadcast storm may quickly consume all link bandwidth and crash network appliances. Because switches flood broadcasts and unicast frames with an unknown destination MAC address out all ports, ARP broadcasts in a looped network will cause a Layer 2 broadcast storm. The ARP broadcast will go down one link to the next switch, which will send the broadcast back up the redundant link. This feedback loop will continue indefinitely until there is manual intervention by an administrator. It will cause network utilization to go to near maximum capacity, and the CPU utilization of the switches to jump to 80 percent or more. This makes the switched segment effectively unusable until the broadcast storm stops.

Layer 2 loops are prevented using the **Spanning Tree Protocol (STP)**, defined in the **IEEE 802.1D MAC Bridges** standard.

SPANNING TREE PROTOCOL (STP)

Spanning tree is a means for the bridges to organize themselves into a hierarchy. The bridge at the top of the hierarchy is the **root bridge**. The switch with the lowest bridge ID, comprising a priority value and the MAC address, will be selected as the root. An administrator can (and should) set the priority value to make the choice of one bridge over another more likely. The root bridge will usually be part of a high-bandwidth backbone or core switch group; performance will suffer if a switch on a low-bandwidth segment becomes root.

Note: If a switch supports STP (not all do), it should operate by default without configuration. It is usually a good idea to configure the root bridge priority, however.

Each bridge then determines the shortest path to the root bridge by exchanging information with other bridges. This STP information is packaged as **bridge protocol data unit (BPDU)** multicast frames. A port that forwards "up" to the root bridge, possibly via intermediate bridges, is identified as a **root port**. Ports that can forward traffic "down" through the network with the least cost are identified as **designated ports**. A port that would create a loop is identified as a **blocking** or **non-designated port**. Subsequently, bridges exchange **Topology Change Notifications** if devices are added or removed, enabling them to change the status of forwarding/blocked ports appropriately.

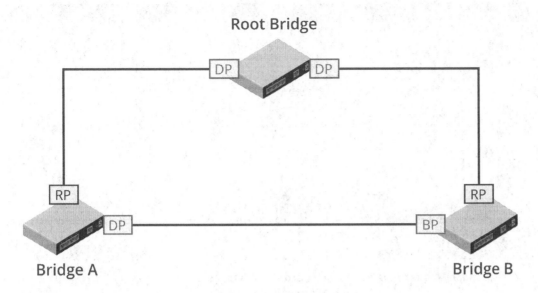

Spanning tree configuration. (Image © 123RF.com.)

This image shows the minimum configuration necessary to prevent loops in a network with three bridges or switches. The root bridge has two designated ports (DP) connected to Bridge A and Bridge B. Bridges A and B both have root ports (RP) connected back to the interfaces on the root bridge. Bridges A and B also have a connection directly to one another. On Bridge A, this interface is active and traffic for Bridge B can be forwarded directly over it. On Bridge B, the interface is blocked (BP) to prevent a loop, and traffic for Bridge A must be forwarded via the root bridge.

The following table shows the different states that a port can be in:

State	Forwards Frames?	Learns MACs?	Notes
Blocking	No	No	Drops all frames other than BPDUs.
Listening	No	No	Port is listening for BPDUs to detect loops.
Learning	No	Yes	The port discovers the topology of the network and builds the MAC address table.
Forwarding	Yes	Yes	The port works as normal.
Disabled	No	No	The port has been disabled by the administrator.

When all ports on all bridges are in forwarding or blocking states, the network is **converged**. When the network is not converged, no communications can take place. Under the original 802.1D standard, this made the network unavailable for extended periods—tens of seconds—during configuration changes. STP is now more likely to be implemented as 802.1D-2004/802.1w or **Rapid STP (RSTP)**. The rapid version creates outages of a few seconds or less. In RSTP, the blocking, listening, and disabled states are aggregated into a discarding state.

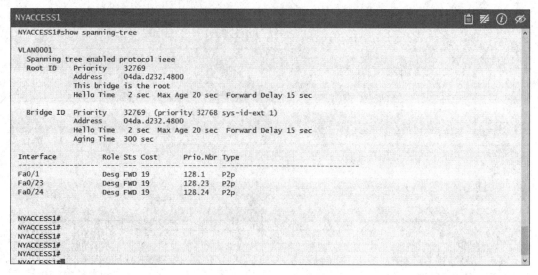

Viewing spanning tree configuration on a Cisco switch. (Image © and Courtesy of Cisco Systems, Inc. Unauthorized use not permitted.)

BPDU AND ROOT GUARD

A switch keeps a cache of MAC addresses associated with each port to enable it to forward traffic quickly. This cache is periodically flushed to ensure it is up to date. When the switch does not know the correct port to use for a particular destination MAC address (if the cache has just been flushed for instance), it **floods** the frame out to all ports, even if the frame is unicast and not broadcast. Topology changes in STP (and especially RSTP) can cause a switch to flush the cache more frequently and to start flooding unicast traffic more frequently, which can have a serious impact on network performance.

To minimize the effects of unicast flooding, ensure that access ports—ports used to connect a host computer—are excluded from topology change notifications. On a Cisco switch, this is accomplished by configuring **PortFast** on the switch port. The equivalent command on switches from other vendors is usually some variant of **edge-port**. In some circumstances, you might want to prevent a switch port from using STP. Some commands that can be used to filter STP traffic include:

- **BPDU Guard**—This causes a port configured with PortFast that receives a BPDU to become disabled. BPDUs are not expected on access ports so this protects against misconfiguration or a possible malicious attack.
- **BPDU Filter**—This causes the port to drop all BPDUs. This could cause traffic to loop if used improperly. You might configure this on a link between two separately administered switching fabrics or use it when joining physical and virtual switch fabrics.
- **Root Guard**—This setting means that a switch will not accept attempts from switches connected to the guarded port to become the root. For example, you might have a group of high-performing "core" switches from which you want the root bridge to be selected. Low-performing access switches would be connected to these "downstream"; they still need to participate in STP but should not be able to become the root. Using Root Guard would prevent a misconfiguration or malicious traffic from making a "downstream" switch or rogue host become root.

 Caution: Do not configure PortFast on switch ports that are used to connect to switches, bridges, or hubs, or you risk creating a switching loop. PortFast must be configured only on ports used to attach host computer devices.

Note: *A virtual switch is different from a virtual LAN. Also, the principal virtual switch vendor (VMware) implements a **BPDU Filter** feature (dropping STP traffic without disabling the port), but calls it **BPDU Guard**.*

POWER OVER ETHERNET (PoE)

Power over Ethernet (PoE) is a means of supplying electrical power from a switch port over ordinary data cabling to a connected **powered device**, such as a VoIP handset or wireless access point. PoE is defined in two IEEE standards (now both rolled into 802.3-2018):

- 802.3af—Powered devices can draw up to about 13 W over the link. Power is supplied as 350mA@48V and limited to 15.4 W, but the voltage drop over the maximum 100 feet of cable results in usable power of around 13 W.
- 802.3at (PoE+)—Powered devices can draw up to about 25 W, with a maximum current of 600 mA. Various proprietary schemes were used prior to the ratification of 802.3at.

PoE switches are referred to as endspan (or endpoint) **power sourcing equipment (PSE)**. If an existing switch does not support PoE, a device called a **power injector** (or midspan) can be used. Power can either be supplied over pairs 1/2 and 3/6 (referred to as Mode A or phantom power, as these are the ones also used for data in 10/100BASE) or over 4/5 and 7/8 (Mode B). Gigabit Ethernet only uses the Mode A method.

When a device is connected to a port on a PoE switch, the switch goes through a detection phase to determine whether the device is PoE-enabled. If not, it does not supply power over the port and, therefore, does not damage non-PoE devices. If so, it determines the device's power consumption and sets the supply voltage level appropriately.

Powering these devices through a switch is more efficient than using a wall-socket AC adapter for each appliance. It also allows network management software to control the devices and apply schemes, such as making unused devices go into sleep states and power capping.

Note: *To learn more, watch the related **Video** on the course website*

Activity 3-2
Discussing Switch Configuration

SCENARIO
Answer the following questions to test your understanding of the content covered in this topic.

---

1. **What is microsegmentation?**

2. **How does a switch keep track of the hardware addresses of hosts connected to its ports?**

3. **What is happening if a switch is flooding?**

4. **True or False? Switch ports should normally be set to autonegotiate speed and duplex settings.**

5. **What is the function of STP?**

6. **Under STP, if a host port is working as normal, what state is it in?**

7. **What mechanisms protect the switching infrastructure from malicious STP traffic?**

8. **What is PoE?**

Topic C
Compare and Contrast Network Topologies

 EXAM OBJECTIVES COVERED
1.5 Compare and contrast the characteristics of network topologies, types, and technologies.

In this topic, you will identify the primary physical and logical network topologies. Network topologies determine the flow of data through a network. Getting to know the different topologies is essential to designing or troubleshooting a network. No matter what your specific role in network implementation and management, you will need to understand the characteristics of the network topology you are working with and identify how the topology affects network performance and troubleshooting.

LOGICAL VS. PHYSICAL NETWORK TOPOLOGIES

A network **topology** can describe the physical or logical structure of the network. This topology is described in terms of nodes and links.

- The **physical network topology** describes the placement of nodes and how they are connected by the network media. For example, in one network, nodes might be directly connected via a single cable; in another network, each node might connect to a switch via separate cables. These two networks have different physical topologies.
- The **logical topology** describes the flow of data through the network. For example, given the different physical network topologies described previously, if in each case the nodes can send messages to one another, the logical topology is the same. The different physical implementations (directly connected via a cable versus connected to the same switch) achieve the same logical layout.

POINT-TO-POINT LINKS

In the simplest type of topology, a single link is established between two nodes. This is called a **point-to-point** (or **one-to-one**) connection. Because only two devices share the connection, they are guaranteed a level of bandwidth.

Router   Router   Router   Router

Point-to-point links—The routers on the left are physically connected via a cable, while the dashed line connecting the routers on the right represents a logical link (not necessarily a single cable). (Image © 123RF.com.)

A point-to-point link can be a physical or logical topology. For example, on a WAN, two routers might be physically linked via multiple intermediate networks and physical devices but still share a logical point-to-point link, where each can address only the other router. With either a physical or logical topology, it is the 1:1 relationship that defines a point-to-point link.

BUS TOPOLOGY

A **physical bus** topology with more than two nodes is a shared access topology, meaning that all nodes share the bandwidth of the media. Only one node can be active at any one time, so the nodes must contend to put signals on the media. All nodes attach directly to a single cable segment via cable **taps**. A signal travels down the bus in both directions from the source and is received by all nodes connected to the segment. The bus is terminated at both ends of the cable to absorb the signal when it has passed all connected devices.

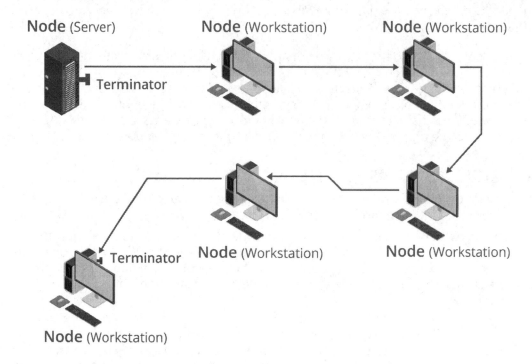

Physical bus topology. (Image © 123RF.com.)

 *Note: A bus network does allow cables to be connected using a device called a **repeater**. Two lengths of cable joined by a repeater is considered one length of cable for the purpose of the bus topology. A repeater is a passive device and is not considered a network node in the way that a switch or router would.*

This type of **physical bus** topology is the basis of the earliest Ethernet networks but is no longer in widespread use. Bus networks are comparatively difficult to reconfigure (adding or removing nodes can disrupt the whole network), impose limitations on the maximum number of nodes on a segment of cable, and are difficult to troubleshoot (a cable fault could be anywhere on the segment of cable). Perhaps most importantly, a fault anywhere in the cable means that all nodes are unable to communicate.

A **logical bus** topology is one in which nodes receive the data transmitted all at the same time, regardless of the physical wiring layout of the network. Because the transmission medium is shared, only one node can transmit at a time. Nodes within the same logical bus segment are in the same collision domain.

STAR TOPOLOGY

In a **star** network, each endpoint node is connected to a central forwarding node, such as a hub, switch, or router. The central node mediates communications between the endpoints. The star topology is the most widely used physical topology. For example, a typical **small office/home office (SOHO) network** is based around a single Internet router appliance that clients can connect to with a cable or wirelessly. The star topology is easy to reconfigure and easy to troubleshoot because all data goes through a central point, which can be used to monitor and manage the network. Faults are automatically isolated to the media, node (network card), or the hub, switch, or router at the center of the star.

You may also encounter the **hub and spoke** topology. This is the same layout as a star topology. The hub and spoke terminology is used when speaking about WANs with remote sites.

PHYSICAL STAR-LOGICAL BUS TOPOLOGY

A **physical star** network can be used to implement a **logical bus** topology. Each node in a **star-wired logical bus** topology behaves as though it will be sharing the network medium with other nodes. When a device such as a **hub** is used at the center of the star, transmissions are still repeated to each node. Logically, the topology works like a single cable bus and the bandwidth is still shared between all nodes, which are all contending for the same network media. This means that some of the limitations of a physical bus topology are retained.

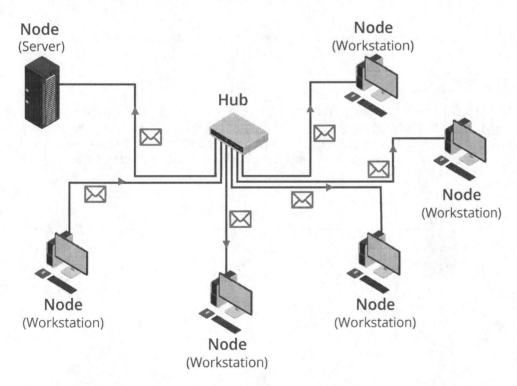

Star topology with a hub at the center of the star. (Image © 123RF.com.)

PHYSICAL STAR-LOGICAL STAR TOPOLOGY

When a device such as a switch is used at the center of the star, the bus element is reduced to the link between each node and its switch port. Taking the network as a whole, both the physical and logical topology is a star. The switch mediates all forwarding between the nodes attached to it. The way the switch operates allows each node to use the full bandwidth of the network media, and it allows nodes to communicate on the network simultaneously, rather than contending for access. Faults are isolated to the link between a node and the switch or to the switch itself.

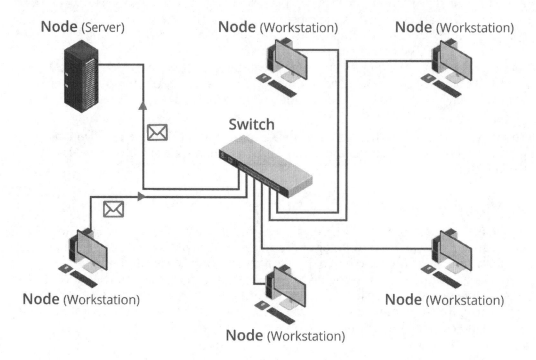

Star topology with a switch at the center of the star. (Image © 123RF.com.)

RING TOPOLOGY

In a **physical ring** topology, each node is wired to its neighbor in a closed loop. A node receives a transmission from its upstream neighbor and passes it to its downstream neighbor until the transmission reaches its intended destination. Each node can regenerate the transmission, improving the potential range of the network.

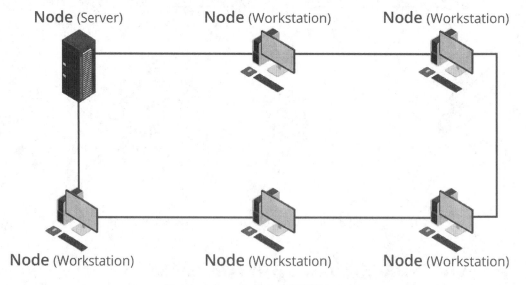

Ring topology. (Image © 123RF.com.)

The physical ring topology is no longer used on LANs, but it does remain a feature of many WANs. Two ring systems (dual counter-rotating rings) can be used to provide fault tolerance. These dual rings allow the system to continue to operate if there is a break in one ring.

Historically, there have been LAN products, such as IBM Token Ring, that implement both pure ring and star-wired rings. In a physical star-logical ring Token Ring implementation, each node is wired to a central device called a multistation access unit (MAU). The internal wiring of the MAU creates the ring topology. Token Ring is no longer used as a mainstream LAN product, but there are still a few deployments in networks with special requirements, such as legacy systems that would be costly to upgrade.

MESH TOPOLOGY

Mesh network topologies are commonly used in WANs, especially public networks like the Internet. In theory, a mesh network requires that each device has a point-to-point link with every other device on the network (**fully connected**). This approach is normally impractical, however. The number of links required by a full mesh is expressed as $n(n-1)/2$, where n is the number of nodes. For example, a network of just four nodes would require six links, while a network of 40 nodes would need 780 links! Consequently, a **hybrid** approach is often used, with only the most important devices interconnected in the mesh, perhaps with extra links for fault tolerance and redundancy. In this case, the topology is referred to as a **partial mesh**.

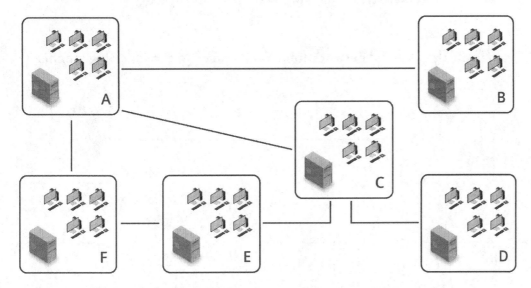

Partial mesh—Each site is linked, but not always directly to every other site. (Image © 123RF.com.)

Mesh networks provide excellent redundancy, because other routes, via intermediary devices, are available between locations if a link failure occurs.

Activity 3-3
Discussing Network Topologies

SCENARIO
Answer the following questions to test your understanding of the content covered in this topic.

1. **What term is used to describe a topology in which two nodes share a single link?**

2. **What is characteristic of the bandwidth of a bus topology?**

3. **Identify the physical network topology depicted in the following graphic.**

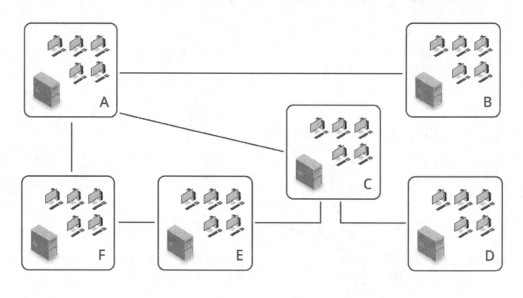

   - ○ Star.
   - ○ Bus.
   - ○ Mesh.
   - ○ Ring.

4. **What type of device is used to implement a physical star topology?**

5.   **You need operations to continue if one link fails. How many links does it take to connect three sites?**

Topic D
Compare and Contrast Network Types

EXAM OBJECTIVES COVERED
1.3 Explain the concepts and characteristics of routing and switching.
1.5 Compare and contrast the characteristics of network topologies, types, and technologies.

Ethernet and switching are the principal technologies used to implement cabled local networks. There are many types and sizes of network, however, and many different ways of using the basic switching function to suit the requirements of large and small organizations and budgets. While you might not be responsible for network design at this stage of your career, it is important that you be able to classify network types and select appropriate technologies to meet the needs of both small and large networks.

LOCAL AREA NETWORKS (LANs)

To categorize the size and nature of individual networks, the industry has developed terms that broadly define the scope of different types of networks. A **local area network (LAN)** covers a wide range of different sizes of networks but is mostly confined to a single geographical location. In a LAN, all nodes and segments are directly connected with cables or short-range wireless technologies. It does not require a leased telecommunication system to function. Most of the network infrastructure in a LAN would be directly owned and managed by a single organization. Some typical examples of LANs include:

- **Home/residential networks**—with an Internet router and a few computers, plus **mobile devices**, gaming consoles, and printers.
- **Small office/home office (SOHO) networks**—A business-oriented network possibly using a centralized server in addition to client devices and printers, but often still using a single Internet router/switch/access point to provide connectivity.
- **Small and medium sized enterprise (SME) networks**—A network supporting dozens of users. Such networks would use structured cabling and multiple switches and routers to provide connectivity.
- **Enterprise LANs**—A larger network with hundreds or thousands of servers and clients. Such networks would require multiple enterprise-class switch and router appliances to maintain performance levels.

The term **campus area network (CAN)** is sometimes used for a LAN that spans multiple nearby buildings. The term **wireless local area network (WLAN)** is used for networks based on Wi-Fi. Open (public) WLANs are often referred to as **hotspots**.

A **storage area network (SAN)** is one that interconnects storage devices such as RAID arrays or tape drives to make "pools" of shared storage capacity available to servers.

WIDE AREA NETWORKS (WANs)

A **wide area network (WAN)** is a network of networks, connected by long-distance links. A typical **enterprise WAN** would connect multiple sites, possibly in different countries. A WAN could link two or more large LANs or could be used for remote workers connecting to an enterprise network via a public network such as the Internet.

WANs are likely to use leased network devices and links, operated and managed by a service provider.

You should also be familiar with the terminology of Internet, intranet, and extranet.

- The **Internet** is a worldwide network of networks based on the TCP/IP protocol. The uncapitalized term *internet* (or *internetwork*) is also used to describe any series of interconnected networks running Internet Protocol (IP).
- An **intranet** uses the same technologies as the Internet, but it is owned and managed by a company or organization. An intranet could be implemented as a LAN or WAN.
- An **extranet** is an intranet that is also accessible to selected third parties, such as customers or suppliers.

The term **metropolitan area network (MAN)** is sometimes used for something a bit smaller than a WAN: a city-wide network encompassing multiple buildings.

PERSONAL AREA NETWORKS (PANs)

The terms **personal area network (PAN)** and **wireless PAN (WPAN)** have gained some currency over the last few years. They refer to the fact that a person might establish close-range network links between a variety of devices, such as smartphones, tablets, headsets, and printers. As digital and network functionality continues to be embedded in more and more everyday objects, appliances (the Internet of Things), and clothing, the use of PANs will only grow.

ENTERPRISE CAMPUS NETWORKS

The terms **campus LAN** and **enterprise network** cover a wide range of different types of site: a whole building, a floor in a building, multiple buildings close together, or multiple buildings some distance apart. Consequently, Cisco (for instance) no longer attempts to define a campus network based on the properties of the site but as "the integrated elements that comprise the set of services used by a group of users and end-station devices that all share the same high-speed switching communications fabric."

The job of a network designer is to select the most appropriate technology given the customer requirements (such as business objective and budget) and network design goals (such as scalability, availability, and security). Other factors might affect the choice of technology. For example, the customer may have existing equipment from one vendor. Selecting a different vendor might cause problems with interoperability and require extra staff training.

Installing or upgrading network infrastructure such as cabling and switches is expensive. Consequently, it is important that infrastructure design be scalable and adaptable.

- **Scalability** means that additional users or devices can be added to the network without having to significantly re-design or re-engineer the existing infrastructure. For example, if a department expands to require two floors, network traffic within the expanded department can be accommodated by the existing cable and switching infrastructure without reducing performance.
- **Adaptability** (or flexibility) means that new or changed services and applications can be accommodated with minimum disruption to the existing physical and logical topology. For example, if the customer wants to switch from a traditional telephone system to Voice over IP, an adaptable network will be able to accommodate this without requiring the installation of new cable.

NETWORK HIERARCHY AND DISTRIBUTED SWITCHING

To accommodate the design goals of adaptability and scalability, a hierarchical model is often adopted. A hierarchical model breaks down a large and complex network design into smaller sections based on the functions performed. Each function can be assessed by network designers to identify the most efficient hardware and software to implement.

One common hierarchical model uses **distributed switching**. This model is especially useful for medium to large networks. Systems can be grouped by location, with the smaller groups each attached to an **access switch**. The access switches form the bottom level of the hierarchy. Access switches are not directly connected to one another. Each access switch forwards traffic to switches in a **distribution layer**. Switches at the distribution layer are highly interconnected, with redundant paths for **failover**. Policies can be implemented at the distribution level to prioritize traffic for optimal network performance. This model also assists with isolating issues that may occur within the network.

As a practical example of this type of model, Cisco recommends designing a large enterprise network with *four* layers of hierarchy: access, distribution, core, and data center.

ACCESS LAYER

The **access layer** allows end-user devices, such as computers, printers, and smartphones to connect to the network. Another important function of the access layer is to prevent the attachment of unauthorized devices. The access layer is implemented for each site using structured cabling and wall ports for wired access and access points for wireless access. Both are ultimately connected to **workgroup switches**. Switches deployed to serve the access layer might also be referred to as LAN switches or data switches.

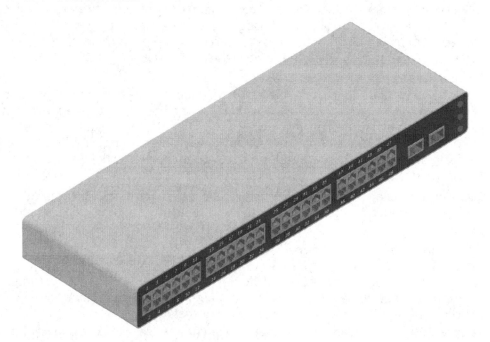

A workgroup switch provides 48x1GbE POE-capable ports plus 2x40GbE uplink ports. (Image © 123RF.com.)

DISTRIBUTION LAYER

The **distribution layer** provides fault-tolerant interconnections between different access blocks and either the core or other distribution blocks. The distribution layer is often used to implement traffic policies, such as routing boundaries, filtering, or quality of service (QoS).

CORE LAYER

The **core layer** provides a highly available network backbone. Devices such as client and server computers should not be attached directly to the core. Its purpose should be kept simple: provide redundant traffic paths for data to continue to flow around the access and distribution layers of the network.

You can think of a network design with a core as a star (or hierarchical star) topology. A "flat" design with only distribution and access layers is more like a mesh (or partial mesh). It is more complex to grow a mesh-like network, because the number of interconnections required grows exponentially as you add sites. Connections between the distribution layer are made via the core layer, rather than interconnecting distribution layer switches directly.

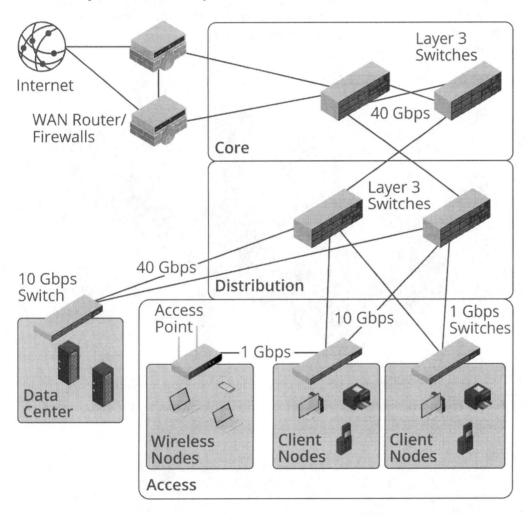

Simplified enterprise network distributed switching hierarchy.

DATA CENTER

The **data center** is a network area that hosts network services (such as authentication, addressing, and name resolution), application servers, and storage area networks (SANs).

CORE AND DISTRIBUTION LAYER SWITCH TYPES

The distribution and core layers provide switching and routing between different access layer locations and server groups. This function can be implemented by several device types:

- **Routers**—Provide connectivity between subnetworks based on their IP addresses.
- **Layer 3 switches**—Router appliances are capable of many different types of routing, such as routing over WANs, but tend not to have as many port interfaces as switches. On a campus Ethernet network, the internal routers will typically be moving traffic between VLANs and have no need to perform WAN routing. Switches with the ability to route traffic efficiently between VLANs are called layer 3 switches.
- **Aggregation switches**—These are functionally similar to layer 3 switches, but the term is often used for very high-performing switches deployed to aggregate links in a large enterprise or service provider's routing infrastructure. Rather than 1 Gbps access ports and 10 Gbps uplink ports, as would be typical of a workgroup switch, basic interfaces on an aggregation switch would be 10 Gbps and uplink/backbone ports would be 40 Gbps (or possibly 40 Gbps/100 Gbps).

An example of a core/distribution switch. (Image © 123RF.com.)

- **Top-of-rack (ToR) switches**—Models designed to provide high-speed connectivity to a rack of server appliances.

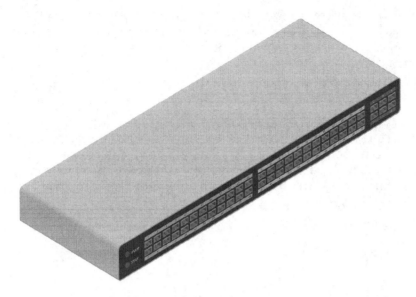

An example of a top-of-rack switch. (Image © 123RF.com.)

MODULAR DESIGN

At each layer of the hierarchy, functions are provided as **modular** blocks, each of which should be capable of being specified and designed separately from the overall network. For example, you might have access and distribution blocks for client devices for each floor of a building, blocks for application and storage services within the data center, others for WAN access, Internet access, or remote access, and a block for network management and administration functions.

Developing these functions using standard modules makes them easier to secure, easier to manage, and easier to troubleshoot. Each module starts with a list of the requirements it must fulfill. This allows for the development of a logical network topology. The implementation of each module in a physical network topology (the placement of cabling and selection and placement of devices) can then be developed from the logical topology taking account of site, environmental, and budgetary factors.

 Note: *View Cisco's series of campus design guides at cisco.com/c/en/us/td/docs/ solutions/Enterprise/Campus/campover.html for more information on this topic.*

SOFTWARE DEFINED NETWORKING (SDN)

As networks become more complex—perhaps involving thousands of physical and virtual computers and appliances—it becomes more difficult to implement network policies, such as ensuring security and managing traffic flow. With so many devices to configure, it is better to take a step back and consider an abstracted model about how the network functions. In this model, network functions can be divided into three "planes":

*   Control plane—makes decisions about how traffic should be prioritized and secured and where it should be switched.
*   Data plane—handles the actual switching and routing of traffic and imposition of access control lists (ACLs) for security.
*   Management plane—monitors traffic conditions and network status.

A **software defined networking (SDN)** application (or suite of applications) can be used to define policy decisions on the control plane. These decisions are then implemented on the data plane by a **network controller** application, which interfaces with the network devices using application programming interfaces (APIs). The interface between the SDN applications and the SDN controller is described as the "northbound" API, while that between the controller and appliances is the "southbound" API.

At the device level, SDN can use virtualized appliances or physical appliances. The appliances just need to support the southbound API of the network controller software.

This architecture saves the network administrator the job and complexity of configuring each appliance with appropriate settings to enforce the desired policy. It also allows for fully automated deployment (or **provisioning**) of network links, appliances, and servers. This makes SDN an important part of the latest software deployment and disaster recovery technologies.

 Note: To learn more, watch the related **Video** on the course website.

GUIDELINES FOR DEPLOYING DISTRIBUTED SWITCHING

UNDERSTAND DESIGN PRINCIPLES

While you might not be responsible for network design at this state in your career, it helps to understand design principles to provide support for existing networks.

- Determine whether to implement a core and distribution layer or a single distribution layer, based on network size and projected requirements for future expansion.
- Determine bandwidth requirements within the core/distribution layer (typically 10 Gbps+) and provision appropriate switch modules, transceivers, and cabling (typically fiber optic).
- Provision redundant trunk links within the core and between the core and distribution layer (or just within the distribution layer).
- Determine bandwidth requirements for the access layer (typically 1 Gbps) and provision appropriate workgroup/LAN switches based on media type.
- Provision redundant trunk links between distribution layer switches and access layer switches.
- Enable spanning tree to prevent loops around redundant circuits and ensure the selection of a root bridge within the core or distribution layer as appropriate.
- Determine bandwidth requirements for a data center segment and provision appropriate access layer switches to support servers.
- Enable appropriate PortFast guards on all access layer ports.
- Connect access points to access layer switches to facilitate wireless networking.
- Connect client devices (PCs, VoIP endpoints, and printers) and non-data center servers to access layer switches.

Activity 3-4
Discussing Network Types

SCENARIO

Answer the following questions to test your understanding of the content covered in this topic.

1. **What is a WLAN?**

2. **What network infrastructure implementation is larger than a LAN but smaller than a WAN?**

3. **What is the purpose of a SAN?**

4. **What types of devices are connected in a PAN?**

5. **What four layers can be used to conceptualize distributed switching hierarchy?**

6. **What is the function of a network controller?**

Activity 3-5
Designing a Switch Topology

SCENARIO

Janice, the IT and network manager, has been given the job of planning the Ethernet switch infrastructure for a new building that her company is moving into.

The building has three floors with a reasonably even spread of network-connected devices across them.

She initially decided on the layout shown in the following image, with two switches on each floor to give the necessary number of ports and some expansion capacity. The main core switch is connected to the building's router, which will provide access to the company's other sites and to the Internet.

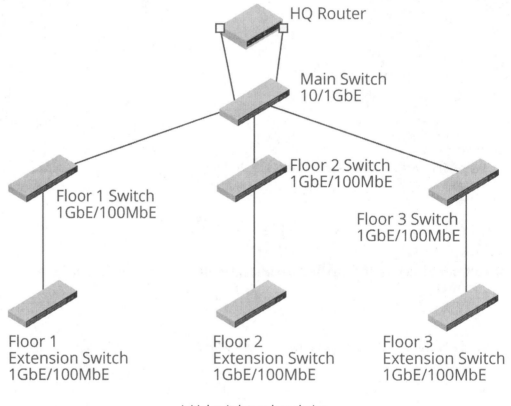

Initial switch topology design.

1. **Looking at this design, what are its potential weaknesses and strengths?**

2. Having re-evaluated the requirements of the occupants of the building and looking at the expected network traffic between the occupants of floor 2 and 3, she comes up with a revised design. She is also mindful of resilience.

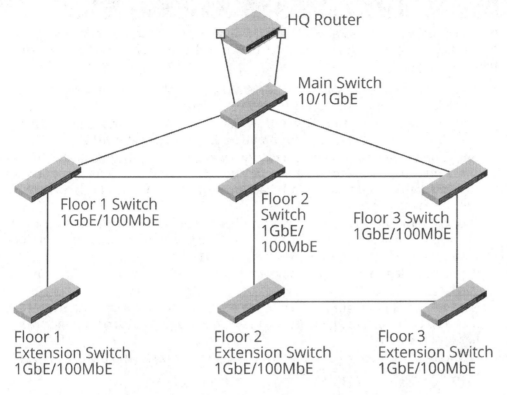

Revised switch topology design.

3. **What would Janice need to ensure about the configuration of the switches, given the revised network layout?**

4. **Assuming the switches are configured with suitable protocols, what would determine which switch became the root bridge? How could this be changed to ensure that the main switch was root?**

5. **Given this design and assuming all switch connections were in place, how many links would be placed in a blocking state by the STP algorithm?**

Summary

In this lesson, you learned about the placement and configuration of connectivity devices such as hubs, bridges, and switches. You also learned some basic principles of network design.

- Hubs are legacy devices used as the network concentrator to implement a star topology (a multiport repeater). Hubs work at layer 1.
- Bridges could be deployed with hubs to divide a network into smaller collision domains, reducing the effect of contention. Bridges work at layer 2.
- Hubs and bridges have been replaced by layer 2 switches in almost all networks. These principally work to eliminate the effect of collisions (each port is a separate collision domain and switches can have many more ports than bridges) but can also come with many advanced features.
- The Spanning Tree Protocol is used to prevent loops in a switched network with multiple paths. If flooded traffic is put in a loop, it will cause a broadcast storm because there is no way to retire layer 2 frames.
- Physical and logical network topologies include point-to-point, star, bus, ring, and mesh.
- Networks can be categorized by size as LAN/CAN, MAN, WAN, or PAN. Networks may also be designated by type, such as wireless LAN (WLAN) or storage area network (SAN).
- Be aware of the design principles for enterprise networks and the use of distributed switching hierarchies and SDN.

Have you encountered switching loops in your network? If so, what did you do to resolve the problem? If not, how did your network ensure they did not occur?

What category (or categories) of networks have you used (such as LAN, WAN, CAN, MAN, PAN, etc.)? Which have you been responsible for managing?

 Practice Questions: Additional practice questions are available on the course website.

Lesson 4

Configuring IP Networks

LESSON INTRODUCTION

In this lesson, you will identify the addressing and data delivery methods of the Internet Protocol (IP). IP is at the heart of most modern networks, and consequently one of the most important topic areas for a network professional to master. This lesson will cover the basic format of IPv4 addresses and how they are used to identify networks and hosts. The lesson will also cover IPv6 and methods of assigning an IP address to hosts automatically.

LESSON OBJECTIVES

In this lesson, you will:

- Configure IPv4 addressing components.
- Test IP interfaces with command line tools.
- Configure IPv4 addressing components.
- Configure private and public IPv4 addressing schemes.
- Configure IPv6 addressing components.
- Configure DHCP services.

Topic A

Configure IPv4 Addressing Components

EXAM OBJECTIVES COVERED
1.1 Explain the purposes and uses of ports and protocols.
1.4 Given a scenario, configure the appropriate IP addressing components.

TCP/IP consists of a suite of complementary protocols and standards that work together to provide the functionality on TCP/IP networks. The Internet Protocol (IP) stands at the heart of this protocol suite, providing logical addressing and packet forwarding between different networks. In this topic, you will start by examining the structure of IPv4 packets and the format of IPv4 addresses.

LAYER 3 ADDRESSING AND FORWARDING

Technologies such as Ethernet work at the Physical and Data Link layers of the OSI model (layers 1 and 2). At the Network layer (layer 3), the **Internet Protocol (IP)** provides logical host and network addressing and routing. IP provides best-effort delivery of an unreliable and connectionless nature. Delivery is not guaranteed, and a packet might be lost, delivered out of sequence, duplicated, or delayed.

There are two versions of IP; version 4 is currently in widespread use and is the version discussed in the following few topics. IPv6 introduces a much larger address space and different means of configuring clients and is discussed later in the lesson.

IPv4 DATAGRAM STRUCTURE

IP **packets** (or **datagrams**) encapsulate data from the Transport layer, adding several fields as a header.

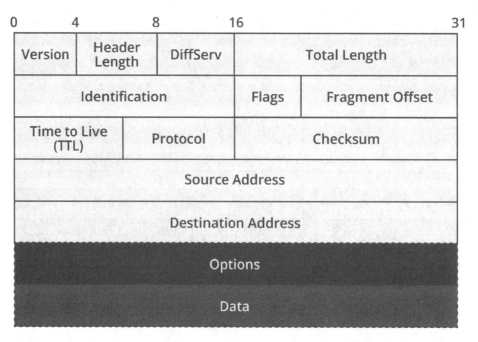

IPv4 header.

IPv4 HEADER FIELDS

The Version field indicates the version of Internet Protocol in use (4), while the Length fields indicate the size of the header and the total packet size (including the payload). The maximum theoretical size is 65,535 bytes, but actual packets would typically be much smaller.

Some of the other header fields are described in the following sections.

PROTOCOL FIELD

The Protocol field describes what is contained (encapsulated) in the payload so that the receiving host knows how to process it. For most packets, the value in the Protocol field will indicate a Transmission Control Protocol (TCP/6) segment or a User Datagram Protocol (UDP/17) datagram. The values assigned to protocols (such as 6 for TCP and 17 for UDP) are managed by IANA.

Note: *Those are the values in decimal. You are also likely to see them in their hex forms (0x06 and 0x11). Both formats ultimately represent 8-bit binary values (00000110 and 00010001).*

Some protocols that run directly on IP (rather than over TCP or UDP) include the following:

- Internet Control Message Protocol (ICMP/1) is used for status messaging and connectivity testing.
- Internet Group Messaging Protocol (IGMP/2) is used with multicasting.
- Generic Routing Encapsulation (GRE/47) is used to tunnel packets across an intermediate network. This is used (for example) in some virtual private network (VPN) implementations.
- Encapsulating Security Payload (ESP/50) and Authentication Header (AH/51) are used with the encrypted form of IP (IPSec).
- Enhanced Interior Gateway Routing Protocol (EIGRP/88) and Open Shortest Path First (OSPF/89) are protocols used by routers to exchange information about paths to remote networks.

DIFFSERV FIELD

The **Differentiated Services Code Point (DSCP)** field is used to indicate a priority value for the packet. This can be used with class of service (CoS) and quality of service (QoS) mechanisms to facilitate better quality real-time data transfers, such as video streaming or Voice over IP calling. The 6-byte DSCP value can be combined with a 2-byte Explicit Congestion Notification (ECN).

TIME TO LIVE FIELD

The **Time to Live (TTL)** is nominally the number of seconds a packet can stay on the network before being discarded; otherwise packets could endlessly loop around an internet. While TTL is defined as a unit of time (seconds), in practice, it is interpreted as a maximum **hop** count. Each router will decrease the TTL by at least 1 when it handles the packet, so the hop count is effectively the number of routers between the source and destination hosts.

ID, FLAGS, AND FRAGMENT OFFSET FIELDS

The ID, Flags, and Fragment Offset fields are used to indicate whether the IP datagram has been split between multiple packets for transport over the underlying Data Link protocol. For example, the Maximum Transmission Unit (MTU) of an Ethernet frame is usually 1500 bytes. An IP datagram larger than 1500 bytes would have to be fragmented across more than one Ethernet frame. A datagram passing over an internetwork might have to be encapsulated in different Data Link frame types, each with different MTUs.

Most systems try to avoid IP fragmentation. Instead, the host performs MTU path discovery to work out the MTU supported by each hop and crafts IP datagrams that will fit the smallest MTU.

IPv4 ADDRESS STRUCTURE

All networks must have a way of uniquely identifying individual computers. This identifier may be in the form of a name or number. At the Data Link layer, each interface is identified by using a MAC or hardware address. This type of address can be used only for local delivery of frames. At the TCP/IP Internet layer (the OSI Network layer), an **IP address** is used to identify each host. The IP address provides two pieces of information:

- The network number (network ID)—This number is common to all hosts on the same IP network.
- The host number (host ID)—This number identifies a host within an IP network.

An IPv4 address is 32 bits long and is used within an IP packet to define the source and destination of the packet. In its raw form, it appears as follows:

```
11000110001010010001000000001001
```

The 32 bits are subdivided into four groups of 8 bits (1 byte) known as **octets**. The previous IP address could therefore be written as:

```
11000110 00101001 00010000 00001001
```

This representation of an IP address makes human memorizing of the number almost impossible, much less entering it correctly into configuration dialog boxes. To make IP addresses easier to use, they are usually displayed in **dotted decimal notation**. This notation requires each octet to be converted to a decimal value. The decimal numbers are separated using a period. Converting the previous number to this notation gives:

```
198.41.16.9
```

BINARY/DECIMAL CONVERSION

The following examples demonstrate the process of converting between binary and decimal notation. The **base** of any number system tells you two things: how many different values any given digit can have and the factor by which the value of a digit increases as you move from right to left in a number. Thus, in **base 10** (or **decimal**) numbers, a digit can take any one of ten different values (0 through 9), and the values of the different place positions within a number, moving from right to left, are units (ones), tens, hundreds, thousands, and so on.

In base 2 (**binary**), digits can take one of two different values (0 and 1). The place values are powers of 2 (2^1=2, 2^2=4, 2^3=8, 2^4=16, and so on). Consider the octet 11101101 represented in base 2. This image shows the octet in the third row, the representation of the place value of each digit of the octet in the fourth row, and the decimal equivalent in the last row

2^7	2^6	2^5	2^4	2^3	2^2	2^1	2^0	
128	64	32	16	8	4	2	1	
1	1	1	0	1	1	0	1	
128*1	64*1	32*1	16*0	8*1	4*1	2*0	1*1	
128	+64	+32	+0	+8	+4	+0	+1	=237

You can use the same columnar method to convert from decimal to binary. For example, the number 199 can be converted as follows:

	2^7	2^6	2^5	2^4	2^3	2^2	2^1	2^0
	128	64	32	16	8	4	2	1
199=	128	+64	+0	+0	+0	+4	+2	+1
	128*1	64*1	32*0	16*0	8*0	4*1	2*1	1*1
	1	1	0	0	0	1	1	1

If all the bits in an octet are set to 1, the number obtained is 255 (the maximum possible value). Similarly, if all the bits are set to 0, the number obtained is 0 (the minimum possible value). Therefore, theoretically an IPv4 address may be any value between 0.0.0.0 and 255.255.255.255. However, some addresses are not permitted or are reserved for special use.

 Note: *To learn more, watch the related **Video** on the course website.*

SUBNET MASKS

An IP address represents both a **network ID** and a **host ID**. A **subnet mask** (or **netmask**) is used to distinguish these two components within a single IP address. It is used to "mask" the host ID portion of the IP address and thereby reveal the network ID portion.

Wherever there is a binary 1 in the mask, the corresponding binary *digit* in the IP address is part of the network ID. The relative sizes of the network and host portions determine how many networks and hosts per network an addressing scheme can support. The 1s in the mask are always contiguous. For example, this mask is valid:

11111111 11110000 00000000 00000000

But the following string is not a valid mask:

11111111 00000000 11110000 00000000

Because the 1s in a mask are always contiguous, each octet in decimal in a subnet mask will always be one of the following.

Octet Mask Bits	Binary Octet	Decimal Equivalent
1	10000000	128
2	11000000	192
3	11100000	224
4	11110000	240
5	11111000	248
6	11111100	252
7	11111110	254
8	11111111	255

For example, a binary mask with 12 bits can be converted to decimal as follows:

```
11111111 11110000 00000000 00000000
   255       240        0         0
```

A longer netmask with 26 bits could use all the octets:

```
11111111 11111111 11111111 11000000
   255       255       255       192
```

There are also default subnet masks that align with the octet boundaries. For example, the default 16-bit mask is as follows:

```
11111111 11111111 00000000 00000000
   255       255        0         0
```

 Note: *Some configuration dialog boxes require you to enter the mask in dotted decimal format, but try to think in terms of the number of mask bits when you are performing subnet calculations.*

IPv4 ADDRESS MASKING PROCESS (ANDing)

The network ID portion of an IP address is revealed by ANDing the subnet mask to the IP address. The rules for a logical AND are shown in this table.

1	AND	1	=	1
1	AND	0	=	0
0	AND	1	=	0
0	AND	0	=	0

When two 1s are ANDed together, the result is a 1. **Any** other combination produces a 0.

For example, to determine the network ID of the IP address 172.30.15.12 with a subnet mask of 255.255.0.0, the dotted decimal notation of the IP address and subnet mask must first be converted to binary notation. The next step is to AND the two binary numbers. The result can be converted back to dotted decimal notation to show the network ID (172.30.0.0).

```
172. 30.15.12 => 10101100 00011110 00001111 00001100
255.255. 0. 0 => 11111111 11111111 00000000 00000000
172. 30. 0. 0 => 10101100 00011110 00000000 00000000
```

IPv4 ROUTING DECISIONS

When two hosts attempt to communicate via IPv4, the protocol compares the source and destination address in each packet against the netmask. If the masked portions of the source and destination IP addresses match, then the destination interface is assumed to be on the same IP network. For example:

```
172. 30. 15. 12 => 10101100 00011110 00001111 00001100
255.255.  0.  0 => 11111111 11111111 00000000 00000000
172. 30. 16.101 => 10101100 00011110 00010000 01100101
```

In this example, IP concludes the destination IPv4 address is on the same IP network and tries to deliver the packet locally, using the Address Resolution Protocol (ARP) to identify the MAC address of the interface associated with the destination IP address.

If the masked portion does not match, IP assumes the packet must be routed to another IP network. For example:

```
172. 30. 15. 12 => 10101100 00011110 00001111 00001100
255.255.  0.  0 => 11111111 11111111 00000000 00000000
172. 31. 16.101 => 10101100 00011111 00010000 01100101
```

In this case, IP concludes the destination IPv4 address is on a different IP network and forwards the packet to a router (its default gateway), rather than trying to deliver it locally.

IPv4 ROUTING BASICS

The netmask is used by IP to identify whether the source and destination addresses in a packet are on the same IP network. If the destination address has a different network ID, the packet must be sent via one or more **routers**. The **default gateway** is the IP address of a router on the same IP network as the host. Messages destined for other IP networks are sent to the default gateway address by the source host.

When a message is sent using IP, the following steps occur:

1. IP tries to establish a connection with the destination host by IP address:
   - The subnet mask of the host is applied to the source IP address to determine the network address of the source host.
   - The subnet mask of the host is applied to the destination IP address to determine the network address of the destination host.
2. The destination network address is compared with that of the source:
   - If the two hosts are on the same IP network, IP uses ARP messaging to locate the destination interface. The response to this broadcast includes the hardware (MAC) address of the destination interface and the message can then be delivered.
   - If the two machines are on different IP networks, IP uses ARP messaging to locate the default gateway (router). This machine responds with its MAC address and the message is then sent to the gateway.
3. It is possible that due to limitations in the underlying network, IP may fragment the packet into more manageable pieces (to fit within the MTU of the Data Link protocol frame).

   If this is the case, IP assigns a new header to each fragment containing:
   - A **flag** to indicate whether more fragments follow.
   - A **fragment identifier** to help group fragments together.
   - An **offset** to assist the destination host in reconstructing the fragments into the original packet.
4. IP then calculates a **checksum** (to use for error detection) and sends the datagram. A Data Link protocol (such as Ethernet) encapsulates this into one or more frames and transmits them over the network.
5. If the packet has been routed, at the gateway, the Time to Live (TTL) is decreased by at least one. This could be greater if the router is congested. When the TTL is zero, the packet will not be forwarded to another router. This prevents badly addressed packets from permanently circulating the network.
6. The router then determines what to do with the packet by repeating the steps described from the second step on. If the message is destined for yet another network, the process is repeated to take it to the next stage, and so on.

Routes to other IP networks can be manually configured or learned by a **dynamic routing protocol**. Discovered routes are held in a **routing table**. The more sophisticated routers can share information about known networks and possible paths to them. This information allows them to choose the best routes to any given destination and select alternate routes if one of these is unavailable.

As well as determining the best path, a router is able to encapsulate the packet in the appropriate frame format. For example, a router might receive an Ethernet frame from a host on the local network. It strips the frame and examines the IP datagram. It determines that the datagram must be sent over a WAN interface, so it encapsulates the packet in the appropriate WAN frame format and transmits it over the wire.

 Note: An IP host must be configured with an IP address and subnet mask. A default gateway is required to communicate beyond the local subnet. The address of a DNS server is essential to most networks, but it is not a mandatory requirement.

Activity 4-1

Discussing IPv4 Addressing Components

SCENARIO

Answer the following questions to test your understanding of the content covered in this topic.

---

1. **What is the function of the Protocol field in an IPv4 header?**

2. **Convert the decimal value 72 into binary.**

3. **Convert the binary value 11110010 to decimal.**

4. **What is the dotted decimal representation of an 8-bit netmask?**

5. **What is the dotted decimal representation of an 18-bit netmask?**

6. **Given an 18-bit netmask, are the IP addresses 172.16.1.10 and 172.16.54.10 on the same network?**

7. **Given the subnet mask 255.255.255.128, are the IP addresses 192.168.0.1 and 192.168.1.1 on the same network?**

8. **Given the subnet mask 255.255.255.128, are the IP addresses 192.168.0.1 and 192.168.0.65 on the same network?**

9. **True or False? A router will not forward a packet when the TTL field is 0.**

10. **Which TCP/IP parameters must be defined for a host to be able to communicate with hosts on a remote network?**

Topic B

Test IP Interfaces with Command Line Tools

EXAM OBJECTIVES COVERED
1.1 Explain the purposes and uses of ports and protocols.
5.2 Given a scenario, use the appropriate tool.

TCP/IP command line utilities enable you to gather information about how your systems are configured and how they communicate over an IP network. When used for troubleshooting, these utilities can provide critical information about communication issues and their causes.

ipconfig

The **ipconfig** command, `ipconfig`, is used to verify the IP configuration on Windows-based systems. `ipconfig` includes the following options:

*   `ipconfig` without any switches will display the IP address, subnet mask, and default gateway (router) for all network interfaces to which TCP/IP is bound.
*   `ipconfig /all` displays complete TCP/IP configuration parameters for each interface to which TCP/IP is bound, including whether the Dynamic Host Configuration Protocol (DHCP) is enabled for the interface and the interface's hardware (MAC) address.
*   `ipconfig /renew interface` forces a DHCP client to renew the lease it has for an IP address.
*   `ipconfig /release interface` releases the IP address obtained from a DHCP Server so that the interface(s) will no longer have an IP address.
*   `ipconfig /displaydns` displays the Domain Name System (DNS) resolver cache.
*   `ipconfig /flushdns` clears the DNS resolver cache.
*   `ipconfig /registerdns` registers the host with a DNS server (if it supports dynamic updates).

Note: *There are also* `/release6` *and* `/renew6` *switches for use with DHCPv6 (a DHCP server supporting IPv6).*

```
C:\Users\administrator>ipconfig /all

Windows IP Configuration

   Host Name . . . . . . . . . . . . : PC1
   Primary Dns Suffix  . . . . . . . : corp.515support.com
   Node Type . . . . . . . . . . . . : Hybrid
   IP Routing Enabled. . . . . . . . : No
   WINS Proxy Enabled. . . . . . . . : No
   DNS Suffix Search List. . . . . . : corp.515support.com

Ethernet adapter Ethernet:

   Connection-specific DNS Suffix  . : corp.515support.com
   Description . . . . . . . . . . . : Microsoft Hyper-V Network Adapter
   Physical Address. . . . . . . . . : 00-15-5D-01-CA-93
   DHCP Enabled. . . . . . . . . . . : Yes
   Autoconfiguration Enabled . . . . : Yes
   Link-local IPv6 Address . . . . . : fe80::a4e7:7155:7f44:dcc6%7(Preferred)
   IPv4 Address. . . . . . . . . . . : 10.1.0.101(Preferred)
   Subnet Mask . . . . . . . . . . . : 255.255.255.0
   Lease Obtained. . . . . . . . . . : Sunday, May 19, 2019 1:29:56 PM
   Lease Expires . . . . . . . . . . : Monday, May 27, 2019 1:29:56 PM
   Default Gateway . . . . . . . . . : 10.1.0.254
   DHCP Server . . . . . . . . . . . : 10.1.0.2
   DHCPv6 IAID . . . . . . . . . . . : 67114333
   DHCPv6 Client DUID. . . . . . . . : 00-01-00-01-24-52-58-FA-00-15-5D-01-CA-93
   DNS Servers . . . . . . . . . . . : 10.1.0.1
   NetBIOS over Tcpip. . . . . . . . : Enabled

C:\Users\administrator>
```

Identifying the current IP configuration with ipconfig. (Screenshot used with permission from Microsoft.)

ifconfig

UNIX® and Linux® hosts provide the **ifconfig** command, `ifconfig`, which provides similar output to the Windows® `ipconfig` program.

```
[centos@lx1 ~]$ ifconfig
eth0: flags=4163<UP,BROADCAST,RUNNING,MULTICAST>  mtu 1500
        inet 10.1.0.10  netmask 255.255.255.0  broadcast 10.1.0.255
        inet6 fe80::1744:5c69:7e04:19f3  prefixlen 64  scopeid 0x20<link>
        ether 00:15:5d:01:ca:55  txqueuelen 1000  (Ethernet)
        RX packets 302  bytes 24723 (24.1 KiB)
        RX errors 0  dropped 0  overruns 0  frame 0
        TX packets 51  bytes 6607 (6.4 KiB)
        TX errors 0  dropped 0 overruns 0  carrier 0  collisions 0

lo: flags=73<UP,LOOPBACK,RUNNING>  mtu 65536
        inet 127.0.0.1  netmask 255.0.0.0
        inet6 ::1  prefixlen 128  scopeid 0x10<host>
        loop  txqueuelen 1000  (Local Loopback)
        RX packets 797  bytes 240635 (234.9 KiB)
        RX errors 0  dropped 0  overruns 0  frame 0
        TX packets 797  bytes 240635 (234.9 KiB)
        TX errors 0  dropped 0 overruns 0  carrier 0  collisions 0
```

Using ifconfig.

Here are some differences between the Windows and Linux commands:

- `ifconfig` can also be used to bind an address to an adapter interface, set up communications parameters, and enable or disable the adapter.

- The Windows switches for configuring the adapter with DHCP and DNS are not supported by `ifconfig`.

 Note: *On most versions of Linux, the* `dhclient` *tool is used to release and renew a DHCP-configured interface.*

- The `ifconfig` command output does not show the default gateway (use `route` instead). It does show traffic statistics, though.

ip

Going forward, the **ip** command, `ip`, is intended to replace `ifconfig`. `ip` is a more powerful tool, with options for managing routes as well as the local interface configuration. The basic functionality of `ifconfig` (show the current address configuration) is performed by running `ip a`

```
[centos@lx1 ~]$ ip a
1: lo: <LOOPBACK,UP,LOWER_UP> mtu 65536 qdisc noqueue state UNKNOWN group defaul
t qlen 1000
    link/loopback 00:00:00:00:00:00 brd 00:00:00:00:00:00
    inet 127.0.0.1/8 scope host lo
       valid_lft forever preferred_lft forever
    inet6 ::1/128 scope host
       valid_lft forever preferred_lft forever
2: eth0: <BROADCAST,MULTICAST,UP,LOWER_UP> mtu 1500 qdisc mq state UP group defa
ult qlen 1000
    link/ether 00:15:5d:01:ca:55 brd ff:ff:ff:ff:ff:ff
    inet 10.1.0.10/24 brd 10.1.0.255 scope global noprefixroute dynamic eth0
       valid_lft 690985sec preferred_lft 690985sec
    inet6 fe80::1744:5c69:7e04:19f3/64 scope link noprefixroute
       valid_lft forever preferred_lft forever
```

Using the ip a command.

INTERNET CONTROL MESSAGE PROTOCOL (ICMP)

The **Internet Control Message Protocol (ICMP)** is used to report errors and send messages about the delivery of a packet. It can also be used to test and troubleshoot connectivity issues on IP networks. ICMP messages are generated under error conditions in most types of unicast traffic, but not for broadcast or multicast packets.

ICMP MESSAGE TYPES
An ICMP message is encapsulated within a single IP packet. ICMP messages are categorized into various types. The most commonly encountered are described here.

ECHO REQUEST/REPLY
These are used for testing a connection with the ping utility. If a request message reaches the destination host, it generates a reply and sends it back to the source. If the request message does not reach its destination, an appropriate error message is generated.

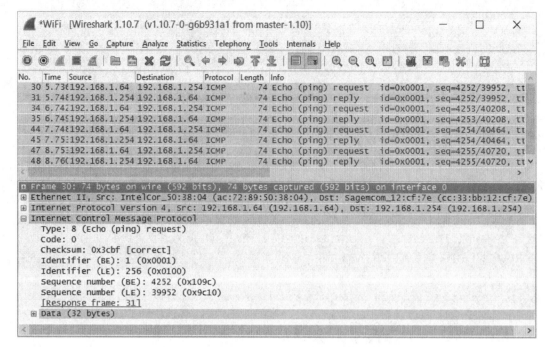

Exchange of ICMP requests and replies. (Screenshot courtesy of Wireshark.)

DESTINATION UNREACHABLE

This class of message indicates that a local host or a host on a remote network (or a protocol or port on a host) cannot be contacted. This might be caused by some sort of configuration error or by a host or router not being available.

TIME EXCEEDED

This is used when the **Time to Live (TTL)** of a packet reaches 0. The TTL field in a packet has a maximum value of 255, and this value is reduced by one every time the packet crosses a router. The TTL is eventually reduced to 0 if the packet is looping (because of a corrupted routing table) or when congestion causes considerable delays. The router then discards the packet and a warning packet is sent back to the source host.

REDIRECT

Most hosts channel all remote communications through the default gateway. If there are in fact multiple routers and a more efficient route can be identified, the default gateway can send a redirect message to the host to update its routing table. The router still delivers the original message.

ping

The `ping` utility sends a configurable number and size of ICMP packets to a destination host. This can be used to perform a basic connectivity test that is not dependent on the target host running any higher-level applications or services. To use `ping`, open a command prompt and enter this command: `ping` *HostName or IPAddress* where *HostName* and *IPAddress* refer to the remote computer.

If `ping` is successful (as in the first attempts shown in the screen capture), it responds with the message "Reply from *IPAddress*" and the time it takes for the server's response to arrive. The millisecond measures of **Round Trip Time (RTT)** can be used to diagnose latency problems on a link.

```
C:\Users\localadmin>ping 127.0.0.1

Pinging 127.0.0.1 with 32 bytes of data:
Reply from 127.0.0.1: bytes=32 time<1ms TTL=128
Reply from 127.0.0.1: bytes=32 time<1ms TTL=128
Reply from 127.0.0.1: bytes=32 time<1ms TTL=128
Reply from 127.0.0.1: bytes=32 time<1ms TTL=128

Ping statistics for 127.0.0.1:
    Packets: Sent = 4, Received = 4, Lost = 0 (0% loss),
Approximate round trip times in milli-seconds:
    Minimum = 0ms, Maximum = 0ms, Average = 0ms

C:\Users\localadmin>ping 192.168.1.1

Pinging 192.168.1.1 with 32 bytes of data:
Reply from 192.168.1.1: bytes=32 time<1ms TTL=64
Reply from 192.168.1.1: bytes=32 time<1ms TTL=64
Reply from 192.168.1.1: bytes=32 time<1ms TTL=64
Reply from 192.168.1.1: bytes=32 time<1ms TTL=64

Ping statistics for 192.168.1.1:
    Packets: Sent = 4, Received = 4, Lost = 0 (0% loss),
Approximate round trip times in milli-seconds:
    Minimum = 0ms, Maximum = 0ms, Average = 0ms

C:\Users\localadmin>ping 10.0.0.1

Pinging 10.0.0.1 with 32 bytes of data:
Reply from 192.168.1.1: Destination host unreachable.
Reply from 192.168.1.1: Destination host unreachable.
Reply from 192.168.1.1: Destination host unreachable.
Reply from 192.168.1.1: Destination host unreachable.

Ping statistics for 10.0.0.1:
    Packets: Sent = 4, Received = 4, Lost = 0 (0% loss),

C:\Users\localadmin>
```

Using ping in Windows. (Screenshot used with permission from Microsoft.)

The TTL output field shows the value of the TTL counter when the packet arrived at its destination. To work out the number of hops it took, you need to know the initial value. Different operating systems and OS versions use different default values. For example, if you ping a remote host from a Windows 10 host and the TTL value in the output is 52, then you know the packet took 12 hops (64-52) to reach its destination. You can set the initial TTL value manually using the `-i` switch in Windows or `-t` switch in Linux.

Note: Use `ping` for a basic connectivity test. The path between two remote hosts is better investigated using the `tracert`, `traceroute`, `mtr`, and `pathping` utilities.

If `ping` is unsuccessful, one of two messages are commonly received:

- **Destination host unreachable**—There is no routing information (that is, the local computer does not know how to get to that IP address). If the host is on the same IP network, check physical cabling, infrastructure devices such as the switch, and IP configuration. If the host is on another IP network, check the IP configuration and router.
- No reply (**Request timed out.**)—The host is unavailable or cannot route a reply to your computer.

Note: Be aware that ICMP traffic is often blocked by firewalls, making a response such as **Request timed out.** inevitable.

ping OUTPUT ANALYSIS

The following steps outline the procedures for verifying a host's configuration and for testing router connections:

1. Ping the loopback address (`ping 127.0.0.1`) to verify TCP/IP is installed and loaded correctly. The loopback address is a reserved IP address used for testing purposes.
2. Ping the IP address of your workstation to verify it was added correctly and to verify that the network adapter is functioning properly.
3. Ping the IP address of the default gateway to verify it is up and running and that you can communicate with a host on the local network.
4. Ping the IP address of a remote host to verify you can communicate through the router.

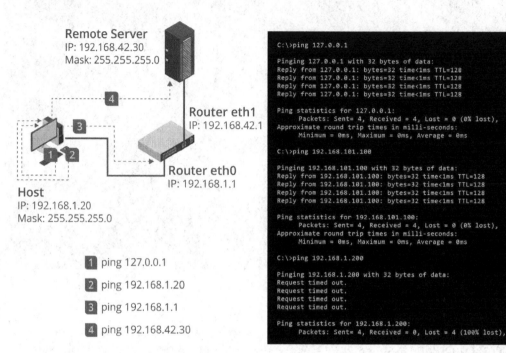

Troubleshooting with ping. (Image © 123RF.com. Screenshot used with permission from Microsoft.)

The trick with `ping` is understanding the messages that you receive when there is a problem.

- If you cannot ping the loopback address, the protocol is not correctly installed on the local system.
- If you cannot ping your own address, there might have been a configuration error, or the network adapter or adapter driver could be faulty.
- If a local host cannot be pinged, then verify the sending host's IP configuration—IP address, subnet mask, and so on.
- If the previous tests are successful, but a remote IP address cannot be contacted, check the default gateway parameter on the local host. If correct, use the **tracert** command, `tracert`, to investigate the route being taken. Also, consider manually adding the route by using the `route` command.
- If you can successfully perform all tests by IP address, but cannot ping by computer name, then this suggests a name resolution problem.

 Note: *To learn more, watch the related **Video** on the course website.*

ping SWITCHES

`ping` can be used with several switches. In Windows, you can adjust the TTL (`-i`) and timeout (`-w`) and force the use of IPv4 (`-4`) or IPv6 (`-6`) when pinging by host name. With IPv4, you can also use loose (`-j`) or strict (`-k`) source routing (sending packets via a predetermined route). The `-a` switch performs name resolution. Also, `-t` continues to ping the host until interrupted (by pressing **Ctrl+C**).

> **Note:** `ping` *has different syntax when used under Linux. By default, the command executes until manually halted, unless run with the number of packets appended at the end. Also, use* `ping6` *rather than* `ping  -6` *to force the use of IPv6 communications in Linux.*

> **Note:** *To learn more, watch the related **Video** on the course website.*

Activity 4-2
Discussing IP Interface Testing Tools

SCENARIO
Answer the following questions to test your understanding of the content covered in this topic.

---

1. **Once it is installed, how would you check the TCP/IP configuration at the command line?**

2. **Which of the protocols included with TCP/IP reports messages and errors regarding packet delivery?**

3. **True or False? Receiving an echo reply message indicates that the link between two hosts is operational.**

4. **True or False? The ipconfig utility can be used to empty the DNS cache.**

5. **If you have a workstation that cannot connect to a server, what is the first test you could perform to establish whether the cabling is OK?**

Activity 4-3
Configuring IPv4 Networking

BEFORE YOU BEGIN

Start the VMs used in this activity in the following order, adjusting the memory allocation first if necessary, and waiting at the ellipsis for the previous VMs to finish booting before starting the next group. You do not need to connect to a VM until prompted to do so in the activity steps.

1. **RT1-LOCAL** (256 MB)
2. **LAMP** (512—1024 MB)
3. **DC1** (1024—2048 MB)
4. ...
5. **MS1** (1024—2048 MB)
6. ...
7. **PC1** (1024—2048 MB)

 Note: *If you can allocate more than the minimum amounts of RAM, prioritize **DC1** and **LAMP**.*

SCENARIO

In this activity, you will investigate ways to configure Windows and Linux hosts with IP addresses and learn the use of the status and troubleshooting tools `ipconfig`/`ifconfig`/`ip` and `ping`. This activity is designed to test your understanding of and ability to apply content examples in the following CompTIA Network+ objectives:

• 1.1 Explain the purposes and uses of ports and protocols.
• 5.2 Given a scenario, use the appropriate tool.
• 5.5 Given a scenario, troubleshoot common network service issues.

---

1. Examine the Windows Server TCP/IP configuration dialog box, and experiment with some invalid IP configurations.

   The Windows VMs are attached to a virtual switch called **vLOCAL**. In this activity, you will also be using the Linux VM **LAMP**. This VM is not attached to the vLOCAL network yet.

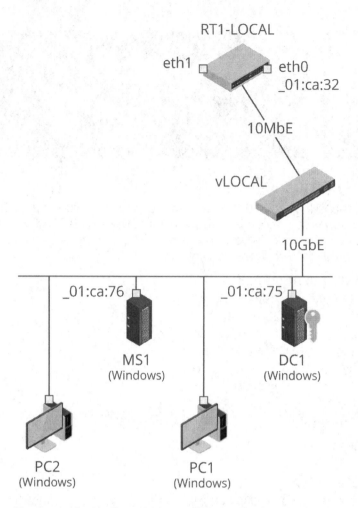

Topology of hosts attached to the vLOCAL switch. (Image © 123RF.com.)

a) When the **DC1** VM has booted, open a connection window and sign in with the username ***Administrator*** and the password ***Pa$$w0rd***

b) Right-click the **Start** button and select **Network Connections**.

c) In the **Network Connections** window, double-click the **Ethernet** icon.

This shows you the status and speed of the link. You can select the **Details** button to see the same information as `ipconfig /all`.

d) In the **Ethernet Status** dialog box, select the **Properties** button. In the **Ethernet Properties** dialog box, double-click **Internet Protocol Version 4 (TCP/IPv4)**.

e) In the **IP address** box, try to change the last octet to ***256***. What happens?

An error message is displayed. 256 is outside the range of possible values for an octet.

f) Select **OK** to close the **Error** dialog box. In the **IP address** box, change the last octet to ***255***, select **OK**. Can you explain the error message?

255 is the broadcast address of the subnet, so you can't use it as a host ID.

g) Select **OK** to close the error message.

h) In the **IP address** box, try to change the last octet to ***0*** then select **OK**. Can you explain the error message?

0 is the network address of the subnet, so you can't use it as a host ID.

i) Select **OK** to close the error message.

j) Select **Cancel** to close the two properties dialog boxes, then select **Close** to close the **Ethernet Status** dialog box. Close the **Network Connections** window.

2. Use Wireshark to examine an IP datagram header.

a) On the desktop, double-click the **Wireshark** icon.

b) In the **Capture** window, type *ip* in the **Enter a capture filter** box, then select the

Start capture button.

The filter limits the capture to IPv4 traffic. On your network, the primary effect of this is to filter out IPv6 traffic.

c) If necessary, select the **AutoScroll** button to turn off autoscrolling.

d) Open a command prompt, and run the following command:

```
ping 10.1.0.254
```

e) Leave the command prompt open. Switch back to Wireshark and look for an **Echo (ping) request** frame in the top pane, and select it.

This frame is a message from DC1 (note the source IP 10.1.0.1) to the router (with destination IP 10.1.0.254).

No.	Time	Source	Destination	Protocol	Length	Info
20	18.190211	10.1.0.2	10.1.0.1	DNS	77	Standard query 0x60db AAA
21	19.131998	10.1.0.1	10.1.0.254	ICMP	74	Echo (ping) request id=0
22	19.133783	10.1.0.254	10.1.0.1	ICMP	74	Echo (ping) reply id=0
23	20.139974	10.1.0.1	10.1.0.254	ICMP	74	Echo (ping) request id=0
24	20.140736	10.1.0.254	10.1.0.1	ICMP	74	Echo (ping) reply id=0
25	20.198314	10.1.0.2	10.1.0.1	DNS	77	Standard query 0x1e35 A o
26	20.198315	10.1.0.2	10.1.0.1	DNS	77	Standard query 0x60db AAA
27	21.249289	10.1.0.1	10.1.0.254	ICMP	74	Echo (ping) request id=0
28	21.249871	10.1.0.254	10.1.0.1	ICMP	74	Echo (ping) reply id=0

```
> Frame 21: 74 bytes on wire (592 bits), 74 bytes captured (592 bits) on interface 0
> Ethernet II, Src: Microsof_01:ca:75 (00:15:5d:01:ca:75), Dst: Microsof_01:ca:32 (00:15:5d:01:ca:32)
v Internet Protocol Version 4, Src: 10.1.0.1, Dst: 10.1.0.254
      0100 .... = Version: 4
      .... 0101 = Header Length: 20 bytes (5)
   > Differentiated Services Field: 0x00 (DSCP: CS0, ECN: Not-ECT)
      Total Length: 60
      Identification: 0x32ed (13037)
   > Flags: 0x0000
      Time to live: 128
      Protocol: ICMP (1)
      Header checksum: 0x0000 [validation disabled]
      [Header checksum status: Unverified]
      Source: 10.1.0.1
      Destination: 10.1.0.254
> Internet Control Message Protocol
```

```
0000  00 15 5d 01 ca 32 00 15  5d 01 ca 75 08 00 45 00   ··]··2·· ]··u··E·
0010  00 3c 32 ed 00 00 80 01  00 00 0a 01 00 01 0a 01   ·<2····· ········
0020  00 fe 08 00 4d 5a 00 01  00 01 61 62 63 64 65 66   ····MZ·· ··abcdef
0030  67 68 69 6a 6b 6c 6d 6e  6f 70 71 72 73 74 75 76   ghijklmn opqrstuv
0040  77 61 62 63 64 65 66 67  68 69                     wabcdefg hi
```

Examining fields in the IP datagram header. With the source address field selected in the middle pane, the hex value of the field is selected in the lowest pane. You should be able to make out the MAC addresses in the top line of the hex output too. (Screenshot courtesy of Wireshark.)

f) In the middle pane, expand the **Internet Protocol Version 4** datagram header.

Some of the fields include:

- **Time to live**—This prevents the datagram from being forwarded continually. At the moment, everything on your network is a single hop, so there is no chance of routing loops.

- **Protocol**—The value in this field (**1**) identifies the protocol contained within the datagram's payload (an ICMP message).

g) In the middle pane, expand the **Internet Control Message Protocol** datagram header.

You are now looking at the payload of the IP datagram. It has its own header; in this case, an ICMP header. ICMP response fields simply codify the type of message and for each type the code returned. There is also a checksum.

h) In the top pane, locate a DNS frame and select it. Expand the **Internet Protocol Version 4** datagram header again.

- Note the source and destination IP addresses. Can you match these to VMs or is an Internet host being contacted?

- Note the ID and fragmentation fields—These frames do not require fragmentation as the payloads are relatively short, but if a datagram must be split up to fit the MTU (the maximum size of the layer 2 frame payload), these fields are used to reassemble it.

- This time the protocol in the payload is identified as the User Datagram Protocol (UDP/17).

i) Optionally, scroll through the rest of the output to try to locate a frame containing a TCP payload. What protocol ID is assigned to TCP?

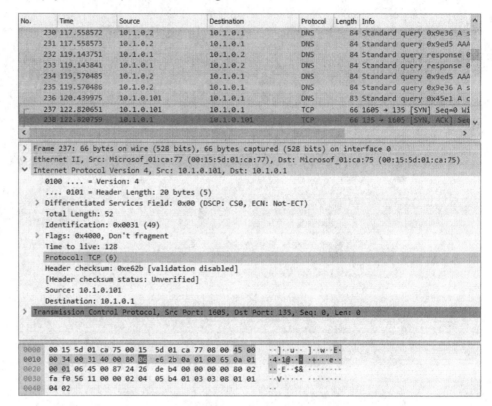

A TCP payload is identified by the value 6 in the Protocol field. Note the position of the field in the hex output. (Screenshot courtesy of Wireshark.)

j) Select the **Stop Capture** button.

k) In the Wireshark window, select the **Close** button. At the **Unsaved packets** prompt, select **Quit without Saving**.

Next, you will compare the different command-line tools used to report on the IP configuration.

3. Use `ipconfig` to report the adapter configuration on **DC1** and **MS1**.

a) Still on the **DC1** VM, in the command prompt, type *ipconfig* and press **Enter**.

Make a note of the IPv4 address: _____

b) At the command prompt, type *ipconfig /all* and then press **Enter**.

More detailed information about the IP configuration (and the Windows network configuration) is displayed.

The **DHCP Enabled** setting of **No** indicates that the address has been statically assigned. The MAC address (physical address) is also listed.

c) Open a connection window for the **MS1** VM, and sign in with the username *515support\Administrator* and the password *Pa$$w0rd*

d) Open a command prompt, type *ipconfig /all* and press **Enter**.

Record the IPv4 address: _____

4. Use the `ifconfig` and `ip` tools to report the adapter configuration on the **LAMP** Linux host.

a) Open a **LAMP** VM console window. Enter the username *lamp* and then the password *Pa$$w0rd*

> **Note:** *You might not see a prompt. You can type the username even though the prompt is not shown.*

In Linux, command-line input is case-sensitive.

> **Note:** *You can type the username even when the prompt is not shown.*

b) Type *ifconfig* and press **Enter**. What do you notice compared to the Windows ipconfig command?

- The output doesn't include the default gateway, but there is information about the MTU and packet stats.
- One key difference between the Linux and Windows versions is that `ifconfig` allows the reconfiguration of adapter properties.

> **Note:** *In Windows, you can configure adapter properties from the command line by using either `netsh` or PowerShell v3 commandlets.*

c) Run the following commands and enter the password *Pa$$w0rd* when prompted:

```
sudo ifconfig eth0 192.168.1.2

sudo ifconfig eth0 down

ifconfig
```

`eth0` is no longer listed in the command results, as the default behavior of the command is to show active interfaces only.

> **Note:** *Configuration changes made in this step will be lost when the system reboots.*

d) Run the following commands:

```
ifconfig -a

ifconfig eth0
```

The first command shows inactive and active interfaces. Using the adapter name filters the output to that interface only.

e) Run the following command (and enter the password *Pa$$w0rd* if prompted):

```
sudo ifconfig eth0 up
```

Though `ifconfig` remains widely supported and used, the `ip` command is designed to replace it.

f) Run the following commands:

```
sudo ip addr del 192.168.1.2/24 dev eth0

sudo ip addr add 192.168.1.1/24 dev eth0

ip addr show eth0
```

This command sequence deletes the existing address from the adapter (or device) `eth0` then assigns a new address and reports the updated configuration.

Note: *You can shorten the commands as well. For example,* `ip a` *is equivalent to* `ip addr show` *and* `ip a d` *is equivalent to* `ip addr del`.

g) Run the following commands:

```
arp

ip neigh
```

Both commands display the ARP cache (equivalent to `arp -a` in Windows). The output shows an entry for 192.168.1.254 and lists it as **FAILED** or possibly **INCOMPLETE**. This is the interface that **LAMP** expects to use as a router (or default gateway), but the interface is not responding to ARP queries (because you haven't started the appropriate VM).

5. Use `ping` to test TCP/IP functionality and links.

a) On the **LAMP** VM, run the following command. What does this tell you?

```
ping 127.0.0.1
```

Pinging the loopback address just confirms that the TCP/IP stack is implemented correctly by the host OS. If you can't ping the loopback address, you will need to reinstall TCP/IP.

b) Press **Ctrl+C** to stop pinging. Run the following command. What does this tell you?

```
ping 192.168.1.1 -c4
```

Pinging the IP address assigned to the local host tests that the network adapter driver is processing TCP/IP correctly. If this doesn't work, try reinstalling the adapter or updating the driver. The switch `-c4` sets the number of ping requests to 4, rather than pinging continually.

c) Run the following command. What does this tell you?

```
ping 192.168.1.254 -c4
```

Pinging another host on the local network would normally test that the link from the local machine to the network is good (no cable, connector, or port problems). In this case, though, the machine you are trying to ping isn't running. The error message is **Host Unreachable** because the destination IP address is local to your IP address.

d) Run the following command. What does this tell you?

```
ping 10.1.0.1 -c4
```

In this case, the error message **Network is unreachable** is self-explanatory. You need to provision both a physical link to the destination network and a logical route to the IP network.

6. Reconfigure IP on the **LAMP** VM and the Hyper-V network settings to allow **LAMP** to communicate with the Windows VMs.

a) In the **LAMP** VM console window, select **File→Settings**.

b) Select the **eth0** node. From the **Virtual switch** box, select **vLOCAL** and select **OK**.

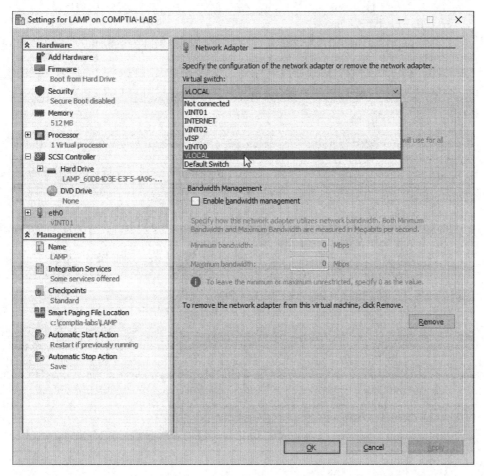

Moving the LAMP VM to a different switch. (Screenshot used with permission from Microsoft.)

In effect, this setting means that the **LAMP** VM and Windows VMs are plugged into the same physical network, as though you had unplugged a network cable from one switch and plugged it into a port on another switch.

c) Run the following command. What does the result tell you?

```
ping 10.1.0.1 -c4
```

LAMP is configured with the IP address of a different subnet, so even though you know the machine with that IP address is attached, **LAMP** still needs a route from the 192.168.1.0 subnet to the 10.1.0.0 subnet to communicate. Using different subnets on the same network segment is not usually a good idea though, so you will take the simpler and more practical approach: adjusting the interface properties to use an IP address on the same subnet as the Windows VMs.

d) Run the following commands and enter the password **Pa$$w0rd** when prompted.

```
sudo ip addr del 192.168.1.1/24 dev eth0

sudo ip addr add 10.1.0.2/24 dev eth0

ip addr show eth0
```

e) Record the **link/ether** address (yet another way of referring to the MAC address) assigned to eth0: _____

f) Run the following command to verify connectivity:

```
ping 10.1.0.1 -c4
```

7. Somewhere in the last few steps, you introduced a configuration problem into this IP network. Use the `ping`, `arp`, and `ip` tools to diagnose and fix the IP address configuration issue.

    a) Switch to the **DC1** VM. Run the following command to test connectivity with the **LAMP** VM:

    ```
    ping 10.1.0.2
    ```

    b) Run the following command—Is there anything to suggest that there is a problem?

    ```
    arp -a
    ```

    Your answer will vary depending on whether the MAC address is that of **LAMP** (_01:CA:5A) or that of **MS1** (varies).

    c) Run the following command to attempt to resolve the host name associated with that IP address:

    ```
    ping -a 10.1.0.2
    ```

    d) Right-click the **Start** button and select **Run**. In the **Run** dialog box, type ***http:// MS1.corp.515support.com*** and press **Enter**.

    The **515 Support User Portal** web page should open. Duplicate IP addresses are not necessarily catastrophic, but they should be avoided and corrected when they are discovered.

    e) Run `arp -a` again—Has the entry for 10.1.0.2 changed?

    f) Switch to the **MS1** VM and inspect the network connection status icon—Is there any warning or event notification suggesting an IP conflict?

    If two Windows machines try to use the same IP address, the second machine will detect the conflict and disable itself. This process does not work with Linux, however. When you are using static IP addresses, you need to consult up-to-date documentation about the IP address space before making changes (and update the documentation after making the change).

    g) Run the following command and record the MAC address—Does it match the one in DC1's ARP cache?

    ```
    ipconfig /all
    ```

8. Use the `ip` command to assign a valid address to the **LAMP** VM.

    a) Switch back to the **LAMP** VM again.

    b) Run the following commands (entering the password ***Pa$$w0rd*** if prompted):

    ```
    sudo ip addr del 10.1.0.2/24 dev eth0

    sudo ip addr add 10.1.0.11/24 dev eth0

    ip addr show eth0

    ping 10.1.0.1 -c1

    ping 10.1.0.2 -c1

    ip neigh
    ```

    This command sequence issues **LAMP** a valid (unused) IP address and tests connectivity with the Windows VMs. You should see that the ARP cache is populated with the correct MAC addresses for 10.1.0.1 and 10.1.0.2.

    c) Run the following command (entering the password ***Pa$$w0rd*** if prompted)—Can you explain what this command attempts and why no replies are received?

    ```
    ping 10.1.0.255 -bc4
    ```

    The `-b` switch confirms pinging the broadcast address of the local network. A broadcast transmission is received by every computer on the same local network. Most machines are configured not to reply to broadcast pings, as these are often used maliciously (to map out used IP address spaces or perform a denial of service attack).

    d) Run the following command to perform a ping sweep:

```
for i in {1..254}; do ping -c1 10.1.0.$i; done
```

This will take some time to complete, so you may want to cancel it before the end (press **Ctrl+Z**), but if you leave it running long enough you should discover the IP address assigned to **PC1**.

*Note: Remember that you can use **Shift+Page Up** and **Shift+Page Down** to scroll the terminal output.*

9. Discard changes made to the VM in this activity.

    a) Switch to Hyper-V Manager.

    b) Use the **Action** menu or the right-click menu in the **Hyper-V Manager** console to revert the **PC1** VM to its saved checkpoint.

*Note: Reverting the VM discards changes to the VM settings too, so **LAMP** will be reconnected to the **vINT01** switch.*

Topic C

Configure IPv4 Subnets

EXAM OBJECTIVES COVERED
1.4 Given a scenario, configure the appropriate IP addressing components.

Organizations with large networks need to divide those networks up into smaller segments to improve performance and security. A network segment is represented at the Network layer by a subnet. Designing and supporting subnet addressing schemes is fundamental to network operations, and a topic you will certainly need to master to progress in your career.

BROADCAST, MULTICAST, AND UNICAST TRAFFIC

IPv4 uses several mechanisms with which to communicate with other hosts. When an IPv4 host wants to send a packet to a single recipient, it uses a **unicast** packet, addressed to the IP address of the destination host. If, however, the local host needs to communicate with multiple hosts, it can do so either by using a **broadcast**, in which the destination address is one specially configured to be delivered to all hosts on the local network, or by using a **multicast** address, which represents a group of computers, programmed to respond to a particular address.

IPv4 BROADCAST DOMAINS

A **broadcast domain** is one where all the hosts receive the same broadcast packets. Broadcast domain boundaries are established at the Network layer (layer 3) by routers. Routers do not forward broadcasts, except in some specially configured circumstances. Consequently, each IP network is a separate broadcast domain. The last address in any IP network is the broadcast address, or put another way, the address in any IP network where all the host bits are set to 1.

For example, if the network ID is 192.168.1.0 and the subnet mask is 255.255.255.0, the last octet in the IP address is the host ID portion. If this last octet is set to all 1s, the last address, and therefore the network broadcast address, is 192.168.1.255.

```
192.168.  1.  0 11000000 10101000 00000001 00000000
255.255.255.  0 11111111 11111111 11111111 00000000
192.168.  1.255 11000000 10101000 00000001 11111111
```

As with unicast traffic, IP packets must be delivered to hosts using layer 2 MAC addresses. At layer 2, broadcasts are delivered using the group MAC address (ff:ff:ff:ff:ff:ff). This means that there is also a broadcast domain scope at layer 2. With legacy devices such as hubs and bridges, every port on all physically connected nodes is part of the same layer 2 broadcast domain. This is also the case with a basic or unmanaged switch. By default, a switch floods broadcasts out of every port except the source port.

Having lots of ports in the same broadcast domain is inefficient because the amount of broadcast traffic uses up more and more bandwidth. It would be very inefficient to solve this problem by provisioning separate switches for every IP network that you wanted to use in your logical network topology. This sort of problem can be addressed by configuring **virtual LANs (VLANs)** on the switch (or switches). With VLANs, each port is assigned a VLAN ID. Each VLAN ID is a separate broadcast domain. VLAN IDs can be communicated across multiple switches, which means that users attached to different switches but the same VLAN can be in the same broadcast domain. VLANs allow the layer 2 topology to match the layer 3 IP network topology.

IPv4 MULTICAST

IPv4 multicasting allows one host on the Internet (or private IP network) to send content to other hosts that have identified themselves as interested in receiving the originating host's content (that have joined a multicast **group**). Multicast packets are sent to a destination IP address from a special range configured for use with that multicast group. The **Internet Group Management Protocol (IGMP)** is typically used to configure group memberships and IP addresses. At layer 2, multicasts are delivered using a special range of MAC addresses. The switch must be multicast capable. If the switch is not multicast-capable, it will treat multicast like a broadcast and flood the multicast transmissions out of all ports.

CLASSFUL ADDRESSING

The combination of an IP address and netmask can be used to describe a **network ID** and a **host ID**. These parameters allow an internetwork to be divided into logically separate IP networks. Addressing schemes describe different ways of configuring IP addressing to suit different types and sizes of networks.

Classful addressing allocates a network ID based on the first octet of the IP address. The classful addressing scheme was employed in the 1980s, before the use of subnet masks to identify the network ID portion of an address was developed.

CLASS A, CLASS B, AND CLASS C ADDRESSES

Under classful addressing, the network IDs are divided into three classes, defining different sizes of IP network.

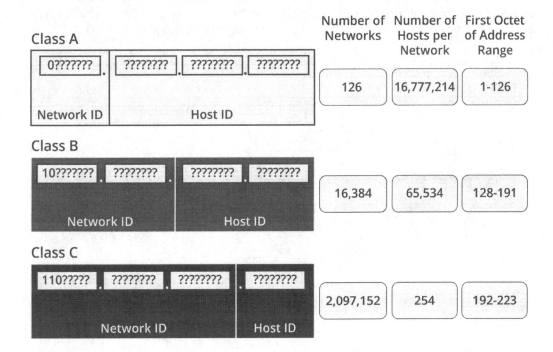

Choosing an address class.

Class A network addresses support large numbers of hosts—over 16 million. However, there are only 126 Class A network addresses. There are 16 thousand **Class B**

networks, each containing up to about 65,000 hosts. Finally, **Class C** networks support only 254 hosts each, but there are over 2 million of them.

When considering classful addressing, you need to identify the address class from the first octet of the IP address. This table shows how to identify an address class from the first octet of the IP address in decimal.

First Octet	Class
1-126	Class A
128-191	Class B
192-223	Class C

 Note: Alternatively, rather than worry about different address class ranges (i.e., A is 1 to 126), just remember the rule that all Class A networks start with a binary 0, all Class B start with a binary 10, and Class C start with a binary 110.

CLASS D AND CLASS E ADDRESSES

There are two additional classes of IP address (D and E) that use the remaining numbers:

* Class D addresses (224.0.0.0 through 239.255.255.255) are used for multicasting.
* Class E addresses (240.0.0.0 through 255.255.255.255) are reserved for experimental use and testing.

SUBNET DESIGN

Subnetting is the process of logically dividing a network into smaller subnetworks (subnets), with each subnet having a unique address.

For example, the following subnet design allocates separate subnets (10.0.1.0 and 10.0.2.0) for the two VLANs configured on Switch A and for the serial WAN links configured between Router A and Routers B and C (10.0.3.0 and 10.0.4.0). Routers B and C also have a subnet each for their local networks (10.0.5.0 and 10.0.6.0).

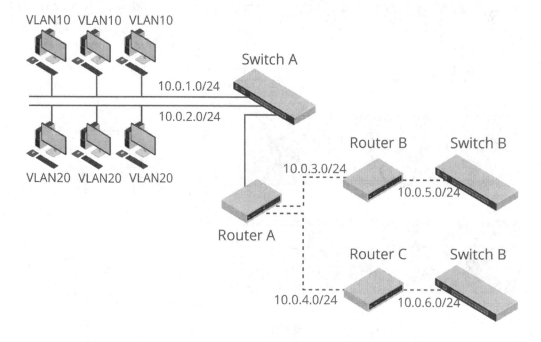

Subnet design. (Image © 123RF.com.)

An organization might divide a large IP network into logically distinct subnets for several reasons:

- It is inefficient to have very large numbers of hosts on the same IP network. A single IP network in this sense is a single broadcast domain; excessive broadcast traffic is created when there are many hosts on the same network. Large networks use VLANs to isolate broadcast domains and create subnets to map to each VLAN.
- Networks that use different physical and data link technologies, such as Token Ring and Ethernet, should be logically separated as different subnets.
- Many organizations have more than one site with WAN links between them. The WAN link normally forms a separate subnet.
- It is useful to divide a network into logically distinct zones for security and administrative control.

DEFAULT SUBNET MASKS AND SUBNET IDS

The conventional addressing technique has IP addresses with two hierarchical levels, namely the network ID and host ID. In subnet addressing, the host portion is further subdivided into the subnet ID and host ID, so subnet addressing is designed with three hierarchical levels: a network ID, subnet ID, and host ID. You should understand, however, that there is only one subnet mask applied to the IP address on each host. The mask containing the subnet is only used within an IP network. External IP networks continue to address the whole network by its network ID.

The **default** subnet masks correspond to the three classes of unicast IP address (A, B, and C). The default masks comprise whole octets:

- Class A: 255.0.0.0
- Class B: 255.255.0.0
- Class C: 255.255.255.0

Using these default masks as examples, you can see how they can be modified to allow a single IP network to be divided into several subnets. To do this, additional bits of the IP address must be allocated as a subnetwork address, rather than part of the host ID.

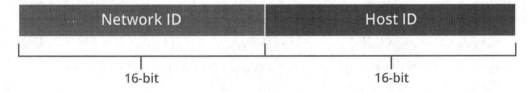

Internetwork addressing (Class B address).

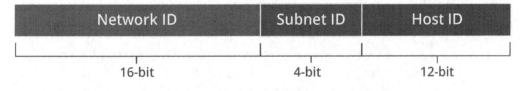

Subnet addressing.

The whole network is still referred to by the network ID (by routers external to the network) and the default mask; 172.30.0.0/255.255.0.0 for example. However, routers and hosts within the network add bits to the mask to differentiate the subnets. For example, if the network designer added 4 bits to the mask, it would mean a subnet mask of 20 bits—the 16 bits of the default Class B mask plus the 4 bits you added. In dotted decimal, the mask would be 255.255.240.0.

```
172. 30.  0. 0 10101100 00011110 00000000 00000000
```

```
255.255.  0. 0 11111111 11111111 00000000 00000000
255.255.240. 0 11111111 11111111 11110000 00000000
```

This leaves fewer bits (12) available for host IDs, but the purpose of subnetting is to create segments with fewer hosts. The trick with subnet design is to fit the scheme to the requirements for number of subnetworks and number of hosts per subnet. Each bit added to the mask approximately halves the number of available host addresses.

 Note: Wherever a 1 appears in the binary mask, the corresponding digit in the IP address is part of the network or subnet address. When you are planning what your mask will be, remember this rule. Allocate more bits in the mask if you need more subnets. Allocate fewer bits in the mask if you need more hosts per subnet.

CLASSLESS ADDRESSING

With a **classless addressing** scheme, the concept of address classes and default masks is abandoned in favor of representing the address with an appropriately sized **network prefix**. The idea that the netmask should align along an octet boundary is discarded completely. For example, when expressed in binary, the subnet mask 255.255.240.0 contains 20 ones followed by 12 zeroes. Therefore, the network prefix, expressed in **slash notation**, is 172.30.0.0/20.

 Note: Most configuration dialog boxes require you to input a subnet mask in dotted decimal format. Some may require you to enter the network address and prefix in slash notation, however.

While routers have performed classless routing for years, the class terminology is still very widely used. Even under classless addressing, the old classes are often used as names for the netmasks that align to whole octet boundaries; a Class A network is /8, a Class B network is /16, and a Class C network is /24.

IPv4 ADDRESS SCHEME DESIGN PLANNING

A network designer will need to plan the IP network addressing scheme carefully. Before choosing a scheme, consider the following factors:

- The number of IP networks and subnetworks required.
- The number of hosts per subnet that must be supported.

There are some additional constraints to consider when planning an addressing scheme:

- The network ID must be from a valid public or a private range (not from the loopback, link-local reserved range, multicast range, or reserved/experimental range, for instance).
- The network and/or host IDs cannot be all 1s in binary—this is reserved for broadcasts.
- The network and/or host ID cannot be all 0s in binary; 0 means "this network."
- Each host ID must be unique on the IP network or subnet.
- The network ID must be unique on the Internet (if you are using a public addressing scheme) or on your internal system of internetworks (if you are using a private addressing scheme).

When you are performing subnet calculations, it helps to remember that each power of 2 is double the previous one:

2^2	2^3	2^4	2^5	2^6	2^7	2^8
4	8	16	32	64	128	256

The process of designing the scheme is as follows:

1. Work out how many subnets are required (remembering to allow for future growth), then round this number up to the nearest power of 2. For example, if you need 12 subnets, the next nearest power of 2 is 16. The exponent is the number of bits you will need to add to your default mask. For example, 16 is 2^4 (2 to the power of 4), so you will need to add 4 bits to the network prefix. In dotted decimal format, the mask becomes 255.255.240.0.

2. Work out how many hosts each subnet must support and whether there is enough space left in the scheme to accommodate them. For example, if your network address (172.30.0.0, for instance) is in the /16 range and you use 4 bits for subnetting, you have 32-20 = 12 bits for hosts in each subnet. The number of hosts per subnet can be expressed using the formula 2^n-2, where *n* is the number of bits you have allocated for the host ID. 12 bits is enough for 4094 hosts in each subnet.

> **Note:** *You subtract 2 because each subnet's network address and broadcast address cannot be assigned to hosts.*

Just for comparison, if you have a /24 (or Class C) network address and try to allocate 16 subnets, there will be enough space left for only 14 hosts per subnet (2^4-2).

3. Work out the subnets. The easiest way to find the first subnet ID is to deduct the least significant octet in the mask (240 in this example) from 256. This gives the first subnet ID, which, in full, is 172.30.16.0/20.

4. The subsequent subnet IDs are all the lowest subnet ID higher than the one before—32, 48, 64, and so on.

5. Work out the host ranges for each subnet. Take the subnet address and add a binary 1 to it for the first host. For the last host, take the next subnet ID and deduct two binary digits from it. In this case, this is 172.30.16.1 and 172.30.31.254, respectively. Repeat for all subnets.

> **Note:** *To learn more, watch the related **Video** on the course website.*

Activity 4-4

Discussing IPv4 Subnetting

SCENARIO

Answer the following questions to test your understanding of the content covered in this topic.

---

1. **What technology or technologies can you use to isolate broadcast domains?**

2. **What is a Class D address?**

3. **Which of the following are Class C IP addresses? (Choose four.)**

    ☐ 195.243.67.51

    ☐ 165.247.220.100

    ☐ 190.234.24.6

    ☐ 11001101 01110100 00000100 00101110

    ☐ 11001111 10000001 01111110 10010010

    ☐ 213.54.53.52

    ☐ 233.168.24.6

4. **Which of the following IP addressing rules is true? (Choose two.)**

    ☐ The host ID must be unique on the network.

    ☐ Network and host IDs cannot be all zeroes.

    ☐ A network ID can be any number.

    ☐ A network ID can be 255.

5. **If a host is configured with the IP address 10.0.10.22 and mask 255.255.255.192, what is the broadcast address of the subnet?**

6.   **A host is configured with the IP address 10.0.10.22 and subnet mask 255.255.255.192. How many hosts per subnet would this addressing scheme support?**

7.   **A technician is troubleshooting a network and has asked your advice. He is trying to ping 192.168.16.192. The network has been subnetted with the custom mask 255.255.255.224. Why might this return a "Destination host unreachable" message?**

8.   **If the IP address 10.0.10.22 were used with an /18 mask, how many subnets and hosts per subnet would be available?**

Activity 4-5
Designing an IP Subnet

SCENARIO

At the Greene City Interiors branch office, you have been asked to implement an IP network. Your network ID is currently 192.168.1.0/24. You need to divide this in half (two subnets) to accommodate hosts on two separate floors of the building, each of which is served by managed switches. The whole network is served by a single router.

1. **To divide the network in half, what subnet mask do you need to use?**

2. **What are the subnet IDs for each network?**

3. **What is the broadcast address for each subnet?**

4. **What is the range of assignable IP addresses for each subnet?**

5. **Your manager has considered his original plan and realized that it does not accommodate the need for a WAN link to the head office or a separate segment for a team that works with sensitive data. What mask will you need to accommodate this new requirement, and how many hosts per subnet will it allow?**

6. **Your manager is not satisfied with the new scheme and wants to reduce the number of subnets to make more host addresses available in each subnet. Is there a way to use the same subnet for the two floors of the office?**

_____

Activity 4-6

Configuring IPv4 Subnets

BEFORE YOU BEGIN

Start the VMs used in this activity in the following order, adjusting the memory allocation first if necessary. You do not need to connect to a VM until prompted to do so in the activity steps.

1. **RT1-LOCAL** (256 MB)
2. **DC1** (1024 to 2048 MB)
3. **MS1** (1024 to 2048 MB)

SCENARIO

In this activity, you will discover the effect on connectivity when you adjust the subnet mask applied to an IP configuration. Recall the logical topology of the local network, as correctly configured:

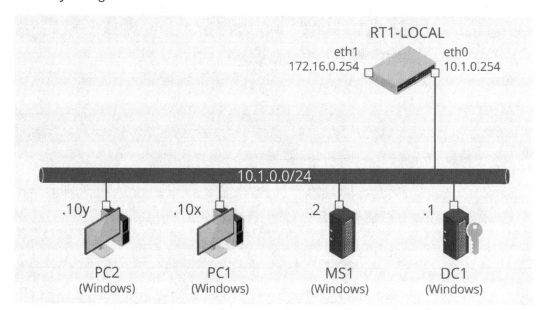

Logical topology of the local network. (Image © 123RF.com.)

This activity is designed to test your understanding of and ability to apply content examples in the following CompTIA Network+ objectives:

- 1.4 Given a scenario, configure the appropriate IP addressing components.
- 5.5 Given a scenario, troubleshoot common network service issues.

---

1. Test connectivity between **MS1** and **DC1**, observing the ICMP traffic in a Wireshark capture.

    a) When the **MS1** VM has booted, open a connection window and sign in with the username **515support\Administrator** and the password **Pa$$w0rd**

b) On the desktop, double-click the **Wireshark** icon.

c) In the **Capture** window, in the **Enter a capture filter** box, type *arp or icmp* then

select the **Start capture** button.

d) If necessary, select the **AutoScroll** button to turn off autoscrolling.

DC1 is configured with an IP address of 10.1.0.1 and a subnet mask of 255.255.255.0, while **MS1** has the IP address 10.1.0.2. In CIDR notation, these addresses can also be expressed as 10.1.0.1/24 and 10.1.0.2/24.

e) Open a command prompt as administrator.

f) Run `ping 10.1.0.1` to verify the link. Observe the Wireshark packet capture. You should see a sequence of four request/reply pairs.

g) Open a connection window for the **DC1** VM and sign in with the username *Administrator* and the password *Pa$$w0rd*

h) On the desktop, double-click the **Wireshark** icon.

i) In the **Capture** window, in the **Enter a capture filter** box, type *icmp* then select the

Start capture button.

j) If necessary, select the **AutoScroll** button to turn off autoscrolling.

k) Open a command prompt as administrator.

l) Run `ping 10.1.0.2` to verify the link.

m) Leave Wireshark running and the command prompts open on both machines.

2. Introduce a configuration problem by changing **DC1**'s subnet mask to **255.255.0.0**.

a) On the **DC1** VM, right-click the **Start** button and select **Network Connections**.

b) In the **Network Connections** window, right-click **Ethernet** and select **Properties**. Double-click **Internet Protocol Version 4 (TCP/IPv4)**.

c) Set the **Subnet mask** field to *255.255.0.0*

d) Select **OK** twice to close the **IPv4 Properties** and **Ethernet Properties** dialog boxes.

Note that the CIDR notation for this IP address is 10.1.0.1/16.

e) In the command prompt, run `ping 10.1.0.2`. Does it still work?
It does work. From the point of view of **DC1**, 10.1.0.2 is still on the same network.

```
10.   1.   0.   1   00001010 00000001 00000000 00000001

255.255.   0.   0   11111111 11111111 00000000 00000000

10.   1.   0.   2   00001010 00000001 00000000 00000010
```

f) Switch to the **MS1** VM and run `ping 10.1.0.1` again. Are you surprised this works? What do you notice about the captured frames on both machines?

MS1 can reply to **DC1** and **DC1** can reply to **MS1**, as the network IDs match one another regardless of which of the two masks is used. The frames show that each request receives a reply.

```
10.   1.   0.   2 00001010 00000001 00000000 00000010

255.255.255.   0 11111111 11111111 11111111 00000000

10.   1.   0.   1 00001010 00000001 00000000 00000001
```

3. Change the IP address of **MS1** to **10.1.254.2**, and test the effect.

a) Run the following command to change the IP address of **MS1** to **10.1.254.2** (ignore any line break and type as a single command followed by **Enter**):

```
netsh interface ip set address "Ethernet" static
10.1.254.2 255.255.255.0 10.1.254.254
```

b) Still on the **MS1** VM, what happens if you ping 10.1.0.1 now? Can you explain the error message(s)?

MS1 needs to use a router to reach a 10.1.0.0/16 subnet from a 10.1.254.0/24 subnet, but it cannot reach the router configured as its default gateway (unsurprisingly, as it doesn't exist). This can produce a mix of **Request timed out** errors (because ARP cannot identify the default gateway) and **Destination unreachable** errors (because there is no other route in the local routing table).

```
10.  1.254.  2    00001010 00000001 11111110 00000010

255.255.255.  0    11111111 11111111 11111111 00000000

10.  1.  0.  1    00001010 00000001 00000000 00000001
```

4. Change the subnet mask of **MS1** to **255.255.0.0**, and test the effect.

   a) Run the following command to change the subnet mask to **255.255.0.0**, leaving the IP address set to **10.1.254.2** (ignore any line break and type as a single command followed by **Enter**):

   ```
   netsh interface ip set address "Ethernet" static
   10.1.254.2 255.255.0.0 10.1.254.254
   ```

   b) What happens if you ping 10.1.0.1 now?

   The first couple of attempts may fail, but subsequently this works as they are within the same /16 subnet.

   ```
   10.  1.254.  2    00001010 00000001 11111110 00000010

   255.255.  0.  0    11111111 11111111 00000000 00000000

   10.  1.  0.  1    00001010 00000001 00000000 00000001
   ```

   c) Switch back to the **DC1** VM. Check that `ping 10.1.254.2` works.

5. Change the subnet mask of **DC1** back to **255.255.255.0**, and test the effect.

   a) Still on the **DC1** VM, run the following command to change the subnet mask back to **255.255.255.0**, leaving the IP address set to **10.1.0.1** (ignore any line break and type as a single command followed by **Enter**):

   ```
   netsh interface ip set address "Ethernet" static 10.1.0.1
   255.255.255.0 10.1.0.254
   ```

   b) Try to ping 10.1.254.2 again.

   This will fail, with **Destination host unreachable** messages. If you ran the command quickly, you may also see a **General failure** message. This is a transitory error because the new configuration isn't properly initialized.

   c) Switch back to the **MS1** VM. Try to ping 10.1.0.1 again. What do you notice about the captured packets? Can you explain the error message?

   Now **MS1** can send to **DC1** as it thinks both are on the 10.1.0.0/16 network, but **DC1** cannot deliver replies to **MS1** as it has no route to a 10.1.254.0/24 network.

   ```
   10.  1.  0.  1 00001010 00000001 00000000 00000001

   255.255.255.  0 11111111 11111111 11111111 00000000

   10.  1.254.  2 00001010 00000001 11111110 00000010
   ```

d) Consequently, **MS1** generates a **Request timed out** error because it thinks the network path is valid, but the host is not responding. In the captures, you should be able to see that **DC1** receives Echo Requests and generates Echo Reply packets but that no replies are received by **MS1**.

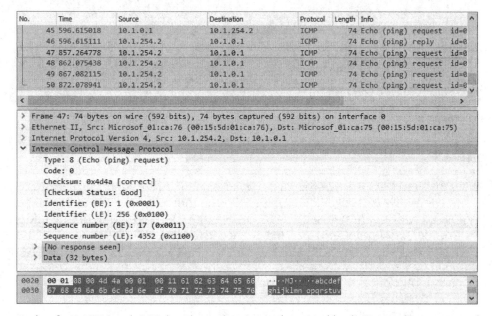

No.	Time	Source	Destination	Protocol	Length	Info
45	596.615018	10.1.0.1	10.1.254.2	ICMP	74	Echo (ping) request id=0
46	596.615111	10.1.254.2	10.1.0.1	ICMP	74	Echo (ping) reply id=0
47	857.264778	10.1.254.2	10.1.0.1	ICMP	74	Echo (ping) request id=0
48	862.075438	10.1.254.2	10.1.0.1	ICMP	74	Echo (ping) request id=0
49	867.082115	10.1.254.2	10.1.0.1	ICMP	74	Echo (ping) request id=0
50	872.078941	10.1.254.2	10.1.0.1	ICMP	74	Echo (ping) request id=0

```
> Frame 47: 74 bytes on wire (592 bits), 74 bytes captured (592 bits) on interface 0
> Ethernet II, Src: Microsof_01:ca:76 (00:15:5d:01:ca:76), Dst: Microsof_01:ca:75 (00:15:5d:01:ca:75)
> Internet Protocol Version 4, Src: 10.1.254.2, Dst: 10.1.0.1
v Internet Control Message Protocol
    Type: 8 (Echo (ping) request)
    Code: 0
    Checksum: 0x4d4a [correct]
    [Checksum Status: Good]
    Identifier (BE): 1 (0x0001)
    Identifier (LE): 256 (0x0100)
    Sequence number (BE): 17 (0x0011)
    Sequence number (LE): 4352 (0x1100)
  > [No response seen]
  > Data (32 bytes)

0020  00 01 08 00 4d 4a 00 01  00 11 61 62 63 64 65 66   ··MJ·· ··abcdef
0030  67 68 69 6a 6b 6c 6d 6e  6f 70 71 72 73 74 75 76   ghijklmn opqrstuv
```

Probes from MS1 reach DC1, but the replies cannot be routed back. (Screenshot courtesy of Wireshark.)

Applying inconsistent subnet masks may or may not break communications between hosts and can sometimes be difficult to identify. Hosts in the same subnet should be configured with the same mask, ideally from an autoconfiguration service such as DHCP.

6. Discard changes made to the VM in this activity.

a) Switch to Hyper-V Manager.

b) Use the **Action** menu or the right-click menu in the **Hyper-V Manager** console to revert all the VMs to their saved checkpoints.

Topic D

Configure Private and Public IPv4 Addressing Schemes

 EXAM OBJECTIVES COVERED
1.4 Given a scenario, configure the appropriate IP addressing components.

Now that you are aware of the basic concepts of IP addressing, you can start identifying ways to assign IP addresses. On the Internet, TCP/IP addresses must be regulated with a common scheme to ensure that there are no duplicate addresses worldwide. Companies and Internet Service Providers (ISPs) often lease addresses for their networks and customers to gain Internet access, but it can be expensive for a company to lease IP addresses for every client that needs Internet access. Consequently, other addressing schemes are available for private networks.

PRIVATE VS. PUBLIC ADDRESSING

A **public** IP network or host address is one that can establish a connection with other public IP networks and hosts over the Internet. The allocation of public IP addresses is governed by IANA and administered by regional registries and Internet Service Providers (ISPs). Hosts communicating with one another over a local area network (LAN) could use a public addressing scheme, but will more typically use **private addressing**. Private IP addresses can be drawn from one of the pools of addresses defined in *RFC 1918* as non-routable over the Internet:

*   10.0.0.0 to 10.255.255.255 (Class A private address range).
*   172.16.0.0 to 172.31.255.255 (Class B private address range).
*   192.168.0.0 to 192.168.255.255 (Class C private address range).

Any organization can use private addresses on its networks without applying to a registry or ISP, and multiple organizations can use these ranges simultaneously. Internet access can be facilitated for hosts using a private addressing scheme in two ways:

*   Through a router configured with a single or block of valid public IP addresses; the router translates between the private and public addresses using a process called **Network Address Translation (NAT)**.
*   Through a proxy server that fulfills requests for Internet resources on behalf of clients. The proxy server itself must be configured with a public IP address on the external-facing interface.

LOOPBACK ADDRESSES

While nominally part of Class A, the range 127.0.0.0 to 127.255.255.255 (or 127.0.0.0/8) is reserved. This range is used to configure a **loopback address**, which is a special address typically used to check that TCP/IP is correctly installed on the local host. The loopback interface does not require a physical interface to function. A packet sent to a loopback interface is not processed by a network adapter, but is otherwise processed as normal by the host's TCP/IP stack. (It is sent by and received by the local host.) Every IP host is automatically configured with a default loopback address, typically 127.0.0.1.

On some hosts, such as routers, more than one loopback address might be configured. Loopback interfaces can also be configured with an address from any suitable IP range, as long as it is unique on the network (again, often of use in routing).

RESERVED ADDRESS RANGES

Apart from loopback, private addressing, and Class D and Class E, a few other IPv4 address ranges are reserved for special use and are not publicly routable:

- 0.0.0.0/8—Used when a specific address is unknown. This is typically used as a source address by a client seeking a DHCP lease.
- 255.255.255.255—Used to broadcast to the local network when the local network address is not known.
- 169.254.0.0 to 169.254.255.255—Used by hosts for automatic private IP addressing (APIPA or link-local addressing).
- 100.64.0.0/10, 192.0.0.0/24, 192.88.99.0/24, 198.18.0.0/15—Set aside for a variety of special purposes.
- 192.0.2.0/24, 198.51.100.0/24, 203.0.113.0/24—Set aside for use in documentation and examples.

CLASSLESS INTER-DOMAIN ROUTING (CIDR)

Classless addressing was designed to solve two major problems of the classful addressing scheme as more and more networks joined the Internet through the early 1990s. The first was that network addresses, specifically, Class B addresses, were becoming very scarce and the second was near exponential growth in Internet routing tables.

Classless Inter-Domain Routing (CIDR) is described in *RFC 4632*. Essentially, it uses bits normally assigned to the network ID to mask the complexity of the subnet and host addressing scheme within that network. CIDR is also sometimes described as **supernetting**.

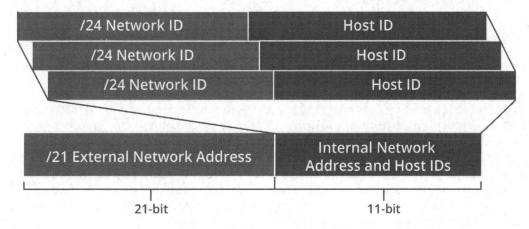

Classless Inter-Domain Routing (CIDR).

For example, rather than allocate a Class B (or /16) network address to a company, several contiguous Class C (or /24) addresses could be assigned. Eight /24 network addresses gives 2,032 hosts. However, this would mean complicated routing with many entries in the routing tables to represent eight IP networks at the same location. Using CIDR collapses these routing entries into one single entry.

If the network addresses assigned to a company were 192.32.168.0 through to 192.32.175.0 and you wanted to view this as one network, just consider the first 21 bits of the address.

```
192.32.168.0    11000000.00100000.10101  000.00000000
192.32.169.0    11000000.00100000.10101  001.00000000
192.32.170.0    11000000.00100000.10101  010.00000000
192.32.171.0    11000000.00100000.10101  011.00000000
192.32.172.0    11000000.00100000.10101  100.00000000
192.32.173.0    11000000.00100000.10101  101.00000000
192.32.174.0    11000000.00100000.10101  110.00000000
192.32.175.0    11000000.00100000.10101  111.00000000
```

The network address could also be expressed in classless or CIDR notation as 192.32.168.0/21, meaning that the network prefix contains 21 bits (count the 1s in the mask following example).

As with subnetting, an ANDing process is used to determine whether to route. If the ANDed result reveals the same network ID as the destination address, then it is the same network. In this next example, the first two IP addresses belong to the same network (the second is the broadcast address for the network), but the third is on a different one:

```
Mask 255.255.248.  0    11111111.11111111.11111000.00000000
IP   192. 32.168.  1    11000000.00100000.10101000.00000001
IP   192. 32.175.255    11000000.00100000.10101111.11111111
IP   192. 32.176.  1    11000000.00100000.10110000.00000001
```

Routers external to the network just use the /21 prefix, so the complexity of the LAN subnets is hidden and doesn't need to clog up their routing tables. The LAN's internal routers use the /24 prefix or even multiple prefixes to create subnets of different sizes, which is called **variable length subnet masking (VSLM)**.

CIDR allows for a more flexible, hierarchical system of network addressing, with efficient routing between networks on the Internet.

VARIABLE LENGTH SUBNET MASKS (VLSMs)

The IPv4 address space is close to being exhausted, making it difficult for ISPs to allocate public addresses to the companies that want them. To mitigate this, more efficient methods of allocating IP addresses must be used. Supernetting simplifies the information Internet routers need to locate IP networks. A complementary technique, called **variable length subnet masking (VLSM)**, allows a network designer to allocate ranges of IP addresses to subnets that match the predicted need for numbers of subnets and hosts per subnet more closely. Without VLSM, you have to allocate subnetted ranges of addresses that are the same size and use the same subnet mask throughout the network. This typically means that some subnets have many wasted IP addresses or additional routing interfaces must be installed to connect several smaller subnets together within a single building or department.

VLSM allows different length netmasks to be used within the same IP network, allowing more flexibility in the design process. VLSM was originally defined in *RFC 1812*.

VLSM ADDRESS SCHEME DESIGN

For this example, consider a company that is part of a multinational organization with many hundreds of subnetworks worldwide. This scenario has six major offices, each with differing network sizes and IP address requirements. There are also two subnets connecting the regional routers with the headquarters router, which provides access to the Internet.

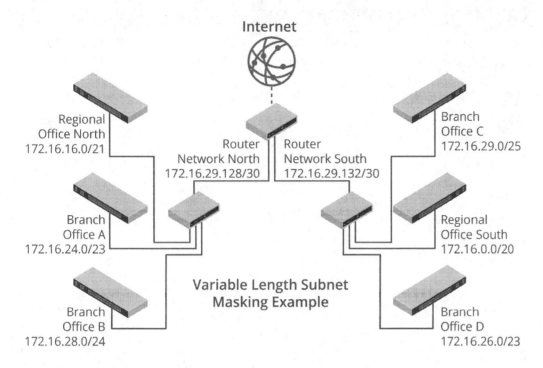

VLSM example. (Image © 123RF.com.)

VLSM design usually proceeds by identifying the largest subnets and organizing the scheme in descending order. Even though VLSM allows more precise allocation of address space, don't forget the requirement to design for growth and allow space in each subnet for additional hosts. Note also the use of router subnets with just two host addresses. As these are point-to-point links, no more than two addresses will ever be required.

The requirements for the subnetted network are listed in the following table, along with the actual number of IP addresses that would be provided by the VLSM design.

Office/Subnet	Required Number of IP Addresses	Actual Number of IP Addresses
Regional Office South	2060	4094
Regional Office North	1200	2046
Branch Office A	420	510
Branch Office D	300	510
Branch Office B	180	254
Branch Office C	70	126
Router Subnet North	2	2
Router Subnet South	2	2

The actual IP address ranges generated by the VLSM design are show in this table.

Office	Subnet	Useable Subnet Address Range
Regional Office South	172.16.0.0/20	172.16.0.1—172.16.15.254
Regional Office North	172.16.16.0/21	172.16.16.1—172.16.23.254
Branch Office A	172.16.24.0/23	172.16.24.1—172.16.25.254
Branch Office D	172.16.26.0/23	172.16.26.1—172.16.27.254
Branch Office B	172.16.28.0/24	172.16.28.1—172.16.28.254
Branch Office C	172.16.29.0/25	172.16.29.1—172.16.29.126

Office	Subnet	Useable Subnet Address Range
Router Subnet North	172.16.29.128/30	172.16.29.129—172.16.29.130
Router Subnet South	172.16.29.132/30	172.16.29.133—172.16.29.134

Note: *To learn more, watch the related* **Video** *on the course website.*

Activity 4-7

Discussing Private and Public IPv4 Addressing Schemes

SCENARIO

Answer the following questions to test your understanding of the content covered in this topic.

1. **True or False? The IP address 172.24.0.1 is routable over the Internet.**

2. **What two methods can an organization use to facilitate Internet access for hosts configured with private addresses?**

3. **What is the significance of the address 127.0.0.1?**

4. **A company has four networks, using the addresses 192.168.0.0/24, 192.168.1.0/24, 192.168.2.0/24, and 192.168.3.0/24. What network prefix and subnet mask can be used to summarize a supernet route to these networks?**

5. **True or False? VLSM means using more than one mask to subnet an IP network.**

Activity 4-8
Designing VLSM Subnets

SCENARIO

In this activity, you will be designing an IP subnetting plan for an organization using VLSM. This division of the company must use the 172.30.0.0/16 network address range and subnet this down to develop an address scheme for the network displayed in the topology diagram. You should be as efficient as possible when designing your VLSM ranges, as additional branch offices may be added in the future.

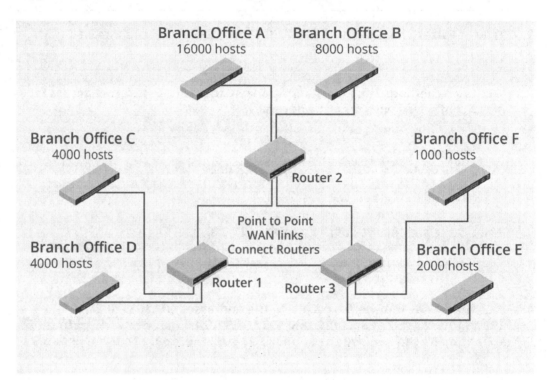

Network topology. (Image © 123RF.com.)

1. **How large will each of the subnets that join the three routers together need to be?**

2. **Which is the largest subnet in the topology? What is the minimum number of bits that will be needed for that number of hosts? How many IP addresses will that subnet provide? What would be the VLSM and address range for the largest subnet?**

3. **What is the next largest subnet in the design? How many host bits will be needed for that subnet? How many IP addresses will that subnet provide and what is the VLSM?**

4. **Work out the remaining subnets, remembering to ensure that subnet ranges do not overlap, but equally that you do not waste IP addresses. Complete the table.**

Subnet Name	Number of Hosts	VLSM Subnet ID	Number of IP Addresses
Branch A			
Branch B			
Branch C			
Branch D			
Branch E			
Branch F			
Router 1 to 2			
Router 2 to 3			
Router 1 to 3			

Topic E

Configure IPv6 Addressing Components

EXAM OBJECTIVES COVERED
1.3 Explain the concepts and characteristics of routing and switching.
1.4 Given a scenario, configure the appropriate IP addressing components.

In the previous topics, you learned about IPv4, which is the original version of the protocol and is in use on thousands of networks. In contrast, IP version 6 (IPv6) is a newer standard that has more limited adoption on networks but is expected to eventually replace IPv4. In this topic, you will describe IPv6 addressing. As a network professional who supports TCP/IP networking, you should be aware of the limitations of the IPv4 addressing scheme. IPv6 is an addressing scheme available to network administrators who need to overcome these limitations. If you support or configure networks that include the IPv6 addressing scheme, you need to understand its characteristics as well as how it can interoperate with existing IPv4 implementations.

USES FOR IPv6

In IPv4, the addressing scheme is based on a 32-bit binary number. 32 bits can express 2^{32} unique addresses (in excess of four billion). However, the way in which addresses have been allocated has been inefficient, leading to waste of available addresses. Inefficiencies in the addressing scheme and growing demand for addresses in Asia mean that the available IPv4 address supply is close to exhaustion.

Network address translation (NAT) and private addressing have provided a stopgap solution to the problem. **IP version 6 (IPv6)** provides a long-term solution to the problem of address space exhaustion. Its 128-bit addressing scheme has space for 340 undecillion unique addresses. Even though only a small part of the scheme can currently be allocated to hosts, there is still enough address space within that allocation for every person on the planet to own approximately 4,000 addresses. As well as coping with the growth in ordinary company networks and Internet access subscribers, IPv6 is designed to meet the demands of billions of handheld and personal devices with Internet connectivity. Currently, that principally means tablets and phones, but the designers of IPv6 envisage a world of wireless Internet connectivity for a huge range of appliances, or the **Internet of Things (IoT)**. For example, an advertising billboard could be made active, so you can link to the product via your phone.

Despite being in development for well over two decades, it is only in the last few years that IPv6 has started to be deployed in certain sections of public and corporate networks. While IPv6 has been a standard installed feature in the last few versions of both desktop and Server versions of common operating systems, it is only in the core network that IPv6 has typically been implemented. However, as the problems with existing IPv4 solutions multiply (especially with regards to security), the next couple of years are almost certain to see IPv6 become more mainstream for corporate networks down to the desktop and the web in general.

Note: This blog explains why we have jumped from IPv4 to IPv6: colocationamerica.com/blog/ipv4-ipv6-what-happened-to-ipv5.htm.

HEXADECIMAL NUMBERING

To interpret IPv6 addresses, you must understand hexadecimal notation and the concept of base numbering systems. To start with the familiar; **decimal numbering** is also referred to as **base 10**. Base 10 means that each digit can have one of ten possible values (0 through 9). A digit positioned to the left of another has 10 times the value of the digit to the right. For example, the number 255 can be written out as follows:

```
(2x10x10)+(5x10)+5
```

Binary is **base 2**, so a digit in any given position can only have one of two values (0 or 1), and each place position is the next power of 2. The binary value 11111111 can be converted to the decimal value 255 by the following sum:

```
(1x2x2x2x2x2x2x2)+(1x2x2x2x2x2x2)+(1x2x2x2x2x2)+(1x2x2x2x2)+(1x2x2
x2)+(1x2x2)+(1x2)+1
```

Many values in computing, such as IPv4 addresses, are represented in **octets** (or bytes). 1 octet (or byte) is 8 bits, which can be represented in decimal as the values 0 through 255. Because IPv6 addresses are so long (128 bits), dotted decimal conversions are not practical. **Hexadecimal** notation (or hex) is a more convenient way of referring to the long sequences of bytes used in IPv6. Hex is **base 16** with the possible values of each digit represented by the numerals 0 through 9 and the characters A, B, C, D, E, and F. Use the following table to help to convert between decimal, binary, and hexadecimal values.

Decimal	Hexadecimal	Binary	Decimal	Hexadecimal	Binary
0	0	0000	8	8	1000
1	1	0001	9	9	1001
2	2	0010	10	A	1010
3	3	0011	11	B	1011
4	4	0100	12	C	1100
5	5	0101	13	D	1101
6	6	0110	14	E	1110
7	7	0111	15	F	1111

As you can see from the table, every hex digit lines up neatly with four binary digits (a nibble), so conversion is a straightforward matter of dividing the binary digits into groups of four, then converting each group individually.

Note: *To avoid confusion with decimal values, hex values can be written with a leading 0x (0xFF for instance). This is not the case with IPv6 notation, however.*

IPv6 ADDRESS STRUCTURE

IPv6 addresses contain eight 16-bit numbers (double-byte or double-octet), with each double-byte number expressed as 4 hex digits. For example, the binary address:

```
0010 0000 0000 0001 : 0000 1101 1011 1000 : 0000 0000 0000 0000 :

0000 0000 0000 0000 : 0000 1010 1011 1100 : 0000 0000 0000 0000 :

1101 1110 1111 0000 : 0001 0010 0011 0100
```

can be represented in hex notation as:

```
2001:0db8:0000:0000:0abc:0000:def0:1234
```

Even this is quite cumbersome, so where a double byte contains leading 0s, they can be ignored. In addition, one contiguous series of 0s can be replaced by a double colon place marker. Thus, the prior address would become:

`2001:db8::abc:0:def0:1234`

You can only use double colon compression **once** in a given address. For example, 2001:db8::abc::def0:1234 is not valid as it is unclear which of the following two addresses is represented:

`2001:db8:0000:0abc:0000:0000:def0:1234`

`2001:db8:0000:0000:0abc:0000:def0:1234`

Where IPv6 addresses are used as part of a URL (web address), because both formats use colon delimiters to mean different things, the IPv6 address must be contained within brackets. For example: **http://[2001:db8::abc:0:def0:1234]/index.htm**.

 Note: *The IPv6 address format and addressing schemes are fully described in RFC 4291.*

IPv6 HEADER FIELDS

An IPv6 packet consists of two or three elements: the main header, which is a fixed length (unlike in IPv4), one or more optional extension headers, and the payload. The IPv6 packet format is detailed in *RFC 2460*, but the key features are:

Field	Size	Explanation
Version	4 bits	Used to indicate which version of IP is being used (0110 or 0x06 for IPv6).
Traffic Class	8 bits	Describes the packet's priority.
Flow Label	20 bits	Used for QoS management, such as for real-time streams. This is set to 0 for packets not part of any delivery sequence or structure.
Payload Length	16 bits	Indicates the length of the packet payload, up to a maximum of 64 KB; if the payload is bigger than that, this field is 0 and a special Jumbo Payload (4 GB) option is established.
Next Header	8 bits	Used to describe what the next extension header (if any) is, or where the actual payload begins.
Hop Limit	8 bits	Replaces the TTL field in IPv4, but performs the same function.
Source Address	128 bits	The originating address.
Destination Address	128 bits	The target address.

Extension headers replace the Options field in IPv4. There are several pre-defined extension headers to cover functions such as fragmentation and reassembly, security (IPSec), source routing, and so on.

IPv6 ADDRESSING SCHEMES

An IPv6 address is divided into two parts: the first 64 bits are used as a network ID, while the second 64 bits designate a specific interface. Unlike in IPv4, the interface address (or host ID portion) is always the same 64-bit length.

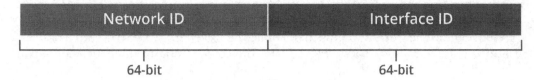

Network ID	Interface ID
64-bit	64-bit

In IPv6, the interface identifier is always the last 64 bits. The first 64 bits are used for network addressing.

Network addresses are written using CIDR notation, where /*nn* is the length of the routing prefix in bits. Within the 64-bit network ID, as with CIDR, the length of any given **network prefix** is used to determine whether two addresses belong to the same IP network. For example, if the prefix is /48, then if the first 48 bits of an IPv6 address were the same as another address, the two would belong to the same IP network. This means that a given organization's network can be represented by a network prefix 48 bits long, and they then have 16 bits left in the network ID to subnet their network. For example,

```
2001:db8:3c4d::/48
```

would represent a network address, while:

```
2001:db8:3c4d:01::/64
```

would represent a subnet within that network address.

Like IPv4, IPv6 can use unicast addressing and multicast addressing. Unlike IPv4, there is no broadcast addressing.

IPv6 UNICAST ADDRESSING

As with IPv4, a **unicast address** identifies a single network interface. IPv6 unicast addressing is **scoped**; a **scope** is a region of the network. Global scopes provide the equivalent of public addressing schemes in IPv4, while link-local schemes provide private addressing.

IPv6 GLOBAL ADDRESSING

Globally scoped unicast addresses are routable over the Internet and are the equivalent of public IPv4 addresses. The parts of a global address are:

- The first 3 bits (001) indicate that the address is within the global scope. Most of the IPv6 address space is unused. The scope for globally unique unicast addressing occupies just 1/8th of the total address space. In hex, globally scoped unicast addresses will start with a 2 (0010) or 3 (0011).
- The next 45 bits are allocated in a hierarchical manner to regional registries and from them to ISPs and end users.
- The next 16 bits identify site-specific subnet addresses.
- The final 64 bits are the interface ID.

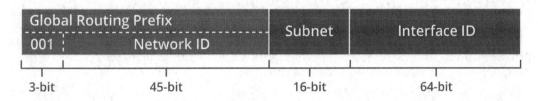

Global Routing Prefix		Subnet	Interface ID
001	Network ID		
3-bit	45-bit	16-bit	64-bit

IPv6 global unicast address format.

INTERFACE ID/EUI-64

The interface ID can be determined by using two techniques.

- One is by using the interface's MAC address. This is known as a **MAC-derived address** or **interface identifier**. As a MAC address is currently 48 bits (6 bytes), a (relatively) simple translation mechanism allows driver software to create a 64-bit interface ID (an EUI-64) from these 48 bits. The conversion mechanism is defined in *RFC 4291*.

  Essentially, the digits `fffe` are added in the middle of the address and the U/L bit is flipped. For example, the MAC address `00608c123abc` would become the EUI-64 address `02608cfffe123abc`, which (when expressed in double-bytes) becomes `0260:8cff:fe12:3abc`, or (without the leading 0) `260:8cff:fe12:3abc`.

- In the second technique, referred to as **privacy extensions** and described in *RFC 4941*, the client device uses a pseudorandom number for the interface ID. This is known as a **temporary interface ID** or **token**. There is some concern that using interface identifiers would allow a host to be identified and closely monitored when connecting to the Internet, and using a token mitigates this to some degree.

IPv6 LINK-LOCAL ADDRESSING

Link-local addresses are used by IPv6 for network housekeeping traffic. Link-local addresses span a single subnet (they are not forwarded by routers). Nodes on the same link are referred to as **neighbors**. Link-local addresses start with a leading `fe80`, with the next 54 bits set to 0, and the last 64 bits are the interface ID.

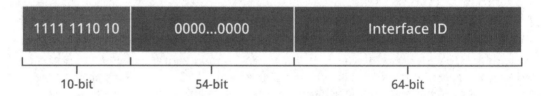

IPv6 link-local unicast address format.

The equivalent in IPv4 is **Automatic Private IP Addressing (APIPA)** and its 169.254.0.0 addresses. However, unlike IPv4, an IPv6 host is always configured with link-local addresses (one for each link), even if it also has a globally unique address.

A link-local address is also appended with a **zone index** (or **scope id**) of the form **%1** (Windows) or **%eth0** (Linux). This is used to define the source of the address and make it unique to a particular link. For example, a given host may have links to a loopback address, Ethernet, and a VPN. Each of these links may use the same link-local address, so each is assigned a zone ID to make it unique. Zone indices are generated by the host system, so where two hosts communicate, they may be referring to the link using different zone IDs.

IPv6 UNIQUE LOCAL ADDRESSING

Unique local addressing (ULA) assigns addresses that are only routable within a site (or collection of sites). ULA addresses are not routable over the Internet. Unlike IPv4's private address ranges, no system such as NAT is envisaged for IPv6, so ULA is designed for hosts that will never access the Internet.

The prefix for ULA is `fc00::/7`, but it is more typical to see addresses of the form `fd00::/8` because the eighth bit should be set to 1 to indicate local addressing. The next 40 bits should be generated by a pseudorandom **algorithm** and used for a single site only. While ULA is designed for site-local addressing, it is global in scope, which means that no organization should assign the same ULA prefix. The remaining 16 bits can be used for subnetting.

Note: *ULA replaces an earlier scheme called site-local addressing, which used the prefix fec0::/10. Site-local addressing is deprecated by the current RFCs.*

IPv6 MULTICAST ADDRESSING

A **multicast address** identifies multiple network interfaces. Unlike IPv4, IPv6 routers must support multicast. The parts of a multicast address are subdivided as follows:

- The first 8 bits indicate that the address is within the multicast scope (1111 1111 or ff).
- The next 4 bits are used to flag types of multicast if necessary; otherwise, they are set to 0.
- The next 4 bits determine the scope; for example, 1 is node-local (to all interfaces on the same node) and 2 is link-local.
- The final 112 bits define multicast groups within that scope.

Broadcast addresses are not implemented in IPv6. Instead, hosts use an appropriate multicast address for a given situation. The well-known multicast addresses are ones reserved for these types of broadcast functionality. They allow an interface to transmit to all interfaces or routers on the same node or local link. Some of the well-known multicast addresses are shown in the following table (the complete list is at *iana.org/assignments/ipv6-multicast-addresses/ipv6-multicast-addresses.xhtml*).

Address	Target
ff02::1	All link-local nodes
ff02::2	All link-local routers
ff02::1:2	All link-local DHCP servers and relay agents

In IPv4, IP address resolution to a specific hardware interface is performed using ARP. ARP is *chatty* and requires every node to process its messages, whether they are relevant to the node or not. IPv6 replaces ARP with the **Neighbor Discovery (ND)** protocol.

Each unicast address for an interface is configured with a corresponding solicited-node multicast address. It has the prefix `ff02::1:ff` plus the last 24 bits of the unicast address. The solicited-node address is used by ND to perform address resolution. It greatly reduces the number of hosts that are likely to receive ND messages (down to one in most cases) and is therefore much more efficient than the old ARP broadcast mechanism.

IPv6 ADDRESS PREFIXES

Use the following table to help you recognize some of the commonly used classes of IPv6 address by prefix notation or leading hex digits.

Type	Prefix	Leading Hex Characters
Global unicast	2000::/3	2
		3
Link-local unicast	fe80::/64	fe80
ULA	fd00::/8	fd00
Multicast	ff00::/8	ff

Type	Prefix	Leading Hex Characters
Multicast (local-link)	ff02::/16	ff02::1 (all nodes)
		ff02::2 (all routers)
		ff:02::1:2 (DHCP)
Solicited-node	ff02::1:ff00:0/104	ff02::1:ff
Unspecified	::/128	::
		0::0
Loopback	::1/128	::1
Teredo	2001::/32	2001
6to4	2002::/16	2002
Documentation/Examples	2001:db8::/32	2001:db8

Globally unique unicast addresses are also widely referred to as **/48s**.

The 0000::/8 block (that is, IPv6 addresses where the first bits are 0000 0000) is reserved for special functions. Within this block, there are two special addresses defined:

- Unspecified address (0:0:0:0:0:0:0:0)—A host that has not obtained a valid address. This is often expressed as ::.
- Loopback address (0:0:0:0:0:0:0:1)—Used for testing (for the host to send a packet to itself). This is often expressed as ::1.

IPv6 INTERFACE AUTOCONFIGURATION

In IPv6, an interface must always be configured with a link-local address. One or more routable addresses can be assigned to the interface *in addition to* the link-local address. As with IPv4, you can either assign a routable IPv6 address statically or use an automatic addressing scheme. Static address configuration would generally be reserved to routers and possibly servers.

 Note: While it is relatively uncommon for an interface to have more than one IPv4 address, in IPv6 it is typical for an interface to have multiple addresses.

NEIGHBOR DISCOVERY PROTOCOL AND ROUTER ADVERTISEMENTS

The **Neighbor Discovery (ND)** protocol performs some of the functions on an IPv6 network that ARP and ICMP perform under IPv4. ND is defined in *RFC 4861*. The main functions of ND are:

- Address autoconfiguration—Enables a host to configure IPv6 addresses for its interfaces automatically and detect whether an address is already in use on the local network, by using neighbor solicitation (NS) and neighbor advertisement (NA) messages.
- Prefix discovery—Enables a host to discover the known network prefixes that have been allocated to the local segment. This also allows next-hop determination (whether a packet should be addressed to a local host or a router). Prefix discovery uses **router solicitation (RS)** and **router advertisement (RA)** messages. An RA contains information about the network prefix(es) served by the router, information about autoconfiguration options, plus information about link parameters, such as the MTU and hop limit. Routers send RAs periodically and in response to a router solicitation initiated by the host.
- Local address resolution—Allows a host to discover other nodes and routers on the local network (neighbors). This process also uses neighbor solicitation (NS) and neighbor advertisement (NA) messages.

- Redirection—Enables a router to inform a host of a better route to a particular destination.

STATELESS ADDRESS AUTOCONFIGURATION

IPv4 has a system for generating link-local addresses, but these are not routable outside the local network. Consequently, IPv4 depends heavily on the **Dynamic Host Configuration Protocol (DHCP)** for address autoconfiguration. IPv6 uses a more flexible system of address autoconfiguration called **stateless address autoconfiguration (SLAAC)**. This process is fully described in *RFC 4862* but is generally:

1. The host generates a link-local address and tests that it is unique by using the **Neighbor Discovery (ND)** protocol.
2. The host listens for a **router advertisement (RA)** or transmits a **router solicitation (RS)** using ND protocol messaging. Routers send out advertisements periodically and will respond to a solicitation request to enable clients to determine in which network they reside. The router can either provide a network prefix, direct the host to a DHCPv6 server to perform stateful autoconfiguration, or perform some combination of stateless and stateful configuration.

MULTICAST LISTENER DISCOVERY PROTOCOL

The **Multicast Listener Discovery (MLD)** protocol allows nodes to join a multicast group and discover whether members of a group are present on a local subnet. MLD is defined in *RFC 3810*.

ICMPv6

IPv6 uses an updated version of ICMP, defined in *RFC 4443*. The key new features are:

- Error messaging—ICMPv6 supports the same sort of destination unreachable and time exceeded messaging as ICMPv4. One change is the introduction of a **Packet Too Big** class of error. Under IPv6, routers are no longer responsible for packet fragmentation and reassembly, so the host must ensure that they fit in the MTUs of the various links used.
- Informational messaging—Again, ICMPv6 supports ICMPv4 functions, such as echo and redirect, plus a whole new class of messages designed to support ND and MLD, such as router and neighbor advertisements and solicitations.

DUAL-STACK IPv4 AND IPv6 ROUTING

Given the number of devices currently running IPv4, switching to IPv6 is not going to be simple. However, there are two strategies to help make the transition easier.

Dual-stack hosts can run both IPv4 and IPv6 simultaneously and communicate with devices configured with either type of address. Most modern desktop and server operating systems implement dual-stack IP.

A dual-stack router can translate between IPv6 and IPv4. One technology is **Intra-Site Automatic Tunnel Addressing Protocol (ISATAP)**. Under ISATAP, a dual-stack router takes an IPv6 packet and rewrites it as an IPv4 packet. The ISATAP router allows for a network with mixed IPv4 and IPv6 hosts, but it cannot be used for routing between networks. ISATAP hosts use the link-local range `fe80::5efe:w.x.y.z`, where *w.x.y.z* is a dotted decimal IPv4 address.

```
C:\Windows\system32>ipconfig /all

Windows IP Configuration

   Host Name . . . . . . . . . . . . : PC1
   Primary Dns Suffix  . . . . . . . : corp.515support.com
   Node Type . . . . . . . . . . . . : Hybrid
   IP Routing Enabled. . . . . . . . : No
   WINS Proxy Enabled. . . . . . . . : No
   DNS Suffix Search List. . . . . . : corp.515support.com

Ethernet adapter Ethernet:

   Connection-specific DNS Suffix  . : corp.515support.com
   Description . . . . . . . . . . . : Microsoft Hyper-V Network Adapter
   Physical Address. . . . . . . . . : 00-15-5D-01-CA-93
   DHCP Enabled. . . . . . . . . . . : Yes
   Autoconfiguration Enabled . . . . : Yes
   IPv6 Address. . . . . . . . . . . : fdab:cdef:0:1:8f0:5e6a:2f0f:9a25(Preferred)
   Lease Obtained. . . . . . . . . . : Monday, May 20, 2019 3:04:51 PM
   Lease Expires . . . . . . . . . . : Saturday, June 1, 2019 3:05:40 PM
   Link-local IPv6 Address . . . . . : fe80::a4e7:7155:7f44:dcc6%7(Preferred)
   IPv4 Address. . . . . . . . . . . : 10.1.0.201(Preferred)
   Subnet Mask . . . . . . . . . . . : 255.255.255.0
   Lease Obtained. . . . . . . . . . : Monday, May 20, 2019 2:59:05 PM
   Lease Expires . . . . . . . . . . : Tuesday, May 28, 2019 2:59:05 PM
   Default Gateway . . . . . . . . . : fe80::215:5dff:fe01:ca32%7
                                       10.1.0.254
   DHCP Server . . . . . . . . . . . : 10.1.0.2
   DHCPv6 IAID . . . . . . . . . . . : 67114333
   DHCPv6 Client DUID. . . . . . . . : 00-01-00-01-24-52-58-FA-00-15-5D-01-CA-93
   DNS Servers . . . . . . . . . . . : fdab:cdef:0:1::1
                                       10.1.0.1
   NetBIOS over Tcpip. . . . . . . . : Enabled
   Connection-specific DNS Suffix Search List :
                                       corp.515support.com
```

Dual-stack IP in Windows. (Screenshot used with permission from Microsoft.)

Dual-stack hosts may also make use of **IPv4 mapped addresses**. An IPv4 mapped address is expressed ::ffff:192.168.0.1 (that is, 80 0s followed by 16 1s and then the 32-bit IPv4 address, expressed by convention in dotted decimal). This sort of address is never assigned to hosts, but it is used by IPv4/IPv6 routers to forward traffic between IPv4 and IPv6 networks.

IPv6 TUNNELING

As an alternative to dual-stack routing, **tunneling** can be used to deliver IPv6 packets across the IPv4 Internet. In **6to4** automatic tunneling (*RFC 3056*), no host configuration is necessary to enable the tunnel. 6to4 addresses start with a leading 2002. Essentially, when 6to4 is implemented, the IPv6 packets are inserted into IPv4 packets and routed over the IPv4 network to their destination. Routing decisions are based on the IPv4 address until the packets approach their destinations, at which point the IPv6 packets are stripped from their IPv4 carrier packets and forwarded according to IPv6 routing rules.

6to4 supports only public IPv4 addresses (that is, those **not** behind a NAT device). Microsoft also provides support for **Teredo** tunneling by Windows hosts. Teredo tunnels IPv6 packets as IPv4-based UDP messages over port 3544. Using UDP rather than TCP allows tunneling through NAT devices. A compatible open source implementation of Teredo, known as **Miredo**, is available for UNIX/Linux operating systems.

Another form of tunneling is **Generic Routing Encapsulation (GRE)**. GRE was developed by Cisco and is supported by many Linux distributions and by Microsoft since Windows Server 2012 R2 (with hotfixes). GRE allows a wide variety of Network layer protocols to be encapsulated inside virtual point-to-point links. This protocol has the advantage that because it was originally designed for IPv4, it is considered a mature mechanism and can carry both v4 and v6 packets over an IPv4 network. GRE also has the advantage (like Teredo) of not requiring public IPv6 addresses.

It is also possible to tunnel IPv4 through an IPv6 network, in which case the process is known as **4to6** or 4in6 tunneling, as defined in *RFC 2473*. However, given that the most likely transit network for tunneling between sites is the Internet, which is based on IPv4, this type of tunnel is currently of limited use.

 Note: *To learn more, watch the related **Video** on the course website.*

Activity 4-9

Discussing IPv6 Addressing Components

SCENARIO

Answer the following questions to test your understanding of the content covered in this topic.

---

1. **Convert the binary value 1010 0001 1000 1100 to hex.**

2. **Which of the following IPv6 addresses is a valid unicast host address?**

    ○ fe80::218:8bff:fea7:bd37

    ○ fe80::219:d2ff::7850

    ○ ff02::219:d2ff:fea7:7850

    ○ ::/128

3. **What is an EUI-64, and how might it be used by IPv6?**

4. **In IPv6, how is the loopback address best expressed?**

5. **In IPv6, how could you distinguish a unicast address with global scope from other addresses?**

6. **With a single global IPv6 address prefix, how many bits are available for subnetting?**

7. **What type of IPv6 unicast addresses are not routable over the Internet?**

8. **In IPv6, how can a client obtain a routable IPv6 address without requiring manual configuration?**

9. **What is 6to4?**

Activity 4-10

Configuring IPv6 Networking

BEFORE YOU BEGIN

Start the VMs used in this activity in the following order, adjusting the memory allocation first if necessary, and waiting at the ellipsis for the previous VMs to finish booting before starting the next group. You do not need to connect to a VM until prompted to do so in the activity steps.

1. **RT1-LOCAL** (256 MB)
2. **DC1** (1024—2048 MB)
3. **MS1** (1024—2048 MB)

Start the following VM only when prompted during the activity steps.

- **PC1** (1024—2048 MB)

SCENARIO

In this activity, you will observe the use of IPv6 neighbor discovery in your VMs, configure static IPv6 addresses, and configure Router Advertisements. This activity is designed to test your understanding of and ability to apply content examples in the following CompTIA Network+ objective:

- 1.3 Explain the concepts and characteristics of routing and switching.

---

1. On **DC1**, view the IPv6 configuration dialog box for Windows.
   a) Open a connection window for the **DC1** VM and sign in with the username **Administrator** and the password **Pa$$w0rd**
   b) Right-click the **Start** button and select **Network Connections**.
   c) In the **Network Connections** applet, right-click the **Ethernet** icon and select **Properties**.
   d) In the **Ethernet Properties** dialog box, double-click **Internet Protocol Version 6 (TCP/IPv6)**.

e) Observe the properties of the static IP address that has been configured.

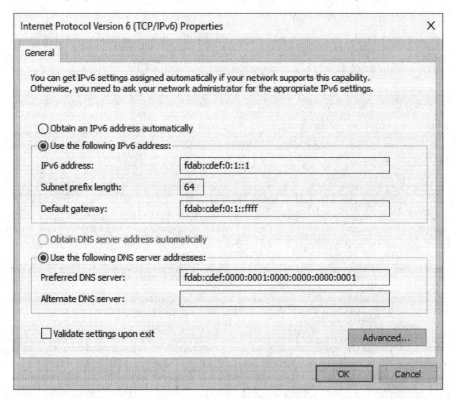

Configuration dialog box for IPv6 in Windows Server. (Screenshot used with permission from Microsoft.)

- The address uses the fd00::/8 prefix defined in RFC 4192 for unique local addressing (ULA). This is the equivalent of RFC 1918 private addressing for IPv4. The prefix is supposed to be appended with a pseudorandom 40-bit value to create the full 48-bit routing prefix, but to simplify this activity, a string of easily readable characters (fdab:cdef:0) is used.

 Note: *Using a memorable string is **not** best practice. Generate a pseudorandom prefix for a production network. This reduces the risk of problems if two private networks have to be internetworked later.*

- There are 16 bits remaining within the network portion to use for a subnet ID. In this example, the subnet ID is 1.
- The remaining bits are the host ID. For this VM, the host ID is also 1.
- The default gateway is identified by the host portion ::ffff.
- The DNS server is identified as the local interface.

f) Select **OK** twice to close the two dialog boxes.

2. Verify the IPv6 configuration of **MS1**.

a) Open a connection window for the **MS1** VM and sign in with the username *515support\Administrator* and the password *Pa$$w0rd*

b) Right-click the **Start** button and select **Network Connections**.

c) In the **Network Connections** applet, right-click the **Ethernet** icon and select **Properties**. In the **Ethernet Properties** dialog box, double-click **Internet Protocol Version 6 (TCP/IPv6)**.

The host ID for this VM is 2, and the DNS server is the IPv6 address of **DC1**.

d) Select **OK** twice to close the two property dialog boxes.

3. Use Wireshark to examine IPv6 datagram headers.

a) Still on the **MS1** VM, from the desktop, double-click the **Wireshark** icon.

b) In the **Capture** window, in the **Enter a capture filter** box, type *ip6*, then select the **Start capture** button.

The filter limits the capture to IPv6 traffic.

c) Open a command prompt as administrator.

d) Run the following command:

```
ping -6 DC1
```

You should see reply packets from fdab:cdef:0:1::1.

e) Switch to the **Wireshark** capture, and look for an **Echo (ping) request** frame. Select the frame in the top pane, then expand the **Internet Protocol Version 6** header in the middle pane.

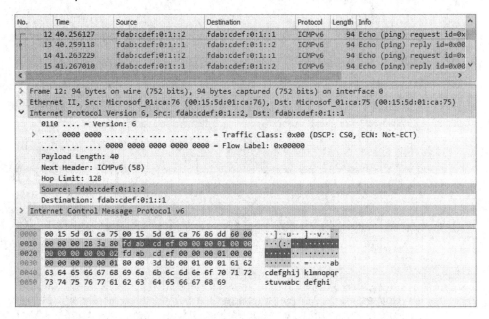

Viewing an IPv6 header in Wireshark. (Screenshot courtesy of Wireshark.)

As with IPv4, the key fields are the source and destination addresses. TTL is renamed **Hop Limit**, and the fields that support QoS are also renamed. Unlike IPv4, there is no **Protocol** field as such; instead the **Next Header** field points to the header for the payload protocol (ICMPv6, in this case).

f) Observe the ICMPv6 neighbor solicitation and advertisement messages in the Wireshark capture as the VMs perform link-layer address resolution.

The advertisements allow a host to map an IPv6 destination address to a destination MAC or link address.

 Note: There is no ARP traffic (ARP is unused in IPv6) and no broadcast traffic of any kind—this has been replaced with specific multicast addresses, such as targeting routers using ff02::2.

g) Select the **Stop Capture** button.

4. Test IPv6 forwarding by experimenting with different network prefix lengths and subnet IDs.

a) On the **MS1** VM, use the following command to remove the existing IP address (ignore any line break and type as a single command followed by pressing **Enter**):

```
netsh interface ipv6 delete address "Ethernet" fdab:cdef:
0:1::2
```

b) Now set the address again using the same command, but use a different number for the subnet ID (ignore any line break and type as a single command followed by pressing **Enter**):

```
netsh interface ipv6 add address "Ethernet" fdab:cdef:
0:fe::2
```

c) Run the following command to test connectivity. It will fail because the hosts are now on different subnets.

```
ping -6 DC1
```

The request times out (as opposed to returning **Destination unreachable**) because **MS1** cannot contact its IPv6 gateway.

5. Configure the router properly so that it sends router advertisements.

   a) On the **HOST** computer, switch to the **Hyper-V Manager** console and select the **RT1-LOCAL** VM icon to open a connection window.

   b) Log on with the username **vyos** and password **Pa$$w0rd**

   VyOS simulates the command environment of a typical network appliance. To change the configuration, you must enter configuration mode first.

   c) Run the following sequence of commands to configure the local interface with an IPv6 address and enable router advertisements (ignore any line break in the commands):

```
conf

edit interfaces ethernet eth0

set ipv6 router-advert send-advert true

set ipv6 router-advert max-interval 10

set ipv6 router-advert prefix fdab:cdef:0:1::/64

set ipv6 router-advert prefix fdab:cdef:0:1::/64
on-link-flag true

set ipv6 router-advert prefix fdab:cdef:0:1::/64
autonomous-flag true

set ipv6 router-advert other-config-flag false

set ipv6 router-advert managed-flag false

set ipv6 router-advert default-preference medium

commit

save

exit
```

   The flags determine what type of address autoconfiguration to perform. The values you set will enforce the following behavior:

   - Managed (M-bit)—Set to false, telling hosts that there is no DHCP service.
   - Other Config (O-bit)—Again, set to false, telling hosts that there is no DHCP service.
   - On-link (L-bit)—The prefix issued by the router can be used over the same local network (rather than relying on link-local addressing).
   - Autonomous (A-bit)—The host should perform stateless address autoconfiguration (SLAAC).

6. Test the router advertisement configuration by booting **PC1**.

   a) On the **HOST**, in **Hyper-V Manager**, right-click **PC1** and select **Start**. Double-click the icon to open a connection window.

   b) Sign in with the username **515support\Administrator** and the password **Pa$$w0rd**

c) Open a command prompt and run `ipconfig` to check the IPv6 addresses that have been configured:
- IPv6 Address: fdab:cdef:0:1:
- Temporary IPv6 Address: fdab:cdef:0:1:

```
C:\Users\administrator>ipconfig

Windows IP Configuration

Ethernet adapter Ethernet:

   Connection-specific DNS Suffix  . : corp.515support.com
   IPv6 Address. . . . . . . . . . . : fdab:cdef:0:1:c134:6500:a68e:de92
   Temporary IPv6 Address. . . . . . : fdab:cdef:0:1:7cfe:337c:303d:44a6
   Link-local IPv6 Address . . . . . : fe80::c134:6500:a68e:de92%8
   IPv4 Address. . . . . . . . . . . : 10.1.0.101
   Subnet Mask . . . . . . . . . . . : 255.255.255.0
   Default Gateway . . . . . . . . . : fe80::215:5dff:fe01:ca32%8
                                       10.1.0.254

Ethernet adapter Npcap Loopback Adapter:

   Connection-specific DNS Suffix  . :
   Link-local IPv6 Address . . . . . : fe80::7149:f79e:5a11:d4f9%13
   Autoconfiguration IPv4 Address. . : 169.254.212.249
   Subnet Mask . . . . . . . . . . . : 255.255.0.0
   Default Gateway . . . . . . . . . :
```

Checking IPv6 configuration using the ipconfig command. (Screenshot used with permission from Microsoft.)

The default gateway is set to the link-local IPv6 address of the VyOS router, not its global address. Router advertisements need to use link-local addressing.

d) Run the following two commands to check connectivity:

`ping fdab:cdef:0:1::1`

`ping fdab:cdef:0:1::ffff`

e) Switch to the **DC1** VM and run the following command:

`ping -6 PC1`

f) Which IPv6 address is used?

fdab:cdef:0:1:

The temporary address is used when an application requests privacy extensions, which is not the case here. The idea is to prevent a website from being able to track a host through use of a persistent host ID portion in the IPv6 address.

7. Optionally, on **PC1**, start a **Wireshark** capture on the Ethernet adapter (filter for *ip6*) and view the router advertisements. Note the link-local source address, derived from the VyOS adapter's MAC address, and the destination multicast address (`ff02::1`).

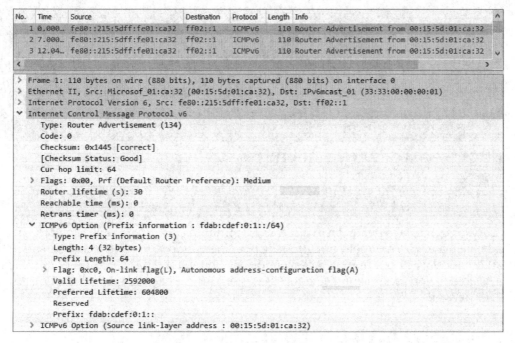

Viewing router advertisements. (Screenshot courtesy of Wireshark.)

8. Discard changes made to the VM in this activity.

    a) Switch to Hyper-V Manager.

    b) Use the **Action** menu or the right-click menu in the **Hyper-V Manager** console to revert all the VMs to their saved checkpoints.

Topic F

Configure DHCP Services

EXAM OBJECTIVES COVERED
1.1 Explain the purposes and uses of ports and protocols.
1.4 Given a scenario, configure the appropriate IP addressing components.
1.8 Explain the functions of network services.

Every host interface needs an IP address to communicate on a TCP/IP network. An administrator can manually assign these IP addresses, or the assignment can be done automatically without manual intervention. By understanding the different methods available to you for assigning IP addresses, you can choose the method that best suits your network.

IPv4 INTERFACE AUTOCONFIGURATION

Originally, all parameters required by TCP/IP were configured manually. This can be referred to as **static IP addressing**. Each host must be allocated an appropriate IP address and subnet mask, plus the IP address of the default gateway (router) for its network. Configuring hosts with a valid static IP address is a complex management task. If any of the values are entered incorrectly, communications are affected, and the cause of the problem must be isolated, which can be difficult.

For example, a common problem is accidental configuration of duplicate IP addresses. When TCP/IP loads on a Windows host, it checks that there is no other machine with the same IP address on the local network. If it encounters a duplicate, it disables the protocol and the machine will be unable to communicate. Ensuring each machine is configured with a unique IP address can become a tedious responsibility for the administrator of a large network. Errors are disastrous for the network users as only the first machine holding the duplicate IP address can connect to the network.

Over the years, several mechanisms have been employed to provide a client autoconfiguration service for IP.

REVERSE ARP (RARP) AND BOOTSTRAP PROTOCOL (BOOTP)

One of the first autoconfiguration mechanisms was **Reverse ARP (RARP)**. This allows a host to obtain an IP address from a server configured with a list of MAC:IP address mappings. RARP can be used to obtain only an IP address, which is inadequate for most implementations of IP. Consequently, the **Bootstrap Protocol (BOOTP)** was developed as a means of supplying a full set of configuration parameters—IP address, subnet mask, default gateway, DNS server addresses, and so on—to a host. The additional parameters are provided in an executable boot file downloaded to the host by using **Trivial File Transfer Protocol (TFTP)**.

BOOTP is still used in some circumstances to provide addressing information to diskless workstations and print devices. The main drawback of BOOTP is that it depends on a static configuration file mapping IP addresses to MAC addresses. This drawback was addressed by the development of BOOTP into the **Dynamic Host Configuration Protocol (DHCP)**.

DYNAMIC HOST CONFIGURATION PROTOCOL (DHCP)

The **Dynamic Host Configuration Protocol (DHCP)** provides an automatic method for allocating an IP address, subnet mask, and optional parameters, such as the **Default gateway** and **DNS server** addresses. DHCP is defined in *RFC 2131*. All the major operating systems provide support for DHCP clients and servers. **DHCP servers** are also embedded in many SOHO routers and modems.

A host is configured to use DHCP by specifying in the TCP/IP configuration that it should automatically obtain an IP address.

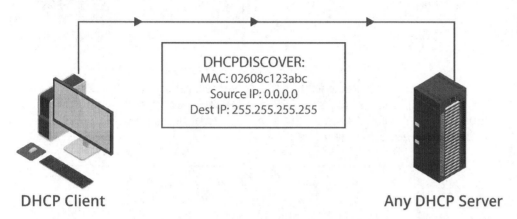

DHCPDISCOVER. (Image © 123RF.com.)

1. When a DHCP client initializes, it broadcasts to find a DHCP server. This is called a DHCPDISCOVER packet. All communications are sent using UDP, with the server listening on port 67 and the client on port 68.

2. The DHCP server responds to the client with an IP address and other configuration information, as long as it has an appropriate IP address available. The IP addressing information is offered for a period of time. This packet is also broadcast and is called a DHCPOFFER.

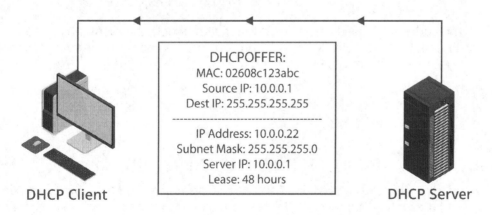

DHCPOFFER. (Image © 123RF.com.)

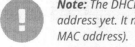 **Note:** *The DHCPOFFER is broadcast at layer 3 because the client doesn't have an IP address yet. It may be delivered as unicast at layer 2, however (using the client's MAC address).*

3. The client may choose to accept the offer using a DHCPREQUEST packet—also broadcast onto the network.

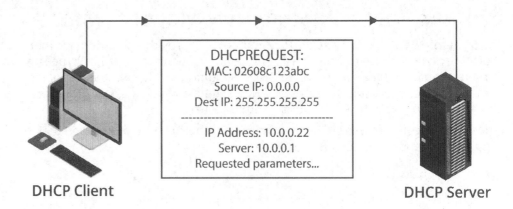

DHCPREQUEST. (Image © 123RF.com.)

4. Assuming the offer is still available, the server will respond with a DHCPACK packet. The client broadcasts an ARP message to check that the address is unused. If so, it will start to use the address and options; if not, it declines the address and requests a new one.

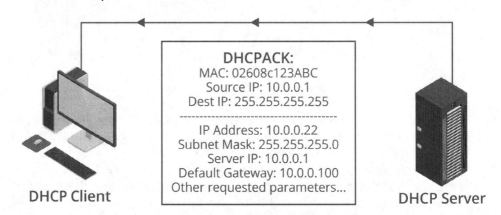

DHCPACK. (Image © 123RF.com.)

The address is leased and, after a designated period, the client must theoretically release the IP addressing information. This process does not normally take place since the client can renew or rebind the lease.

Note: *Sometimes, the DHCP lease process is called the DORA process: Discover, Offer, Request, and* **Ack(nowledge)**.

AUTOMATIC PRIVATE IP ADDRESSING (APIPA)

Automatic Private IP Addressing (APIPA) was developed by Microsoft as a means for clients that could not contact a DHCP server to communicate on the local network anyway. If a Windows host does not receive a response to a DHCPDISCOVER broadcast within a given time frame, it randomly selects an address from the range 169.254.1.1 to 169.254.254.254. It then performs an ARP broadcast to check that the address is currently unused; if it is in use, the host selects another address, and repeats the broadcast, and so on.

Note: *These addresses are from one of the address ranges reserved for private addressing (169.254.0.0/16). The first and last subnets are supposed to be unused.*

This type of addressing is referred to as **link-local** in standards documentation (*RFC 3927*). Link-local addressing mechanisms can also be implemented on other operating systems, such as Bonjour® for the macOS® platform or Avahi for Linux®.

DHCP SERVER CONFIGURATION

DHCP is normally provided as part of the network operating system or through an appliance such as a switch or router. A DHCP server must be allocated a static IP address and configured with the following information:

- A range (or pool) of IP addresses and subnet masks to allocate.
- A lease period plus renewal (T1) and rebinding (T2) timers.
- Other optional information to allocate, such as default gateway and DNS server address(es).

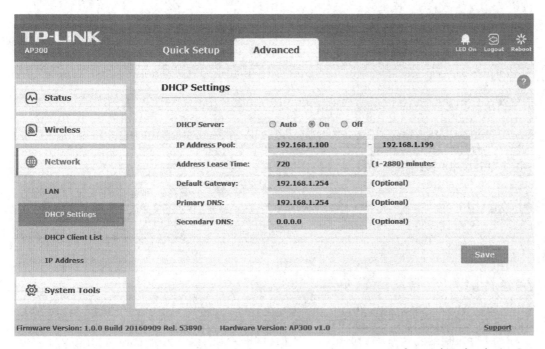

Configuring DHCP on a TP-LINK wireless access point. (Screenshot courtesy of TP-Link Technologies Co., Ltd.)

Not all DHCP servers support the same capabilities. The multi-function device shown only supports a single IP address range, while the Windows DHCP service supports far more options, including creating static and dynamic address reservations.

DHCP ADDRESS POOL

The **address pool** is the range of IP addresses that a DHCP server can allocate to clients on a particular subnet, which Microsoft refers to as a **scope**. A pool is defined within the scope because some addresses might be excluded. For example, if IP addresses have been used for static configuration of some hosts, the DHCP server must not try to assign those addresses to other hosts. To define an address pool, you must provide a start and end IP address along with a subnet mask. The subnet mask given must be such that the entire range of addresses is contained within the scope of a single subnet.

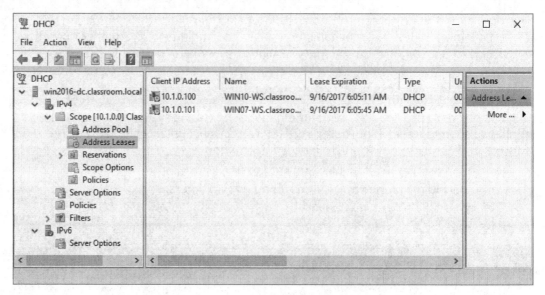

Windows Server DHCP management console. (Screenshot used with permission from Microsoft.)

The server maintains a one-to-one mapping of pools to subnets. That is, no pool can cover more than one subnet and no subnet can contain more than one pool. This is because in situations where a server provides IP configuration for multiple subnets/scopes, it must choose the pool to service each request based on the subnet from which the request originated.

 Note: *There is no mechanism for a client to choose between multiple servers. Therefore, if multiple DHCP servers are deployed—for fault tolerance, for instance—they must be configured with non-overlapping pools. DHCP for multiple subnets is usually handled by configuring relay agents to forward requests to a central DHCP server.*

DHCP LEASE TIME/TTL

Along with an address pool, you also need to define a **lease time**. A long lease period means the client does not have to renew the lease as frequently, but the DHCP server's pool of IP addresses is not replenished. Where IP addresses are in short supply, a short lease period enables the DHCP server to allocate addresses from computers that are not in use.

The client can **renew** the lease when at least half the lease's **Time to Live** (TTL) period has elapsed (T1 timer) so that it keeps the same IP addressing information. If the original DHCP server does not respond to the request to renew the lease, the client attempts to **rebind** the same lease configuration with any available DHCP server. By default, this happens after 87.5% of the lease duration is up (T2 timer). If this fails, the client reinitializes and continues to broadcast to discover a server.

 Note: *A Windows client can be forced to release a lease by issuing a command such as* `ipconfig`. *In Linux, the utility* `dhclient` *is often used for this task.*

DHCP OPTIONS

When the DHCP server provides IP settings to a client, at a minimum it must supply an IP address and subnet mask. Depending on the configuration of the network, it may also provide other IP-related settings, known as **DHCP options**. Each option is identified by a tag byte or decimal value between 0 and 255 (though neither 0 nor 255 can be used as option values). Some widely used options include:

- The default gateway (IP address of the router).
- The IP address(es) of DNS servers.
- The DNS suffix (domain name) to be used by the client.
- Other useful server options, such as time synchronization (NTP), file transfer (TFTP), or VoIP proxy.

A set of **default (global)** options can be configured on a server-wide basis. Default options can be overridden by setting **scope-specific** options. It is also possible to set user-specific options based on a **class ID**. Different options can also be set for **reserved** IP addresses.

DHCP RESERVATIONS AND EXCLUSIONS

While DHCP provides central management of IP configuration, a disadvantage is that the standard **dynamic allocation** method does not guarantee that any given client will retain the same IP address over time. In most cases this is not a problem; for example, as long as a desktop PC has a valid IP address for its subnet, it does not generally matter what that IP address actually is. However, there are some cases where it would be advantageous for certain hosts, such as network printers or wireless access points, to retain their IP addresses.

One solution is to configure these devices statically, using IP addresses outside the DHCP pool. Alternatively, statically assigned addresses can be **excluded** from the pool (though not all DHCP servers support exclusions). While this solution works, it loses the advantages of central configuration.

An alternative approach is to create a **MAC reservation** (or **IP reservation**, depending on which way you want to look at it). A reservation is a mapping of a MAC address to a specific IP address within the DHCP server's address pool. When the DHCP server receives a request from the given MAC address, it always provides the same IP address. This is also referred to as **static** or **fixed** address assignment. **Automatic allocation** refers to an address that is leased permanently to a client. This is distinct from static allocation as the administrator does not pre-determine which IP address will be leased.

DHCP RELAY AND IP HELPER

Normally, routers do not forward broadcast traffic. To contact a DHCP server, each broadcast domain must be served by its own DHCP server. On a large network, this would mean provisioning and configuring many DHCP servers. To avoid this scenario, a **DHCP relay agent** can be configured to provide forwarding of DHCP traffic between subnets. Routers that can provide this type of forwarding are described as *RFC 1542* compliant.

The DHCP relay intercepts any broadcast BOOTP/DHCP frames, applies a unicast address for the appropriate DHCP server, and forwards them on the interface for the subnet containing the server. It also performs the reverse process of directing responses from the server to the appropriate client subnet.

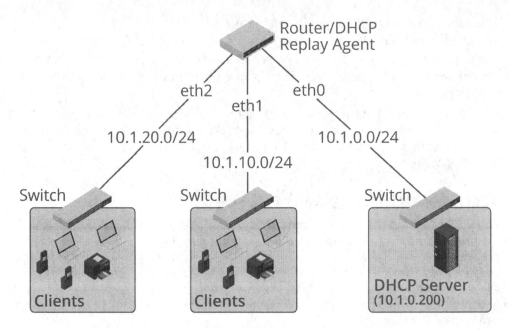

Configuring a DHCP relay agent.

The `ip helper` command can be configured on Cisco routers to allow set types of broadcast traffic (including DHCP) to be forwarded to an interface. This supports the function of the DHCP relay agent. For example, in the diagram, hosts in the 10.1.20.0/24 and 10.1.10.0/24 subnets need to use a DHCP server for autoconfiguration, but the DHCP server is located in a different subnet. The router is configured as a DHCP relay agent, using the following commands to enable forwarding of DHCP broadcasts on the interfaces serving the client subnets:

```
interface eth1

ip helper-address 10.1.0.200

interface eth2

ip helper-address 10.1.0.200
```

DHCPv6

IPv6 can locate routers (default gateways) and generate a host address with a suitable network prefix automatically as part of **Stateless Address Autoconfiguration (SLAAC)**. In this context, the role of a DHCP server in IPv6 is different. In an IPv6 network, DHCPv6 is often just used to provide additional option settings, rather than leases for host IP addresses.

DHCPv6 is defined in *RFC 3315*. The format of messages is different, but the process of DHCP server discovery and address leasing (if offered) is fundamentally the same. As IPv6 does not support broadcast, clients use the multicast address ff:02::1:2 to discover a DHCP server. DHCPv6 uses ports 546 (clients) and 547 (servers), rather than ports 68 and 67 as in DHCPv4.

DHCPv6 STATELESS

In stateless mode, a client obtains a network prefix from a Router Advertisement and uses it with the appropriate interface ID. The router can also set a combination of flags to tell the client that a DHCP server is available. If so configured, the client solicits a DHCPv6 server using the multicast address ff:02::1:2 and requests additional configuration information.

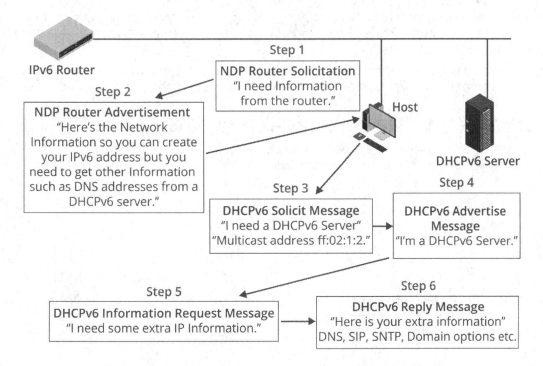

DHCPv6 stateless mode. (Image © 123RF.com.)

The DHCPv6 server responds with options such as addresses for DNS resolvers, SIP (telephony), or SNTP (time synchronization).

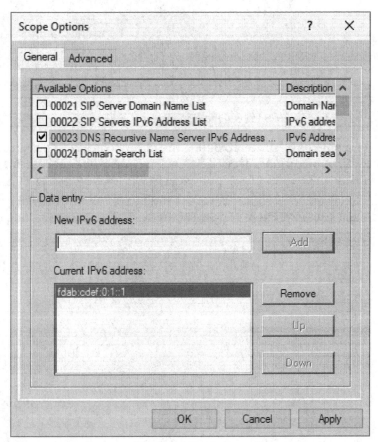

Example DHCPv6 scope options. (Screenshot used with permission from Microsoft.)

This is the most common implementation, although there can be issues with security due to the automatic nature of the mode, which can cause administrators to choose stateful implementations.

It is also possible to configure some clients so that they automatically solicit a DHCPv6 server for additional options, regardless of how the router has been configured.

DHCPv6 STATEFUL AND PREFIX DELEGATION (PD)

Stateful mode means that a host can also obtain a routable IP address from a DHCPv6 scope, plus any other options (like with DHCP for IPv4).

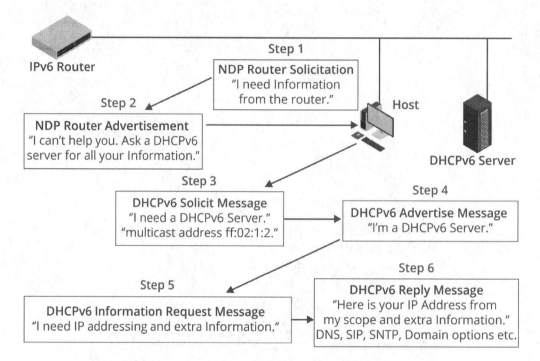

DHCPv6 stateful mode. (Image © 123RF.com.)

Configuring the scope requires you to define the network prefix and then any IP addresses that are to be *excluded* from being offered. All other addresses that are not explicitly excluded can be offered.

The host must still listen for a router advertisement to obtain the network prefix and configure a default gateway. There is no mechanism in DHCPv6 for setting the default route.

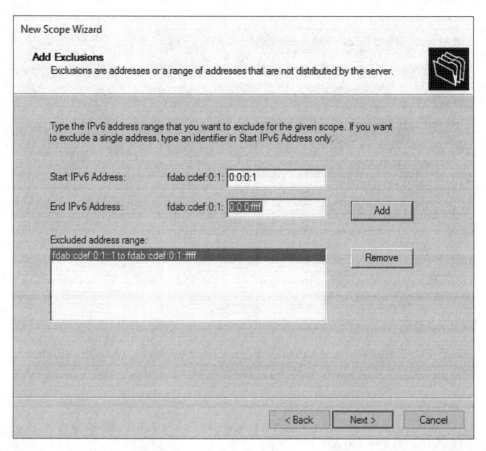

Configuring a DHCPv6 scope in Windows Server. (Screenshot used with permission from Microsoft.)

DHCPv6 Prefix Delegation (PD) is used by ISPs to provide routable address prefixes to a SOHO router, installed as **customer premises equipment (CPE)**. With PD, the CPE router obtains a prefix from a delegating router, installed upstream on the ISP's network. The CPE router then uses the prefix to assign devices on the customer's network with IPv6 addressing information by using router advertisements or DHCPv6, or both.

 Note: *To learn more, watch the related **Video** on the course website.*

Activity 4-11
Discussing DHCP Services

SCENARIO
Answer the following questions to test your understanding of the content covered in this topic.

---

1. **What is the advantage of having a DHCP server in a TCP/IP network?**

2. **What port should be open on the client for it to negotiate with a DHCP server?**

3. **True or False? If a client accepts a DHCPOFFER, the DHCPREQUEST packet is broadcast on the network.**

4. **If a network adapter is using the address 169.254.1.10 on a host connected to the LAN, what would you suspect?**

5. **On the DHCP server, what is a range of IP addresses that are available to be leased or assigned to clients called?**

6. **When configuring multiple DHCP servers for redundancy, what should you take care to do?**

7. **True or False? DHCP options can be configured on a per-scope basis.**

8. **What is an RFC 1542 compliant router?**

9. **What address is used to contact a DHCPv6 server?**

10. **In a stateless environment, what sort of information does DHCPv6 provide?**

Activity 4-12

Configuring Address Assignments

BEFORE YOU BEGIN

Start the VMs used in this activity in the following order, adjusting the memory allocation first if necessary, and waiting at the ellipsis for the previous VMs to finish booting before starting the next group. You do not need to connect to a VM until prompted to do so in the activity steps.

1. **RT1-LOCAL** (256 MB)
2. **DC1** (1024—2048 MB)
3. ...
4. **MS1** (1024—2048 MB)
5. ...

Start the following VMs only when prompted in the activity steps:

1. **PC1** (1024—2048 MB)
2. **PC2** (512—1024 MB)

 Note: *If you can allocate more than the minimum amounts of RAM, prioritize **MS1**.*

SCENARIO

Very few hosts are configured with static IP addresses. Almost all networks use the DHCP service to allocate IP addressing information automatically. This activity is designed to test your understanding of and ability to apply content examples in the following CompTIA Network+ objectives:

- 1.1 Explain the purposes and uses of ports and protocols.
- 1.4 Given a scenario, configure the appropriate IP addressing components.
- 1.8 Explain the functions of network services.
- 5.5 Given a scenario, troubleshoot common network service issues.

---

1. To observe how a DHCP-configured client behaves when no DHCP server is available, disable the **DHCP server** on **MS1**.

   a) Connect to the **MS1** VM and sign in as ***515support\Administrator*** with the password ***Pa$$w0rd***

   b) When Server Manager has loaded, select **Tools→DHCP**.

   c) In the **DHCP** management console, expand **MS1.corp. 515support.com→IPv4→Scope (10.1.0.0)**.

   d) Right-click **Scope [10.1.0.0] 515 Support Scope** and select **Deactivate**. Confirm the warning by selecting **Yes**.

   e) Start the **PC1** and **PC2** VMs. When **PC2** has finished booting, open a connection window and sign in as ***515support\Administrator*** with password ***Pa$$w0rd***

*Note: When you are prompted to press **Ctrl+Alt+Delete**, press **Ctrl+Alt+End** or use the **Ctrl+Alt+Delete** button on the VM Connection window toolbar.*

f) Point to the **network status** icon in the Notification Area to observe the tooltip. Its status will be shown as **Identifying** for a minute or two before being listed as **Unidentified network**.

g) Open a command prompt and enter this command:

```
ipconfig /all
```

Observe what type of **IPv4** address has been assigned to the adapter **Ethernet**. Also, make a note of the interface's **MAC address** so that you can identify it in packet captures:

- IP Address: _____
- MAC Address: 0 0 - 1 5 - 5 D -

Output from ipconfig /all. (Screenshot used with permission from Microsoft.)

This is an APIPA address in the range 169.254.x.y. There is no default gateway, as APIPA is for local-link connectivity only.

2. View the network traffic generated by the APIPA configuration.

a) On the **PC2** VM, start **Wireshark**.

b) Select the **Local Area Connection** adapter. Enter ***arp or icmp or port 67 or port 68*** in the **Capture Filter** box and start the capture.

 Note: Port 67 and port 68 capture DHCP traffic. Wireshark does not support the use of DHCP as capture filter criteria.

c) At some point, you should see that **PC1** and **PC2** (look at the source MAC address to distinguish them) start broadcasting unanswered **DHCP Discover** packets. If you don't see any, run this command:

```
ipconfig /renew
```

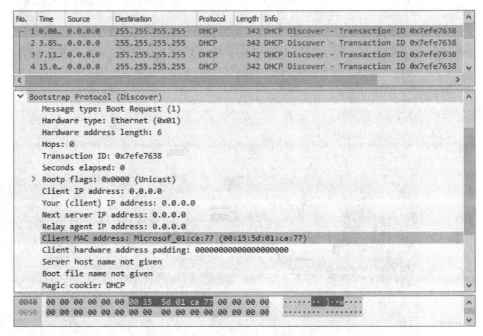

Hosts broadcasting for a DHCP server without reply. (Screenshot courtesy of Wireshark.)

Examine the way that broadcast works. The source IP is 0.0.0.0 (or this network) and the destination is 255.255.255.255 (or any host on this network). At the Data Link layer, the source address is the VM's MAC address and the destination is ff:ff:ff:ff:ff:ff. These frames are flooded by the switch and accepted by all interfaces that receive them.

d) Leave the packet capture running.

e) Switch to the command prompt and run the following connectivity tests:

```
ping -4 PC1

ping -4 DC1
```

You can ping **PC1** because it is using the same link-local address range. The host name is resolved using a protocol called Link Local Multicast Name Resolution (LLMNR). You cannot ping the DC because it has a static IP address and cannot route to hosts with APIPA addresses.

 *Note: You could configure an **Alternate Configuration** address in the correct IP subnet, but this requires a lot of administrative overhead and risks causing problems with duplicate IP addresses and configuration errors. Generally, if DHCP is failing, it is better to find that out and fix it.*

3. Re-enable the DHCP scope on the **MS1** VM, and observe the DHCP lease negotiation.

a) Switch to the **MS1** VM and select or open the **DHCP** management console again.

b) In the **DHCP** management console, expand **MS1.corp. 515support.com→IPv4→Scope [10.1.0.0] 515 Support Scope**.

c) Right-click **Scope [10.1.0.0] 515 Support Scope** and select **Activate**.

d) Switch to the **PC2** VM, and observe the Wireshark capture as the DHCP scope is activated. If nothing happens, run `ipconfig /renew`.

You may see **PC1** negotiate a lease first.

e) Observe the Offer, Request, and Ack sequence that follows the Discover packet now that DHCP is operating normally again.

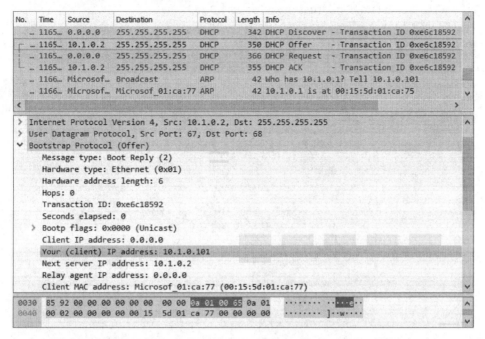

No.	Time	Source	Destination	Protocol	Length	Info
...	1165...	0.0.0.0	255.255.255.255	DHCP	342	DHCP Discover - Transaction ID 0xe6c18592
...	1165...	10.1.0.2	255.255.255.255	DHCP	350	DHCP Offer - Transaction ID 0xe6c18592
...	1165...	0.0.0.0	255.255.255.255	DHCP	366	DHCP Request - Transaction ID 0xe6c18592
...	1165...	10.1.0.2	255.255.255.255	DHCP	355	DHCP ACK - Transaction ID 0xe6c18592
...	1166...	Microsof...	Broadcast	ARP	42	Who has 10.1.0.1? Tell 10.1.0.101
...	1166...	Microsof...	Microsof_01:ca:77	ARP	42	10.1.0.1 is at 00:15:5d:01:ca:75

> Internet Protocol Version 4, Src: 10.1.0.2, Dst: 255.255.255.255
> User Datagram Protocol, Src Port: 67, Dst Port: 68
∨ Bootstrap Protocol (Offer)
    Message type: Boot Reply (2)
    Hardware type: Ethernet (0x01)
    Hardware address length: 6
    Hops: 0
    Transaction ID: 0xe6c18592
    Seconds elapsed: 0
  > Bootp flags: 0x0000 (Unicast)
    Client IP address: 0.0.0.0
    Your (client) IP address: 10.1.0.101
    Next server IP address: 10.1.0.2
    Relay agent IP address: 0.0.0.0
    Client MAC address: Microsof_01:ca:77 (00:15:5d:01:ca:77)

```
0030  85 92 00 00 00 00 00 00  00 00 0a 01 00 65 0a 01   ···········e··
0040  00 02 00 00 00 00 00 00  15 5d 01 ca 77 00 00 00 00 00   ·········]··w·····
```

Obtaining a lease from the DHCP server. (Screenshot courtesy of Wireshark.)

f) Stop the packet capture.

g) Use `ipconfig` on the **PC2** VM to confirm the new configuration.

4. Browse the DHCP server on **MS1** to identify the configuration options.

a) Switch back to the **MS1** VM and, if it is not already open, open the **DHCP** management console.

b) Under the **Scope** node, select the **Address Pool** node.
This is the range of addresses that the server is configured to allocate. No machines should be manually assigned static addresses from this pool or you risk IP conflicts. Similarly, the pool should be large enough to cope with the number of hosts on the network.

c) Select the **Address Leases** node.
You should see **PC1** and **PC2** listed. (If you don't, select the **Refresh** button on the toolbar.)

d) Select **Reservations**. You can see two records have been set up. The VMs that use these reservations aren't part of this activity, though. Right-click a record and select **Properties** to see how it is configured. The IP address is allocated based on the host's MAC address. Select **Cancel**.

e) Select **Scope Options**.
These records configure additional options. In this example, the options set the router (default gateway), primary DNS server, and the connection-specific DNS suffix.

5. Re-configure the scope to use the range **10.1.0.201-10.1.0.239**.

a) Right-click the **Scope** node and select **Properties**.

b) Change the **Start IP address** value to *10.1.0.201*

c) Change the **End IP address** value to *10.1.0.239*

d) Select **OK**. Read the error message and select **OK**.
Windows DHCP does not support changing the address pool to omit previously allocated addresses. You would have to delete the scope and re-create it.

e) Select **Cancel**.

f) Right-click the existing scope and select **Delete**. Confirm the warning by selecting **Yes**.

g) Right-click the **IPv4** node and select **New Scope**.

h) On the first page of the **New Scope Wizard**, select **Next**.

i) In the **Name** box, enter ***515support 10.1.0.201-239 Scope*** and then select **Next**.

j) In the **Start IP address** box, type ***10.1.0.201***

k) In the **End IP address** box, type ***10.1.0.239***

l) Change the value in the **Length** box to ***24***

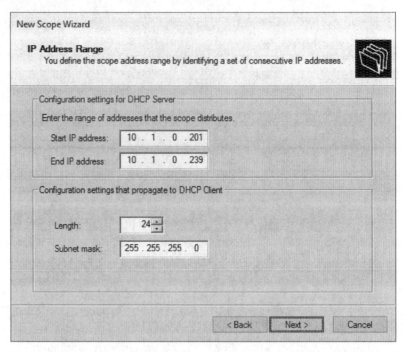

Configuring a DHCP scope on Windows Server. (Screenshot used with permission from Microsoft.)

m) Select **Next**. You could enter exclusions on this page, but for this activity just select **Next** again.

n) Select **Next** to accept the default lease duration.

o) With **Yes, I want to configure these options now** selected, select **Next**.

p) In the **IP address** box, type ***10.1.0.254*** then select the **Add** button.

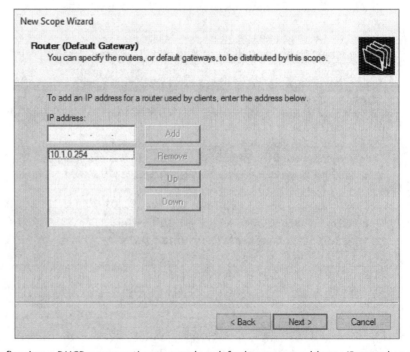

Configuring a DHCP scope option to supply a default gateway address. (Screenshot used with permission from Microsoft.)

q) Select **Next**.

r) The DNS parent domain and server address should be added already (as shown earlier). Select **Next**.

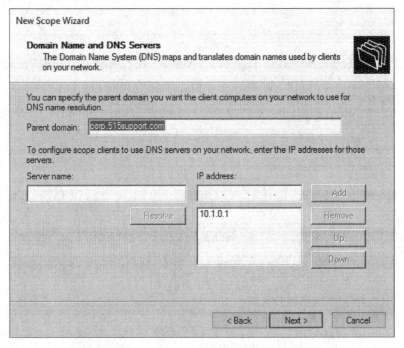

Configuring a DHCP scope option to supply a DNS server address and parent domain suffix. (Screenshot used with permission from Microsoft.)

s) WINS is a name resolution service for legacy clients (pre-Windows 2000). There is rarely any need to configure it on modern networks. Select **Next**.

t) With **Yes, I want to activate this scope now** selected, select **Next**.

u) Select **Finish**.

6. Test the new scope by obtaining a lease on the **PC1** VM.

a) Open a connection window for the **PC1** VM and sign in as *515support\Administrator* with password *Pa$$w0rd*

b) Open a command prompt as administrator.

c) Run the following commands to check the configuration and verify connectivity:

```
ipconfig
```

```
ping 10.1.0.1
```

The IP configuration is unchanged, even though the server scope has been changed. This is now an expired IP address. In this situation, it doesn't really affect network access, but on a network that depended on ACLs, having an IP address outside of the valid DHCP range might block the host from accessing firewalled services.

d) Enter the following command:

```
ipconfig /release
```

This command clears the current IP configuration. **PC1** autoconfigures an APIPA address in the 169.254.x.y range.

e) Run the following command:

```
ipconfig /renew "Ethernet"
```

The VM will obtain a lease for the new scope.

7. Configure the DHCP server with an IPv6 scope, and configure a router to respond to Router Solicitation requests. Start by configuring an IPv6 scope on **MS1**.

a) On the **MS1** VM, in the **DHCP** management console, select the **IPv6** node then right-click **IPv6** and select **New Scope**.

 Note: *One of the oddities of Windows Server management consoles is that you must select a node before the shortcut menu options become available.*

b) On the first page of the **New Scope Wizard**, select **Next**.

c) On the **Scope Name** page, in the **Name** box, type *515support fdab:cdef:0:1 Scope* and then select **Next**.

d) In the **Prefix** box, type *fdab:cdef:0:1::*

e) Leave the **Preference** value set to 0 (most preferred) and select **Next**.

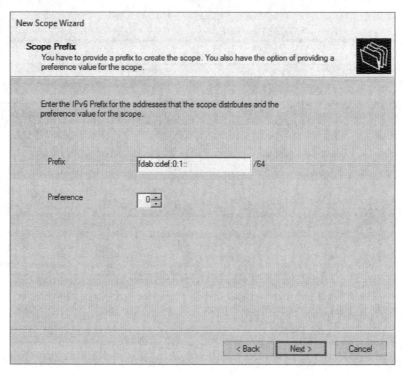

Configuring an IPv6 scope on Windows Server. (Screenshot used with permission from Microsoft.)

f) On the **Add Exclusions** page, in the **Start IPv6 Address** box, type *0:0:0:1*

g)   In the **End IPv6 Address** box, type *0:0:0:ffff* and then select the **Add** button.

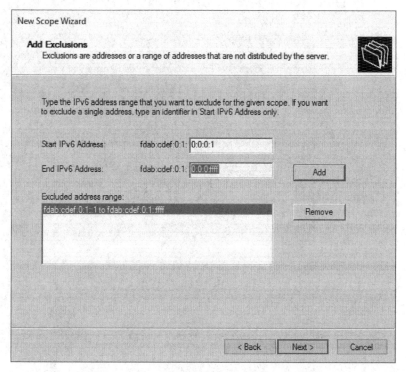

Adding excluded addresses to an IPv6 scope on Windows Server. (Screenshot used with permission from Microsoft.)

You don't want the scope to include any addresses that have been assigned statically, as is the case with the **DC1**, **MS1**, and **RT1-LOCAL** hosts.

h)   Select **Next** twice.

i)   Select **Finish**.

j)   Under the new scope node, select **Scope Options** then right-click **Scope Options** and select **Configure Options**.

k) Check the **00023 DNS Recursive Name Server IPv6 Address** check box. In the **New IPv6 address** box, type *fdab:cdef:0:1::1* and then select **Add**.

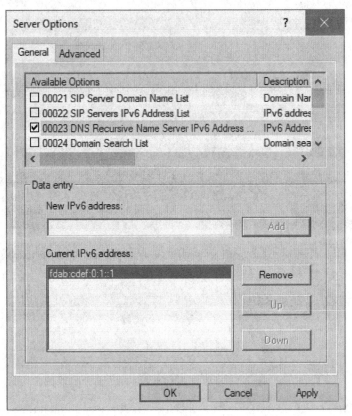

Configuring IPv6 scope options. (Screenshot used with permission from Microsoft.)

l) Check the **00024 Domain Search List** check box. In the **New value** box, type *corp. 515support.com* and then select **Add**.

m) Select **OK**.

8. With IPv6, hosts expect to receive configuration instructions from a router, or use link-local addressing if no router is present. Configure the **RT1-LOCAL** VyOS router to issue Router Advertisements (RA).

These will advertise the routing prefix and default route in use on the local network, but direct the client to obtain a full address and other configuration information from the DHCPv6 server.

 Note: *Because most hosts ship with IPv6 enabled out of the box, it is important to set up a valid IPv6 routing infrastructure even if it is not really used to access application services. If no valid router advertisements are configured, the network can be vulnerable to rogue services and man-in-the-middle attacks.*

a) On the **HOST**, switch to the **Hyper-V Manager** console and double-click the **RT1-LOCAL** VM icon to open a connection window.

b) Log on with the username *vyos* and password *Pa$$w0rd*

c) Run the following sequence of commands to configure the local interface with an IPv6 address and enable router advertisements. (Ignore any line break in the commands):

```
conf

edit interfaces ethernet eth0

set ipv6 router-advert send-advert true

set ipv6 router-advert max-interval 10

set ipv6 router-advert prefix fdab:cdef:0:1::/64
```

```
set ipv6 router-advert prefix fdab:cdef:0:1::/64 on-link-
flag true

set ipv6 router-advert prefix fdab:cdef:0:1::/64
autonomous-flag false

set ipv6 router-advert other-config-flag true

set ipv6 router-advert managed-flag true

set ipv6 router-advert default-preference medium

commit

save

exit
```

The flags determine what type of address autoconfiguration to perform. In this scenario, the flags you are setting work as follows:

- Managed (M-bit)—The client should use a DHCPv6 server to obtain its address (stateful DHCP).
- Other Config (O-bit)—The client should use a DCHPv6 server to obtain other link parameters (such as DNS server addresses). If the M-bit is set, the O-bit is redundant, but you can have the situation where M=false and O=true and the client will use the RA to generate an address and DHVPv6 to obtain other parameters (stateless DHCP).
- Autonomous (A-bit)—You have disabled this option to use stateful configuration via DHCPv6 instead of SLAAC. If both M-bit and A-bit are set to true, then the host will generate an address from the RA and receive a lease from the DHCP server.

9. Use **PC1** to obtain a lease from the newly configured scope.

   a) Press **Ctrl+Alt+Left Arrow** to release the cursor from the **RT1-LOCAL** VM. On the **PC1** VM, at the command prompt, run the following command:

```
ipconfig /renew6 "Ethernet"
```

b) Verify the configuration by running the following command:

```
ipconfig /all
```

```
C:\Windows\system32>ipconfig /all

Windows IP Configuration

    Host Name . . . . . . . . . . . . : PC1
    Primary Dns Suffix  . . . . . . . : corp.515support.com
    Node Type . . . . . . . . . . . . : Hybrid
    IP Routing Enabled. . . . . . . . : No
    WINS Proxy Enabled. . . . . . . . : No
    DNS Suffix Search List. . . . . . : corp.515support.com

Ethernet adapter Ethernet:

    Connection-specific DNS Suffix  . : corp.515support.com
    Description . . . . . . . . . . . : Microsoft Hyper-V Network Adapter
    Physical Address. . . . . . . . . : 00-15-5D-01-CA-93
    DHCP Enabled. . . . . . . . . . . : Yes
    Autoconfiguration Enabled . . . . : Yes
    IPv6 Address. . . . . . . . . . . : fdab:cdef:0:1:8f0:5e6a:2f0f:9a25(Preferred)
    Lease Obtained. . . . . . . . . . : Monday, May 20, 2019 3:04:51 PM
    Lease Expires . . . . . . . . . . : Saturday, June 1, 2019 3:05:40 PM
    Link-local IPv6 Address . . . . . : fe80::a4e7:7155:7f44:dcc6%7(Preferred)
    IPv4 Address. . . . . . . . . . . : 10.1.0.201(Preferred)
    Subnet Mask . . . . . . . . . . . : 255.255.255.0
    Lease Obtained. . . . . . . . . . : Monday, May 20, 2019 2:59:05 PM
    Lease Expires . . . . . . . . . . : Tuesday, May 28, 2019 2:59:05 PM
    Default Gateway . . . . . . . . . : fe80::215:5dff:fe01:ca32%7
                                        10.1.0.254
    DHCP Server . . . . . . . . . . . : 10.1.0.2
    DHCPv6 IAID . . . . . . . . . . . : 67114333
    DHCPv6 Client DUID. . . . . . . . : 00-01-00-01-24-52-58-FA-00-15-5D-01-CA-93
    DNS Servers . . . . . . . . . . . : fdab:cdef:0:1::1
                                        10.1.0.1
    NetBIOS over Tcpip. . . . . . . . : Enabled
    Connection-specific DNS Suffix Search List :
                                        corp.515support.com
```

Configuration obtained from DHCPv6 service. (Screenshot used with permission from Microsoft.)

c) Run the following command to test connectivity:

```
ping -6 DC1
```

10. Discard changes made to the VM in this activity.

a) Switch to the **Hyper-V Manager** window.

b) From the **Action** menu, select **Revert** then select the **Revert** button (or use the right-click menu in the **Hyper-V Manager** console) to revert the VM to its saved checkpoint.

Summary

In this lesson, you learned about the operation of IP in terms of addressing hosts and defining logical networks and subnets.

- The Internet Protocol provides layer 3 addressing, allowing for logically distinct networks.
- IPv4 clients are configured with a 32-bit IP address and subnet mask—The subnet mask defines the network and host ID portions of the IP address.
- An IPv4 address is expressed using dotted decimal notation. The netmask can either be expressed using dotted decimal or as a network prefix (slash notation).
- Hosts with the same network ID transmit packets locally (using ARP). A packet addressed to a host with a different network ID must be sent via a router.
- ipconfig/ifconfig is used for various troubleshooting and configuration tasks—There are differences between the Windows and Linux versions.
- ICMP delivers status message and allows for connectivity testing (ping utility).
- IPv4 traffic can be addressed to unicast, broadcast, or multicast.
- Classful addressing uses a system of fixed network IDs based on the first octet of the IP address. Classless addressing, where the mask is defined by a network prefix, allows for subnetting and supernetting (CIDR), plus variable length subnet masks (VLSMs).
- Make sure you can calculate the numbers of networks and hosts available for an addressing scheme and work out the network ID, valid host addresses, and broadcast address of an IP network.
- IPv4 provides public and private addressing schemes. Privately addressed hosts can use some type of NAT or proxy to communicate over the Internet.
- IPv6 uses 128-bit addresses with variable length network prefixes and a 64-bit host ID derived from the MAC address or randomly assigned.
- IPv6 supports global and link-local address schemes and unicast and multicast addressing.
- In IPv6, SLAAC, ND, MLD, ICMPv6, and DHCPv6 are used for autoconfiguration and neighbor discovery.
- Communications can take place between IPv4 and IPv6 by using dual-stack hosts or tunneling.
- DHCP is a method for a client to automatically request IP configuration information from a server.
- A DHCP service can be configured to run on a Windows/Linux server, or it can be provided by most types of switches and routers.
- In Windows, if a client cannot contact a DHCP server, it uses an APIPA (link-local) address that allows for communications on the local network.
- DHCPv6 is principally used to provide optional information, such as DNS server addresses. Router advertisements can be used to direct a client to use a stateless or stateful autoconfiguration.

Where would you expect to use custom subnet masks?

What measures have you taken to prepare for implementing IPv6?

Practice Questions: *Additional practice questions are available on the course website.*

Lesson 5

Installing and Configuring Routed Networks

LESSON INTRODUCTION

In the previous lesson, you learned how the TCP/IP protocol suite uses IP addressing on networks to enable communication. To facilitate communication across internetworks, including the Internet, you will need to use routers and routing techniques. It is not enough to just know how millions of networks across the globe connect to form an internetwork. You should also know how these interconnected networks talk to each other and share data. Because routers are the workhorses of all internetworks, you will need to understand routing basics no matter what kind of network you support.

LESSON OBJECTIVES

In this lesson, you will:

- Explain routing characteristics.

- Install and configure routers.

Topic A

Explain Characteristics of Routing

 EXAM OBJECTIVES COVERED
1.3 Explain the concepts and characteristics of routing and switching.

As a network professional, you should understand the way routers make forwarding decisions and how you can implement them so that you can support routed environments of all sizes and types. This will ensure that each host is properly identified on the network. In this topic, you will examine both static and dynamic routing. You will compare the benefits and features of each method, as well as the protocols used to implement them.

ROUTING DECISIONS

The process of **routing** takes place when a host needs to communicate with a host on a different IP network or a different subnet. By masking the full IP address against a network prefix or subnet mask, IP derives the network IDs of the source and destination addresses, and determines whether the target host is on a different IP network. In IPv4, the network prefix can be increased—to make more network numbers available—at the expense of the number of host IDs left available for each network. The network prefix can be expressed in slash notation as the number of bits (172.30.0.0/20 for instance) or as a dotted decimal subnet mask (255.255.240.0 for instance). In IPv6, the interface ID is always 64 bits, and the network prefix is given only in slash notation. Prefixes are allocated in a hierarchical manner, with the smaller prefix blocks, which contain more networks, going to Internet registries, who then allocate mid-size blocks to ISPs, who then allocate the blocks with the largest network prefixes to end users. End users are left with a block to use to subnet their network.

END SYSTEMS AND INTERMEDIATE SYSTEMS

All IP hosts are capable of functioning as routers, but most workstation and server computers are configured with a single network adapter connected to only one network. Although potentially capable of routing, they are not equipped with the necessary interfaces and knowledge of the location of other networks. Hosts with no capacity to forward packets to other IP networks are referred to as **end systems (ESs)**. Routers that interconnect IP networks and can perform this packet forwarding process are known as **intermediate systems (ISs)**.

ROUTING AND SWITCHING COMPARISON

Both switches and routers provide a forwarding function. Make sure that you are clear on the different ways these devices make forwarding decisions.

Switches	Routers
Ethernet switches make forwarding decisions based on layer 2 MAC addresses.	Routers make forwarding decisions based on layer 3 network addresses. These are typically IP addresses, although they can also include other types of layer 3 protocol addresses.

Switches	Routers
When devices communicate with different network segments through switches, they are limited to hosts within the same broadcast domain (link-local).	Routers are designed to interconnect networks and support connectivity to distant networks. • They use a routing table to determine the next hop interface to use to forward a packet. • They can connect dissimilar layer 2 network segments. A router strips the layer 2 header of an incoming packet and replaces it with the appropriate layer 2 header for the destination interface.
Switches flood broadcast traffic.	Each router interface is a separate broadcast domain. Routers do not typically forward broadcast traffic, though this can be overridden by configuring specific router settings (to allow DHCP relay, for instance).

ROUTING TABLES AND PATH SELECTION

On a router, information about the location of other IP networks and hosts is stored in a **routing table**. Each entry in the routing table represents an available route to a destination network or host, and contains (at least) the following parameters:

- **Destination IP address and netmask**—Routes can be defined to specific hosts but are more generally directed to network IDs.
- **Gateway/next hop**—The IP address of the next router along the path.
- **Interface**—The local port to use to forward a packet along the chosen route.
- **Metric**—A preference value assigned to the route, with low values being preferred over high ones. The value of the metric may be determined by different parameters, such as how far the next hop router is, how long it will take to route a packet to the subsequent routers, what bandwidth is available on the selected path, how large a packet can be sent without fragmentation, and so on.

Routing table entries fall into four general categories:

- Direct network routes, for subnets to which the router is directly attached.
- Remote network routes, for subnets and IP networks that are not directly attached.
- Host routes, for routes to a specific IP address.
- Default routes, which are used when a better network or host route is not found.

Early routers were manually configured with this routing information. These days, almost all routers use some sort of **dynamic routing protocol** to learn about remote networks and the most efficient route to those networks. Different routing **algorithms**, as implemented in the various protocols, may use different metrics and make comparisons of available paths in different ways. However, the desired result is always the same—to choose the optimal path for a specific packet at a given moment.

ROUTING TABLE EXAMPLES

As examples of the entries that might appear in a routing table, you can look at an ES host and two routers on a simple network.

END SYSTEM HOST ROUTING TABLE

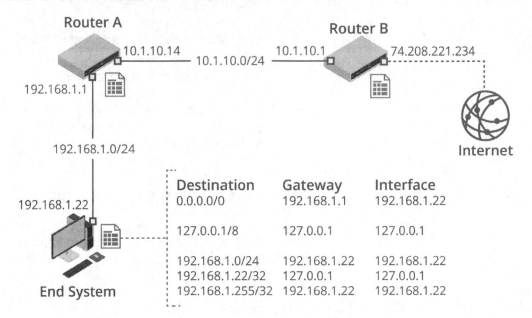

Router A

10.1.10.14

10.1.10.0/24

Router B

10.1.10.1   74.208.221.234

192.168.1.1

Internet

192.168.1.0/24

192.168.1.22

Destination	Gateway	Interface
0.0.0.0/0	192.168.1.1	192.168.1.22
127.0.0.1/8	127.0.0.1	127.0.0.1
192.168.1.0/24	192.168.1.22	192.168.1.22
192.168.1.22/32	127.0.0.1	127.0.0.1
192.168.1.255/32	192.168.1.22	192.168.1.22

End System

Routing table for an end system host. (Image © 123RF.com.)

First, consider the routing table of the ES host computer, located on the 192.168.1.0/24 network.

- 0.0.0.0/0—This is the all 0s default route. If a packet's destination address does not match any of the other entries, this is the route that will be used. The gateway for this route is Router A (192.168.1.1), and the host uses its local interface (192.168.1.22) to communicate with the gateway.
- 127.0.0.1/8—This is the loopback address for directing any communications back to the same host. This is used mostly for troubleshooting.
- 192.168.1.0/24—This represents the host's local IP network, so it uses its 192.168.1.22 interface as the gateway to deliver packets to hosts on the same subnet, resolving IP addresses to MAC addresses by using ARP.
- 192.168.1.22/32—This is the host's own address, so any traffic for it, is directed to the loopback interface.
- 192.168.1.255/32—This is the broadcast address for the 192.168.1.0/24 IP network.

ROUTER A ROUTING TABLE

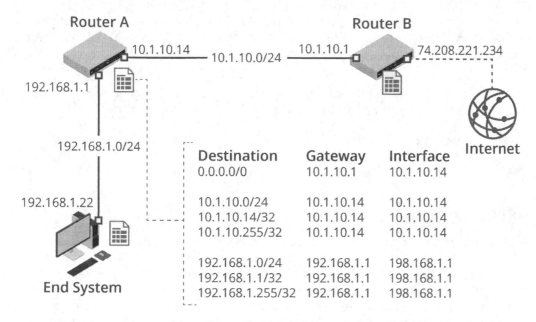

Routing table for Router A. (Image © 123RF.com.)

Router A connects the 192.168.1.0/24 network to a different IP network (10.1.10.0/24). For these directly connected IP networks, the gateway is the same as the local interface. This router also has a default route, pointing to the 10.1.10.0/24 network. Any traffic not addressed to 192.168.1.0 or a specific host on 10.1.10.0/24 is going to be forwarded to router B.

ROUTER B ROUTING TABLE

Router B connects the 10.1.10.0/24 network (which does not contain any end systems) with the Internet. Its 74.208.221.234 interface uses an IP address assigned by the company's Internet service provider (ISP). The gateway for the default route via this network (74.208.221.1) is one of the ISP's routers (not shown on the diagram).

Destination	Gateway	Interface
0.0.0.0/0	74.208.221.1	74.208.221.234
10.1.10.0/24	10.1.10.1	10.1.10.1
10.1.10.1/32	10.1.10.1	10.1.10.1
10.1.10.255/32	10.1.10.1	10.1.10.1
74.208.221.0/24	74.208.221.234	74.208.221.234
74.208.221.234/32	74.208.221.234	74.208.221.234
74.208.221.255/32	74.208.221.234	74.208.221.234
192.168.1.0/24	10.1.10.14	10.1.10.1

Routing table for Router B. (Image © 123RF.com.)

Like router A, router B has entries for its directly connected networks (74.208.221.234/24 and 10.1.10.0/24). Router B is also configured with a route to 192.168.1.0/24, the gateway for which is Router A. This is important, as if a route to this IP network was not present, any incoming traffic addressed to it would not match any rule and be directed back out using the default route.

 Note: *This example is simplified. The local addressing schemes used (192.168.x.y and 10.x.y.z) are not routable over the Internet. Router B would normally be using some sort of Network Address Translation (NAT).*

 Note: *If there are two (or more) available routes, the metric value (not shown in the examples) is used to favor one over the other.*

PACKET DELIVERY

When a router receives a packet, it goes through the same process that the source host did to calculate if the packet needs to be routed to another router or it can be delivered locally to another interface (a **directly connected** route). In the case of a directly connected route, the router uses ARP (IPv4) or Neighbor Discovery (ND in IPv6) to determine the interface address of the destination host and encapsulates the packet in the appropriate frame format for delivery over the interface. If there is no directly connected route, the router consults its routing table to determine the next hop router. It inserts the **next hop** router's MAC address into a new frame (containing the original IP packet) and merges it onto the wire attached to the appropriate interface for the next hop router.

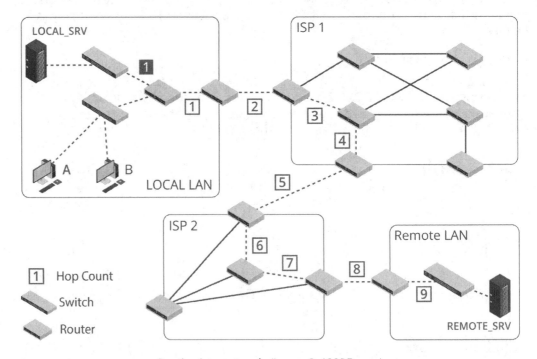

Routing internetwork. (Image © 123RF.com.)

For example, in the network shown, host A takes 1 hop to communicate with LOCAL_SRV via a directly connected interface on the LAN router. Note that the switches do not count as hops. Host B takes multiple hops (9) to communicate with REMOTE_SRV, with traffic routed via two ISP networks. Also, observe the alternative routes that could be taken. Do any have a lower hop count?

If no route exists, the packet is either forwarded to the default gateway of the router (also referred to as the **default route** or **gateway of last resort**) or dropped (and the source host is notified that it was undeliverable). If the packet has been routed, the **Time to Live (TTL)** is decreased by at least 1. This could be greater if the router is congested. When the TTL is 0, the packet is discarded. This prevents badly addressed packets from permanently circulating the network.

STATIC AND DEFAULT ROUTES

The routing protocol you implement depends upon a variety of factors. As different protocols support different routing algorithms, it is worth spending some time considering the different algorithms used.

STATIC ROUTES

Static routing means that you manually add routes to a routing table, and they change only if you edit them. Configuring static routing entries can be useful in some circumstances, but it can be problematic if the routing topology changes often, as each route on each affected router needs to be updated manually.

 Note: Static routes can be configured either as non-persistent or persistent. A non-persistent route is removed from the routing table if the router is rebooted.

DEFAULT ROUTE

A **default route** is a special type of static route that identifies the next hop router for an unknown destination. The destination address 0.0.0.0/0 (IPv4) or ::/0 (IPv6) is used to represent the default route. The default route is used only if there are no matches for the destination in the rest of the routing table. Most end systems are configured with a default route (pointing to the default gateway). This may also be the simplest way for an edge router to forward traffic to an ISP's routers.

LEARNED ROUTES AND ALGORITHMS

A **learned route** is one that was communicated to the router by another router by using a **dynamic routing protocol**. Routers use these protocols to exchange information about connected networks periodically and select the best available route to a destination. The algorithms used for path selection can be categorized according to the topology and metrics that they use to build and update routing tables.

CONVERGENCE

Convergence is the process whereby routers running dynamic routing algorithms agree on routes through the internetwork. As the internetwork topology changes constantly (with router failures, addressing changes, and unforeseen events), routers must be capable of adapting to these changes and communicating them *quickly* to other routers to avoid loops and black holes. A **black hole** means that a packet is discarded without notification back to the source; a **loop** causes a packet to be forwarded around the network until its TTL expires. A network where all the routers share the same topology is described as **steady state**. The time taken to reach steady state is a measure of a routing protocol's convergence performance.

 *Note: A **flapping interface** is one that frequently changes from online to offline and offline to online. Similarly, **route flapping** refers to a router changing the properties of a route it is advertising quickly and often. Flapping can cause serious convergence problems.*

HIERARCHICAL VS. FLAT

In **hierarchical** routing systems, certain routers form a routing backbone. Other routers are grouped into logical collections, sometimes called areas or domains. Backbone or border routers can communicate with routers in other domains, while internal routers are limited to communications with routers within the current domain or the border router(s) serving it. The hierarchical approach allows for route summarization (discussed later).

Non-hierarchical systems are referred to as **flat**—a situation where all routers can inter-communicate with one another. Each network ID requires a separate entry in the routing table, which can be problematic in very large internetworks.

DISTANCE VECTOR VS. LINK-STATE

Distance vector algorithms require that routers periodically propagate their entire routing table to their immediate neighbors. Distance vector algorithms provide for slower convergence than link-state algorithms. This is the general process for distance-vector routing:

1. Each router passes a copy of its routing table to its neighbors and maintains a table of minimum distances to every node.
2. The neighbors add the route to their own tables, incrementing the metric to reflect the extra distance to the end network. The distance is given as a hop count; the vector component specifies the address of the next hop.
3. When a router has two routes to the same network, it selects the one with the lowest metric, assuming that it is faster to route through fewer hops.

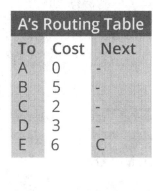

A's Routing Table		
To	Cost	Next
A	0	-
B	5	-
C	2	-
D	3	-
E	6	C

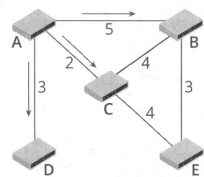

B's Routing Table		
To	Cost	Next
A	5	-
B	0	-
C	4	-
D	8	A
E	3	-

D's Routing Table		
To	Cost	Next
A	3	-
B	8	A
C	5	A
D	0	-
E	9	A

C's Routing Table		
To	Cost	Next
A	2	-
B	4	-
C	0	-
D	5	A
E	4	-

E's Routing Table		
To	Cost	Next
A	6	C
B	3	-
C	4	-
D	9	C
E	0	-

Each router maintains a table of minimum costs. (Image © 123RF.com.)

Routers implementing a **link-state** algorithm propagate information about only their own links to other routers on the internetwork. Routers update each other only when one of their links changes state. Otherwise, they do not communicate except for sending a periodic "hello" packet to assure their neighboring routers that they are still functioning on the network. These smaller, frequent updates lead to more rapid convergence and more efficiently support larger networks. However, link-state algorithms can be more expensive to implement because they require more power and memory.

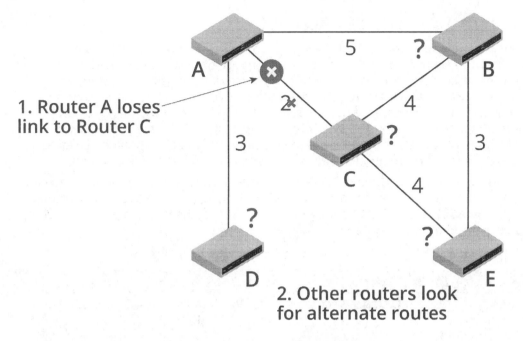

Link-state routing. (Image © 123RF.com.)

Some protocols use a **hybrid** of different methods to perform path selection more efficiently.

ROUTING ALGORITHM METRICS

Each routing algorithm uses different metrics to help determine the appropriate path to use. These metrics might include:

- **Path length**—The end-to-end cost of using a route (**hop count**). You might assign a value to a path between router A and B and between B and C. The end-to-end path length is the sum of A-to-B and B-to-C.
- **Reliability**—Over time, it might become obvious that some links between routers are more reliable than others. You can assign a value for this reliability that routers can assess when determining an effective path.
- **Latency**—It takes time for a packet to traverse an internetwork. Delay-based metrics measure transit time. This metric is most important if the route is used to carry time-sensitive data, such as voice or video.
- **Bandwidth**—Metrics based on bandwidth look at the maximum achievable bandwidth on a link and do not consider the available bandwidth. This is a less efficient metric than delay-based metrics.
- **Load (link utilization)**—A metric that bases routing decisions on how busy a route is.
- **Maximum Transmission Unit (MTU)**—How large a packet can be sent without the need for fragmentation.

> **Note:** *In IPv4, routers can be made responsible for calculating the MTU, based on packet size, for a given interface and fragmenting and reassembling packets that are too big. In IPv6, the host is responsible for determining the MTU, and routers cannot perform fragmentation.*

- **Price/costs**—You can assign a monetary cost to various links, and the router using a cost metric will try to select the cheapest link available. This is useful for organizations routing on a budget.

DYNAMIC ROUTING PROTOCOLS

For larger organizations, it is simply not practical to configure routing tables manually. Aside from anything else, routing information is seldom static as routers are reconfigured, taken temporarily offline, and even decommissioned. While many organizations can manage to maintain routing tables for these internal changes, when connected to the Internet, it becomes almost impossible. Consequently, router vendors provide support for **dynamic routing protocols**. These protocols use various algorithms and metrics to build and maintain routing tables to provide reasonably current routing information about the networks to which they are connected.

An **Interior Gateway Protocol (IGP)** is one that performs routing within a network under the administrative control of a single owner, also referred to as an **Autonomous System (AS)**. An **Exterior Gateway Protocol (EGP)** is one that can perform routing between autonomous systems.

Some of the most popular protocols are listed in the following table.

Protocol	Type	Class	Transport
Routing Information Protocol (RIP)	Distance-vector	Interior Gateway Protocol (IGP)	UDP (port 520 or 521)
Enhanced Interior Gateway Routing Protocol (EIGRP)	Distance-vector (Hybrid)	Interior Gateway Protocol (IGP)	Native IP (88)
Open Shortest Path First (OSPF)	Link-state	Interior Gateway Protocol (IGP)	Native IP (89)
Border Gateway Protocol (BGP)	Distance-vector (Hybrid)	Exterior Gateway Protocol (EGP)	TCP (port 179)

ROUTING INFORMATION PROTOCOL (RIP)

Routing Information Protocol (RIP) is a long-established distance vector-based routing protocol. It uses a hop count metric to determine the distance to the destination network. Generally speaking, each router is assigned a hop count value of 1. RIP considers only one route to a given destination network—that with the lowest hop count.

To help prevent looping, the maximum hop count allowed is 15. Consequently, this limits the maximum size of a RIP network, since networks that have a hop count of 16 or higher are unreachable. RIP sends regular updates about the routing table to neighboring routers, plus ad hoc updates whenever changes occur. When a router receives an update from a neighbor, it updates the appropriate route in its own routing table, increases the hop count by 1, and indicates the originator of the update as the next hop to the specified network. The router then propagates the update.

RIP uses the User Datagram Protocol (UDP port 520) for routers to exchange messages.

There are, in fact, three implementations of RIP. RIPv2 provides for a level of authentication between RIP routers and uses more efficient multicast transmissions, rather than broadcasting updates. In addition, RIPv2 packets carry a subnet mask field and, therefore, support classless addressing. RIPng is an update to support IPv6. RIPng uses UDP port 521.

Because it is widely adopted, well understood, and simple, RIP is ideally suited to small networks with limited failover routes. For more complex networks with redundant paths, other network routing protocols should be considered.

ENHANCED INTERIOR GATEWAY ROUTING PROTOCOL (EIGRP)

The **Interior Gateway Routing Protocol (IGRP)** was developed by Cisco to provide a routing protocol for routing within a domain or autonomous system. Limitations in IGRP, such as lack of support for classless addressing, led to the development of **Enhanced IGRP (EIGRP)**. There are versions for IPv4 and IPv6. IGRP itself is now obsolete.

Like RIP, EIGRP is usually classed as a distance vector-based routing protocol. Unlike RIP, which is based on a simple hop count metric, EIGRP uses a metric composed of several administrator weighted elements, including reliability, bandwidth, delay, and load. EIGRP also supports multiple paths to the destination network; again, unlike RIP. EIGRP may also, therefore, be described as an advanced distance vector protocol or as a hybrid routing protocol. EIGRP builds on the strengths of RIP while providing for more efficient route selection, better administrative control, and better fault tolerance.

Unlike RIP, EIGRP is a native IP protocol, which means that it is encapsulated directly in IP datagrams, rather than using TCP or UDP. It is tagged with the protocol number 88 in the Protocol field of the IP header.

OPEN SHORTEST PATH FIRST (OSPF)

The hierarchical link-state routing protocol **Open Shortest Path First (OSPF)** is suited to large organizations with multiple redundant paths between networks. It has high convergence performance compared to RIP. It was designed from the outset to support classless addressing.

Networks and their connected hosts and routers within an autonomous system are grouped into OSPF **areas**. Routers within a given area share the same topological database of the networks they serve.

Routers that can connect to multiple areas are known as **area border routers**. A **backbone** (always called Area 0) is created by the collection of border routers. This backbone is only visible to the border routers and invisible to the routers within a specific area. Routers use a **Link State Advertisement (LSA)** to update their routing tables. In a given area, routers exchange OSPF "hello" messages, both as a form of a keep-alive packet and in order to acquire neighbors with which to exchange routing information. These exchanges of routing information enable the routers to each build a topological routing tree (a **shortest path tree**) and keep it up to date. The use of areas to subdivide the network minimizes the amount of routing traffic that must be passed around the network as a whole, improving convergence performance.

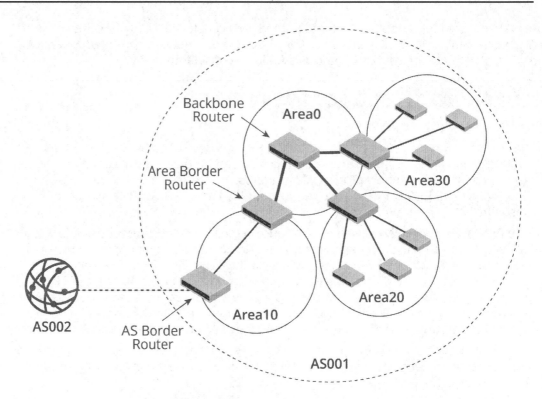

Typical OSPF topology. (Image © 123RF.com.)

Messages are sent using OSPF's own datagram format. This is tagged as protocol number 89 in the IP datagram's Protocol field. There are various packet types and mechanisms to ensure sequencing and reliable delivery and to check for errors. OSPF also supports **plaintext** or cryptographic authentication.

BORDER GATEWAY PROTOCOL (BGP)

The **Border Gateway Protocol (BGP)** is designed to be used between routing domains, or **Autonomous Systems (ASes)**, and as such is used as the routing protocol on the Internet, primarily between ISPs.

All the protocols discussed so far have been classed as interior gateway protocols (IGPs) used for communications between routers within an AS. BGP is a type of exterior gateway protocol (in fact, it replaced a protocol named EGP) for communications between routers in diverse ASes. When BGP is used within an AS, it is referred to as Interior BGP (IBGP), and when implemented between ASes, it is referred to as Exterior BGP (EBGP).

The uses of ASes are discussed in *RFC 1930*. ASes are designed to hide the complexity of private networks from the public Internet. If all Internet locations had to be propagated to all Internet routers, the routing tables would become too large to process. Border (or edge) routers for each AS exchange only as much network-reachability information as is required to access other autonomous systems (the **AS path**), rather than networks and hosts within each AS. **Autonomous System Numbers (ASN)** are allocated to ISPs by IANA via the various regional registries.

BGP works with CIDR IP network prefixes called **Network Layer Reachability Information (NLRI)**. Route selection is based on multiple metrics, including hop count, weight, local preference, origin, and community. BGP is not a pure distance-vector algorithm but uses a **hybrid** approach. In fact, BGP is more usually classed as a **path vector** routing protocol.

BGP works over TCP on port 179.

Note: *Remember that both subnetting and supernetting require the use of a classless routing protocol (one that does not determine the network mask based on the first octet in the IP address). Dynamic routing protocols that support classless addressing include RIPv2, EIGRP, OSPF, and BGPv4.*

IPv4 AND IPv6 INTERNET ROUTING

Internet routers must be able to locate any host on the Internet. As there are millions of networks and hosts, it is impossible to do this by storing routes to each of them. Instead, an Internet core router will consolidate the route to a group of networks, as identified by their shared **network routing prefix**, to a single routing table entry. This is referred to as **route aggregation** or **route summarization**.

Classless IPv4 routing uses a mix of flat and hierarchical structures to make more efficient use of the limited address space compared to the old method of classful address allocation. The system is based on the **Classless Inter-Domain Routing (CIDR)** specification.

High-level network routing prefixes (or CIDR blocks), which are 8 bits in length (/8s), are allocated by IANA to Regional Internet Registries (RIR), such as ARIN (America) and RIPE (Europe). A few are still held privately by companies such as IBM, Xerox, HP, and AT&T, or by government agencies such as the DoD. You can view the assignments at *iana.org/assignments/ipv4-address-space/ipv4-address-space.xhtml*.

The registries then allocate blocks to national and local registries. Actual ISPs are generally allocated blocks with prefixes of 20 bits or less. Any routing over that boundary (that is, a /21 network or higher) takes place solely within the ISP's network, rather than over the general Internet. The ISP's network is referred to as an **Autonomous System**. The ISPs subdivide their allocations into different sized blocks for different customer requirements, ranging from dynamically allocated addresses for home users, to fixed single IP addresses for small businesses, to smaller and larger ranges for medium-sized and large enterprises. At each level, a router serving a group of networks needs only to be advertised by a routing prefix of a given length, greatly reducing the number of routes that need to be stored in memory.

IPv6 follows the same hierarchical structure, with the advantage of planning an efficient addressing topology from the start and having a larger address space to work with. The full network prefix of an IPv6 address is 64 bits long. This is divided up into the following general hierarchy:

- The globally unique unicast address range is indicated by the 2000::/3 address space (the first 3 bits). Ranges from this address space are allocated to regional registries in blocks from /3 to /32, as listed at *iana.org/assignments/ipv6-unicast-address-assignments/ipv6-unicast-address-assignments.xhtml*.
- ISPs receive allocations from their registry in the space from /32 to /35.
- End users receive allocations from their ISP in the /48 to /64 range.
- End users can subnet their networks using the remainder of the network prefix left to them (if any).

Note: *To learn more, watch the related* **Video** *on the course website.*

Activity 5-1
Discussing Characteristics of Routing

SCENARIO
Answer the following questions to test your understanding of the content covered in this topic.

1. **What is a directly connected route?**

2. **An entry in a routing table will list the destination network address and netmask plus a gateway and metrics. What other piece of information is required?**

3. **If a routing protocol carries a subnet mask field for route updates, what feature of IP routing does the routing protocol support?**

4. **True or False? A router would normally have more than one network interface.**

5. **Referring to the routing table in the previous question, to which IP address would packets be sent if they were going to the Internet or another network?**

6. **What does it mean if a routing protocol converges to a steady state quickly?**

7. **Which general class of dynamic routing protocol provides the best convergence performance?**

8. **If forced to pick just one, which routing metric might you prioritize for a VoIP application?**

9. **Refer to the following routing table to answer the question. Which route determines the destination for packets to the 172.16.0.0 network? What adapter will they be delivered to?**

```
IPv4 Route Table
===========================================================================
Active Routes:
Network Destination        Netmask          Gateway       Interface  Metric
          0.0.0.0          0.0.0.0    192.168.1.200    192.168.1.11     276
        127.0.0.0        255.0.0.0         On-link        127.0.0.1     306
        127.0.0.1  255.255.255.255         On-link        127.0.0.1     306
  127.255.255.255  255.255.255.255         On-link        127.0.0.1     306
       172.16.0.0      255.255.0.0         On-link       172.16.0.1     286
       172.16.0.1  255.255.255.255         On-link       172.16.0.1     286
   172.16.255.255  255.255.255.255         On-link       172.16.0.1     286
      192.168.1.0    255.255.255.0         On-link     192.168.1.11     276
     192.168.1.11  255.255.255.255         On-link     192.168.1.11     276
    192.168.1.255  255.255.255.255         On-link     192.168.1.11     276
        224.0.0.0        240.0.0.0         On-link        127.0.0.1     306
        224.0.0.0        240.0.0.0         On-link       172.16.0.1     286
        224.0.0.0        240.0.0.0         On-link     192.168.1.11     276
  255.255.255.255  255.255.255.255         On-link        127.0.0.1     306
  255.255.255.255  255.255.255.255         On-link       172.16.0.1     286
  255.255.255.255  255.255.255.255         On-link     192.168.1.11     276
===========================================================================
```

10. **What is an ASN and how does it assist route aggregation?**

Activity 5-2

Designing a Branch Office Internetwork

SCENARIO

Helpful Help is a charitable organization that operates out of numerous small offices spread all over the country. Each office has a team of 10-20 people who currently use a network of PCs and Apple Macs running various applications. Each office is connected back to a main site, which has a connection to the Internet via an ISP. Staff at each local office uses the link for web access and to access an online email service. Each office has a 192.168.x.0/24 subnet allocated to it. The East region is shown in the graphic.

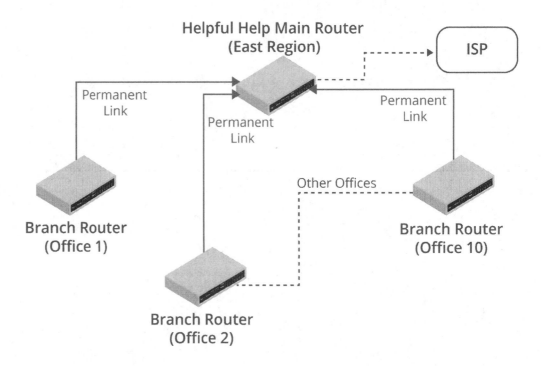

Helpful Help East region branch office internetwork. (Image © 123RF.com.)

1. **Given the current scenario of the charity, how would the routers at each local office be configured?**

2. Presently, each local office has several PSTN (landline) telephones. The plan is to replace these with a unified communications system for VoIP, conferencing, and messaging/information. This will require devices in each local office to be able to contact devices in other offices for direct media streaming. It is also anticipated that additional links may be added between branch offices where larger numbers

of users are situated due to the increased bandwidth required by the new applications at this site. Here is the revised diagram:

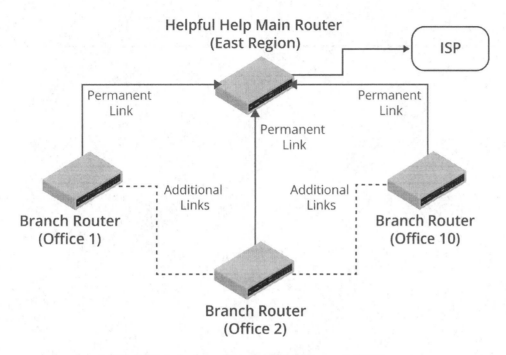

Additional links between branch offices. (Image © 123RF.com.)

3. **With this new infrastructure in place, what changes would need to be made to the router's configuration?**

4. **Which protocol would be best here?**

5. If the new system works well in the East region (the smallest), the plan is to roll out the system to the three other regions (North, South, and West). This will involve connecting the main routers for each region together, plus some additional links for redundancy. The other regions use different IP numbering systems and some use VLSM.

6. **Considering the potential changes a successful pilot in the East region might bring about in the whole organization, would your router configuration options change?**

7. **What might you do to manage the much larger number of IP subnets?**

Topic B

Install and Configure Routers

EXAM OBJECTIVES COVERED
1.4 Given a scenario, configure the appropriate IP addressing components.
2.2 Given a scenario, determine the appropriate placement of networking devices on a network and install/configure them.
5.2 Given a scenario, use the appropriate tool.

As well as understanding the different types of routing algorithms, as a network professional you must also be able to install routing devices to an appropriate place in the network. This topic will help you to install and configure routers, and to use command-line tools to test the routing infrastructure.

NETWORK OPERATING SYSTEM (NOS) AND APPLIANCE ROUTERS

A router can be implemented as hardware or software. The relatively complex tasks performed by a router mean that they tend to be processing intensively. A router may be a dedicated appliance with a port to each of the networks, or it may be a network operating system (NOS) server with multiple interface cards (**multi-homed**). Routers very often also support the functions of a firewall. A router designed to connect a private network to the Internet is called an **edge router** or **border router**. These routers can perform framing to repackage data from the private LAN frame format to the WAN Internet access frame format. Edge routers designed to work with DSL or cable modems are called small office/home office (SOHO) routers.

An integrated services router. This type of device combines DSL Internet access with Ethernet switch, Wi-Fi, and VoIP for a "one box" solution for remote sites and branch offices. (Image © 123RF.com.)

Routers designed to service medium to large networks are complex and expensive appliances. They feature specialized processors to handle the routing and forwarding processes, and memory to buffer data. Most routers of this class will also support plug-in cards for WAN interfaces.

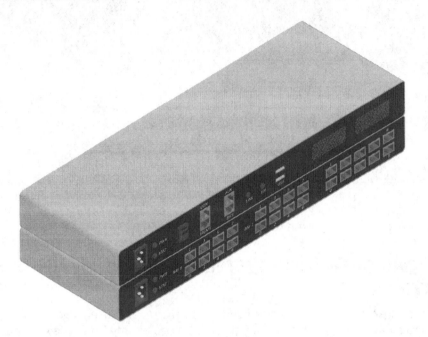

An advanced services router. This type of device provides network edge connectivity over Carrier Ethernet networks. (Image © 123RF.com.)

 Note: *Although they may be combined in the same appliance, the layer 1 and 2 framing and modem/WAN interface capability are separate functions from the layer 3 forwarding capability. Routers are always described as working at layer 3, even if they contain modules that work at layers 1 and 2 as well.*

ROUTER PLACEMENT

Routers serve both to join physically remote networks and subdivide autonomous IP networks into multiple subnets. **Border** or **edge** routers are typified by distinguishing external (Internet-facing) and internal interfaces. These devices are placed at the network **perimeter**.

The following figure shows a simplified example of a typical network configuration. A WAN router provides access to the Internet. Basic switches provide ports and virtual LANs (logical groupings of clients) for wired and wireless (via an access point) devices. Traffic between logical networks is controlled by a LAN router (or layer 3 switch).

Traffic between VLANs must be routed. In this scenario, it is possible to use a router with a single interface (a one-armed router or router on a stick) with the interface configured to be part of all the VLANs it serves. Passing traffic between a router appliance and the switches is relatively inefficient, however. Consequently, enterprise networks usually use a layer 3 switch, which is an appliance that can establish the VLANs and perform routing between them.

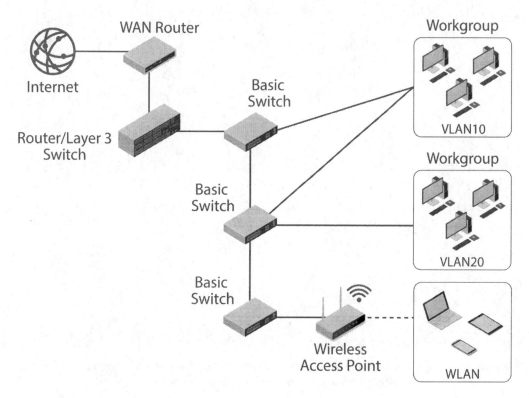

Typical network configuration. (Image © 123RF.com.)

ROUTER CONFIGURATION AND LOOPBACK INTERFACES

As router appliances do not have a screen or keyboard, they are configured locally either via a serial connection known as a console port or (more usually) remotely over the network by using a protocol such as Secure Shell (SSH). SSH can be used to communicate with the router via the IP address of any configured interface. However, as any given physical interface could suffer a hardware fault or be temporarily unavailable for various reasons, it is considered best practice to create a virtual interface, known as a **loopback interface**, in the router's operating system and assign it an IP address for use in remotely managing the router. This is a way of giving the router an internal IP address, not connected to any physical network, that is therefore not reliant on a specific network being available.

A software router is configured using the appropriate tools in the underlying NOS. As well as the configuration of the routing functions, the performance and security of the underlying server should also be considered.

```
protocols {
    bgp 65537 {
        neighbor 172.16.1.254 {
            remote-as 65536
        }
        network 10.1.0.0/24 {
        }
        network 172.16.0.252/30 {
        }
        parameters {
            router-id 172.16.0.253
        }
    }
    static {
        route 10.1.0.0/24 {
            next-hop 172.16.0.254 {
                distance 1
            }
        }
    }
}
service {
    ssh {
        port 22
:
```

Configuring routing protocols on a VyOS-based software router. The host can be configured at a local terminal or from a remote computer over Secure Shell (SSH).

route

A host's **routing table** contains information about routes to other hosts. A router for a complex network would normally have a large routing table populated dynamically by one or more routing protocols. An end system will usually have a simple routing table configured with a few default entries. For example, the default entries for a Windows® host are:

- Default route (0.0.0.0/0).
- Loopback address.
- Host's subnet address.
- Host's own address.
- Multicast address.
- Broadcast address.

```
IPv4 Route Table
===========================================================================
Active Routes:
Network Destination        Netmask          Gateway       Interface  Metric
          0.0.0.0          0.0.0.0       10.1.0.254      10.1.0.101     15
         10.1.0.0    255.255.255.0         On-link       10.1.0.101    271
       10.1.0.101  255.255.255.255         On-link       10.1.0.101    271
       10.1.0.255  255.255.255.255         On-link       10.1.0.101    271
        127.0.0.0        255.0.0.0         On-link        127.0.0.1    331
        127.0.0.1  255.255.255.255         On-link        127.0.0.1    331
  127.255.255.255  255.255.255.255         On-link        127.0.0.1    331
      169.254.0.0        255.255.0.0       On-link   169.254.252.237    281
  169.254.252.237  255.255.255.255         On-link   169.254.252.237    281
  169.254.255.255  255.255.255.255         On-link   169.254.252.237    281
        224.0.0.0        240.0.0.0         On-link        127.0.0.1    331
        224.0.0.0        240.0.0.0         On-link   169.254.252.237    281
        224.0.0.0        240.0.0.0         On-link       10.1.0.101    271
  255.255.255.255  255.255.255.255         On-link        127.0.0.1    331
  255.255.255.255  255.255.255.255         On-link   169.254.252.237    281
  255.255.255.255  255.255.255.255         On-link       10.1.0.101    271
===========================================================================
Persistent Routes:
  None

IPv6 Route Table
===========================================================================
Active Routes:
 If Metric Network Destination       Gateway
  1    331 ::1/128                    On-link
 14    281 fe80::/64                  On-link
  7    271 fe80::/64                  On-link
  7    271 fe80::a4e7:7155:7f44:dcc6/128
                                      On-link
 14    281 fe80::dd5c:a7d0:925b:fced/128
                                      On-link
  1    331 ff00::/8                   On-link
 14    281 ff00::/8                   On-link
  7    271 ff00::/8                   On-link
===========================================================================
Persistent Routes:
  None
```

IPv4 and IPv6 routing tables for a Windows host. For IPv4, the host uses 10.1.0.254 as its default gateway. The IPv6 configuration has no route from the local network. (Screenshot used with permission from Microsoft.)

On a Windows or Linux/UNIX host, the **route** command, `route`, is used to view and modify the routing table. In Windows, to show the routing table, run `route print`. To add a route, the syntax for the Windows version of the tool is:

```
route [-f -p] add DestinationIP mask Netmask GatewayIP metric
MetricValue if Interface
```

The variables in the syntax are defined as:

- *DestinationIP* is a network or host address.
- *Netmask* is the subnet mask for *DestinationIP*.
- *GatewayIP* is the router to use to contact the network or host.
- *MetricValue* is the cost of the route.
- *Interface* is the adapter the host should use (used if the host is multi-homed).

For example:

```
route add 192.168.3.0 mask 255.255.255.0 192.168.5.1 metric 2
```

Routes added in this manner are **non-persistent** by default. This means that they are stored in memory and will be discarded if the machine is restarted. A route can be permanently configured (stored in the registry) using the `-p` switch. The tool also allows for routes to be deleted (`route delete`) and modified (`route change`).

The Linux version of `route` performs the same function, but the syntax is different. The routing table is shown by entering `route` with no parameters. The `change` parameter is not supported, and the command cannot be used to add **persistent** routes. A non-persistent route can be added using the following general syntax:

```
route add -net 192.168.3.0 netmask 255.255.255.0 metric 2 dev eth0
```

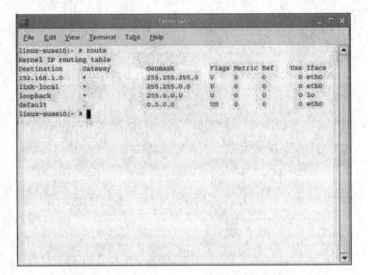

Output of Linux route and ip route show commands.

 Note: The `ip` suite of tools is designed to replace deprecated legacy command-line tools in Linux. You can use `ip route show` and `ip route add` to achieve the same ends.

tracert AND pathping

The `tracert` ICMP utility is used from a Windows host to trace the route taken by a packet as it hops to the destination host on a remote network. It can be used either with an IP address or a host and domain name. It returns the IP address (or name) of each router used by the packet to reach its destination.

If the host cannot be located, the command will eventually timeout, but it will return every router that was attempted.

The output shows the number of hops, the ingress interface of the router or host (that is, the interface from which the router receives the ICMP packet), and the time taken to respond to each probe in milliseconds (ms). If no acknowledgement is received within the timeout period, an asterisk is shown against the probe.

`tracert` can be used with several switches, which must precede the target IP address or host.

```
tracert -6 www.microsoft.com
```

You can use the `-d` switch to suppress name resolution, `-h` to specify the maximum number of hops (the default is 30), and `-w` to specify a timeout in ms (the default is 4000). If, after increasing the value, destinations are then reachable, you probably have a bandwidth issue to resolve. The `-j` option allows you to specify preferred routers (loose source routing). When used with host names (rather than IP addresses), `tracert` can be forced to use IPv6 instead of IPv4 by adding the `-6` switch.

```
C:\Users\James>tracert www.comptia.org

Tracing route to www.comptia.org [198.134.5.6]
over a maximum of 30 hops:

  1    <1 ms    <1 ms    <1 ms  ARCHER_VR900 [192.168.0.254]
  2     1 ms    <1 ms    <1 ms  router.broadband [192.168.1.254]
  3     7 ms     8 ms     7 ms  host-212-158-250-33.dslgb.com [212.158.250.33]
  4    10 ms    10 ms    10 ms  63.130.127.221
  5    10 ms    10 ms    10 ms  ae15-xcr1.slo.cw.net [195.2.2.217]
  6    78 ms    77 ms    77 ms  ae2-xcr1.nyh.cw.net [195.2.28.169]
  7    77 ms    77 ms    77 ms  ae13-xcr2.nyk.cw.net [195.2.25.69]
  8    79 ms    79 ms    81 ms  ae-36.a02.nycmny01.us.bb.gin.ntt.net [128.241.2.153]
  9    94 ms    93 ms    93 ms  ae-13.r07.nycmny01.us.bb.gin.ntt.net [129.250.6.50]
 10    81 ms    78 ms    78 ms  ae-2.r25.nycmny01.us.bb.gin.ntt.net [129.250.3.97]
 11    99 ms    96 ms    98 ms  ae-1.r20.chcgil09.us.bb.gin.ntt.net [129.250.2.166]
 12    97 ms    96 ms    96 ms  ae-6.r07.chcgil09.us.bb.gin.ntt.net [129.250.6.61]
 13   115 ms    96 ms    96 ms  ae-30.a00.chcgil09.us.bb.gin.ntt.net [129.250.3.145]
 14    96 ms    96 ms    96 ms  ae-0.windstream.chcgil09.us.bb.gin.ntt.net [129.250.203.6]
 15    98 ms    97 ms    98 ms  be1-agr02.chcg02-il.us.windstream.net [40.136.99.47]
 16    96 ms    95 ms    95 ms  be3.pe03.chcg02-il.us.windstream.net [40.138.80.61]
 17    96 ms    95 ms    97 ms  h229.201.129.40.static.ip.windstream.net [40.129.201.229]
 18    97 ms    96 ms    98 ms  h207.201.129.40.static.ip.windstream.net [40.129.201.207]
 19    98 ms    98 ms    98 ms  unassigned.norlight.net [209.83.91.205]
 20    98 ms    98 ms    98 ms  63-250-233-14.ord.bobbroadband.com [63.250.233.14]
 21    98 ms    98 ms    97 ms  198.134.5.6
 22    97 ms    97 ms    97 ms  198.134.5.6

Trace complete.
```

Using tracert in Windows to plot the path from a host in the UK to CompTIA's web server. (Screenshot used with permission from Microsoft.)

`pathping` performs a trace route, then it pings each hop router a given number of times for a given period to determine the Round Trip Time (RTT) and measure link latency more accurately. The output also shows packet loss at each hop.

```
Computing statistics for 550 seconds...
             Source to Here   This Node/Link
Hop  RTT     Lost/Sent = Pct  Lost/Sent = Pct  Address
  0                                             COMPTIA-LABS [192.168.0.103]
                                0/ 100 =  0%    |
  1    0ms    0/ 100 =  0%     0/ 100 =  0%    ARCHER_VR900 [192.168.0.254]
                                0/ 100 =  0%    |
  2    0ms    0/ 100 =  0%     0/ 100 =  0%    router.broadband [192.168.1.254]
                                0/ 100 =  0%    |
  3   73ms    0/ 100 =  0%     0/ 100 =  0%    host-212-158-250-33.dslgb.com [212.158.250.33]
                                0/ 100 =  0%    |
  4   ---   100/ 100 =100%   100/ 100 =100%    63.130.127.221
                                0/ 100 =  0%    |
  5   12ms    0/ 100 =  0%     0/ 100 =  0%    ae15-xcr1.slo.cw.net [195.2.2.217]
                                0/ 100 =  0%    |
  6   78ms    0/ 100 =  0%     0/ 100 =  0%    ae2-xcr1.nyh.cw.net [195.2.28.169]
                                0/ 100 =  0%    |
  7   78ms    0/ 100 =  0%     0/ 100 =  0%    ae13-xcr2.nyk.cw.net [195.2.25.69]
                                0/ 100 =  0%    |
  8   81ms    0/ 100 =  0%     0/ 100 =  0%    ae-36.a02.nycmny01.us.bb.gin.ntt.net [128.241.2.153]
                                0/ 100 =  0%    |
  9   79ms    0/ 100 =  0%     0/ 100 =  0%    ae-13.r07.nycmny01.us.bb.gin.ntt.net [129.250.6.50]
                                0/ 100 =  0%    |
 10   79ms    0/ 100 =  0%     0/ 100 =  0%    ae-2.r25.nycmny01.us.bb.gin.ntt.net [129.250.3.97]
                                0/ 100 =  0%    |
 11  100ms    0/ 100 =  0%     0/ 100 =  0%    ae-1.r20.chcgil09.us.bb.gin.ntt.net [129.250.2.166]
                                0/ 100 =  0%    |
 12   97ms    0/ 100 =  0%     0/ 100 =  0%    ae-6.r07.chcgil09.us.bb.gin.ntt.net [129.250.6.61]
                                0/ 100 =  0%    |
 13   99ms    0/ 100 =  0%     0/ 100 =  0%    ae-30.a00.chcgil09.us.bb.gin.ntt.net [129.250.3.145]
```

pathping output for the same trace. You can see 100% packet loss in the fourth hop. This could indicate some sort of routing issue or it could just be because that interface doesn't respond to ICMP probes. (Screenshot used with permission from Microsoft.)

Note: *ICMP is often blocked by firewalls and routers, so the output from tools such as* `tracert` *and* `pathping` *is not always completely accurate.*

traceroute, mtr, AND LOOKING GLASS SITES

`traceroute` is supported on Linux and router OSes (such as IOS) but not on Windows. `traceroute` performs a similar function to `tracert` but it uses UDP probes instead of ICMP by default. An ICMP probe can be performed by using `traceroute -I` (this command is case-sensitive). The **traceroute** commands, `traceroute -6` or `traceroute6`, are used for IPv6 networks.

The **mtr** command (short for My Trace Route) , `mtr`, provides similar functionality to `pathping` for Linux-based OSes. The `StDev` field in the output shows standard deviation in the latency measurements. Standard deviation is a measure of how dispersed the highest and lowest values are from the mean (or average) sample value. If `StDev` is high, latency values vary widely across the samples. This sort of inconsistent latency is called jitter.

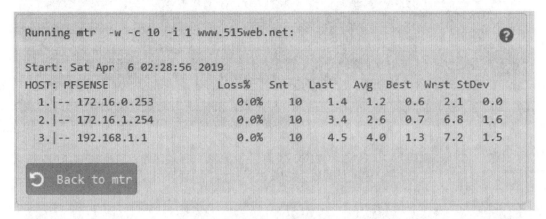

Running mtr—The output updates continually to show route statistics over time [packet loss and latency or Round Trip Time (RTT) statistics].

A **looking glass site** is one that hosts a server that exposes its routing table to public queries via HTTP. Some looking glass servers can be accessed via Telnet.

An ISP can use these to verify that information about routes to its networks is being properly propagated to the routers of other ISPs. You could also use a looking glass server to troubleshoot problems accessing a particular website. If a site is available from one location but not another, you can use the looking glass server to work out the route(s) from the site to an IP address.

HIGH AVAILABILITY ROUTING AND VIRTUAL IP

Routers are vital to the connectivity of a network, so their failure can lead to loss of service. In many environments, this constitutes an unacceptable risk, and systems must be implemented in order to ensure that the network can continue to operate in the event of a router failure. In a mesh network topology, alternate routes can be found to bypass failed routers or faulty connections. However, routing protocols take time to converge, and during this convergence time, packets may be dropped. Also, end sites are typically served by a single router configured as the default gateway. While it is possible to configure hosts with multiple default gateways for fault tolerance, this does not work well in practice, as it requires a greater degree of complexity in the hosts' routing algorithms than is typically implemented on an end system host.

HOT STANDBY ROUTER PROTOCOL (HSRP)

To address this problem, Cisco developed the proprietary **Hot Standby Router Protocol (HSRP)**, standardized in 1998 as *RFC 2281*. HSRP allows for multiple physical routers to serve as a single default gateway for a subnet. To do this, each router must have an interface connected to the subnet, with its own unique MAC address and IP address. In addition, they also need to be configured to share a common **virtual IP address** and a common MAC address. The group of routers configured in this way is known as a **standby group**. They communicate among themselves using IP multicasts and choose an active router based on priorities configured by an administrator. The active router responds to any traffic sent to the virtual IP address. Of the remaining routers in the standby group, the router with the next highest priority is chosen as the standby router. The standby router monitors the status of the active router and takes over the role if the active router becomes unavailable, also triggering the selection of a new standby router from the remaining routers in the group.

VIRTUAL ROUTER REDUNDANCY PROTOCOL (VRRP)

An open standard protocol known as **Virtual Router Redundancy Protocol (VRRP)** was developed in 2004. The current version is VRRP version 3, defined in *RFC 5798*, which adds support for IPv6. VRRC is very similar to HSRP, the differences mainly being in terminology and packet formats. In VRRP, the active router is known as the **master**, and all other routers in the group are known as **backup routers**. There is no specific standby router; instead, all backup routers monitor the status of the master, and in the event of a failure, a new master router is selected from the available backup routers based on priority.

One advantage of VRRP over HSRP is that it does not require each router interface to be assigned a unique IP address. It is possible to configure VRRP routers to use only the virtual IP address. This can be useful on subnets where address space utilization is high.

 *Note: To learn more, watch the related **Video** on the course website.*

Activity 5-3
Discussing Router Configuration

SCENARIO
Answer the following questions to test your understanding of the content covered in this topic.

1. **How would you view the routing table on a Linux PC?**

2. **If you receive a Request timed out error message when using ping, what would you attempt next?**

3. **What tool(s) could you use to measure link statistics over time?**

4. **What is a looking glass site?**

5. **What is the purpose of HSRP and VRRP?**

Activity 5-4
Configuring Routing

BEFORE YOU BEGIN

Start the VMs used in this activity in the following order, adjusting the memory allocation first if necessary, and waiting at the ellipses for the previous VMs to finish booting before starting the next group. You do not need to connect to a VM until prompted to do so in the activity steps.

1. **RT1-LOCAL** (256 MB)
2. **RT2-ISP** (256 MB)
3. **RT3-INT** (256 MB)
4. **DC1** (1024—2048 MB)
5. ...
6. **MS1** (1024—2048 MB)
7. ...
8. **PC1** (1024—2048 MB)
9. **PC2** (512—1024 MB)

Start the following VM only when prompted during the activity:

- **LAMP** (1024—2048 MB)

 Note: *If you can allocate more than the minimum amounts of RAM, prioritize **DC1** and **PC1**.*

SCENARIO

In this activity, you will configure the VyOS VMs to act as routers between different types of network, each represented by a different Hyper-V switch.

- **vLOCAL**—A private local network hosting the Windows VMs.
- **vISP**—A network representing an Internet Service Provider's access network allowing the LAN to join the Internet.
- **vINT00/vINT01/vINT02**—Switches representing a public Internet.

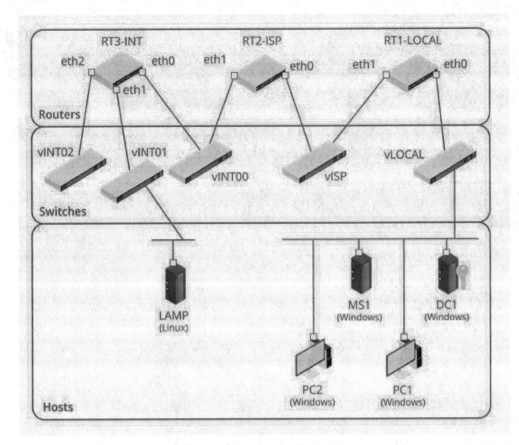

Physical network topology for the activity. (Image © 123RF.com.)

This activity is designed to test your understanding of and ability to apply content examples in the following CompTIA Network+ objectives:

- 1.3 Explain the concepts and characteristics of routing and switching.
- 2.2 Given a scenario, determine the appropriate placement of networking devices on a network and install/configure them.
- 5.2 Given a scenario, use the appropriate tool.

1. In the default activity configuration, routing between the networks has already been set up for you. Use `ping`, `pathping`, and `tracert` to test links and paths between hosts on different networks from the **PC1** VM.

    a) Connect to the **PC1** VM and sign in as ***515support\Administrator*** with password ***Pa$$w0rd***

    b) Open a command prompt and run the following commands to test connectivity:

    ```
    ping www.515web.net
    ```

    ```
    ping 192.168.1.1
    ```

    ```
    ping 192.168.1.254
    ```

    The **Destination host unreachable** message says that a network path to 192.168.1.1 is known, but the host cannot be contacted. A quick check will reveal this is because the host isn't started.

    c) On the **HOST**, in Hyper-V Manager, right-click the **LAMP** VM and select **Start**. Double-click the icon to show the connection window.

    d) When **LAMP** has finished booting (**Ubuntu 16.04.2 LTS LAMP tty1** will be shown), switch to the **PC1** VM.

    e) Run the following command:

```
ping www.515web.net
```

This command should now be successful.

f) Run the following command:

```
tracert 192.168.1.1
```

g) Examine the output to identify the interfaces used in the route:

- 10.1.0.254—The default gateway for the LAN (the eth0 interface on **RT1-LOCAL**).
- 172.16.0.253—The interface on **RT2-ISP** that **RT1-LOCAL** uses to reach the Internet. On a real network, this would be some type of WAN link (DSL or Metro Ethernet, for instance).
- 172.16.1.254—An interface on the router representing your Internet core. There would be much more complexity in real life of course, but in this example the router is directly connected to the destination network.
- 192.168.1.1—The end station (the **LAMP** VM hosting the **515web.net** HTTP server).

Observe the different subnets that are used. Again, this is greatly simplified, as they all use private address ranges.

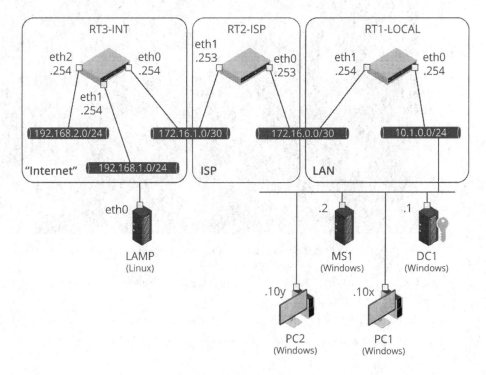

Layer 3 (IP) logical network topology. (Image © 123RF.com.)

h) Run the following command:

```
pathping 192.168.1.1
```

You can reduce the amount of time `pathping` takes by setting the number of pings using the `-q` switch. Using `-n` to suppress name resolution will also speed up execution.

```
C:\Users\administrator>tracert 192.168.1.1

Tracing route to 192.168.1.1 over a maximum of 30 hops

  1    <1 ms    <1 ms     1 ms  10.1.0.254
  2     1 ms     2 ms     3 ms  172.16.0.253
  3    <1 ms     4 ms     4 ms  172.16.1.254
  4     3 ms     2 ms     4 ms  192.168.1.1

Trace complete.

C:\Users\administrator>pathping 192.168.1.1

Tracing route to 192.168.1.1 over a maximum of 30 hops

  0  PC1.corp.515support.com [10.1.0.101]
  1  10.1.0.254
  2  172.16.0.253
  3  172.16.1.254
  4  192.168.1.1

Computing statistics for 100 seconds...
                Source to Here   This Node/Link
Hop  RTT    Lost/Sent = Pct   Lost/Sent = Pct   Address
  0                                                  PC1.corp.515support.com [10.1.0.101]
                                 0/ 100 =  0%   |
  1   0ms    0/ 100 =  0%       0/ 100 =  0%   10.1.0.254
                                 0/ 100 =  0%   |
  2   2ms    0/ 100 =  0%       0/ 100 =  0%   172.16.0.253
                                 0/ 100 =  0%   |
  3   3ms    0/ 100 =  0%       0/ 100 =  0%   172.16.1.254
                                 0/ 100 =  0%   |
  4   5ms    0/ 100 =  0%       0/ 100 =  0%   192.168.1.1

Trace complete.
```

tracert and pathping output. (Screenshot used with permission from Microsoft.)

2. Test the link from the **LAMP** VM to the Windows Server network by using the `ping` and `mtr` tools.

a) Switch to the **LAMP** VM, and log in with the username *lamp* and password *Pa$$w0rd*

 Note: *You can type the username even if no prompt is shown.*

b) Run the following command:

```
ping updates.corp.515support.com -c4
```

Although name resolution is configured, for the rest of this activity, you will use IP addresses.

c) Run the following command:

```
mtr 10.1.0.2
```

mtr output on LAMP.

Unlike `tracert/traceroute`, `mtr` runs continually to monitor the link state. Compared to `pathping`, it shows results more quickly.

d) Examine the output to identify the interfaces used in the route:

- 192.168.1.254—This is LAMP's default gateway (the eth1 interface on the **RT3-INT** router).
- 172.16.1.253—The entry point for the ISP network.
- 172.16.0.254—The external interface (eth1) of the **RT1-LOCAL** router.
- 10.1.0.2—The end station (the **MS1** VM).

e) Press **Ctrl+C** to quit.

3. Before you configure the routers, look at the routing tables for end systems and intermediate systems, and examine the routing protocol traffic exchanged between the routers.

a) On the **LAMP** VM, run the command `route`
As you can see, the routing table couldn't be much simpler. There is one entry for the default route (to any network or 0.0.0.0) and no router (*) required for the local subnet (192.168.1.0).

b) Switch to the **PC1** VM and run the following command:

```
route -4 print
```

This routing table is superficially more complex but essentially performs the same function as the Linux end host—use the local interface for the 10.1.0.0 subnet, and broadcast and multicast traffic and the 10.1.0.254 default gateway for any other network.

c) Open a connection window for the **RT1-LOCAL** VM and log on using the username **vyos** and password **Pa$$w0rd**

d) Run the following command:

```
show ip route
```

```
vyos@RT1-LOCAL:~$ show ip route
Codes: K - kernel route, C - connected, S - static, R - RIP, O - OSPF,
       I - ISIS, B - BGP, > - selected route, * - FIB route

S>* 0.0.0.0/0 [1/0] via 172.16.0.253, eth1
C>* 10.1.0.0/24 is directly connected, eth0
C>* 127.0.0.0/8 is directly connected, lo
C>* 172.16.0.252/30 is directly connected, eth1
vyos@RT1-LOCAL:~$
```

Output from the show ip route command on an intermediate system.

Ignoring the loopback interface, the entries in the routing table are:

- 0.0.0.0/0—This is the default route, forwarding traffic to the upstream router over the eth1 interface. This route has been statically configured (S).
- 10.1.0.0/24—This is the interface connected to the **vLOCAL** switch and subnet.
- 172.16.0.252/30—This is the interface connected to the upstream router (on a real network this would be over a WAN link). This uses a 2 host /30 netmask, leaving plenty of the address space available for VLSM, should it be needed. This is typical of the way point-to-point WAN interfaces are configured.

e) Open a connection window for the **RT2-ISP** VM and log on using the username *vyos* and password *Pa$$w0rd*

 Note: *Remember, you might need to press **Ctrl+Alt+Left Arrow** to release the cursor from the **RT1** VMs.*

f) Run the following command:

```
show ip route
```

```
vyos@RT2-ISP:~$ show ip route
Codes: K - kernel route, C - connected, S - static, R - RIP, O - OSPF,
       I - ISIS, B - BGP, > - selected route, * - FIB route

S>* 10.1.0.0/24 [1/0] via 172.16.0.254, eth0
C>* 127.0.0.0/8 is directly connected, lo
C>* 172.16.0.252/30 is directly connected, eth0
C>* 172.16.1.252/30 is directly connected, eth1
B>* 192.168.1.0/24 [20/1] via 172.16.1.254, eth1, 00:35:56
B>* 192.168.2.0/24 [20/1] via 172.16.1.254, eth1, 00:35:56
vyos@RT2-ISP:~$
```

Output from the show ip route command showing routes learned from BGP added to the routing table.

This router has no default route. Ignoring the loopback interface, the entries in the routing table are:

- 10.1.0.0/24—The route to the LAN subnet has been configured statically.
- 172.16.x.252/30—The directly connected interfaces link the **vISP** switch (eth0) and the **vINT01** switch (eth1).
- 192.168.x.0/24—The router has learned these routes via the Border Gateway Protocol (BGP). The route to them is via the upstream router over the eth1v/**INT01** switch link.

g) Open a connection window for the **RT3-INT** VM and log on using the username *vyos* and password *Pa$$w0rd*

h) Run the following command:

```
show ip route
```

Hopefully, you can now interpret the entries you are looking at. This router services three directly connected switches/subnets and has discovered routes to the 10.1.0.0/24 network and 172.16.0.252/30 network via the Border Gateway Protocol (BGP).

4. Load a blank configuration file to erase the current settings for each router, and then re-create the static routes used to implement the internetwork.

a) For each **VyOS** VM, complete the following command sequence:

```
conf

load config.bare

commit

save

exit
```

 Note: *Don't be concerned about the syslog error notification.*

5. Configure the **RT1-LOCAL** router with the appropriate IP addresses for its interfaces and set the default route.

a) Switch to **RT1-LOCAL** and run the command `show conf`
As you can see, the interfaces no longer have IP addresses configured.

b)   Press **q** to quit the rest of the configuration output.

c)   Consulting the network diagram, make a note of what IP address and netmask you should be assigning to each interface:

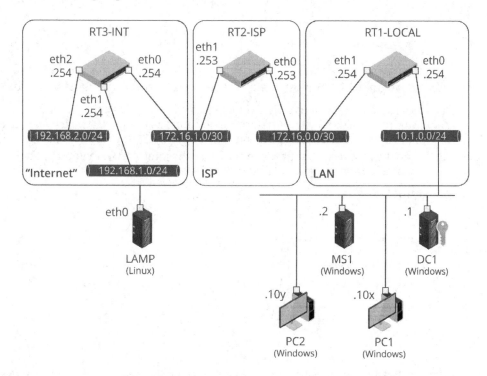

Layer 3 (IP) logical network topology. (Image © 123RF.com.)

d)   Run the following commands and ignore any line break in the commands:

```
conf

set interfaces ethernet eth0 description PRIVATE

set interfaces ethernet eth0 address 10.1.0.254/24

set interfaces ethernet eth1 description PUBLIC

set interfaces ethernet eth1 address 172.16.0.254/30

commit

save

exit

show interfaces
```

e)   Verify the configuration using the output from `show interfaces`

f)   Switch to **PC1** and run the following commands to test connectivity:

```
ping 10.1.0.254

ping 172.16.0.254
```

Check that you understand what is happening here:

- **PC1** has no specific route to 172.16.0.0/24 but uses the default gateway to try to contact it.
- No route needs to be configured between the two subnets on **RT1-LOCAL** because they are both directly connected.

RT1-LOCAL has a simple job: Process packets for the local network and forward everything else to the Internet. You can accomplish this by simply configuring a default route.

g)   Switch back to the **RT1-LOCAL** VM. Run the following commands to configure the static default route and ignore any line break in the commands:

```
conf

set protocols static route 0.0.0.0/0 next-hop 172.16.0.253

commit

save

exit
```

6. Configure the **RT2-ISP** interfaces, and set a static route to the LAN subnet.

    a) Switch to **RT2-ISP** and run the command `show interfaces`
This router also has two interfaces; eth0 connects to the **vISP** switch and makes the link to **RT1-LOCAL**, while eth1 connects to the **vINT00** switch.

    b) Run the following commands to configure the interfaces with appropriate IP addresses and ignore any line break in the **set** commands:

```
conf

set interfaces ethernet eth0 description 'vISP Switch'

set interfaces ethernet eth0 address 172.16.0.253/30

set interfaces ethernet eth1 description 'vINT00 Switch'

set interfaces ethernet eth1 address 172.16.1.253/30

commit

save

exit
```

As **RT1-LOCAL** does not run a dynamic routing protocol with **RT2-ISP**, you need to configure the route to the 10.1.0.0/24 network statically.

    c) Run the following commands on **RT2-ISP** and ignore any line breaks:

```
conf

set protocols static route 10.1.0.0/24 next-hop
172.16.0.254 distance 1

commit

save

exit

show interfaces

show ip route
```

    d) Verify that the routing table matches the configuration you looked at previously.

    e) Run the following command to test the route:

```
traceroute 10.1.0.254
```

    f) On the **PC1** VM, run the following command to test the route:

```
ping 172.16.1.253
```

7. To complete the configuration, configure Border Gateway Protocol (BGP) on the **RT2-ISP** and **RT3-INT** routers.

BGP depends on the concept of Autonomous Systems (ASes). Each routing domain is allocated its own AS Number (ASN), which allows routers to differentiate between internal and external peers. In this example, the network operated by the ISP is distinct from that operated by the wider Internet, so you should configure each router with different ASNs.

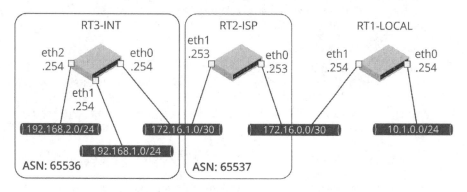

BGP ASNs in the activity topology. (Image © 123RF.com.)

a) Switch to the **RT2-ISP** VM and run the following commands, and ignore any line breaks:

```
conf

set protocols bgp 65537 neighbor 172.16.1.254 remote-as
65536

set protocols bgp 65537 parameters router-id 172.16.0.253

set protocols bgp 65537 network 10.1.0.0/24

commit

save

exit
```

These commands perform the following functions:
- Define the ASN for this routing domain as 65537.
- Identify a peer or neighbor domain with the ASN 65536 at the IP address 172.16.1.254.
- Uniquely identify this router by arbitrarily using the IP of one of its interfaces.
- Add the network 10.1.0.0/24 to the list of routes to propagate to BGP peers.

8. Configure the **RT3-INT** router.

a) Switch to the **RT3-INT** VM and run the following command:

```
show interfaces
```

b) Run the following commands to configure the interfaces with appropriate IP addresses and ignore any line breaks:

```
conf

set interfaces ethernet eth0 description 'vINT00 Switch'

set interfaces ethernet eth0 address 172.16.1.254/30

set interfaces ethernet eth1 description 'vINT01 Switch'

set interfaces ethernet eth1 address 192.168.1.254/24

set interfaces ethernet eth2 description 'vINT02 Switch'

set interfaces ethernet eth2 address 192.168.2.254/24

commit

save

exit

show interfaces
```

c) On the **PC1** VM, run the following command to test the current state of the routing infrastructure. Can you explain the error?

```
ping 172.16.1.254
```

The route to 172.16.0.254 is known by way of the default route but **RT3-INT** does not have a route back to the sending host. This is why the request times out, rather than being described as unreachable.

d) Switch to the **RT3-INT** VM and run the following command to test the route:

```
traceroute 10.1.0.254
```

You must configure the peer before it will accept any routing updates from its neighbor.

e) Run the following commands to configure BGP on this router, ignoring any line breaks:

```
conf

set protocols bgp 65536 neighbor 172.16.1.253 remote-as
65537

set protocols bgp 65536 parameters router-id 172.16.1.254

set protocols bgp 65536 network 192.168.1.0/24

set protocols bgp 65536 network 192.168.2.0/24

commit

save

exit
```

f) Run the following commands to verify the configuration:

```
show interfaces

show ip route
```

g) You should be able to complete `pings` or `traceroutes` between any of the interfaces. Name resolution will not work, as you have not restored that bit of the configuration.

Note: Refer back to the logical network topology in step 5c to verify in the diagram.

9. Discard changes made to the VMs in this activity.

a) Switch to the **Hyper-V Manager** window.

b) Select one of the running VMs. From the **Action** menu, select **Revert** then select the **Revert** button (or use the right-click menu in the **Hyper-V Manager** console). Select another VM and revert it, continuing to revert all the VMs to their saved checkpoints.

Summary

In this lesson, you covered the core protocols and technologies used to enable routing.

- Routers allow the interconnection of networks or the division of a single network into subnets.
- Routers perform path selection and forwarding between networks, storing information about networks in a routing table.
- Path selection can be configured statically, but is more likely to be determined by a dynamic routing protocol, working with defined routing metrics.
- Dynamic routing protocols can be classed as distance-vector (RIP, EIGRP), link-state (OSPF), or hybrid (BGP).
- A single autonomous system uses an Interior Gateway Protocol. Extra-AS routing uses an Exterior Gateway Protocol (BGP).
- Routers can be implemented by software running on Windows/Linux servers or as dedicated appliances.
- The `route` command allows for static configuration of Windows/Linux routing while `tracert`/`traceroute`, `pathping`, and `mtr` are used to compile statistics about loss and latency as a packet traverses a network.

At your workplace, what situations might you use static routing for?

What dynamic routing protocol do you think you would recommend for implementation? Why?

Practice Questions: *Additional practice questions are available on the course website.*

Lesson 6

Configuring and Monitoring Ports and Protocols

LESSON INTRODUCTION

Layers 1 through 3 of the OSI model are concerned with addressing and packet forwarding and delivery. This basic connectivity is established for the purpose of transporting application data. In this lesson, you will start to look at layer 4 and higher to describe the transport and name resolution services that network applications depend upon.

LESSON OBJECTIVES

In this lesson, you will:

- Explain the uses of ports and protocols.

- Use port scanners and protocol analyzers.

- Explain the use of name resolution services.

- Configure DNS and IPAM services.

Topic A

Explain the Uses of Ports and Protocols

 EXAM OBJECTIVES COVERED
1.1 Explain the purposes and uses of ports and protocols.

You have seen how IP provides addressing and delivery at layer 3 of the OSI model. At layer 4, the TCP/IP protocol suite also defines how applications on separate hosts establish a connection and track communications. Understanding how applications use ports to establish connections is critical to being able to configure and support network services and devices.

TRANSMISSION CONTROL PROTOCOL (TCP)

Transport protocols work at the OSI model layer above the Network layer. IP provides addressing and routing functionality for internetworks. Protocols at the Transport layer (layer 4) are concerned with effective delivery of multiplexed application data.

In the TCP/IP suite, the **Transmission Control Protocol (TCP)** provides a **connection-oriented**, **guaranteed** method of communication using **acknowledgements** to ensure delivery. TCP takes data from the Application layer as a stream of bytes and divides it up into **segments**, each of which is given a header. The TCP segments become the payload of the underlying IP datagrams.

TCP requires that a **connection** be established before hosts can exchange data. A connection uses the following features to ensure reliability:

- Orderly connection establishment and teardown—The client and server perform a **handshake** to establish and end connections. Under normal circumstances, a single connection is created between hosts. However, multiple connections can be established by a single application process to improve throughput.
- **Segmentation**—TCP breaks PDUs from the Application layer into a segment format and uses sequence numbers to allow the receiver to rebuild the message correctly. This allows the connection to deal with out-of-order packets.
- Acknowledgements (ACKs)—Packets might be out-of-order because they are delayed, but they could also be lost completely or arrive in a damaged state. In the first case, the lack of acknowledgement results in the retransmission of 0 data and, in the second case, a **Negative Acknowledgement (NAK or NACK)** forces retransmission.
- **Flow control**—Enables one side to tell the other when the sending rate must be slowed.

TCP THREE-WAY HANDSHAKE AND FLOW CONTROL

A TCP connection is typically established to transfer a single file, so a client session for something like a web page (HTTP) might involve multiple TCP connections being opened with the server. A connection is established using a **three-way handshake**:

No.	Time	Source	Destination	Protocol	Length	Info
1	0.0...	10.1.0.101	10.1.0.2	TCP	66	1624 → 80 [SYN] Seq=0 Win=65535 Len=0 MSS=1460 WS=25(
2	0.0...	10.1.0.2	10.1.0.101	TCP	66	80 → 1624 [SYN, ACK] Seq=0 Ack=1 Win=8192 Len=0 MSS=;
3	0.0...	10.1.0.101	10.1.0.2	TCP	54	1624 → 80 [ACK] Seq=1 Ack=1 Win=262144 Len=0
4	0.0...	10.1.0.101	10.1.0.2	HTTP	433	GET / HTTP/1.1
5	0.0...	10.1.0.2	10.1.0.101	TCP	54	80 → 1624 [ACK] Seq=1 Ack=380 Win=2102272 Len=0
6	0.2...	10.1.0.2	10.1.0.101	TCP	1514	80 → 1624 [ACK] Seq=1 Ack=380 Win=2102272 Len=1460 [

```
> Internet Protocol Version 4, Src: 10.1.0.101, Dst: 10.1.0.2
˅ Transmission Control Protocol, Src Port: 1624, Dst Port: 80, Seq: 1, Ack: 1, Len: 0
    Source Port: 1624
    Destination Port: 80
    [Stream index: 0]
    [TCP Segment Len: 0]
    Sequence number: 1    (relative sequence number)
    [Next sequence number: 1    (relative sequence number)]
    Acknowledgment number: 1    (relative ack number)
    0101 .... = Header Length: 20 bytes (5)
  > Flags: 0x010 (ACK)
    Window size value: 1024
    [Calculated window size: 262144]
    [Window size scaling factor: 256]
```

```
0000  00 15 5d 01 ca 76 00 15  5d 01 ca 77 08 00 45 00   ··]··v·· ]··w··E·
0010  00 28 16 49 40 00 80 06  00 00 0a 01 00 65 0a 01   ·(·I@··· ·····e··
0020  00 02 06 58 00 50 61 ff  66 ce 99 26 04 92 50 10   ···X·Pa· f··&··P·
0030  04 00 14 83 00 00                                  ······
```

Observing the 3-way handshake with the Wireshark protocol analyzer. (Screenshot courtesy of Wireshark.)

1. The client sends a SYN segment to the server with a randomly generated sequence number. The client enters the SYN-SENT state.
2. The server, currently in the LISTEN state (assuming it is online), responds with a SYN/ACK segment, containing its own randomly generated sequence number. The server enters the SYN-RECEIVED state.
3. The client responds with an ACK segment. The client assumes the connection is ESTABLISHED.
4. The server opens a connection with the client and enters the ESTABLISHED state.

 Note: *Servers can (usually) support thousands or even millions of TCP connections simultaneously.*

The sending machine expects regular acknowledgements for segments it sends and, if a period elapses without an acknowledgement, it assumes the information did not arrive and automatically resends it. This overhead makes the system relatively slow. Connection-oriented transmission is suitable when reliability and data **integrity** are important.

Another important function of TCP is handling **flow control** to make sure the sender does not inundate the receiver with packets. The main mechanism used for this is called the **sliding window**. The window field in the header represents the number of bytes starting from the last acknowledged byte that a host is prepared to receive before it will send an acknowledgement.

 Note: *To learn more, watch the related **Video** on the course website.*

TCP HEADER FIELDS

The main fields in the header of a TCP segment are:

Field	Explanation
Source port	TCP port of sending host.
Destination port	TCP port of destination host.
Sequence number	The ID number of the current segment (the sequence number of the last byte in the segment).
Ack number	The sequence number of the next segment expected from the other host (that is, the sequence number of the last segment received +1).
Data length	Length of the TCP segment.
Flags	Type of content in the segment (ACK, SYN, FIN, and so on).
Window	The amount of data the host is willing to receive before sending another acknowledgement (used for flow control).
Checksum	Ensures validity of the segment. The checksum is calculated on the value of not only the TCP header and payload but also part of the IP header, notably the source and destination addresses. Consequently, the mechanism for calculating the checksum is different for IPv6 (128-bit addresses) than for IPv4 (32-bit addresses).
Urgent Pointer	If urgent data is being sent, this specifies the end of that data in the segment.
Options	Allows further connection parameters to be configured. The most important of these is the Maximum Segment Size. This allows the host to specify how large the segments it receives should be, minimizing fragmentation as they are transported over data link frames.

TEARDOWN

There are also functions for resetting a connection and (in some implementations) keeping a connection alive if no actual data is being transmitted (hosts are configured to timeout unused connections). To close a connection, also referred to as **teardown**, the following basic steps are performed:

1. The client sends a FIN segment to the server and enters the FIN-WAIT1 state.
2. The server responds with an ACK segment and enters the CLOSE-WAIT state.
3. The client receives the ACK segment and enters the FIN-WAIT2 state. The server sends its own FIN segment to the client and goes to the LAST-ACK state.
4. The client responds with an ACK and enters the TIME-WAIT state. After a defined period, the client closes its connection.
5. The server closes the connection when it receives the ACK from the client.

Some implementations may use one less step by combining the FIN and ACK responses into a single segment operation.

```
Microsoft Windows [Version 10.0.14393]
(c) 2016 Microsoft Corporation. All rights reserved.

C:\Users\administrator>netstat -ano

Active Connections

  Proto  Local Address          Foreign Address        State           PID
  TCP    0.0.0.0:135            0.0.0.0:0              LISTENING       652
  TCP    0.0.0.0:445            0.0.0.0:0              LISTENING       4
  TCP    0.0.0.0:5985           0.0.0.0:0              LISTENING       4
  TCP    0.0.0.0:47001          0.0.0.0:0              LISTENING       4
  TCP    0.0.0.0:49664          0.0.0.0:0              LISTENING       428
  TCP    0.0.0.0:49665          0.0.0.0:0              LISTENING       912
  TCP    0.0.0.0:49666          0.0.0.0:0              LISTENING       864
  TCP    0.0.0.0:49669          0.0.0.0:0              LISTENING       1996
  TCP    0.0.0.0:49670          0.0.0.0:0              LISTENING       524
  TCP    0.0.0.0:49703          0.0.0.0:0              LISTENING       516
  TCP    0.0.0.0:49706          0.0.0.0:0              LISTENING       524
  TCP    10.1.0.100:139         0.0.0.0:0              LISTENING       4
  TCP    10.1.0.100:49764       10.1.0.192:3000       ESTABLISHED     4280
  TCP    [::]:135               [::]:0                LISTENING       652
  TCP    [::]:445               [::]:0                LISTENING       4
  TCP    [::]:5985              [::]:0                LISTENING       4
  TCP    [::]:47001             [::]:0                LISTENING       4
```

Observing TCP connections with the netstat tool. (Screenshot used with permission from Microsoft.)

A host can also end a session abruptly using a reset (RST) segment. This would not be typical behavior and might need to be investigated. A server or security appliance might refuse connections using RST, a client or sever application might be faulty, or there could be some sort of suspicious scanning activity ongoing.

USER DATAGRAM PROTOCOL (UDP)

The **User Datagram Protocol (UDP)** also works at the Transport layer, but unlike TCP, it is a **connectionless, non-guaranteed** method of communication with no sequencing or flow control. There is no guarantee regarding the delivery of messages or the sequence in which packets are received. When you are using UDP, the Application layer must control delivery reliability, if this is required.

UDP is suitable for applications that send small amounts of data in each packet and do not require acknowledgement of receipt. It is used by Application layer protocols that need to send multicast or broadcast traffic (TCP supports unicast only). It may also be used for applications that transfer time-sensitive data but do not require complete reliability, such as voice or video. The reduced overhead means that delivery is faster.

This table shows the structure of a UDP datagram.

Field	Explanation
Source port	UDP port of sending host.
Destination port	UDP port of destination host.
Message length	The size of this UDP message.
Checksum	Verify the datagram.

The header size is 8 bytes, compared to 20 bytes (or more) for TCP.

TCP VS. UDP

The following table summarizes the differences between TCP and UDP.

TCP	UDP
Connection-oriented, reliable delivery with error correction.	Connectionless, non-guaranteed delivery. Reliability and error correction must be processed at the Application layer.
20-byte header and connection control mechanisms add substantial overhead to data transmissions (slower).	8-byte header and no connection control means less bandwidth is consumed by overheads (faster).
Hosts must use resources to track connections in a state table.	No connection control.
Can be used only for unicast transmission.	Can be used for unicast, broadcast, and multicast transmission.
Used by applications where reliability is paramount (for example, HTTP, FTP, SMTP, and IMAP).	Used by applications where speed is paramount (such as Voice over IP and media streaming) and for multicast/broadcast communication (for example, DHCP and router traffic).

TCP AND UDP PORTS

A TCP/IP host may be running multiple services or communicating with multiple servers, clients, or peers in parallel. This means that incoming packets must be directed to the appropriate service or application. Any application or process that uses TCP or UDP for its transport is assigned a unique identification number called a **port**. Ports are logically assigned to provide a communications channel between a server application on one host and a client application on another host, allowing them to send and receive data.

Port numbers for some server application protocols are pre-assigned by the **Internet Assigned Numbers Authority (IANA)**. IANA assigns protocols to port numbers 0 through 1023. These port assignments are documented at *iana.org/assignments/service-names-port-numbers/service-names-port-numbers.xhtml*. Vendors can **register** ports 1024 through 49,151. The following table contains some of the well-known and registered port numbers.

Port Number	Transport Protocol	Service or Application	Description
20	TCP	ftp-data	File Transfer Protocol—Data
21	TCP	ftp	File Transfer Protocol—Control
22	TCP	ssh/sftp	Secure Shell/FTP over SSH
23	TCP	telnet	Telnet
25	TCP	smtp	Simple Mail Transfer Protocol
53	TCP/UDP	domain	Domain Name System
67	UDP	bootps	BOOTP/DHCP Server
68	UDP	bootpc	BOOTP/DHCP Client
69	UDP	tftp	Trivial File Transfer Protocol
80	TCP	http	HTTP
110	TCP	pop	Post Office Protocol
123	UDP	ntp	Network Time Protocol
143	TCP	imap	Internet Mail Access Protocol
161	UDP	snmp	Simple Network Management Protocol

Port Number	Transport Protocol	Service or Application	Description
162	UDP	snmp-trap	Simple Network Management Protocol Trap
443	TCP	https	HTTP-Secure
445	TCP	smb	Server Message Block
546	UDP	dhcpv6-client	DHCPv6 Client
547	UDP	dhcpv6-server	DHCPv6 Server
587	TCP	smtps	SMTP-Secure
636	TCP	ldaps	LDAP Secure
993	TCP	imaps	IMAP-Secure
995	TCP	pop3s	POP3-Secure
1720	TCP	h323hostcall	H.323 Call Signaling
3389	TCP	rdp	Remote Desktop Protocol
5004	UDP	rtp	Real-Time Protocol
5005	UDP	rtcp	Real-Time Control Protocol
5060	TCP/UDP	sip	Session Initiation Protocol
5061	TCP/UDP	sips	Session Initiation Protocol Secure

The remaining ports (up to 65,535) are designated for **private** or **dynamic** use. A client application or process is dynamically assigned a port number greater than 1024 by the operating system when there is a request for service. Client ports are also referred to as **ephemeral** ports.

The port number is used in conjunction with an IP address to form a **socket**. A socket provides an endpoint to a connection, and two sockets form a complete path. A socket works as a bi-directional pipe for incoming and outgoing data. Examples of socket numbers are shown in the following table.

IP Address	Port Number	Socket Number
10.155.22.99	1028	10.155.22.99:1028
172.16.16.10	21	172.16.16.10:21

Activity 6-1

Discussing the Uses of Ports and Protocols

SCENARIO

Answer the following questions to test your understanding of the content covered in this topic.

1. **Why would a developer choose to use unreliable delivery over reliable, connection-oriented delivery?**

2. **What is the purpose of the window field in a TCP segment?**

3. **If the client is in the TIME-WAIT state, is the connection with the server still open?**

4. **What are the sizes of TCP and UDP headers?**

5. **A function of TCP is to handle flow control. What is the purpose of the flow control function?**

6. **True or False? User Datagram Protocol (UDP), like TCP, uses flow control in the sending of data packets.**

7. **Which port is used by the Network Time Protocol (NTP)?**

Topic B

Use Port Scanners and Protocol Analyzers

 EXAM OBJECTIVES COVERED
3.3 Explain common scanning, monitoring and patching processes and summarize their expected outputs.
5.2 Given a scenario, use the appropriate tool.

One of the critical tasks for network administrators is to identify and analyze the traffic passing over network links. This information is used to troubleshoot network services, and to verify the security of the network.

PORT SCANNERS

A **port scanner** is software designed to report on the status and activity of TCP and UDP ports. Some port scanners work on the local machine; others are designed to probe remote hosts. Some scanners are designed for legitimate auditing by system engineers, system analysts, network engineers, and network security consultants, while others are focused on penetration testing or intrusion, where there is a need for the scan to be stealthy (not detected by the target). A port scanner may be operated by a malicious user attempting to discover hosts and services to exploit.

netstat

The `netstat` **command** allows you to check the state of ports on the local host. You can use `netstat` to check for service misconfigurations—perhaps a host is running a web or FTP server that a user installed without authorization? You may also be able to identify suspect remote connections to services on the local host or from the host to remote IP addresses. If you are attempting to identify malware, the most useful `netstat` output is to show which process is listening on which ports. You may also be able to identify connections to suspicious IP address ranges.

On Windows®, used without switches, the command outputs active TCP connections, showing the local and foreign addresses and ports. The following additional switches can be used:

- `-a` displays all connections (active TCP and UDP connections plus ports in the listening state).
- `-o` shows the Process ID (PID) number that has opened the port.
- `-b` shows the process name that has opened the port.
- `-n` displays ports and addresses in numerical format. Skipping name resolution speeds up each query.
- `-s` shows per protocol statistics (such as packets received, errors, discards, unknown requests, port requests, failed connections, and so on).
- `-p` *proto* displays connections by protocol (TCP or UDP or TCPv6/UDPv6). When used with `-s`, this switch can also filter the statistics shown by IP, IPv6, ICMP, and ICMPv6.

- -r shows the routing table.
- -e displays Ethernet statistics.

The utility can also be set to run in the background by entering `netstat  nn`, where *nn* is the refresh interval in seconds (press **Ctrl+C** to stop).

```
C:\Users\Administrator>netstat | findstr "10.1.0"
  TCP    10.1.0.1:80            ROGUE:1415             TIME_WAIT
  TCP    10.1.0.1:80            GATEWAY:49161          ESTABLISHED
  TCP    10.1.0.1:135           ROGUE:1417             TIME_WAIT
  TCP    10.1.0.1:135           ROGUE:ms-sql-s         TIME_WAIT
  TCP    10.1.0.1:139           ROGUE:1418             TIME_WAIT
  TCP    10.1.0.1:445           10.1.0.134:49226       ESTABLISHED
  TCP    10.1.0.1:49154         ROGUE:1467             ESTABLISHED
  TCP    10.1.0.1:49155         ROGUE:1468             ESTABLISHED
  TCP    10.1.0.1:49158         ROGUE:1469             ESTABLISHED
  TCP    10.1.0.1:49159         ROGUE:1470             ESTABLISHED
  TCP    10.1.0.1:49163         ROGUE:1471             ESTABLISHED

C:\Users\Administrator>_
```

netstat command running on Windows showing activity during an Nmap scan. The findstr function is being used to filter the output (to show only connections from IPv4 hosts on the same subnet). (Screenshot used with permission from Microsoft.)

Linux® supports a similar utility with some different switches. Used without switches, it shows active connections of any type. If you want to show different connection types, you can use the switches for Internet connections for TCP (-t) and UDP (-u), raw connections (-w), and UNIX® sockets/local server ports (-x). For example, the following command shows Internet connections (TCP and UDP) only: `netstat -tu`

```
administrator@lamp:~$ netstat -tua | more
Active Internet connections (servers and established)
Proto Recv-Q Send-Q Local Address          Foreign Address         State
tcp        0      0 localhost:mysql        *:*                     LISTEN
tcp        0      0 *:pop3                 *:*                     LISTEN
tcp        0      0 *:imap2                *:*                     LISTEN
tcp        0      0 *:http                 *:*                     LISTEN
tcp        0      0 lamp.web.com:domain    *:*                     LISTEN
tcp        0      0 localhost:domain       *:*                     LISTEN
tcp        0      0 *:ftp                  *:*                     LISTEN
tcp        0      0 *:ssh                  *:*                     LISTEN
tcp        0      0 *:telnet               *:*                     LISTEN
tcp        0      0 localhost:953          *:*                     LISTEN
tcp        0      0 *:imaps                *:*                     LISTEN
tcp        0      0 *:pop3s                *:*                     LISTEN
tcp        0      0 lamp.web.com:http      10.1.0.128:49405        ESTABLISHED
tcp        0      0 lamp.web.com:http      10.1.0.128:49407        ESTABLISHED
tcp        0      0 lamp.web.com:http      10.1.0.128:49406        ESTABLISHED
tcp6       0      0 [::]:pop3              [::]:*                  LISTEN
tcp6       0      0 [::]:imap2             [::]:*                  LISTEN
tcp6       0      0 [::]:ssh               [::]:*                  LISTEN
tcp6       0      0 [::]:imaps             [::]:*                  LISTEN
tcp6       0      0 [::]:pop3s             [::]:*                  LISTEN
udp        0      0 lamp.web.com:domain    *:*
udp        0      0 localhost:domain       *:*
udp        0      0 lamp.web.com:15454     202.12.27.33:domain     ESTABLISHED
udp        0      0 lamp.web.com:53222     202.12.27.33:domain     ESTABLISHED
udp        0      0 lamp.web.com:31693     192.203.230.10:domain   ESTABLISHED
administrator@lamp:~$ _
```

Linux netstat output showing active and listening TCP and UDP connections.

Some of the other switches are as follows:

- -a includes ports in the listening state in the output. -l shows only ports in the listening state (omits established connections).
- -p shows the Process ID (PID) number that has opened the port (similar to -o on Windows).
- -r shows the routing table.
- -s displays protocol statistics (as in Windows).

- -i displays interface statistics (similar to -e on Windows).
- -e displays extra information.
- -c sets output to update continuously.

```
administrator@lamp:~$ netstat -i
Kernel Interface table
Iface   MTU Met   RX-OK RX-ERR RX-DRP RX-OVR   TX-OK TX-ERR TX-DRP TX-OVR Flg
eth0    1500 0     560      0      0 0         1301      0      0      0 BMRU
lo     16436 0     315      0      0 0          315      0      0      0 LRU
administrator@lamp:~$
```

Linux netstat interface statistics showing receive and transmit packets numbers plus errors and dropped packets.

Nmap HOST DISCOVERY

The **Nmap Security Scanner** (*nmap.org*) is widely used for scanning remote hosts and networks, both as an auditing and a penetration testing tool. The tool is open source software with packages for most versions of Windows, Linux, and macOS®. It can be operated with a command line or via a GUI (Zenmap). As well as port scanning, Nmap is used to discover hosts and map out the network topology. Nmap can use diverse methods of host discovery, some of which can operate stealthily and serve to defeat security mechanisms such as firewalls and intrusion detection.

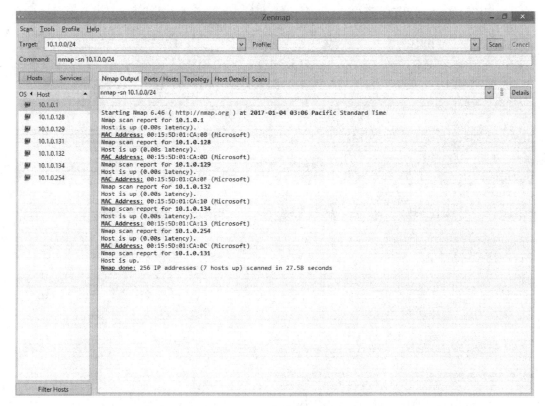

Nmap discovery scan. (Screenshot used with permission from Nmap.)

The basic syntax of an Nmap command is to give the IP subnet (or IP address) to scan. When used without switches like this, the default behavior of Nmap is to ping and send a TCP ACK packet to ports 80 and 443 to determine whether a host is present. On a local network segment, Nmap will also perform ARP and Neighbor Discovery (ND) sweeps. If a host is detected, Nmap performs a port scan against that host to determine which services it is running. This OS fingerprinting can be time consuming on a large IP scope and is also non-stealthy. If you want to perform only host discovery, you can use Nmap with the `-sn` switch (or `-sP` in earlier versions) to suppress the port scan.

Nmap PORT SCANNING

When Nmap completes a host discovery scan, it will report on the state of each port scanned for each IP address in the scope. At this point, you can run port discovery scans against one or more of the active IP addresses. The following represent some of the main types of scanning that Nmap can perform:

- TCP SYN (`-sS`)—This is a fast technique (also referred to as half-open scanning) as the scanning host requests a connection without acknowledging it. The target's response to the scan's SYN packet identifies the port state.

- TCP connect (`-sT`)—A half-open scan requires Nmap to have privileged access to the network driver so that it can craft packets. If privileged access is not available, Nmap must use the OS to attempt a full TCP connection. This type of scan is less stealthy.

- UDP scans (`-sU`)—Scan UDP ports. As these do not use ACKs, Nmap needs to wait for a response or timeout to determine the port state, so UDP scanning can take a long time. A UDP scan can be combined with a TCP scan.

- Port range (`-p`)—By default, Nmap scans 1,000 commonly used ports. Use the `-p` argument to specify a port range. You can also use `--top-ports` *n*, where *n* is the number of commonly used ports to scan. The frequency statistics for determining how commonly a port is used are stored in the nmap-services configuration file.

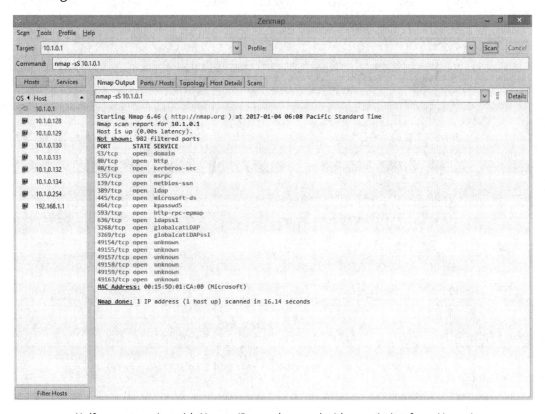

Half-open scanning with Nmap. (Screenshot used with permission from Nmap.)

Nmap OS AND SERVICE FINGERPRINTING

When services are discovered, you can use Nmap with the ‑sV or ‑A switch to probe a host more intensively to discover the software or software version operating each port. The process of identifying an OS or software application from its responses to probes is called **fingerprinting**.

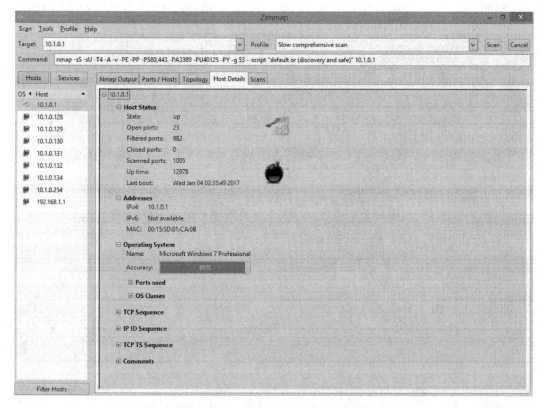

The responses to network probes can be used to identify the type and version of the host operating system. (Screenshot used with permission from Nmap.)

Nmap comes with a database of application and version fingerprint signatures, classified using a standard syntax called **common platform enumeration (CPE)**. Unmatched responses can be submitted to a web URL for analysis by the community.

PROTOCOL ANALYZERS

A **protocol analyzer** (or **packet analyzer**) works in conjunction with a packet sniffer. You can either analyze a live capture or open a saved capture (.pcap) file. Protocol analyzers can decode a captured frame to reveal its contents in a readable format. You can choose to view a summary of the frame or choose a more detailed view that provides information on the OSI layer, protocol, function, and data.

Analyzing protocol data at the packet level will help to identify protocol or service misconfigurations. You can also perform **traffic analysis** to monitor statistics related to communications flows, such as bandwidth consumed by each protocol or each host, identifying the most active network hosts, monitoring link utilization and reliability, and so on.

The capabilities of different products vary widely, but in general terms, protocol analyzers can perform the following functions:

- Filter traffic and capture packets meeting certain criteria (capturing traffic to and from a particular device, for instance).
- Isolate hosts producing erroneous packets and rectify the problem.

- Identify malicious or unauthorized use of the network.
- Establish a network activity baseline. The baseline provides a comparison against activity when a problem is suspected or as a basis for network expansion plans.

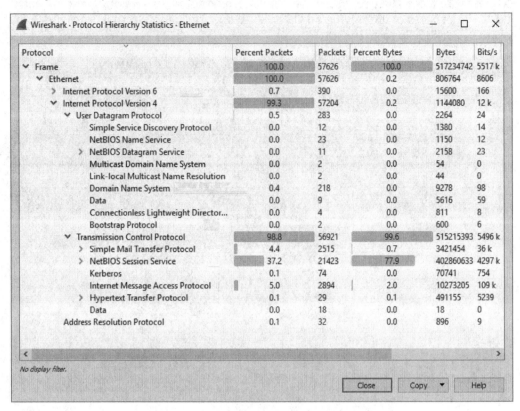

Using the Protocol Hierarchy tool in Wireshark to view the most active protocols on a network link. This sort of report can be used to baseline network activity. (Screenshot courtesy of Wireshark.)

- Identify the most active hosts on the network, which aids in balancing traffic on networks.
- Monitor bandwidth utilization by hosts, applications, and protocols.
- Trigger alarms when certain network conditions fall outside normal levels.
- Generate frames and transmit them onto the network to test network devices and cabling.

WIRESHARK

Wireshark (*wireshark.org*) is an open source graphical packet capture and analysis utility, with installer packages for most operating systems. Having chosen the interfaces to listen on, the output is displayed in a three-pane view, with the top pane showing each frame, the middle pane showing the fields from the currently selected frame, and the bottom pane showing the raw data from the frame in hex and ASCII.

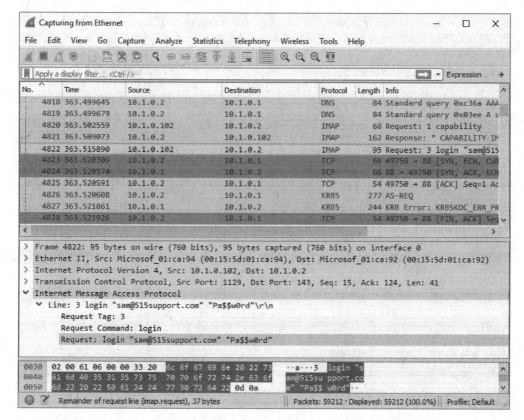

Wireshark protocol analyzer. (Screenshot courtesy of Wireshark.)

Wireshark is capable of parsing (interpreting) the headers of hundreds of network protocols. You can apply a capture filter using the same expression syntax as `tcpdump`. You can also apply display filters by using a different and more powerful set of expressions (a query can be built via the GUI tools, too). Another useful option is to use the **Follow TCP Stream** context command to reconstruct the packet contents for a TCP session. Use the **Statistics** menu to access traffic analysis tools.

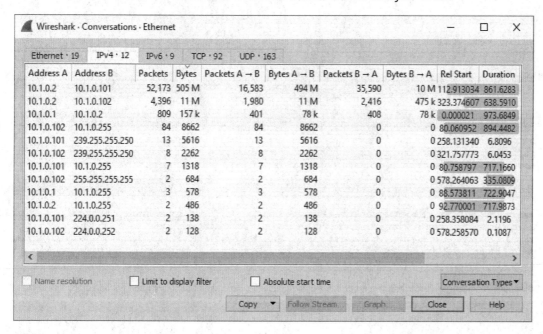

Using the Conversations option from Wireshark's Statistics tools. (Screenshot courtesy of Wireshark.)

Note: *To learn more, watch the related* **Video** *on the course website.*

Activity 6-2

Discussing Port Scanners and Protocol Analyzers

SCENARIO

Answer the following questions to test your understanding of the content covered in this topic.

1. **If you wanted to investigate connections on your machine, which built-in utility could you use?**

2. **What is CPE?**

3. **You need to audit services made publicly available on a web server. What command-line tool could you use?**

4. **You need to analyze the information saved in a .pcap file. What type of command-line tool or other utility is best suited to this task?**

Activity 6-3
Using Port Scanning Tools

BEFORE YOU BEGIN

Start the VMs used in this activity in the following order, adjusting the memory allocation first if necessary, and waiting at the ellipsis for the previous VMs to finish booting before starting the next group. You do not need to connect to a VM until prompted to do so in the activity steps.

- **RT1-LOCAL** (256 MB)
- **DC1** (1024—2048 MB)
- ...
- **MS1** (1024—2048 MB)
- ...
- **PC1** (1024—2048 MB)
- **PC2** (512—1024 MB)

SCENARIO

In this activity, you will examine the establishment of a TCP session and use some tools to analyze TCP connections. This activity is designed to test your understanding of and ability to apply content examples in the following CompTIA Network+ objectives:

- 1.1 Explain the purposes and uses of ports and protocols.
- 5.2 Given a scenario, use the appropriate tool.

---

1. Use Wireshark on **PC1** to record and analyze a TCP session as you browse the **updates.corp.515support.com** website.

   a) Sign in on the **PC1** VM as ***515support\Administrator*** with the password ***Pa$$w0rd***

   b) Start **Wireshark**. In the **Welcome** pane, select the **Ethernet** adapter. Enter `port http` in the **Enter a capture filter** box and start the capture.

   c) Right-click the Windows **Start** button and select **Run**, then type the following command in the **Run** dialog box and select **OK**:

   ```
   http://updates.corp.515support.com
   ```

d) Switch back to **Wireshark**. Leave the capture running, but scroll to the top and observe the first three packets—this is the TCP handshake.

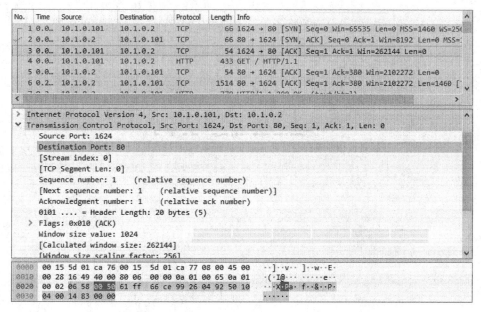

Observing the TCP handshake. (Screenshot courtesy of Wireshark.)

e) Expand the packet contents, and observe the following:
- The SYN→SYN/ACK→ACK sequence of packets.
- The client assigns the connection an ephemeral source port.
- The destination port on the server is 80 (the well-known port for HTTP).
- The server responds to the client's ephemeral port.
- The sequence and acknowledgement numbers.
- The Seq/Ack Analysis performed by Wireshark.

f) Now observe the HTTP packets—Observe that they are interspersed with ACK packets from the client to the server and the server to the client.

g) At the end of the packet capture, observe the exchange of FIN/ACK packets to close the TCP connection (you might have to wait for a minute or two for these to appear).

h) Stop the packet capture.

i) Right-click any **HTTP** packet and select **Follow**→**TCP Stream**.

This option reconstructs all the payload data exchanged in the HTTP session. Most of the information is recoverable in plain text. The unreadable text later in the capture is a binary image file.

j) Select **Close** to close the Follow TCP Stream window.

k) Select **Clear** to remove the filter.

2. Another use for Wireshark is to analyze traffic statistics. While you have not captured much data, you can still view the sort of tools available for analysis. Use the **Statistics** menu to analyze the traffic you just captured.

a) From the **Statistics** menu, select **Protocol Hierarchy**.

This tool shows you which protocols are most active on the network link. In this example, the view is very simple, with just TCP/HTTP traffic (unsurprisingly, given the capture filter you applied). Most of the bandwidth was used to transfer the JPEG image.

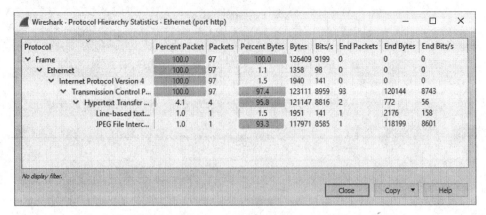

Observing per-protocol statistics. (Screenshot courtesy of Wireshark.)

b) Select **Close** and then select **Statistics→Endpoints**.

This report shows you the top talkers and top listeners on the link.

c) Select **Close** and then select **Statistics→Conversations**.

This view is like that of endpoints but shows you the most active sessions. You can view, and sort by, the packets, bytes, and duration for each session.

d) Explore any other options in the **Statistics** menu as time allows. Note the options at the bottom for listing protocols, ports, and addresses.

3. Use the `netstat` tool to monitor open connections from the **MS1** VM.

a) Sign in on the **MS1** VM as ***515support\Administrator*** with the password ***Pa$$w0rd***

b) Open a command prompt as administrator.

c) Type `netstat` and press **Enter**.

Without switches appended to the command, the Windows version of `netstat` shows active TCP connections and the foreign hosts connected to them, using name resolution if possible. The state of each connection is also listed (Established, Time Wait, and so on).

d) If the **PC1** VM is not listed in the output, switch to it and open the **http://updates.corp.515support.com** site in the browser again. Refresh the page to ensure you are not viewing cached content.

Note: *Repeat this step whenever* `netstat` *doesn't show any active connections.*

e)   Back on **MS1**, run `netstat -n`

```
C:\Windows\system32>netstat

Active Connections

   Proto  Local Address          Foreign Address        State
   TCP    10.1.0.2:49734         DC1:epmap              TIME_WAIT
   TCP    10.1.0.2:49735         DC1:49666             ESTABLISHED
   TCP    10.1.0.2:49737         DC1:49687             TIME_WAIT

C:\Windows\system32>netstat -n

Active Connections

   Proto  Local Address          Foreign Address        State
   TCP    10.1.0.2:80            10.1.0.101:1638        ESTABLISHED
   TCP    10.1.0.2:49734         10.1.0.1:135           TIME_WAIT
   TCP    10.1.0.2:49735         10.1.0.1:49666         ESTABLISHED
   TCP    10.1.0.2:49737         10.1.0.1:49687         TIME_WAIT

C:\Windows\system32>_
```

netstat output. (Screenshot used with permission from Microsoft.)

This time, the command executes much more quickly. The `-n` switch suppresses name resolution, so foreign hosts are shown by IP address.

f)   Run `netstat -ano`

This switch combination shows all active ports. Those with no connections are listed as **Listening**. The `-o` switch displays the Process ID (**PID**) of the service or application that opened the port.

g)   Now run the command with the following switches: `netstat -anbo`

The `-b` switch tries to resolve each process' image name. This will make the command slower to execute. Some names cannot be resolved; processes running under PID 4 have system-level privileges.

h)   You can also use `netstat` to gather interface and per-protocol statistics. Run the following command to view both sets of statistics: `netstat -es`

i)   If you want to filter statistics by a protocol, use the `-p` switch. For example, the following command shows IPv4 statistics only: `netstat -sp ip`

 Note: You can also use `netstat -r` to view the routing table.

j)   Run the following command to start netstat in persistent mode: `netstat -no 10`

k)   Use the **PC1** VM to re-establish the browser session or connect to a file share, such as **\\MS1\admin$**. Optionally, you could open connections from **PC2** too.

l)   On **MS1**, observe the `netstat` output. Note the different ports used for the clients. If you opened a file share, you will see connections to server port 445.

m)   After a minute or two, the server should start to timeout connections. You might observe port status on the server change to **Time Wait** but more likely the connection will just disappear from the output.

n)   Leave `netstat` running while you complete the next step.

4.   `netstat` is used to monitor connections on the local host. Network auditing and techniques such as penetration testing and vulnerability scanning require tools to discover and probe hosts remotely. Nmap (*nmap.org*) is one of the principal tools used for network host discovery and scanning.

a)   Switch to the **PC1** VM.

b) Select the **Zenmap-GUI** desktop shortcut.

Nmap has many uses and functions, but one of its main uses is to scan a target system to determine what services and software it is running.

The first step is to select a target. This can be a single host, expressed as an IP address or host name/FQDN, or it can be a range of hosts, expressed as a range of IP addresses (such as 10.1.0.0/24).

c) In the **Target** box, type *10.1.0.2*

This activity uses the GUI tool instead of the command-line version, but you can see the command that will be run in the **Command** box. Notice that the text you entered in the **Target** box has been added to the **Command** box. The switches implement the **Intense scan** option selected in the **Profile** box.

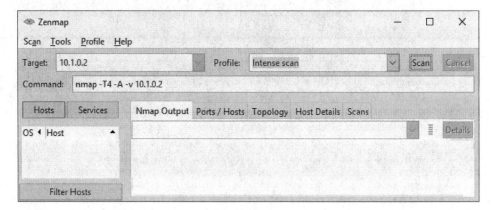

Configuring a scan target in Zenmap. (Screenshot used with permission from Nmap.)

The default **Intense scan** will attempt to determine the OS, open ports from commonly used ranges, and the software operating any services it finds. Other types of scans can be used to probe more deeply (but they take longer).

d) Select some of the different scan profiles, and observe how the command switches change.

e) Select **Intense scan** again then select the **Scan** button.

f) Switch to **MS1** (or arrange the VM windows) so that you can watch the `netstat` output as `Nmap` performs its scan.

You should see uncommon port states, such as **SYN received**.

5. Analyze the output of the Nmap scan.

a)   Switch back to **PC1**, and observe the results report.

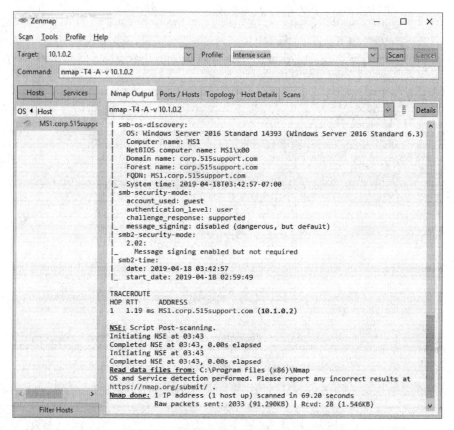

Nmap's scanning activity is complete when the "Nmap done" message is printed. (Screenshot used with permission from Nmap.)

b)   Select the **Ports/Hosts** tab.

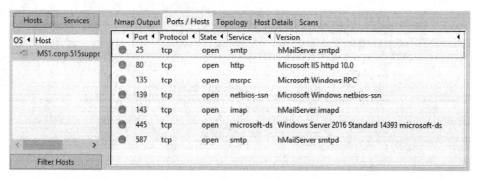

Results shown on the Ports/Hosts tab in Nmap. (Screenshot used with permission from Nmap.)

c)   Observe the ports open on this VM.

- Port 25—This is the default port for SMTP servers to use to relay messages. Nmap has identified the software application/service operating the port.
- Port 80—The default port for HTTP. Again, Nmap has identified the server as IIS 10.
- Ports 135, 139, and 445—These are the NetBIOS and SMB (Server Message Block) ports used by Windows networking and file sharing.
- Port 143—This is used by another mail protocol, Internet Message Access Protocol (IMAP). IMAP is used by a client email application to access a server message box and download and manage received emails.
- Port 587—By common practice, an SMTP server uses this port, rather than port 25, to accept messages from mail clients. Port 25 is reserved for relaying messages with other SMTP servers.

d) Select the **Topology** tab.

This tab shows the number of hops to the target. In this case, the first and only ring represents the single hop to a target on the same local network.

e) Select the **Host Details** tab.

This shows the results of Nmap's OS fingerprinting scripts. As you can see, the scripts have correctly identified Server 2016.

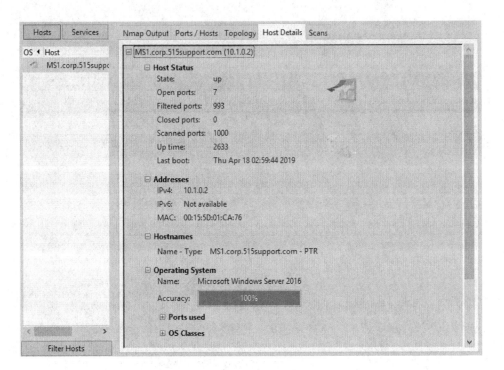

Results shown on the Host Details tab in Nmap. (Screenshot used with permission from Nmap.)

6. Discard changes made to the VMs in this activity.

a) Switch to Hyper-V Manager.

b) Use the **Action** menu or the right-click menu in the **Hyper-V Manager** console to revert each of the VMs to their saved checkpoints.

Topic C

Explain the Use of Name Resolution Services

EXAM OBJECTIVES COVERED
1.8 Explain the functions of network services.

Each node that has an IP address assigned to it can also have a descriptive name. This makes it easier for human users to identify and access it on the network. Almost all networks depend on this functionality to operate smoothly and securely, so it is important to understand how it works. In this topic, you will identify methods for host name resolution for TCP/IP networks.

HOST NAMES AND FULLY QUALIFIED DOMAIN NAMES (FQDNs)

The Internet Protocol uses a binary IP address to locate a host on an internetwork. The dotted decimal (IPv4) or hex (IPv6) representation of this IP address is used for configuration purposes, but it is not easy for people to remember. For this reason, a "friendly" name is also typically assigned to each host. There are two types of names: host names and Fully Qualified Domain Names (FQDNs).

A **host name** is assigned to a computer by the administrator, usually when the OS is installed. The host name needs to be unique on the local network. To avoid the possibility of duplicate host names on the Internet, a **fully qualified domain name (FQDN)** is used to provide a unique identity for the host belonging to a particular network. An example of an FQDN might be **nut.widget.com**.

An FQDN is made up of the **host name** and a **domain suffix**. In the example, the host name is **nut** and the domain suffix is **widget.com.** This domain suffix consists of the domain name **widget** within the **top-level domain (TLD) .com**. A domain suffix could also contain **subdomains** between the host and domain name. The trailing dot or period represents the root of the hierarchy.

When you are configuring name records, an FQDN must include the trailing period to represent the root, but this can be omitted in most other use cases.

Domain names must be registered with a registrar to ensure they are unique within a top-level domain. Once a domain name has been registered, it cannot be used by another organization. The same domain name may be registered within different top-level domains, however—**widget.com.** and **widget.co.uk.** are distinct domains, for instance.

Numerous hosts may exist within a single domain. For example: **nut**, **bolt**, and **washer** might all be hosts within the **widget.com.** domain. Given that, FQDNs must follow certain rules:

- The host name must be unique within the domain.
- The total length of an FQDN cannot exceed 253 characters, with each label (part of the name defined by a period) no more than 63 characters (excluding the periods).

- A DNS label should use letter, digit, and hyphen characters only. A label should not start with a hyphen. Punctuation characters such as the period (.) or forward slash (/) should not be used.
- DNS labels are not case sensitive.

Additionally, Internet registries may have their own restrictions.

In Windows, you can use the command `ipconfig /all` to display the FQDN of the local host. In Linux, you can use the command `hostname --fqdn`.

NAME RESOLUTION USING THE HOSTS FILE

To make use of these friendly names, there must be a system for resolving a host name or FQDN to an IP address. This process is called **name resolution**. Modern networks and the Internet use a system called the **Domain Name System (DNS)**, but before DNS was available, a **HOSTS file** was used.

 Note: Even though they seem to provide quite low-level functionality, name resolution protocols such as DNS sit at layer 7 (Application layer) in terms of the OSI model.

The first method for resolving host names to IP addresses involved the InterNIC central authority—now operated by ICANN (*icann.org*)—maintaining a text file of host name to IP address mappings. This file was called HOSTS. Whenever a site wanted to add a new host to the Internet, the site administrator sent an email to InterNIC giving the new host name to IP address mapping. This information was manually entered into the file.

An example HOSTS file is shown here.

```
# Sample
10.1.0.201 nut #web server
10.1.0.202 bolt #mail server
10.1.0.203 washer #ftp server
```

Any text preceded by the **#** symbol in a HOSTS file is a comment and will not be processed.

Network administrators were required to download a copy of the latest HOSTS file at regular intervals and install it on each host at their site. Each host could then perform name resolution by looking up a host name in the local copy of the HOSTS file and locating the corresponding IP address. The default location under Windows is %SystemRoot%\system32\drivers\etc\, while under Linux it is usually placed in the /etc directory.

The HOSTS file approach to naming became impractical as the number of hosts connected to the Internet grew; maintaining completeness and accuracy of the file became too difficult. Therefore, in the mid-1980s, the **Domain Name System (DNS)** was developed.

 Note: The HOSTS file is now primarily of use in troubleshooting.

DOMAIN NAME SYSTEM (DNS)

The **Domain Name System (DNS)** is a hierarchical system of distributed **name server** databases that contain information on domains and hosts within those domains. The system's distributed nature has the twin advantages that maintenance is delegated and loss of one DNS server does not necessarily prevent name resolution from being performed. At the top of the DNS hierarchy is the **root**, which is represented by the null label, consisting of just a **period** (.). There are 13 root level servers (A to M).

Immediately below the root lie the **top-level domains (TLDs)**. There are several types of top-level domains, but the most prevalent are generic (.com, .org, .net, .info, .biz), sponsored (.gov, .edu), and country code (.uk, .ca, .de).

DNS is operated by ICANN (*icann.org*), which also manages the generic TLDs. Country codes are generally managed by an organization appointed by the relevant government. Each domain name must be registered with a Domain Name Registry for the appropriate top-level domain.

Information about a domain is found by tracing records from the root down through the hierarchy. The root servers have complete information about the top-level domain servers. In turn, these servers have information relating to servers for the second level domains.

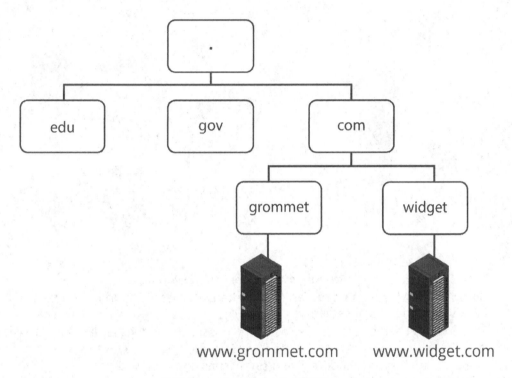

DNS hierarchy. (Image © 123RF.com.)

No name server has complete information about all domains. Records within the DNS tell them where the missing information is found. FQDNs reflect the hierarchy, from most specific (the host) to least specific (the TLD followed by the root). For example: **www.widget.com**.

NAME RESOLUTION USING DNS

The signal for the name resolution process to commence occurs when a user presents an FQDN (often within a URL) to an application program, such as a web browser. The client application, referred to as a **stub resolver**, checks its local cache for the mapping. If no mapping is found, it forwards the query to its local name server. The IP addresses of primary and secondary (backup) name servers are usually set in the TCP/IP configuration. The resolution process then takes place as follows:

1. The client **grommet.co.uk** queries its local name server for the IP address of the host **www.widget.com**.
2. The Grommet name server checks its own zone database for the record.
3. It is not authoritative for the domain, and it has no record of the domain in its own cache, so the Grommet name server queries a root server for the required IP address.

4. The root server checks its zone, finds that it is not authoritative for the requested record, and passes the Grommet name server the IP address of a name server in the .com domain.
5. The Grommet name server queries the designated name server in .com, which doesn't have the required information.
6. However, it does have the IP addresses of name servers in the **widget.com** domain. It passes these to the Grommet name server.

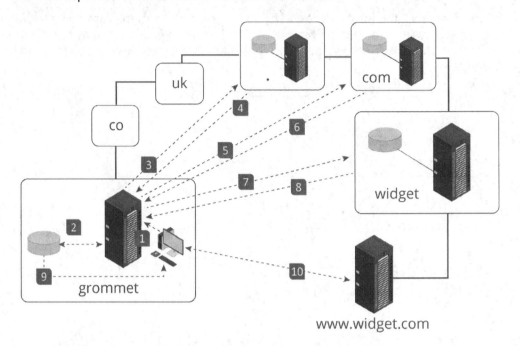

Resolving a name. (Image © 123RF.com.)

7. Because the Widget name server is authoritative, it passes the required record back to the originating server.
8. The Grommet server caches the result and passes the requested IP address to the client.
9. The client caches the IP address and establishes a session with the **www.widget.com** host.

Most queries between name servers are **iterative**; a name server responds to a query with whatever information it has. In the previous example, at steps 4 and 5, the root server and .com name server simply pass the querying server the address of an authoritative name server. They do not take on the task of resolving the original query for **www.widget.com**. A **recursive** query means that if the queried server is not authoritative, it does take on the task of referring to other name servers. The primary and secondary name servers in a client's TCP/IP configuration will almost always be recursive resolvers. This is the type of querying performed by the **grommet.co.uk** name server.

> **Note:** *A DNS server may be configured to perform recursive querying (a resolver) only, maintain zone records only, or perform both recursive querying and maintain zone records. Usually the roles are split, especially if the servers are open to the Internet. Most Internet-accessible DNS servers disable recursive queries. Recursive resolvers are typically only accessible by authorized clients—subscribers within an ISP's network or clients on a private LAN, for instance.*

> **Note:** *To learn more, watch the related* **Video** *on the course website.*

Activity 6-4
Discussing Name Resolution Services

SCENARIO
Answer the following questions to test your understanding of the content covered in this topic.

1. **What is a generic top-level domain?**

2. **What characters are allowed in a DNS host name?**

3. **What is the location of the HOSTS file?**

4. **Why would the following HOSTS file entry not affect name resolution?**
   `#198.134.5.6 www.comptia.org`

5. **When you configure name server addresses as part of a host's IP settings, do you need to specify servers perform iterative queries only or ones that accept recursive queries?**

Topic D

Configure DNS and IPAM Services

EXAM OBJECTIVES COVERED
1.1 Explain the purposes and uses of ports and protocols.
1.8 Explain the functions of network services.
5.2 Given a scenario, use the appropriate tool.

The name resolution process performed by DNS servers is a critical service for almost all types of networks. As a network technician, you will often be involved in configuring name servers and troubleshooting name resolution services.

DNS SERVER CONFIGURATION

DNS is essential to the function of the Internet. Windows **Active Directory**® and most Linux networks also require a DNS service to be running and correctly configured. It is important to realize that there are different kinds of DNS servers however, fulfilling different roles in network architecture.

A DNS server is usually configured to listen for queries on **UDP port 53**. Some DNS servers are also configured to allow connections over **TCP port 53**, as this allows larger record transfers (over 512 bytes). Larger transfers might be required if IPv6 is deployed on the network or if the DNS servers are using a security protocol (**DNSSEC**).

DNS name servers maintain the DNS namespace in **zones**. A name server can maintain primary and secondary zones:

- **Primary** means that the zone can be edited.
- **Secondary** means a read-only copy of the zone. This is maintained through a process of replication known as a **zone transfer** from the zone master (usually a primary zone). A secondary zone would typically be provided on two or more separate servers to provide fault tolerance and load balancing.

A name server that holds complete records for a domain can be defined as **authoritative**. This means that a record in the zone identifies the server as a name server for the domain. Both primary and secondary name servers are authoritative.

Servers that don't maintain a zone (primary or secondary) are referred to as **cache-only servers**. A **non-authoritative answer** from a server is one that derives from a cached record, rather than directly from the zone records. Caching servers are usually deployed as DNS resolvers. The function of a resolver is to perform recursive queries in response to requests from client systems (stub resolvers).

It is possible for the same DNS server instance to perform in both name server and resolver roles, but more typically these functions are separated to different servers for security reasons.

As well as making sure that resource records for the managed domain(s) are accurate, administrators should ensure that DNS services are **highly available** and **secure**, to prevent DNS spoofing, where an attacker is able to supply false name resolutions to clients.

INTERNAL VS. EXTERNAL DNS

A company will use primary and secondary name servers to maintain authoritative zone records for the domains that it manages. **Internal DNS zones** refer to the domains used on the private network only. These name records should only be available to internal clients. For example, a company might run a Windows Active Directory network using the domain name **corp.widget.com**. The zone records for **corp.widget.com** would be served from internal name servers. This would allow a client PC (**pc1.corp.widget.com**) to contact a local application server (**crm.corp.widget.com**). The name servers hosting these internal domain records must not be accessible from the Internet.

External DNS zones refer to records that Internet clients must be able to access. For example, the company might run web and email services on the domain **widget.com**. In order for Internet hosts to use a web server at **www.widget.com** or send email to an **@widget.com** address, the zone records for **widget.com** must be hosted on a name server that is accessible over the Internet.

DNS FORWARDERS

Companies must also provide name resolution services to support their internal clients contacting other domains. If a server is not authoritative for the requested domain, it can either perform a **recursive query** to locate an authoritative name server or it can **forward** the request to another name server. A recursive resolver must be configured with a root hints file so that it can query the whole DNS hierarchy from the root servers down. DNS servers should allow recursive queries only from authorized internal clients. It is also a good idea to separate the DNS servers used to host zone records from ones used to service client requests for non-authoritative domains.

As an alternative to recursion (or to supplement it), name servers can be configured to resolve queries via forwarding. A **forwarder** transmits a client query to another DNS server and routes the replies it gets back to the client. A **conditional forwarder** performs this task for certain domains only. For example, you might configure a DNS server that is authoritative for the local private network (internal DNS), but that forwards any requests for Internet domains to an external DNS resolver run by your ISP.

THIRD-PARTY AND CLOUD-HOSTED DNS

Third-party DNS means that another organization is responsible for hosting your DNS records. Typically, this would be for external domains, rather than local network ones. The DNS hosting provider must ensure the reliability and availability of services. A hosting provider might use **cloud-based servers** to do this, replicating the DNS information to multiple physical servers accessible using different Internet routes.

Whether you host your own public name servers or use a third party, you should set up a system for monitoring DNS and ensure that your public name servers are working. This might be provided as part of a hosting service. Otherwise, there are numerous monitoring services, such as Site24x7 (*site24x7.com/dns-monitoring.html*), that can check that your website host, mail, and other critical records are available and resolving correctly at different geographic locations. Such systems can be configured to send a notification if service is interrupted.

Companies and residential customers will also usually depend on their ISP's DNS infrastructure for resolving client queries. It is possible to configure your clients with any trusted DNS resolvers, however. Google's public DNS servers (8.8.8.8 and 8.8.4.4) are quite widely used for instance. Another option is Quad9, sponsored by IBM. Quad9 has a special focus on blocking domains known to host malicious content. There is a filtered service (9.9.9.9 and 149.112.112.112) and a non-secured service (9.9.9.10 and 149.112.112.10).

Note: *Name resolution is a critical process. Compromising name resolution enables a wide range of attacks against network services. You must ensure the use of trustworthy external DNS resolvers.*

RESOURCE RECORDS

A DNS zone will contain numerous **resource records**. These records allow the DNS server to resolve queries for names and services hosted in the domain into IP addresses. Resource records can be created and updated manually (statically) or dynamically from information received from client and server computers on the network. It is important to understand that multiple different named resource records can refer to the same IP address (and vice versa in the case of load balancing). It is also possible for a resource record to point to an incorrect IP address, many examples of which have occurred over the years on the Internet and have caused major network outages.

There are many different resource records, but the main ones are discussed in the next few sections.

START OF AUTHORITY (SOA) AND NAME SERVER (NS) RECORDS

The **Start of Authority (SOA)** record identifies the primary DNS name server that is authoritative for the zone and is therefore responsible for resolving names in the domain (plus any subdomains).

The SOA also includes contact information for the zone and a serial number (for **version control**).

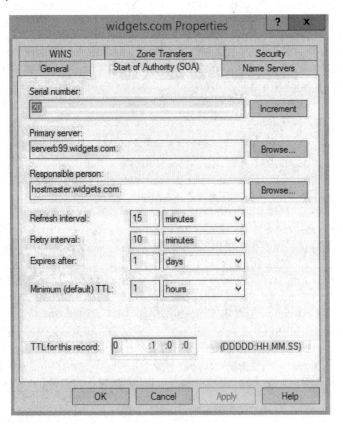

Configuring a Start of Authority record in Windows DNS. (Screenshot used with permission from Microsoft.)

Name Server (NS) records identify authoritative DNS name servers for the zone. In most enterprise networks, each zone will have several (at least two) DNS servers holding a replicated copy of the zone. Therefore, two or more NS records are configured for redundancy.

_msdcs			
_sites			
_tcp			
_udp			
DomainDnsZones			
ForestDnsZones			
(same as parent folder)	Start of Authority (SOA)	[30], serverb99.widgets.co...	static
(same as parent folder)	Name Server (NS)	99servera.widgets.com.	static
(same as parent folder)	Name Server (NS)	serverb99.widgets.com.	static

Start of Authority and Name Server records in Windows Server DNS. (Screenshot used with permission from Microsoft.)

ADDRESS (A), AAAA, AND CANONICAL NAMES (CNAME) RECORDS

A host address or **A record** is used to resolve a host name to an IPv4 address. This is the most common type of record in a DNS zone. In a lot of infrastructures, there will be an A record for every client on the network, plus servers, printers, and other connected devices. However, in some environments, client workstations will not be listed as A records—only servers, printers, and other shared resources.

An **AAAA record** performs the same function as an A record, but for resolving a host name to an IPv6 address.

 Note: DNS uses the UDP transport protocol by default, which has a maximum packet size of 512 bytes. Due to the much larger address sizes of IPv6, AAAA records can often exceed this size. This can result in UDP packets being fragmented into several smaller packets, which may be blocked by firewalls if they are not configured to expect them. Network administrators should check that their DNS servers can accept these transmissions and that intermediary components are not blocking them.

A **Canonical Name (CNAME)** (or **alias**) record is used to represent an alias for a host. For example, the true name of a web server could be masked as the alias **www**. CNAME records are also often used to make DNS administration easier. For example, an alias can be redirected to a completely different host temporarily during system maintenance.

(same as parent folder)	Host (A)	192.168.0.102	30/12/2017
99servera	Host (A)	192.168.0.188	static
FileServer1	Host (A)	192.168.0.178	static
MailServer1	Mail Exchanger (MX)	[10] serverb99.widgets.co...	static
MailServer2	Mail Exchanger (MX)	[10] servera99.widgets.co...	static
ServerA99	Host (A)	192.168.0.12	static
serverb99	Host (A)	192.168.0.102	static
ServerC99	Host (A)	192.168.0.34	static
TestServer	IPv6 Host (AAAA)	2001:0001:3dfe:0001:0000:...	static
www	Alias (CNAME)	serverc99.widgets.com.	static

Both types of host records (A and AAAA) plus a CNAME record in Windows Server DNS. (Screenshot used with permission from Microsoft.)

MAIL EXCHANGER (MX), SERVICE (SRV), AND TXT RECORDS

A **Mail Exchanger (MX)** record is used to identify an email server for the domain. In a typical network, multiple servers are installed to provide redundancy, and each one will be represented with an MX record. Each server record is given a preference value with the lowest numbered entry preferred.

While most DNS records are used to resolve a name into an IP address, a **Service (SRV) record** is used to identify a record that is providing a network service or protocol. SRV records are often used to locate VoIP or media servers. SRV records are also an essential part of the infrastructure supporting Microsoft's Active Directory; they are used by clients to locate **domain controllers**, for instance. As with MX, SRV records can be configured with a priority value.

_gc	Service Location (SRV)	[0][100][3268] serverb99.w...	30/12/2017 14:00:00
_kerberos	Service Location (SRV)	[0][100][88] serverb99.wid...	30/12/2017 14:00:00
_kpasswd	Service Location (SRV)	[0][100][464] serverb99.wi...	30/12/2017 14:00:00
_ldap	Service Location (SRV)	[0][100][389] serverb99.wi...	30/12/2017 14:00:00

SRV records in Windows Server DNS. (Screenshot used with permission from Microsoft.)

A **TXT record** is used to store any free-form text that may be needed to support other network services. A single domain name may have many TXT records, but most commonly they are used as part of **Sender Policy Framework (SPF)** and **DomainKeys Identified Mail (DKIM)**. An SPF record is used to list the IP addresses or names of servers that are permitted to send email from a particular domain and is used to combat the sending of **spam**. DKIM records are used to decide whether you should allow received email from a given source, preventing spam and mail spoofing. DKIM can use encrypted signatures to prove that a message really originated from the domain it claims.

POINTER (PTR) RECORDS

A DNS server may have two types of zones: forward lookup and reverse lookup. **Forward lookup zones** contain most of the resource records you are looking at here— Given a name record, a forward lookup returns an IP address. A **PTR record** is found in **reverse lookup zones** and is used to resolve an IP address to a host name.

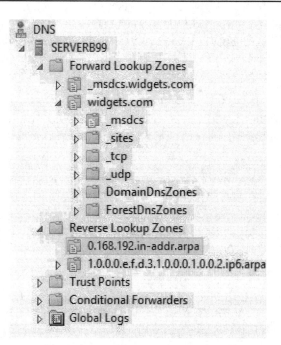

Reverse lookup zone and pointer records in Windows Server DNS. (Screenshot used with permission from Microsoft.)

Reverse name resolution uses a special domain called **in-addr.arpa**. The name server would hold a zone mapped to the first three octets of the IP address in reverse order; the final octet is a PTR record in this subdomain. For example, the reverse lookup FQDN for **comptia.org** is:

```
6.5.134.198.in-addr.arpa
```

This resolves to the IP address 198.134.5.6. IPv6 uses the **ip6.arpa** domain; each of the 32 hex characters in the IPv6 address is expressed in reverse order as a subdomain. For example, the IPv6 address:

```
2001:0db8:0000:0000:0bcd:abcd:ef12:1234
```

is represented by the following pointer record:

```
4.3.2.1.2.1.f.e.d.c.b.a.d.c.b.0.0.0.0.0.0.0.0.0.8.b.d.
0.1.0.0.2.ip6.arpa
```

Reverse lookup zones are not mandatory and are often omitted from DNS servers, as they can be used by hackers to sequentially work through a range of IP addresses to discover useful or interesting device names, which can then be targeted by other hacking mechanisms.

DYNAMIC DNS

In modern networks, DNS is used not only to resolve the IP addresses of hosts on the Internet, but also those on the local network. This presents a challenge, as IP addresses on the LAN are typically assigned by DHCP, so the IP address of any given host cannot be guaranteed to remain the same from one day to the next.

Dynamic DNS solves this problem by allowing either individual clients or the DHCP server to notify the DNS server of any IP address changes. In Windows this can be triggered manually using the `ipconfig /registerdns` command. The DNS server updates its A and PTR records based on the information provided, ensuring that the host name will resolve to the new IP address.

Dynamic DNS is also used by SOHO Internet routers. If the ISP does not provide a static IP address, the user can sign up with a Dynamic DNS (DDNS) service and then configure the DDNS host and credentials on the SOHO router. Whenever the router IP is changed by the ISP, it will update the records at the DDNS provider so that the router remains addressable by FQDN on the Internet.

nslookup

In a Windows environment, you can troubleshoot DNS with the **nslookup** command, `nslookup`, either interactively or from the command prompt.

```
nslookup -Option Host Server
```

Host can be either a host name, a domain name, a Fully Qualified Domain Name (FQDN), or an IP address. *Server* is the DNS server to query; the default DNS server is used if this argument is omitted. *-Option* specifies an `nslookup` subcommand. For example, the following command queries Google's public DNS server (8.8.8.8) for information about widget.com's mail records:

```
nslookup -type=mx widget.com 8.8.8.8
```

If `nslookup` is run without any arguments (or with just the argument *-Server*), the tool is started in interactive mode. You can perform specific query types and output the result to a text file for analysis. When in interactive mode, keep the following points in mind:

- To interrupt interactive commands at any time, press **Ctrl+C**.
- To view subcommands, type **help** or **?**
- By default, host name (A) records will be returned; use the `set type=xx` command to display different records (for example, `set type=mx` returns mail server records for the domain).
- The command line length must be less than 256 characters.
- An unrecognized command is interpreted as a host name. To treat a built-in command as a host name, precede it with the escape character (\).

```
C:\Users\Admin>nslookup -type=mx comptia.org 8.8.8.8
Server:  dns.google
Address:  8.8.8.8

Non-authoritative answer:
comptia.org      MX preference = 10, mail exchanger = comptia-org.mail.protection.outlook.com

C:\Users\Admin>nslookup -type=ns comptia.org 8.8.8.8
Server:  dns.google
Address:  8.8.8.8

Non-authoritative answer:
comptia.org      nameserver = ns2.comptia.org
comptia.org      nameserver = ns1.comptia.org

C:\Users\Admin>nslookup -type=mx comptia.org ns1.comptia.org
Server:  UnKnown
Address:  209.117.62.56

comptia.org      MX preference = 10, mail exchanger = comptia-org.mail.protection.outlook.com

C:\Users\Admin>
```

The first two nslookup commands identify comptia.org's MX and primary name server records using Google's public DNS resolver (8.8.8.8). Note that the answers are non-authoritative. The third command queries CompTIA's name server for the MX record. This answer is authoritative. (Screenshot used with permission from Microsoft.)

POWERSHELL NAME RESOLUTION

The Windows **PowerShell** environment provides a much more sophisticated, scripted environment that you can use to issue **cmdlets** to test DNS name resolution (and change DNS settings as well, if required).

PowerShell® provides a cmdlet called `Resolve-DnsName`, which allows a more flexible method of testing name resolution than `nslookup`, as it allows testing of the different methods of name resolution (HOSTS file, DNS cache, and DNS server). There are several parameters that can be used with the cmdlet to control how it works. After entering PowerShell, the following examples show the different options:

`Resolve-DnsName` *host*

This will resolve *host* using the same method as the Windows client.

`Resolve-DnsName` *host* `-NoHostsFile`

This will resolve *host* but without using any entries from the HOSTS file in the local cache.

`Resolve-DnsName` *host* `-DnsOnly`

This resolves *host* using only the DNS server (not the client-side cache). A specific DNS server can be chosen (rather than the default) using the additional parameter:

`-Server` *IPofDNSserver*

It is also possible to search DNS for records other than A or AAAA records. For example, to show only Mail Exchange records in a specific domain, use the cmdlet:

`Resolve-DnsName` *domain* `-Type MX`

```
Windows PowerShell
Copyright (C) Microsoft Corporation. All rights reserved.

PS C:\Users\James> Resolve-DNSName comptia.org

Name                                      Type   TTL     Section    IPAddress
----                                      ----   ---     -------    ---------
comptia.org                               A      35107   Answer     6.6.6.6
                                                 8

PS C:\Users\James> Resolve-DNSName comptia.org -NoHostsFile

Name                                      Type   TTL     Section    IPAddress
----                                      ----   ---     -------    ---------
comptia.org                               A      60      Answer     198.134.5.6
```

Using Resolve-DnsName. (Screenshot used with permission from Microsoft.)

In this example, you can see the effect of adding the `-NoHostsFile` option. This host has a malicious HOSTS entry for comptia.org pointing to a different address from the DNS server.

dig

Domain Information Groper (dig) is a command-line tool for querying DNS servers that ships with the BIND DNS server software published by the Internet Systems Consortium (ISC) (*isc.org/downloads/bind*).

`dig` can be much more useful than `nslookup`, as it can operate in batch mode (using a text file) as well as the normal interactive mode from the command line. `dig` can be run pointing at a specific DNS server; otherwise, it will use the default resolver. Without any specific settings, it queries the DNS root zone.

A simple query uses the syntax:

```
dig host
```

Which will search for the host, domain, FQDN, or IP address and display any information using the default DNS settings mentioned earlier.

The following command example directs the resolve request to the specific DNS server after the @ symbol. This can be an FQDN or IP address.

```
dig @ns1.isp.com host
```

Other examples of `dig` are to display all the resource records about a domain or just specific ones such as Mail Exchange.

```
dig @ns1.isp.com host all
```

```
dig @ns1.isp.com host MX
```

`dig` often generates a lot of information, so it is possible to add parameters to the end of the command like `+nocomments` or `+nostats`, which will reduce the output.

```
[centos@lx1 ~]$ dig @9.9.9.9 comptia.org MX

; <<>> DiG 9.9.4-RedHat-9.9.4-72.el7 <<>> @9.9.9.9 comptia.org MX
; (1 server found)
;; global options: +cmd
;; Got answer:
;; ->>HEADER<<- opcode: QUERY, status: NOERROR, id: 40334
;; flags: qr rd ra; QUERY: 1, ANSWER: 1, AUTHORITY: 0, ADDITIONAL: 1

;; OPT PSEUDOSECTION:
; EDNS: version: 0, flags:; udp: 512
;; QUESTION SECTION:
;comptia.org.                   IN      MX

;; ANSWER SECTION:
comptia.org.            60      IN      MX      10 comptia-org.mail.protection.o
utlook.com.

;; Query time: 110 msec
;; SERVER: 9.9.9.9#53(9.9.9.9)
;; WHEN: Thu May 23 13:52:35 PDT 2019
;; MSG SIZE  rcvd: 95

[centos@lx1 ~]$
```

Using dig to locate comptia.org's MX records using IBM's Quad9 DNS service as a resolver. Note that the response is non-authoritative.

 Note: *You can install `dig` on Windows by downloading the BIND DNS server package (isc.org/downloads) and installing it using the tools-only option.*

IP ADDRESS MANAGEMENT (IPAM)

An enterprise network or ISP will have to manage hundreds or even thousands of IPv4 and IPv6 networks and subnets across a wide range of physical infrastructure. Maintaining visibility into IP address assignments and name resolution across physical, virtualized, and cloud infrastructure and incorporating network appliances, servers and clients, plus mobile devices and Internet of Things (IoT) devices, is a challenging task. Historically, IT departments might have tracked IP usage in static files such as spreadsheets. The demands of modern networks require software solutions, however, and that is what the **IP address management (IPAM)** sector provides.

The core function of IPAM is to scan DHCP and DNS servers and log IP address usage to a database. Most suites can scan IP address ranges to detect use of statically assigned addresses. Some IPAM software may also be able to scan the hardware associated with an IP address (device fingerprinting) and save the information to an asset inventory. IPAM software can often be used to manage and reconfigure DHCP and DNS servers remotely.

The software also provides analysis tools to allow administrators to identify overloaded DHCP scopes or to make more valuable public IP addresses available.

Apart from managing and configuring the IP address space, IPAM also performs valuable incident response and forensics functions. IPAM may reveal unauthorized use of IP addresses or address ranges and can track the use of an IP address over time. This means that if a forensics investigation needs to identify the host associated with an IP address some months ago, the IPAM database will have recorded it.

Windows Server ships with a basic IPAM tool, though it is only suitable for managing Windows-based servers. Cisco has their Prime Network Registrar (*cisco.com*). Other popular IPAM vendors include Infoblox (*infoblox.com*) and Efficient IP (*efficientip.com*).

 Note: *To learn more, watch the related* **Video** *on the course website.*

GUIDELINES FOR DEPLOYING DNS

DEPLOY DNS SERVICES

DNS is a critical service for almost all networks. Follow these guidelines for deploying internal and external DNS services:

- Set up primary and secondary name servers to host records for your LAN. These name services should be accessible only by authorized clients.
- Configure the appropriate host, MX, and service records for the forward lookup zone on the primary server.
- Optionally, configure a reverse lookup zone to allow clients to resolve IP addresses to host names.
- Optionally, configure dynamic DNS to allow hosts and DHCP servers to update their host records. Ensure that only secure updates from authorized clients are allowed.
- Configure the secondary server to obtain up-to-date records periodically through a zone transfer with the primary server.
- To resolve client Internet queries, set up a forwarder to pass queries to trusted resolvers on the Internet, such as your ISP's DNS server or trusted public services such as those from Google or Quad9.
- For external DNS, consider using a third-party provider, ideally with a cloud service, to ensure high availability. Without public DNS, your customers will not be able to browse your websites or send you email.
- Set up a process for checking that your external DNS records are accurate and working correctly.

Activity 6-5

Discussing DNS and IPAM Services

SCENARIO

Answer the following questions to test your understanding of the content covered in this topic.

---

1. **What type of DNS record resolves IPv6 addresses?**

2. **What use is a PTR DNS record?**

3. **What types of DNS records have priority or preference values?**

4. **What type of DNS record is used to prove the valid origin of email?**

5. **What type of DNS enables clients to report a change of IP address to a DNS server?**

6. **What is the function of the command** `nslookup - 8.8.8.8`**?**

7. **What is the function of a** `dig` **subcommand such as** `+nostats`**?**

8. **What type of server infrastructure is IPAM designed to monitor?**

Activity 6-6
Configuring DNS Servers

BEFORE YOU BEGIN

Start the VMs used in this activity in the following order, adjusting the memory allocation first if necessary, and waiting at the ellipsis for the previous VMs to finish booting before starting the next group. You do not need to connect to a VM until prompted to do so in the activity steps.

1. **RT1-LOCAL** (256 MB)
2. **RT2-ISP** (256 MB)
3. **RT3-INT** (256 MB)
4. **LAMP** (512—1024 MB)
5. **PC1** (1024—2048 MB)
6. **PC2** (512—1024 MB)

Start the following VM only when prompted during the activity:

1. **DC1** (1024—2048 MB)
2. ...
3. **MS1** (1024—2048 MB)

> **Note:** *If you can allocate more than the minimum amounts of RAM, prioritize **PC1**.*

SCENARIO

In this activity, you will explore different ways of addressing machines by a friendly name, rather than an IP address. This activity is designed to test your understanding of and ability to apply content examples in the following CompTIA Network+ objectives:

- 1.1 Explain the purposes and uses of ports and protocols.
- 1.8 Explain the functions of network services.
- 5.2 Given a scenario, use the appropriate tool.

---

1. Run some of the VMs without making a DNS server available, and test the effect on name resolution.

   a) Open a connection window for the **PC1** VM and log on as ***515support\Administrator*** with the password ***Pa$$w0rd***

   b) Start **Wireshark**. Select the **Ethernet** adapter and then start a capture.

   c) Open a command prompt as administrator and enter `hostname`

      The computer's host name is the same as the name of the VM.

   d) At the command prompt, enter ***ping PC1***. What do you notice about the replies?

      ping uses IPv6 by default. Also, the address resolves to a link-local range (fe80). Finally, the FQDN of the machine is returned (**PC1.corp.515support.com**).

   e) At the command prompt, enter ***ping -4 PC2***. Does it work? What is the host name resolved to? What do you notice about the replies?

The IPv4 address is in the APIPA range. Note also that no domain suffix is appended to the host name.

f) Look at the **Wireshark** capture, and locate the query frames that **PC1** uses to perform name resolution.

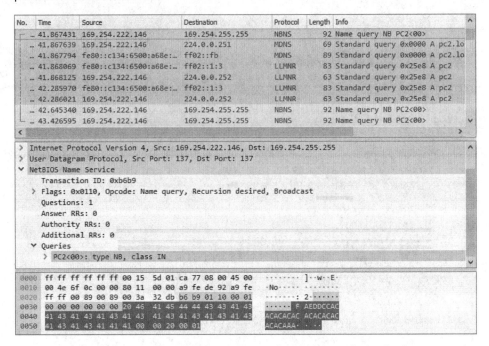

Name resolution without DNS. (Screenshot courtesy of Wireshark.)

PC1 is using DHCP to try to locate its proper IP configuration and DNS server, but as neither are running, it falls back to Multicast DNS (MDNS), Link Local Multicast Name Resolution (LLMNR), and NetBIOS Name Service (NBNS).

g) Leave the capture running.

2. Create a HOSTS file, place a host record into it, and test the effect on name resolution.

a) On the **PC1** VM, right-click the **Start** button and select **Run**, then type the following command in the **Run** dialog box:

```
notepad c:\windows\system32\drivers\etc\hosts
```

b) Press **Ctrl+Shift+Enter** to run the command as administrator. Confirm the **UAC** prompt by selecting **Yes**.

c) In **Notepad**, go to the end of the file and type the following (pressing the **Tab** key between the IP address and the host name):

```
10.1.0.102      PC2
```

d) Save the file but do not close it—leave it open in Notepad.

e) At the command prompt, enter ***ping -4 PC2***

f) Can you explain the error message? Look at the packet capture to see if the command generated any activity.
   The HOSTS file entries added to the name cache override other name resolution methods, so **PC1** does not attempt to send out any queries. As the IP mapping it has for 10.1.0.102 is on a different subnet from its current APIPA range and it has no default gateway, it makes no attempt to ping the host.

g) Run `ipconfig /displaydns`. Observe the entries in the name cache.

```
C:\Users\administrator>ipconfig /displaydns

Windows IP Configuration

    102.0.1.10.in-addr.arpa
    ----------------------------------------
    Record Name . . . . . : 102.0.1.10.in-addr.arpa.
    Record Type . . . . . : 12
    Time To Live  . . . . : 86400
    Data Length . . . . . : 8
    Section . . . . . . . : Answer
    PTR Record  . . . . . : PC2


    pc2
    ----------------------------------------
    Record Name . . . . . : PC2
    Record Type . . . . . : 1
    Time To Live  . . . . : 86400
    Data Length . . . . . : 4
    Section . . . . . . . : Answer
    A (Host) Record . . . : 10.1.0.102


    pc2
    ----------------------------------------
    No records of type AAAA


C:\Users\administrator>
```

Viewing the local DNS name cache. (Screenshot used with permission from Microsoft.)

 Note: *Not all applications use the Windows DNS name cache. Browsers such as Firefox maintain their own cache, for instance.*

h) Modify the **HOSTS** file to change the IP address of **PC2** to **169.254.1.102**. Save the file, but keep it open in Notepad.

i) Does **ping -4 PC2** work now? What is different about the error message?
PC1 knows that the IP address is local, so it tries that. It is the wrong IP address for **PC2**, however, so no replies are received. Looking at the Wireshark capture, note the unanswered ARP queries for 169.254.1.102.

j) Leave Notepad, Wireshark, and the command prompt open.

3. Bring the DNS and DHCP servers online, and use some tools to query name services.

a) Start the **DC1** VM and watch the thumbnail in **Hyper-V Manager**.

b) When the **DC1** thumbnail shows the login screen, start the **MS1** VM.

c) Switch back to the **PC1** VM, and wait for **PC1** to obtain an IP address in the **10.1.0.0/24** range from the DHCP server. You should see the relevant traffic in **Wireshark**. If **PC1** doesn't obtain a lease, run the following command: `ipconfig /renew "Ethernet"`

d) At a command prompt, run the following commands:

```
ping -4 PC2

ping -4 DC1
```

The test for **PC2** will fail, but there should be replies from **DC1**. Remember that the HOSTS mapping for **PC2** that you configured is still active.

e) Observe the DNS queries generated in **Wireshark**.

f) Still on **PC1**, run `ipconfig /displaydns` and observe the entries in the name cache.

The only record for **PC2** is the data cached from the HOSTS file. The name cache entries derived from HOSTS override DNS. This is why it was often targeted (and still is targeted to some extent) by malicious applications trying to subvert name resolution.

g) Switch to **Notepad**, and delete the line you added to the **HOSTS** file. Save and close the file, and then close Notepad.

h) At the command prompt, run the following commands. Is the host name correctly resolved now?

```
ipconfig /flushdns

ping -4 PC2
```

The test should work and **PC2** should be resolved to 10.1.0.10*x*.

4. Use the `nslookup` tool to query the domain's DNS records.

a) On the **PC1** VM, run `nslookup`

Your DNS server's IP address is returned, and `nslookup` starts in interactive mode.

b) At the **>** prompt, enter ***set type=A***

c) Enter ***www.corp.515support.com***

Your DNS name server and address are returned, followed by the result of your query. The A or host record for **www** is 10.1.0.10 (you do not have the relevant VM running).

d) Enter ***set type=MX***

e) Enter ***corp.515support.com*** to query it.

```
C:\Windows\system32>nslookup
Default Server:  DC1.corp.515support.com
Address:  10.1.0.1

> set type=A
> www.corp.515support.com
Server:  DC1.corp.515support.com
Address:  10.1.0.1

Name:    www.corp.515support.com
Address:  10.1.0.10

> set type=MX
> corp.515support.com
Server:  DC1.corp.515support.com
Address:  10.1.0.1

corp.515support.com      MX preference = 10, mail exchanger = mail.corp.515support.com
mail.corp.515support.com          internet address = 10.1.0.2
>
```

nslookup queries. (Screenshot used with permission from Microsoft.)

The **MX** type attempts to return servers used to deliver email to the domain (SMTP servers). Email for the zone is handled by the alias **mail.corp.515support.com** on IP address **10.1.0.2** (the **MS1** VM).

f) Enter `ls -t any corp.515support.com` to attempt to perform a zone transfer (obtain all the information about a zone).

If you have the right to perform a zone transfer, you can use `-t` with a specific record type to return a subset of the zone's records. This server has been purposefully misconfigured to allow this. On a real domain server, it would be an unnecessary security risk.

g) Enter **exit** to quit `nslookup`.

5. Use `nslookup` in command mode, and have it output the results to a file.

   a) Run the following command.

      ```
      echo ls -d corp.515support.com | nslookup > 515support.txt
      ```

      The `-d` switch is another way of specifying all records.

   b) Enter **notepad 515support.txt** to open the file.

   c) Close Notepad.

   d) To query records hosted in a foreign domain, run the following queries:

      ```
      nslookup www.515web.net

      nslookup -query=ns 515web.net

      nslookup www.515web.net 192.168.1.1
      ```

```
C:\Windows\system32>nslookup www.515web.net
Server:  DC1.corp.515support.com
Address:  10.1.0.1

Non-authoritative answer:
Name:    lamp.515web.net
Address:  192.168.1.1
Aliases:  www.515web.net


C:\Windows\system32>nslookup -query=ns 515web.net
Server:  DC1.corp.515support.com
Address:  10.1.0.1

Non-authoritative answer:
515web.net      nameserver = ns.515web.net

ns.515web.net   internet address = 192.168.1.1

C:\Windows\system32>nslookup www.515web.net 192.168.1.1
Server:  mail.515web.net
Address:  192.168.1.1

Name:    LAMP.515web.net
Address:  192.168.1.1
Aliases:  www.515web.net
```

Non-authoritative and authoritative responses. (Screenshot used with permission from Microsoft.)

The last command uses the DNS server at 192.168.1.1 to perform the query. The first two queries use the default resolver, which is getting query responses by forwarding. The responses to these queries are consequently identified as non-authoritative. The last response is authoritative because you are querying the name server directly. When you are troubleshooting, you might query a specific DNS server to check whether it is configured correctly or if your updated DNS records are propagating to other servers.

6. Connect to the **LAMP** VM and use the `dig` utility to query DNS servers.

   a) Open a connection window for the **LAMP** VM and log on with the username **lamp** and password **Pa$$w0rd**

    Note: *If there is no prompt, just type **lamp** and press **Enter**.*

b) Run the following commands to return the complete domain records, pipe the output from the command to a file, then open the file for viewing:

```
dig 515web.net axfr > 515web.txt

nano 515web.txt
```

c) Verify that the server resolving these queries is at **192.168.1.254**. Press **Ctrl+X** to close the text editor.

d) To query the local name server directly, run the following command:

```
dig 515web.net axfr @192.168.1.1
```

The @ option sets the DNS server to use to perform the query.

e) You can use the following syntax to query specific record types. For example, run the following commands to return MX and NS records:

```
dig 515web.net MX

dig 515web.net NS +noall +answer
```

The second command uses options to control the output, displaying only the answer section. `dig` has many more options available—use `dig -h` to browse them.

f) Run the following command to view the complete domain records for **corp. 515support.com**:

```
dig corp.515support.com axfr
```

This works, but the domain administrator has made a serious error in allowing this to work!

7. Examine the configuration of the three DNS servers that you have been querying using the Berkeley InterNet Daemon (BIND) software available on most Linux name servers.

a) Run the following command:

```
nano /etc/bind/named.conf.local
```

```
//
// Do any local configuration here
//

// Consider adding the 1918 zones here, if they are not used in your
// organization
//include "/etc/bind/zones.rfc1918";

zone "515web.net" {
        type master;
        file "/etc/bind/db.515web.net";
        allow-transfer { "any"; };
};
zone "1.168.192.in-addr.arpa" {
        type master;
        file "/etc/bind/db.192";
};
zone "515support.com" {
        type master;
        file "/etc/bind/db.515support.com";
};
zone "corp.515support.com" {
        type forward;
        forward only;
        forwarders { 10.1.0.1; };
};
zone "0.1.10.in-addr.arpa" {
        type forward;
        forward only;
        forwarders { 10.1.0.1; };
};
```

BIND local zones and forwarders configuration.

b) Review the text file.

The first part of this file configures a forward zone (**515web.net**) for which the server is responsible (primary master) and a corresponding reverse lookup zone (used to obtain a host name given an IP address). The forward zone allows full transfers of all records to any other host.

c) Press **Ctrl+X** to close the text editor.

d) To test that there are no errors in the configuration file, run the following command:

```
named-checkconf
```

If there are no errors (and there shouldn't be), the command will execute with no output.

e) The actual zone information is configured in the zone database files at the locations specified in the configuration file. Run the following command to view the **web.net** zone database:

```
nano /etc/bind/db.515web.net
```

The @ character represents the domain defined in the named.conf.local file. The SOA record declares that this name server is authoritative for this domain (**515web.net.**). **ns.515web.net** is the machine hosting the domain record and **hostmaster. 515web.net.** is a contact email address for the domain. The rest of the information in this first record is for controlling caching and updates.

 Note: *Notice the periods at the end of each FQDN. Also note that as @ has special meaning in the configuration file (a placeholder for the zone name from named.conf.local), the hostmaster email address uses a period delimiter after the mailbox name, rather than @.*

The other records configure the primary name server (NS) in the zone (192.168.1.1) and the web server LAMP (192.168.1.1). The CNAME **www** is also configured to point to 192.168.1.1 as is the blank domain name, represented by the @ character. There is also an MX record.

```
;
; BIND data file for 515web.net domain
;
$TTL        604800
@           IN      SOA     ns.515web.net. lamp.515web.net. (
                                    1           ; Serial
                                 604800         ; Refresh
                                  86400         ; Retry
                                2419200         ; Expire
                                 604800 )       ; Negative Cache TTL
            IN      A       192.168.1.1
@           IN      NS      ns.515web.net.
@           IN      A       192.168.1.1
ns          IN      A       192.168.1.1
LAMP        IN      A       192.168.1.1
mail        IN      A       192.168.1.1
@           IN      MX  10  mail.515web.net.
www         IN      CNAME   lamp.515web.net.
```

Configuring DNS records.

f) Press **Ctrl+X** to close the text editor.

g) To test that there are no errors in the configuration file, run the following command:

```
named-checkzone 515web.net /etc/bind/db.515web.net
```

h) Finally, run the following command to view the reverse lookup zone configuration file:

```
nano /etc/bind/db.192
```

There is only one host configured.

i) Press **Ctrl+X** to close the text editor.

8. Remember that this machine is not actually using the local domain server to resolve queries. Its default name server is at 192.168.1.254. This is hosted on the **RT3-INT** VM. Examine the configuration of this server.

   a) Open a connection window for the **RT3-INT** VM and log on using the username *vyos* and password *Pa$$w0rd*

   b) Run the command `show conf` and use the **Page Down** or **Down Arrow** key to scroll to the **service > dns** section.

      This server is configured as a forwarder only and has been configured with the three zones in use on your network.

9. Examine the configuration of the Windows DNS server on **DC1**.

   a) Open a connection window for the **DC1** VM and log on as *515support\Administrator* with the password *Pa$$w0rd*

   b) In **Server Manager**, select **Tools→DNS**.

   c) In the **DNS** snap-in, expand **DC1→Forward Lookup Zones→corp.515support.com**. Right-click the **corp.515support.com** zone and select **Properties**.

      On the **General** tab, observe the option to limit dynamic updates to secure only. A Windows domain allows domain-joined computers configured via DHCP to register with DNS but prevents changes to other records.

   d) Select the **Start of Authority** tab.

      The information here is the same sort of information that was configured in the server configuration text file in BIND.

   e) Select the **Zone Transfers** tab. Change the **Allow zone transfers** option to **Only to servers listed on the Name Servers tab**. Select **OK**.

      That should prevent unwanted zone transfers. On a production network you might want to allow more management stations to access this information, though. You can use the **Only to the following servers** option to configure an ACL.

   f) Look through the subfolders added by Active Directory. You will find several SRV records that allow domain clients to locate services such as Kerberos (authentication) and LDAP (directory information).

10. Discard changes made to the VMs in this activity.

    a) Switch to Hyper-V Manager.

    b) Use the **Action** menu or the right-click menu in the **Hyper-V Manager** console to revert each of the VMs to their saved checkpoints.

Summary

In this lesson, you covered the core protocols and technologies used to enable host-to-host communications. You also learned about how the DNS service supports name resolution and the main configuration parameters for DNS servers.

- TCP provides connection-oriented, guaranteed delivery, while UDP provides connectionless, non-guaranteed delivery.
- TCP and UDP client and server processes use numbered ports. Well-known server ports up to 1023 and registered ports up to 49,151 are maintained by IANA.
- `netstat` can be used to investigate listening and active connections on the local machine, while Nmap is widely used for probing networks and hosts remotely.
- Protocol analysis is critical to network monitoring and troubleshooting.
- A computer can be configured with a host name to provide a simpler means for users to address the system on the network.
- An FQDN provides a unique identity for hosts communicating on an Internet.
- Name resolution services, such as DNS, map IP addresses to host names and FQDNs. DNS provides other record types to allow for the discovery of services such as email or SIP.
- `nslookup` and `dig` can be used to troubleshoot DNS.
- IPAM tools give administrators visibility into IP address allocation and usage.

How do you see yourself using the tools covered in this lesson (like `netstat`, Nmap, Wireshark, `nslookup`, and `dig`)?

Will your organization host its own DNS servers or rely on third-party DNS servers? Why?

 Practice Questions: *Additional practice questions are available on the course website.*

Lesson 7

Explaining Network Application and Storage Services

LESSON INTRODUCTION

You have identified the Physical, Data Link, Network, and Transport layer technologies and protocols that underpin basic connectivity. The TCP/IP protocol suite also includes application protocols that implement network services. The delivery of these services can be supported by technologies such as load balancing, virtualization, and storage networks. In this lesson, you will identify common network applications and service platforms.

LESSON OBJECTIVES

In this lesson, you will:

- Explain the uses of network applications.

- Explain the uses of voice services and advanced networking devices.

- Explain the uses of virtualization and network storage services.

- Summarize the concepts of cloud services.

Topic A

Explain the Uses of Network Applications

EXAM OBJECTIVES COVERED
1.1 Explain the purposes and uses of ports and protocols.
1.8 Explain the functions of network services.
5.5 Given a scenario, troubleshoot common network service issues.

So far, you have looked at lower-layer services that enable basic connectivity between nodes. Above these are the services that provide useful functions to users, such as email and web browsing. The services that form part of the TCP/IP protocol suite are mostly client-server protocols and applications. Client-server applications are based around a centralized server that stores information and waits for requests from clients. You need a good understanding of how these protocols are used so that you can support them on your networks.

SERVER MESSAGE BLOCK (SMB)

On a Windows® network, the **File/Print Sharing Service** is provided by the **Server Message Block (SMB)** protocol. SMB allows a machine to share its files and printers to make them available for other machines to use. Support for SMB in UNIX- or Linux-based machines and **network attached storage (NAS)** appliances is provided by using the Samba software suite, which allows a Windows client to access a UNIX® or Linux® host as though it were a Windows file or print server.

On legacy networks, SMB ran as part of the **NetBIOS** API on TCP port 139. If no legacy client support is required, however, SMB is more typically run directly over TCP port 445. SMB should be restricted to use only on local networks. It is important that any traffic on the NetBIOS port ranges (137-139 and 445) be blocked by a perimeter firewall.

NETWORK TIME PROTOCOL (NTP)

Many applications on networks are time-dependent and time-critical, such as authentication and security mechanisms, scheduling applications, and backup software. The **Network Time Protocol (NTP)** enables the synchronization of these time-dependent applications.

NTP works over UDP on port 123.

Top-level NTP servers (stratum 1) obtain the Coordinated Universal Time (UTC) from a highly accurate clock source, such as an atomic clock accessed over the **General Positioning System (GPS)**. Lower-tier servers then obtain the UTC from multiple stratum 1 servers and sample the results to obtain an authoritative time. Most organizations use one of these stratum 2 servers to obtain the time for use on their LANs. Examples include **time.google.com**, **time.windows.com**, **time.apple.com**, **time.nist.gov**, and **pool.ntp.org**.

Servers at lower tiers may then perform the same sort of sampling operation, adjust for the delay involved in propagating the signal, and provide the time to clients. Clients themselves usually obtain the time by using a modified form of the protocol called **Simple NTP (SNTP)**. SNTP works over the same port as NTP. In Windows, the Time

Service can be configured by using the `w32tm` command. In Linux, the ntp package can be configured via `/etc/ntp.conf`.

If a server or host is configured with the **incorrect time**, it may not be able to access network services. Authentication, and other security mechanisms will often fail if the time is not synchronized on both communicating devices. In this situation, errors are likely to be generic **failed** or **invalid token** type messages. Always try to rule out time synchronization as an issue early in the troubleshooting process.

HYPERTEXT TRANSFER PROTOCOL (HTTP)

Websites and web applications are perhaps the most useful and ubiquitous of network services. Web technology can be deployed for a huge range of functions and applications, in no way limited to the static pages of information that characterized the first websites. The foundation of web technology is the **HyperText Transfer Protocol (HTTP)**. HTTP enables clients (typically web browsers) to request resources from an HTTP server. A client connects to the HTTP server using an appropriate TCP port (the default is port 80) and submits a request for a resource, using a **Uniform Resource Locator (URL)**. The server acknowledges the request and responds with the data (or an error message).

 Note: *Technically, Uniform Resource Indicator (URI) is the preferred term. The use of URL is deprecated in standards documentation, though it's still widely used by the public. Refer to Daniel Miessler's blog (danielmiessler.com/study/url-uri) for more information.*

The response and request formats are defined in the HTTP header. The HTTP payload is usually used to serve HTML web pages, which are plain text files with coded tags (HyperText Markup Language) describing how the page should be formatted. A web browser can interpret the tags and display the text and other resources associated with the page, such as binary picture or sound files linked to the HTML page.

As with other early TCP/IP application protocols, HTTP communications are not secured.

HTTP also features a forms mechanism (POST) that enables a user to submit data from the client to the server. HTTP is a **stateless protocol**; this means that the server is not required to preserve information about the client during a session. However, the basic functionality of HTTP servers is also often extended by support for scripting and programmable features (web applications). Servers can also set text file **cookies** to preserve session information. Technologies such as **Java**™, ASP, and integration with databases increase flexibility and interactivity, but they also significantly increase security risks.

WEB SERVERS

Most organizations have an online presence, represented by a website. In order to run a website, it must be hosted on an HTTP server connected to the Internet. Larger organizations or SMEs with the relevant expertise may host websites themselves, but more typically, an organization will lease a server or space on a server from an ISP. The following types of hosting packages are common:

- Dedicated server—The ISP allocates your own private server computer. This type of service is usually unmanaged (or management comes at additional cost).
- Virtual Private Server (VPS)—The ISP allocates you a **virtual machine (VM)** on a physical server. This is isolated from other customer instances by the **hypervisor**.
- Cloud hosting—Your website is run on a cloud over several hardware computers, allowing more scalability if demand patterns change.

- Shared hosting—Your website is hosted within a private directory on a shared server. Performance can be severely affected by other sites hosted on the server, because all the sites are competing for the same resources.

When you are using an ISP, the degree to which the server may be customized, responsibility for security, and amount of technical support will all vary according to the contract terms. Greater flexibility may mean greater responsibility for securing the server.

 Note: *As with any third-party service, analyze the Service Level Agreement (SLA) to confirm what the ISP is contracted to do and satisfy yourself that these obligations are being met (for example, demand reports of backup operations, security patch management, effective account management, and so on).*

Running your own website gives complete control over the configuration of the server, but it also give you complete responsibility for its security (and the security of the private network behind it). The main web server platforms are:

- **Apache®**—Open source software and powerful, robust features combine to make this server the most popular. It is available for UNIX, Linux, Mac OS X®, and Windows, but it is most widely deployed on Linux. Apache accounts for about 50% of the most active websites.
- **Microsoft Internet Information Server (IIS)**—Bundled with Windows Server® (and client versions of Windows). IIS accounts for about 12% of busy sites.
- **nginx**—An open source web server and load balancer specially designed to cope with very high traffic. nginx ("Engine X") accounts for about 17% of the active sites.
- **Apache Tomcat®**—Used to host Java-based applications.

SECURE SOCKETS LAYER/TRANSPORT LAYER SECURITY (SSL/TLS)

One of the critical problems for the provision of early e-commerce sites was the lack of security in HTTP. Under HTTP, all data is sent unencrypted, and there is no authentication of client or server. **Secure Sockets Layer (SSL)** was developed by Netscape in the 1990s to address these problems. SSL proved very popular with the industry. **Transport Layer Security (TLS)** was developed from SSL and ratified as a standard by the IETF.

SSL/TLS works as a layer between the Application and Transport layers of the TCP/IP stack, or, in OSI terms, at the Session or Presentation layer. It's normally used to encrypt TCP connections. When it is used with the HTTP application, it is referred to as **HTTPS** or **HTTP Over SSL** or **HTTP Secure**, but it can also be used to secure other TCP application protocols, such as Telnet, FTP, NNTP, SMTP, and LDAP.

 Note: *TLS can also be used with UDP, referred to as **Datagram Transport Layer Security (DTLS)**, most often in virtual private networking (VPN) solutions.*

HTTP SECURE (HTTPS)

HTTP Secure (HTTPS) is a subset of HTTP that allows for a secure dialog between the client and server using SSL/TLS. To implement HTTPS, the web server is assigned a **digital certificate** by some trusted **certificate authority (CA)**. The **certificate** proves the identity of the server, assuming that the client also trusts the CA. The certificate is a wrapper for a public/private encryption key pair. The **private key** is kept a secret known only to the server; the **public key** is given to clients via the digital certificate.

The server and client use the key pair in the digital certificate and a chosen cipher suite within the SSL/TLS protocol to set up an encrypted tunnel. Even though someone else might know the public key, they cannot decrypt the contents of the tunnel without obtaining the server's private key. This means that the communications cannot be read or changed by a third party.

Encrypted traffic between the client and server is sent over TCP port 443 (by default), rather than the open and unencrypted port 80. A web browser will open a secure session to a server providing this service by using a URL starting with **https://** and it will also show a padlock icon in the address bar to indicate that the connection is secure. A website can be configured to require a secure session.

HTTPS padlock icon. (Screenshot used with permission from Microsoft.)

UNTRUSTED CERTIFICATE ISSUES

If the certificate presented by a subject (server or user) is not trusted by the client application (such as a browser), the client will notify the user. The most common reason for a certificate not to be trusted is that the certificate issuer is not trusted. For example, say Widget's web server receives a certificate signed by MyCA. Unless MyCA's own certificate is stored in the browser's trusted root store, the client application will not trust the Widget server. The user can usually choose to ignore this warning and add an exception, but this should be done only if the cause of the lack of a trust relationship is understood.

If you trust the issuer, you can add their certificate to the client device's **root certificate** store. In Windows, you can use the `certmgr.msc` console to manage user certificates and the `certlm.msc` console to manage machine certificates. You also use these consoles to manage certificates used by the computer or its **user accounts**.

One complication here is that different applications may have different stores of trusted certificates. For example, there is a Windows certificate store, but the Firefox® browser does not trust it by default and maintains its own certificate stores. The various Linux distributions store trusted root certificates in several different locations.

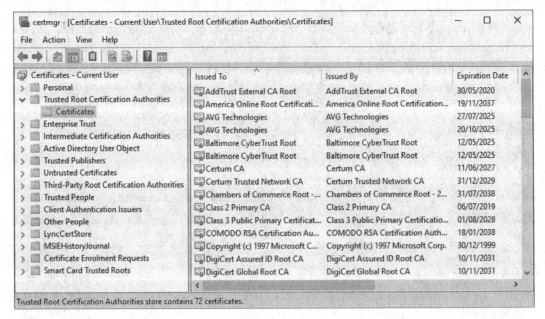

Certificate Management console. The Trusted Root CA contains all Microsoft and enterprise trusts, plus the third-party CA trusts. (Screenshot used with permission from Microsoft.)

Frequently, certificates are untrusted because they are **self-signed** (the certificate holder is both the issuer and the subject of the certificate). This is often the case with the certificates used to protect the web management interfaces of budget appliances and server applications. You might be able to replace the default certificate with one trusted by the enterprise.

Some other causes of untrusted certificates are:

- The certificate's subject name does not match the URL. This is usually a configuration error on the part of the web server manager, but it could indicate malicious activity. You should confirm the certificate's common name and access the website by using that URL.
- The certificate is not being used for its stated purpose. For example, a certificate issued to sign email is being used on a web server. In this circumstance, you should *not* add an exception. The service owner or subject should obtain a correctly formatted certificate.
- The certificate is expired or revoked. Again, unless there are explainable circumstances, you should not allow an exception. If you are managing a legacy appliance (a SOHO router or NAS drive, for instance), it is likely that the certificate installed on it will have expired. If you know that the appliance has not been tampered with, you can proceed.
- Time is not correctly synchronized between the server and client.

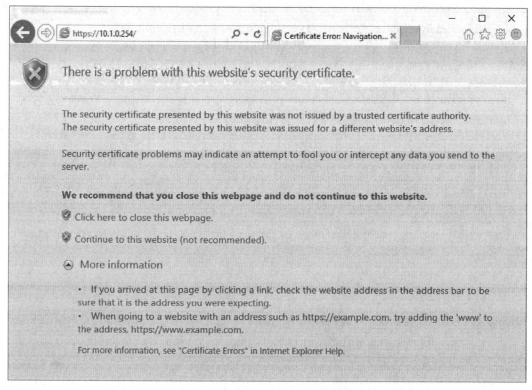

This certificate is not trusted because it is self-signed and because it does not match the subject name (because it is using an IP address instead of an FQDN). (Screenshot used with permission from Microsoft.)

Note: *Browsers and email applications usually display informative error messages. In other contexts, such as VPN authentication, it might not be so obvious that the certificate is the cause of the failure or why the certificate is being rejected. Inspect the logs recording the connection for clues.*

SIMPLE MAIL TRANSFER PROTOCOL (SMTP)

Electronic mail enables a person to compose a message and send it to another user on their own network (intranet) or anywhere in the world via the Internet.

The **Simple Mail Transfer Protocol (SMTP)** specifies how email is delivered from one system to another. It is a relatively straightforward protocol that makes the connection from the sender's server to that of the recipient and then transfers the message. The SMTP server of the sender discovers the IP address of the recipient SMTP server by using the domain name part of the email address. The SMTP server for the domain is registered in DNS using a **Mail Exchanger (MX)** record.

SMTP is not used for transferring the message from the recipient's SMTP server to its email client because it requires that both source and destination are online to make a connection. The SMTP server retries at regular intervals before timing out and returning a **non-delivery report (NDR)** to the sender. The NDR will contain an error code indicating the reason the item could not be delivered.

SMTP communications can (and should) be secured using the SSL/TLS version of the protocol (SMTPS). This works much like HTTPS with a certificate on the SMTP server and a negotiation between client and server about which cipher suites to use. There are two ways for SMTP to use TLS:

- STARTTLS—This is a command that upgrades an existing unsecure connection to use TLS. This is also referred to as **explicit TLS** or **opportunistic TLS**.

- SMTPS—This establishes the secure connection before any SMTP commands (HELO, for instance) are exchanged. This is also referred to as **implicit TLS**.

The STARTTLS method is generally more widely implemented than SMTPS. Typical SMTP configurations use the following ports and secure services:

- Port 25—Used for message relay between SMTP servers, or message transfer agents (MTAs). If security is required and supported by both servers, the STARTTLS command can be used to set up the secure connection.
- Port 587—Used by mail clients or message submission agents (MSAs) to submit messages for delivery by an SMTP server. Servers configured to support port 587 should use STARTTLS and require authentication before message submission.
- Port 465—Some providers and mail clients use this port for message submission over implicit TLS (SMTPS), though this usage is now deprecated by standards documentation.

 Note: Mail clients can use port 25 to submit messages to the server for delivery, but this is not best practice. Use of port 25 is typically reserved for relay between servers.

MAILBOX ACCESS PROTOCOLS

SMTP is useful only to deliver mail to hosts that are permanently available. Mail users require the convenience of receiving and reading their mail when they choose. A **mailbox** access protocol is designed to allow mail to be downloaded to the recipient's email client at his/her convenience.

POST OFFICE PROTOCOL (POP)

The **Post Office Protocol (POP)** is an early example of a mailbox protocol. POP is often referred to as **POP3** because the active version of the protocol is version 3. A POP client application, such as Microsoft Outlook® or Mozilla Thunderbird®, establishes a connection to the POP server on TCP port 110. This can be a different service running on the same machine as the SMTP server. The user is authenticated (by username and password), and the contents of his or her mailbox are downloaded for processing on the local PC. Generally speaking, the messages are deleted from the server when they are downloaded, though some clients have the option to leave messages on the server.

Like other TCP application protocols, unless an encryption service is configured, POP transfers all information as cleartext. This means anyone able to monitor the session would be able to obtain the user's credentials. POP can be secured by using SSL/TLS. The default TCP port for secure POP (POP3S) is port 995.

INTERNET MESSAGE ACCESS PROTOCOL (IMAP)

POP has some significant limitations, some of which are addressed by the **Internet Message Access Protocol (IMAP)**. Clients connect to an IMAP server over TCP port 143. They authenticate themselves and then retrieve messages from the designated folders. SMTP is still needed to support mail delivery. Like POP, IMAP is a mail retrieval protocol, but with mailbox management features lacking in POP.

POP is primarily designed for **dial-up** access; the client contacts the server to download its messages, and then disconnects. IMAP supports permanent connections to a server and connecting multiple clients to the same mailbox simultaneously. It also allows a client to manage the mailbox on the server (to organize messages in folders and to control when they are deleted, for instance) and to create multiple mailboxes.

As with the other email protocols, the connection can be secured by establishing an SSL/TLS tunnel. The default port for IMAPS is TCP port 993.

```
GNU nano 2.2.2          File: /etc/dovecot/dovecot.conf              Modified

protocols = imap imaps
#protocols = none

# A space separated list of IP or host addresses where to listen in for
# connections. "*" listens in all IPv4 interfaces. "[::]" listens in all IPv6
# interfaces. Use "*, [::]" for listening both IPv4 and IPv6.
#
# If you want to specify ports for each service, you will need to configure
# these settings inside the protocol imap/pop3/managesieve { ... } section,
# so you can specify different ports for IMAP/POP3/MANAGESIEVE. For example:
  protocol imap {
    listen = *:143
    ssl_listen = *:943
  }
#  protocol pop3 {
#    listen = *:10100
#    ..
#  }
#  protocol managesieve {
#    listen = *:12000
#    ..
#  }
#listen = *

# Disable LOGIN command and all other plaintext authentications unless
                          [ Read 1280 lines ]
^G Get Help   ^O WriteOut   ^R Read File   ^Y Prev Page   ^K Cut Text    ^C Cur Pos
^X Exit       ^J Justify    ^W Where Is    ^V Next Page   ^U UnCut Text  ^T To Spell
```

Configuring mailbox access protocols on a server. (Screenshot courtesy of Mozilla Foundation.)

Note: *To learn more, watch the related* **Video** *on the course website.*

Activity 7-1

Discussing the Uses of Network Applications

SCENARIO

Answer the following questions to test your understanding of the content covered in this topic.

1. **What is SNTP?**

2. **What must be installed on a server to use secure (HTTPS) connections?**

3. **What happens if a message sent via SMTP cannot be delivered?**

4. **What protocol would enable a client to manage mail subfolders on a remote mail server?**

Activity 7-2

Configuring Application Protocols

BEFORE YOU BEGIN

Start the VMs used in this activity in the following order, adjusting the memory allocation first if necessary, and waiting at the ellipsis for the previous VMs to finish booting before starting the next group. You do not need to connect to a VM until prompted to do so in the activity steps.

1. **RT1-LOCAL** (256 MB)
2. **RT2-ISP** (256 MB)
3. **RT3-INT** (256 MB)
4. **LAMP** (512—1024 MB)
5. **DC1** (1024—2048 MB)
6. ...
7. **MS1** (1024—2048 MB)
8. ...
9. **PC1** (1024—2048 MB)
10. **PC2** (512—1024 MB)

 Note: *If you can allocate more than the minimum amounts of RAM, prioritize* **PC1** *and* **PC2**.

SCENARIO

In this activity, you will configure a mail client and examine the effect of using unsecured protocols. This activity is designed to test your understanding of and ability to apply content examples in the following CompTIA Network+ objective:

- 1.1 Explain the purposes and uses of ports and protocols.

---

1. Configure the mail client (Mozilla Thunderbird) on the **PC1** VM for the domain account **Sam**, and examine the connection process in Wireshark.

   The mail server on **MS1** does not have any connection security configured.

   a) Open a connection window for the **PC1** VM, and log on with the credentials **Sam** and **Pa$$w0rd**

   b) Start a **Wireshark** capture on the **Ethernet** interface with the following filter:

   ```
   port 25 or port 143 or port 587 or port 465 or port 993 or
   port 53
   ```

   These are the default ports for secure and unsecure SMTP and IMAP, plus DNS.

   c) On the desktop, double-click the **Mozilla Thunderbird** icon.

   d) When Thunderbird starts, if prompted, select **Set as Default** at the prompt (you may only see this dialog box after configuring the account).

   e) In the **Set Up an Existing Email Account** dialog box, for **Email address**, type **sam@515support.com** and for **Password**, type **Pa$$w0rd**

   f) Select **Continue**.

g) When the mail servers are discovered, select the **Done** button.

 Note: *If there are problems configuring mail, verify that the DHCP and hMailServer services on **MS1** are started.*

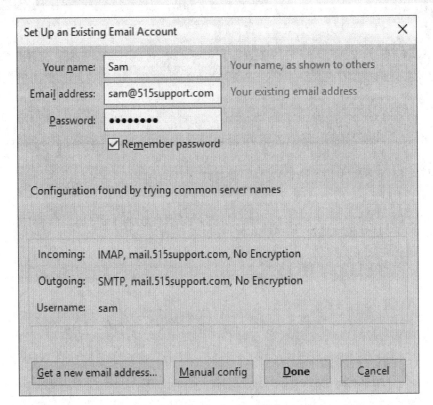

An email client can try to guess the server for a domain by querying common names such as mail, imap, pop, and smtp. In this case, mail is the correct choice! (Screenshot courtesy of Mozilla Foundation.)

h) Read the warning message, then check the **I understand the risks** check box and select **Done**.

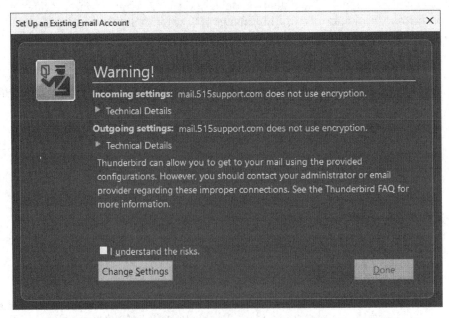

Unsecure connection warning. (Screenshot courtesy of Mozilla Foundation.)

i)   In **Thunderbird**, in the **System Integration** dialog box, select **Set as Default**, then select the **Inbox**, and then select the **Write** button. Create a message addressed to ***sam@515support.com*** with the subject ***test*** and send it.

The self-addressed message should come through.

2.   Analyze the traffic captured by Wireshark to identify the risks from running unsecure protocols.

a)   Stop the Wireshark capture, and view the first part of the output.

You should see:

- DNS queries to locate the mail servers. The client is looking for A (host) records, not MX records, because this is to configure an account, not transfer email. You should see quite a lot of extra traffic as Thunderbird tries to locate the various Internet sites that it can normally contact.
- DNS responses from 10.1.0.1 identifying that the host record **mail. 515support.com** can be found at **10.1.0.2**.
- An SMTP session where the mail client says **hello** (or more technically **EHLO**) to the SMTP server at 10.1.0.2 to verify it is available and to figure out the configuration parameters. This connection takes place on server port 25.
- A similar exchange established with the IMAP server.
- Further SMTP and IMAP sessions where the client authenticates with the servers to process the mail message that was composed and sent. These connections to SMTP use port 587.

b)   Right-click the first non-DNS packet and select **Follow→TCP Stream**. Select the **Up arrow** on the **Stream** spin box in the bottom-right to browse through the series of connections (some will be blank, as there is no application data exchange).

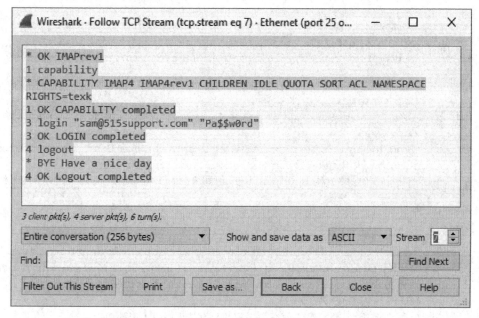

Browsing the TCP sessions established with the mail server. (Screenshot courtesy of Wireshark.)

You should discover that, for one thing, the IMAP server is unfailingly polite, and for another, the account credentials are easily discoverable. You are sniffing your own host's traffic here, but there are means for attackers to sniff the same packets. With account passwords, you must also consider the possibility of rogue administrators.

Regardless of how protected you think a private network is, credentials should **never** be exchanged in cleartext like this. You will configure connection security later in the activity.

c)   Select the **Close** button. In the **Filter** bar, select the **Clear** button.

d)   Leave the Wireshark window open.

e) In **Thunderbird**, compose and send another **Test** message, but address it to **hostmaster@515web.net**

3. Configure the mail client on the **PC2** VM to connect to the mail services hosted by **LAMP**.

In this case, the connections are protected by TLS. You will be using the PC2 VM as a client on the "internet." Recall the activity topology, summarized here:

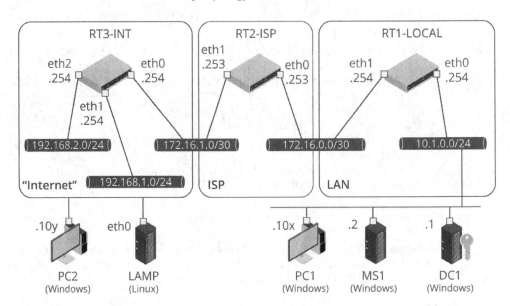

Activity environment topology. The LAMP web and email server hosting a 515web.net domain is located on the 192.168.1.0/24 subnet, while the MS1 VM provides email services for the 515support.com email domain. There are no firewalls to worry about. (Image © 123RF.com.)

a) Open a connection window for the **PC2** VM. In the **PC2** VM console window, select **File→Settings**.

b) Select the **Network Adapter** node. From the **Virtual switch** box, select **vINT02**. Select **OK**.

c) From the log on screen, select **Switch User** then **Other User**. Log on as **.\Admin** with the password **Pa$$w0rd**

d) Start a **Wireshark** capture on the **Local Area Connection** adapter with the following filter:

```
port 25 or port 143 or port 587 or port 465 or port 993
```

e) On the desktop, double-click the **Mozilla Thunderbird** icon.

f) When Thunderbird starts, if displayed, select **Set as Default** at the prompt.

g) In the **Set Up an Existing Mail Account** dialog box, type **hostmaster** in the **Your name** box—note that this is case-sensitive. For **Email address**, type **hostmaster@515web.net**

h) Leaving the **Password** text box blank, select **Continue**.

i) When the mail servers are discovered, select the **Done** button.

j)   In the **System Integration** dialog box, select **Set as Default**.

The mail server presents a certificate to identify itself and encrypt the communications channel. This certificate is encountered on port 143.

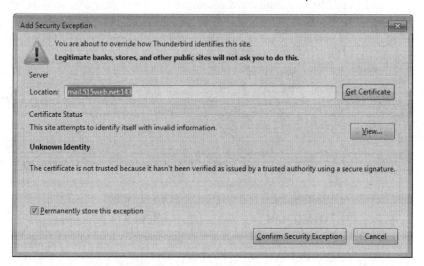

Thunderbird does not automatically trust the certificate presented by the LAMP mail server.
(Screenshot courtesy of Mozilla Foundation.)

k)   In the **Add Security Exception** dialog box, select the **View** button.

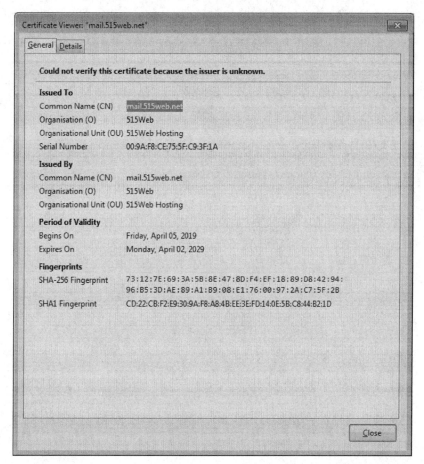

Certificate details—The owner and issuer are the same entity (self-signed). (Screenshot
courtesy of Mozilla Foundation.)

Since the certificate is self-signed, you would have to use an out-of-band method to determine whether it is trustworthy.

l) Select **Close** then, in the **Add Security Exception** dialog box, select **Confirm Security Exception**.

m) Select the **Inbox** folder. In the **Mail Server Password Required** box, type *Pa$$w0rd* and check the **Use Password Manager to remember this password** check box, and then select **OK**.

n) The **Test** message from the sam@515support.com account should come through. Send a **reply** to the message.

   At first, the message will not be sent.

o) In the **Send Message Error** dialog box, review the message, then select **OK**. Switch to the **Inbox - Mozilla Thunderbird** window where the **Add Security Exception** dialog box is open, and select **Confirm Security Exception**.

   This is the same certificate, but this time it is for port 25 (SMTP).

p) Switch back to the message window and send the message. When you are prompted by the **SMTP Server Password Required** dialog box, provide the password *Pa$$w0rd*

   Mail servers shouldn't really accept submissions from clients on this port.

q) Switch to **Wireshark** and stop the capture.

r) View the **TCP streams** to compare the capture to what you saw before. The first part is much the same as the client works out the connection parameters in cleartext. When it comes to exchanging credentials, though, the **STARTTLS** command is used and an encrypted session set up. None of the data exchange is decipherable.

4. Discard changes made to the VMs in this activity.

a) Switch to Hyper-V Manager.

b) Use the **Action** menu or the right-click menu in the **Hyper-V Manager** console to revert all the VMs to their saved checkpoints.

Topic B

Explain the Uses of Voice Services and Advanced Networking Devices

EXAM OBJECTIVES COVERED
1.1 Explain the purposes and uses of ports and protocols.
1.3 Explain the concepts and characteristics of routing and switching.
2.2 Given a scenario, determine the appropriate placement of networking devices on a network and install/configure them.
2.3 Explain the purposes and use cases for advanced networking devices.
5.3 Given a scenario, troubleshoot common wired connectivity and performance issues.

The use of IP voice and video services is now common in homes and in many workplaces. These real-time applications bring their own challenges for network architecture, and you will often need to implement advanced networking devices to support them.

VOICE OVER IP (VoIP)

Voice over IP (VoIP), **web conferencing**, and **video teleconferencing (VTC)** solutions have become the standard method for the provision of business communications over the last decade, as the network technologies that support them have become faster, more reliable, and cheaper. The main challenges that these applications have in common is that they transfer real-time data and must create point-to-point links between hosts on different networks. **Real-time services** are those that require response times measured in milliseconds (ms), because delayed responses will result in poor call or video quality. This type of data can be one-way, as is the case with media streaming, or two-way, as is the case with VoIP and VTC.

VoIP can provide both short-range and long-haul communications, so it can replace traditional telephone links by converting and then transmitting analog voice communications to digital signals sent over data cabling. As in a typical packet-switched network, digital signals are broken down into packets, to transmit voice as data. After reassembling the packets, the digital signals are reconverted into audio signals. Because voice communications are time-sensitive, the system must ensure that packets arrive complete and in sequence.

Using VoIP, voice software interfaces with an analog voice device, such as a microphone, to convert the analog voice into a data signal and to translate the dialing destination into a network address. When you make a telephone call, the network connection transmits signals over data networks, and transfers them to the standard phone system if the called party does not have a VoIP service. Conversely, when you dial a number that maps to a VoIP device, VoIP routes the call to the IP host. VoIP relies on the existing, robust infrastructure of IP networks and the near-universal implementation of IP. It also eliminates per-call costs, especially for long-distance calls, because it uses data channels to transmit voice signals

There are numerous ways of implementing VoIP. In the past, proprietary protocols specific to the software vendor were used, but most modern IP telephony solutions use Session Initiation Protocol (SIP) both for internal and public (trunk) telephone calls.

Note: *To learn more, watch the related **Video** on the course website.*

PRIVATE BRANCH EXCHANGES (PBX/VoIP PBX)

A residential telephone installation would be serviced by a simple box providing a one- or two-line analog interface to the local exchange. Each line provides a single channel for an incoming or outgoing call. A typical business requires tens or hundreds of lines for voice communications, let alone capacity for data communications. Historically, this requirement would have been facilitated by a digital trunk line, also referred to as a Time Division Multiplexing (TDM) circuit. A TDM can multiplex separate voice and data channels for transmission over a single cable.

A **private branch exchange (PBX)** is an automated switchboard providing a single connection point for an organization's voice lines. A TDM-based PBX connects to the telecommunications carrier over a digital trunk line, which will support multiple channels (inward and outward calls). The PBX allows for the configuration of the internal phone system to direct and route calls to local extensions, and provides other telephony features such as call waiting, music on hold, and voice mail.

This type of PBX is being replaced by hybrid and fully IP/VoIP PBX. A VoIP PBX maintains a list of the internal accounts assigned to user endpoint devices. For internal calls and conferences, the PBX establishes the connection between local VoIP endpoints with data transmitted over the local Ethernet network. A VoIP PBX can also route incoming and outgoing calls with external networks. This might involve calls between internal and external VoIP endpoints, or with voice telephone network callers and receivers. A VoIP PBX will also support features such as music on hold and voice mail.

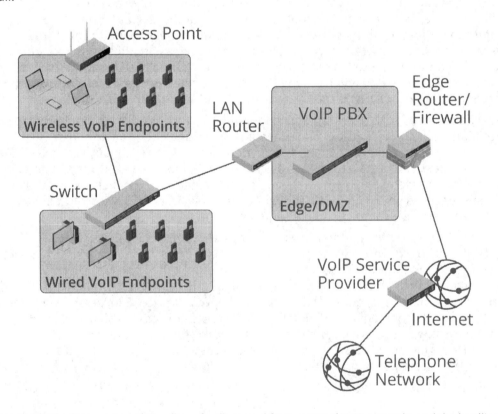

A VoIP PBX facilitates internal IP calls and calls to and from external VoIP networks and the landline and cellular telephone networks.

A TDM PBX is supplied as vendor-specific hardware. A VoIP PBX can be implemented as software running on a Windows or Linux server. Examples of software-based solutions include 3CX (*3cx.com*) and Asterisk (*asterisk.org*). There are also hardware solutions, where the VoIP PBX runs on a router, such as Cisco Unified Communications Manager (*cisco.com/c/en/us/products/unified-communications/unified-communications-manager-callmanager/index.html*).

A VoIP PBX would normally be placed at the network edge and be protected by a firewall. Internal clients connect to the PBX over Ethernet data cabling and switching infrastructure, using Internet Protocol (IP) at the Network layer for addressing. The VoIP PBX uses the organization's Internet link to connect to a VoIP service provider, which facilitates inward and outward dialing to voice-based telephone networks.

VoIP GATEWAYS

While many implementations depend on a service provider to facilitate connections between the local VoIP system and the voice telephone network, there can also be requirements for on-premise integration between data and voice networks and equipment. A **VoIP gateway** is a means of translating between a VoIP system and voice-based equipment and networks, such as public switched telephone network (PSTN) lines. There are many types of VoIP gateways, serving different functions. For example, a company may use VoIP internally, but connect to the telephone network via a gateway. To facilitate this, you could use a hybrid or hardware-based VoIP PBX with a plug-in or integrated VoIP gateway, or you could use a separate gateway appliance. There are analog and digital types to match the type of incoming landline. An analog version of this type of gateway is also called a **Foreign Exchange Office (FXO) gateway**.

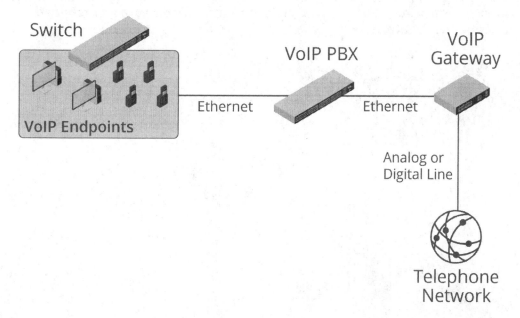

VoIP gateway connecting a local network using VoIP calling to the ordinary telephone network.

A VoIP gateway can also be deployed to allow a legacy analog or digital internal phone system to use a VoIP service provider to place calls. In this type of setup, low rate local and national calls might be placed directly, while international calls that would attract high charges if placed directly are routed via the VoIP service provider.

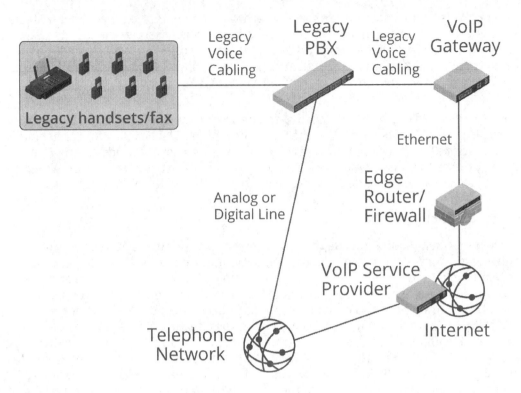

VoIP gateway connecting a local network using legacy PBX and handsets to a VoIP service provider.

Finally, a VoIP gateway or adapter can be used to connect legacy analog handsets and fax machines to a VoIP PBX. This type of device is also called a **Foreign Exchange Subscriber (FXS) gateway**.

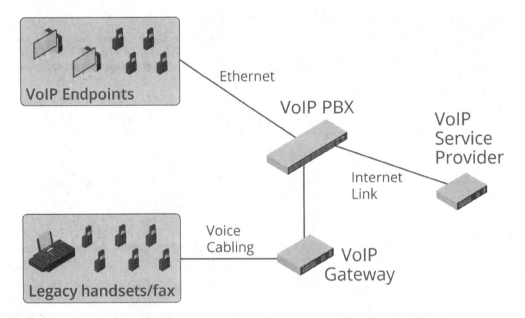

VoIP gateway connecting legacy handsets to a VoIP PBX.

REAL-TIME SERVICES PROTOCOLS

The protocols designed to support real-time services cover one or more of the following functions:

- Session control—Used to establish, manage, and disestablish communications sessions. They handle tasks such as user discovery (locating a user on the network), availability advertising (whether a user is prepared to receive calls), negotiating session parameters (such as use of audio/video), and session management and termination.
- Data transport—Handles the delivery of the actual video or voice information.
- **Quality of Service (QoS)**—Provides information about the connection to a QoS system, which in turn ensures that voice or video communications are free from problems, such as dropped packets, delay, or jitter.

SESSION INITIATION PROTOCOL (SIP) AND VoIP ENDPOINTS

The **Session Initiation Protocol (SIP)** is one of the most widely used session control protocols. SIP endpoints are the end-user devices (also known as **user agents**), such as IP-enabled handsets or client and server web conference software. Each device, conference, or telephony user is assigned a unique SIP address known as a SIP Uniform Resource Indicator (URI). Examples of SIP URIs include:

- sip:bob.dobbs@comptia.org
- sip:2622136227@comptia.org
- sip:bob.dobbs@2622136227
- meet:sip:organizer@comptia.org;ms-app=conf;ms-conf-id=subg42

*Note: There is also a **tel:** URI scheme allowing SIP endpoints to dial a landline or cell phone. A **tel:** URI can either use the global (E.164) format (such as tel:+1-866-8358020) or a local format (for internal extensions).*

SIP typically runs over UDP or TCP ports 5060 (unsecured) and 5061 (SIP-TLS). SIP has its own reliability and retransmission mechanisms and can thus be seen to benefit most from the lower overhead and reduced latency and jitter of UDP. Some enterprise SIP products use TCP anyway.

A **VoIP/SIP endpoint** can be implemented as software running on a computer or smartphone or as a dedicated hardware handset. SIP endpoints can establish communications directly in a peer-to-peer architecture, but it is more typical to use intermediary servers, **directory** servers, and VoIP gateways. Many VoIP/SIP handsets are connected to the corporate network over "normal" data ports but assigned to separate virtual LANs (VLAN) than other data traffic. In many cases, VoIP has been implemented into network infrastructures that were originally designed for just desktop and laptop computers, with limited numbers of network access ports. Most SIP endpoints use VLAN tagging to ensure that the SIP control and Real Time Transport (RTP) media protocols can be segregated from normal data traffic. Handsets use Power over Ethernet (PoE), if available, to avoid the need for separate power cabling or batteries. There are also wireless handsets that work over 802.11 Wi-Fi networks.

Connection security for VoIP works in a similar manner to HTTPS. To initiate the call, the secure version of SIP (SIPS) uses digital certificates to authenticate the endpoints and establish an SSL/TLS tunnel. The secure connection established by SIPS can also be used to generate a master key to use with the secure versions of the transport and control protocols.

When you are installing a new handset, you should also test that the connection works and that the link provides sufficient call quality. Most service providers have test numbers to verify basic connectivity and perform an echo test call, which replays a message you record so that you can confirm voice quality.

REAL-TIME TRANSPORT PROTOCOL (RTP) AND RTP CONTROL PROTOCOL (RTCP)

While SIP provides session management, the actual delivery of real-time data uses different protocols. The principal one is **Real-time Transport Protocol (RTP)**. RTP enables the delivery of a stream of media data via UDP, while implementing some of the reliability features usually associated with TCP communications. The data is packetized and tagged with control information (sequence numbering and timestamping). UDP is used to minimize overhead and because some of the reliability features of TCP could adversely affect the quality of a media stream. For example, if a single packet from a voice stream is lost, the effect of simply ignoring the lost data (which may only correspond to a small fraction of a second) is less noticeable than pausing the entire stream while waiting for a retransmit.

RTP does not guarantee reliability or real-time delivery. In fact, depending on the underlying network technology, this may be impossible to achieve. Instead, RTP works closely with the **RTP Control Protocol (RTCP)**. Each RTP stream uses a corresponding RTCP session to monitor the quality of the connection and to provide reports to the endpoints. These reports can then be used by the applications to modify codec parameters or by the network stacks to tune **Quality of Service (QoS)** parameters.

RTP and RTCP use a sequential pair of UDP ports, with RTP using an even numbered port and the corresponding RTCP session using the next higher odd numbered port. UDP ports 5004 (RTP) and 5005 (RTCP) are reserved for this purpose, although in practice RTP typically uses an even-numbered ephemeral UDP port, with RTCP again using the next higher port number. This is to allow for multiple streams on a single endpoint, which would not be possible with a fixed port number.

H.323

H.323 is an alternative session control protocol to SIP. It predates SIP, having been first standardized by the ITU-T in 1996, although the current version was published in 2009. In the H.323 model, endpoints (known as **terminals**) connect to gatekeepers in order to request services. When used for standard VoIP communications, the respective gatekeepers of the two endpoints communicate to establish whether the connection will be allowed, and then the endpoints communicate directly with one another to establish the session. When used in videoconferencing, devices known as Multipoint Control Units (MCUs) provide conference facilities such that one or more gatekeepers can enable sessions from multiple terminals to be established to a multipoint conference on a single MCU.

The H.323 architecture also allows for gateways. These gateways enable non-H.323 networks, such as the telephone network, to connect to the H.323 network and access the services provided.

H.323 primarily uses TCP port 1720, although UDP ports 1718 and 1719 are used for associated functions.

QUALITY of SERVICE (QoS), LATENCY, AND JITTER

Quality of Service (QoS) protocols and appliances are designed to support real-time services on packet-switched networks. Applications such as voice and video that carry real-time data have different network requirements to the sort of data represented by file transfer. With "ordinary" data, it might be beneficial to transfer a file as quickly as possible, but the sequence in which the packets are delivered and the variable intervals between packets arriving do not materially affect the application. This type of data transfer is described as **bursty**.

While streaming video applications (and especially High Definition video) can have a high bandwidth requirement in terms of the sheer amount of data to be transferred, bandwidth on modern networks is typically less of a problem than packet loss, latency, and jitter.

 Note: *Bandwidth required for video is determined by image resolution (number of pixels), color depth, and the frame rate, measured in frames per second (fps). Bandwidth for audio depends on the sampling frequency (Hertz) and bit depth of each sample. Bandwidth consumption can be reduced by compressing the data stream, but most effective compression routines reduce quality.*

LATENCY AND JITTER

Problems with the timing and sequence of packet delivery are defined as latency and jitter. **Latency** is the time it takes for a transmission to reach the recipient, measured in milliseconds (ms). **Jitter** is defined as being a variation in the delay. Jitter manifests itself as an inconsistent rate of packet delivery. Jitter is also measured in milliseconds, using an algorithm to calculate the value from a sample of transit times.

Latency and jitter are not significant problems when data transfer is bursty, but real-time applications are much more sensitive to their effects because they manifest as echo, delay, and video slow down. If packets are delayed, arrive out of sequence, or are lost, then the receiving host must buffer received packets until the delayed packets are received. If packet loss or delay is so excessive that the buffer is exhausted, then noticeable audio or video problems (artifacts) are experienced by users.

LATENCY AND JITTER TROUBLESHOOTING

You can test the latency of a link using tools such as `ping`, `pathping`, and `mtr`. You can also use `mtr` to calculate jitter. When assessing latency, you need to consider the Round Trip Time (RTT). VoIP is generally expected to require an RTT of less than 300 ms. Jitter should be 30 ms or less. The link should also not exhibit more than 1% packet loss. Bandwidth requirements for voice calling can vary, but allowing 100 Kbps per call upstream and downstream should be sufficient in most cases.

On a local network, latency and jitter are caused by congestion. This means that the network infrastructure is not capable of meeting the demands of peak load. You can either provision higher bandwidth links and/or faster switches and routers, or you can use some sort of traffic prioritization. Latency and jitter on the Internet are much more difficult to control because of the number of different parties that are involved (both caller networks plus any ISP transit networks).

DiffServ/IEEE 802.1p

Latency and jitter might be caused by transient cable or interference problems. It may also be the case that link bandwidth is simply insufficient for the voice or video application being deployed. Rather than invest in an upgraded link, it may be possible to mitigate performance problems by using **Quality of Service (QoS)** mechanisms.

If you are running VoIP over your network and someone decides to copy a 40 GB file down from a server, the file transfer has the potential to wreak havoc with VoIP call quality. Without QoS, switches and routers forward traffic based on best effort or first-in, first-out, meaning that frames or packets are forwarded in the order in which they arrive. A QoS system identifies the packets or traffic streams belonging to a specific application, such as VoIP, and prioritizes them over other applications, such as file transfer.

The **Differentiated Services (DiffServ)** framework (*RFC 2474*) classifies each packet passing through a device. Router policies can then be defined to use the packet classification to prioritize delivery. DiffServ is an IP (layer 3) service tagging mechanism. It uses the **Type of Service** field in the IPv4 header (**Traffic Class** in IPv6) and renames it the **Differentiated Services** field. The field is populated with a 6-byte **DiffServ Code Point (DSCP)** by either the sending host or by the router. Packets with the same DSCP and destination are referred to as **Behavior Aggregates** and allocated the same Per Hop Behavior (PHB) at each DiffServ-compatible router.

While DiffServ works at layer 3, IEEE 802.1p can be used at layer 2 (independently or in conjunction with DiffServ) to classify and prioritize traffic passing over a switch or wireless access point. 802.1p defines a tagging mechanism within the 802.1Q VLAN field (it also often referred to as 802.1Q/p). The 3-bit priority field is set to a value between 0 and 7. 7 is reserved for network infrastructure (routing table updates), 6-5 for 2-way communications, 4-1 for streaming multimedia, and 0 for "ordinary" best-effort delivery.

 Note: *As well as invoking the priority tag, VLAN infrastructure is often used for traffic management on local networks. For example, voice traffic might be allocated to a different VLAN than data traffic.*

While DSCP allows for far more traffic classes (64) than 802.1p (8), most vendors map DSCP values to 802.1p ones. DiffServ traffic classes are typically grouped into three types:

- Best Effort;
- Assured Forwarding (which is broken down into sub-levels); and
- Expedited Forwarding (which has the highest priority).

When setting up QoS, you need to ensure that router and layer 3 switches that forward based on DiffServ values have mapping or forwarding tables that match the options being used, otherwise priority traffic can be handled as Best Effort. SIP traffic is typically tagged as Assured Forwarding, while RTP is normally tagged as Expedited Forwarding.

QUALITY OF SERVICE (QoS) VS. CLASS OF SERVICE (CoS) AND TRAFFIC SHAPING

There is a distinction to be made between **Quality of Service (QoS)** and **Class of Service (CoS)**. CoS mechanisms such as DiffServ and 802.1p just categorize protocols into groups that require different service levels and provide a tagging mechanism to identify a frame or packet's class. QoS allows fine-grained control over traffic parameters. For example, if a network link is congested, there is nothing that DiffServ and 802.1p can do about it, but a protocol such as **Multiprotocol Label Switching (MPLS)** with QoS functionality can reserve the required bandwidth and pre-determine statistics such as acceptable packet loss and maximum latency and jitter when setting up the link.

In terms of QoS, network functions are commonly divided into three planes:

- **Control plane**—makes decisions about how traffic should be prioritized and where it should be switched.
- **Data plane**—handles the actual switching of traffic.
- **Management plane**—monitors traffic conditions.

Protocols, appliances, and software that can apply these three functions can be described as **traffic shapers** or **bandwidth shapers**. Traffic shapers enable administrators to closely monitor network traffic and to manage that network traffic. The primary function of a traffic shaper is to optimize network media throughput to get the most from the available bandwidth. Simpler devices, performing traffic **policing**, do not offer the enhanced traffic management functions of a shaper. For example, typical traffic policing devices will simply fail to deliver packets once the configured traffic threshold has been reached (this is often referred to as **tail drop**). Consequently, there will be times when packets are being lost, while other times when the network is relatively idle, and the bandwidth is being under-utilized. A smoothing device will store packets until there is free bandwidth available. Hopefully, this leads to consistent usage of the bandwidth and few lost packets.

 Note: It is essential that the selected device is capable of handling high traffic volumes. As these devices have a limited buffer, there will be situations when the **buffer overflows***. Devices can either drop packets and in essence provide traffic policing, or else they must implement a dropping algorithm. Random Early Detection (RED) is one of several algorithms that can be implemented to help manage traffic overflow on the shaper.*

Traffic shapers delay certain packet types—based on their content—to ensure that other packets have a higher priority. This can help to ensure that latency is reduced for critical applications. This traffic management function can take place on the originating host, or source, but is more usually implemented at the network edge—that is, the perimeter network.

ISPs implement traffic shaping in order to provide premium services to consumers, such as low-latency gaming or a guarantee of a defined QoS. Shaping can also be used to help identify undesirable traffic and drop those packets. This will reduce the overall load on the network. Shaping can help ISPs manage file sharing download activities, for instance. These high throughput activities can be detrimental to applications that require low latency. By implementing bandwidth shaping, ISPs can reduce excessive bandwidth consumption during peak times and allow for more download bandwidth during less busy times.

BOTTLENECKS AND LOAD BALANCERS

Where a network has high bandwidth requirements or applications that are sensitive to latency, performance problems could be exacerbated by a **bottleneck**. A bottleneck is a link or forwarding/processing node that becomes overwhelmed by the volume of traffic. This means that systems behind the bottleneck are underutilized compared to 100% utilization of the bottleneck link or system. As well as measuring utilization statistics, you can identify a bottleneck using a tool such as `pathping` or `mtr`. Hops within the local network that exhibit slower response times should be investigated as bottlenecks.

A bottleneck could be eased by upgrading the affected link or system, but if this is not possible, additional links and systems can be added and the service managed by a load balancer. A **load balancer** distributes client requests across available server nodes in a farm or pool. Clients use the single name/IP address of the load balancer to connect to the servers in the farm. This provides for higher throughput or supports more connected users. A load balancer also provides fault tolerance. If there are multiple servers available in a farm, all addressed by a single name/IP address via a load balancer, then if a single server fails, client requests can be routed to another server in the farm.

You can use a load balancer in any situation where you have multiple servers providing the same function. Examples include web servers, front-end email servers, and web conferencing, A/V conferencing, or streaming media servers. Each server node or instance needs its own IP address, but externally, the service is advertised using a **virtual IP (VIP) address** (or addresses). There are different protocols available to handle VIP addresses, and they differ in the ways that the VIP responds to ARP and ICMP and in compatibility with services such as NAT and DNS. One of the most widely used protocols is the **Common Address Redundancy Protocol (CARP)**. There is also Cisco's proprietary **Gateway Load Balancing Protocol (GLBP)**.

There are two main types of load balancers:

- Layer 4 load balancer—Early instances of load balancers would base forwarding decisions on IP address and TCP/UDP port values (working at up to layer 4 in the

OSI model). This type of load balancer is stateless; it cannot retain any information about user sessions.

- Layer 7 load balancer (content switch)—As web applications have become more complex, modern load balancers need to be able to make forwarding decisions based on Application-level data, such as a request for a set of URLs or data types like video or audio streaming. This requires more complex logic, but the processing power of modern appliances is sufficient to deal with this.

Most load balancers need to be able to provide some or all of the following features:

- Configurable load—The ability to assign a specific server in the farm for certain types of traffic or a configurable proportion of the traffic.
- Prioritization—To filter and manage traffic based on its priority.
- TCP offload—The ability to group HTTP packets from a single client into a collection of packets assigned to a specific server.
- SSL offload—When you implement SSL/TLS to provide for secure connections, this imposes a load on the web server (or another server). If the load balancer can handle the processing of authentication and encryption/decryption, this reduces the load on the servers in the farm.
- Caching—As some information on the web servers may remain static, it is desirable for the load balancer to provide a caching mechanism to reduce load on those servers.
- URL writing—Changing the URL requested by a client on the fly can be performed to disguise the actual location of content, make a complex URL more readable, perform Search Engine Optimization (SEO), and disguise active content to make attacking the server more difficult (rewriting .php file extensions to .html, for instance).

A load balancer could be implemented as software running on a Windows or Linux host, but because of the performance demands placed on these devices, it is much more common for them to be implemented as advanced switching devices.

MULTILAYER SWITCHES

The basic function of an Ethernet switch is **microsegmentation**: that is, putting each port in its own collision domain so that the effect of contention on the network is eliminated and two hosts can in effect establish point-to-point, full-duplex links. Microsegmentation describes switching at layer 2 of the OSI model. Many switches can perform routing between subnets mapped to virtual LANs (VLANs), operating at layer 3.

Load balancing switches and **content switches** (or **multilayer switches**) provide switching functionality higher up the OSI model, at layer 4 or at layers 4-7, respectively. In TCP/IP terms, these are the Transport (TCP) and Application (HTTP) layers. A content switch may also be referred to as a web or application switch. Layer 4 or 4-7 switches are used for load balancing applications, typically for the web (HTTP and HTTPS) or SSL-based VPNs, although they can be used to switch for any specified TCP or UDP port. The operation of the switch is typically transparent to the clients and servers. To ensure that the client workstations connecting through a content switch are unaware of which server they are connected to, most content switches perform some sort of address translation (NAT).

In a common scenario, a multilayer switch would be the interface for a server farm. The switch facilitates connections between clients and servers to optimize performance. This load balancing can take place using defined metrics and rule sets. A layer 4 switch applies these rules by inspecting the TCP segment while a layer 4-7 switch can be configured with rules relating to the headers and possibly content of application-layer packets. For example, rich media such as pictures or Flash video could be served from a separate server pool than the basic HTML. Layer 7 switching allows more fine-grained control but is consequently more difficult to configure, slower, and requires more expensive hardware.

While layer 2 and 3 switches are measured by frame or packet throughput, layer 4 and content switches deal with **sessions**. The key performance criteria are the number of sessions per second that can be established and the number of simultaneous sessions that can be supported. As sessions tend to be short-lived, the first factor is typically more important.

Note: *Remember that a connection is usually established for the transfer of a single file, so downloading a typical web page would require several connections to be established by a single client. However, many content switches can perform TCP multiplexing to consolidate multiple connection requests from individual clients.*

A content switch may be implemented as a standalone appliance or as a plug-in module for an enterprise-class layer 2/3 switch.

Activity 7-3

Discussing the Uses of Voice Services and Advanced Networking Devices

SCENARIO

Answer the following questions to test your understanding of the content covered in this topic.

1. **True or False? SIP enables the location of user agents via a specially formatted URI.**

2. **Which component in a VoIP network allows calls to be placed to and from the voice telephone or public switched telephone network (PSTN)?**

3. **How is jitter mitigated by a VoIP application?**

4. **How many different traffic classes can be defined by 802.1Q/p?**

5. **How does a traffic shaper benefit real-time data applications?**

6. **What would be a typical scenario for implementing a content switch?**

Topic C

Explain the Uses of Virtualization and Network Storage Services

EXAM OBJECTIVES COVERED
2.4 Explain the purposes of virtualization and network storage technologies.

Virtualization technology is now a mainstream feature of networks. There are different types of virtualization and several methods of networking with virtualized components. It is important to understand them if you want to implement virtualization in your environment. You will also describe various network storage technologies. Different technologies of varying scope can be used for implementing network storage. When planning a network storage solution, you need to understand the strengths of each type to ensure you select the solution that best fits your needs.

VIRTUALIZATION TECHNOLOGIES

For most of the history of the microcomputer, a single computer has been able to run a single operating system at any one time. This makes multiple applications available on that computer (whether it be a workstation or server), but the applications must all share a common environment. **Virtualization** means that multiple operating systems can be installed and run simultaneously on a single computer. There are many ways of implementing this and many different reasons for doing so. A virtual platform requires at least three components:

- Host(s)—The platform that will host the virtual environment. Optionally, there may be multiple computers networked together.
- Hypervisor or virtual machine monitor (VMM)—Manages the virtual environment and facilitates interaction with the computer hardware and network.
- Guest operating systems or virtual machines (VMs)—Operating systems installed under the virtual environment. The number of operating systems is generally only restricted by hardware capacity.

The presence of other guest operating systems can be completely transparent to any single OS. Each OS is allocated CPU time and memory space, which it uses as though they were physical components. The guest is allocated a hard disk, which is actually an image file on the host. The guest will also have one or more virtualized network adapters, which are configured in much the same way as regular NICs. The guest operating systems can be networked together or may be able to share data directly through the hypervisor, though for security reasons, this is not commonly allowed.

Virtualization technologies can serve several purposes:

- Server consolidation—A typical hardware server may have resource utilization of about 10%. This implies that you could pack the server computer with another 8 or 9 server software instances and obtain the same performance. This saves on equipment costs and can reduce energy consumption.
- **Virtual Desktop Infrastructure (VDI)**—Provision client desktop instances as VMs. This allows low-cost thin client PC hardware to be deployed and provides better management over desktop configuration and **updates**.

- Application virtualization—Software is run on the server and either accessed by a remote desktop client or streamed to the client PC.
- Legacy/development/test environment—VMs can be deployed to support test and development environments that should not be allowed access to the main data network. It can also be used to run legacy applications on older OS versions.

HYPERVISOR TYPES

One basic distinction that can be made between virtual platforms is between host and bare metal methods of interacting with the host hardware. In a **guest OS** (or **host-based**) system, the hypervisor application (known as a **Type II hypervisor**) is itself installed onto a **host operating system**.

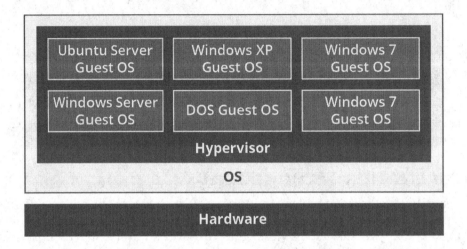

Guest OS virtualization (Type II hypervisor). The hypervisor is an application running within a native OS, and guest OSes are installed within the hypervisor.

Examples of host-based hypervisors include VMware Workstation™, Oracle® Virtual Box, and Parallels® Workstation. The hypervisor software must support the host OS.

A **bare metal** virtual platform means that the hypervisor (**Type I hypervisor**) is installed directly onto the computer and manages access to the host hardware without going through a host OS.

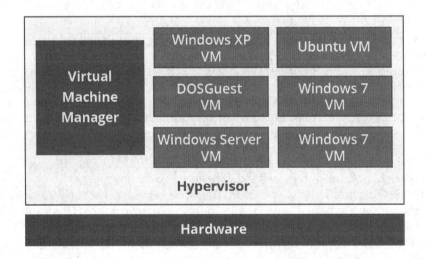

Type I bare metal hypervisor. The hypervisor is installed directly on the host hardware along with a management application, then VMs are installed within the hypervisor.

Examples include VMware ESXi® Server, Microsoft's Hyper-V®, and Citrix's XEN Server. The hardware needs to support only the base system requirements for the hypervisor plus resources for the type and number of guest OSes that will be installed.

VIRTUAL NICs AND SWITCHES

Where multiple VMs are running on a single platform, virtualization provides a means for these VMs to communicate with each other and with other computers on the network (both physical and virtual) by using standard networking protocols. The guest OS running in each virtual machine is presented with an emulation of a standard hardware platform and for the most part is unaware that it is not running on an actual physical machine. Among the hardware devices emulated will be one or more network adapters. The number of adapters and their connectivity can typically be configured within the hypervisor.

Within the VM, the **virtual NIC** will look exactly like an ordinary network adapter and will be configurable in the same way. For example, protocols and services can be bound to it, and it can be assigned an IP address. In other words, a virtual NIC functions identically to a physical NIC for data transmission; it is just wholly software-based instead of being a combination of physical hardware, **firmware**, and driver software.

Typically, a hypervisor will implement network connectivity by means of one or more **virtual switches** (or vSwitch in VMware's terminology). These perform the same function as layer 2 physical switches, except that they are implemented in software instead of hardware. Connectivity between the virtual network adapters in the guest VMs and the virtual switches is configured via the hypervisor. This is analogous to connecting patch cables between real computers and real switches. Multiple VMs may be connected to the same virtual switch or to separate switches. The number of virtual switches supported varies from one hypervisor to another.

In this networking model, the VMs and the virtual switch can all be contained within a single hardware platform, so no actual network traffic is generated; instead, data is moved from buffers in one VM to another. It is also possible to configure connectivity with a virtual switch that bridges the virtual and physical networks via the host computer's physical NIC. For example, in Microsoft's Hyper-V virtualization platform, three types of virtual switches can be created:

- External—Binds to the host's NIC to allow the VM to communicate on the physical network via a bridge.
- Internal—Creates a bridge that is usable only by VMs on the host and the host itself. This type of switch does not permit access to the wider physical network.
- Private—Creates a switch that is usable only by the VMs. They cannot use the switch to communicate with the host.

 Note: When the VMs are permitted to interact with a "real" network, the host must support a high bandwidth, high availability network link. Any failure of the physical link will affect multiple VMs.

Virtual switches can be as simple or complex as the hypervisor software makes them. As you can see from the screenshot, they can be used to implement VLANs. In a more advanced network, such as VMware's vSphere, you could also have virtual switches that can connect guests running on multiple hosts and configure advanced switching, such as QoS and traffic shaping.

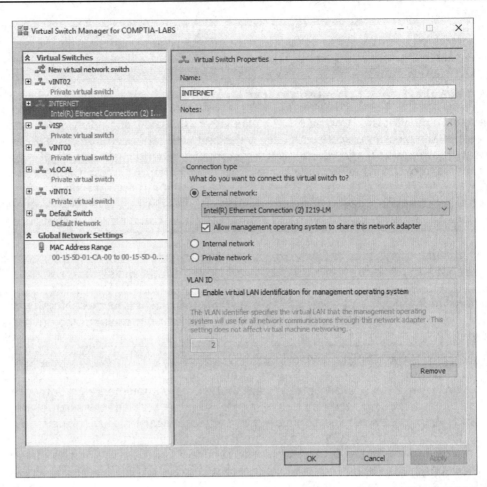

Configuring a virtual switch in Microsoft's Hyper-V hypervisor. The external switch allows the VM to use the physical network via the host's NIC. The private switches have no external access. (Screenshot used with permission from Microsoft.)

VIRTUAL ROUTERS AND FIREWALLS

When a VM is joined to a virtual switch, the MAC address for its virtual NIC is configured via the hypervisor. The VM must be configured with an appropriate IP address for the subnet it is in. If the VM needs a link to other networks, it must be assigned a default gateway. You might also want to configure security for the network link, such as implementing a firewall. None of the requirements of a virtual network are different than physical networks.

You can configure the VM's IP parameters statically, or you can use DHCP. You could provision a DHCP server as a VM on the virtual network, or the VM could use the physical network's ordinary DHCP server. With some types of virtual switch that bridge VMs to the physical network, the hypervisor can implement a DHCP and/or network address translation (NAT) service to VMs.

 Note: *You must also provision DNS and time synchronization services for the virtual network.*

Any guest Linux or Windows Server VM can be configured as a router for a VM network. Similarly, either OS (or third-party software installed under the guest VM) could be used to implement a firewall. The VMs have the same functionality as software installed on real computers.

It is also possible to provision virtual appliances. With a virtual appliance, the vendor either develops a software product that emulates the functions of an existing hardware appliance (router, firewall, packet shaper, or malware/intrusion detection, for instance) or creates software that implements that kind of functionality in a new product.

A virtual firewall that is deployed into the virtualized infrastructure as a logical network object is described as working in **bridged mode**. This replicates the way a firewall might be deployed on a physical network. Traffic passing over the virtual network logically passes through the virtual firewall. A virtual firewall can also be deployed in kernel or hypervisor mode. This means that the firewall is inspecting data directly as it is being processed, by being granted privileged access to the hypervisor's kernel processes. This type of access is faster, and it can be considered more secure, as the firewall is completely abstracted from the network environment.

STORAGE VIRTUALIZATION

Another element in a virtual platform is **storage virtualization**. In a virtual storage platform, a software layer is inserted between client OSes and applications and the physical storage medium—a **storage area network (SAN)**. This abstraction makes it easier to expand or shrink storage capacity allocated to any given client without having to reconfigure the client. It can also simplify operations such as backup, replication, and migration by consolidating data storage in one physical location.

One of the problems in data storage is data duplication. This refers to the way a single data file may get duplicated in multiple locations, through user file copy actions, attaching the file to email, and making backups. Each instance of the file takes up a chunk of storage space. **Data deduplication** refers to techniques to consolidate multiple copies of the same file in a single location. Data deduplication is greatly facilitated by storage virtualization, as each user reference to a file can point to the same physical file location (without the user having to track where this might be).

Storage virtualization also assists the implementation of tiered storage hierarchies. The principle here is of where to store archived information. An **offline storage** medium might require physical interaction to access the data, such as putting a tape into a drive. **Nearline storage** refers to technology such as tape loaders or "slow" hard disk media that can operate in low-power states.

NETWORK STORAGE TYPES

Traditional server-based (or direct-attached) storage means that the data a server hosts is stored on its internal hard drives or on a USB or eSATA external device connected only to that server. Such **direct-attached storage** creates certain problems:

- It is resource-inefficient because while some servers have space free, others may be running low on storage capacity.
- Traditional storage creates unplanned redundancy, because multiple instances of files can exist on multiple servers.
- Cross-platform sharing of data (for example, Linux and Windows) can be complex because the file system may only be accessible to one type of client.

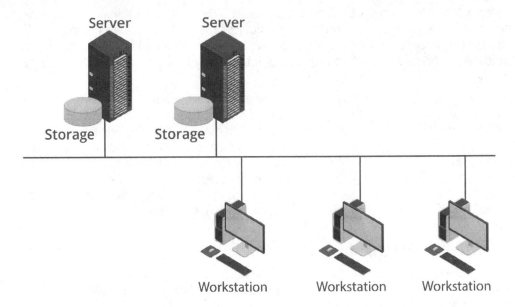

Traditional server direct attached storage. (Image © 123RF.com.)

Vendors have been coming up with methods for attaching storage devices to the network for shared use by servers and clients. These are usually divided into **network attached storage (NAS)** solutions and **storage area networks (SAN)** solutions.

NETWORK ATTACHED STORAGE (NAS)

A **network attached storage (NAS)** appliance is a hard drive (or RAID array) with a cut-down server board, usually running some form of Linux, that provides network access, various file sharing protocols, and a web management interface. The appliance is accessed over the network, either using a wired Ethernet port—in a SOHO network, you would plug it into an Ethernet port on the Internet router—or Wi-Fi. At layer 3, the NAS device is allocated an IP address. The device may also be allocated a host name and DNS host record to make it easier for users to connect to the device.

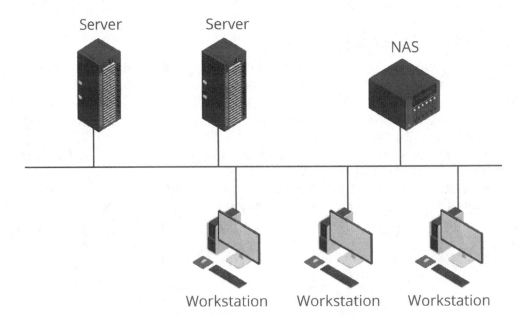

Network attached storage. (Image © 123RF.com.)

The principal characteristic of NAS is that it uses file-based protocols such as Network File System (NFS), Server Message Block/Common Internet File System (SMB/CIFS), Apple Filing Protocol (AFP), File Transfer Protocol (FTP), and HyperText Transport Protocol (HTTP). Each network host accesses the NAS independently.

STORAGE AREA NETWORKS (SANs)

Where NAS is typified as providing access to clients at **file level** (File I/O), in a **storage area network (SAN)**, access is provided at **block level**. Each read or write operation addresses the actual location of data on the media (Block I/O). This is much more efficient for database applications, as it does not mean copying the whole file across the network to access a single record.

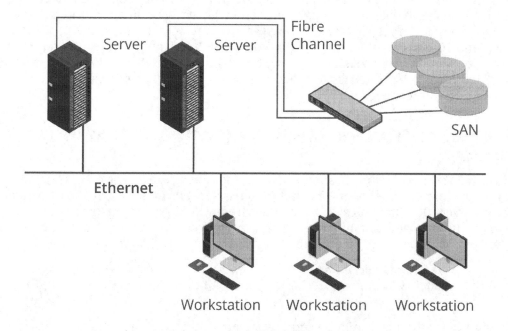

Storage area network. (Image © 123RF.com.)

A SAN can integrate different types of storage technology—RAID arrays and tape libraries, for instance. It can contain a mixture of high-speed and low-cost devices, allowing for tiered storage to support different types of file access requirements without having to overprovision high-cost, fast drives. Unlike NAS, the SAN is isolated from the main network. It is only accessed by servers, not by client workstations. A SAN can be implemented using a variety of technologies, but the most popular are high bandwidth Fibre Channel and InfiniBand fiber optic networks.

A SAN can provide robust and extensible storage solutions for local networks and for remote storage but at greater cost than NAS. NAS provides a cheap storage solution and is very easy to set up. Consequently, SANs are typically deployed in enterprise networks and data centers, while NAS is more of a small office or workgroup solution.

FIBRE CHANNEL (FC)

A SAN based on a **Fibre Channel (FC) Switched Fabric (FC-SW)** involves three main types of components:

- Initiator—This is a host bus adapter (HBA) installed in the file or database server.
- Target—The network port for a storage device. Typical devices include single drives, RAID drive arrays, tape drives, and tape libraries. Space on the storage devices is divided into logical volumes, each identified by a 64-bit logical unit number (LUN). The initiator will use SCSI, Serial Attached SCSI (SAS), or SATA commands to operate

the storage devices in the network, depending on which interface they support. Most devices have multiple ports for load balancing and fault tolerance.

The initiators and targets are identified by 64-bit WorldWide Names (WWN), similar to network adapter MAC addresses. Collectively, initiators and targets are referred to as **nodes**. Nodes can be allocated their own WWN, referred to as a WWNN (WorldWide Node Name). Also, each port on a node can have its own WorldWide Port Name (WWPN).

- FC switch—This provides the interconnections between initiators and targets (a **fabric**). The switch topology and interconnections would be designed to provide multiple paths between initiators and targets, allowing for fault tolerance and load balancing. High performance FC switches are often referred to as directors.

Fibre Channel is defined in the T11 ANSI standard. The spelling "fibre" is deliberately used to distinguish the standard from fiber optic cabling, which it often uses but on which it does not rely. The standard **transfer rates** are 1GFC (1 Gbps), 2GFC, 4GFC, 8GFC, and 16GFC. Two other rates (10GFC and 20GFC) use different encoding and are incompatible with devices supporting only the standard rates. Using fiber optic cabling, an FC fabric can be up to 10 km (6 miles) in length using single mode cable or 500 m (1640 ft) using multimode cable.

FIBRE CHANNEL over ETHERNET (FCoE) AND JUMBO FRAMES

Provisioning separate Fibre Channel adapters and cabling is expensive. As its name suggests, **Fibre Channel over Ethernet (FCoE)** is a means of delivering Fibre Channel packets over 10G Ethernet cabling, NIC/HBAs [referred to as converged network adapters (CNAs)], and switches. FCoE uses a special frame type, identified by the EtherType value 0x8096. The protocol maps WWNs onto MAC addresses.

 Note: FCoE does not quite run on standard Ethernet. It requires QoS mechanisms to ensure flow control and guaranteed delivery. FCoE compliant products are referred to as lossless Ethernet, Data Center Ethernet, or Converged Enhanced Ethernet.

Ordinarily, an Ethernet frame can carry a data payload or maximum transmission unit (MTU) of up to 1,500 bytes. When you are transferring data around a SAN with a 10 Gbps switching fabric, a 1500-byte limit means using a lot of frames. A **jumbo frame** is one that supports a data payload of up to around 9,000 bytes. This reduces the number of frames that need to be transmitted, which can reduce the amount of processing that switches and routers need to do. It also reduces the bandwidth requirement somewhat, as fewer frame headers are being transmitted. The benefits of jumbo frames are somewhat disputed, however.

When implementing jumbo frames, it is critical that all hosts and appliances (switches and routers) along the communications path be able and configured to support them. It is also vital to ensure that each device supports the same MTU. Also, it can be complex to calculate the MTU if any additional headers are used (for IPSec, for instance).

InfiniBand

InfiniBand is a high-speed switching fabric representing another way to create a SAN and a direct competitor to FC and Ethernet-based technologies. The latest Enhanced Data Rate (EDR) adapters support up to 100 Gbps unidirectional throughput. As it was designed from the outset as a switched fabric (where Ethernet has evolved from a shared access medium), InfiniBand has delivered faster port speeds, is lower latency, and provides better support for QoS mechanisms.

Hosts connect to the fabric via a Host Channel Adapter (HCA), while storage devices are attached using Target Channel Adapters (TCA).

iSCSI

Internet Small Computer System Interface (iSCSI) is an IP tunneling protocol that enables the transfer of SCSI data over an IP-based network. iSCSI works with ordinary Ethernet network adapters and switches. It could be deployed with bonded Gigabit links or with Ethernet 10G adapters and switches.

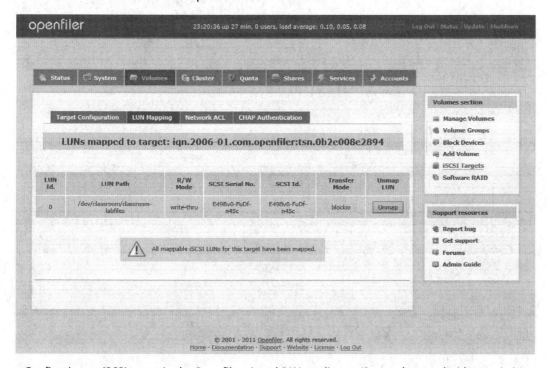

Configuring an iSCSI target in the Openfiler virtual SAN appliance. (Screenshot used with permission from Openfiler LTD.)

iSCSI can be used to link SANs but is also seen as an alternative to Fibre Channel itself, as it does not require FC-specific switches or adapters.

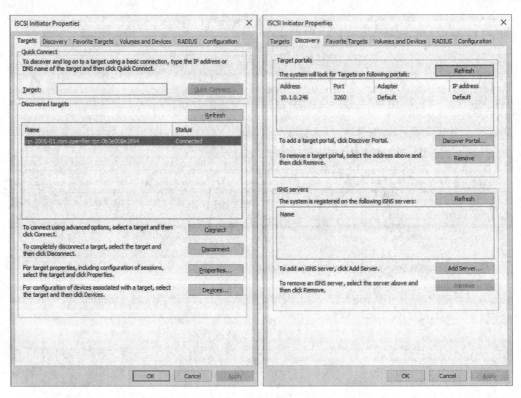

Connecting to the iSCSI target using an iSCSI initiator in Windows Server. (Screenshot used with permission from Microsoft.)

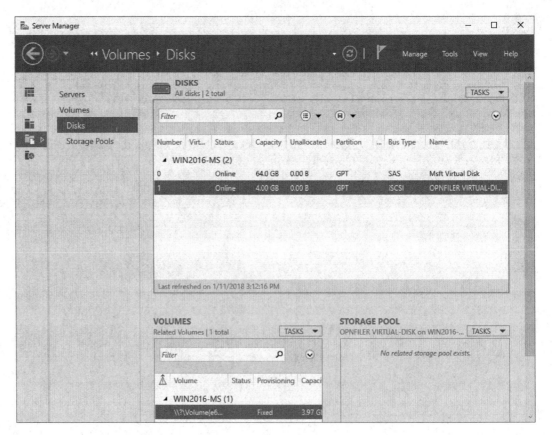

Once connected, the OS can use the storage just like a disk drive. Here is a volume formatted with NTFS. (Screenshot used with permission from Microsoft.)

Note: *To learn more, watch the related* **Video** *on the course website.*

Activity 7-4

Discussing the Uses of Virtualization and Network Storage Services

SCENARIO
Answer the following questions to test your understanding of the content covered in this topic.

1. **What is a hypervisor?**

2. **If a VM is connected to a bridged virtual switch, what sort of network access does it have?**

3. **What are the main differences between NAS and SAN?**

4. **What protocol can be used to implement a SAN without provisioning dedicated storage networking adapters and switches?**

5. **Is InfiniBand a competitor technology to Fibre Channel or an upgrade path allowing integration with legacy infrastructure?**

6. **What is the MTU of a jumbo frame compared to a regular Ethernet frame?**

Topic D

Summarize the Concepts of Cloud Services

EXAM OBJECTIVES COVERED
1.7 Summarize cloud concepts and their purposes.

Cloud services allow companies to outsource computing power and network/application infrastructure and are becoming more popular all the time. Cloud computing encompasses different implementations and services. If you plan to use a cloud service, you need to know what the choices are and the advantages and disadvantages. Having a solid grasp of these choices will enable you to better manage and implement these technologies in your environment.

CLOUD COMPUTING

From the consumer point of view, **cloud computing** is a service that provides on-demand resources—server instances, data storage, databases, or applications—over a network, typically the Internet. The service is a **cloud** because the end user is not aware of or responsible for any details of the procurement, implementation, or management of the infrastructure that underpins those resources. The end user is interested in and pays for only the services provided by the cloud.

Among other benefits, the cloud provides **rapid elasticity**. This means that the cloud can scale quickly to meet peak demand. For example, a company may operate a single web server instance for most of the year but provision additional instances for the busy-period and then release them again in the New Year. This example also illustrates the principles of **on-demand** and **pay-per-use**; key features of a cloud service, as opposed to a hosted service. On-demand implies that the customer can initiate service requests and that the cloud provider can respond to them immediately. Pay-per-use implies a **measured service**, so that the customer is paying for the CPU, memory, disk, and network bandwidth resources they are actually consuming, rather than paying a monthly fee for a particular service level.

From the provider point of view, provisioning a cloud is like provisioning any other type of large-scale data center. Cloud computing almost always uses one or more methods of virtualization to ensure that resources are quickly and easily provisioned to the client who requires them. The security implications of virtualization are therefore closely tied to the security implications of the cloud. In order to respond quickly to changing customer demands, cloud providers must be able to provision resources quickly. This is achieved through **resource pooling** and **virtualization**. Resource pooling means that the hardware making up the cloud provider's data center is not dedicated or reserved to a single customer account. The layers of virtualization used in the cloud architecture allow the provider to provision more CPU, memory, disk, or network resource using management software, rather than (for instance) having to go to the data center floor, unplug a server, add a memory module, and reboot.

Note: *The NIST Definition of Cloud Computing (nvlpubs.nist.gov/nistpubs/Legacy/SP/nistspecialpublication800-145.pdf) provides an authoritative definition of what is a cloud service (and what isn't).*

CLOUD DELIVERY MODELS

In most cases, the **cloud**—that is, the hardware and/or software hosting the service—will be **offsite** relative to the organization's users. The cloud users will typically require an Internet link to access the cloud services. There can be different ownership and access arrangements for clouds, however, which can be broadly categorized as:

- Public (or multi-tenant)—Hosted by a third party and shared with other subscribers. This is what many people consider cloud computing to be. As a shared resource, there are risks regarding performance and security.
- Hosted Private—Hosted by a third party for the exclusive use of the organization. This is more secure and can guarantee a better level of performance, but it is correspondingly more expensive.
- Private—Cloud infrastructure that is completely private to and owned by the organization. In this case, there is likely to be one business unit dedicated to managing the cloud while other business units make use of it. With private cloud computing, organizations can exercise greater control over the privacy and security of their services. This type of delivery method is geared more toward banking and governmental services that require strict access control in their operations.

   This type of cloud could be on-premise or offsite relative to the other business units. An onsite link can obviously deliver better performance and is less likely to be subject to outages (loss of an Internet link, for instance). On the other hand, a dedicated offsite facility may provide better shared access for multiple users in different locations.
- Community—This is where several organizations share the costs of either a hosted private or fully private cloud. This is usually done in order to pool resources for a common concern, like standardization and security policies.
- Hybrid—A cloud computing solution that implements some sort of hybrid public/private/community/hosted/onsite/offsite solution. For example, a travel organization may run a sales website for most of the year using a private cloud but "break out" the solution to a public cloud at times when much higher utilization is forecast. As another example, a hybrid deployment may be used to provide some functions via a public cloud, but keep sensitive or regulated infrastructure, applications, and data on-premises. Flexibility is a key advantage of cloud computing, but the implications for data risk must be well understood when you are moving data between private and public storage environments.

 *Note: It is important to understand that the term **cloud** is a reference to an abstraction layer over a set of computing resources. When discussing systems as being on-premise, hosted, or in the cloud, there is a very similar set of infrastructures behind it all. A single server farm could be sold to one (internal) customer as an on-premise offering, another customer as a hosted offering, and yet another customer as a cloud offering. This terminology is all a matter of perspective and access to these resources, and the cloud is not any more inherently secure than the servers in the data center down the hall or the hosting company next door.*

CLOUD SERVICE TYPES

As well as the ownership model—public, private, hybrid, or community—cloud services are often differentiated on the level of complexity and pre-configuration provided. These models are referred to as **Something as a Service (*aaS)**, where the *something* can refer to infrastructure, platform, or software.

INFRASTRUCTURE AS A SERVICE

Infrastructure as a Service (IaaS) is a means of provisioning IT resources such as servers, load balancers, and storage area network (SAN) components quickly. Rather than purchase these components and the Internet links they require, you rent them on an as-needed basis from the service provider's data center. Examples include Amazon Elastic Compute Cloud (*aws.amazon.com/ec2*), Microsoft® Azure® Virtual Machines (*azure.microsoft.com/services/virtual-machines*), and OpenStack® (*openstack.org*).

SOFTWARE AS A SERVICE

Software as a Service (SaaS) is a different model of provisioning software applications. Rather than purchasing software licenses for a given number of seats, a business would access software hosted on a supplier's servers on a pay-as-you-go or lease arrangement (on-demand). Virtual infrastructure allows developers to provision on-demand applications much more quickly than previously. The applications can be developed and tested in the cloud without the need to test and deploy on client computers. Examples include Microsoft Office 365® (*support.office.com*), Salesforce® (*salesforce.com*), and Google G Suite™ (*gsuite.google.com*).

PLATFORM AS A SERVICE

Platform as a Service (PaaS) provides resources somewhere between SaaS and IaaS. A typical PaaS solution would provide servers and storage network infrastructure (as per IaaS) but also provide a multi-tier web application/database platform on top. This platform could be based on Oracle® or MS SQL or PHP and MySQL™. Examples include Oracle Database (*cloud.oracle.com/paas*), Microsoft Azure SQL Database (*azure.microsoft.com/services/sql-database*), and Google App Engine™ (*cloud.google.com/appengine*).

As distinct from SaaS though, this platform would not be configured to actually do anything. Your own developers would have to create the software (the CRM or e-commerce application) that runs using the platform. The service provider would be responsible for the integrity and availability of the platform components, but you would be responsible for the security of the application you created on the platform.

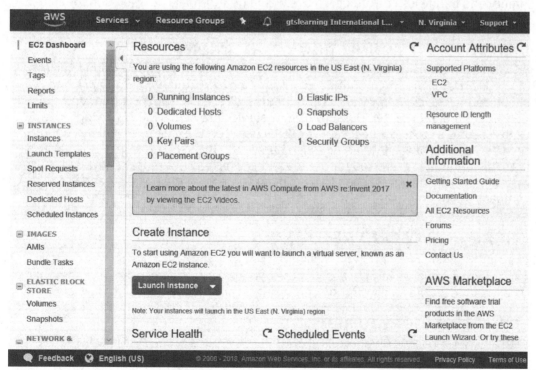

Dashboard for Amazon Web Services Elastic Compute Cloud (EC2) IaaS/PaaS. (Screenshot courtesy of Amazon.)

CLOUD STORAGE

Cloud storage is a type of SaaS where the vendor provides reliable data storage and backup. Many cloud storage solutions are combined with content management tools that offer document permission, version history, and collaborative editing features.

CONNECTIVITY WITH THE CLOUD

The last decade has seen a massive growth in cloud computing. This also presents many challenges to administrators integrating cloud services into an enterprise network infrastructure. One of these issues is the mechanism by which clients connect to the cloud service. As with any contracted service, cloud computing is a means of transferring responsibilities from the organization's own infrastructure and, therefore, some of the risks. However, these resources must also be accessible in a timely, secure fashion to ensure business operations are not affected.

Connectivity with cloud-based services is always going to involve some tradeoffs but should consider price, bandwidth, latency (delay), and availability. In practical terms, there are a few options for connecting an organization's staff with cloud-based services.

INTERNET/VIRTUAL PRIVATE NETWORK (VPN)

The simplest way of interfacing with a cloud service is to use the provider's website or application programming interface (API) over the Internet. This type of connection can also be implemented as a virtual private network (VPN), if this is supported by the cloud service provider. The VPN method has the advantages of being cost-effective and straightforward to set up wherever there is Internet connectivity, which is ideal for organizations that have a fragmented or distributed network structure. However, any connection running over the public Internet can suffer from poor performance due to latency and bandwidth throttling, so this would not normally be a solution for a mission critical or high-volume application.

DIRECT/PRIVATE CONNECTION/CO-LOCATION

Co-location within a data center offers a higher bandwidth solution by providing a direct or private link. The customer establishes infrastructure within a data center supported by the cloud provider or provisions a direct link from his or her enterprise network to the data center, possibly using a service provider's MPLS network. The data center installs a cross-connect cable or VLAN between the customer and the cloud provider, establishing a low latency, high bandwidth (typically up to 10 Gbps), secure link. This solution is preferred for organizations which have a more centralized operation where the connection to the cloud can be from the main HQ and the company's own enterprise network is used to allow branch locations access.

LOCAL AND CLOUD RESOURCES

One of the challenges with a cloud solution is managing local and cloud-based data. This topic can cover several issues, but the two fundamental ones are deciding what data must be stored locally and synchronizing locally cached data with the cloud.

LOCAL STORAGE REQUIREMENTS

With any cloud-based solution, it is likely that some parts of the system will require data to be stored and accessed within the company's enterprise network. So, while the applications may be run as a SaaS, the data these applications work with never leaves the company network. This would typically apply where the data is too sensitive to consider having it leave the company's private network/equipment or where a **risk assessment** has determined that the threats to this data and the management of it cannot be entrusted to the service provider.

SYNCHRONIZATION AND VERSION CONTROL

Most cloud-based systems, while typically storing both software and data on a remote service provider's network, still use local CPU, RAM, and disk cache resources to help smooth out any latency or network connectivity issues. Without these facilities, cloud services would suffer from pauses and interruptions. The problem is that caching can cause issues with data and file synchronization and version control, especially where files are accessible to several users simultaneously.

Similar issues can also occur where some information is stored in the remote cloud and some within the enterprise network. This can often be the case with large database systems. SQL Data Sync, which is part of Microsoft's Azure SQL Database, is an example of a facility that helps to achieve this.

Any cloud-based solution must offer robust **document management**, marking, and versioning to ensure that data is not updated or overwritten with an older version. Many systems also have background synchronization services which ensure local cached copies are synchronized with the cloud copy in as timely a fashion as possible.

SECURITY AND RESILIENCE

One of the risks of using a cloud-based solution is that potentially confidential or commercially secret data may be transferred on connection links that extend beyond the enterprise's infrastructure and direct control. As such, it is imperative to identify precisely which risks you are transferring; to identify which responsibilities the service provider is undertaking, and which remain with you. This should be set out in a **service level agreement (SLA)**.

For example, in a SaaS solution, the provider may be responsible for the **confidentiality**, integrity, and availability of the software. They would be responsible for configuring a fault tolerant, clustered server service; for firewalling the servers and creating proper authentication, authorization, and accounting procedures; for scanning for intrusions and monitoring network logs; applying OS and software **patches**; and so on. You may or may not be responsible for some or all of the software management functions, such as ensuring that administrators and users practice good password management, configuring system privileges, making backups of data, and so on. Where critical tasks are the responsibility of the service provider, you should try to ensure that there is a reporting mechanism to show that these tasks are being completed, that their disaster recovery plans are effective, and so on.

Another provision is that your company is likely to remain directly liable for serious security breaches. If customer data is stolen, for instance, or if your hosted website is hacked and used to distribute malware, the legal and regulatory "buck" still stops with you. You might be able to sue the service provider for damages, but your company would still be the point of investigation. You may also need to consider the legal implications of using a cloud provider if its servers are in a different country.

You must also consider the risk of **insider threat**, where the insiders are administrators working for the service provider. Without effective security mechanisms, such as separation of duties, it is possible that they would be able to gain privileged access to your data. Consequently, the service provider must be able to demonstrate to your satisfaction that they are prevented from doing so. There is also the risk that your data is in proximity to other, unknown virtual servers and that some sort of attack could be launched on your data from another virtual server.

As with any contracted service, with any *aaS solution you place a large amount of trust in the service provider. The more important the service is to your business, the more risk you are investing in that trust relationship.

CLOUD ACCESS SECURITY BROKER (CASB)

A **Cloud Access Security Broker (CASB)** is enterprise management software designed to mediate access to cloud services by users across all types of devices. CASB vendors include Blue Coat™, now owned by Symantec™ (*symantec.com/products/cloud-application-security-cloudsoc*), and SkyHigh Networks, now owned by MacAfee® (*skyhighnetworks.com*). Some of the functions of a CASB are:

- Enable single-sign on authentication and enforce access controls and authorizations from the enterprise network to the cloud provider.
- Scan for malware and rogue or non-compliant device access.
- Monitor and audit user and resource activity.
- Mitigate **data exfiltration** by preventing access to unauthorized cloud services from managed devices.

The interface between the CASB software, the cloud service, and users/devices can be created in several ways:

- Proxy—Each client must be configured to contact the cloud service via a CASB proxy. The problems with this approach are that not all cloud applications have proxy support, and users may be able to evade the proxy and connect directly.
- API—The CASB software uses the cloud provider's application programming interface (API). This depends on the API supporting the range of functions that the CASB and access and authorization policies demand.

 Note: *To learn more, watch the related* **Video** *on the course website.*

Activity 7-5

Discussing the Concepts of Cloud Services

SCENARIO

Answer the following questions to test your understanding of the content covered in this topic.

---

1. **What is the key difference between purchasing cloud web server instances and a virtual hosted server?**

2. **What is meant by a public cloud?**

3. **What type of cloud solution would be used to implement a SAN?**

4. **What are the main options for implementing connections to a cloud service provider?**

5. **What is a Cloud Access Security Broker?**

Summary

In this lesson, you learned about network applications and services, such as web and file transfer services, email, VoIP, and conferencing. You also learned about the way modern networks can provide different platforms for network services, such as virtualization, storage networks, and cloud.

- SMB implements file sharing on Windows networks, while NTP provides time synchronization, which is critical to many applications and services.
- Websites and applications use HTTP to transfer data and are accessed via URLs. Communications can be secured using SSL/TLS and digital certificates (HTTPS).
- SMTP is used for mail delivery, while POP and IMAP are means of accessing a mailbox on a remote server. Client access to these servers should be protected by connection security (SSL/TLS).
- Real-time services such as VoIP and VTP use session protocols such as SIP along with data transfer protocols such as RTP.
- Packet shaping and load balancing protocols and appliances allow a network to be tuned to support QoS for real-time services and provide high availability.
- A multilayer switch can provide layer 3 routing and/or layer 4/7 content-based path selection.
- Virtualization allows swift deployment of clients and servers and also virtual switches, routers, and firewalls to implement virtualized networks.
- SAN solutions allow different types of storage technology to be mixed. They are usually provisioned using Fibre Channel networks.
- Cloud computing allows the lease of infrastructure and software on an as-needed basis but carries the same risks as other contracted services.

Which *aaS do you plan to implement? Why?

Describe common roadblocks you might encounter while trying to implement virtualization.

 Practice Questions: *Additional practice questions are available on the course website.*

Lesson 8
Monitoring and Troubleshooting Networks

LESSON INTRODUCTION

So far in this course, you have learned about all the different components, technologies, and protocols that go towards building network connectivity and services. In this lesson, you will investigate some tools and management methods that will help you determine your network's baseline, optimize your network's performance, and troubleshoot connectivity issues.

LESSON OBJECTIVES

In this lesson, you will:

- Monitor network interfaces and logs.
- Explain network troubleshooting methodologies.
- Troubleshoot common network services issues.

Topic A
Monitor Network Interfaces and Logs

EXAM OBJECTIVES COVERED
1.1 Explain the purposes and uses of ports and protocols.
3.3 Explain common scanning, monitoring, and patching processes and summarize their expected outputs.

Managing your network for optimal performance is an essential task for network technicians to understand and be able to perform. By monitoring your network, determining your network's baseline, and optimizing your network to perform at its peak performance, your network can provide reliable service to your users. An effectively managed network has low downtime and improved availability of services no matter what the network size is.

MONITORING PROCESSES

When you install network infrastructure and applications for a given purpose, you will have tried to anticipate user demand for the service you wish to provide and will have installed a network with the appropriate link bandwidth, appliances, and servers. As time goes by, users' demands on the system will increase, making additional demands on the network's resources until a point is reached where service availability and/or throughput is compromised to such an extent that users begin to experience problems. You then add resources to the network and the cycle begins again. **Performance monitoring** allows you to determine when resources are being stretched before the point is reached where service function is impaired.

A **bottleneck** is a point of poor performance that reduces the productivity of the whole network. A bottleneck may occur because a device is underpowered or faulty. It may also occur because of user or application behavior. To identify the cause of a bottleneck, you need to identify where and when on the network overutilization or excessive errors occur. If the problem is continual, it is likely to be device-related; if the problem only occurs at certain times, it is more likely to be user- or application-related.

BASELINES

A **baseline** establishes the performance metrics at a point-in-time, such as when the system was first installed. This provides a comparison to measure system responsiveness later. For example, if a company is expanding a remote office that is connected to the corporate office with an ISP's basic tier package, the baseline can help determine if there is enough reserve bandwidth to handle the extra user load, or if the basic package needs to be upgraded to support higher bandwidths.

Reviewing baselines is the process of evaluating whether a baseline is still fit for purpose or whether a new baseline should be established. Changes to the system usually require a new baseline to be taken. Some examples when this should be done are:

- Hardware or software upgrade.
- Reconfiguration of network.
- Installation of new devices/services.
- Changed user access volume or patterns.

• Changed server role.

PERFORMANCE AND HEALTH MONITORING TOOLS

Network monitoring tools fulfill a wide range of functions. They can capture and analyze traffic, create logs, alert you to events you define, monitor interface and device metrics, indicate areas of traffic congestion, help you construct baselines, determine upgrade and forecast needs, and generate reports for management. A **performance monitor** can be used to provide real-time charts of server system and network resources or to log information to a file for review. By monitoring different resources at different times of the day, you can detect when performance is stretched and why.

It may be that a server providing a database service is having problems coping with the number of queries being sent to it during the day. This could be caused by several things. Perhaps the processor is too slow, which would cause the requests to take longer. Perhaps the hard disk is too slow, which would mean that it takes too long for the server to pull the database files from the disk. The performance of this server could be increased by upgrading any or all of these components, but monitoring key metrics will help you decide which is critical.

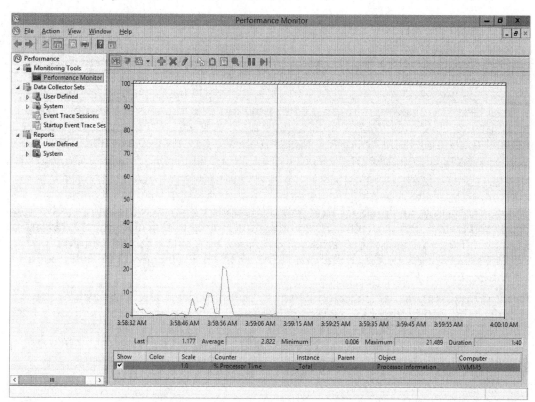

Using Performance Monitor for system monitoring in Windows. (Screenshot used with permission from Microsoft.)

Statistics can also be gathered from network appliances. Stand-alone devices may have a web console to use for monitoring. Devices may also be able to report performance metrics to a management console using the **Simple Network Management Protocol (SNMP)**.

Tools can be used to alert administrators to (and provide early warning of) problems with servers or appliances, such as device temperature, fan speeds, voltage fluctuations, disk failure, chassis intrusion, component failure, network link failure, and so on.

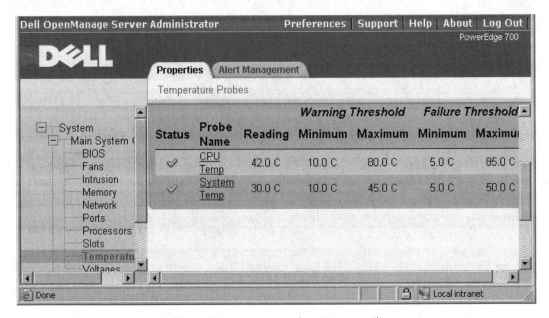

Dell OpenManage Server Administrator utility.

Finally, you can gather statistics (or metadata) about network traffic, perhaps by attaching a network monitor or packet analyzer to a mirrored port. Collecting just the packet metadata, rather than the whole packet payload, greatly reduces the bandwidth required by the monitoring application. The statistics can be collated by technologies such as Cisco's NetFlow to perform **packet flow monitoring**. This allows the administrator to identify routes, applications, and interfaces that might be over-utilized or that are creating bottlenecks. An enterprise network might deploy traffic shapers to provide advanced control over network utilization.

NetFlow (*cisco.com/c/en/us/products/ios-nx-os-software/ios-netflow/index.html*) is a Cisco-developed means of reporting network flow information to a structured database. While SNMP allows an appliance to report basic statistics, such as the number of bytes processed by an interface, NetFlow allows better understanding of IP traffic flows as used by different network applications and hosts. A traffic flow can be defined by packets sharing the same characteristics, such as IP source and destination addresses and protocol type.

Cisco® produces their own collector software, and there are many other traffic analysis products supporting NetFlow—NetScout TruView (*enterprise.netscout.com/apps/truview*), HP® Intelligent Management Center (*hpe.com/us/en/networking/management.html*), IBM Tivoli Network Manager (*ibm.com/support/knowledgecenter/en/SSSHRK_4.2.0/overview/concept/ovr_product.html*), and Plixer Scrutinizer (*plixer.com/products/scrutinizer*), for instance.

There are other open source and commercial alternatives to NetFlow, including sFlow and jFlow (used by Juniper) (*juniper.net/documentation/en_US/junos/topics/concept/sflow-qfx-series-understanding.html*). Additionally, IP Flow Information Export (IPFIX) is an IETF-sponsored open standard, derived principally from NetFlow v9.

TRAFFIC ANALYSIS TOOLS

Network analysis tools will help you to perform the following kinds of tests.

THROUGHPUT TESTERS

One fairly simple way to measure network **throughput** is to transfer a large file between two appropriate hosts. Appropriate in this sense means an appropriate subnet and representative of servers and workstations that you want to measure. It is also important to choose a representative time. There is not much point in measuring the throughput when the network is carrying no other traffic.

To determine your network throughput using this method, simply divide the file size by the amount of time taken to copy the file. For example, if you transfer a 1 GB file in half an hour, the throughput can be calculated as follows:

- 1 gigabyte is 10243 bytes (1,073,741,824 bytes or 8,589,934,592 bits).
- 8,589,934,592 bits in 1,800 seconds is 4,772,186 bits per second or 4.55 Mbps.

This method derives a value that is different from the nominal data rate. Because two hosts are transferring the files between one another, it is the Application layers that handle the file transfer. The intervening layers on both hosts add complexity (headers) and introduce inaccuracy, such as corrupt frames that have to be retransmitted.

 Note: *The value recorded using this method (ignoring overhead introduced by packet headers) is often referred to as the* **goodput** *of the network.*

Several software utilities, such as iperf (*iperf.fr*), Ttcp (*linux.die.net/man/1/ttcp*), and bwping (*bwping.sourceforge.io*), can be used to measure network throughput.

SPEED TEST SITES

In addition to testing performance on a local network, you may also want to test Internet links. There are many Internet tools available for checking performance. The two main classes are:

- **Broadband speed checkers**—These test how fast the local broadband link to the Internet is. They are mostly designed for SOHO use. The tool will test downlink and uplink speeds, test latency using `ping`, and can usually compare the results with neighboring properties and other users of the same ISP.
- **Website performance checkers**—These query a nominated website to work out how quickly pages load. One of the advantages of an online tool is that you can test your site's response times from the perspective of customers in different countries.

TOP TALKERS/LISTENERS

One of the functions of a network analyzer may be to identify the most active interfaces on the network. **Top talkers** are interfaces generating the most outgoing traffic (in terms of bandwidth), while **top listeners** are the interfaces receiving the most incoming traffic. Identifying these hosts and the routes they are using is useful in identifying and eliminating performance bottlenecks. Most network analyzer software comes with filters or built-in reporting to identify top talkers or top listeners.

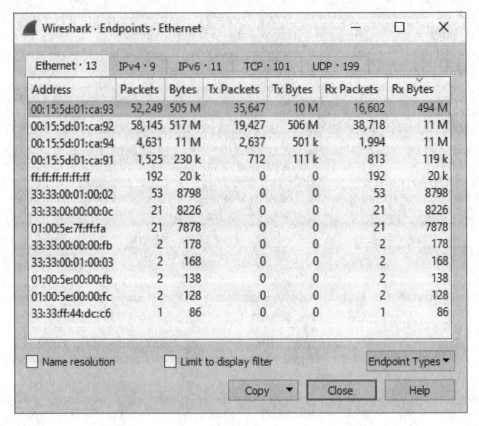

Address	Packets	Bytes	Tx Packets	Tx Bytes	Rx Packets	Rx Bytes
00:15:5d:01:ca:93	52,249	505 M	35,647	10 M	16,602	494 M
00:15:5d:01:ca:92	58,145	517 M	19,427	506 M	38,718	11 M
00:15:5d:01:ca:94	4,631	11 M	2,637	501 k	1,994	11 M
00:15:5d:01:ca:91	1,525	230 k	712	111 k	813	119 k
ff:ff:ff:ff:ff:ff	192	20 k	0	0	192	20 k
33:33:00:01:00:02	53	8798	0	0	53	8798
33:33:00:00:00:0c	21	8226	0	0	21	8226
01:00:5e:7f:ff:fa	21	7878	0	0	21	7878
33:33:00:00:00:fb	2	178	0	0	2	178
33:33:00:01:00:03	2	168	0	0	2	168
01:00:5e:00:00:fb	2	138	0	0	2	138
01:00:5e:00:00:fc	2	128	0	0	2	128
33:33:ff:44:dc:c6	1	86	0	0	1	86

The Endpoints report in Wireshark can be used to identify top talkers and top listeners. (Screenshot courtesy of Wireshark.)

LOAD TESTING

Network administrators must be able to test their systems under load to simulate working conditions or test higher loads for assessing likely future problems. This can also be described as a **stress test**. Test frame and packet generator systems allow frames or packets for a variety of networking technologies (such as Ethernet or Wi-Fi) and protocols (TCP/IP) to be defined and placed on the network at a desired level. The frames or packets are used to test network devices such as servers, switches, and routers. The generators collect the results of tests and analyze network device performance.

 Note: *Reserve stress testing for non-business hours only!*

HOST MONITORING METRICS

When you are monitoring a network host or intermediate system, several parameters can tell you whether the host is operating normally:

- **Bandwidth/throughput**—This is the rated speed of all the interfaces available to the device, measured in Mbps or Gbps. For wired Ethernet links, this will not usually vary, but the bandwidth of WAN and wireless links can change over time.
- **CPU and memory**—Devices such as switches and routers perform a lot of processing. If CPU and/or system memory utilization (measured as a percentage) is very high, an upgrade might be required. High CPU utilization can also indicate a problem with network traffic.

- **Storage**—Some network devices require persistent storage (typically, one or more flash drives) to keep configuration information and logs. Storage is measured in MB or GB. If the device runs out of storage space, it could cause serious errors.

INTERFACE MONITORING METRICS

You can also collect data and configure alerts for metrics related to an interface, whether on a network adapter or switch or router port.

- **Link Status**—Measures whether an interface is working (up) or not (down). You would want to configure an alert if an interface goes down so that it can be investigated immediately. You may also want to track the uptime percentage so that you can assess a link's reliability over time.
- **Resets**—The number of times an interface has restarted over the counter period. Interfaces may be reset manually or could restart automatically if traffic volume is very high or a large number of errors are experienced. Anything but occasional resets should be closely monitored and investigated. An interface that continually resets is described as **flapping**.
- **Speed**—This is the rated speed of the interface, measured in Mbps or Gbps. For wired Ethernet links this will not usually vary, but the bandwidth of WAN and wireless links may change over time. For Ethernet links, the interface speed should match both the host and switch ports.
- **Duplex**—Most ports now operate in full-duplex mode. If an interface is operating in half-duplex mode, there is likely to be some sort of problem, unless you are supporting a legacy device.
- **Utilization**—The data transferred over a period. This can either be measured as the amount of data both sent and received (measured in bps or a multiple thereof) or calculated as a percentage of the available bandwidth.

> *Note: You also need to differentiate between overall utilization and peak utilization. If overall utilization is around 80%, it may appear that there is sufficient bandwidth. However, if peak utilization often spikes to 100%, then that will manifest as delay and packet loss and may require that you upgrade the link.*

- **Error rate**—The number of packets per second that cause errors. Errors may occur as a result of interference or poor link quality causing data corruption in frames. In general terms, error rates should be under 1%; very high error rates may indicate a driver problem, if a network media problem can be ruled out.
- **Discards/drops**—An interface may discard (drop) incoming and/or outgoing frames for several reasons, including checksum errors, mismatched MTUs, packets that are too small (runts) or too large (giants), high load, or **permissions**— the sender is not on the interface's access control list (ACL) or there is some sort of VLAN configuration problem, for instance. Each interface is likely to class the type of discard or **drop** separately to assist with troubleshooting the precise cause of high discard rates.

> *Note: Some vendors may use the term **discard** for frames that are rejected because of errors or security policies and **drop** for frames that are lost due to high load, but often the terms are used interchangeably.*

- **Retransmissions**—Errors and discards/drops mean that frames of data are lost during transmission between two devices. As a result, the communication will be incomplete, and the data will, therefore, have to be re-transmitted to ensure application data integrity. If you observe high levels of retransmissions (as a percentage of overall traffic), you must analyze and troubleshoot the specific cause of the underlying packet loss, which could involve multiple aspects of network configuration and connectivity.

```
C:\Users\James>netstat -ps TCP

TCP Statistics for IPv4

    Active Opens                    = 26193
    Passive Opens                   = 447
    Failed Connection Attempts      = 1506
    Reset Connections               = 2082
    Current Connections             = 51
    Segments Received               = 5114972
    Segments Sent                   = 4573238
    Segments Retransmitted          = 1623
```

Using netstat to measure retransmissions. (Screenshot used with permission from Microsoft.)

SIMPLE NETWORK MANAGEMENT PROTOCOL (SNMP)

The **Simple Network Management Protocol (SNMP)** is a widely used framework for management and monitoring remote devices. It is part of the TCP/IP protocol suite, operating at the Application layer of the OSI model. SNMP consists of **agents** and a **monitoring system**.

SNMP AGENTS

The **agent** is a process (software or firmware) running on a switch, router, server, or other SNMP-compatible network device. This agent maintains a database called a **Management Information Base (MIB)** that holds statistics relating to the activity of the device, such as the number of frames per second handled by a switch. Each parameter stored in a MIB is referred to by a numeric **Object Identifier (OID)**. OIDs are stored within a tree structure. Part of the tree is generic to SNMP, while part can be defined by the device vendor.

SNMP MONITOR

An **SNMP monitor** is management software that provides a location from which you can oversee network activity. The monitor polls agents at regular intervals for information from their MIBs and displays the information for review. It also displays any trap operations as alerts for the network administrator to assess and act upon as necessary. The monitor can retrieve information from a device in two main ways:

- **Get**—The software queries the agent for a single OID. This command is used by the monitor to perform regular polling (obtaining information from devices at defined intervals).
- **Trap**—The agent informs the monitor of a notable event (port failure, for instance). The threshold for triggering traps can be set for each value.

The monitor can be used to change certain variables using the **Set** command. It can also **walk** an MIB subtree by using multiple **Get** and **Get Next** commands. This is used to discover the complete layout of an MIB. Device queries take place over UDP port 161; traps are communicated over UDP port 162.

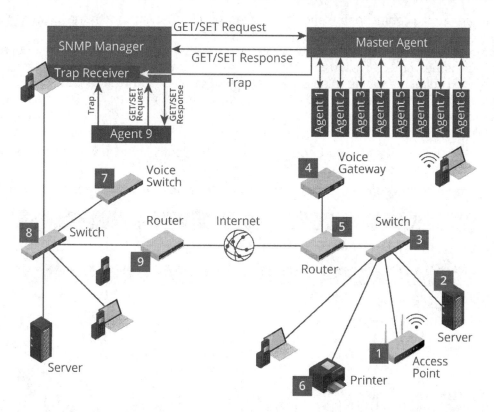

SNMP collects information from network devices for diagnostic purposes.

SNMP AGENT CONFIGURATION

The method of configuring the SNMP agent on a device or component depends on the software or firmware installed on the device. On a Windows Server®, you configure the agent via **SNMP Service Properties**. To do so, open the **Services** applet in **Computer Management**, right-click the **SNMP Service**, and select **Properties**.

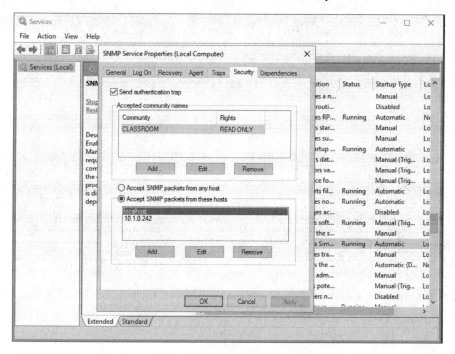

SNMP Service—Agent properties. (Screenshot used with permission from Microsoft.)

You can input a contact name and physical location for the computer and choose what services are running on the machine. On the **Traps** tab, you should input the **Community Name** of the computers allowed to manage the agent and the IP address or host name of the server running the management system. The community name acts as a rudimentary type of password. An agent can pass information only to management systems configured with the same community name. There are usually two community names; one for read-only access and one for read-write access (or privileged mode).

On a device such as a hardware router, UPS, or RAID controller, you would use the device's management interface to set agent properties.

Thresholds for triggering trap alerts are configured using the management system.

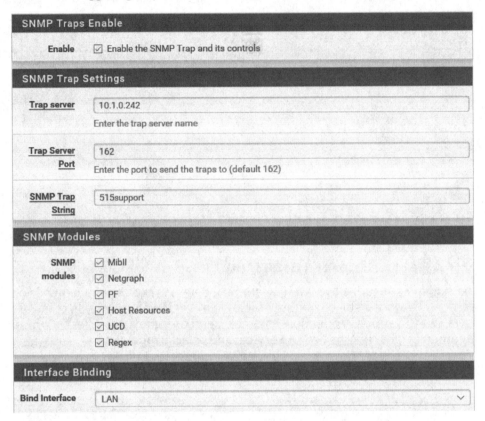

Configuring SNMP traps on a pfSense security appliance. (Screenshot courtesy of pfSense.)

LOGS

Logs are one of the most valuable sources of performance, troubleshooting, and security (auditing) information. A single logged event consists of metadata, such as the date and time, category, and event ID, plus a description and possibly contents of error output. For example, you can use a system log to troubleshoot an IP conflict by looking for TCP/IP events or to determine when (or why) a system was shut down.

Logs can be categorized into the following sorts of functions:

- **System** logs record the initial configuration (setup) and subsequent changes to the configuration.
- **Application** (or **General**) logs record system- or application-initiated incidents.
- **History** (or **Security** or **Audit**) logs record user activity.

Note: *Audit logs typically associate an action with a particular user. This is one of the reasons that it is critical that users not share logon details. If a user account is compromised, there is no means of tying events in the log to the actual attacker.*

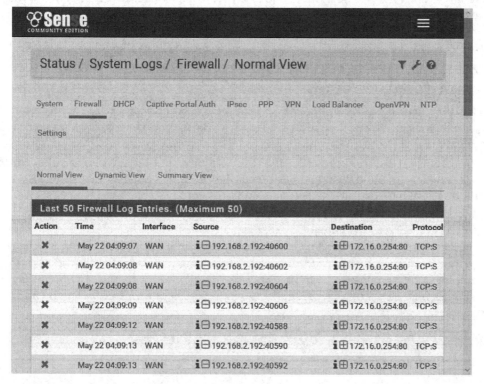

Viewing audit logs on a pfSense security appliance. (Screenshot courtesy of pfSense.)

• **Performance** logs record defined metrics over a period.

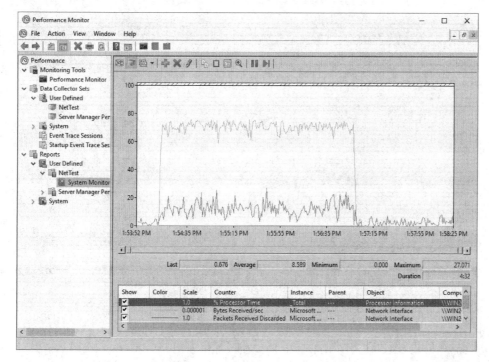

Data retrieved from a performance log file. (Screenshot used with permission from Microsoft.)

A network logging system may be able to aggregate the logs from numerous devices into a central control panel, using a protocol such as SNMP. Alternatively, the logs from appliances such as switches and routers can typically be transferred using FTP, TFTP, or SSH.

Windows operating systems store system logs internally, and these logs can be viewed through Event Viewer. The standard logs (**System**, **Application**, and **Security**) may be supplemented by other software-specific logs, as additional services and applications are installed.

SYSLOG AND SECURITY INFORMATION AND EVENT MANAGEMENT (SIEM)

Prior to Windows Vista®/Windows 7, one limitation of Windows logs was that they only logged local events; that is, each computer was responsible for logging its own events. This meant that third-party tools were required in order to gain an overall view of messaging for the entire network. However, the development of **event subscriptions** in Windows Vista/7 allows logging to be configured to forward all events to a single computer, enabling a holistic view of network events.

The equivalent system in UNIX® and Linux® is usually **SYSLOG**. This was designed to follow a client-server model and so allows for centralized collection of events from multiple sources. It also provides an open format for event logging messages and as such, has become a de facto standard for logging events from distributed systems. For example, SYSLOG messages can be generated by Cisco® routers and switches, as well as servers and workstations, and collected in a central database for viewing and analysis.

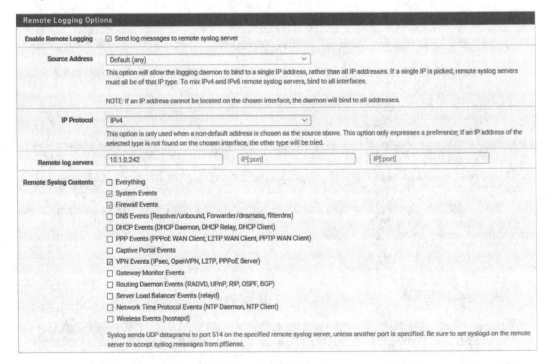

Configuring a pfSense security appliance to transmit logs to a remote SYSLOG server. (Screenshot courtesy of pfSense.)

Software designed to assist with security logging and alerting is often described as **Security Information and Event Management (SIEM)**. The core function of a SIEM tool is to **aggregate** logs from multiple sources. In addition to logs from Windows and Linux-based hosts, this could include switches, routers, firewalls, IDS sensors, vulnerability scanners, malware scanners, and databases.

The second critical function of SIEM (and the principal factor distinguishing it from basic log management) is that of **correlation**. This means that the SIEM software can link individual events or data points (observables) into a meaningful indicator of risk, or **indicator of compromise (IOC)**. Correlation can then be used to drive an **alerting** system. Finally, SIEM can provide a long-term retention function and be used to demonstrate regulatory compliance.

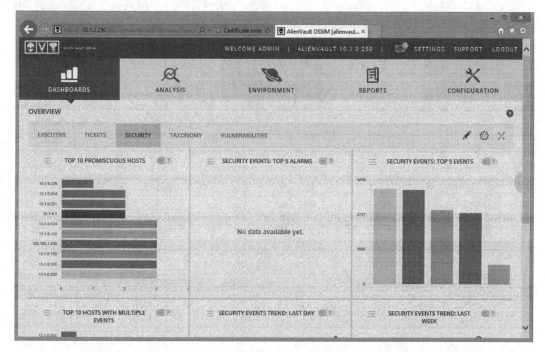

OSSIM SIEM dashboard. Configurable dashboards provide the high-level status view of network security metrics. (Screenshot used with permission from AT&T Cybersecurity.)

There are very many SIEM vendors. Some of the major suites include AlienVault OSSIM (*https://www.alienvault.com/products/ossim*), Micro Focus (previously HPE) ArcSight (*https://www.microfocus.com/en-us/products/siem-security-information-event-management/overview*), IBM QRadar (*https://www.ibm.com/us-en/marketplace/ibm-qradar-siem*), Splunk (*https://www.splunk.com/*), and SolarWinds (*https://www.solarwinds.com/security-event-manager*).

EVENT MANAGEMENT

Most logging systems categorize each event. For example, in Windows, system and application events are defined as Informational, Warning, or Critical, while audit events are categorized as Success or Fail. An automated event management system can be configured to generate some sort of **alert** when certain event types of a given severity are encountered. Alerts can also be generated by setting **thresholds** for performance counters. Examples include **packet loss**, link bandwidth drops, number of sessions established, delay/jitter in real-time applications, and so on. Most network monitors also support **heartbeat** tests so that you can receive an alert if a device or server stops responding to probes.

Setting alerts is a matter of balance. On the one hand, you do not want performance to deteriorate to the point that it affects user activity; on the other hand, you do not want to be overwhelmed by alerts.

You can also make a distinction between alerts and **notifications**. An alert means that the system has matched some sort of pattern or filter that should be recorded and highlighted. A notification means that the system sends a message to advertise the occurrence of the alert. A low priority alert may simply be displayed in the system dashboard. A high priority alert might use some sort of active notification messaging, such as emailing a system administrator, sending a text message (**SMS**) to a phone, or triggering a physical alarm signal.

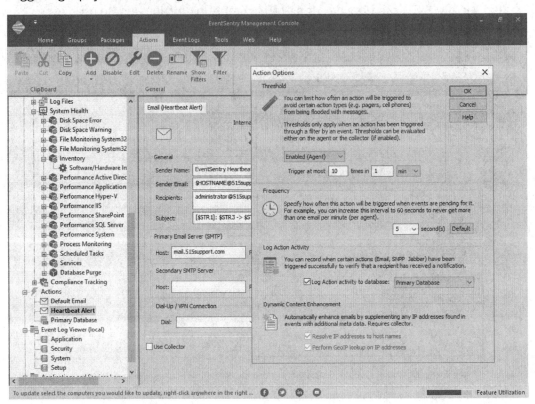

Configuring alert and notification settings in EventSentry SIEM. (Screenshot courtesy of NETIKUS.NET ltd.)

There should be some process for acknowledging and dismissing alerts as they are raised. A serious alert may need to be processed as an incident and assigned a job ticket for formal investigation. If an alert is a false positive, it can be dismissed. If the management system or dashboard is allowed to become cluttered with old alerts, it is much more difficult to identify new alerts and gauge the overall status of the network.

LOG REVIEWING

Monitoring involves viewing traffic, protocols, and events in real time. Network and log reviewing or analysis involves later inspection and interpretation of captured data to determine what the data shows was happening on the network during the capture. Monitoring is more aligned with identifying problems. Analysis is more aligned with investigating the cause of the identified problems. It is important to perform performance analysis and log review continually. Referring to the logs only after a major incident is missing the opportunity to identify threats and vulnerabilities or performance problems early and to respond proactively.

Not all performance incidents will be revealed by a single event. One of the features of log analysis and reporting software should be to identify **trends**. A trend is difficult to spot by examining each event in a log file. Instead, you need software to chart the incidence of types of events and show how the number or frequency of those events changes over time.

Plotting data as a graph is particularly helpful as it is easier to spot trends or spikes or troughs in a visualization of events, rather than the raw data. Most performance monitors can plot metrics in a graph.

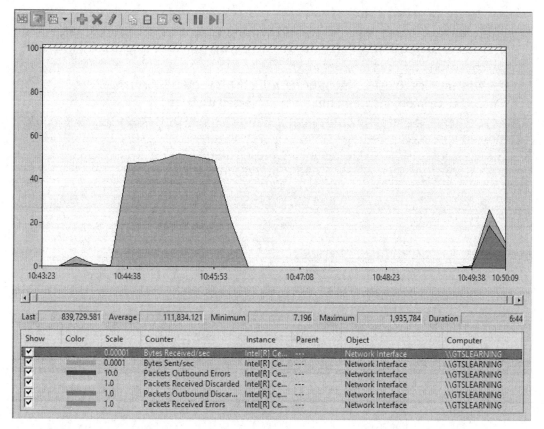

Graphing performance information. (Screenshot used with permission from Microsoft.)

 Note: *To learn more, watch the related **Video** on the course website.*

GUIDELINES FOR CONFIGURING MONITORING AND LOGGING

SET UP A MANAGEMENT AND MONITORING SYSTEM

Setting up a management and monitoring system for a network can be a complex process, involving the evaluation and testing of different products. Follow these guidelines for the general steps to complete:

1. Select a systems management or SIEM system that will provide the best compatibility with the endpoints used on your network, plus the reporting and management features that you require.
2. Install the systems management software to a secure server or workstation, ensuring that it meets the processor and storage requirements for the number of hosts you are monitoring and the expected event volume.
3. Configure accounts with the rights to monitor endpoints, and (optionally) perform remote management and deployment of agent-based tools.
4. Configure endpoints to provide information to the SIEM. This could involve one or more different methods, such as:

- Configure SNMP traps.
- Configure remote logging to the SIEM using SYSLOG or a similar protocol.
- Deploy agents to the endpoints to perform log and performance counter collection and measurement.

5. Identify metrics to use to monitor network health and performance.
6. Record baseline measurements for the selected metrics.
7. Set up filters to alert and notify administrators when key thresholds are exceeded or when hosts fail heartbeat tests.
8. Set up a process for reviewing and managing alerts.
9. Set up a process for reviewing events and diagnosing trends.

Activity 8-1

Discussing Network Interface and Log Monitoring

SCENARIO

Answer the following questions to test your understanding of the content covered in this topic.

1. **Gathering systems' statistics regularly allows system administrators to identify bottlenecks. Why do they want to do this?**

2. **What is a top listener in terms of network monitoring?**

3. **You suspect that a network application is generating faulty packets. What interface metric(s) might help you to diagnose the problem?**

4. **What sort of log would you inspect if you wanted to track web server access attempts?**

5. **What is the function of a SIEM?**

6. **How does an SNMP agent report an event to the management system?**

7. **What would be the purpose of configuring thresholds in network monitoring software?**

Activity 8-2

Using Event Management and Performance Monitors

BEFORE YOU BEGIN

Start the VMs used in this activity in the following order, adjusting the memory allocation first if necessary, and waiting at the ellipsis for the previous VMs to finish booting before starting the next group. You do not need to connect to a VM until prompted to do so in the activity steps.

1. **PFSENSE** (512—1024 MB)
2. **DC1** (1024—2048 MB)
3. ...
4. **MS1** (1024—2048 MB)
5. ...
6. **PC1** (1024—2048 MB)
7. **PC2** (512—1024 MB)

 Note: *If you can allocate more than the minimum amounts of RAM, prioritize **PC1**.*

SCENARIO

In this activity, you will use tools to log system configuration and performance data, monitor performance counters, and test network and host bandwidth. This activity is designed to test your understanding of and ability to apply content examples in the following CompTIA Network+ objectives:

- 1.1 Explain the purposes and uses of ports and protocols.
- 3.3 Explain common scanning, monitoring and patching processes and summarize their expected outputs.
- 4.5 Given a scenario, implement network device hardening.

---

1. To explore the features of an event management tool, you will install EventSentry Light, created by NETIKUS.NET ltd (*eventsentry.com*). Configure **PC1** as a management station to host the software. To make monitoring simpler, assign a static IP address (**10.1.0.242**) and disable the firewall. Also, configure an email account to receive notifications.

    Note: *It is better to configure specific access rules to allow monitoring software to work through host firewalls. Disabling the firewall completely is bad practice, but this isn't a firewall configuration activity, so you'll take this shortcut this time.*

   a) Open a connection window for the **PC1** VM and log on as *515support\Administrator* with the password *Pa$$w0rd*
   b) Right-click the **Start** button and select **Network Connections**. Select the **Change adapter options** link.
   c) In the **Network Connections** applet, right-click **Ethernet** and select **Properties**.

---

d) Double-click **Internet Protocol Version 4 (TCP/IPv4)**.

e) Select **Use the following IP address** and in the **IP address** box, type *10.1.0.242*

f) In the **Subnet mask** box, type *255.255.255.0*

g) In the **Default gateway** box, type *10.1.0.254*

h) Select **Use the following DNS server addresses**.

i) In the **Preferred DNS server** box, type *10.1.0.1*

j) Select **OK** to close each dialog box. Close the **Network Connections** window.

k) In the **Settings** window, select the **Windows Firewall** link.

l) Select the **Domain network** link. Select the **On** toggle button and confirm the UAC prompt by selecting **Yes**.

m) Close each **Settings** window.

n) On the desktop, double-click the **Mozilla Thunderbird** icon.

o) When Thunderbird starts, select **Set as Default** at the prompt. (You may only see this dialog box after configuring the account.)

p) In the **Set Up an Existing Email Account** dialog box, enter *Administrator* as **Your name** and *administrator@515support.com* as the **Email address**. For **Password**, type *Pa$$w0rd*

q) Select **Continue**.

r) When the mail servers are discovered, select the **Done** button.

s) Read the warning message, then check **I understand the risks** and select **Done**.

t) In the **System Integration** dialog box, select **Set as Default**.

u) Open the **c:\LABFILES** folder in File Explorer and double-click **essysadmintools_v2_4_2_0_windows_setup.exe**. Confirm the UAC prompt by selecting **Yes**.

v) Complete the setup wizard. Select **Finish** when complete.

w) Double-click **eventsentrylight_v4_0_3_6_windows_setup.exe**. Confirm the UAC prompt.

x) Complete the setup wizard. Select **Finish** when complete.

y) Leave the **Configuration Assistant** dialog box open. You will complete this after configuring SNMP agents.

2. Complete the following steps on **MS1** (and optionally also on **DC1**) to configure an SNMP agent.

a) Open a connection window and sign in on the **MS1** VM as *515support\Administrator* with the password *Pa$$w0rd*

b) In **Server Manager**, select **Tools**→**Services**.

c) Right-click the **SNMP Service** and select **Properties**.

d) Select the **Agent** tab.

e) Check only the following items: **Physical**, **Applications**, **End-to-end**. Select the **Apply** button.
   You would select the **Datalink** and **Internet** options if the host functioned as a bridge or as a router, respectively. As the server acts as an endpoint only, the **End-to-end** option is more appropriate.

f) Select the **Traps** tab. In the **Community name** box, type *515support* and then select the **Add to list** button.

 Note: The community name functions as a password and is case-sensitive. Make sure you enter the same value wherever it is required.

g) Under **Trap destinations**, select the **Add** button.

h) Enter *10.1.0.242* and select **Add**. Select the **Apply** button.

i) Select the **Security** tab.

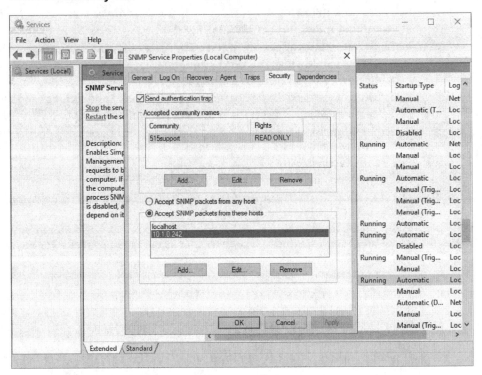

Configuring the SNMP service. (Screenshot used with permission from Microsoft.)

j) Under **Send authentication trap**, select the **Add** button.

Rights are set to READ ONLY by default.

k) In the **Community Name** text box, enter **515support** and select **Add**.

l) Under **Accept SNMP packets from these hosts**, select the **Add** button.

m) Enter **10.1.0.242** and select **Add**.

n) Select **OK**.

o) In Server Manager, select the **Local Server** node. Select the **Domain: On** link next to **Windows Firewall**.

p) Select the **Turn Windows Firewall on or off** link.

q) Under **Domain network settings**, select **Turn off Windows Firewall**. Select **OK**.

3. You can use SNMP and event logging software to monitor other host types, such as the pfSense router/firewall appliance. Configure the appliance to send log and SNMP messages to the monitoring host **10.1.0.242**.

a) Switch to the **PC1** VM and run `http://10.1.0.254`

b) When the web administration app loads in the browser, log in using the credentials **admin** and **Pa$$w0rd**. You can select **Save** when prompted to save the password.

c) From the **Status** menu, select **System Logs**. Select the **Settings** tab.

 Note: *If the window is too small, the menu is shown as three lines on the right side of the window. You can either select this menu or enlarge the window to see the menu items.*

d) Scroll to the bottom of the page, and then check the **Enable Remote Logging** check box.

e) From the **Source Address** box, select **LAN**.

f) In the first **Remote log servers** box, type **10.1.0.242:514**

g) For **Remote Syslog Contents**, check the **System Events** and **Firewall Events** check boxes.

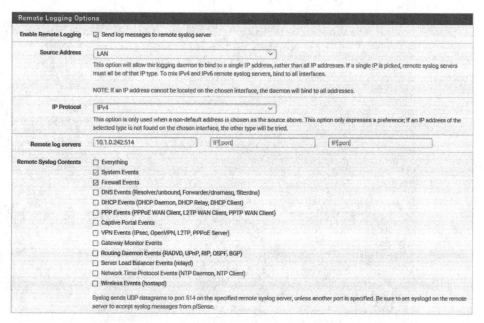

Configuring remote logging (SYSLOG) settings. (Screenshot courtesy of pfSense.)

h) Select the **Save** button.

i) From the **Services** tab, select **SNMP**. Check the **Enable** check box.

j) In the **Read community string** box, enter *515support*

k) Under **SNMP Traps Enable**, check the **Enable** check box.

l) In the **Trap server** box, type *10.1.0.242* and in the **SNMP Trap String** box, type *515support*

m) From the **Bind interface** box, select **LAN**.

n) Select the **Save** button.

4. Before configuring the SIEM monitoring server, test the SNMP agents using the **snmpinfo** tool. Also, capture SNMP and SYSLOG traffic in Wireshark so you can observe the connection.

Snmpinfo is part of the SysAdmin Tools kit developed by NETIKUS.NET ltd (*eventsentry.com/sysadmintools*).

a) On the **PC1** VM, start **Wireshark**, select the **Ethernet** adapter, and enter a capture filter of *not ip6 and (icmp or port snmp or port snmptrap or port syslog)* and start the capture.
After a few moments, you should see SYSLOG messages generated by PFSENSE. 10.1.0.242 is responding with ICMP **Port unreachable** messages because you have not yet configured the SYSLOG server.

b) Select **Start**, type *snmpinfo*, and then select the **Snmpinfo** icon that appears in the search results.

 Note: *You can also access Snmpinfo on the* **Start** *menu under* **EventSentrySysAdmin Tools**.

c) Run the following command:

```
snmpinfo 10.1.0.254 /u 515support
```

Output from the snmpinfo tool. (Screenshot used with permission from NETIKUS.NET ltd.)

A lot of information about the configuration of the device is revealed. Ideally, you would not want this information to be available to unauthorized users.

d) Run the following command to observe the information reported by a Windows server:

```
snmpinfo 10.1.0.2 /u 515support
```

The report shows the same sort of information. You can set platform type, CPU usage, network adapters and disks, and process information.

e) Close the command prompt.

f) In **Wireshark**, locate an SNMP response and view the packet details.
    You can view the community name in cleartext. Each **get** operation returns an OID. If you were to load the relevant MIBs into Wireshark, the analyzer would be able to decode the OID as a plain text string.

g) Also observe that remote logging creates a *lot* of network activity. Leave the Wireshark capture running, though.

5. Configure the **EventSentry** SIEM with your account details.

a) In the **Event Sentry Configuration Assistant**, select **Next**.

b) Select the **HIGH** option button and select **Next**.

c) In the **SMTP Server** box, type *mail.515support.com*

d) In the **Username** box, type *administrator@515support.com*

e) In the **Password** box, type *Pa$$w0rd*

f) Select **Next**.

g) In the **Sender Email** box, type *administrator* and in the **@** box, type *515support.com*

h) In the **Recipient(s)** box, type *administrator@515support.com* and select **Next**.

i) Select **Next** at each remaining page of the wizard to accept the default values. Select **Finish** to complete the wizard.

At the **Summary** page of the wizard as the items are being installed and configured, it will take some time. You will see the screen flash periodically as well. When the items have been installed and configured, the **Setup Complete** page is displayed where you can select **Finish**.

6. Configure the **EventSentry Light** SIEM with details of the hosts on your network.

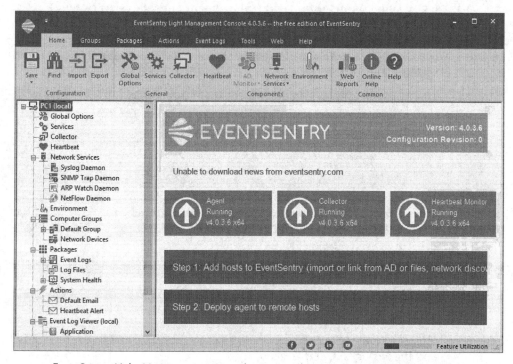

EventSentry Light Management Console. (Screenshot courtesy of NETIKUS.NET ltd.)

a) After a few moments, the **EventSentry Light Management Console** opens. In the main console, select the **Step 1: Add hosts** box.

b) Select the **Network scan** option button.

c) In the **Please specify a subnet** box, type *10.1.0.0/24* and select **Next**.

d) When the scan completes, press **Ctrl+click** to select all the hosts except **PC1**. Select **Next**. Select **Finish**.

e) In the main console, in the navigation pane, select **Computer Groups**.

f) Right-click **Computer Groups** and select the **Add Group** option. In the dialog box, type *Server Group* and select **OK**.

g) In the navigation pane, expand the **Default Group**, and then drag **DC1** and **MS1** into the **Server** group and **10.1.0.254** into the **Network Devices** group.

h) Expand **Network Devices**. Right-click **10.1.0.254** and select **Set as Router**.

i) Select **Router for one or more subnets** and type *10.1.0.0/24* in the box. Select **OK**.

j) Right-click the **Server Group** node and select **Deploy Agent(s)**. On the toolbar, select the **Go** button.

k) When the **Agent installed successfully** message is shown for both hosts, on the toolbar, select the **Home** tab and then select the **Save** button.

7. Test the event alerting system by disconnecting **PFSENSE** from the network temporarily.

a) On the **HOST**, in **Hyper-V Manager**, right-click **PFSENSE** and select **Settings**.

b) Select the **hn0** node. In the **Virtual switch** list box, select **Not connected**. Select the **Apply** button. Leave the dialog box open.

c) After a minute or two, this should generate an email notification that 10.1.0.254's heartbeat monitoring is in error status. If you do not see a message, select **Services** in the navigation pane and select the **Restart** button for the **Heartbeat Monitor**.

d) On the **HOST**, in the **Settings for PFSENSE** dialog box, select **vLOCAL** again and select **OK**.
    You do not need to wait for it, but at some point, a notification that 10.1.0.254 is back up should arrive.

8. Configure the SNMP and SYSLOG daemons to collect data from the **PFSENSE** VM.

a) On **PC1**, in the **EventSentry Light Management Console**, select **Network Services→Syslog Daemon**.

The SIEM is configured to listen on TCP and UDP ports 514 and will accept packets from any host. You can also configure a threshold to prevent the server from being inundated with log entries.

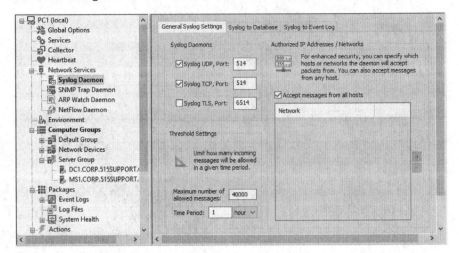

SYSLOG daemon settings in EventSentry Light. (Screenshot courtesy of NETIKUS.NET ltd.)

b) Select the **Syslog to Event Log** tab.

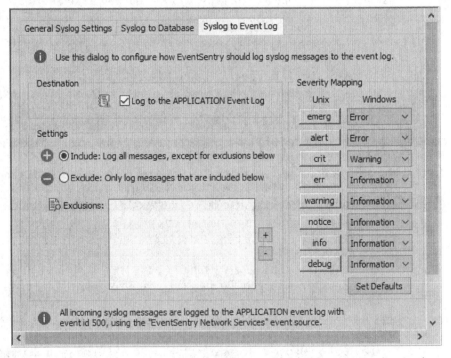

Configuring EventSentry to write SYSLOG events to the local system's Application log. (Screenshot courtesy of NETIKUS.NET ltd.)

The full version of EventSentry can log to a database, and that would usually be the preferred option, but you will simply direct messages to the local computer's event log.

c) Check the **Log to the APPLICATION Event Log** check box, and select the **Include** option button.

Observe the options for mapping Unix/Linux severity levels to Windows event categories, but do not change any of the settings.

d) In the navigation pane, select the **SNMP Trap Daemon** node.

e) Select the **Mibs, Communities & Users** tab. Under **Communities**, select the **+** button. Type ***515support*** in the box and select **OK**.

f) Select the **Traps to Event Log** tab.

g) Check the **Log to the APPLICATION Event Log** check box, and select the **Information** option from the **Log as** list box. Select the **Include** option button.

h) In the navigation pane, expand **Network Devices** and then right-click **10.1.0.254** and select **Set Authentication**.

i) In the **Authentication Manager** dialog box, select the **+** button. In the **Account name** box, type ***515support***. Select the **SNMP** tab. In the **Username / Community** box, type ***515support***.

j) Select the **Add** button and select **OK**.

k) On the toolbar, select the **Home** tab and then select the **Save** button.

9. EventSentry defines information to collect as a package, including packages for collecting event logs from different types of hosts and System Health packages that can read Windows and SNMP performance counters. Add the package tailored for the **pfSense** appliance and assign it to the **10.1.0.254** host.

a) In the navigation pane, expand **Packages**.
Optionally, take a few moments to browse the packages installed by default. More packages, including log file parsers and compliance tracking, are available with the full edition.

b) Expand **System Health→Performance System→Performance / SNMP**. Select the **Import** button and then select **Yes** when prompted to save the configuration.

c) Check the **pfSense** package box and select the **Import Now** button.

d) In the navigation pane, expand **Packages→System Health**. Right-click **pfSense** and select **Assign**. In the dialog box, check the **Network Devices** group check box and then select **OK**.

e) In the navigation pane, select **pfSense→Performance / SNMP**. Double-click the **pfStateTableCount** item in the table. The dialog box allows you to configure how often to sample data from the counter. Select the **Test** button.

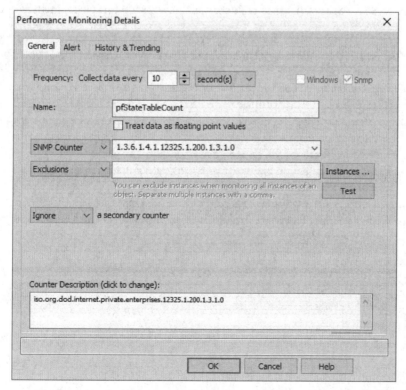

Browsing an SNMP counter defined for the pfSense router/firewall appliance. (Screenshot courtesy of NETIKUS.NET ltd.)

f) In the dialog box, enter *10.1.0.254* and select **OK**.
A panel at the bottom shows a reading for the states table counter (tracking how many sessions are established with the device).

g) Select the **Alert** tab. Check the **Enable Event Log Alert** check box. Set the value to something that will get triggered—use the **Min** readout at the bottom of the dialog box as a baseline. Select **OK**.
You will configure some generic counters with low settings so as to generate notifications.

h) Expand **Performance System→Performance / SNMP**. Double-click **CPU**.

i) On the **Alert** tab, configure a low threshold, such as 5% for 1 minute. Select **OK**.

j) Double-click **Network Utilization**. On the **Alert** tab, configure a low threshold, such as 2% for 30 seconds.

k) On the toolbar, select the **Home** tab and then select the **Save** button.

10. To supplement the SIEM, configure the **Performance Monitor** tool to measure network interface statistics.

a) On **MS1**, in Server Manager, select **Tools→Performance Monitor**.

b) Expand **Performance→Monitoring Tools→ Performance Monitor**.

c) Select the **Add** button ⊞ and select the **Network Interface** object.

d) From the **Instances of selected object** box, select **Microsoft Hyper-V Network Adapter**.

e) Add the following counters:

- **Bytes Received/sec**
- **Packets Received Discarded**
- **Packets Received Errors**

f) Select the **Add>>** button. Select **OK**.

g) Right-click **Performance Monitor** and select **New→Data Collector Set**.

h) On the first page of the wizard, enter the name *NetTest* and select **Next**.

i) Accept the default save location by selecting **Next**.

j) Select **Start this data collector set now**, and then select **Finish** to complete the wizard.

11. You will use the network throughput tester NetStress (from *nutsaboutnets.com*) and a web server stress tester (from *paessler.com*) to simulate some network load. Like most throughput test tools, you need to configure the network throughput software on both endpoints.

a) On the **MS1** VM, double-click the **NetStress** icon on the desktop. Confirm the UAC prompt.

b) In the **Select Network Interface** dialog box, select **OK**.

c) Open a connection window for the **PC2** VM and log on as *515support\Administrator* with the password *Pa$$w0rd*

d) Double-click the **NetStress** icon on the desktop. Confirm the UAC prompt.

e) In the **Select Network Interface** dialog box, select **OK**. Select **Allow access** to all the firewall prompts.

f)   In the toolbar, select the **0.0.0.0** address next to **Remote Receiver IP**. In the **Select Remote Receiver** dialog box, the IP of **MS1 (10.1.0.2)** should be present. Select **OK**.

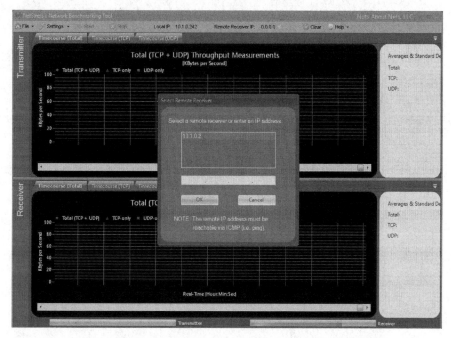

Configuring NetStress. (Screenshot courtesy of Nuts About Nets.)

g)   Select **Settings→TCP & UDP Settings→Packets Per Second**. Under **Network Rating**, select **1-Gigabits/sec**.

h)   From **Number of TCP data streams**, select **8**. Move the slide to around the **20318** mark.

i)   From **Number of UDP data streams**, select **8**. Move the slide to around the **20318** mark. Select **OK**.
     Of course, it does not really matter what you choose here as you cannot test an actual network link; just the ability of the host CPU to move data between buffers. On a real network, you could use TCP to test an HTTP application server and UDP to simulate VoIP load.

j)   Select **Settings→Data Flow**. Note that you can choose between Uplink and Downlink (but not both). Select **OK**.

k)   Select **Start**. Select **Allow access** to all the firewall prompts. Leave the NetStress window open with the test running.

l)   From the desktop, double-click the **Webserver Stress Tool** icon. Confirm the UAC prompt.

m)   Select the **RAMP** option and type *5* in the **minutes** box.

Configuring Webserver Stress Tool. (Screenshot courtesy of Paessler.)

n)   In the **Number of Users** box, type *100*

o)   Check the **Random Click Delay** check box.

p)   Select the **URLs** node. Select in the **URL** box and enter ***http://updates.corp.515support.com***
     Observe the option to use a custom script. You would use this with a test site to set up a more realistic test scenario.

q)   Select the **Start Test** button.
     The log shows the average click time as the simulated load increases. You are unlikely to witness substantial delays however!

12.   Observe the effect of the simulated network activity in **Performance Monitor**.

a)   Switch to **MS1** and observe the activity in **Performance Monitor**.
     You might see some processor time spikes. Bytes received should remain constant. You should not see any errors or discards.

b)   To view a counter more clearly, right-click and select **Scale Selected Counters**.
     You can also format the line type to distinguish them.

c)   Switch back to **PC2** and wait for the web server test to complete (or select **Abort Test** if you are short of time). In **NetStress**, select **Stop**.

d)   On **MS1**, observe the drop-off in activity in **Performance Monitor**.

e)   In **Performance Monitor**, expand **Data Collector Sets**→**User Defined**→**NetTest**. Right-click **NetTest** and select **Stop**.

f)   Expand **Reports**→**User Defined**→**NetTest**.

g)   Double-click the **System Monitor Log** icon to view the report.

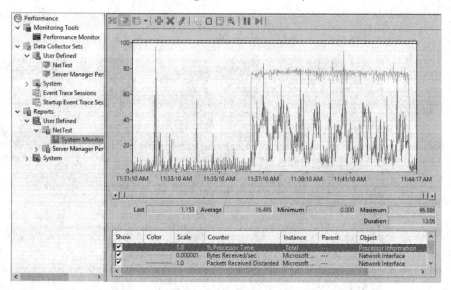

Graphing interface statistics in Performance Monitor. (Screenshot used with permission from Microsoft.)

13.   Check the number and type of notifications that the activity has generated.

a)   Switch to the **PC1** VM and view **Thunderbird**.

b)   Browse the emails to distinguish the type and number of notifications.

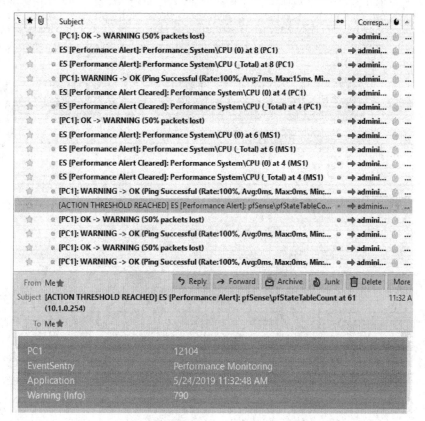

Viewing alerts that have triggered the notification threshold. (Screenshot used with permission from NETIKUS.NET ltd.)

You should see performance thresholds exceeded for **PFSENSE** (10.1.0.254) and **MS1**, and probably other VMs. You are also likely to see **Threshold Reached** notifications, informing you that notifications will be paused for that alert.

c) Examine the following screenshot.

The full trial version of the product (*eventsentry.com/downloads/trial*) comes with a customizable dashboard tool. This is used to monitor the events and alerts being logged to the database in real time.

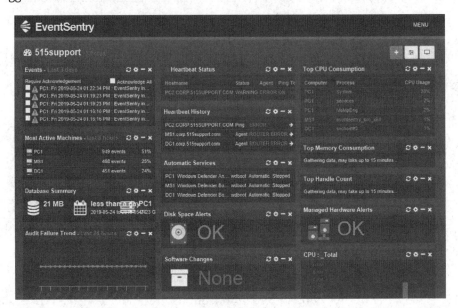

EventSentry dashboard. (Screenshot used with permission from NETIKUS.NET ltd.)

In the top-left corner, there is a widget for acknowledging events. Tuning an event management system can be a complex process. If you configure thresholds that are too low, it is very easy to overwhelm the reporting and notification system.

d) Another section of the web reports feature allows you to view network and service status reports.

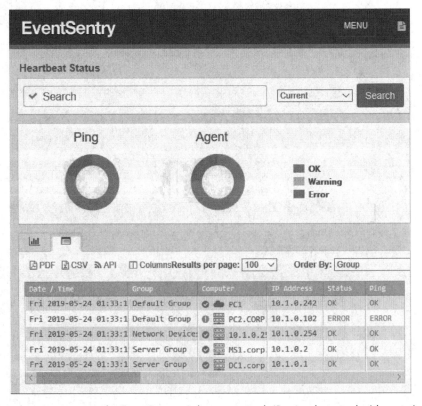

Network status page in the EventSentry web reports tool. (Screenshot used with permission from NETIKUS.NET ltd.)

e)	You can also use the reports to identify trends in network bandwidth usage or server hardware utilization.

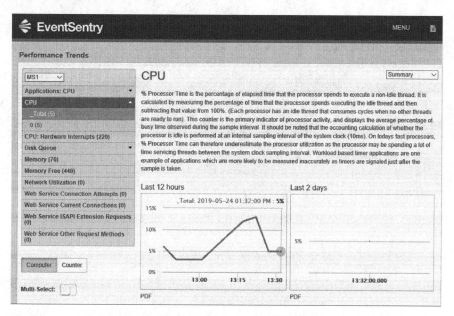

Performance trends page in the EventSentry web reports tool. (Screenshot used with permission from NETIKUS.NET ltd.)

14.	Discard changes made to the VMs in this activity.

a)	Switch to the **Hyper-V Manager** window.

b)	From the **Action** menu, select **Revert** then select the **Revert** button (or use the right-click menu in the **Hyper-V Manager** console) to revert all the VMs to their saved checkpoints.

Topic B

Explain Network Troubleshooting Methodology

EXAM OBJECTIVES COVERED
5.1 Explain the network troubleshooting methodology.

While you can hope that monitoring and management processes will forestall most network problems, unforeseen issues do arise on a network that require you, as a network professional, to identify and troubleshoot issues. Because troubleshooting network problems is such a big part of a network professional's job, you should always use a systematic approach to problem solving. Troubleshooting models provide you with processes on which to base your troubleshooting techniques. Learning and using a troubleshooting methodology can help you resolve problems speedily and effectively.

NETWORK TROUBLESHOOTING METHODOLOGY

When you encounter a network problem, you must try to get it resolved as quickly as you reasonably can. However, you must also take enough time to determine what has caused the problem, so that you can avoid a recurrence.

You should make sure you familiarize yourself with the order of the steps in the CompTIA® Network+® troubleshooting methodology. These steps are explained in more detail in the following topics.

1. Identify the problem:
   - Gather information.
   - Duplicate the problem, if possible.
   - Question users.
   - Identify symptoms.
   - Determine if anything has changed.
   - Approach multiple problems individually.
2. Establish a theory of probable cause:
   - Question the obvious.
   - Consider multiple approaches.
   - Top-to-bottom/bottom-to-top OSI model.
   - Divide and conquer.
3. Test the theory to determine cause:
   - Once theory is confirmed, determine next steps to resolve problem.
   - If theory is not confirmed, re-establish new theory or escalate.
4. Establish a plan of action to resolve the problem and identify potential effects.
5. Implement the solution or escalate as necessary.
6. Verify full system functionality, and if applicable, implement preventive measures.
7. Document findings, actions, and outcomes.

Note: *To learn more, watch the related* **Video** *on the course website.*

IDENTIFY THE PROBLEM

The first step in the troubleshooting process is to establish what the best sources of information about the problem may be.

GATHER INFORMATION

At the outset, define the scope of the problem (that is, the area affected). This is helpful in two ways. First, if it's a single user, then it's not as urgent as the other outstanding call you have. But if it's the whole third floor, then it's more urgent. In addition, the fact that the problem affects a wider area means that it is unlikely to be a problem with one user's workstation. Knowing the scope of the problem can help to identify its source and prioritize the issue in relation to other incidents.

As well as the information gathering techniques discussed here, consider what indirect sources of information there may be:

- Check the system documentation, such as installation or maintenance logs, for useful information.
- Check recent job logs or consult any other technicians who might have worked on the system recently or might be working on some related issue.
- Use vendor support sites (knowledge bases) and forums.

Information gathering is the first step in troubleshooting. (Image by rawpixel © 123RF.com.)

QUESTION USERS

The first report of a problem will typically come from a user or another technician, and they will be one of the best sources of information, if you can ask the right questions. The basis of getting troubleshooting information from users is asking good questions. Questions are commonly divided into two types:

- **Open questions** invite someone to explain in their own words. Examples are: "What is the problem?" or "What happens when you try to switch the computer on?" Open questions are good to start with, as they help to avoid making your own assumptions about what is wrong, and they encourage the user to give you all the information they can.
- **Closed questions** invite a Yes/No answer or a fixed response. Examples include: "Can you see any text on the screen?" or "What does the error message say?" Closed questions can be used to drill down into the nature of the problem and guide a user toward giving you information that is useful.

IDENTIFY SYMPTOMS AND DUPLICATE THE PROBLEM

Of course, you cannot always rely on the user to let you know everything that has happened. To diagnose a problem, you may also need to use the following techniques:

- Make a physical inspection; look for something out of the ordinary.
- Duplicate the problem on the user's system or a test system. You will need to try to follow the same steps as the user. Issues that are transitory or difficult to reproduce are often the hardest to troubleshoot.
- Check system logs or diagnostic software for information.

DETERMINE IF ANYTHING HAS CHANGED

There are two key questions to ask when trying to identify the cause of a problem:

- **Did it ever work?** Hopefully, your users will answer the question truthfully, because the correct answer is important—two different approaches are required. If the system worked before 9:00 a.m., you must ask what happened at 9:00 a.m. If the system never worked, then you are not looking for something that stopped working, but for something which was never working in the first place.
- **What has changed since it was last working?** The change that caused the problem may not be obvious. Maybe the window cleaners were in the building, and one of them tripped over a cable and now the user can't login. Maybe someone has moved the user's workstation from one end of his desk to another and plugged the cable into a different port. Check for documented changes using the system inventory, but if this does not reveal anything, look for undocumented changes in the local area of the incident.

APPROACHING MULTIPLE PROBLEMS

When you start to investigate symptoms, you might discover symptoms of more than one problem. Perhaps a user has reported that a machine has lost Internet connectivity, and you discover that it has also not been receiving maintenance updates. The issues could be related, or one might be incidental to the other.

If the problems do not seem to be related, treat each issue as a separate case. If they seem to be related, check for outstanding support or maintenance tickets that might indicate existing problems.

It may also be the case that a user reports two different problems at the same time, often preceded by "While you're on the line..." sort of statements. Treat each problem as a separate case. In most cases, you should advise the user to initiate a separate support ticket.

ESTABLISH A PROBABLE CAUSE

If you obtain accurate answers to your initial questions, you will have determined the severity of the problem (how many users or systems are affected), a rough idea of where to look (workstation or server end), and whether to look for a recent change or an oversight in configuration.

You diagnose a problem by identifying the symptoms. From knowing what causes such **symptoms**, you can test each **possible cause** until you find the right one. Sometimes symptoms derive from more than one cause; while this type of problem is rarer, it is much harder to troubleshoot.

A network system comprises many components. Fault finding needs to identify which component is causing the issue. For difficult problems, be prepared to consider multiple approaches. If one approach does not identify the problem, use a different one. For example, you could consider two different styles of approaching troubleshooting:

- Question the obvious. Step through what *should* happen, and identify the point at which there is a failure or error. This approach can quickly identify obvious oversights, such as a network cable not being plugged in.
- Methodically prove the functionality of each component in sequence. This approach is more time consuming, but may be necessary for a difficult problem.

TOP-TO-BOTTOM/BOTTOM-TO-TOP OSI MODEL APPROACH

Methodical validation of network components can be approached by testing at each layer of the OSI model in sequence. There are many components which go to make up a network.

Some, or several, of these components may be at fault when a problem is reported to you. It is important that you tackle the problem logically and methodically. Unless a problem is trivial, break the troubleshooting process into compartments or categories, using the OSI model as a guide. Start from either the top or bottom and only move up or down when you have discounted a layer as the source of the problem. For example, when troubleshooting a client workstation, you might work as follows:

1. Decide whether the problem is hardware or software related (Hardware).
2. Decide which hardware subsystem is affected (NIC or cable).
3. Decide whether the problem is in the NIC adapter or connectors and cabling (cabling).
4. Test your theory (replace the cable with a **known good** one).

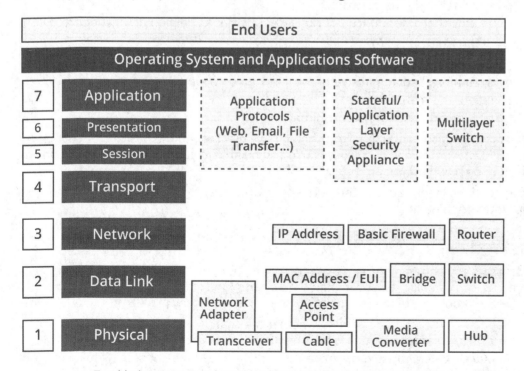

Troubleshooting top-to-bottom or bottom-to-top using the OSI model.

When you have drilled down like this, the problem should become obvious. Of course, you could have made the wrong choice at any point, so you must be prepared to go back and follow a different path.

 Note: *If you are really unlucky, two (or more) components may be faulty. Another difficulty lies in assessing whether a component itself is faulty or if it is not working because a related component is broken.*

DIVIDE AND CONQUER APPROACH

In a divide and conquer approach, rather than starting at the top or bottom, you start with the layer *most likely* to be causing the problem and then work either down or up depending on what your tests reveal. For example, if you start diagnosis at layer 3 and cannot identify a problem, you would then test at layer 4. Conversely, if you discovered a problem at layer 3, you would first test layer 2. If there is no problem at layer 2, you can return to layer 3 and work from there up.

TEST A PROBABLE CAUSE

By questioning the obvious or by using one or more methodical diagnostic approaches, hopefully you will have gathered enough data to come to an initial theory about the probable cause. Remember that you might be wrong! Without jumping to conclusions, set out to prove or disprove your suspicions by using your troubleshooting skills and toolkit.

If you cannot prove the cause of the problem, you will either need to develop and test a new theory or decide to **escalate** the problem. **Escalation** means referring the problem to a senior technician, manager, or third party. You may need to escalate a problem for any of these reasons:

- The problem is beyond your knowledge or ability to troubleshoot.
- The problem falls under a system warranty and would be better dealt with by the supplier.
- The scope of the problem is very large and/or the solution requires some major reconfiguration of the network.
- A customer becomes difficult or abusive or demands help on an unsupported item.

Some of the alternatives for escalation include:

- Senior staff, knowledge experts, subject matter experts, technical staff, developers, programmers, and administrators within your company.
- Suppliers and manufacturers.
- Other support contractors/consultants.

When you escalate a problem, you should have established the basic facts, such as the scope of the problem and its likely cause and be able to communicate these clearly to the person to whom you are referring the incident.

If you can prove the cause of the problem, you can start to investigate the most appropriate solution.

ESTABLISH A PLAN OF ACTION

Assuming you choose not to escalate the issue, the next step in the troubleshooting process is to establish an action plan. An **action plan** sets out the steps you will take to solve the problem. There are typically three solutions to any problem:

- **Repair**—You need to determine whether the cost of repair/time taken to reconfigure something makes this the best option.
- **Replace**—Often, this is more expensive and may be time-consuming if a part is not available. There may also be an opportunity to **upgrade** the device or software.

Note: *A basic technique when you are troubleshooting a cable, connector, or device is to have a **known good** duplicate on hand (that is, another copy of the same cable or device that you know works) and to test by substitution.*

- **Ignore**—As any software developer will tell you, not all problems are critical. If neither repair nor replace is cost-effective, it may be best either to find a workaround or just to document the issue and move on.

When you consider solutions, you must assess the cost and time required. Another consideration is potential effects on the rest of the system. A typical example is applying a software patch, which might fix a given problem but cause other programs not to work. This is where an effective configuration management system comes into play, as it should help you to understand how different systems are interconnected and cause you to seek the proper authorization for your plan.

IMPLEMENT THE SOLUTION

The solution to a problem might just involve resetting a system to its baseline configuration. Perhaps a user installed some unauthorized software, disabled a necessary service, or unplugged a cable. If you are reverting to a **known good** configuration, you may be able to implement the solution directly. If the solution requires a change to the system or the network environment, you are likely to have to follow a change management plan.

If you do not have authorization to implement a solution, you will need to escalate the problem to more senior personnel. If applying the solution is disruptive to the wider network, you also need to consider the most appropriate time to schedule the reconfiguration work and plan how to notify other network users. When you change a system as part of implementing a solution, test after each change. If the change does not fix the problem, reverse it and then try something else. If you make a series of changes without recording what you have done, you could find yourself in a tricky position.

VERIFY FULL SYSTEM FUNCTIONALITY AND IMPLEMENT PREVENTIVE MEASURES

When you apply a solution, validate that it fixes the reported problem and that the system as a whole continues to function normally. In other words, identify the results and effects of the solution. Ensure that you were right and that the problem is resolved. Can the user now log in properly? Is there any way you can induce the problem again?

Before you can consider a problem closed, you should be satisfied in your own mind that you have resolved it *and* you should get the customer's acceptance that it has been fixed. Restate what the problem was and how it was resolved, then confirm with the customer that the incident log can be closed.

To fully solve a problem, you should try to eliminate any factors that may cause the problem to recur. For example, if a user plugs his or her laptop into the wrong network jack, ensure that the jacks are clearly labeled to help users in the future. If a faulty server induces hours of network downtime, consider implementing failover services to minimize the impact of the next incident.

DOCUMENT FINDINGS, ACTIONS, AND OUTCOMES

Most troubleshooting takes place within the context of a ticket system. This shows who is responsible for any given problem and what its status is. This gives you the opportunity to add a complete description of the problem and its solution, including findings, actions, and outcomes.

This is massively useful for future troubleshooting, as problems fitting into the same category can be reviewed to see if the same solution applies. It also helps to analyze IT infrastructure by gathering statistics on what type of problems occur and how frequently.

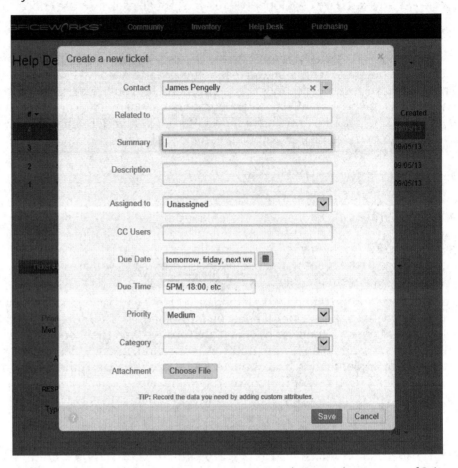

Creating a ticket in the Spiceworks IT Support management tool. (Screenshot courtesy of Spiceworks.)

When you complete a problem log, remember that people other than you may come to rely on it. Also, logs may be presented to customers as proof of troubleshooting activity. Write clearly and concisely, checking for spelling and grammar errors.

Activity 8-3

Discussing Network Troubleshooting Methodology

SCENARIO

Answer the following questions to test your understanding of the content covered in this topic.

1. Use the following list of activities to answer the question:
   - Gather information
   - Duplicate the problem, if possible
   - Question users
   - Identify symptoms
   - Determine if anything has changed

   Which step has been omitted from the list of activities related to identifying the problem?

2. **After asking the three basic questions of anyone reporting a problem, what should you have determined? (Choose three.)**

   ☐ Whether to look for recent change or an oversight in configuration.

   ☐ Where to look for the problem.

   ☐ The severity of the problem.

   ☐ If the problem should be escalated.

3. **Which three means of establishing a theory of probable cause refer to the OSI model?**

4. **When should you escalate a problem?**

5. **Which step follows "Implement the solution or escalate as necessary" in the troubleshooting methodology?**

6. **True or False? Documentation should be created only at the end of the troubleshooting process.**

Topic C

Troubleshoot Common Network Services Issues

EXAM OBJECTIVES COVERED
5.3 Given a scenario, troubleshoot common wired connectivity and performance issues.
5.5 Given a scenario, troubleshoot common network service issues.

Network problems can arise from a variety of sources outside your control. As a network professional, your users, your managers, and your colleagues will all look to you to identify and resolve those problems efficiently. To do that, you will need a strong fundamental understanding of the tools and processes involved in troubleshooting a network. Being able to resolve problems in these areas is a crucial skill for keeping your network running smoothly.

END-TO-END CONNECTIVITY TROUBLESHOOTING

When you are using the CompTIA Network+ troubleshooting model, it is wise to rule out physical hardware failure and Data Link layer issues before diagnosing a service issue.

When you are troubleshooting end-to-end connectivity between two hosts, you need to consider the topology of the network between them. Most LANs are wired in a star configuration, perhaps with switches connected in some cascading backbone structure. You should be aware that different topologies generate potentially different symptoms when there are low-level network problems.

STAR-WIRED TOPOLOGIES

Generally, a failure in a star-wired topology will manifest itself either with one client unable to connect or with all clients unable to connect. This usually makes the location of the problem quite simple to identify. Star-wired topologies tend to be reasonably fault tolerant. If one system is affected, then check the link from switch to host for that system. If more than one system is affected, check the backbone wiring between switches or the switch itself.

BACKBONES

These segments connect switches and routers together; consequently, failures are far more noticeable. Many hosts will have connection problems. Isolating where is a question of determining which hosts can see which other hosts.

MESH TOPOLOGIES AND ROUTING

Mesh topologies are difficult to troubleshoot because all hosts have connections to all others. Your knowledge of routing should help you troubleshoot issues here. If host A and B can communicate using three routes and they used to have four routes, then troubleshoot the fourth route—there may be a wiring problem there, or a routing device might be down.

HARDWARE FAILURE ISSUES

Like any computer system, networks require stable power to operate properly. **Power anomalies**, such as surges and spikes, can damage devices, brownouts (very brief power loss) can cause systems to lockup or reboot, while **power failures** (blackouts) will down everything, including the lights. Enterprise sites have systems to protect against these issues. **Uninterruptible power supplies (UPSs)** can keep servers, switches, and routers running for a few minutes. This provides time to either switch in a secondary power source (a generator) or shut down the system gracefully, hopefully avoiding data loss. Most power problems will have to be escalated to an electrician or to the power company, depending on where the fault lies.

If power is not the issue, consider other components that might have experienced **hardware failure**, including host network adapters, switch/router/modem appliances, and the cabling between them. You can test for specific cabling faults using specialist tools, discussed later in the course. Complete hardware failure is relatively uncommon, so if you can rule out power and cabling problems, then for a network adapter, verify the driver. Perhaps it has become corrupted. You could use packet monitoring software to record the number of **interface errors** generated. The easiest thing to do is to replace the driver (in Windows®, use **Device Manager** to do this). For a network appliance, use status LEDs to confirm operation and check that things like plug-in cards and modules are seated correctly. You should also consider **overheating** as a potential cause of hardware issues. Make sure there is good airflow around the intake and outlet vents. Check that fans and internal components are not clogged with dust and that systems are not exposed to direct sunlight.

NETWORK INTERFACE ISSUES

If there are no obvious hardware failure issues, you should verify the settings on the switch port and NIC. Most adapters and switches successfully autonegotiate port settings. If this process fails, the adapter and port can end up with **mismatched speed or duplex settings**.

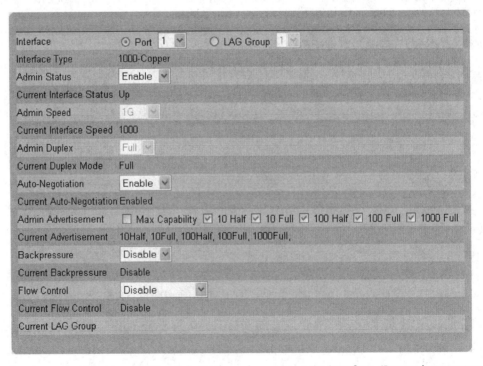

Configuring port settings on a Dell switch via the web management interface. (Screenshot courtesy of Dell.)

In most cases, this will be because either the adapter or the switch port has been manually configured. If a host is set to a fixed configuration and the switch is set to autonegotiate, the switch will default to 10 Mbps/half-duplex because the host will not negotiate with it! So, if the host is manually configured to 100 Mbps/full-duplex, the link will fail. Setting both to autonegotiate will generally solve the problem. A speed mismatch will cause the link to fail, while a duplex mismatch will slow the link down (it will cause high packet loss and late collisions).

IP CONFIGURATION ISSUES

If you can rule out a problem at the Physical and Data Link layers, the next thing to check is basic addressing and protocol configuration. If a host cannot perform neighbor discovery to contact any other nodes on the local network (and you can discount power, cable, and other hardware issues), first use `ipconfig` or `ifconfig` and `route` to check for a misconfiguration.

- Is the IP address appropriate for the local subnet?
- Is the netmask (subnet mask or network prefix) appropriate for the local subnet?

> *Note: Many private network addressing schemes use one of the default netmasks, which are often referred to by the old classful addressing terminology. Remember that these are 255.0.0.0 (or /8 or Class A), 255.255.0.0 (or /16 or Class B), and 255.255.255.0 (or /24 or Class C).*

- Is the address of the default gateway correct?
- Are there any static routes in the routing table of a host?
- Are the DNS server IP addresses configured correctly?

If there are errors, either correct them (if the interface is statically configured) or investigate the automatic addressing server.

DUPLICATE IP AND MAC ADDRESS ISSUES

Two systems could end up with the **same IP address** because of a configuration error; perhaps both addresses were statically assigned, or one was assigned an address that was part of a DHCP pool. If Windows detects a duplicate IP address, it will display a warning and disable IP. Linux® does not typically check for duplicate IP addresses. If there are two systems with duplicate IPs, a sort of race condition will determine which receives traffic. Obviously, this is not a good way for the network to be configured, and you should identify and fix the machines. To do this, obtain the MAC addresses of both interfaces using `ping` and `arp -a` or using a scanning tool such as Nmap. Once identified, configure each host to use a unique address.

A **duplicate MAC address** will cause a problem similar to a duplicate IP address. Both hosts will contend to respond to ARP queries, and communications could be split between them or reach only one of the hosts. Duplicate MAC addresses are unlikely to arise unless the network uses locally administered addressing, which is almost never a good idea. Issues with MAC addressing are more likely to be a sign that someone is attempting to perform an ARP spoofing attack.

To diagnose MAC address issues, use the `arp` utility to verify the MAC addresses recorded for each host and `ipconfig` or `ifconfig` to check the MAC address assigned to the interface. Also check the MAC address and ARP tables on any switches and routers involved in the communications path. You can use a protocol analyzer to examine ARP traffic and identify which IP hosts are attempting to claim the same MAC address.

NETMASK AND GATEWAY ISSUES

If the interface IP configuration seems correct, you can complete a series of connectivity tests using `ping` to determine where the fault lies.

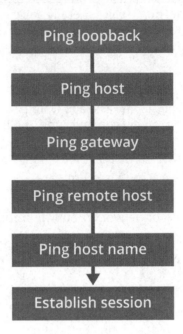

A general ping sequence for identifying connectivity issues.

1. First, ping the local loopback address. If that works, you can be sure that IP is installed, although it doesn't prove much else.

2. Next, test that the machine can discover **neighboring devices or nodes** by pinging a local IP address—perhaps the nearest router interface. Remember, choose something in the same subnet that you know is online and available. If the ping operation is unsuccessful, then view the error carefully.

   If the error returned is **Request Timed Out**, this might suggest that the local computer is configured correctly but cannot access the host. If the error returned is **Destination Unreachable**, this suggests a routing problem. If you are pinging a host in the same subnet, it is likely that either the IP address of this host is wrong or that the **netmask/subnet mask is incorrect**, leading IP to believe that the target host is in a different subnet. Check the IP configuration on the host (if IP is configured statically) or the lease obtained from a DHCP server.

   Another issue that might arise if a netmask is incorrect, is that the host can receive communications, but misroutes its replies, thinking that the hosts communicating with it are on a different subnet. The replies may still get through, though they may go via the default gateway (router), rather than directly. If the IP address is wrong, the host will probably not receive any communications, as no other hosts will be able to locate a route to it.

   When performing tests using ping, always be aware that ICMP could be blocked by a firewall or other security software.

3. If you can ping a local address, try pinging a remote host. If that doesn't work, check that the **default gateway** parameter is correct. View the host's routing table to verify that the default route (0.0.0.0/0 for IPv4 or ::/0 for IPv6) is configured correctly.

4. If the default gateway is correct and you can ping it, start investigating the router.

```
C:\Users\administrator>ping 10.1.0.101

Pinging 10.1.0.101 with 32 bytes of data:
Reply from 10.1.0.101: bytes=32 time<1ms TTL=128
Reply from 10.1.0.101: bytes=32 time<1ms TTL=128
Reply from 10.1.0.101: bytes=32 time<1ms TTL=128
Reply from 10.1.0.101: bytes=32 time<1ms TTL=128

Ping statistics for 10.1.0.101:
    Packets: Sent = 4, Received = 4, Lost = 0 (0% loss),
Approximate round trip times in milli-seconds:
    Minimum = 0ms, Maximum = 0ms, Average = 0ms

C:\Users\administrator>ping 10.1.0.2

Pinging 10.1.0.2 with 32 bytes of data:
Request timed out.
Request timed out.
Request timed out.
Request timed out.

Ping statistics for 10.1.0.2:
    Packets: Sent = 4, Received = 0, Lost = 4 (100% loss),

C:\Users\administrator>ping 10.2.0.1

Pinging 10.2.0.1 with 32 bytes of data:
Reply from 172.16.0.253: Destination net unreachable.
Reply from 172.16.0.253: Destination net unreachable.
Reply from 172.16.0.253: Destination net unreachable.
Reply from 172.16.0.253: Destination net unreachable.

Ping statistics for 10.2.0.1:
    Packets: Sent = 4, Received = 4, Lost = 0 (0% loss),

C:\Users\administrator>
```

Completing a series of ping tests. (Screenshot used with permission from Microsoft.)

SWITCHING ISSUES

Having eliminated cabling, the network interface card and driver, and a host's IP configuration as potential sources of the problem, you need to know who else experiences the problem. If several users are affected, try connecting them to another switch. If this works, check the suspect switch's connections to other switches, and verify obvious things like power, complete hardware failure, and so on.

If you suspect a device like a switch, look at the logical topology of your network. You should be able to view those users who are suffering the problem, identify which part of the network is affected, and identify the problem bridging or switching device. When you have narrowed the problem to a device, you must determine what the nature of the problem is. It is always worth resetting the switch to see if that resolves the problem. Often, restarting network devices can clear any errors.

When you have verified the physical configuration of the switches, determine whether it is applicable or relevant to update the switch software. It could be that the vendor has firmware or software updates that you must apply to resolve your problem. If you have still not resolved the problem, it will be necessary to check the vendor product documentation or support service to progress your troubleshooting.

ROUTING ISSUES

Forwarding issues can also occur at layer 3. If you can ping a host's default gateway and ping some, but not all, hosts on remote networks, then there is a route problem. In most cases, this will be because a router has gone offline and there is no alternative path to that network. If routes between networks have been configured statically, it is possible that a certain IP route is missing or incorrectly configured. Use the `route` command to investigate the router's routing table.

A **routing loop** is a routing process in which two routers discover different routes to the same location that include each other but have incorrect information, and therefore never reach the endpoint. Data caught in a routing loop circles around until its TTL expires. Routing loops can be difficult to detect and to troubleshoot; the best prevention is proper router configuration.

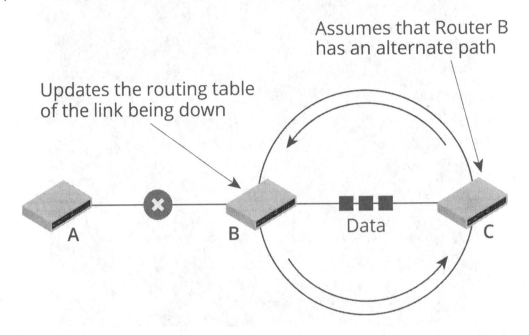

A routing loop created between routers B and C.

For example, Routers A, B, and C are connected in a line. When the link between A and B goes down, it prompts B to update its routing table. But this update does not reach C on time, and it sends its regular update to B. This leads B to assume that C has found an alternate path to reach A. An endless loop is created because B tries to send packets addressed to A via C, which redirects the packets to B. This routing loop continues until the TTL of the data expires.

Another possibility is that a security appliance such as a firewall is blocking communications.

DHCP ISSUES

The **Dynamic Host Configuration Protocol (DHCP)** provides IP addressing autoconfiguration to hosts without static IP parameters. If Windows machines are failing to obtain an IP configuration, the symptom will be the inability to connect to other hosts. Upon closer inspection, you should verify the hosts' IP configurations. If APIPA (169.254.0.0/16) is being used, the client has failed to obtain a configuration from the server. You will need to establish why. Possible reasons include:

- The DHCP server is offline. Restart the server.
- No more addresses available (exhausted DHCP scope). Create a new scope with enough addresses, or reduce the lease period. Remember that IP Address Management (IPAM) software suites can be used to track address usage across a complex DHCP infrastructure.

- The router between the client and DHCP server doesn't support BOOTP forwarding. Either install *RFC 1542*-compliant routers, or add another type of DHCP relay agent to each subnet or VLAN.
- If your DHCP servers go offline, users will continue to connect to the network for a period and then start to lose contact with network services and servers. They may appear to connect to the network, but they will be restricted to the local subnet.
- If you reconfigure your DHCP servers and their scopes, the clients will gradually get reconfigured. You will need to ensure that you plan for the fact that not all clients' IP configurations will be updated when the server scopes are edited and could be left with an expired IP address. You could lower the lease duration in advance of changes, force all clients to renew, or run parallel settings for a period.
- If device time is not set correctly, when the lease reaches the halfway point and tries to renew, the IP address shows as expired because the other device shows that the time to renew has passed.
- Rogue DHCP. Clients have no means of preferring a DHCP server if a lease has expired. If two DHCP servers are running on the same subnet, clients could end up with an incorrect IP configuration because they have obtained a lease from a **rogue server**. A rogue server may be deployed accidentally (forgetting to disable a DHCP server in an access point or router, for instance) or may be used by a malicious attacker to subvert the network.

NAME RESOLUTION ISSUES

If you can ping a local and a remote IP address, then basic connectivity is not the issue. The next step may be to try pinging by name, thus testing name resolution. It is important that you know the order of name resolution for the operating system that you are troubleshooting; otherwise, you cannot determine which step failed. Bear in mind that different operating systems do things differently. A client will perform name resolution in a prescribed order.

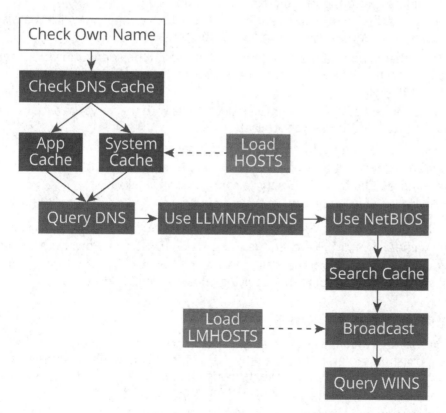

Name resolution order for a Windows client (Vista and later).

Link-Local Multicast Name Resolution (LLMNR) and **multicastDNS (mDNS)** are modified forms of DNS that allow clients to perform name resolution on a local link without needing a server. NetBIOS is a protocol used for Microsoft workgroup networking. WINS is a server that can provide name resolution for NetBIOS clients along the same lines as DNS.

Linux does not use the NetBIOS protocol, and therefore if the name to be resolved is not in the **/etc/hosts** file or DNS cache, it will be sent to the DNS servers specified in the **/etc/resolv.conf** file. If none of these can successfully resolve the name to an IP address, a failure is reported to the application making the request. Linux can also implement mDNS, using the Avahi package.

DNS CONFIGURATION ISSUES

Linux and Windows systems all rely on DNS for name resolution and **service discovery**. In the absence of DNS servers, network client machines will be unable to log on or connect to services or servers. The symptoms will appear quite quickly, as the name cache of clients is defined in DNS and is usually set to timeout after one hour. Reconfiguration of DNS should be planned and implemented carefully, as the service is such a cornerstone of any network that its absence, or misconfiguration, will undoubtedly cause major problems.

If your hosts are experiencing DNS problems, symptoms will include the inability to connect to a server by name, despite it being accessible by IP address. To verify a name resolution problem, edit the **HOSTS** file and place the correct name and IP address record in the file for the test host. When you ping, if that is successful, it suggests a name resolution problem.

If a single client is unable to resolve names, the issue is likely to lie with the client configuration.

- The client has been configured either with no DNS server address or the wrong DNS server address. Reconfigure the DNS server address.
- The client has the incorrect DNS suffix. Verify the DNS domain in which the client is supposed to be, and verify the Windows settings match.

Bear in mind that in both of these situations, DHCP might be configuring these settings incorrectly. Therefore, check the server options or scope options configuration on the DHCP server as well.

If multiple clients are affected, the issue is likely to lie with the server service (or the way a subnet accesses the server service).

- The DNS server is offline. Check and restart if necessary.
- If some DNS queries work from the client and others don't, then the problem is more complex. Check the DNS service configuration itself. Use the `nslookup` or `dig` utilities to check that the service is working.

You can use `nslookup` in Windows to check if the default or a specific DNS server is resolving names correctly. However, the `Resolve-DNSName` PowerShell® cmdlet or the `dig` utility packaged with the BIND server can often give a more complete picture of what is happening regarding the resolving of names to IP addresses.

UNRESPONSIVE SERVICE ISSUES

If you can rule out connectivity problems with a local client or subnet, the issue may be with an application server, rather than the client. Such **unresponsive service issues** will usually manifest with multiple clients being unable to connect. There can be any number of underlying causes, but consider some of the following:

- The application or OS hosting the service has crashed (or there is a hardware or power problem).

- The server hosting the service is overloaded (high CPU/memory/disk I/O utilization/ disk space utilization). Try throttling client connections until the server resources can be upgraded (or supported by cloud-based infrastructure).
- There is congestion in the network, either at the client or server end (or both). Use `pathping` or `mtr` to check the latency experienced over the link and compare to a baseline. Again, throttling connections or bandwidth may help to ease the congestion until higher bandwidth links can be provisioned.
- A broadcast storm is causing loss of network bandwidth. Switching loops cause broadcast frames to circulate the network perpetually, as each switch repeatedly floods each frame. A broadcast storm may quickly consume all link bandwidth and crash network appliances (check for excessive CPU utilization on switches and hosts). The Spanning Tree Protocol (STP) is supposed to prevent such loops, but this can fail if STP communications between switches do not work correctly, either because of a fault in cabling or a port/transceiver or because of a misconfiguration.
- Network congestion may also be a sign that the service is being subject to a **Denial of Service (DoS)** attack. Look for unusual access patterns (for example, use GeoIP to graph source IP addresses by country and compare to baseline access patterns).

> **Note:** *If users on a LAN cannot connect to an external service, such as a cloud application, you can use a site such as https://www.isitdownrightnow.com/ to test whether the issue is local to your network or a problem with the service provider site.*

- A misconfigured firewall or other security appliance is blocking access. Check the logs and configuration settings of the security appliance. Remember that a firewall's access control list (ACL) may be blocking a port (in which case, all clients passing the firewall should be unable to connect) or a particular source IP address or subnet (so that only particular clients are unable to connect). There could also be more complex filtering rules applied somewhere.

> **Note:** *Be proactive in monitoring service availability so that you can resolve problems before they affect large numbers of clients.*

> **Note:** *To learn more, watch the related **Video** on the course website.*

Activity 8-4

Discussing Common Network Services Issues

SCENARIO

Answer the following questions to test your understanding of the content covered in this topic.

1. You have connected a new computer to a network port and cannot get a link. You have tested the adapter and cable and can confirm that there are no problems. No other users are experiencing problems. The old computer also experienced no problems. What cause would you suspect, and what is a possible next step?

2. Users on a floor served by a single switch cannot get a network connection. What is the best first step?

3. You have pinged the router for the local subnet and confirmed that there is a valid link. The local host cannot access remote hosts, however. No other users are experiencing problems. What do you think is the cause?

4. Following maintenance on network switches, users in one department cannot access the company's internal web and email servers. You can demonstrate basic connectivity between the hosts and the servers by IP address. What might the problem be?

5. Users on a network segment have been experiencing poor performance. The cause has been identified as a broadcast storm. What is often the cause of broadcast storms?

6. You are planning to reconfigure static and DHCP-assigned IP addresses across the network during scheduled downtime. What preliminary step should you take to minimize connectivity issues when the network is re-opened?

Activity 8-5

Troubleshooting Network Issues

SCENARIO

You are staffing the network help desk and dealing with support requests as they arrive. Your network uses four access switches to support four subnets. One subnet contains network servers (authentication, directory services, DNS, and DHCP) and another contains Line of Business (LoB) application servers, for sales and order processing. There are two client subnets, serving different floors in the building.

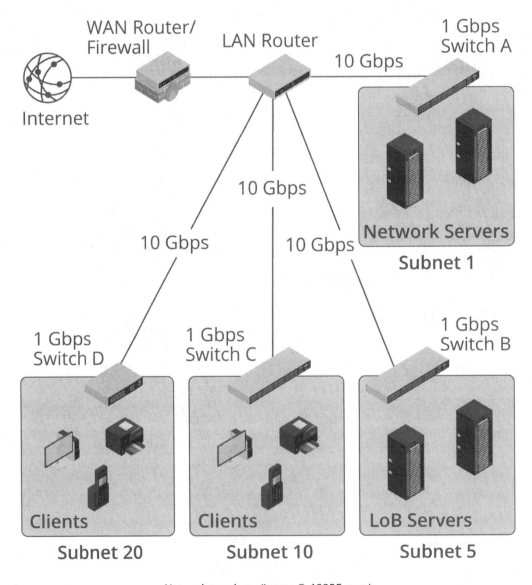

Network topology. (Image © 123RF.com.)

1. **You receive a call from the user of host A who has always been able to connect to the LoB application servers, but today she is unable to connect. You verbally check with other users and discover that none of the hosts on subnet 20 can connect, but that users in subnet 10 report no problems. What tests should you perform to narrow down the cause of the problem?**

2. **You send a junior technician to the equipment room to fix the problem. Some time later, another user from subnet 20 calls complaining that he cannot connect to the Internet. What questions should you ask to begin troubleshooting?**

3. **You asked a junior technician to step in because your manager had asked you to deploy a wireless access point on the network to support a sales event due to start the next day. There will be lots of guests, and your manager wants them all to have Internet access. You did not have much time, so you simply added the access point to the switch supporting subnet 10. The next day arrives, and some time after the sales event starts, multiple employees in subnet 10 report that when they attempt to connect to the network, they get a message that the Windows network has limited connectivity. What might be the cause and what test should you use to confirm the issue?**

Summary

In this lesson, you learned about network monitoring, plus troubleshooting procedures for basic connectivity issues.

- Documenting baselines and establishing thresholds underpins effective performance monitoring and alerting.
- Load and throughput testing can be used to determine whether a network is meeting its performance goals or deviating from its baseline.
- Analysis of logs and device and interface metrics can identify faults and bottlenecks. Logs and performance information can be aggregated by SYSLOG and SIEM servers.
- SNMP is used to monitor and manage network devices from a central location.
- Make sure you know how to interpret network interface metrics, such as error rate and utilization.
- Troubleshooting should be completed against a checklist of best practice actions (identify the problem, establish and test a theory, establish and implement an action plan, verify functionality, and document the solution).
- Taking a layered approach can help to troubleshoot specific connectivity scenarios.
- Learn the symptoms and causes of common connectivity and configuration issues.

What network monitoring tasks have you used in your organization?

What method do you use when troubleshooting? Is it a formalized model documented within your organization?

 Practice Questions: *Additional practice questions are available on the course website.*

Lesson 9

Explaining Networking Attacks and Mitigations

LESSON INTRODUCTION

You have identified the basic components and concepts for implementing a network, but a network implementation is not complete without security mechanisms. In this lesson, you will describe basic concepts related to network security. As a networking professional, it is part of your responsibility to understand these fundamental concepts so that you can ensure appropriate security levels in your organization.

LESSON OBJECTIVES

In this lesson, you will:

- Summarize common networking attacks.

- Explain the characteristics of VLANs.

- Explain the characteristics of NAT and port forwarding.

Topic A
Summarize Common Networking Attacks

 EXAM OBJECTIVES COVERED
4.4 Summarize common networking attacks.

In this lesson, you will describe basic concepts related to network security. It's important to have a solid foundation and awareness of the industry terminology used when you are discussing network security. There are many ways in which networks can be attacked and just as many ways for making networks more secure. You will need a basic understanding of the security risks, and security methods and tools, in order to protect your network.

SECURITY BASICS

Establishing computer and network security means developing processes and controls that protect data assets and ensure business continuity by making network systems and hosts resilient to different kinds of attack.

THE CIA TRIAD

One of the foundational principles of computer security is that the systems used to store, transmit, and process data must demonstrate three properties, often referred to as the **CIA Triad**.

- **Confidentiality**—Certain information should only be known to certain people.
- **Integrity**—The data is stored and transferred as intended, and any modification is authorized.
- **Availability**—Information is accessible to those authorized to view or modify it.

Many tools and techniques are available to ensure that network systems demonstrate these three key properties.

SECURITY POLICIES

Security policies ensure that an organization has evaluated the risks it faces and has put **security controls** in place to mitigate those risks. Making a system more secure is also referred to as **hardening**. Different security policies should cover every aspect of an organization's use of computer and network technologies, from procurement and change control to acceptable use.

EXPLOITS VS. VULNERABILITIES

In IT security, it is important to distinguish between the concepts of **vulnerability**, **threat**, **exploit**, and **risk**:

- **Vulnerability**—A weakness that could be accidentally triggered or intentionally exploited to cause a security breach.
- **Threat**—The potential for a **threat agent** or **threat actor** (something or someone that may trigger a vulnerability accidentally or exploit it intentionally) to exercise a vulnerability (that is, to breach security). The path or tool used by the threat actor can be referred to as the **threat vector**.

- **Exploit**—A specific means of using a vulnerability to gain control of a system or damage it in some way.
- **Risk**—The likelihood and impact (or consequence) of a threat actor exercising a vulnerability.

To understand network security, you need to understand the types of threats and vulnerabilities to which a network is exposed and how they can be used in actual attacks via an exploit.

Vulnerabilities can exist because of misconfigurations or poor practice, but many people understand the term to mean faults in software specifically. This type of software vulnerability is a design flaw that can cause the application security system to be circumvented or that will cause the application to crash. The most serious vulnerabilities allow the attacker to execute arbitrary code on the system, which could allow the installation of malware. Typically, applications such as web servers, web browsers, web browser plug-ins, email clients, and databases are targeted. The code or method by which an attacker uses a vulnerability is called an **exploit**.

Typically, software vulnerabilities can be exploited only in quite specific circumstances, but because of the complexity of modern software and the speed with which new versions must be released to market, almost no software is free from vulnerabilities. Most software vulnerabilities are discovered by software and security researchers, who notify the vendor to give them time to patch the vulnerability before releasing details to the wider public. A vulnerability that is exploited before the developer knows about it or can release a patch is called a **zero-day exploit**. These can be extremely destructive, as it can take the vendor a lot of time to develop a patch, leaving systems vulnerable for days, weeks, or even years.

While some zero-day attacks can be extremely destructive, they are relatively rare. A greater threat is the large number of unpatched or legacy systems in use. An **unpatched** system is one that its owner has not updated with OS and application patches; a **legacy** system is one where the software vendor no longer provides support or fixes for problems.

 Note: *This issue does not just affect PCs. Network appliances can also be vulnerable to exploits. The risks to embedded systems have become more obvious over the last few years, and the risks posed by unpatched mobile devices and the Internet of Things is likely to grow.*

NETWORK RECONNAISSANCE ATTACKS

A network can be attacked by many kinds of intruders or adversaries for many different reasons. The goals of most types of adversaries will either be to steal (exfiltrate) information from the network, to misuse network services (for fraud, for instance), or to damage it. Insider threat-type attacks may be launched with privileged access to the network, while external threats must find some way of accessing the network, perhaps by installing malware on a host system. Network attacks can then proceed in several ways.

 Note: *Attacks become less effective when they are well known, so new threats and exploits appear all the time. To keep up to date, you should monitor websites and newsgroups. Apart from the regular IT magazines, some good examples include cert.org, sans.org, schneier.com, and grc.com. The SANS "Top 20" security controls is one of the most useful starting points (sans.org/top20).*

Footprinting is a process of information gathering, in which the attacker attempts to learn about the configuration of the network and security systems. Footprinting can be done by **social engineering** attacks—persuading users to give information or locating information that has been thrown out as trash, for instance. **Port scanning** specifically aims to enumerate the TCP or UDP application ports that are "open" on a host. When a host running a particular operating system responds to a port scan, the syntax of the response might identify the specific operating system. This fact is also true of application servers, such as web servers, FTP servers, and mail servers. The responses these servers make often include headers or banners that can reveal a great deal of information about the server.

Eavesdropping (or **sniffing**) refers to capturing and reading data packets as they move over the network. When an attacker has gained access to the network, he or she can use a packet sniffer, such as Wireshark, to capture live network traffic. Unless the packets are encrypted, the attacker can gain a lot of information about the way the network is designed, as well as intercepting any data transmitted in plaintext. An attack would be limited to data traffic to and from the individual user's computer (as well as broadcast traffic), as network switches will prevent all other traffic from being directed to that host. However, switches can be subverted by various types of **spoofing** attacks.

SPOOFING AND MAN-IN-THE-MIDDLE ATTACKS

The term **spoofing** (or impersonation or masquerade) covers a very wide range of different attacks. Spoofing can include any type of attack where the attacker disguises his or her identity, or in which the source of network information is forged to appear legitimate. Social engineering and techniques such as **phishing** and **pharming**, where the attacker sets up a false website in imitation of a real one, are types of spoofing attacks. It is also possible to **abuse** the way a protocol works or how network packets are constructed to inject false or modified data onto a network. The ARP and DNS protocols are often used as vectors for this type of attack.

In an **IP spoofing** attack, the attacker changes the source address recorded in the IP packet. IP spoofing is done to disguise the real identity of the attacker's host machine. The technique is also used in most **denial of service (DoS)** attacks to mask the origin of the attack and make it harder for the target system to block packets from the attacking system.

A **man-in-the-middle (MitM) attack** is a specific type of spoofing attack where the attacker sits between two communicating hosts and transparently intercepts and relays all communications between them. The MitM might also have the opportunity to modify the traffic before relaying it.

ARP POISONING ATTACKS

An **ARP cache poisoning** attack is a common means of perpetrating a MitM attack. It works by broadcasting *unsolicited* ARP reply packets, also known as gratuitous ARP replies, with a spoofed source address. Because ARP has no security, the receiving devices trust this communication and update their MAC:IP address cache table with the spoofed address. An ARP spoofing attack can be launched by running software such as Dsniff, Cain and Abel, or Ettercap from a host attached to the same broadcast domain as the target.

No.	Time	Source	Destination	Protocol	Length	Info
6	10.022521400	Microsof_01:ca:4a	Microsof_01:ca:76	ARP	42	10.1.0.102 is at 00:15:5d:01
7	10.032593900	Microsof_01:ca:4a	Microsof_01:ca:77	ARP	42	10.1.0.2 is at 00:15:5d:01:c
8	10.032605300	Microsof_01:ca:4a	Microsof_01:ca:76	ARP	42	10.1.0.101 is at 00:15:5d:01
9	18.219200000	10.1.0.101	10.1.0.2	TCP	66	1702 → 80 [SYN] Seq=0 Win=65
10	18.220473400	10.1.0.101	10.1.0.2	TCP	66	[TCP Out-Of-Order] 1702 → 80
11	18.223616200	10.1.0.2	10.1.0.101	TCP	66	80 → 1702 [SYN, ACK] Seq=0 A
12	18.228456800	10.1.0.2	10.1.0.101	TCP	66	[TCP Retransmission] 80 → 17
13	18.228797700	10.1.0.101	10.1.0.2	TCP	54	1702 → 80 [ACK] Seq=1 Ack=1
14	18.229264100	10.1.0.101	10.1.0.2	HTTP	433	GET / HTTP/1.1
15	18.238162600	10.1.0.101	10.1.0.2	TCP	54	1702 → 80 [ACK] Seq=1 Ack=1
16	18.238250400	10.1.0.101	10.1.0.2	TCP	433	[TCP Retransmission] 1702 →
17	18.239342200	10.1.0.2	10.1.0.101	HTTP	412	HTTP/1.1 302 Redirect (text
18	18.244530700	10.1.0.2	10.1.0.101	TCP	412	[TCP Retransmission] 80 → 17
19	18.245021200	10.1.0.101	10.1.0.2	TCP	54	1702 → 80 [ACK] Seq=380 Ack=
20	18.252421600	10.1.0.101	10.1.0.2	TCP	54	[TCP Dup ACK 19#1] 1702 → 80
21	18.255190400	10.1.0.101	10.1.0.2	TCP	66	1703 → 443 [SYN] Seq=0 Win=6
22	18.260593200	10.1.0.101	10.1.0.2	TCP	66	[TCP Retransmission] 1703 →
23	18.261065300	10.1.0.2	10.1.0.101	TCP	66	443 → 1703 [SYN, ACK] Seq=0
24	18.268454800	10.1.0.2	10.1.0.101	TCP	66	[TCP Retransmission] 443 → 1

```
▶ Frame 9: 66 bytes on wire (528 bits), 66 bytes captured (528 bits) on interface 0
▽ Ethernet II, Src: Microsof_01:ca:77 (00:15:5d:01:ca:77), Dst: Microsof_01:ca:4a (00:15:5d:01:ca:4a)
  ▶ Destination: Microsof_01:ca:4a (00:15:5d:01:ca:4a)
  ▶ Source: Microsof_01:ca:77 (00:15:5d:01:ca:77)
    Type: IPv4 (0x0800)
▶ Internet Protocol Version 4, Src: 10.1.0.101, Dst: 10.1.0.2
▶ Transmission Control Protocol, Src Port: 1702, Dst Port: 80, Seq: 0, Len: 0
```

```
0000  00 15 5d 01 ca 4a 00 15  5d 01 ca 77 08 00 45 00   ..].. J.. ]..w..E.
0010  00 34 1c ca 40 00 80 06  c9 91 0a 01 00 65 0a 01   .4..@... .....e..
0020  00 02 06 a6 00 50 dc 52  ee 41 00 00 00 00 80 02   .....P.R .A......
0030  ff ff 89 1d 00 00 02 04  05 b4 01 03 03 08 01 01   ........ ........
0040  04 02                                              ..
```

Destination Hardware Address (eth.dst), 6 bytes   Packets: 286 · Displayed: 286 (100.0%)   Profile: Default

Observing ARP poisoning in a Wireshark packet capture. (Screenshot courtesy of Wireshark.)

The usual target will be the subnet's default gateway (the router that accesses other networks). If the attack is successful, all traffic destined for the remote network will be sent to the attacker. The attacker can then monitor the communications and continue to forward them to the router to avoid detection. The attacker could also modify the packets before forwarding them. ARP poisoning could also perform a DoS attack by not forwarding the packets. ARP poisoning can be difficult to detect without closely monitoring network traffic. However, attempts at ARP poisoning are likely to cause sporadic communications difficulties, such as an unreachable default gateway. In such cases, performing network captures and examining ARP packets may reveal the poison packets, as will examining local ARP caches for multiple IP addresses mapping to the same MAC address.

Note: *While IPv6 does not use ARP, it is also vulnerable to layer 2 spoofing if the unencrypted Neighbor Discovery (ND) protocol is used.*

Note: *To learn more, watch the related* **Video** *on the course website.*

DNS POISONING ATTACKS

DNS poisoning is an attack that compromises the name resolution process. Typically, the attacker will replace the valid IP address for a trusted website, such as **mybank.com**, with the attacker's IP address. The attacker can then intercept all the packets directed to **mybank.com** and bounce them to the real site, leaving the victim unaware of what is happening (referred to as **pharming**). Alternatively, DNS spoofing could be used for a DoS attack by directing all traffic for a particular FQDN to an invalid IP address (a black hole).

One way to attack DNS is to corrupt the client's name resolution process by changing the servers used for resolving queries, intercepting and modifying DNS traffic, or polluting the client's name cache (by modifying the HOSTS file, for instance). DNS server cache poisoning (or pollution) is another redirection attack, but instead of trying to subvert the name service used by the client, it aims to corrupt the records held by the DNS server itself.

```
  HOSTNAME    www.web.local      yes      Hostname to hijack
  INTERFACE                      no       The name of the interface
  NEWADDR     192.168.2.192      yes      New address for hostname
  RECONS      192.168.2.254      yes      The nameserver used for reconnaissance
  RHOST       192.168.1.1        yes      The target address
  SNAPLEN     65535              yes      The number of bytes to capture
  SRCADDR     Real               yes      The source address to use for sending t
he queries (Accepted: Real, Random)
  SRCPORT     0                  yes      The target server's source query port (
0 for automatic)
  TIMEOUT     500                yes      The number of seconds to wait for new d
ata
  TTL         46348              yes      The TTL for the malicious host entry
  XIDS        0                  yes      The number of XIDs to try for each quer
y (0 for automatic)

msf auxiliary(bailiwicked_host) > run

[-] Failure: This hostname is already in the target cache: www.web.local
[-]          Cache entry expires on 2017-09-17 09:08:17 -0700... sleeping.
^C[-] Auxiliary interrupted by the console user
[*] Auxiliary module execution completed
msf auxiliary(bailiwicked_host) > set hostname updates.web.local
hostname => updates.web.local
msf auxiliary(bailiwicked_host) > run

[*] Targeting nameserver 192.168.1.1 for injection of updates.web.local. as 192.
168.2.192
[*] Querying recon nameserver for web.local.'s nameservers...
[*]  Got an NS record: web.local.             604800   IN     NS     ns.web.lo
cal.
[*]    Querying recon nameserver for address of ns.web.local....
[*]    Got an A record: ns.web.local.          604800   IN     A      192.168.
1.1
[*]    Checking Authoritativeness: Querying 192.168.1.1 for web.local....
[*]    ns.web.local. is authoritative for web.local., adding to list of nameser
vers to spoof as
[*] Calculating the number of spoofed replies to send per query...
[*]  race calc: 100 queries | min/max/avg time: 0.0/0.0/0.0 | min/max/avg repli
es: 0/1/0
[*] The server did not reply, giving up.
[*] Auxiliary module execution completed
msf auxiliary(bailiwicked_host) > 
```

Attempting to poison a DNS server cache—This attack has failed.

DENIAL of SERVICE (DoS) ATTACKS

A **denial of service (DoS) attack** causes a service at a given host to fail or to become unavailable to legitimate users. Typically, DoS attacks focus on overloading a service by using up CPU, system RAM, disk space, or network bandwidth (**resource exhaustion**). It is also possible for DoS attacks to exploit design failures or other vulnerabilities in application software. An example of a physical DoS attack would be cutting telephone lines or network cabling or switching off the power to a server. DoS attacks may simply be motivated by the malicious desire to cause trouble. They may also be part of a wider attack, such as the precursor to a MitM or data exfiltration attack.

DoS can assist these attacks by diverting attention and resources away from the real target. For example, a **blinding** attack attempts to overload a logging or alerting system with events. It is crucial to understand the different motives attackers may have.

Many DoS attacks attempt to deny bandwidth to Internet web and DNS servers. They focus on exploiting historical vulnerabilities in the TCP/IP protocol suite. TCP/IP was never designed for security; it assumes that all hosts and networks are trusted. Other application attacks do not need to be based on consuming bandwidth or resources. Attacks can target known vulnerabilities in software to cause them to crash; **worms** and **viruses** can render systems unusable or choke network bandwidth.

All these types of DoS attack can have severe impacts on service availability, with a consequent effect on the productivity and profitability of a company. Where a DoS attack disrupts customer-facing services, there could be severe impacts on the company's reputation. An organization could also be presented with threats of blackmail or extortion.

DISTRIBUTED DoS (DDoS) ATTACKS AND BOTNETS

Most bandwidth-directed DoS attacks are **distributed**. This means that the attacks are launched from multiple, compromised computers. Typically, an attacker will compromise one or two machines to use as **handlers**, **masters**, or **herders**. The handlers are used to compromise hundreds or thousands or millions of **zombie** (agent) PCs with DoS tools (**bots**) forming a **botnet**. To compromise a computer, the attacker must install a backdoor application that gives them access to the PC. The attacker can then use the backdoor application to install DoS software and trigger the zombies to launch the attack at the same time.

 Note: *Any type of Internet-enabled device is vulnerable to compromise. This includes web-enabled cameras, SOHO routers, and smart TVs and other appliances. This is referred to as an Internet of Things (IoT) botnet.*

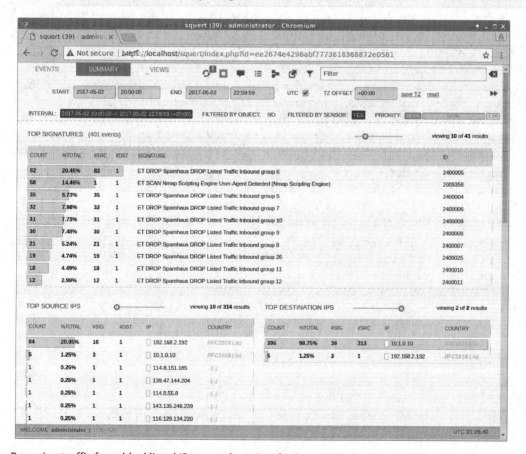

Dropping traffic from blacklisted IP ranges by using the Security Onion Network Security Monitoring (NSM) appliance. (Screenshot courtesy of Security Onion.)

DoS attacks might be **coordinated** between groups of attackers. There is growing evidence that nation states are engaging in "cyber warfare," and terrorist groups have also been implicated in DoS attacks on well-known companies and government institutions. There are also "hacker collectives" who might target an organization as part of a campaign.

Some types of attacks simply aim to consume network bandwidth, denying it to legitimate hosts. Others cause **resource exhaustion** on the hosts processing requests, consuming CPU cycles and memory. This delays processing of legitimate traffic and could potentially crash the host system completely. For example, a **SYN flood** attack works by withholding the client's ACK packet during TCP's three-way handshake. The client's IP address is spoofed, meaning that an invalid or random IP is entered so the server's SYN/ACK packet is misdirected. A server can maintain a queue of pending connections. When it does not receive an ACK packet from the client, it resends the SYN/ACK packet a set number of times before "timing out" and giving up on the connection. The problem is that a server may only be able to manage a limited number of pending connections, which the DoS attack quickly fills up. This means that the server is unable to respond to genuine traffic.

Servers can suffer the effects of a DDoS even when there is no malicious intent. For instance, the Slashdot effect is a sudden, temporary surge in traffic to a website that occurs when another website or other source posts a story that refers visitors to the victim website. This effect is more noticeable on smaller websites, and the increase in traffic can slow a website's response times or make it impossible to reach altogether.

AMPLIFICATION ATTACKS (DRDoS)

A more powerful TCP SYN flood attack is a type of **distributed reflection DoS (DRDoS)** or **amplification attack**. In this attack, the adversary spoofs the victim's IP address and attempts to open connections with multiple servers. Those servers direct their SYN/ACK responses to the victim server. This rapidly consumes the victim's available bandwidth.

A similar type of amplification attack can be performed by exploiting other protocols. For example, in a **Smurf attack**, the adversary spoofs the victim's IP address and pings the broadcast address of a third-party network (one with many hosts; referred to as the "amplifying network"). Each host directs its echo responses to the victim server.

The same sort of technique can be used to bombard a victim network with responses to **bogus DNS queries**. One of the advantages of this technique is that while the request is small, the response to a DNS query can be made to include a lot of information, so this is a very effective way of overwhelming the bandwidth of the victim network with much more limited resources on the attacker's botnet.

The **Network Time Protocol (NTP)** can be abused in a similar way. NTP helps servers on a network and on the Internet to keep the correct time. It is vital for many protocols and security mechanisms that servers and clients be synchronized. One NTP query (monlist) can be used to generate a response containing a list of the last 600 machines that the NTP server has contacted. As with the DNS amplification attack, this allows a short request to direct a long response at the victim network.

Activity 9-1

Discussing Common Networking Attacks

SCENARIO

Answer the following questions to test your understanding of the content covered in this topic.

---

1. **Response time on the website that hosts the online version of your product catalog is getting slower and slower. Customers are complaining that they cannot browse the catalog items or search for products. What type of attack do you suspect?**

   ○ Trojan horse attack.

   ○ Spoofing attack.

   ○ Social engineering attack.

   ○ DoS attack.

2. **The network administrator at your organization analyzes a network trace capture file and discovers that packets have been intercepted and retransmitted to both a sender and a receiver during an active session. This could be a(n):**

   ○ IP spoofing attack.

   ○ Session hijacking attack.

   ○ Replay attack.

   ○ Man-in-the-middle attack.

3. **What type of activity is often a prelude to a full-scale network attack?**

4. **What is the usual goal of an ARP spoofing attack?**

5. **Why are most network DoS attacks distributed?**

6. **What means might an attacker use to redirect traffic to a fake site by abusing DNS name resolution?**

7. **What type of DoS is a DNS amplification attack, and how is it perpetrated?**

8. **Greene City Interiors IT staff discovered an entry when reviewing their audit logs showing that a junior employee from the R&D department had logged into the network at 3:00 a.m. Further review of the audit logs show that he had changed his timecard on the HR server. Which security factor was breached, and did the attack exploit a software vulnerability or a configuration vulnerability?**

Topic B
Explain the Characteristics of VLANs

EXAM OBJECTIVES COVERED
1.3 Explain the concepts and characteristics of routing and switching.
4.4 Summarize common networking attacks.
4.6 Explain common mitigation techniques and their purposes.
5.3 Given a scenario, troubleshoot common wired connectivity and performance issues.

One of the primary benefits of using switches is to implement the concept of **virtual LANs (VLANs)** to segment a network. Most networks make use of VLANs, both to improve network security and network performance, so they are an important concept for you to understand. In this topic, you will identify the benefits of network segmentation and the characteristics and functions of VLANs.

NETWORK SEGMENTATION

One means of mitigating network attacks is through **network segmentation**. This is the process of determining which parts of the network are accessible to other parts. Segmentation can mitigate an attack by restricting it to a smaller group of network hosts. The technologies that can be used to enforce network segmentation include **virtual LANs (VLANs)**, subnets, virtual private networks (VPNs), and host virtualization. All these types of systems enforce network segmentation by deploying **access controls** of different types. The networks are not physically separate, but they are logically separate. For example, when a host is assigned to a VLAN, the switch restricts it to communications designated for that VLAN. To communicate outside the VLAN, the host must use a router, and a router equipped with a **firewall** can apply additional rules to what it allows in and out.

*Note: A highly secure network or single host computer may have to be physically separated from any other network. This is also referred to as an **air gap**. Air gapping creates many management issues, however, and so is rarely implemented.*

VIRTUAL LANs (VLANs)

Modern local networks are built using switches. In its default configuration, every port on a switch will be in the same local segment or, put another way, in the same broadcast domain. Any host within a broadcast domain can contact any other host using the same logical addressing scheme (IP subnet) and by hardware/MAC addressing. With too many hosts attached to the same switch, broadcast traffic can become excessive and reduce performance. Also, nodes within the same broadcast domain can be vulnerable to attacks such as ARP spoofing and worm malware. Breaking up the broadcast domains helps to limit the scope of these kinds of attacks. **Virtual LANs (VLANs)** are a means of addressing these issues. A VLAN means that different groups of computers on the same cabling and attached to the same switch(es) can appear to be in separate LAN segments. Nodes in each VLAN are in separate broadcast domains.

Note: : *If a VLAN were to contain multiple IP networks or subnets, nodes would receive broadcast traffic for all the subnets. This would be a very complex configuration, however. Normally, the network would be designed with a 1:1 mapping between VLANs and subnets.*

Implementing VLANs can reduce broadcast traffic when a network has expanded beyond a certain number of hosts or users. As well as reducing the impact of broadcast traffic, from a security point of view, each VLAN can represent a separate zone. These zones would typically be configured to protect the integrity and confidentiality of different departments within the organization. For example, the finance department can be its own VLAN, and marketing could be its own VLAN. If something like a virus or worm were introduced in one VLAN, it should not be able to spread to other VLANs. You also can prevent unauthorized users from accessing the data in a particular VLAN. For example, it is common practice to isolate server-to-server traffic from client-server traffic and to isolate administration/management traffic (channels used for inbound management of appliances and servers). Another standard configuration option is to create a "null" VLAN that is non-routable to the rest of the network. This VLAN is used for any physical ports that do not have authorized connected equipment.

VLANs also overcome the problem that building local networks that are limited by the number of ports available on a single switch is inefficient and inflexible. You might want a zone that contains hosts on different floors or even in different buildings. VLANs help to overcome these limitations imposed by the physical location of a host and assign them to the appropriate logical group of hosts.

VLANs are also used to separate nodes based on traffic type and the need for Quality of Service. For example, it is commonplace to put all VoIP phones on their own VLAN, so there is no interference coming from nodes that are sending email or downloading large files on the same network. The switches and routers can then be configured to give the VoIP VLAN priority over other VLANs.

Note: *VLANs and host virtualization (running multiple OS instances on a single physical server) are completely different technologies that just happen to share the word "virtual."*

When VLANs are deployed to segment large networks, a lot of bandwidth can be wasted pushing traffic from the switches to a router and back again. Layer 3 switches address this problem by using hardware optimized for this specific routing job. They work on the principle of "route once, switch many," which means that once a route is discovered, it is cached with the destination MAC address and subsequent communications are switched without invoking the routing lookup. While a router uses a generic processor and firmware to process incoming packets, a layer 3 switch uses **Application-Specific Integrated Circuits (ASICs)**. This can have an impact on the relative performance of the two types of devices. Layer 3 switches can be far faster, but they are not always as flexible. Layer 3 switches cannot usually perform WAN routing and work with interior routing protocols only. Often layer 3 switches support Ethernet only.

STATIC AND DYNAMIC VLAN MEMBERSHIP

The simplest means of assigning a node to a VLAN is by configuring the port interface on the switch. For example, from the switch management interface, ports 1 through 10 could be configured as a VLAN with the ID **10** and ports 11 through 20 could be assigned to VLAN **20**. Host A connected to port 2 would be in VLAN 10, and host B connected to port 12 would be in VLAN 20. Host A and Host B would not be able to communicate directly, even though they are connected to the same switch. Each VLAN is typically configured with its own subnet address and IP address range. Communications between VLANs must go through an IP router.

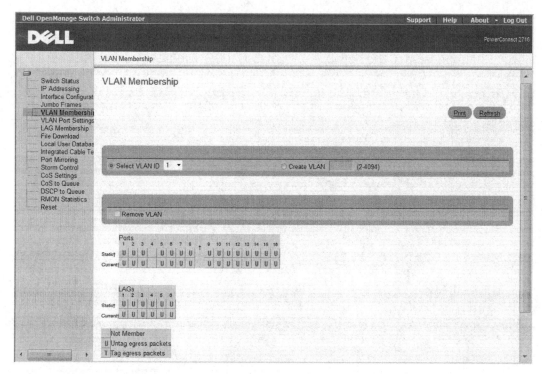

Configuring VLANs on a Dell switch using the web management interface. (Screenshot courtesy of Dell.)

This type of port-based assignment is described as a **static VLAN**. Nodes or hosts can also be assigned to **dynamic VLANs** using some feature of the host, such as its MAC address or authentication credentials supplied by the user.

VLAN ASSIGNMENT ISSUES

When you partition a network into separate VLANs, as each VLAN is a discrete broadcast domain, you must ensure that services, such as name resolution and IP autoconfiguration, are properly available to all VLANs. Otherwise, users will complain that "the Internet is down," when it transpires that there is no local DNS server available to handle their name resolution requests. Perhaps the most important thing that a network troubleshooter should have is an accurate and up-to-date map of both the logical and physical network infrastructure. This should identify what VLANs exist and which servers are located where. It's no good simply looking at the ports on the switch—they won't tell you anything about how the VLANs are configured. You may see a link light on the port and on the NIC, but if the interface is assigned to the wrong VLAN, it won't be able to access network resources.

Configuration errors can cause ports to isolate (that is, a host connected to the port will not be joined to the network). Problems can include trunking configuration, layer 3 (routing) configuration, and incorrect device or host placement. Make sure all devices are placed into the appropriate VLAN as per your network maps. If they are not, network performance will degrade or fail. VLAN assignments can be configured manually by assigning the switch port, and the administrator may have made a mistake. VLAN assignments can also be configured automatically, using parameters such as the host MAC address or authentication credentials.

If devices are not in the same VLAN and must communicate, ensure that routing has been configured to enable VLAN-to-VLAN communications. You may also need to configure services such as DHCP relay to allow hosts to contact a DHCP server. Also, if a device is placed in a designated VLAN, its IP configuration must be appropriate in terms of IP address, subnet mask, default gateway, and DNS servers.

TRUNKING AND IEEE 802.1Q

On a large network, one switch will not provide enough ports for all the hosts that need to be connected to the network. This means that multiple switches must be interconnected to build the network fabric. Multiple switches may also be deployed to provide redundant links. The interconnections between switches are referred to as **trunks**. One of the ports on each switch would be configured as a **trunk port** for this purpose.

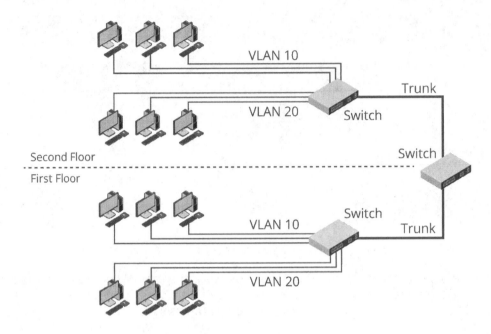

VLAN trunk link. (Image © 123RF.com.)

 Note: You can connect VLANs on different switches without using a trunk, but each VLAN requires its own link port on each switch, so this solution does not scale well.

When frames designated for different VLANs are transported across a trunk, the VLAN ID (VID) of each frame must be preserved for the receiving switch to forward it correctly. While Cisco's proprietary **Inter-Switch Link (ISL)** was once widely used to accomplish this, VIDs are now normally defined by the **IEEE 802.1Q** standard. Under 802.1Q, traffic is identified by a **VLAN tag** inserted in the Ethernet frame between the Source Address and EtherType fields. The tag contains information about the VID (from 1 to 4094) and priority (used for QoS functions). The EtherType value is set to identify the frame as 802.1Q.

Construction of an 802.1Q (VLAN tagged) Ethernet frame.

TAGGED AND UNTAGGED PORTS

If a port will only ever participate in a single VLAN, that port can be configured as **untagged**. This is also referred to as an **access port** or **host port**. An untagged/access port uses the following logic:

- If a frame is addressed to a port in the same VLAN on the same switch, no tag needs to be added to the frame.
- If the frame needs to be transported over a trunk link, the switch adds the relevant 802.1Q tag to identify the VLAN, and then forwards the frame over the trunk port.
- If the switch receives an 802.1Q tagged frame on an access port, it strips the tag before forwarding it.

Conversely, a **tagged port** will normally be one that is operating as a trunk; that is, capable of transporting traffic addressed to multiple VLANs. A trunk might be used to connect switches or to connect to a router. In some circumstances, a host attached to a port might need to be configured to use multiple VLANs and would need to be attached to a trunk port, rather than an access port. Consider a virtualization host with multiple guest operating systems. The virtual servers might need to be configured to use different VLANs.

DEFAULT VLAN AND NATIVE VLAN

The VLAN with ID 1 is referred to as the **default VLAN**. This cannot be changed. Unless configured differently, all ports on a switch default to being in VLAN 1. When you are implementing VLANs, you should avoid sending user data traffic over the default VLAN. It should remain unused or used only for inter-switch protocol traffic, where necessary. For example, spanning tree traffic would be permitted to run over the default VLAN. Make sure that unused ports are not assigned to VLAN 1.

> **Note:** *Unused ports should normally be disabled and assigned to a **black hole VLAN**, which is a VID set up so that the rest of the network is not accessible from it (no route is configured to or from that network). 666 and 999 are popular choices for a black hole VID.*

A **native VLAN** is one into which any untagged traffic is put when receiving frames over a trunk port. When a switch receives an untagged frame over a trunk, it assigns the frame to the native VLAN. Untagged traffic might derive from legacy devices such as hubs or older switches that do not support 802.1Q encapsulated frames. The native VLAN is initially set with the same VID as the default VLAN (VID 1). You can **and should** change this, however, to make the native VID any suitable ID. This should not be the same as any VLAN used for any other data traffic.

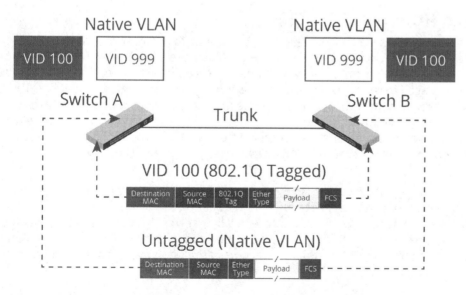

The native VLAN allows untagged frames to be transported across the trunk. The same native VLAN ID (VID) should be configured for the trunk port on both switches.

Note: *The traffic assigned to a native VLAN is usually untagged, but to improve security, newer switches allow the option of tagging these frames.*

The native VID can be configured per port. Switch ports participating in a trunk link should be configured with the same native VID. A **VLAN mismatch error** occurs where the native VID is set differently at either end of a trunk link. The switches will usually identify this situation, block traffic on that VID, and log an error. This avoids bridging the broadcast domains for each VLAN and potentially creating a loop. To correct the mismatch error, make sure the same native VID is configured for the trunk ports on both switches.

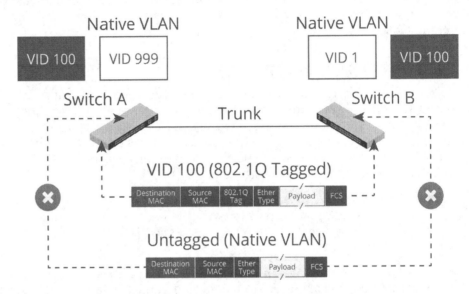

Mismatched native VLAN IDs—On Switch A, the native VID is configured as 999, but on Switch B it is still the default (1). Most switches will detect the mismatch and block frames for that VLAN from the trunk. Considerable problems may occur if the default VLAN is blocked, which is why you should never leave the native VLAN set to the default VID 1.

VLAN HOPPING ATTACKS

VLAN hopping is an attack designed to send traffic to a VLAN other than the one the host system is in. This exploits the native VLAN feature of 802.1Q. Native VLANs are designed to provide compatibility with non-VLAN capable switches. The attacker, using a device placed in the native VLAN, crafts a frame with two VLAN tag headers. The first trunk switch to inspect the frame strips the first header, and the frame gets forwarded to the target VLAN. Such an attack can only send packets one way but could be used to perform a DoS attack against a host on a different VLAN. Double tagging can be mitigated by ensuring that the native VLAN uses a different ID to any user accessible VLAN.

A VLAN hopping attack can also be launched by attaching a device that spoofs the operation of a switch to the network and negotiating the creation of a trunk port. As a trunk port, the attacker's device will receive all inter-VLAN traffic. This attack can be mitigated by ensuring that ports allowed to be used as trunks are pre-determined in the switch configuration and that access ports are not allowed to auto-configure as trunk ports.

VLAN TRUNKING PROTOCOL (VTP)

Trunking means that VLANs can be configured across more than one switch device without having to configure the VLANs on each device manually. This means that hosts connected to different switches (and perhaps in completely different locations) can be part of the same local network. The VLANs can be used to define organizational boundaries without having to put hosts in the same physical location.

The protocol governing this exchange of VLAN information between switches is either Cisco's **VLAN Trunking Protocol (VTP)** or the standards-based **Multiple VLAN Registration Protocol (MVRP)**. Under VTP, switches can be grouped into **management domains**, identified by a domain name. Within these groups, switches are assigned the roles of either **VTP server** or **VTP client**. Modifications to the VLAN topology of the network can be made on any switch that has been assigned the VLAN server role, and these changes are replicated to all switches in the management domain. In a small network with only a few switches, all switches may be configured as VTP servers. However, in a large network, it is more efficient to limit the number of switches that are assigned this role.

Pruning refers to removing transmissions related to designated VLANs from a trunk to preserve bandwidth. If a VLAN is not associated with a given trunk link, pruning it from the trunk reduces the amount of broadcast traffic passing over the link. There may also be security reasons for removing a VLAN from a trunk link. Pruning can either be done via VTP or by configuring the trunk manually.

You also need to consider how spanning tree works over trunks with VLANs configured. A modified version of Spanning Tree Protocol (STP) must be used with VLANs. If a trunk port to multiple VLANs were to be blocked, all the VLANs on that trunk would be denied access to the rest of the network. Some means must be established to disable links on a per-VLAN basis. Originally, this was accomplished using Cisco's **Per-VLAN STP Protocol (PVST)**, but is now implemented using **Multiple Spanning Trees Protocol (MSTP)**, defined in 802.1Q.

 Note: *To learn more, watch the related* **Video** *on the course website.*

GUIDELINES FOR PLANNING VLAN INFRASTRUCTURE

IMPLEMENT VLANS

Follow these general guidelines for implementing VLANs:

- Determine the organizational principles that will guide VLAN assignment. There are no rules to govern what these principles should be, but some commonly followed practices include:

  - Assign devices to VLANs by type (wired workstations, VoIP endpoints, wireless clients, printers, servers, and SAN). This should be governed by the performance and security requirements of each device type.
  - Use VLANs for distinct security zones, such as management traffic, guest network access, and Internet edge/Demilitarized Zones (DMZs).
  - Aim for 250 as the maximum number of hosts in a single VLAN (/24 subnet). Use VLANs for separate building floors to minimize traffic that must pass over a trunk.

- Consider using VLANs to represent departmental boundaries and functions, but don't create VLANs just for the sake of it. Physical location will generally override function, as moving more traffic over trunk links will affect performance.
- Design IP subnets for each VLAN, and design a VLAN numbering system. Do not use VLAN 1.
- Map the logical topology to the physical switch topology and identify trunk links. Tag the interfaces that will participate in trunk links with the VLANs they are permitted to carry.
- Assign the same native VID on each trunk port.
- Configure other interfaces as untagged/access ports within the appropriate VLAN.
- Ensure that hosts in each VLAN can obtain leases from DHCP servers, route to other network segments (as permitted), and contact DNS servers.

Activity 9-2
Discussing the Characteristics of VLANs

SCENARIO
Answer the following questions to test your understanding of the content covered in this topic.

1. **Why should VLANs be carefully planned before implementing them?**

2. **What methods can you use to allocate a host to a VLAN?**

3. **When you are connecting an ordinary client workstation to a switch and assigning it to a VLAN, should the switch port be tagged or untagged?**

4. **What distinguishes a layer 3 switch from a router?**

5. **What is a trunk port?**

6. **How do you correct a VLAN mismatch error?**

Topic C

Explain the Characteristics of NAT and Port Forwarding

EXAM OBJECTIVES COVERED
1.3 Explain the concepts and characteristics of routing and switching.
4.6 Explain common mitigation techniques and their purposes.

While VLANs are used to segment areas of a network at layer 2, you also need to consider the logical security topology at layer 3. At the Network layer, parts of the network with different security requirements are conceived as different zones. You can use characteristics of routing such as ACLs, NAT, and port forwarding to control communications between different zones.

DEMILITARIZED ZONES (DMZs) AND ACCESS CONTROL LISTS (ACLs)

The main unit of a logically segmented network is a **zone**. A zone is an area of the network where the security configuration is the same for all hosts within it. Network traffic between zones should be strictly controlled using a security device—typically a **firewall**. A firewall is software or hardware that filters traffic passing into and out of a network segment. The firewall bases its decisions on a set of rules called an **access control list (ACL)**. For example, a basic firewall can allow or deny a host access based on its IP address or by the port it is requesting or a combination of both. Different types of firewalls (and other filtering devices) can apply different—often more sophisticated—criteria in their ACLs.

One important distinction between different security zones is whether a host is Internet-facing. An Internet-facing host accepts **inbound** connections from the Internet. These Internet-facing hosts are placed in one or more **demilitarized zones (DMZs)**. A DMZ is also referred to as a **perimeter network**. The idea of a DMZ is that traffic cannot pass through it directly. A DMZ enables external clients to access data on private systems, such as web servers, without compromising the security of the internal network.

If communication is required between hosts on either side of a DMZ, a host within the DMZ acts as a **proxy**. For example, if an intranet host requests a connection with a web server on the Internet, a proxy in the DMZ takes the request and checks it. If the request is valid, it re-transmits it to the destination. External hosts have no idea about what (if anything) is behind the DMZ.

Servers that provide public access services should be placed in a DMZ. These would typically include web servers, mail and other communications servers, proxy servers, and remote access servers. The hosts in the DMZ are not fully trusted by the internal network because of the possibility that they could be compromised from the Internet. They are referred to as **bastion hosts**. A bastion is a defensive structure in a castle. The bastion protrudes from the castle wall and enables the defenders to fire at attackers that have moved close to the wall. A bastion host would not be configured with any services that run on the local network, such as user authentication.

DMZ TOPOLOGIES

To configure a DMZ, two different security configurations must be enabled: one on the external interface and one on the internal interface.

SCREENED SUBNET

One important use of subnets is to implement a DMZ. In a **screened subnet**, two firewalls are placed at either end of the DMZ. One restricts traffic on the external interface; the other restricts traffic on the internal interface.

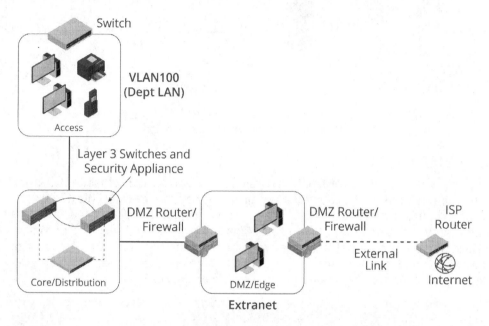

Screened subnet. (Image © 123RF.com.)

THREE-LEGGED FIREWALL

A DMZ can also be established using a single router/firewall appliance. A **three-legged firewall** (or **triple-homed firewall**) is one with three network ports, each directing traffic to a separate subnet.

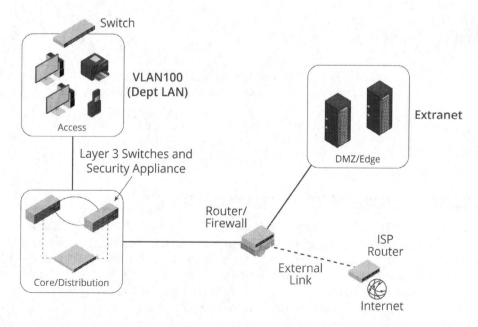

Three-legged firewall. (Image © 123RF.com.)

SCREENED HOST

Smaller networks may not have the budget or technical expertise to implement a DMZ. In this case, Internet access can still be implemented using a dual-homed proxy/ gateway server acting as a **screened host**.

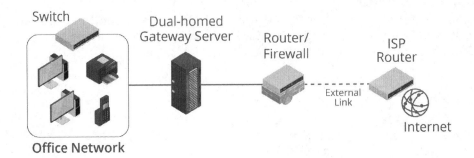

Screened host. (Image © 123RF.com.)

SOHO DMZ/DMZ HOST

Sometimes the term **DMZ** (or **DMZ host**) is used by SOHO Internet router vendors to mean an Internet-facing host or zone not protected by the firewall. This might be simpler to configure and solve some access problems, but it makes the whole network vulnerable to intrusion and DoS. A true DMZ is established by a separate network interface and subnet so that traffic between hosts in the DMZ and the LAN must be routed (and subject to firewall rules). Most SOHO Internet routers do not have the necessary ports or routing functionality to create a true DMZ.

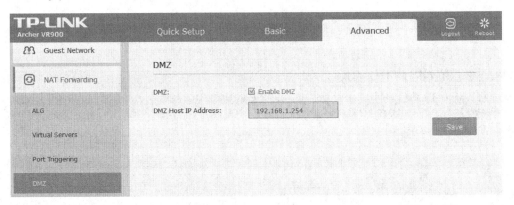

DMZ as configured on a SOHO Internet router. The host specified here is completely exposed to the Internet. (Screenshot used with permission from TP-Link.)

 Note: *To learn more, watch the related **Video** on the course website.*

NETWORK ADDRESS TRANSLATION (NAT)

Network Address Translation (NAT) was devised as a way of freeing up scarce IP addresses for hosts needing Internet access. NAT is a service translating between a **private** (or **local**) addressing scheme used by hosts on the LAN or a DMZ and a **public** (or **global**) addressing scheme used by an Internet-facing device. NAT is configured on a border device, such as a router, proxy server, or firewall. NAT is *not* a security mechanism; security is provided by the router/firewall's ACL.

In a basic NAT static configuration, a simple 1:1 mapping is made between the private (**inside local**) network address and the public (**inside global**) address. If the destination network is using NAT, it is described as having **outside global** and **outside local** addressing schemes.

Basic NAT is useful in scenarios where an inbound connection to a host must be supported. For example, you might position a web server behind a firewall running NAT. The firewall performs 1:1 address translation on the web server's IP address. This means that external hosts do not know the true IP address of the web server, but they can communicate with it successfully. Basic NAT with a static mapping for a single host can be referred to as **static NAT**, sometimes with the acronym SNAT, though this is more usually reserved for **Source NAT**.

 *Note: Just to confuse things further, Cisco use SNAT to mean **stateful NAT**, which is a means for routers to share dynamic NAT state tables. It is a good idea to avoid using acronyms when discussing NAT.*

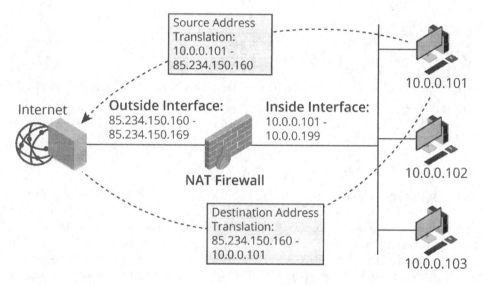

Network Address Translation (NAT). (Image © 123RF.com).

A single static mapping is not very useful in most scenarios. Under **dynamic NAT**, the NAT device exposes a pool of public IP addresses. To support inbound and outbound connections between the private network and the Internet, the NAT service builds a table of public to private address mappings. Each new session creates a new public-private address binding in the table. When the session is ended or times out, the binding is released for use by another host.

Dynamic NAT can be referred to by the acronym DNAT, though DNAT is more usually taken to mean Destination NAT.

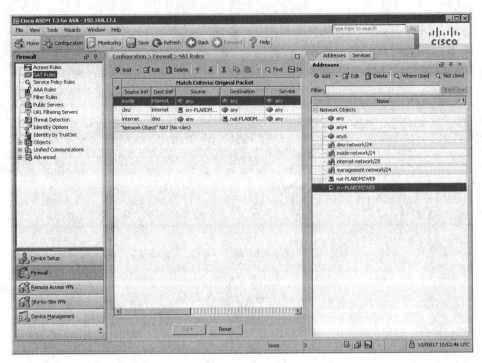

Defining NAT rules in Cisco Adaptive Security Appliance (ASA). (Screenshot used with permission from Cisco.)

PORT ADDRESS TRANSLATION (PAT)

Basic NAT supports multiple simultaneous connections but is still limited by the number of available public IP addresses. Smaller companies may only be allocated a single or small block of addresses by their ISPs. In such cases, a means for multiple private IP addresses to be mapped onto a single public address would be useful. This function is provided by **Port Address Translation (PAT)**. This can be referred to as **Network Address Port Translation (NAPT)** or **NAT overloading** or **one-to-many NAT**.

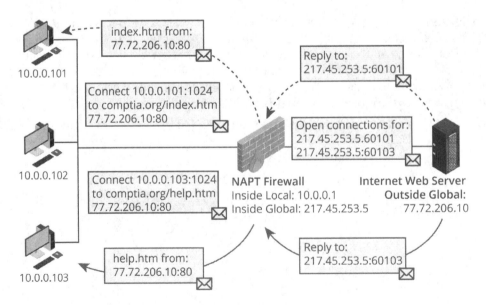

Port Address Translation (PAT). (Image ©123RF.com.)

PAT works by allocating each new connection a high-level TCP or UDP port. For example, say two hosts (10.0.0.101 and 10.0.0.102) initiate a web connection at the same time. The PAT service creates two new port mappings for these requests (10.0.0.101:61101 and 10.0.0.102:61102) in its **state table**. It then substitutes the private IP for the public IP and forwards the requests to the public Internet. It performs a reverse mapping on any traffic returned using those ports, inserting the original IP address and port number, and forwarding the packets to the internal hosts.

 Note: *On SOHO networks, PAT is much more commonly implemented than NAT, because it is typical for this type of network that only a single public IP address is available, and many devices on the local network must share it for Internet access.*

PORT FORWARDING

Basic NAT and PAT involve source addresses from a private range being rewritten with public addresses to facilitate client access to Internet resources or translation between networks using different IP ranges. Because it modifies the source addresses, both these types of address translations can be called **source NAT (SNAT)**.

There are also circumstances where you may want to use the router's public address for something like a web server but forward incoming requests to a different IP. This can be achieved with **destination NAT (DNAT)**, also known as **port forwarding**. Port forwarding means that the router takes requests from the Internet for a specific application (say, HTTP/port 80) and changes the destination address (and optionally destination port too) to send them to a designated host and port on the LAN.

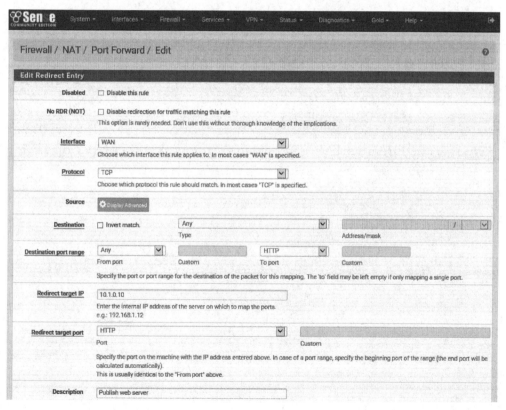

Configuring port forwarding for HTTP traffic. (Screenshot used with permission from pfSense.)

Activity 9-3

Discussing the Characteristics of NAT and Port Forwarding

SCENARIO

Answer the following questions to test your understanding of the content covered in this topic.

1. **What is the purpose of a DMZ?**

2. **How can an enterprise DMZ be implemented?**

3. **What distinguishes PAT from static NAT?**

4. **What is the difference between port forwarding and other types of NAT?**

Summary

In this lesson, you learned about common networking attacks and about some of the network segmentation techniques that can be used to mitigate them.

- The main network attack strategies can be characterized as footprinting (port scanning and eavesdropping), MitM, spoofing, DNS poisoning, and DoS.
- VLANs can be used to aggregate and subdivide networks into a different logical topology and enforce security zones. Each VLAN is a separate broadcast domain.
- Firewalls and addressing schemes can be used to segment a network by implementing a system of security zones. A DMZ is an Internet-facing area of the network outside the firewall protecting the LAN.
- NAT is a means of translating private internal network addresses to one or more public addresses.

Can you describe any exploited network vulnerabilities and/or threats and attacks that you have encountered?

Share your experiences with planning a VLAN infrastructure.

 Practice Questions: *Additional practice questions are available on the course website.*

Lesson 10

Installing and Configuring Security Devices

LESSON INTRODUCTION

Segmentation is a useful security technique, but many other technologies and controls are required to fully protect a network. Each day, the number and complexity of threats against network security increases. In response to these threats, there are more and more security tools and techniques available to increase network security. Because you are a networking professional, your organization and users will be looking to you to deploy these security appliances, without compromising network performance.

LESSON OBJECTIVES

In this lesson, you will:

- Install and configure firewalls and proxies.

- Explain the uses of IDS/IPS and UTM.

Topic A

Install and Configure Firewalls and Proxies

EXAM OBJECTIVES COVERED
2.2 Given a scenario, determine the appropriate placement of networking devices on a network and install/configure them.
2.3 Explain the purposes and use cases for advanced networking devices.
4.6 Explain common mitigation techniques and their purposes.
5.2 Given a scenario, use the appropriate tool.
5.5 Given a scenario, troubleshoot common network service issues.

The firewall is one of the longest serving types of network security control, developed to segregate some of the first Internet networks in the 1980s. Since those early days, firewall types and functionality have both broadened and deepened. As a network professional, a very large part of your workday will be taken up with implementing, configuring, and troubleshooting firewalls, proxies, and content filters.

FIREWALL USES AND TYPES

Firewalls are the devices principally used to implement security zones, such as intranet, DMZ, and Internet. The basic function of a firewall is **traffic filtering**. A firewall resembles a quality inspector on a production line; any bad units are knocked off the line and go no farther. The firewall processes traffic according to **rules**; traffic that does not conform to a rule that allows it access is blocked.

There are many types of firewalls and many ways of implementing a firewall. One distinction can be made between firewalls that protect a whole network (one that is placed inline in the network and inspects all traffic that passes through) and firewalls that protect a single host only (one that is installed on the host and inspects only that traffic destined for that host). Another distinction can be made between border firewalls and internal firewalls. Border firewalls filter traffic between the trusted local network and untrusted external networks, such as the Internet. DMZ configurations are established by border firewalls. Internal firewalls can be placed anywhere within the network, either inline or as host firewalls, to filter traffic flows between different security zones. A further distinction can be made about what parts of a packet a particular firewall technology can inspect and operate on.

PACKET FILTERING FIREWALLS

Packet filtering describes the earliest type of firewall. All firewalls can still perform this basic function. A packet filtering firewall is configured by specifying rules, which are called an **access control list (ACL)**. Each rule defines a specific type of data packet and the appropriate action to take when a packet matches the rule. An action can be either to deny (block or drop the packet, and optionally log an event) or to accept (let the packet pass through the firewall). A packet filtering firewall can inspect the headers of IP packets. This means that rules can be based on the information found in those headers:

- IP filtering—Accepting or denying traffic based on its source and/or destination IP address.

- Protocol ID/type (TCP, UDP, ICMP, routing protocols, and so on).
- Port filtering/security—Accepting or denying a packet based on source and destination port numbers (TCP or UDP application type).

There may be additional functionality in some products, such as the ability to block some types of ICMP (ping) traffic but not others, or the ability to filter by hardware (MAC) address. Packet filtering works mainly at layer 3 (Network) of the OSI model. Packet filtering is a **stateless** technique because the firewall examines each packet in isolation and has no record of previous packets.

 Note: *Port numbers are contained in TCP or UDP headers (layer 4), rather than the IP datagram header, but packet filtering firewalls are still almost always described as working at layer 3. They can inspect only port numbers and not any other layer 4 header information.*

Another distinction that can be made is whether the firewall can control only inbound traffic or both inbound and outbound traffic. This is also often referred to as "ingress" and "egress" traffic or filtering. Controlling outbound traffic is useful because it can block applications that have not been authorized to run on the network and defeat malware, such as backdoors. Ingress and egress traffic is filtered using separate ACLs.

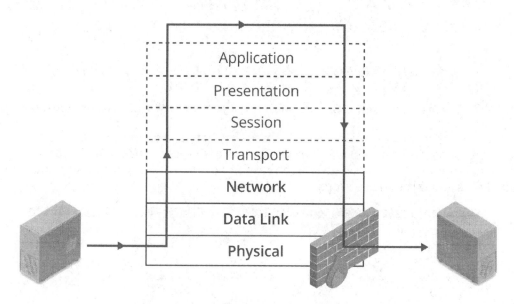

Packet filtering firewall. (Image © 123RF.com.)

A packet filtering firewall is **stateless**. This means that it does not preserve information about the connection between two hosts. Each packet is analyzed independently with no record of previously processed packets. This type of filtering requires the least processing effort, but it can be vulnerable to attacks that are spread over a sequence of packets. A stateless firewall can also introduce problems in traffic flow, especially when some sort of load balancing is being used or when clients or servers need to make use of dynamically assigned ports.

STATEFUL INSPECTION FIREWALLS

A **circuit-level stateful inspection firewall** addresses these problems by maintaining stateful information about the session established between two hosts (including malicious attempts to start a bogus session). Information about each session is stored in a dynamically updated **state table**. A stateful firewall operates at layer 5 (Session) of the OSI model. When a packet arrives, the firewall checks it to confirm whether it belongs to an existing connection. If it does not, it applies the ordinary packet filtering rules to determine whether to allow it. Once the connection has been allowed, the firewall allows traffic to pass unmonitored, in order to conserve processing effort.

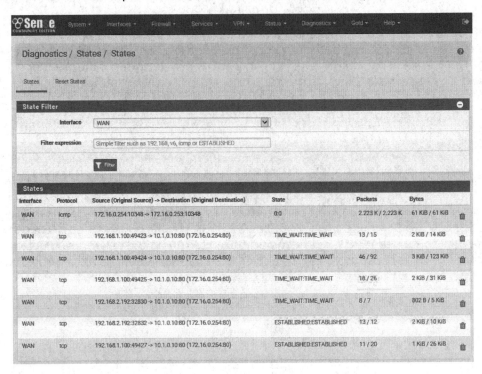

State table in the pfSense firewall appliance. (Screenshot used with permission from pfSense.)

A circuit-level firewall examines the TCP three-way handshake and can detect attempts to open connections maliciously. It also monitors packet sequence numbers and can prevent **session hijacking** attacks. It can respond to such attacks by blocking source IP addresses and throttling sessions.

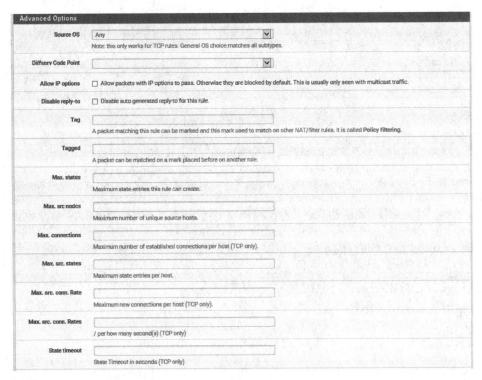

pfSense firewall rule configuration—Advanced settings allow maximums for states and connections to be applied. (Screenshot used with permission from pfSense.)

NGFW/LAYER 7 FIREWALLS

A **next generation firewall (NGFW)** or **layer 7 firewall** is one that can inspect and parse (interpret) the contents of packets at the Application layer. For example, a **web application firewall (WAF)** could analyze the header and the HTML code present in HTTP packets to try to identify code that matches a pattern in its threat database. Layer 7 firewalls have many different names, including **application firewall**, **Application layer gateway**, **stateful multilayer inspection**, or **deep packet inspection**.

> **Note:** *Security appliances working with this level of sophistication often use intrusion detection/prevention system techniques and perform malware scanning too. Such all-in-one appliances are usually referred to as* **Unified Threat Management (UTM)**. *UTM may incorporate other features, such as web content and access control, data loss prevention, spam and email filtering, and so on. UTM devices can often be found in enterprise environments, such as hospitals, credit card processing companies, and government network operations, to prevent malicious intrusions and attacks.*

Application aware devices must be configured with separate filters for each type of traffic (HTTP and HTTPS, SMTP/POP/IMAP, FTP, and so on).

Application aware firewalls are very powerful, but they are not invulnerable. Their very complexity means that it is possible to craft DoS attacks against exploitable vulnerabilities in the firewall firmware. Also, the firewall cannot examine encrypted data packets (unless configured with an SSL inspector).

NETWORK-BASED FIREWALLS

You should also consider how the firewall is implemented (as hardware or software, for instance) to cover a given placement or use on the network. Some types of firewalls are better suited for placement at network or segment borders; others are designed to protect individual hosts.

An **appliance firewall** is a stand-alone hardware firewall that performs only the function of a firewall. The functions of the firewall are implemented on the appliance firmware. This is also a type of network-based firewall and monitors all traffic passing into and out of a network segment. This type of appliance could be implemented with routed interfaces or as a layer 2/virtual wire "transparent" firewall. Nowadays, the role of advanced "firewall" is likely to be performed by an all-in-one or Unified Threat Management (UTM) security appliance, combining the function of firewall, intrusion detection, malware inspection, and web security gateway (content inspection and URL filtering).

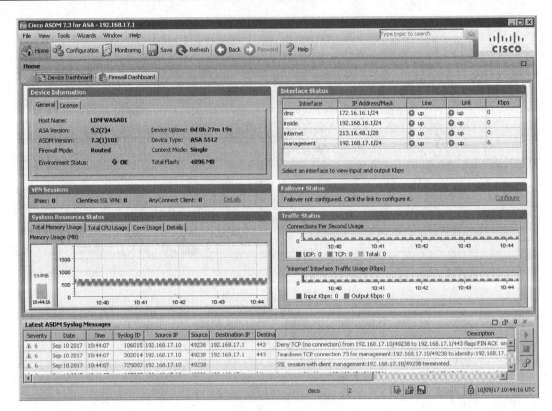

Cisco ASA (Adaptive Security Appliance) ASDM (Adaptive Security Device Manager) interface. (Image © and Courtesy of Cisco Systems, Inc. Unauthorized use not permitted.)

A **router firewall** is similar, except that the functionality is built into the router firmware. Most **SOHO Internet router/modems** have this type of firewall functionality, though they are typically limited to supporting a single subnet within the home network. An enterprise-class router firewall would be able to support far more sessions than a SOHO one. Additionally, some layer 3 switches can perform packet filtering.

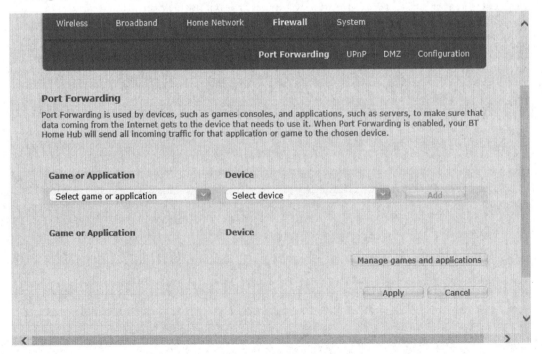

A SOHO router firewall comes with simple tools to configure port forwarding.

APPLICATION-BASED FIREWALLS

A firewall can also run as software on any type of computing host. There are several types of application-based firewalls:

- **Host-based firewall** (or **personal firewall**)—Implemented as a software application running on a single host designed to protect that host only.
- **Application firewall**—Software designed to run on a server to protect a particular type of application, rather than just general access to the host. Examples include a web server firewall, or a firewall designed to protect an SQL Server® database. This type of host-based firewall would typically be deployed in addition to a network firewall.
- **Network Operating System (NOS) firewall**—A software-based firewall running under a network server OS, such as Windows® or Linux®. The server would function as a gateway or proxy for a network segment.

 Note: When you are using a personal firewall on an enterprise network, some thought needs to be given as to how it will interact with network border firewalls. The use of personal firewalls can make troubleshooting network applications more complex.

FORWARD PROXY SERVERS

The basic function of a packet filtering network firewall is to inspect packets and determine whether to block them or allow them to pass. By contrast, a **proxy server** works on a store-and-forward model. Rather than inspecting traffic as it passes through, the proxy deconstructs each packet, performs analysis, then rebuilds the packet and forwards it on, providing it conforms to the rules. In fact, a proxy is a Man-in-the-Middle; but a legitimate one! This is more secure than a firewall that only performs filtering. If a packet contains malicious content or construction that a firewall does not detect as such, the firewall will allow the packet. A proxy would erase the suspicious content in the process of rebuilding the packet. The drawback is that there is more processing to be done than with a firewall.

A basic proxy server provides for protocol-specific outbound traffic. For example, you might deploy a web proxy that enables client hosts to connect to websites and secure websites on the Internet. In this case, you have deployed a proxy server that services TCP ports 80 and 443 for outbound traffic. This type of device is placed at the network edge, usually in some sort of DMZ. Web proxies are often also described as **web security gateways** as usually their primary functions are to prevent viruses or Trojans infecting computers from the Internet, block spam, and restrict web use to authorized sites, acting as a **content filter**.

The main benefit of a proxy server is that clients connect to a specified point within the perimeter network for web access. This provides for a degree of traffic management and security. In addition, most web proxy servers provide **caching engines**, whereby frequently requested web pages are retained on the proxy, negating the need to re-fetch those pages for subsequent requests. Some proxy servers also **pre-fetch** pages that are referenced in pages that have been requested. When the client computer then requests that page, the proxy server already has a local copy.

A proxy server must understand the application it is servicing. For example, a web proxy must be able to parse and modify HTTP and HTTPS commands (and potentially HTML, too). Some proxy servers are application-specific; others are multipurpose. A **multipurpose proxy** is one configured with filters for multiple protocol types, such as HTTP, FTP, and SMTP.

Proxy servers can generally be classed as **non-transparent** or **transparent**. A **non-transparent server** means that the client must be configured with the proxy server address and port number to use it. The port on which the proxy server accepts client connections is often configured as port 8080. A transparent (or "forced" or "intercepting") proxy intercepts client traffic without the client having to be reconfigured. A **transparent proxy** must be implemented on a switch or router or other inline network appliance.

Transparent Proxy Settings	
Transparent HTTP Proxy	☑ Enable transparent mode to forward all requests for destination port 80 to the proxy server. ℹ Transparent proxy mode works without any additional configuration being necessary on clients. **Important:** Transparent mode will filter SSL (port 443) if you enable 'HTTPS/SSL Interception' below. **Hint:** In order to proxy both HTTP and HTTPS protocols **without intercepting SSL connections**, configure WPAD/PAC options on your DNS/DHCP servers.
Transparent Proxy Interface(s)	LAN WAN The interface(s) the proxy server will transparently intercept requests on. Use CTRL + click to select multiple interfaces.
Bypass Proxy for Private Address Destination	☐ Do not forward traffic to Private Address Space (RFC 1918) destinations. Destinations in Private Address Space (RFC 1918) are passed directly through the firewall, not through the proxy server.
Bypass Proxy for These Source IPs	Do not forward traffic from these **source** IPs, CIDR nets, hostnames, or aliases through the proxy server but let it pass directly through the firewall. **Applies only to transparent mode.** Separate entries by semi-colons (;)
Bypass Proxy for These Destination IPs	Do not proxy traffic going to these **destination** IPs, CIDR nets, hostnames, or aliases, but let it pass directly through the firewall. **Applies only to transparent mode.** Separate entries by semi-colons (;)

Configuring transparent proxy settings for the Squid proxy server (squid-cache.org) running on pfSense. (Screenshot used with permission from pfSense.)

CONTENT FILTERS

As firewalls have become effective at blocking unwanted ports, configuring network applications to work with firewalls has become more difficult. Many network applications consequently package all their content as HTTP traffic and send it all over port 80 or port 443 (HTTPS). This means that allowing all HTTP traffic is not particularly secure, as it could be allowing all sorts of malicious applications or management interfaces, in addition to basic web pages.

A **content filter** or **web security gateway** is designed for corporate control over employees' Internet use. It could be implemented as a standalone appliance or proxy server software. Many ISPs implement content filtering as part of their Internet access packages.

Configuring content filter settings for the Squid proxy server (squid-cache.org) running on pfSense (pfsense.org). The filter can apply ACLs, apply time-based restrictions, and use blacklists to prohibit access to URLs. (Screenshot used with permission from pfSense.)

Web security gateways would typically apply content restrictions to web, Instant Messaging, email, FTP, and **P2P** applications. Filtering can be applied to a mix of permitted/restricted URLs, keyword matching, web object matching (looking at usage of plug-ins), time of day use, total usage, and so on. The software may also allow the creation of profiles for different user groups and should feature logging and reporting capabilities.

With an encrypted connection (over HTTPS, for instance), the content filter will not be able to inspect the URL or content of the communications unless it is capable of SSL inspection. This means that the content filter intercepts and decrypts encrypted traffic, inspects it for **policy violations**, and if accepted, re-encrypts the traffic and forwards it to the destination.

REVERSE PROXY SERVERS

A **reverse proxy server** provides for protocol-specific inbound traffic. For security purposes, it is inadvisable to place application servers, such as messaging and VoIP servers, in the perimeter network, where they are directly exposed to the Internet. Instead, you can deploy a reverse proxy and configure it to listen for client requests from a public network (the Internet) and create the appropriate request to the internal server on the corporate network.

Reverse proxies can publish applications from the corporate network to the Internet in this way. In addition, some reverse proxy servers can handle the encryption/decryption and authentication issues that arise when remote users attempt to connect to corporate servers, reducing the overhead on those servers. Typical applications for reverse proxy servers include publishing a web server, publishing IM or conferencing applications, and enabling POP/IMAP mail retrieval.

FIREWALL AND ACL CONFIGURATION

A firewall, proxy, or content filter is an example of **rule-based management**. Firewall and other filtering rules are configured on the principle of **least access**. The aim of this principle is to only allow the minimum amount of traffic required for the operation of valid network services, and no more. The rules in a firewall's ACL are processed top-to-bottom. If traffic matches one of the rules, then it is allowed to pass; consequently, rules that are most specific and that must override other rules (if there is a conflict) are placed at the top. The final default rule is typically to block any traffic that has not matched a rule. This default rule is referred to as **implicit deny**.

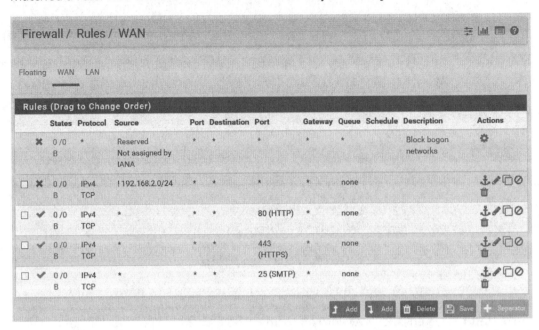

	States	Protocol	Source	Port	Destination	Port		Gateway	Queue	Schedule	Description	Actions
✖	0 / 0 B	*	Reserved Not assigned by IANA	*	*		*	*	*		Block bogon networks	⚙
☐ ✖	0 / 0 B	IPv4 TCP	! 192.168.2.0/24	*	*		*	*	none			⚓✏📋⊘ 🗑
☐ ✔	0 / 0 B	IPv4 TCP	*		*	*	80 (HTTP)	*	none			⚓✏📋⊘ 🗑
☐ ✔	0 / 0 B	IPv4 TCP	*		*	*	443 (HTTPS)	*	none			⚓✏📋⊘ 🗑
☐ ✔	0 / 0 B	IPv4 TCP	*		*	*	25 (SMTP)	*	none			⚓✏📋⊘ 🗑

Sample firewall ruleset configured on pfSense. This ruleset blocks all traffic from bogon networks and a specific private address range, but it allows any HTTP, HTTPS, or SMTP traffic from any other source. (Screenshot used with permission from pfSense.)

Each rule can specify whether to block or allow traffic based on parameters, often referred to as **tuples**. If you think of each rule being like a row in a database, the tuples are the columns. For example, in the screenshot, the tuples include **Protocol**, **Source** (address), (Source) **Port**, **Destination** (address), (Destination) **Port**, and so on.

Even the simplest packet filtering firewall can be complex to configure securely. It is essential to create a written policy describing what a filter ruleset should do and to test the configuration as far as possible to ensure that the ACLs you have set up work as intended. Also test and document changes made to ACLs. Some other basic principles include:

- Block incoming requests on the external interface from internal or private IP addresses (that have obviously been spoofed).
- Block incoming requests on the external interface from protocols that should only be functioning at a local network level, such as DHCP, SMB, or routing protocol traffic.
- Use penetration testing to confirm the configuration is secure. Log access attempts and monitor the logs for suspicious activity.
- Take the usual steps to secure the hardware on which the firewall is running and use of the management interface.

 Note: *To learn more, watch the related **Video** on the course website.*

iptables

`iptables` is a command line utility provided by many Linux distributions that allows administrators to edit the rules enforced by the Linux kernel firewall. `iptables` works with the firewall **chains**, which apply to the different types of traffic passing through the system. The three main chains are:

- `INPUT`—Affecting incoming connections. For example, if a user attempts to SSH into the Linux server, `iptables` will attempt to match the IP address and port to a rule in the input chain.
- `OUTPUT`—For outgoing connections. For example, if you try to ping an FQDN such as **comptia.org**, `iptables` will check its output chain to see what the rules are regarding `ping` and **comptia.org** (or the IP address that **comptia.org** resolves to) before deciding to allow or deny the connection attempt.
- `FORWARD`—Used for connections that are passing through the server, rather than being delivered locally. Unless the Linux system is performing routing, NATing, or something else similar on the system that requires forwarding, this chain will not be used.

Rules can be assigned to these chains, or new chains can be created and then linked to the standard system chains to affect traffic flow. To view the current status of the `iptables` and the volume of traffic using the chains, use the command:

```
iptables -L -v
```

```
lamp@LAMP:~$ sudo iptables -L -v
Chain INPUT (policy ACCEPT 0 packets, 0 bytes)
 pkts bytes target     prot opt in     out     source               destination

Chain FORWARD (policy ACCEPT 0 packets, 0 bytes)
 pkts bytes target     prot opt in     out     source               destination

Chain OUTPUT (policy ACCEPT 4 packets, 288 bytes)
 pkts bytes target     prot opt in     out     source               destination
```

Using iptables to view firewall rules.

To change the firewall rules, commands such as those that follow would be used. These examples allow one IP address from a specific subnet to connect and block all others from the same subnet.

```
iptables -A INPUT -s 10.1.0.1 -j ACCEPT
```

```
iptables -A INPUT -s 10.1.0.0/24 -j DROP
```

When you set least access rules (if both `INPUT` and `OUTPUT` default policy is set to deny all), you must set both `INPUT` and `OUTPUT` rules to allow most types of client/server traffic. For example, to allow a host to operate as an SSH server, configure the following rules:

```
iptables -A INPUT -p tcp --dport 22 -s 10.1.0.0/24 -m state --
state NEW,ESTABLISHED -j ACCEPT
```

```
iptables -A OUTPUT -p tcp --sport 22 -d 10.1.0.0/24 -m state --
state ESTABLISHED -j ACCEPT
```

These commands use the stateful nature of the firewall to differentiate between new and established connections. The first rule allows hosts in the 10.1.0.0/24 net to initiate connections with the SSH server on the local host over port 22. The second rule allows the server to respond to existing connections established by hosts in the same subnet.

Conversely, if you want to allow the local host (10.1.0.254) to ping other hosts (on any network, or 0/0), you must also enable a matching rule on the `INPUT` table to allow the remote hosts to reply to the probes:

```
iptables -A OUTPUT -p icmp -s 10.1.0.254 -d 0/0 -m state --state
NEW,ESTABLISHED,RELATED -j ACCEPT
```

```
iptables -A INPUT -p icmp -s 0/0 -d 10.1.0.254 -m state --state
ESTABLISHED,RELATED -j ACCEPT
```

If you are configuring a remote host, take care not to create a least access ACL that blocks you from accessing the host! Use the following commands to whitelist your host machine (192.168.1.100 say) as the first rule (-I adds the rule to the top of the ACL):

```
iptables -I INPUT -p tcp --dport 22 -s 192.168.1.100 -m state --
state NEW,ESTABLISHED -j ACCEPT

iptables -I OUTPUT -p tcp --sport 22 -d 192.168.1.100 -m state --
state ESTABLISHED -j ACCEPT
```

Note: *Another option is to apply a new ruleset with a timer, meaning that the new rules run for a limited period (5 minutes) before reverting to the previous configuration.*

Note: *To learn more, watch the related **Video** on the course website.*

MISCONFIGURED FIREWALL AND ACL ISSUES

One type of firewall, ACL, or content filter misconfiguration blocks packets that are supposed to be allowed through. This will cause an application or protocol to fail to function correctly. For example, the firewall might be **blocking TCP or UDP ports** that are supposed to be open, or it might be allowing the ports but denying access to an IP network or host that is supposed to be able to connect.

This type of error will usually be easy to identify, as users will report incidents connected with the failure of the data traffic. With such incidents, firewall configuration will always be a likely cause, so will be high on the list to investigate. Diagnosis can be confirmed by trying to establish the connection from both inside and outside the firewall. If it connects from outside the firewall but not from inside, this would confirm the firewall to be the cause of the issue. You also need to consider whether a host firewall is involved (at either end of the connection). To diagnose an issue with a host firewall, attempt the connection with the host firewall disabled. If the connection attempt succeeds, then the network firewall ACL is allowing the packets, but the host firewall is configured to block them. If the connection attempt fails, investigate the network firewall ACL first—do consider the possibility that both the network and the host firewall are blocking the connection. You can also inspect the firewall's log files to discover what rules have been applied to block traffic at a particular time.

The other possible outcome of a badly configured firewall is that packets may be allowed through that should be blocked. This is a more serious outcome because the result is to open the system to security vulnerabilities. It is also not necessarily so easily detected, as it does not typically cause anything to stop functioning. As no incidents usually arise from this outcome (except in the case that a vulnerability is exploited), it is not a scenario that is subject to troubleshooting. Rather, it underlines the need for regular firewall audits and thorough change control processes to deal with firewall change requests.

Activity 10-1

Discussing Firewall and Proxy Configuration

SCENARIO

Answer the following questions to test your understanding of the content covered in this topic.

1. **What parameters can a layer 3 firewall ruleset use?**

2. **What OSI layer does an NGFW work at and why?**

3. **Other than attempting to block access to sites based on content, what security options might be offered by Internet content filters?**

4. **Why would you deploy a reverse proxy?**

5. **What is the default rule on a firewall?**

6. **Using iptables, in which chain would you create rules to block all outgoing traffic not meeting certain exceptions?**

7. **You are troubleshooting a connectivity problem with a network application server. Certain clients cannot connect to the service port. How could you rule out a network or remote client host firewall as the cause of the problem?**

Activity 10-2
Configuring a NAT Firewall

BEFORE YOU BEGIN

Start the VMs used in this activity in the following order, adjusting the memory allocation first if necessary, and waiting at the ellipses for the previous VMs to finish booting before starting the next group.

1. **RT2-ISP** (256 MB)
2. **RT3-INT** (256 MB)
3. **PFSENSE** (512—1024 MB)
4. **DC1** (1024—2048 MB)
5. **LAMP** (512—1024 MB)
6. **KALI** (2048—4096 MB)
7. ...
8. **MS1** (756—2048 MB)
9. ...
10. **PC1** (1024—2048 MB)

 *Note: If you can allocate more than the minimum amounts of RAM, prioritize **KALI** and **PC1**.*

SCENARIO

The networks you have created so far are completely open. Any of the VMs can connect to any of the network servers. This activity demonstrates some of the installation and configuration issues you might face in deploying a typical security appliance to screen a local network from the Internet. You will be using pfSense, an open source UTM created and maintained by Netgate (*pfsense.org*).

The following diagram shows the network layout. The icons at the top represent routers (implemented by the VyOS VMs), while the pipes represent different subnets, each underpinned by a virtual switch (configured via Hyper-V). The **RT3-INT** and **RT2-ISP** routers and the subnets they support represent an internet. The LAN subnet has the Windows VMs (plus others) attached to it. The pfSense firewall is positioned so that it routes and screens all traffic passing between the LAN network and the ISP network. The "Internet" contains two separate subnets, one hosting a **LAMP** Linux web server and the other with the **KALI** Linux penetration testing VM in it.

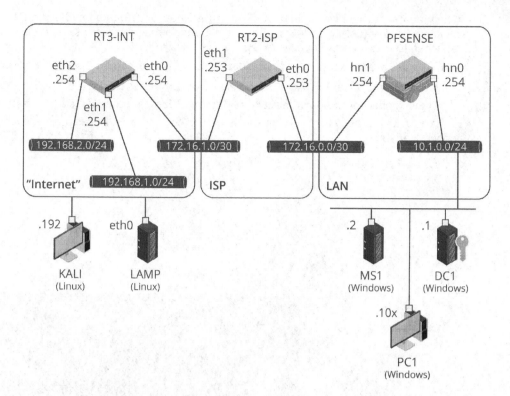

Network topology with pfSense VM protecting the LAN switch.

This activity is designed to test your understanding of and ability to apply content examples in the following CompTIA Network+ objectives:

- 2.2 Given a scenario, determine the appropriate placement of networking devices on a network and install/configure them.
- 2.3 Explain the purposes and use cases for advanced networking devices.
- 4.6 Explain common mitigation techniques and their purposes.
- 5.2 Given a scenario, use the appropriate tool.

---

1. Use the pfSense local console to troubleshoot the installation.

    a) Open a connection window for the **PFSENSE** VM.

```
 Starting /usr/local/etc/rc.d/radiusd.sh...done.
 Starting /usr/local/etc/rc.d/sqp_monitor.sh...done.
pfSense (pfSense) 2.3.3-RELEASE (Patch 1) amd64 Thu Mar 09 07:17:41 CST 2017
Bootup complete

FreeBSD/amd64 (PFSENSE.classroom.local) (ttyv0)

*** Welcome to pfSense 2.3.3-RELEASE-p1 (amd64 full-install) on PFSENSE ***

 WAN (wan)       -> hn1       -> v4: 172.16.0.254/30
 LAN (lan)       -> hn0       -> v4: 10.1.0.254/24
 OPT1 (opt1)     -> hn2       ->

 0) Logout (SSH only)              9) pfTop
 1) Assign Interfaces             10) Filter Logs
 2) Set interface(s) IP address   11) Restart webConfigurator
 3) Reset webConfigurator password 12) PHP shell + pfSense tools
 4) Reset to factory defaults     13) Update from console
 5) Reboot system                 14) Enable Secure Shell (sshd)
 6) Halt system                   15) Restore recent configuration
 7) Ping host                     16) Restart PHP-FPM
 8) Shell

Enter an option:
```

pfSense console.

b) The fundamental configuration option is to assign interfaces (named **hn0** and **hn1**) to the correct zone (LAN and WAN, respectively). Confirm that these interfaces are attached to the correct vSwitches to replace the VyOS router.

You can also reboot or open a command shell (pfSense is based on OpenBSD UNIX).

c) Type *8* and press **Enter** to start the shell, and then run `ifconfig`

d) From the connection window, select **File→Settings**. Compare the MAC address in the `ifconfig` output with the value shown on the **Advanced Features** page of each network adapter.

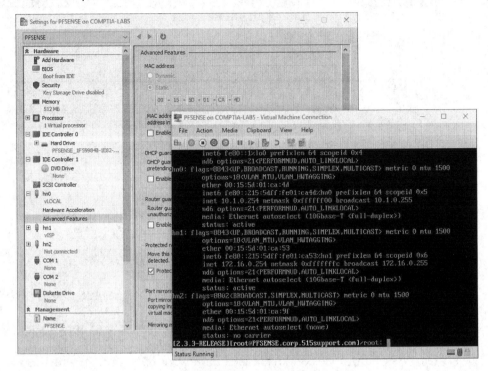

Verifying layer 2 connections.

e) Verify that:
- **hn0** is connected to the **vLOCAL** switch.
- **hn1** is connected to the **vISP** switch.
- **hn2** is not connected.

 Note: *While the Hyper-V configuration sets the MAC address for the virtual adapter, it does not set the adapter name (hn0 or hn1). The same labels have been applied in Hyper-V as in the VM, but this is a convention, not a configuration setting.*

 Note: ***hn2*** *was used to update the VM configuration over the Internet via an external switch and won't be used in the activity.*

f) Select **Cancel**. In the console, type *exit* and press **Enter** to return to the menu from the shell.

g) Close the connection window.

2. Later in the activity, you will use port forwarding to make the Windows web server publicly available. To facilitate this, update the DNS records on **LAMP** to point to the external IP address for the pfSense router/firewall.

a) Open a **LAMP** VM console window. Sign in as *lamp* with the password *Pa$$w0rd*

Unlike in Windows, the username is case-sensitive.

Note: *You can type the username even though there is no prompt showing.*

b) Run the following two commands, ignoring any line breaks, and enter the password **Pa$$w0rd** when you are prompted:

```
sudo mv /etc/bind/named.conf.local.bak /etc/bind/
named.conf.local

sudo service bind9 restart
```

c) Close the connection window.

3. Use the pfSense WebConfigurator application to verify the route to other networks.

a) Open a connection window for the **PC1** VM and sign in with the credentials **515support\Administrator** and **Pa$$w0rd**

b) Run **http://10.1.0.254**

c) Log on using the credentials **admin** and **Pa$$w0rd**. Select **Save** when you are prompted to save the password.

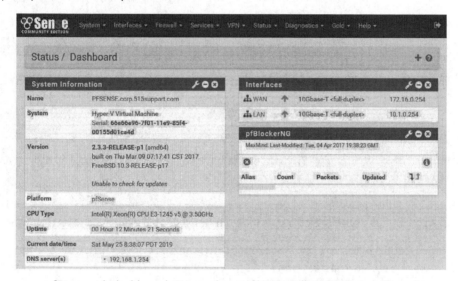

pfSense web dashboard. (Screenshot used with permission from pfSense.)

The dashboard can be configured with different alert and status widgets by using the **Plus** button in the top-right. Observe the IP addresses assigned to the **LAN** and **WAN** interfaces. Locate these addresses in the topology diagram presented in the Scenario for this activity.

d) Select **Diagnostics**→**Routes**. Observe that the default gateway is the IP address of the **RT2-ISP** VM.

 Note: *If the window is not full size, the menu will be shown as three lines on the right side of the window. You can either use this menu or maximize the window to see the menu bar.*

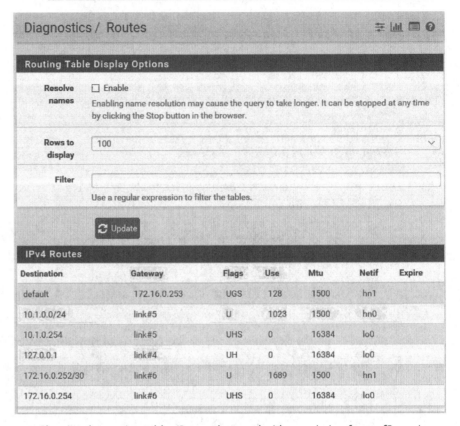

Showing the routing table. (Screenshot used with permission from pfSense.)

You can use the **My Traceroute (mtr)** tool to verify paths to remote hosts.

e) Select **Diagnostics**→**mtr**. In the **IP Address or Hostname** box, type ***www.515web.net*** then select the **Run mtr** button.

The **LAMP** VM is running a web server and DNS for the 515web.net domain.

f) Observe the mtr output then select the **Back to mtr** button.

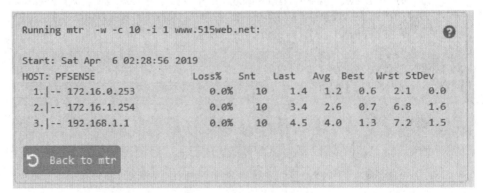

mtr trace—The packet is sent out to the default gateway (172.16.0.253 on RT2-ISP), which is able to discover a route to the host 192.168.1.1 via 172.16.1.254 (RT3-ISP). (Screenshot used with permission from pfSense.)

g) Select **Status**→**System Logs**. The most important logs are

• System—Events affecting the operation of the appliance.

- Firewall—Events triggered by processing firewall rules.

h) On the **System Logs** page, select the **Settings** tab.

i) Check the **Log packets matched from the default block rules in the ruleset** and **Log packets matched from the default pass rules put in the ruleset** check boxes.

j) Select the **Save** button.

4. Use the **KALI** VM to ping the firewall, and test outgoing connectivity by browsing the **www.515web.net** website from **PC1**.

a) Open a connection window for the **KALI** VM. Log on using *root* and *Pa$$w0rd*

b) Start the **Firefox** browser and try to open *http://www.515support.com*

This will fail to connect.

c) Right-click the desktop, and select **Open Terminal**. In the terminal, run the following commands:

```
ping -c4 www.515support.com

ping -c4 172.16.0.254

ping -c4 10.1.0.254

traceroute 172.16.0.254
```

d) Switch back to **PC1**. Open a second browser tab and go to *http://www.515web.net*

The **Apache2 Ubuntu Default Page** should open. The default firewall ruleset is blocking incoming connection requests from external networks to the LAN, but it is allowing outgoing communications.

e) Select the tab for the **pfSense** web interface again. Select the **Firewall** tab.

You should see the pass rule allowing the **PC1** client to access the 515web.net server (plus outgoing DNS traffic) and the block rule dropping pings from **KALI**.

f) Select **Diagnostics→States**. In the **Filter expression** box, type *192.168.1.1* then select the **Filter** button.

You should see a connection on the LAN interface to 192.168.1.1 and a matching WAN connection such as:

```
172.16.0.254:17464 (10.1.0.100:49794) -> 192.168.1.1:80
```

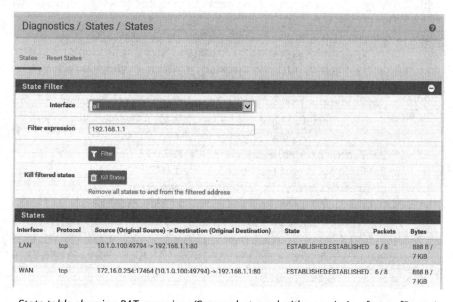

State table showing PAT mapping. (Screenshot used with permission from pfSense.)

This represents the client **PC1** opening a connection to the web server at 192.168.1.1 using the client port 49794. pfSense intercepts this request and forwards it using its own IP address and client port. Any replies received from 192.168.1.1:80 on port 17464 will be forwarded to 10.1.0.100:49794.

g) If you were to run `netstat` on the **LAMP** VM, you would see the connection as follows—note the foreign address and port number:

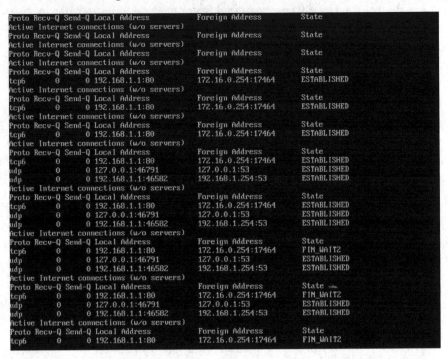

Viewing a NAT connection from the outside network.

5. Configure the firewall to forward external requests for web services to a designated host on the LAN (**MS1**). Also, disable the default block rule matching so that you can inspect the firewall logs more easily.

a) On the **PC1** VM, in the web management app, select **Status**→**System Logs**. On the **System Logs** page, select the **Settings** tab.

b) Uncheck the check box for **Log packets matched from the default block rules in the ruleset**.

c) Select the **Save** button.

d) Scroll down the page, select the **Reset Log Files** button, and select **OK** to confirm.

e) From the main menu, select **Firewall**→**NAT**. On the **Port Forward** tab, select the **Add** button (either one will work).

f) In the **Destination** section, verify that **WAN address** is selected.

This selects the interface on which packets for forwarding will be arriving.

g) In the **Destination port range** section, select **HTTP**.

h) In the **Redirect target IP** section, enter *10.1.0.2*

i) In the **Redirect target port** section, select **HTTP**.

j) In the **Description** section, enter *Web server access*

k) Select the **Save** button, then select **Apply Changes** to confirm.

l) Verify that you can browse **http://www.515support.com** from the **KALI** VM.

You should see the updates page. This is not a great choice of web server to be making available over the "Internet," but you have established that the port forwarding rule works.

m) Switch back to **PC1** and select **Status→System Logs→Firewall** and observe the matched rule that allows this session to take place.

The selected rule shows the router forwarding the HTTP request to the IP address 10.1.0.254 on the LAN. Note that the rule shows PC1's browser connection to the firewall management console. (Screenshot used with permission from pfSense.)

6. In some cases, you may want to restrict access to a service using an access control list (ACL). For example, you might want to block access from certain networks. Configure a firewall rule to block hosts from the **192.168.2.0** net.

a) From the main menu, select **Firewall→ Rules**. Select the **Add rule to the top of the list** button.

You want this rule to be processed before the one that permits HTTP access.

> **Note:** *pfSense operates a non-configurable drop default rule for any traffic that is not explicitly passed. This rule is not shown in the rules table.*

b) From the **Action** box, select **Block**. Read the tip explaining the difference between the block and reject methods.

c) From the **Protocol** box, select **Any**.

d) From the **Source** box, select **Network** and type *192.168.2.0* in the box and select the **24** bit mask.

e) Check the **Log** check box.

f) In the **Description** section, enter *Blacklist 192.168.2.0 net*

g) Select the **Save** button, then select **Apply Changes** to confirm.

h) On the **KALI** VM, refresh the page, and try to browse to ***http://www.515support.com***
It should fail to connect.

i) On the **PC1** VM, view the logs to observe the rules in action.

✔	May 25 09:21:17	LAN	i ⊟ 10.1.0.101:1686	i ⊞ 10.1.0.254:80	TCP:S
✔	May 25 09:22:12	LAN	i ⊟ [fdab:cdef:0:1::1]	i ⊞ [ff02::1.ff00:ffff]	ICMPv6
✔	May 25 09:22:18	► WAN	i ⊟ 172.16.0.254:63571	i ⊞ 192.168.1.254:53	UDP
✔	May 25 09:22:18	► WAN	i ⊟ 172.16.0.254:40991	i ⊞ 192.168.1.254:53	UDP
✔	May 25 09:22:18	► WAN	i ⊟ 172.16.0.254:10462	i ⊞ 192.168.1.254:53	UDP
✔	May 25 09:22:18	► WAN	i ⊟ 172.16.0.254:43891	i ⊞ 192.168.1.254:53	UDP
✘	May 25 09:22:37	WAN	i ⊟ 192.168.2.192:35310	i ⊞ 10.1.0.2:80	TCP:S
✘	May 25 09:22:37	WAN	i ⊟ 192.168.2.192:35312	i ⊞ 10.1.0.2:80	TCP:S
✘	May 25 09:22:38	WAN	i ⊟ 192.168.2.192:35310	i ⊞ 10.1.0.2:80	TCP:S
✘	May 25 09:22:38	WAN	i ⊟ 192.168.2.192:35312	i ⊞ 10.1.0.2:80	TCP:S
✘	May 25 09:22:40	WAN	i ⊟ 192.168.2.192:35310	i ⊞ 10.1.0.2:80	TCP:S
✘	May 25 09:22:40	WAN	i ⊟ 192.168.2.192:35312	i ⊞ 10.1.0.2:80	TCP:S
✘	May 25 09:22:44	WAN	i ⊟ 192.168.2.192:35310	i ⊞ 10.1.0.2:80	TCP:S
✘	May 25 09:22:44	WAN	i ⊟ 192.168.2.192:35312	i ⊞ 10.1.0.2:80	TCP:S
✘	May 25 09:22:52	WAN	i ⊟ 192.168.2.192:35310	i ⊞ 10.1.0.2:80	TCP:S
✘	May 25 09:22:52	WAN	i ⊟ 192.168.2.192:35312	i ⊞ 10.1.0.2:80	TCP:S

Observing the firewall log. KALI's connection requests to the HTTP server are blocked. Above these, you can see outgoing DNS queries and, at the top, the PC1 browser connection to the management interface. (Screenshot used with permission from pfSense.)

j) Select **Firewall →Rules** then select the **Disable** icon on the **Blacklist** rule. Select **Apply Changes** to confirm.

7. If you have time, you can also investigate the use of the Linux firewall (`netfilter`) and the `iptables` command. Netfilter is the packet filtering engine while `iptables` is a means of configuring a ruleset for `netfilter`. Configure the firewall on **RT3-INT** to perform port forwarding for the **LAMP** web server, located on the 192.168.0.0/24 subnet.

a) Open a connection window for the **RT3-INT** VM, and log on with the username ***vyos*** and password ***Pa$$w0rd***

VyOS doesn't use `iptables` to configure the netfilter firewall, but the principles are similar. You will configure port forwarding so that **RT3-INT** passes any HTTP traffic arriving on its eth0 or eth2 interfaces to **LAMP** (connected off the eth1 interface).

b) Run the following commands:

```
conf

edit nat destination rule 008000

set inbound-interface eth0

set protocol tcp

set destination port 80

set translation address 192.168.1.1

commit

up

up

up

edit nat destination rule 008002

set inbound-interface eth2

set protocol tcp

set destination port 80
```

```
set translation address 192.168.1.1

commit

save

exit

show conf
```

c) Press the **Page Down** key to locate the **NAT** section of the configuration file and verify that the configuration matches this screenshot.

```
}
nat {
    destination {
        rule 008000 {
            destination {
                port 80
            }
            inbound-interface eth0
            protocol tcp
            translation {
                address 192.168.1.1
            }
        }
        rule 008002 {
            destination {
                port 80
            }
            inbound-interface eth2
            protocol tcp
            translation {
                address 192.168.1.1
            }
        }
    }
}
```

NAT configuration.

d) Press **q** to quit the configuration output.

e) Switch to the **PC1** VM, and browse to ***http://172.16.1.254*** to test that you can access the **Apache Default Page** site.

f) Switch to the **KALI** VM, and browse to ***http://172.16.1.254*** to test that you can access the **Apache Default Page** site.

8. You have configured port forwarding, but you do not have rules to prevent a host from accessing the internal IP hosts by using other protocols. Configure the firewall to put these access controls in place and accept only traffic necessary for running the web server (HTTP itself plus DNS and routing and ICMP for a bit of troubleshooting).

a) Switch back to the **RT3-INT** VM, and run the following commands (ignore any line breaks in the commands):

```
conf

set firewall state-policy established action accept

set firewall state-policy related action accept

commit
```

These commands configure the firewall to allow established and related connections as a global option. The effect of this is that the firewall applies access controls only to new connection requests.

b) Run the following commands (ignore any line breaks in the commands):

```
edit firewall name FWD_POLICY

set default-action drop

up

up

set interfaces ethernet eth0 firewall in name FWD_POLICY

set interfaces ethernet eth2 firewall in name FWD_POLICY

commit
```

This block configures a ruleset named **FWD_POLICY** with just one rule (drop any traffic) and applies it to the inbound forwarding chain on the eth0 (172.16.1.0/30) and eth2 (192.168.2.0/24) interfaces.

c) Run the following commands (ignore any line breaks in the commands):

```
edit firewall name LOCAL_POLICY

set default-action drop

up

up

set interfaces ethernet eth0 firewall local name
LOCAL_POLICY

set interfaces ethernet eth2 firewall local name
LOCAL_POLICY

commit

save

exit
```

This final block configures an identical ruleset, this time named **LOCAL_POLICY**, and applies it to the local chain on eth0 and eth2.

> **Note:** *It can be easy to get confused by the terminology used to describe traffic directed at the router as a host in itself and traffic that the router is forwarding. The rules configured on "local" will apply (for example) to any traffic directed at 172.16.1.254. In* iptables *terms, this would be referred to as the INPUT chain. The ruleset applied to "in" will act (for example) on any traffic directed at 192.168.1.1 (**LAMP**) or 192.168.2.192 (**KALI**); in* iptables *terms this is a FORWARD chain.*

d) Test the rule by trying to establish a connection to **LAMP** or any of **RT3-INT's** interfaces via ping or HTTP from **PC1** and **KALI**. When you are using the browser, press **Ctrl+F5** to ensure you are viewing a cached version of the page. All attempts to connect should fail.

9. Add rules to the policies you configured earlier to allow inbound forwarding ICMP, DNS, and HTTP requests and local ICMP and BGP (routing protocol) traffic.

a) Switch back to the **RT3-INT** VM. Enter the following series of commands:

```
conf

edit firewall name FWD_POLICY

edit rule 0001

set protocol icmp

set action accept

up
```

```
edit rule 0080

set protocol tcp

set destination port 80

set action accept

up

edit rule 0053

set protocol udp

set destination port 53

set action accept

up

up

edit name LOCAL_POLICY

edit rule 0001

set protocol icmp

set action accept

up

edit rule 0053

set protocol udp

set destination port 53

set action accept

up

edit rule 0179

set protocol tcp

set destination port 179

set action accept

commit

save

exit
```

Remember, the FWD_POLICY rules are being applied to the traffic that **RT3-INT** is receiving on eth0 or eth2 then forwarding out over another interface; the LOCAL_POLICY rules are applied to traffic addressing the host router itself.

b) Test the new rules by trying to establish a connection to **LAMP** or any of **RT3-INT's** interfaces via `ping` or HTTP from **PC1** and **KALI**. You can also try to connect by FQDN (**http://www.515web.net**).

Your tests should succeed.

10. Examine the `iptables` command.

a) Switch to the **LAMP** VM, and run the following command to show the current configuration, inputting **Pa$$w0rd** when prompted:

```
sudo iptables -vL
```

Empty firewall ruleset.

As you can see, no rules are configured for any of the chains.

b) Run the following commands (ignore any line breaks in the commands):

```
sudo iptables -A INPUT -s 192.168.2.0/24 -j DROP
```

```
sudo iptables -vL
```

This creates a rule to block all traffic deriving from the 192.168.2.0/24 subnet.

c) Switch to the **KALI** VM, and try to access the **Apache Default Page** site by browsing **http://www.515web.net**

Remember, press **Ctrl+F5** to ensure you are reconnecting and not viewing a cached page.

d) Try the following command. It should also fail.

```
ping 192.168.1.1 -c4
```

e) Switch back to **LAMP**, and run the following commands (ignore any line breaks in the commands):

```
sudo iptables -L --line-numbers
```

```
sudo iptables -R INPUT 1 -s 192.168.2.0/24 -p TCP --dport 80 -j DROP
```

The first command checks the line numbers of the current ruleset; the second command replaces the existing rule #1 in the INPUT chain with one that only blocks traffic on destination TCP port (--dport) 80.

f) Switch to the **KALI** VM. Web browsing will still be blocked, but you should be able to ping 192.168.1.1 successfully.

g) Switch back to **LAMP**, and run the following commands:

```
sudo iptables -A OUTPUT -d 172.16.0.0/24 -j DROP
```

```
ping 172.16.0.253 -c4
```

The pings should fail, as you have blocked any outgoing communications to that subnet.

h) Run the following commands to disable the OUTPUT rule again:

```
sudo iptables -D OUTPUT -d 172.16.0.0/24 -j DROP

sudo iptables -L
```

Changes made using iptables are **ephemeral** (discarded at reboot). To make permanent changes, you need to save the rules with a tool such as iptables-persistent.

11. Discard changes made to the VM in this activity.

a) Switch to Hyper-V Manager.

b) Use the **Action** menu or the right-click menu in the **Hyper-V Manager** console to revert the VMs to their saved checkpoints.

Topic B

Explain the Uses of IDS/IPS and UTM

EXAM OBJECTIVES COVERED
2.3 Explain the purposes and use cases for advanced networking devices.
4.6 Explain common mitigation techniques and their purposes.

Intrusion detection and prevention and anti-malware systems are mature security technologies and vary widely to protect company networks. While you may not be installing and configuring these devices, it is important that you understand their use on the network.

NETWORK-BASED INTRUSION DETECTION SYSTEMS (NIDSs)

An **intrusion detection system (IDS)** is a means of using software tools to provide real-time analysis of either network traffic or system and application logs. IDS is similar to **anti-virus** software, but it protects against a broader range of threats. A **network IDS (NIDS)** is basically a packet sniffer (referred to as a **sensor**) with an **analysis engine** to identify malicious traffic and a **console** to allow configuration of the system.

Snort open source IDS running on Windows Server. (Screenshot used with permission from Snort.)

The basic functionality of NIDS is to provide **passive detection**; that is, to log intrusion incidents and to display an alert at the management interface or to email the administrator account. This type of passive sensor does not slow down traffic and is undetectable by the attacker (it does not have an IP address on the monitored network segment).

A NIDS will be able to identify and log hosts and applications, and detect attack signatures, password guessing attempts, port scans, worms, backdoor applications, malformed packets or sessions, and policy violations (ports or IP addresses that are not permitted, for instance). You can use analysis of the logs to tune firewall rulesets, remove or block suspect hosts and processes from the network, or deploy additional security controls to mitigate any threats you identify.

NETWORK-BASED INTRUSION PREVENTION SYSTEMS (NIPSs)

Compared to the passive logging of IDSs, an **intrusion prevention system (IPS)** can provide an active response to any network threats that it matches. One typical preventive measure is to end the TCP session, sending a spoofed TCP reset packet to the attacking host. This will not always succeed in preventing an attack, however. Another option is for the sensor to apply a temporary filter on the firewall to block the attacker's IP address (**shunning**). Other advanced measures include throttling bandwidth to attacking hosts, applying complex firewall filters, and even modifying suspect packets to render them harmless. Finally, the appliance may be able to run a script or third-party program to perform some other action not supported by the IPS software itself.

Some IPSs provide inline, "wire-speed" anti-virus scanning. Their rulesets can be configured to provide user content filtering, such as blocking URLs, applying keyword-sensitive blacklists or whitelists, or applying time-based access restrictions.

IPS appliances are positioned like firewalls at the border between two network zones. As with proxy servers, the appliances are "inline" with the network, meaning that all traffic passes through them (also making them a **single point-of-failure (SPoF)** if there is no fault tolerance mechanism). This obviously means that they need to be able to cope with high bandwidths and process each packet very quickly to avoid slowing down the network.

ANTI-VIRUS SCANNERS

An on-access **anti-virus scanner** or intrusion prevention system works by identifying when processes or scripts are executed and intercepting (or hooking) the call to scan the code first. If the code matches a signature of known malware or exhibits malware-like behavior that matches a heuristic profile, the scanner will prevent execution and attempt to take the configured action on the host file (clean, **quarantine**, erase, and so on). An alert will be displayed to the user, and the action will be logged (and an administrative alert might also be generated). The malware will normally be tagged using a vendor proprietary string and possibly by a Common Malware Enumeration (CME) identifier. These identifiers can be used to research the symptoms of, and methods used by, the malware. This may help to confirm the system is fully remediated and to identify whether other systems have been infected. It is also important to trace the source of the infection and ensure that it is blocked to prevent repeat attacks and outbreaks.

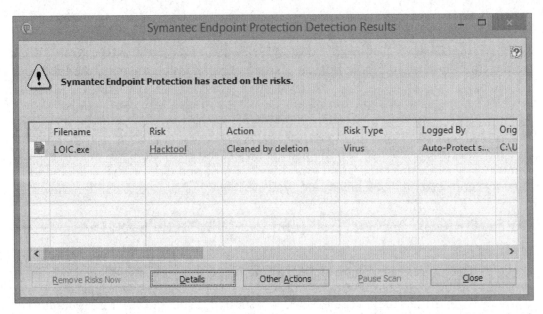

Detecting and remediating a virus infection using Symantec Endpoint Protection. (Screenshot used with permission from Symantec.)

UNIFIED THREAT MANAGEMENT (UTM)

Unified Threat Management (UTM) refers to a system that centralizes various security controls—firewall, anti-malware, network intrusion prevention, spam filtering, content inspection, etc.—into a single appliance. In addition, UTM security appliances usually include a single console from which you can monitor and manage various defense settings. UTM was created in response to difficulties that administrators face in deploying discrete security systems; namely, managing several complex platforms as well as meeting the significant cost requirements. UTM systems help to simplify the security process by being tied to only one vendor and requiring only a single, streamlined application to function. This makes management of your organization's network security easier, as you no longer need to be familiar with or know the quirks of each individual security implementation. Nevertheless, UTM has its downsides. When defense is unified under a single system, this creates the potential for a single point of failure that could affect an entire network. Distinct security systems, if they fail, might only compromise that avenue of attack. Additionally, UTM systems can struggle with latency issues if they are subject to too much network activity.

HOST-BASED IDS (HIDS) AND IPS (HIPS)

A **host-based IDS (HIDS)** captures information from a single host, such as a server, router, or firewall. Some organizations may configure HIDSs on each client workstation. HIDSs come in many different forms with different capabilities. The core ability is to capture and analyze log files, but more sophisticated systems can also monitor OS kernel files, monitor ports and network interfaces, and process data and logs generated by specific applications, such as HTTP or FTP.

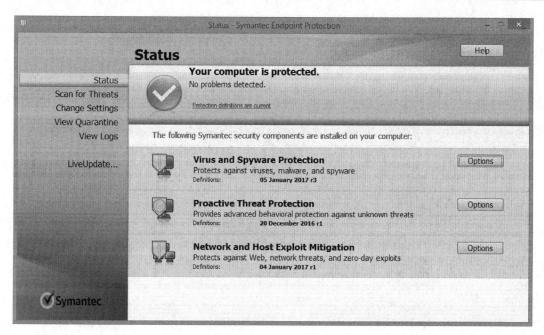

The Symantec Endpoint Protection client application provides malware and intrusion prevention security. (Screenshot used with permission from Symantec.)

Installing HIDS/HIPS is simply a case of choosing which hosts to protect, then installing and configuring the software. There will also normally be a reporting and management server to control the agent software on the hosts.

Note: *Ideally, an IDS host has two network interfaces: one to connect to the normal network, and the other is a management interface to connect to a separate network containing the management server. This could be implemented as a physically separate network infrastructure or as a VLAN.*

A **host-based IPS (HIPS)** with active response can act to preserve the system in its intended state. This means that the software can prevent system files from being modified or deleted, prevent services from being stopped, log off unauthorized users, and filter network traffic.

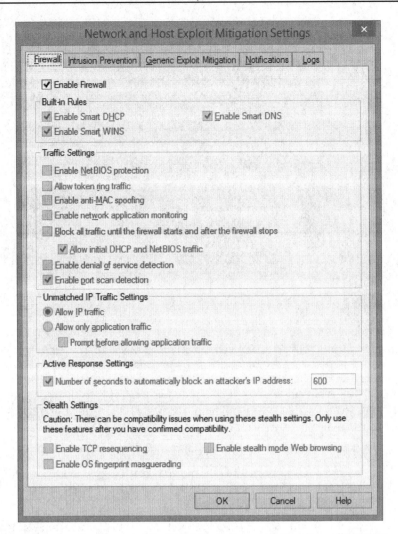

Exploit mitigation settings for Symantec Endpoint Protection suite host firewall/IPS. (Screenshot used with permission from Symantec.)

SIGNATURE MANAGEMENT

An IDS, IPS, anti-malware suite, or UTM appliance can use several methods to detect intrusions. **Signature-based detection** (or pattern-matching) means that the engine is loaded with a database of attack patterns or signatures. If traffic matches a pattern, then the engine generates an incident.

The two principal vulnerabilities of signature detection are that the protection is only as good as the last signature update and that no protection is provided against threats that cannot be matched in the pattern database. Another issue is that it is difficult to configure pattern matching that can detect attacks based on a complex series of communications.

These vulnerabilities are addressed by **behavior-based detection**, which can be effective at detecting previously unknown threats. Heuristic, profile-based detection is usually harder to set up and generates more **false positives** and **false negatives** than 1:1 pattern matching.

 Note: A false positive is where legitimate behavior is identified as an incident. Conversely, a false negative is where malicious traffic is not identified. High volumes of false positives can blind the analysis team, which can also result in attacks going undetected.

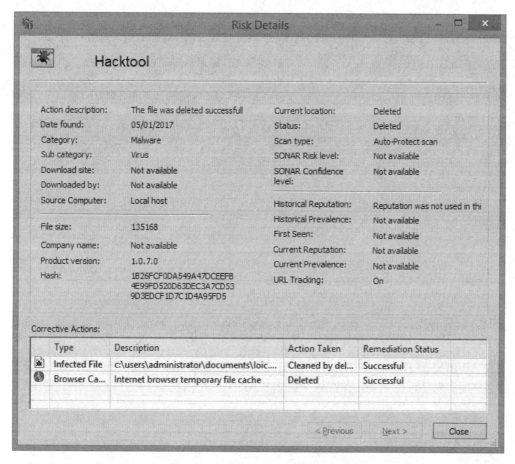

Identifying a malware file signature with Symantec Endpoint Protection. (Screenshot used with permission from Symantec.)

Signature matching can be tuned to the extent of disabling signatures that are not relevant to the network. For example, it would be appropriate to disable Windows-specific threat signatures on a Linux network. Behavior-based detection requires an intensive training period, during which there could be considerable disruption to the network in addition to requiring close monitoring by administrators. Also, re-training may be required as typical network use changes over time and the IDS starts to generate more false positives. Behavior-based detection also requires more processing resources.

FILE INTEGRITY MONITORING (FIM)

File integrity monitoring (FIM) software audits key system files to make sure they match the authorized versions. FIM does this by computing a secure checksum, also known as a hashsum, for the "known-good" version of a file. It periodically scans protected files, re-computing a hashsum for the locally installed version and checking that it matches the "known-good" value. In Windows, the Windows File Protection service runs automatically and the System File Checker (sfc) tool can be used manually to verify OS system files. Tripwire (*tripwire.com*) and OSSEC (*ossec.net*) are examples of multi-platform tools with options to protect a wider range of applications. FIM functionality is built into HIDS suites, too.

Activity 10-3

Discussing the Uses of IDS/IPS and UTM

SCENARIO

Answer the following questions to test your understanding of the content covered in this topic.

1. **What component does a network-based IDS use to scan traffic?**

2. **A company has suffered a data breach. Investigators are able to establish exactly when the data breach occurred, but on checking the IDS logs, no evidence of the breach is present. What type of intrusion detection error condition is this?**

3. **What is shunning?**

4. **What sort of maintenance must be performed on signature-based monitoring software?**

5. **What is the main purpose of UTM?**

Summary

In this lesson, you learned about various security device technologies.

- Firewalls can operate at several different layers, from simple packet filtering, through session control, to deep packet inspection (application). They can be implemented as appliances or software and deployed to protect network segments or individual hosts or applications.
- Make sure you know the basic ways to use the `iptables` command.
- IDS/IPS/UTM can monitor hosts and networks for known attack signatures or heuristic anomaly detection.

How does your organization use firewalls and proxies to protect the network, devices, and users?

What types of intrusion detection have been implemented in your organization?

 Practice Questions: *Additional practice questions are available on the course website.*

Lesson 11

Explaining Authentication and Access Controls

LESSON INTRODUCTION

Each network user and host device must be identified and categorized in certain ways so that you can control their access to your organization's applications, data, and services. In this lesson, you'll explain authentication and authorization solutions to foster a strong access management program.

LESSON OBJECTIVES

In this lesson, you will:

- Explain authentication controls and attacks.

- Explain the uses of authentication protocols and directory services.

- Explain the uses of port security and NAC.

- Implement network device hardening.

- Explain patch management and vulnerability scanning processes.

Topic A

Explain Authentication Controls and Attacks

EXAM OBJECTIVES COVERED
4.2 Explain authentication and access controls.
4.4 Summarize common networking attacks.
4.6 Explain common mitigation techniques and their purposes.

In this topic, you will identify network authentication methods. Strong authentication is the first line of defense to secure network resources. But authentication is not a single process; there are many methods and mechanisms involved. You should also understand the types of attacks that can threaten the secure functioning of authentication mechanisms. As a network professional, to effectively manage authentication on your network, you will need to understand these different systems and what each one can provide for your organization.

AUTHENTICATION AND ACCESS CONTROLS

An **access control** system is the set of technical controls that govern how subjects may interact with objects. **Subjects** in this sense are users, devices, or software processes, or anything else that can request and be granted access to a resource. **Objects** are the resources; these could be networks, servers, databases, files, and so on. In computer security, the basis of access control is usually an **access control list (ACL)**. This is a list of subjects and the rights or permissions they have been granted on the object. An **identity and access management (IAM)** system to mediate use of objects by subjects is usually described in terms of four main processes:

- **Identification**—Creating an account or ID that identifies the user, device, or process on the network.
- **Authentication**—Proving that a subject is who or what it claims to be when it attempts to access the resource.
- **Authorization**—Determining what rights subjects should have on each resource and enforcing those rights.
- **Accounting**—Tracking authorized usage of a resource or use of rights by a subject and alerting when unauthorized use is detected or attempted.

IAM enables you to define the attributes that make up an entity's identity, such as its purpose, function, security clearance, and more. These attributes subsequently enable access management systems to make informed decisions about whether to grant or deny an entity access, and if granted, decide what the entity has authorization to do. For example, an individual employee may have his or her own identity in the IAM system. The employee's role in the company factors into his or her identity, like what department the employee is in, and whether the employee is a manager. For example, if you are setting up an e-commerce site and want to enroll users, you need to select the appropriate controls to perform each function:

- Identification—You need to ensure that customers are legitimate. You might need to ensure that billing and delivery addresses match, for instance, and that they are not trying to use fraudulent payment methods.

- Authentication—You need to ensure that customers have unique accounts and that only they can manage their orders and billing information.
- Authorization—You need rules to ensure customers can only place orders when they have valid payment mechanisms in place. You might operate loyalty schemes or promotions that authorize certain customers to view unique offers or content.
- Accounting—The system must record the actions a customer takes (to ensure that they cannot deny placing an order, for instance).

 Note: *Historically, the acronym* **AAA** *was used to describe Authentication, Authorization, and Accounting systems. The use of* **IAAA** *is becoming more prevalent as the importance of the identification phase is better acknowledged.*

TRUSTED AND UNTRUSTED USERS

Users such as employees and approved partners or contractors are **trusted** to use network resources. The access control system should enforce accountability by identifying these users (requiring them to authenticate to the network), explicitly authorizing what they can do, and auditing (logging) their activities. The process of auditing and logging user activity is essential to the security posture of all networks. This provides documentation of user actions and actionable evidence that can be used during an inspection or investigation or to justify reprimand of users for misusing network services.

A network might also be required to provide access to **untrusted** users. This group might include site visitors, customers, and suppliers. Such users may be authenticated or unauthenticated (guests). Untrusted users will only be granted limited network access.

PRIVILEGED USER ACCOUNTS AND ROLE SEPARATION

Privileges are the rights users are granted over objects in the access control system. Most ordinary user accounts are only granted basic privileges, such as the ability to read or modify documents or adjust superficial properties of the OS or desktop. At the other end of the scale, a **privileged user account** is one that can control the system. Notably, an account with full privileges, such as members of the Windows **Local Administrators** account group, the Windows **Domain Admins** account group, or the Linux **root** account, can control the access control system itself. Such accounts are difficult to audit. You could consider such an account a *super-user* compared to the standard accounts of others within the same network with administrative privileges. These super-users are typically supervisors, managers, executives, or IT professionals.

A well-designed access control system seeks to avoid the use of these all-powerful accounts and delegate role-based responsibilities among different users. This type of **role separation** makes it harder for an insider threat to use a single account to compromise the whole system. For example, you can run logging and auditing under a non-interactive **system** account so that user-operated accounts cannot easily change or modify logging settings without another administrator being notified that such a change has been made. You can create one class of administrator responsible for allocating users to security groups and a different class of administrator responsible for allocating permissions over data files to those security groups.

More generally, role separation, also known as **separation of duties**, is a policy that states that no one person should have too much power or responsibility. Duties and responsibilities should be divided among individuals to prevent ethical conflicts or abuses of power. Duties such as authorization and approval, and design and development, should not be held by the same individual because it would be far too easy for that individual to defraud or otherwise harm an organization. For example, it would be easier for an employee to make sure that the organization only uses specific software that contains vulnerabilities if they are the only one with that responsibility. In many typical IT departments, roles like backup operator, restore operator, and auditor are assigned to different people.

Allocation of rights should also be guided by the principle of **least privilege**. This principle states that an account should only be granted the minimum sufficient permissions, and no more. For example, you can configure a privileged user with account permissions that are much less than those of the superuser or root. The rights should be designed to support the user's role, rather than just indiscriminately allocating the maximum possible rights.

INSIDER THREAT ATTACKS AND LOGIC BOMBS

Role separation and least privilege are necessary for two reasons. The first is that a privileged user's account could be compromised by malware or social engineering, giving an adversary the ability to impersonate that user. The other reason is the risk of insider threat. **Insider threat** means attacks launched by the organization's own trusted users (employees, partners, or contractors). The **Computer Emergency Response Team (CERT)** at Carnegie Mellon University definition of a malicious insider is:

A current or former employee, contractor, or business partner who has or had authorized access to an organization's network, system, or data and intentionally exceeded or misused that access in a manner that negatively affected the confidentiality, integrity, or availability of the organization's information or information systems.

When you are evaluating the risk of insider threat, it is important to identify likely motivations, such as employees who might harbor grievances or those likely to perpetrate fraud. An employee who plans and executes a campaign to modify invoices and divert funds is launching a structured attack; an employee who tries to guess the password on the salary database a couple of times, having noticed that the file is available on the network, is an opportunistic attack. CERT identifies the main motivators for insider threat as sabotage, financial gain, and business advantage. A **logic bomb** is a type of malware that executes in response to a system or user event. A typical example is a disgruntled system administrator who leaves a scripted trap that runs when his or her account is deleted or disabled. Anti-virus software is unlikely to detect this kind of malicious script or program.

SOCIAL ENGINEERING ATTACKS

Adversaries can use a diverse range of techniques to compromise a security system. A prerequisite of many types of attacks is to obtain information about the network and security system. **Social engineering** (or hacking the human) refers to means of getting users to reveal confidential information. **Impersonation** (pretending to be someone else) is one of the basic social engineering techniques. The classic impersonation attack is for the social engineer to phone into a department, claim they have to adjust something on the user's system remotely, and get the user to reveal their password. For this attack to succeed, the approach must be convincing and persuasive.

Social engineering is one of the most common and successful malicious techniques in information security. Because it exploits basic human trust, social engineering has proven to be a particularly effective way of manipulating people into performing actions that they might not otherwise perform. Attackers will generally try one of the following methods:

- Intimidate their target by pretending to be someone senior in rank.
- Intimidate the target by using spurious technical arguments and jargon or alarm him or her with a **hoax**.
- Coax the target by engaging him/her in friendly chat.

PHISHING AND PHARMING ATTACKS

Phishing is a combination of social engineering and **spoofing** (disguising one computer resource as another). In the case of phishing, the attacker sets up a spoof website to imitate a target bank or e-commerce provider's secure website or some other web resource that should be trusted by the target. The attacker then emails users of the genuine website informing them that their account must be updated or with some sort of hoax alert or alarm, supplying a disguised link that actually leads to their spoofed site. When the user authenticates with the spoofed site, their logon credentials are captured. Another technique is to spawn a "pop-up" window when a user visits a genuine banking site to try to trick them into entering their credentials through the pop-up.

Spear phishing refers to a phishing scam where the attacker has some information that makes an individual target more likely to be fooled by the attack. The attacker might know the name of a document that the target is editing, for instance, and send a malicious copy, or the phishing email might show that the attacker knows the recipient's full name, job title, telephone number, or other details that help convince the target that the communication is genuine. A spear phishing attack directed specifically against upper levels of management in the organization (CEOs and other "big beasts") is sometimes called **whaling**. Upper management may also be more vulnerable to ordinary phishing attacks because of their reluctance to learn basic security procedures.

Pharming is another means of redirecting users from a legitimate website to a malicious one. Rather than using social engineering techniques to trick the user, pharming relies on corrupting the way the victim's computer performs Internet name resolution, so that they are redirected from the genuine site to the malicious one. For example, if **mybank.com** should point to the IP address 2.2.2.2, a pharming attack would corrupt the name resolution process to make it point to IP address 6.6.6.6.

RANSOMWARE

Ransomware is a type of malware that tries to extort money from the victim. One class of ransomware will display threatening messages, such as requiring Windows to be reactivated or suggesting that the computer has been locked by the police because it was used to view child pornography or for terrorism. This may block access to the computer by installing a different shell program, but this sort of attack is usually relatively simple to fix.

The **crypto-malware** class of ransomware attempts to encrypt data files on any fixed, removable, and network drives. If the attack is successful, the user will be unable to access the files without obtaining the private encryption key, which is held by the attacker. If successful, this sort of attack is extremely difficult to mitigate unless the user has up-to-date backups of the encrypted files.

Ransomware uses payment methods such as wire transfer, bitcoin, or premium rate phone lines to allow the attacker to extort money without revealing his or her identity or being tracked by local law enforcement. In the context of social engineering, ransomware may give an attacker the opportunity to blackmail or coerce an employee.

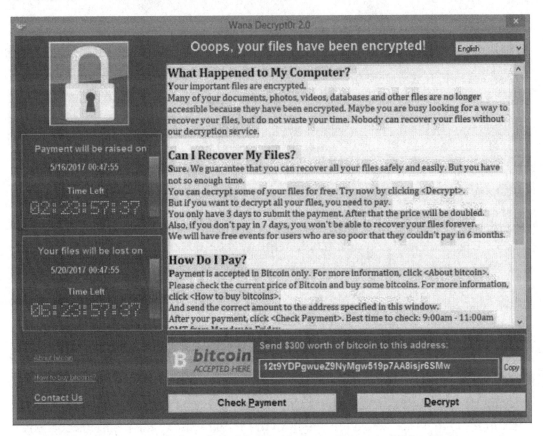

WannaCry ransomware. Wikimedia Public Domain image. (Image by Wikimedia Commons.)

MULTIFACTOR AND TWO-FACTOR AUTHENTICATION

An account defines a subject on the computer or network system. Assuming that an account has been created securely (the identity of the account holder has been verified), **authentication** verifies that only the account holder is able to use the account, and that the system may be used only by account holders. Authentication is performed when the account holder supplies the appropriate **credentials** to the system. These are compared to the credentials stored on the system. If they match, the account is authenticated.

Authentication factors (the data used to perform an authentication) fall into three categories:

- Something you **know** (such as a password).
- Something you **have** (such as a smart card).
- Something you **are** (such as a fingerprint).
- Something you **do** (such as making a signature).
- **Somewhere** you **are** (such as using a mobile device with location services).

An authentication technology or mechanism is considered **strong** if it combines the use of more than one authentication data type (**multifactor**). **Single-factor authentication** systems can quite easily be compromised; a password could be written down or shared or compromised by a social engineering attack, a smart card could be lost or stolen, and a biometric system could be subject to high error rates.

Two-factor authentication combines something like a smart card or biometric mechanism with "something you know," such as a password or PIN. Three-factor authentication combines three of the possible technologies. An example of this would be a smart card with an integrated fingerprint reader. This means that to authenticate, the user must possess the card, the user's fingerprint must match the template stored on the card, and the user must input a PIN.

> *Note: Multifactor authentication requires a combination of different technologies. For example, requiring a PIN along with date of birth may be stronger than entering a PIN alone, but it is not multifactor.*

> *Note: To learn more, watch the related **Video** on the course website.*

SINGLE SIGN-ON (SSO)

Single sign-on (SSO) means that a user has to authenticate to a system only once to gain access to all its resources (that is, all the resources to which the user has been granted rights). An example is the Kerberos authentication and authorization model. In this model, a user who has authenticated with Windows is also authenticated with the Windows **domain's** SQL Server and Exchange Server services.

The advantage of SSO is that each user does not have to manage multiple user accounts and passwords. The disadvantage is that compromising the account also compromises multiple services.

SSO tends to be implemented only on enterprise networks. There have been various initiatives to try to extend the principle to web accounts (Microsoft accounts, Facebook Login, and the PayPal e-commerce model, for instance), but no scheme has achieved the sort of critical mass that would force widespread acceptance. There would also be serious security concerns about using a common logon for different sites, especially where online banking sites are concerned.

> *Caution: It is critical that users do not re-use work passwords or authentication information on third-party sites. Of course, this is almost impossible to enforce, so security managers must rely on effective user training.*

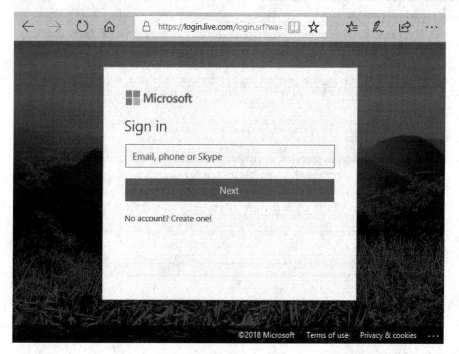

Microsoft accounts allow SSO to multiple Microsoft and third-party services. (Screenshot used with permission from Microsoft.)

SOMETHING YOU KNOW AUTHENTICATION

The typical **something you know** technology is the logon: this comprises a **username** and a **password**. The username is typically not a secret (though it should not be published openly), but the password must be known only to the account holder. A **passphrase** is a longer password comprising several words. This has the advantages of being more secure and easier to remember. A **Personal Identification Number (PIN)** is also something you know, though long PIN codes are hard to remember, and short codes are too vulnerable for most authentication systems. If the number of attempts is not limited, it is simple for password cracking software to try to attempt every combination to "brute force" a 4-digit PIN

Windows sign in screen. (Screenshot used with permission from Microsoft.)

Something you know authentication is also often used for account reset mechanisms. For example, to reset the password on an account, the user might have to respond to challenge questions, such as "What is your favorite color/pet/movie?"

PASSWORD AND BRUTE FORCE ATTACKS

Password- and PIN-based authentication has several vulnerabilities to poor practice and malicious **attacks**. Passwords can be discovered via social engineering or because a user has written one down. It is also possible to capture password packets in transit. If the protocol uses **cleartext** credentials, then the attacker's job is done.

 Note: A password might be sent in an encoded form, such as Base64, which is simply an ASCII representation of binary data. This is not the same as encryption. The password value can easily be derived from the Base64 string.

Most passwords are only sent using some sort of encryption, however. Either the channel can be encrypted, or the password can be encrypted (or both). If the channel is encrypted, the attacker must compromise the encryption keys stored on the server. If the password is encrypted, the attacker might be able to use password cracking software to decipher it.

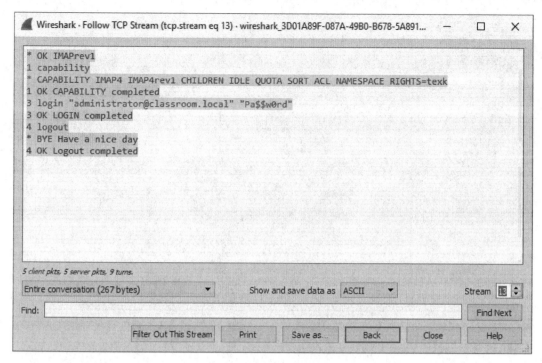

If authentication credentials are transmitted in cleartext, such as the unencrypted version of the IMAP mailbox access protocol, it is a simple matter for the credentials to be intercepted via packet sniffing. (Screenshot courtesy of Wireshark.)

While the precise mechanism is platform-dependent, in general terms, a password is stored securely by making a cryptographic hash of the string entered by the user. A cryptographic hash algorithm, **Secure Hash Algorithm (SHA)** or **Message Digest v5 (MD5)**, produces a fixed length string, called a **message digest**, from a variable length string. The function is designed so that it is impossible to recover the original string from the digest (**one-way**) and so that different strings are unlikely to produce the same digest (a **collision**).

Password cracking software uses different methods to obtain the password from a cryptographic hash of a password string:

- **Dictionary**—The software matches the hash to those produced by ordinary words found in a dictionary. This could also include information such as user and company names, pet names, or any other data that people might naively use as passwords.
- **Brute force**—The software tries to match the hash against one of every possible combination it could be. If the password is short (under seven characters) and non-complex (using only letters, for instance), a password might be cracked in minutes. Longer and more complex passwords increase the amount of time the attack takes to run.

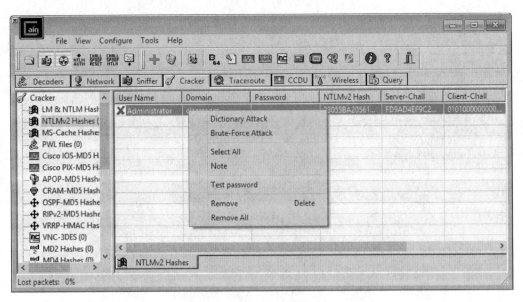

Cain and Abel password cracker. (Screenshot courtesy of Cain and Abel.)

SOMETHING YOU HAVE AUTHENTICATION

There are various ways to authenticate a user based on something they have. Examples include a smart card, USB **token**, or key fob that contains a chip with authentication data, such as a **digital certificate**. The card must be presented to a card reader before the user can be authenticated. A smart card with contactless capability can simply be touched to the reader (a **proximity card**). A USB token can be plugged into a normal USB port. When the card is read, the card software prompts the user for a PIN or password, which mitigates the risk of the card being lost or stolen.

Key fobs are another example of something you have. A key fob is a small object that acts similarly to a proximity card, as it uses contactless technology to authenticate a person through a reader. Some common forms include a small fob to put on your keychain, a tag glued to an ID, or in the form of a wristband.

Another option is a hardware token that generates a **one-time password (OTP)**. The token displays a passcode that either changes periodically or is generated for one-time use. The frequency or sequence of changes are mathematically linked to an algorithm on the authenticating server, so inputting the correct code proves possession of the token.

SOMETHING YOU ARE/DO AUTHENTICATION

Something you are means employing some sort of **biometric** recognition system. Many types of biometric information can be recorded, including fingerprint patterns, iris or retina recognition, or facial recognition. The chosen biometric information (the **template**) is scanned and recorded in a database. When the user wants to access a resource, he or she is re-scanned, and the scan is compared to the template. If the confirmation scan matches the template to within a defined degree of tolerance, access is granted. The main problems with biometric technology generally are:

- Users can find it intrusive and threatening to privacy.
- The technology can be discriminatory or inaccessible to those with disabilities.
- Setup and maintenance costs to provision biometric readers.
- Vulnerability to spoofing methods.

Something you do refers to behavioral biometric recognition. Rather than scan some attribute of your body, a template is created by analyzing a behavior, such as typing or writing a signature. The variations in speed and pressure applied are supposed to uniquely verify an individual. In practice, however, these methods are subject to higher error rates and are much more troublesome for a subject to perform. Something you do authentication is more likely to be deployed as an intrusion detection or continuous authentication mechanism. For example, if a user successfully authenticates using a password and smart card, their use of the keyboard might be subsequently monitored. If this deviates from the baseline, the IDS would trigger an alert.

SOMEWHERE YOU ARE AUTHENTICATION

Location-based authentication measures statistics about where you are. This could be a geographic location, measured using a device's location service and the Global Positioning System (GPS) and/or Indoor Positioning System (IPS), or it could be by IP address. The IP address could also be used to refer to a logical network segment, or it could be linked to a geographic location using a **geolocation** service. Geolocation by IP address works by looking up a host's IP address in a geolocation database, such as GeoIP (*maxmind.com/en/geoip-demo*), IPInfo (*ipinfo.io*), or DB-IP (*db-ip.com*), and retrieving the registrant's country, region, city, name, and other information. The registrant is usually the ISP, so the information you receive will provide an approximate location of a host based on the ISP. If the ISP is one that serves a large or diverse geographical area, you will be less likely to pinpoint the location of the host.

Like something you do, location-based authentication is not used as a primary authentication factor, but it may be used as a continuous authentication mechanism or as an access control feature. For example, if a user enters the correct credentials at a VPN gateway, but his or her IP address shows him/her to be in a different country than expected, access controls might be applied to restrict the privileges granted or refuse access completely.

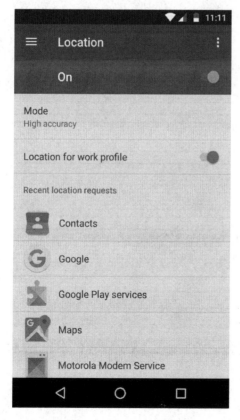

Location services, such as those provided by Android on this smartphone, can support access control systems. (Android is a trademark of Google LLC.)

Activity 11-1
Discussing Authentication Controls and Attacks

SCENARIO
Answer the following questions to test your understanding of the content covered in this topic.

1. **What element is missing from the following list, and what is its purpose? Identification, Authentication, Accounting**

2. **Why do malicious insider threats often pose greater risk than malicious users generally?**

3. **Why is a logic bomb unlikely to be detected by anti-virus software?**

4. **What is the purpose of SSO?**

5. **How do social engineering attacks succeed?**

6. **How might an attacker recover a password from an encrypted hash?**

7. **What are the two main types of tokens that a user can present as part of an authentication mechanism?**

8. **Which factor is missing from the following list? Something You Know, Something You Are, Something You Have, Somewhere You Are.**

Topic B

Explain the Uses of Authentication Protocols and Directory Services

EXAM OBJECTIVES COVERED
1.1 Explain the purposes and uses of ports and protocols.
2.3 Explain the purposes and use cases for advanced networking devices.
4.2 Explain authentication and access controls.

Authentication mechanisms and factors, plus information about network subjects and authorizations, must be implemented by server software and hardware. While you may not be responsible for deploying and configuring these systems at this stage in your career, you should be able to explain the uses of authentication and access controls.

LOCAL AUTHENTICATION

One set of protocols is used to log on locally to a network or host; another class of protocols is used to log on across a potentially unsecure channel (a VPN or wireless network, for instance). **Local authentication** is the primary method of logging into systems when on-site. Local authentication methods typically require username and password credentials, but some will support multifactor methods, such as smart cards or biometric readers.

LAN MANAGER/NTLM

LAN Manager (LM or **LANMAN)** was an NOS developed by Microsoft® and 3Com. Microsoft used the authentication protocol from LM for Windows 9x networking. This protocol was later redeveloped as **NTLM** and NTLMv2. LM is a **challenge/response** authentication protocol using an encrypted hash of the user's password. This means that the user's password is not sent to the server in plaintext and cannot (in theory) be obtained by an attacker. The version of LM used for early versions of Windows® NT (NTLM) fixed some of the problems in LM. A substantially revised version of the protocol appeared in Windows NT4 SP4 (NTLMv2) and continues to provide local logon for current versions of Windows. While the basic challenge/response process is the same, the responses are calculated differently to defeat known attacks against NTLM.

LINUX LOCAL AUTHENTICATION

Linux®, like most operating systems, supports multiple users. These user accounts are linked to a primary group which determines many aspects of security in Linux. User and group settings are stored in the **/etc/passwd** and **/etc/group** files. The user password is typically stored as an encrypted hash in the **/etc/shadow** file, along with other password settings such as age and expiration date.

KERBEROS

Kerberos is a network authentication protocol developed by the **Massachusetts Institute of Technology (MIT)** in the 1980s. The idea behind Kerberos is that it provides SSO. Once authenticated, a user is trusted by the system and does not need to re-authenticate to access different resources. The Kerberos authentication method was selected by Microsoft as the network logon provider for Windows 2000 and later. It provides authentication to Active Directory®, as well as compatibility with other, non-Windows operating systems.

Kerberos was named after the three-headed guard dog of Hades (Cerberus) because it consists of three parts. **Clients** request services from a **server**, which both rely on an intermediary—a **Key Distribution Center (KDC)**—to vouch for their identity.

There are two services that make up a KDC: the **Authentication Service** and the **Ticket Granting Service**. The KDC runs on port 88 using TCP or UDP. The **Authentication Service** is responsible for authenticating user logon requests. More generally, users and services can be authenticated; these are collectively referred to as principals. For example, when you sit at a Windows domain workstation and log on to the domain (Kerberos documentation refers to *realms* rather than domains, which is Microsoft's terminology), the first step of logon is to authenticate with a KDC server (implemented as a domain controller).

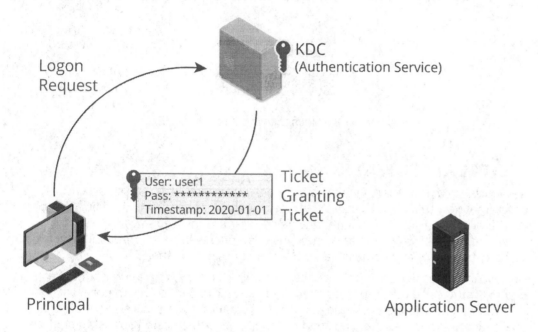

Kerberos Authentication Service. (Image © 123RF.com.)

When authenticated, the KDC server presents the user with a **Ticket Granting Ticket**. To access resources within the domain, the client requests a **Service Ticket** (a token that grants access to a target application server) by supplying the Ticket Granting Ticket to the **Ticket Granting Service (TGS)**.

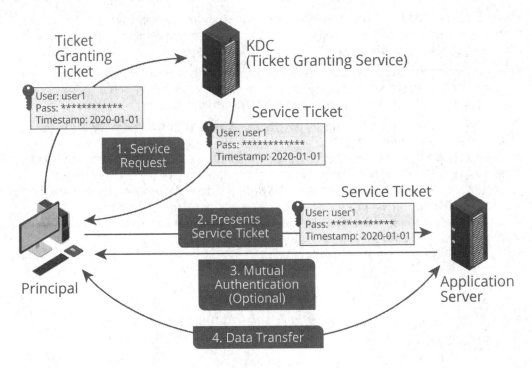

Kerberos Ticket Granting Service. (Image © 123RF.com.)

DIGITAL CERTIFICATES AND PKI

A protocol such as Kerberos can also be used with smart cards. The smart card is programmed with a digital certificate, issued by the authenticating domain. **Digital certificates** are also used to authenticate server machines when using Transport Layer Security (TLS). A certificate can be installed on a web server or email server to validate its identity and establish a secure transmission channel.

Digital certificates depend on the concept of public key **cryptography**. **Public key cryptography**, also referred to as **asymmetric encryption**, solves the problem of distributing encryption keys when you want to communicate securely with others, authenticate a message that you send to others, or authenticate yourself to an access control system. With asymmetric encryption, you generate a key pair. The private key in the pair remains a secret that only you know. The public key can be transmitted to other subjects. The private key cannot be derived from the public key. The key pair can be used in the following ways:

- When you want others to send you confidential messages, you give them your public key to use to encrypt the message. The message can then only be decrypted by your private key, which you keep known only to yourself. Due to the way asymmetric encryption works, the public key cannot be used to decrypt a message, even though it was used to encrypt it in the first place.

 *Note: As encryption using a public key is relatively slow; rather than encrypting the whole message using a public key, more typically, the public key is used to encrypt a **symmetric encryption** key for use in a single session and exchange it securely. The symmetric session key is then used to encrypt the actual message. A symmetric key can perform both encryption and decryption.*

- When you want to authenticate yourself to others, you create a signature and sign it by encrypting the signature with your private key. You give others your public key to use to decrypt the signature. As only you know the private key, everyone can be assured that only you could have created the signature.

The basic problem with public key cryptography is that you may not really know with whom you are communicating. The system is vulnerable to man-in-the-middle attacks. This problem is particularly evident with e-commerce. How can you be sure that a shopping site or banking service is really maintained by whom it claims? The fact that the site is distributing public keys to secure communications is no guarantee of actual identity. How do you know that you are corresponding directly with the site, using its certificate? How can you be sure there isn't a man-in-the-middle intercepting and modifying what you think the legitimate server is sending you?

Public key infrastructure (PKI) aims to prove that the owners of public keys are who they say they are. Under PKI, anyone issuing public keys should obtain a **digital certificate**. The validity of the certificate is guaranteed by a **certificate authority (CA)**. A digital certificate is essentially a wrapper for a subject's (or end entity's) public key. As well as the public key, it contains information about the subject and the certificate's issuer or guarantor. The certificate is digitally signed to prove that it was issued to the subject by a particular CA.

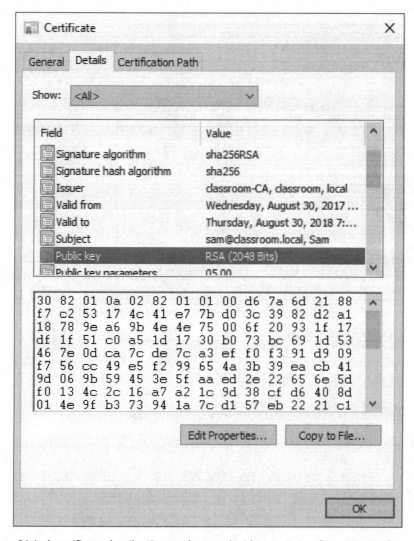

Digital certificate details. (Screenshot used with permission from Microsoft.)

The subject could be a human user (for certificates allowing the signing of messages or authenticating to a network using smart card logon, for instance) or a computer server (for a web server hosting confidential transactions, for instance). The X.509 standard defines the fields (information) that must be present in the certificate. The standard provides interoperability between different vendors.

AUTHENTICATION, AUTHORIZATION, AND ACCOUNTING (AAA) SERVERS

Enterprise networks and ISPs potentially need to support hundreds or thousands of users and numerous different remote and wireless access technologies and devices. The problem arises that each remote access device needs to be configured with authentication information, and this information needs to be synchronized between them. These remote access devices are often placed at the network edge, making them most vulnerable to compromise. Hosting large databases of user credentials directly on these devices is not a good idea. Consequently, an authentication architecture, referred to as **authentication, authorization, and accounting (AAA)**, has been developed to mediate authentication operations between network clients, network access devices, and user authentication and credential management servers.

As well as validating user credentials for authentication, AAA can transmit authorizations for rights and permissions and collect accounting information from the user session.

RADIUS

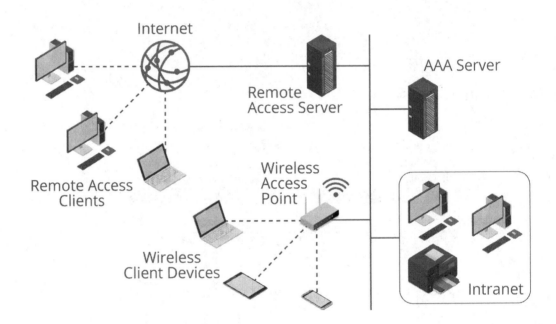

RADIUS. (Image © 123RF.com.)

Remote Authentication Dial-in User Service (RADIUS) is one way of implementing an AAA server. Remote access devices—such as routers, layer 3 switches, wireless access points, or VPN servers and concentrators—function as client devices of the RADIUS server. Rather than storing authentication information, they pass this data between the AAA server and the remote user. The server and clients are identified to one another by configuring the same shared secret on the devices.

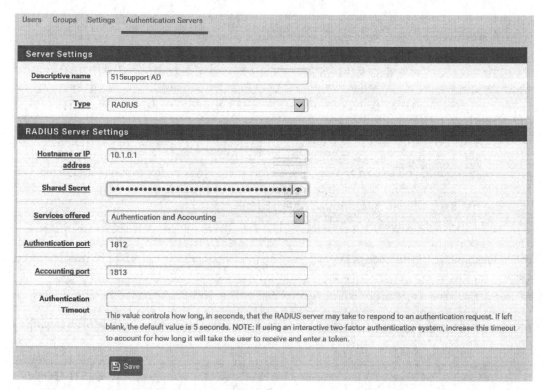

Configuring a pfSense security appliance as a RADIUS client. The pfSense appliance is working as a virtual private network (VPN) access server. It uses the RADIUS server at 10.1.0.1 to authenticate VPN users. The client must be configured with the same shared secret as the server. (Screenshot used with permission from pfSense.)

There are several RADIUS server and client products. Microsoft has the Network Policy Server (NPS) for Windows platforms, and there are open-source implementations for UNIX and Linux, such as FreeRADIUS, as well as third-party commercial products, such as Cisco's Secure Access Control Server, OSC Radiator, and Juniper Networks Steel-Belted RADIUS. Products are not always interoperable, as they may not support the same authentication and accounting technologies (proxy support).

RADIUS typically uses UDP ports 1812 and 1813, but some implementations use UDP ports 1645 and 1646.

TACACS+

Terminal Access Controller Access Control System (TACACS+) is a similar protocol to RADIUS but designed to be more flexible and reliable. TACACS+ was developed by Cisco but is also supported on many of the other third-party and open source RADIUS server implementations. Where RADIUS is often used in VPN implementations, TACACS + is often used in authenticating administrative access to routers and switches. It uses TCP over port 49 and the reliable delivery offered by TCP makes it easier to detect when a server is down. Another feature is that the entire payload in TACACS+ packets is encrypted, rather than just the authentication data.

DIRECTORY SERVICES AND ACCESS CONTROL LISTS

Directory services are the principal means of providing **privilege management** and authorization on an enterprise network. Depending on the sort of access control model used, the **owner** or **systems administrator** can share resources (folders, printers, and other resources) to make them available for network users. The resources can then be protected with a security system based around the **authentication credentials** provided by each user at logon to gain access to a system-defined **account**. Windows and UNIX/Linux systems all provide versions of this type of security.

When logging on to the network, the user must supply logon credentials. This username and password (or other authentication data) are compared with the server's **security database**, and if they match, the user is authenticated. The server security service generates an **access key** for the user. This contains the username and **group memberships** of the authenticated user.

All **resources** on server-based systems have an **access control list (ACL)** that is used to control access to the resource. The access list contains entries for all usernames and groups that have **permission** to use the resource. It also records the level of access available for each entry. For example, an access list may allow a user named **user1** to view the name of a file in a folder but not read the file contents.

Whenever the user attempts to access a resource, his or her access key is provided as identification. The server's security service matches username and group memberships from the access key with entries in the access list, and from this, it calculates the user's access privileges.

All this information is stored in a directory. Most directories are based on the **Lightweight Directory Access Protocol (LDAP)**. As well as enterprise networking directories, LDAP also provides a model for Internet directory access, such as providing contact lists for instant messaging (IM) applications.

LIGHTWEIGHT DIRECTORY ACCESS PROTOCOL (LDAP)

A directory is like a database, where an **object** is like a record, and things that you know about the object (**attributes**) are like fields. For products from different vendors to be interoperable, most directories are based on the same standard. The main directory standard is the **X.500** series of standards, developed by the **International Telecommunications Union (ITU)** in the 1980s. As this standard is complex, most directory services are implementations of the **Lightweight Directory Access Protocol (LDAP)**. LDAP is not a directory standard, but a protocol used to query and update an X.500 directory or any type of directory that can present itself as an X.500 directory. LDAP is widely supported in current directory products (Windows Active Directory®, Novell eDirectory, Apple OpenDirectory, or the open source OpenLDAP). LDAP messaging uses TCP and UDP port 389 by default.

A **distinguished name** is a unique identifier for any given resource within an X.500-like directory. A distinguished name is made up of attribute=value pairs, separated by commas. The most specific attribute is listed first, and successive attributes become progressively broader. This most specific attribute is also referred to as the **relative distinguished name**, as it uniquely identifies the object within the context of successive (parent) attribute values.

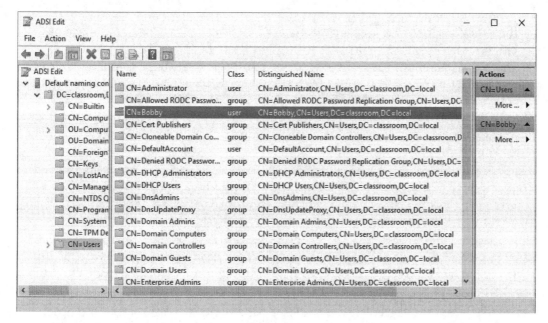

Browsing objects in an Active Directory LDAP schema. (Screenshot used with permission from Microsoft.)

The types of attributes, what information they contain, and the way object types are defined through attributes (some of which may be required and some optional) is described by the directory **schema**. Some of the attributes commonly used are as follows.

Attribute	Field	Usage
CN	Common Name	Identities the person or object.
OU	Organizational Unit	A unit or department within the organization.
O	Organization	The name of the organization.
L	Locality	Usually a city or area.
ST	State	A state, province, or county within a country.
C	Country	The country's two-character ISO code (such as c=US or c=UK).
DC	Domain Component	Components of the object's domain.

For example, the distinguished name of a web server operated by Widget in London might be:

```
CN=WIDGETWEB, OU=Marketing, O=Widget, L=London, ST=London, C=UK,
DC=widget, DC=com
```

LDAP SECURE (LDAPS)

LDAP itself provides no security, and all transmissions are in plaintext, making it vulnerable to sniffing and MitM (spoofing an LDAP server) attacks. Also, a server that does not require clients to authenticate is vulnerable to overloading by DoS attacks. Authentication, referred to as **binding** to the server, can be implemented in the following ways:

- No authentication—Anonymous access is granted to the directory.
- Simple authentication—The client must supply its DN and password, but these are passed as plaintext. This method could be secured if using IPSec for transport across the network.

- Simple Authentication and Security Layer (SASL)—The client and server negotiate the use of a supported security mechanism. Typically, this will mean the use of either Kerberos or TLS to provide strong certificate-based authentication.
- There is also an unofficial way of securing LDAP using SSL/TLS called **LDAPS**. This is very similar to HTTPS and works over TCP port 636. SSL/TLS provide a means for the server to authenticate to the client and configure a secure channel for communications.

If secure access is required, anonymous and simple authentication access methods should be disabled on the server.

Generally, two levels of access will need to be granted on the directory: read-only access (query) and read/write access (update). This is implemented using an access control policy, but the precise mechanism is vendor-specific and not specified by the LDAP standards documentation.

Unless it is hosting a public service, the LDAP directory server should also only be accessible from the private network. This means that LDAP ports (389 over TCP and UDP) should be blocked by a firewall from access over the public interface.

Where LDAP can be queried from some sort of web application, the application design needs to prevent the possibility of **LDAP injection attacks**. For example, if the web application presents a search form to allow the user to query a directory, a malicious user may enter a search string that includes extra search filters. If the input string is not properly validated, this could allow the user to bypass authentication or inject a different query, possibly allowing the attacker to return privileged information, such as a list of usernames or even passwords.

AUDITING AND LOGGING

The accounting function in AAA is generally performed by **logging** subject and object activity. All NOSs and many applications and services can be configured to log events. The main decision is which events to record. Logs serve the following general purposes:

- Accounting for all actions that have been performed by users. Change and version control systems depend on knowing when a file has been modified and by whom. Accounting also provides for **non-repudiation** (that is, a user cannot deny that they accessed or made a change to a file). The main problems are that **auditing** successful access attempts can quickly consume a lot of disk space and analyzing the logs can be very time-consuming.
- Detecting intrusions or attempted intrusions. Here records of failure-type events are likely to be more useful, though success-type events can also be revealing if they show unusual access patterns.

Obviously, the more events that are logged, the more difficult it is to analyze and interpret the logs. Also, logs can take up a large amount of disk space. When a log reaches its allocated size, it will start to overwrite earlier entries. This means that some system of backing up logs will be needed in order to preserve a full accounting record over time. It is also critical that the log files be kept secure so that they cannot be tampered with. Insider threats are particularly pertinent here, as rogue administrators could try to doctor the event log to cover up their actions.

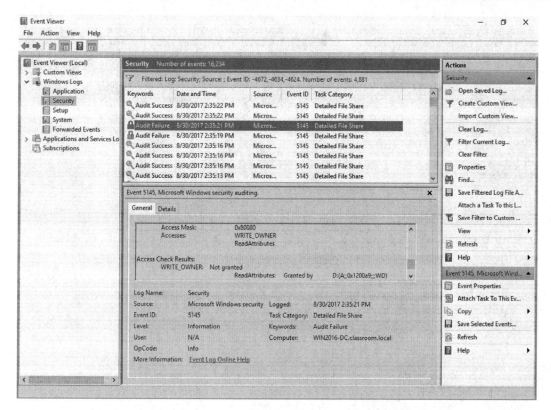

Recording an unsuccessful attempt to take ownership of an audited folder. (Screenshot used with permission from Microsoft.)

Note: *To learn more, watch the related* **Video** *on the course website.*

Activity 11-2

Discussing the Uses of Authentication Protocols and Directory Services

SCENARIO
Answer the following questions to test your understanding of the content covered in this topic.

1. **What are the main features of a digital certificate?**

2. **What authorization feature makes Kerberos a good choice for a network authentication protocol?**

3. **What is a RADIUS client, and how should it be configured?**

4. **What is an LDAP distinguished name?**

Activity 11-3

Securing Appliance Administration Using RADIUS Authentication

BEFORE YOU BEGIN

Start the VMs used in this activity in the following order, adjusting the memory allocation first if necessary, and waiting at the ellipsis for the previous VMs to finish booting before starting the next group. You do not need to connect to a VM until prompted to do so in the activity steps.

1. **PFSENSE** (512—1024 MB)
2. **DC1** (1024—2048 MB)
3. **KALI** (2048—4096 MB)
4. ...
5. **MS1** (1024 MB)
6. ...
7. **PC1** (1024 MB)

> **Note:** *If you can allocate more than the minimum amounts of RAM, prioritize* **KALI** *and* **DC1**.

SCENARIO

In this activity, you will investigate some of the challenges involved in providing secure administrative access to network and security appliances and the solutions available for secure authentication and authorization. This activity is designed to test your understanding of and ability to apply content examples in the following CompTIA Network+ objectives:

- 1.1 Explain the purposes and uses of ports and protocols.
- 2.3 Explain the purposes and use cases for advanced networking devices.
- 4.2 Explain authentication and access controls.
- 4.4 Summarize common networking attacks.
- 4.5 Given a scenario, implement network device hardening.

---

1. Any channel used for administration credentials must be secure. Sniff the password from the unprotected administration interface of the pfSense web admin app.

   a) Open a connection window for the **KALI** VM. Select **File→Settings**.

   b) Select the **eth0** node. In the right-hand pane, under **Virtual switch**, select **vLOCAL**. Select **OK**.

   c) Log on with the credentials *root* and *Pa$$w0rd*

   You will use ARP spoofing to perform a MitM attack. This means that **KALI** will be able to monitor traffic passing between two hosts. You will use the Ettercap tool (*ettercap-project.org*) to perform the attack.

   d) From the Dash, select **Ettercap**.

    e)   From the **Ettercap** menu bar, select **Sniff→Unified Sniffing** and select **OK**.

    f)   Select **Hosts→Scan for hosts**. When complete, select **Hosts→Hosts list**.

    g)   Select **10.1.0.10x** (where *x* completes the DHCP-assigned IP of **PC1**) and select **Add to Target 1** then select **10.1.0.254** and select **Add to Target 2**.

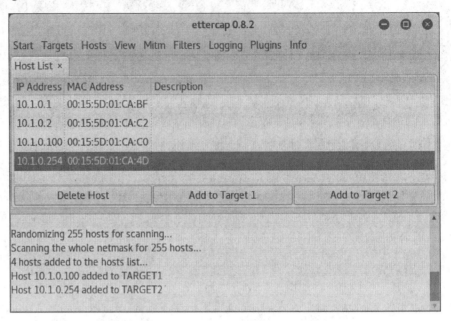

Configuring Ettercap. (Screenshot courtesy of Ettercap.)

    h)   Select **Mitm→Arp Poisoning**. In the dialog box, check the **Sniff remote connections** check box and select **OK**.

2.   Run a packet capture to follow the progress of the ARP poisoning attack.

    a)   From the Dash, select **Wireshark**.

    b)   Select **eth0** and then select the **Start Capture** button.

3.   With the attack in place, perform an action for the **KALI** host to intercept.

    a)   Open a connection window for the **PC1** VM, and log on with the credentials *515support\Administrator* and *Pa$$w0rd*

    b)   Run *http://10.1.0.254*. Log on to the **pfSense web admin console** with the credentials *admin* and *Pa$$w0rd*

    c)   When you are prompted to save the password, select **Never**. Leave the web application open.

    d)   Switch to the **KALI** VM, and stop the packet capture.

    e)   In the **Display filter** box, type *http.request.method == "POST"* and press **Enter**

          Make sure you type two equals signs.

f) Expand the HTML elements to locate the credentials.

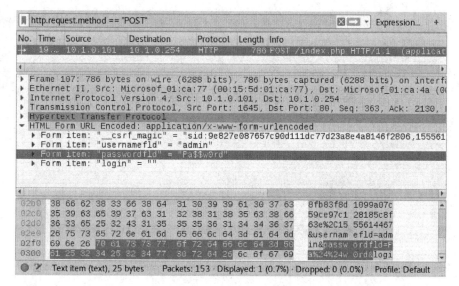

Sniffing credentials over unencrypted HTTP with Wireshark. (Screenshot courtesy of Wireshark.)

g) Switch to **Ettercap**, and select **Mitm→Stop Mitm attack(s)**. Select **OK**.
h) Select **Start→Stop sniffing**.

4. You can use SSL/TLS to protect the log in. Rather than use a self-signed certificate generated by pfSense, you will request a certificate from the domain's certificate authority (CA) and install it to the appliance. This means that the certificate will be trusted by domain computers. To start, register the appliance's host name with the local DNS server.

 Note: In this activity setup, the root CA is running on a domain controller. This is not advisable on a production network. A CA should be installed to a dedicated server under separate administrative control.

a) Switch to the **PC1** VM. Select **Start→Windows Administrative Tools→DNS**. In the dialog box, select **The following computer**. Type *DC1* in the box and select **OK**.
b) Expand **DC1→Forward Lookup Zones→corp.515support.com**.
c) Right-click the **corp.515support.com** node and select **New Host (A or AAAA)**.
d) In the **Name** box, type *pfsense* then in the **IP address** box, type *10.1.0.254*
e) Select the **Add Host** button, then confirm by selecting **OK**.
f) In the **New Host** dialog box, select **Done**.

5. Create a certificate signing request.

a) In the **pfSense web app**, select **System→Cert. Manager**. Select the **Certificates** tab.

 Note: If the window is not maximized, you will need to either maximize the window or use the three-line menu.

b) Select the **Add** button. From the **Method** list box, select **Create a Certificate Signing Request**.
c) In the **Descriptive name** box, type *pfSense Network Security Appliance*
d) Enter any appropriate value for country, state/province, and city.
e) Enter the **Organization** as *515support*
f) In the **Email Address** box, type *administrator@515support.com*
g) In the **Common Name** box, type *pfsense.corp.515support.com*

h)   Select **Save**.

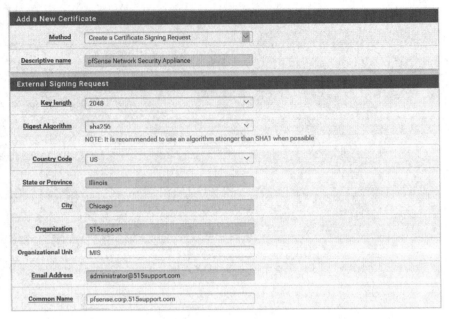

Creating a certificate signing request (CSR). (Screenshot used with permission from pfSense.)

i)   When the request is created, select the **Export Request** button. ⬇ Open the request with **Notepad**, then copy the text of the request. Close Notepad.

j)   Open a new browser tab, then open ***https://DC1.corp.515support.com/certsrv***

k)   Log on with the ***Administrator/Pa$$w0rd*** credentials, then select **Request a certificate**.

l)   Select **Advanced certificate request**.

m)   Paste the certificate request into the **Saved Request** box. From the **Certificate Template** list box, select **Web Server**.

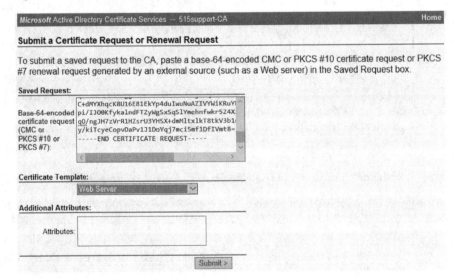

Submitting the CSR to the 515support CA. (Screenshot used with permission from Microsoft.)

n)   Select the **Submit** button.

o)   On the **Certificate Issued** page, select **Base 64 encoded** then select **Download certificate**. Select **Save** to confirm.

p)   Open the **Downloads** folder in **File Explorer** then right-click the **certnew.cer** file and select **Edit with Notepad++**. Copy the text. Close Notepad++.

q) Switch back to the **pfSense web app** and select the **pen** icon 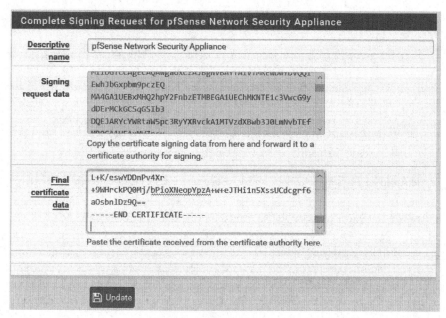 to update the CSR.

Importing the certificate signed by the CA back into pfSense. (Screenshot used with permission from pfSense.)

r) Paste the certificate data into the **Final certificate data** box and select **Update**.

6. Use the certificate you installed to enable HTTPS for the web admin app.

   a) Select **System→Advanced**. From the **Protocol** field, select **HTTPS**.

   b) From the **SSL Certificate** list box, select **pfSense Network Security Appliance**.

   c) Scroll down and select the **Save** button.

   d) When the app restarts, examine the certificate error message. What is the cause of this error?

   Accessing the console by the IP address means that the URL does not match the common name configured in the certificate.

   e) Change the URL to ***https://pfsense.corp.515support.com*** and log back in.

   The login was protected by TLS. Anyone sniffing the network would not be able to view the credentials exchanged.

7. Another significant policy challenge of managing network appliances is the use of shared credentials, such as the **admin** account you have been using to log in. This means that individual administrators are not accountable for their actions and properly auditing changes to the system configuration is impossible. You can solve this problem by authenticating to pfSense by using Active Directory credentials via RADIUS. Active Directory works like LDAP to store information about network users. You can configure accounts to represent different roles/ administration tasks in Active Directory, use RADIUS to authenticate the user credentials when logging on to the pfSense web administration interface, and configure authorizations for the accounts on the pfSense appliance. Install and configure Microsoft's RADIUS implementation Network Policy Server on the **DC1** VM.

   a) Open a connection window for the **DC1** VM, and log on with the credentials ***Administrator*** and ***Pa$$w0rd***

   b) From **Server Manager**, select the **Add roles and features** link. On the **Before you begin** page, select **Next**.

   c) On the **Select installation type** page, ensure **Role-based or feature-based installation** is selected, then select **Next**.

d) On the **Select destination server** page, ensure **Select a server from the server pool** is selected, and **DC1.corp.515support.com** is selected in the **Server Pool** list, then select **Next**.

e) On the **Select server roles** page, check the **Network Policy and Access Services** check box.

f) In the **Add Roles and Features Wizard** dialog box, ensure the **Include management tools (if applicable)** check box is checked, then select the **Add Features** button.

g) On the **Select server roles** page, select **Next** then on the **Select features** page, select **Next**.

h) On the **Network Policy and Access Services** page, select **Next**.

i) On the **Confirm installation options** page, select **Install**.

j) When the installation has completed, select **Close**.

8. Use Network Policy Server to configure the **PFSENSE** VM as an authorized RADIUS client.

a) In **Server Manager**, select **Tools→Network Policy Server**.

b) Expand **RADIUS Clients and Servers** to select **RADIUS Clients**. Right-click **RADIUS Clients** and select **New**.

The RADIUS client is the network appliance accepting the user's credentials (in this case, the **PFSENSE** VM).

c) In the **New RADIUS Client** dialog box, in the **Friendly name** box, enter *pfsense.corp. 515support.com*.

d) In the **Address** box, type *10.1.0.254*

e) Under **Shared Secret**, select the **Generate** radio button, and select **Generate**.

This means that a RADIUS server can trust a RADIUS client and vice versa. This prevents a rogue RADIUS client from requesting authentication information from a legitimate server, provided the shared secret has not been compromised.

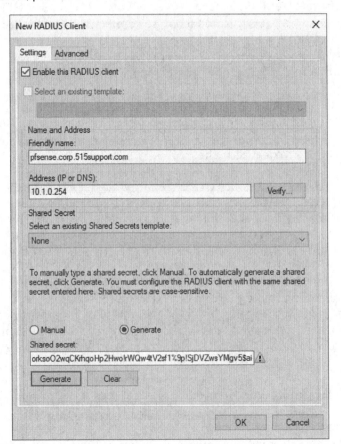

Configuring a RADIUS Client connection on the RADIUS Server. (Screenshot used with permission from Microsoft.)

f)   Copy the shared secret string. Select **OK**.

> **Note:** *You need to keep this value on the Clipboard for a while—alternatively, you can paste it into a Notepad file.*

9.   Configure a policy that allows users in the **LocalAdmin** security group to authenticate with **PFSENSE** by using unencrypted authentication. Use the **Class** attribute to transmit the **LocalGroup** property from the RADIUS server to the RADIUS client when a user authenticates.

a)   Expand **Policies** to select **Network Policies**. Right-click **Network Policies** and select **New**.

b)   In **Policy name**, type *pfSense Network Security Appliance Administration*

c)   Select **Next**. On the **Specify conditions** page, select the **Add** button.

d)   Select **Windows Groups** and select **Add**.

e)   Select the **Add Groups** button then type *localadmin* and select **Check Names**.

f)   Select **OK** then select **OK** again to confirm the **Windows Groups** dialog box.

g)   Select **Next**.

h)   On the **Specify Access Permission** page, leave **Access granted** selected and select **Next**.

i)   Check only the **Unencrypted authentication** check box, as shown in this screenshot.

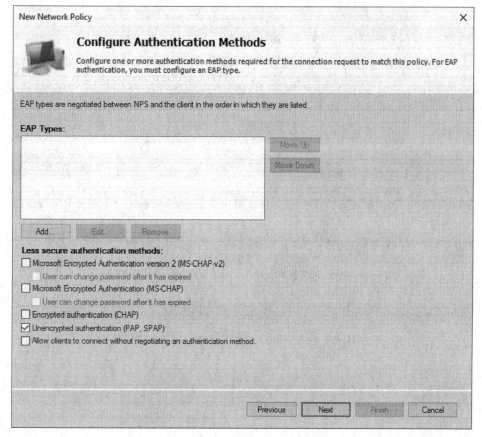

New Network Policy wizard—Configure Authentication Methods. (Screenshot used with permission from Microsoft.)

j)   Select **Next**. Select **No** to confirm without viewing the help topics.

Remember that you are protecting the credentials using HTTPS.

k)   On the **Configure Constraints** page, select **Next**.

l)   On the **Configure Settings** page, with **Standard** selected, select the **Add** button.

m) In the **Add Standard RADIUS Attribute** dialog box, from the **Attributes** box, select **Class**. Select the **Add** button.

n) Type *LocalAdmin* in the box and select **OK**.

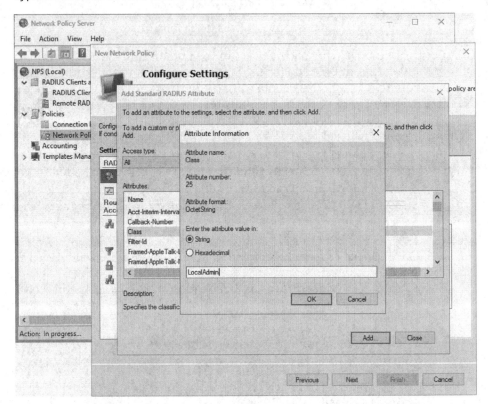

Setting a custom RADIUS attribute. (Screenshot used with permission from Microsoft.)

pfSense uses the **Class** attribute to communicate group membership.

o) Select **Close**.

p) Select **Next** then **Finish**.

10. Configure the **PFSENSE** VM as a RADIUS client by inputting the RADIUS server details.

a) Still on the **DC1** VM, open *https://pfsense.corp.515support.com* in the browser.

b) Log on with the credentials *admin* and *Pa$$w0rd*

c) Select **System→User Manager**. Select the **Authentication Servers** tab, then select the **Add** button.

d) In the **Descriptive name** box, type *515support AD*

e) From the **Type** list, select **RADIUS**.

f) In the **Hostname or IP address** box, enter *10.1.0.1*

g)   In the **Shared Secret** box, paste the Clipboard contents and select **Save**.

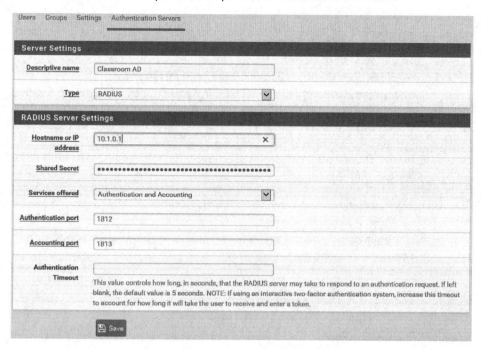

Configuring a RADIUS Server connection on the RADIUS Client. (Screenshot used with permission from pfSense.)

11. Configure a basic least permissions role for the **LocalGroup** security group account so users don't have access to advanced system configuration pages.

a)   Select the **Groups** tab, then select the **Add** button.

b)   In the **Group name** box, type *LocalAdmin*

c)   Select the **Save** button.

d)   Select the pen icon to edit the **LocalAdmin** group.

e)   Under **Assigned Privileges**, select the **Add** button.

f)   Select from **WebCfg—Dashboard (all)** down to **WebCfg—Status: UPnP Status**.

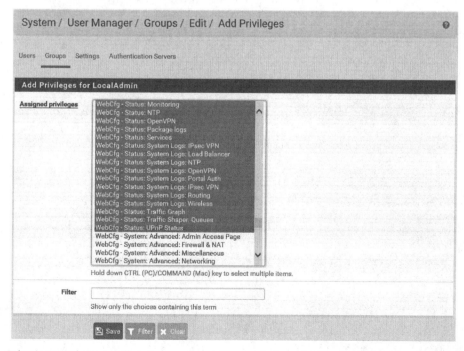

Selecting privileges to allocate to a group. (Screenshot used with permission from pfSense.)

g) Locate the item **WebCfg—pfSense wizard subsystem** and **Ctrl+click** to de-select it.

h) Select the **Save** button.

i) Select the **Settings** tab then from the **Authentication Server** box, select **515support AD**. Select the **Save** button.

j) Select the **Logout** button.

k) Log back on with the credentials *bobby* and *Pa$$w0rd*

Now when you log on, the **PFSENSE** VM passes the credentials you have submitted to the RADIUS server for validation.

l) Observe that you can configure most things but cannot adjust system settings to change the user accounts or **root** admin password.

Ideally, you would create role-based groups with more fine-grained privileges for different tasks.

12. Discard changes made to the VMs in this activity.

a) Switch to Hyper-V Manager.

b) Use the **Action** menu or the right-click menu in the **Hyper-V Manager** console to revert the VMs to their saved checkpoints.

Topic C

Explain the Uses of Port Security and NAC

EXAM OBJECTIVES COVERED
4.2 Explain authentication and access controls.
4.6 Explain common mitigation techniques and their purposes.

So far in this lesson, you have discussed user authentication and access control and their roles in a comprehensive network security implementation. Endpoint and switch port security is another important network security control, providing defense in depth and preventing the attachment of unauthorized devices.

ENDPOINT AND PORT SECURITY

Endpoint security is a set of security procedures and technologies designed to restrict network access at a device level. Endpoint security contrasts with the focus on perimeter security established by topologies such as DMZ and technologies such as firewalls. Endpoint security does not replace these but adds **defense in depth**. The portability of devices, such as removable storage, wireless access points, VoIP phones, cell phones, smartphones, and laptop computers, makes penetrating network perimeter security more straightforward. The security of these devices is often heavily dependent on good user behavior. There is also the circumstance of providing guests with network facilities, such as web access and email. While training and education can mitigate the risks somewhat, new technologies are emerging to control these threats.

Access to the physical switch ports and switch hardware should be restricted to authorized staff, using a secure server room and/or lockable hardware cabinets. To prevent the attachment of unauthorized client devices, a switch port can be disabled using the management software, isolated to a black hole VLAN, or the patch cable can be physically removed from the port. Completely disabling ports in this way can introduce a lot of administrative overhead and scope for error. Also, it doesn't provide complete protection, as an attacker could unplug a device from an enabled port and connect their own laptop. Consequently, more sophisticated methods of ensuring **port security** have been developed.

MAC FILTERING AND SWITCH PORT PROTECTION

Configuring **MAC filtering** on a switch means defining which MAC addresses are permitted to connect to a particular port. This can be done by creating a list of valid MAC addresses or by specifying a **limit** to the number of permitted addresses. For example, if port security is enabled with a maximum of two MAC addresses, the switch will record the first two MACs to connect to that port but then drop any traffic from machines with different network adapter IDs that try to connect. This type of switch port protection feature acts as a **flood guard** against MAC flooding attacks. One use of a MAC flooding attack is to facilitate eavesdropping. The attacker floods MAC addresses to try to overload the switch's MAC port mapping table or **Content Addressable Memory (CAM)**. This causes the switch to start working like a hub and flooding all traffic out of all ports. This allows the attacker to sniff all unicast traffic processed by the switch.

A malicious host may use a spoofed MAC address to try to perform ARP cache poisoning against other hosts on the network and perpetrate a MitM attack. A switch port security feature such as **ARP inspection** prevents a host attached to an untrusted port from flooding the segment with gratuitous ARP replies. ARP inspection maintains a trusted database of IP:ARP mappings. It also ensures that ARP packets are validly constructed and use valid IP addresses.

```
NYCORE1>
NYCORE1#
*Mar  1 00:02:27.991: %SYS-5-CONFIG_I: Configured from console by console
*Mar  1 00:02:46.287: %LINEPROTO-5-UPDOWN: Line protocol on Interface Vlan1, changed state to up
NYCORE1#configure terminal
Enter configuration commands, one per line.  End with CNTL/Z.
NYCORE1(config)#ip arp inspection vlan 1,999
NYCORE1(config)#
*Mar  1 00:07:20.561: %SW_DAI-4-DHCP_SNOOPING_DENY: 1 Invalid ARPs (Req) on Fa1/0/23, vlan 1.([0023.049
0.0000/192.168.16.21/00:07:20 UTC Mon Mar 1 1993])
```

Configuring ARP inspection on a Cisco switch. (Image © and Courtesy of Cisco Systems, Inc. Unauthorized use not permitted.)

Another switch port protection setting is to configure **DHCP snooping**. This inspects DHCP traffic arriving on access ports to ensure that a host is not trying to spoof its MAC address. It can also be used to prevent rogue (or **spurious**) DHCP servers from operating on the network. With DHCP snooping, only DHCP offers from ports configured as trusted are allowed.

IEEE 802.1X PORT-BASED NETWORK ACCESS CONTROL (PNAC)

MAC limiting and filtering and ARP inspection provide some protection against attacks, but they are not a means of ensuring only valid hosts are connecting to the network. The **IEEE 802.1X** standard defines a **Port-Based Network Access Control (PNAC)** mechanism. PNAC means that the switch (or router) performs some sort of authentication of the attached device before activating the port. Under 802.1X, the device requesting access is the **supplicant**. The switch, referred to as the **authenticator**, enables the **Extensible Authentication Protocol over LAN (EAPoL)** protocol only and waits for the device to supply authentication data. Using EAP, this data could be a simple username/password (EAP-MD5) or could involve using a digital certificate or token. The authenticator passes this data to an **authenticating server**, typically a RADIUS server, which checks the credentials and grants or denies access. If access is granted, the switch will configure the port to use the appropriate VLAN and enable it for ordinary network traffic. Unauthenticated hosts may be denied any type of access or be placed in a guest VLAN with only limited access to the rest of the network.

Network Access Control (NAC) also allows administrators to devise policies or profiles describing a minimum-security configuration that devices must meet to be granted network access. This is called a **health policy**. Typical policies check things such as malware infection, firmware and OS patch level, personal firewall status, and presence of up-to-date virus definitions. A solution may also be able to scan the registry or perform file signature verification. The health policy is defined on a NAC management server along with reporting and configuration tools.

ADMISSION CONTROL

Admission control is the point at which client devices are granted or denied access based on their compliance with the health policy. Most NAC solutions work on the basis of **preadmission control** (that is, the device must meet the policy to gain access). **Post-admission** control involves subsequently polling the device to check that it remains compliant. Some solutions only perform post-admission control; some do both.

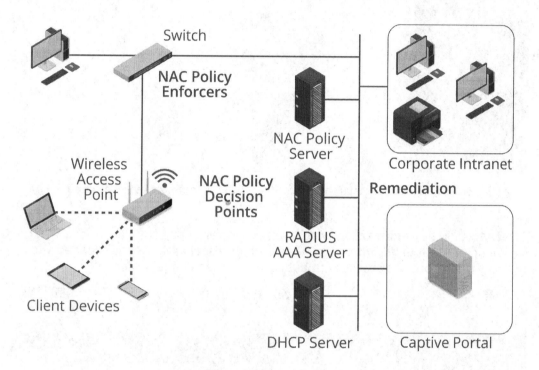

NAC framework (Image © 123RF.com.)

With pre-admission control, supplicant client devices connect to the network via a **NAC Policy Enforcer**, such as a switch, router, or wireless access point. Other options for the location of the policy enforcer include a VPN remote access gateway or a specially configured DHCP server. The policy enforcer checks the client credentials with the **NAC Policy Server** and performs machine and user authentication with a RADIUS AAA Server. The client is allocated a suitable IP address by a DHCP server and assigned to a VLAN by the switch; depending on whether the policy was met, this would allow access to the network or to a quarantine area or captive web portal only.

Post-admission controls would rely on the NAC policy server polling the client device once access has been granted or performing a policy check if the configuration of a client changes or when a client attempts to access a server or service.

HOST HEALTH CHECKS

Posture assessment is the process by which **host health checks** are performed against a client device to verify compliance with the health policy. Most NAC solutions use client software called an **agent** to gather information about the device, such as its anti-virus and patch status, presence of prohibited applications, or anything else defined by the health policy.

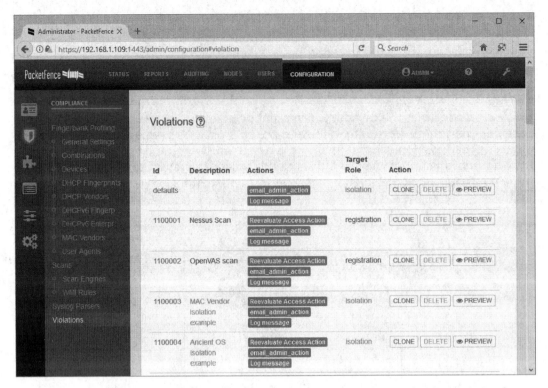

Defining policy violations in PacketFence Open Source NAC. (Screenshot used with permission from PacketFence.)

An agent could be **persistent**, in which case it is installed as a software application on the client, or **non-persistent**. A non-persistent (or **dissolvable**) agent is loaded into memory during posture assessment but is not installed on the device.

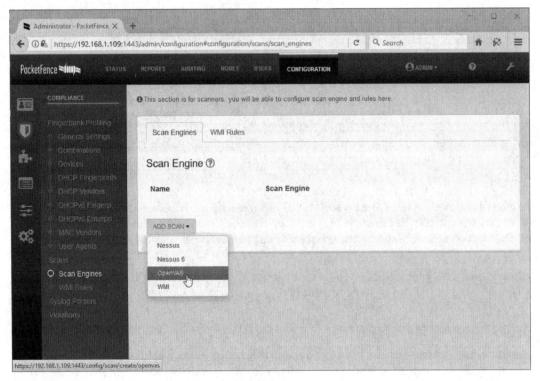

PacketFence supports the use of several scanning techniques, including vulnerability scanners, such as Nessus and OpenVAS, Windows Management Instrumentation (WMI) queries, and log parsers. (Screenshot used with permission from PacketFence.)

Some NAC solutions can perform **agentless** posture assessment. This is useful when the NAC solution must support a wide range of devices, such as smartphones and tablets, but less detailed information about the client is available with an agentless solution.

If it is implemented as a primarily software-based solution, NAC can suffer from the same sort of exploits as any other software. There have been instances of exploits to evade the NAC admission process or submit false scan results. One fruitful line of attack is to use VMs to evade the initial admission policy; one VM is created that complies with the policy and when access is granted, the user switches to a second non-compliant VM. Therefore, post-admission control is an increasingly important requirement for NAC solutions.

Note: *To learn more, watch the related **Video** on the course website.*

REMEDIATION

Remediation refers to what happens if the device does not meet the security profile. A non-compliant device may be refused connection completely or put in a quarantined guest network or captive portal.

- **Guest network**—This would be a VLAN or firewalled subnet (DMZ) granting limited access to network resources. For example, you might allow visitors with non-compliant devices to use your Internet routers to browse the web and view email, but not grant them any access to your corporate network.
- **Quarantine network**—This is another type of restricted network, usually based on a **captive portal**. A captive portal allows only HTTP traffic and redirects the HTTP traffic to a remediation server. The remediation server would allow clients to install OS and anti-virus updates in order to achieve or return to compliance.

Activity 11-4

Discussing the Uses of Port Security and NAC

SCENARIO

Answer the following questions to test your understanding of the content covered in this topic.

---

1. **What type of attack does a switch port flood guard prevent?**

2. **What is the role of EAPoL in implementing port-based network access control?**

3. **What is a dissolvable agent?**

4. **What is meant by remediation in the context of NAC?**

Topic D

Implement Network Device Hardening

EXAM OBJECTIVES COVERED
4.5 Given a scenario, implement network device hardening.
4.6 Explain common mitigation techniques and their purposes.

If you are configuring policies to ensure only authorized devices connect to the network, you also need policies for ensuring that those devices are in a secure configuration. As a network technician, one of your roles will be ensuring that network hosts are put in a secure configuration before being granted access.

DEVICE AND SERVICE HARDENING

As part of a **defense in depth** strategy, you need to think about making each host and network infrastructure device secure against tampering or abuse. Deploying systems in a secure configuration is known as **device hardening**. It can be tempting to think of network devices such as switches and routers as self-contained. In fact, these devices often run quite complex firmware and host numerous services to enable remote management and configuration. Some of the policies that will make up a secure configuration involve the following:

- **Changing default credentials**—Devices such as wireless access points, switches, and routers sometimes ship with a default management password such as **password**, **admin**, or the device vendor's name. These should be changed on installation. Also, the password used should be a strong one—Most devices do not enforce complexity rules, so the onus is on the user to choose something secure.

  Note: It is now standard practice for devices to be shipped with individually configured default credentials, usually placed on a label on the device or in the instruction manual, or for devices to require a change of password as part of their initial setup.

- **Avoiding common passwords**—The number of successful attacks against web servers and company networks has led to huge databases of credentials being posted online. Analysis of these databases shows how many users—even administrative users—rely on trivially simple passwords, such as **123456** or **password**. These password database dumps give attackers a useful dictionary to work with when trying to crack credentials. Any password that could be matched to a dictionary term is completely unsecure and must not be used.

- **Backdoor/default account**—Vendors sometimes deliberately install **backdoors** on devices such as routers and switches (often as a password reset mechanism). Another possibility is for someone with physical access to the device to reset it to the factory configuration. Devices such as access points attached to the network without authorization are called **rogues**. These could create a backdoor through which to attack the network. A rogue device could also be used to capture user logon attempts. Make sure physical access to network appliances is restricted by locked gateways or cabinets. Disable any **default accounts**.

- **Disabling unnecessary services**—Any services or protocols that are not used should be disabled. This reduces the attack surface of a network appliance or OS. **Attack surface** means the range of things that an attacker could possibly exploit in order to compromise the device. It is particularly important to disable unused administration interfaces (and to secure those that are used).

- **Disabling unused IP ports**—Another part of reducing the system attack surface is to limit the ways an attacker could connect to it. Closing services will normally also block TCP and UDP ports on an IP network; alternatively, access to such ports can be controlled by a firewall.

- **Closing unused device ports**—Physical access may allow an attacker to use hardware ports such as USB or a router's console port to gain access. Some network appliance management ports may also be virtualized and made available on the network. Again, these device ports should be disabled or subject to ACLs and secure authentication.

SECURE PROTOCOLS

Eavesdropping attacks can be mitigated by **encrypting** the channel over which communications takes place. This means that even if the eavesdropper can listen to the message, he or she cannot understand it without obtaining the encryption key. It is important to understand which protocols are **unsecure** in terms of using **unencrypted channels**. This is particularly important when using a channel to authenticate. The use of **cleartext credentials** (username and password) sent over the channel will be easy for an eavesdropper to obtain. Consequently, as part of a process of network hardening, unsecure protocols should be deprecated, and secure protocols used instead.

Some examples of unsecure protocols and their secure alternatives are as follows:

- **Telnet**—All communications are in the clear. Telnet is often replaced by Secure Shell (SSH), but this may not be supported by legacy appliances. Another option for establishing a secure tunnel might be available; using IPSec, for instance.

- **HTTP**—This can be made secure by using SSL/TLS (HTTPS), if the appliance supports it.

- **SLIP (Serial Line Internet Protocol)/Point-to-Point Protocol (PPP)**—These encapsulation protocols transmit IP over a serial link. On data networks, PPP is more prevalent (and just as unsecure), but SLIP may still be in use on **embedded systems** networks. More secure VPNs can be established by using TSL or IPSec.

- **FTP/T(rivial)FTP**—FTP can be secured by using SSL (FTPS) or SSH (SFTP), but only if both client and server support it. When FTP or TFTP is used for uploading configuration files to legacy devices, there may be few effective security precautions that can be taken.

- **SNMPv1 and v2**—The original versions of SNMP are unencrypted. SNMPv3 supports encryption. Otherwise, a protocol such as IPSec could be used to encrypt SNMP traffic.

 Note: It is important to encrypt and secure networks as soon as possible. Using secure protocols for remote access over a VPN, such as an SSL VPN, IPSec, or MPLS VPN, allows users to securely tunnel into the network and prevents unauthorized parties from eavesdropping on packets during transmission.

GENERATING NEW KEYS

When you use a secure channel, such as Secure Shell (SSH) or HTTP over SSL/TLS, the communications are protected by the host's private key. This **host key** must be changed if any compromise of the host is suspected. If an attacker has obtained the private key of a server or appliance, they can masquerade as that server or appliance and perform a MitM attack, usually with a view to obtaining other network credentials. You might also change the key to use a longer bit strength.

The method of generating a key is different for SSH and HTTPS:

- SSH—This would typically use a utility such as **ssh-keygen**.
- HTTPS—You would make a certificate signing request (CSR) with new key material and submit it to the CA that issues digital certificates.

In the case of SSH, you might also need to change **user keys**. A user key can be used instead of a password to authenticate with the appliance. In this scenario, the appliance is configured with a list of authorized users' public keys. This means that if the computer storing a user's matching private key is compromised, the attacker could gain access to the appliance too. Recent attacks against web servers have shown that management of keys is very poor, with many keys being left active even when administrators have left the company.

If a user's private key is compromised, delete the public key from the appliance, and then regenerate the key pair on the user's (remediated) client device and copy the public key to the SSH server. Always delete public keys if the user's access permissions have been revoked.

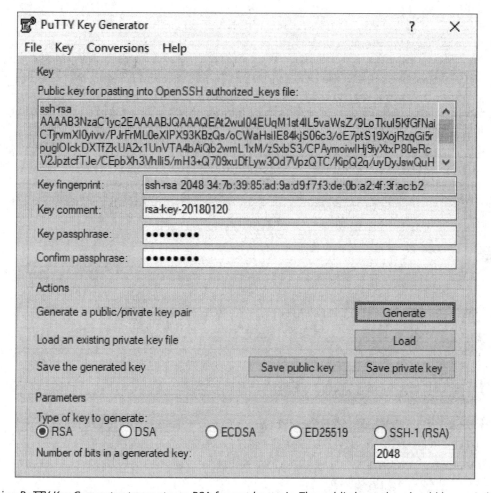

Using PuTTY Key Generator to create an RSA-format key pair. The public key value should be copied to the SSH server in the appliance you are going to access; the linked private key value must be kept secure and secret. (Screenshot used with permission from PuTTY.)

FILE HASHING

A secure hash algorithm, such as the Secure Hash Algorithm (SHA) or Message Digest (MD5), is a means of fingerprinting a file. The algorithm creates a fixed-sized output based on the file contents. The algorithm is designed so that no other input can produce the same hash output. This means that if you want to prove the integrity of a file downloaded from the Internet, you can calculate its hash value and compare it to the hash value published for the file. If they do not match, you should not trust the file. Of course, you must be confident that the published value comes from a respectable source in the first place!

 Note: *It is important to understand that file hashing secures a file so that it is not processed in cleartext. If even one character is changed in a file, the entire hash string for that file will be 100% different from the original one that was generated upon original transmission.*

When software is installed from a legitimate source (using signed code in the case of Windows or a secure repository in the case of Linux), the OS package manager checks the signature or fingerprint of each executable file and notifies the user if there is a problem. A file integrity check can be performed manually using tools such as the following:

- `certutil -hashfile` *`File Algorithm`*—This is a built-in Windows command, where *`File`* is the input and *`Algorithm`* is `MD5`, `SHA1`, `SHA256`, or `SHA512`. You have to compare the value obtained to the published fingerprint manually (or by using a shell script).
- **File Checksum Integrity Verifier** (`fciv`)—This is a downloadable Windows utility that can be used as an alternative to `certutil`. You can use the `-v` switch to compare the target with the value stored in a file or add fingerprints to an **XML** database and check to see if the hash of a target file matches one stored in the database.
- `md5sum` | `sha1sum` | `sha256sum` | `sha512sum`—Linux tools to calculate the fingerprint of a file supplied as the argument. You can also use the `-c` switch to compare the input file with a source file containing the pre-computed hash.
- `gpg`—If a Linux source file has been signed, you need to use the publisher's public key and the `gpg` utility to verify the signature.

 Note: *Security scanners, such as anti-virus software, also use fingerprints to identify malware code signatures.*

 Note: *To learn more, watch the related **Video** on the course website.*

GUIDELINES FOR DEVICE HARDENING

IMPLEMENT DEVICE HARDENING

Follow these guidelines for device hardening:

- Change default device credentials on installation, and ensure that accounts are secured with strong passwords.
- Use only secure channels for administration traffic or any other protocol where credentials need to be submitted.
- Configure services according to the device's baseline and disable any services which are not required. Consider setting up alerting mechanisms to detect service configuration changes.

- Ensure that only the necessary IP ports (TCP and UDP ports) to run permitted services are open and that access to a port is controlled by a firewall ACL if appropriate.
- Ensure any physical ports on a device that could be used to attach unauthorized USB or network devices are protected by secure access (in a locked room or cabinet).
- If a device is decommissioned, ensure that encryption keys stored on that device are archived (if appropriate) and then securely deleted from the device storage.
- Change encryption keys used to access servers and appliances when employees with credentials to access these devices leave the company or change job roles.

Activity 11-5
Discussing Network Device Hardening

SCENARIO

Answer the following questions to test your understanding of the content covered in this topic.

1. **What is a common password?**

2. **Other than completely disabling the protocol, how could you mitigate the risk posed by an open port?**

3. **True or False? Telnet is a secure channel for host administration.**

4. **What type of key allows a user to access an SSH server without a password, and where is it stored?**

Topic E

Explain Patch Management and Vulnerability Scanning Processes

EXAM OBJECTIVES COVERED
3.3 Explain common scanning, monitoring and patching processes and summarize their expected outputs.
4.5 Given a scenario, implement network device hardening.
4.6 Explain common mitigation techniques and their purposes.

In this topic, you will examine how monitoring for vulnerabilities and installing patches and updates can also help ensure network security. Managing patches and updates is another important part of device hardening techniques. The firmware in network devices also needs to be kept current as well.

PATCH MANAGEMENT

Each type of OS and application software has vulnerabilities that present opportunities for would-be attackers. As soon as a vulnerability is identified, vendors will try to correct it. At the same time, attackers will try to exploit it. There can never be a single comprehensive list of vulnerabilities for each OS, so you must stay up to date with the system security information posted on vendor websites and in other security references. **Patch management** refers to the procedures put in place to manage the installation of updates for hardware (firmware) and software. There are two approaches to applying updates:

- Apply all the latest patches to ensure the system is as secure as possible against attacks against flaws in the software.
- Only apply a patch if it solves a particular problem being experienced.

The second approach (completing update tasks manually) obviously requires more work, as the administrator needs to keep up to date with security bulletins, version changes, and updates released by the developer or manufacturer. However, it is well recognized that updates (particularly service releases) can cause problems, especially with software application compatibility, and so the second approach is wisest.

It makes sense to trial an update, especially a service release, on a test system to try to discover whether it will cause any problems. Approach the update like a software installation or upgrade (make a backup and a **rollback** plan). Read the documentation accompanying the update carefully. Updates may need to be applied in order and there may be known compatibility issues or problems listed in the ReadMe file.

Note: Patches are often released in batches, but remember that when testing or troubleshooting a system, it is best to change one thing at a time. If you install several patches at the same time without testing and a problem subsequently occurs, it will be difficult to identify which, if any, of the updates might be linked to the problem.

Caution: It is essential that you verify the author of all patches for authenticity and scan for viruses. Only install patches from trusted sources. Updates published to authorized repositories are usually digitally signed by the vendor to prove their authenticity.

HOST AND NETWORK APPLIANCE UPDATES

Software updates resolve issues that a vendor has identified in the initial release of its product, based on additional testing or customer feedback. The updates are usually provided free of charge. Many updates address security vulnerabilities (problems in the software that could allow an attacker to crash the program or OS, run malware, or steal information).

Updates are also referred to as **patches**, though not by Microsoft. Microsoft categorizes updates as **security updates**, **critical updates**, or just **updates**. A **hotfix** is an update designed for and released to certain customers only, though they may be included in later **service packs**. Service packs may also contain product **improvements**, differentiating them from update rollups, which are simply collections of updates released since the last service pack.

Once you have evaluated a patch and determined the need for it to be applied, you then need to download it and apply it to the device. If you are applying this patch to an enterprise network, you can add the file to a repository to have it automatically run outside of normal business hours, or prompt users to run the program at their convenience if a restart is required during the update.

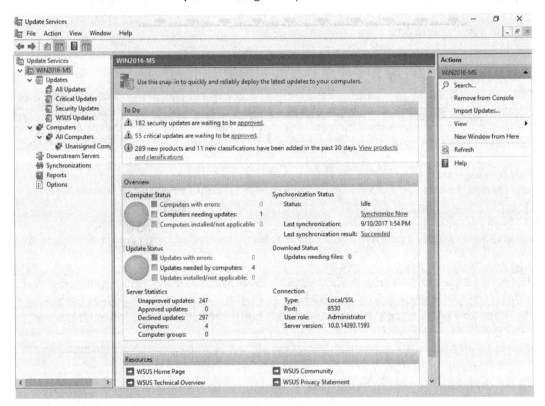

Windows Server Update Services (WSUS) allows administrative control over local deployment of patches. (Screenshot used with permission from Microsoft.)

 Note: *To learn more, watch the related* **Video** *on the course website.*

FIRMWARE AND DRIVER UPDATES

As well as software updates, it is important to keep hardware up to date with the latest patches. There are two main types of updates for hardware devices:

- Driver—This is software that provides an interface between the operating system and the device.
- Firmware—This is software instructions stored in flash memory. This type of chip does not require a power supply, so the data does not have to be moved in and out of disk storage.

The firmware on a device such as a router/firewall may be a very sophisticated piece of software. It is quite common for such software to have known vulnerabilities, so it is vital to use a secure version. Updating firmware is known as **flashing the chip**. This is generally done via a vendor-supplied setup program. It is important to make a backup of the system configuration (especially for a firewall) before performing a firmware update or upgrade.

A host OS, such as Windows, can apply patches individually. An appliance OS, such as Cisco IOS, must be patched to a particular version number by applying a new software image. To address a particular vulnerability, you could use a tool such as the IOS Software Checker (*tools.cisco.com/security/center/softwarechecker.x*) to identify the "first fix" version of IOS for that security advisory. This does mean that other changes could be introduced, so careful testing and impact assessment is required.

Once you have completed environment and compatibility checks and backed up the existing configuration, the basic upgrade process is to copy the new system image to the appliance's flash memory. This can be done over a network (using TFTP or remote file copy) or by using a removable flash memory card. Once the image update is in place, you run a command sequence to replace the old image and load the new one at startup.

DOWNGRADING/ROLLBACK

Most software and firmware version changes and updates are upward, toward newer versions. **Downgrading** (or **rollback**) refers to reverting to a previous version of the software or firmware. This might be necessary to fix a problem caused by a recently upgraded or updated device or software. In some circumstances downgrading might not be possible. A network appliance might not support downgrading to an earlier firmware version, for instance, or an OS might have to be reinstalled completely. When applying a patch or upgrade, it is common practice to make a **configuration backup**, in case settings must be reapplied after the update. When downgrading, a configuration backup might not work because it may involve settings not included in the earlier version.

VULNERABILITY SCANNING

Vulnerability scanning is the process of auditing a network (or application) for known vulnerabilities. Remember that a vulnerability is a weakness that could be triggered accidentally or exploited maliciously by a threat actor to cause a security breach. An unpatched software application, a host with no anti-virus software, and an administrator account with a **weak password** are examples of vulnerabilities. **Vulnerability assessments** might involve manual inspection of security controls, but are more often accomplished through automated **vulnerability scanners**. A vulnerability scanner examines an organization's systems, applications, and devices and compares the scan results to configuration templates plus lists of known vulnerabilities. The result is a report showing the current state of operation and the effectiveness of any security controls. Typical results from a vulnerability scan will identify common misconfigurations, the lack of necessary security controls, and missing patches.

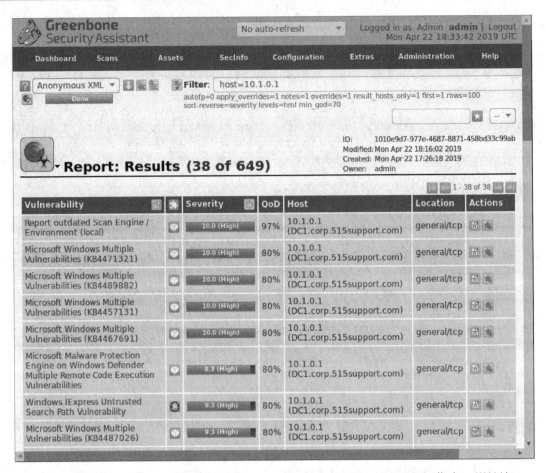

Issues reported by a vulnerability scan performed by Greenbone OpenVAS as installed on KALI Linux.
(Screenshot used with permission from Greenbone Networks.)

The first phase of scanning might be to run a detection scan to discover hosts on an IP subnet. Each scanner is configured with a database of known vulnerabilities. In the next phase of scanning, a target range of hosts is probed to detect running services, patch level, security configuration and policies, network shares, unused accounts, weak passwords, rogue access points and servers, anti-virus configuration, and so on. The tool then compiles a report about each vulnerability in its database that was found to be present on each host. Each identified vulnerability is categorized and assigned an impact warning. Most tools also suggest current and ongoing remediation techniques. This information is highly sensitive, so use of these tools and the distribution of the reports produced should be restricted to authorized hosts and user accounts.

A vulnerability scanner can be implemented purely as software or as a security appliance, connected to the network. One of the best known software scanners is **Tenable Nessus** (*tenable.com/products/nessus/nessus-professional*). As a previously open source program, Nessus also provides the source code for many other scanners. **Greenbone OpenVAS** (*openvas.org*) is open source software, originally developed from the Nessus codebase at the point where Nessus became commercial software. It is available in a Community Edition VM, as an enterprise product called Greenbone Security Manager (*greenbone.net*), and as source code or pre-compiled packages for installation under Linux. Some other vulnerability scanners include SAINT (*saintcorporation.com/security-suite*), BeyondTrust Retina (*beyondtrust.com/resources/datasheets/retina-network-security-scanner*), and Rapid7 NeXpose (*rapid7.com/products/nexpose*).

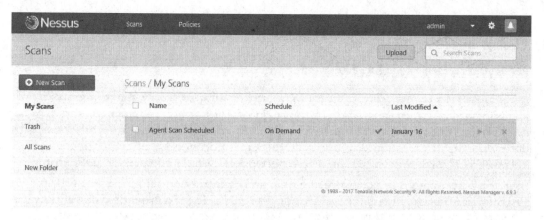

Nessus Manager web management interface. (Screenshot used with permission from Tenable.)

As with anti-malware software, a vulnerability scanner needs to be kept up to date with information about known vulnerabilities, derived from security advisories issued by software vendors, plus the scripts to scan for vulnerabilities on different hosts. This database is supplied by the scanner vendor as a feed or plug-in.

PENETRATION TESTING

A **penetration test** is a more comprehensive assessment of a network's security systems than a basic vulnerability scan. A penetration test (pen test), also referred to as **ethical hacking**, essentially involves thinking like an attacker and trying to demonstrate that the security systems can be compromised. A pen test might involve the following steps:

- Verify that a threat exists—Use surveillance, social engineering, network scanners, and vulnerability scanning tools to identify vulnerabilities that could be exploited.
- Bypass security controls—Look for easy ways to attack the system. For example, if the network is strongly protected by a firewall, is it possible to gain physical access to a computer in the building and run malware from a USB stick?
- Actively test security controls—Probe controls for configuration weaknesses and errors, such as weak passwords or software vulnerabilities.
- Exploit vulnerabilities—Prove that a vulnerability is high risk by exploiting it to gain access to data or install malware.

The key difference to passive vulnerability scanning is that an attempt is made to actively test security controls and exploit any vulnerabilities discovered. Pen testing is an active reconnaissance technique. For example, a vulnerability scan may reveal that an SQL Server has not been patched to safeguard against a known exploit. A penetration test would attempt to use the exploit to perform code injection and compromise and "own" (or "pwn," in hacker idiom) the server. This provides active testing of security controls. For example, even though the potential for the exploit exists, in practice, the permissions on the server might prevent an attacker from using it. This fact would not be identified by a vulnerability scan, but should be proven or not proven to be the case by penetration testing.

 Note: *sectools.org is a useful resource for researching the different types and uses of security assessment tools.*

Penetration tests are often contracted to third parties, following the assumption that it is better to have an independent test of the system security design than to rely on the designer. Alternatively, a large organization may split its security personnel between two teams; a "blue" defense team and a "red" attack team. If you are using third-party penetration testers, it is imperative to specify and scope the project carefully and to use consultants whose trustworthiness is unquestionable.

HONEYPOTS AND HONEYNETS

A **honeypot** is a computer system set up to attract attackers, with the intention of analyzing attack strategies and tools, to provide early warning of attack attempts, or possibly as a decoy to divert attention from actual computer systems. Another use is to detect internal fraud, snooping, and malpractice. A **honeynet** is an entire decoy network. This may be set up as an actual network or simulated using an emulator.

Deploying a honeypot or honeynet can help an organization to improve its security systems, but there is the risk that the attacker can still learn a great deal about how the network is configured and protected from analyzing the honeypot system. Many honeypots are set up by security researchers investigating malware threats, software exploits, and spammers' abuse of **open relay** mail systems. These systems are generally fully exposed to the Internet.

On a production network, a honeypot is more likely to be located in a protected but untrusted area between the Internet and the private network (a DMZ) or on the private network itself (though fully isolated from it). This provides early warning and evidence of whether an attacker has been able to penetrate to a given security zone.

Activity 11-6

Discussing Patch Management and Vulnerability Scanning Processes

SCENARIO

Answer the following questions to test your understanding of the content covered in this topic.

1. **How would a router appliance be patched to protect against a specific vulnerability described in a security advisory?**

2. **How does a configuration backup assist rollback?**

3. **What type of information is updated when a scanner receives a new set of feeds or plug-ins?**

4. **What type of security audit performs active testing of security controls?**

Summary

In this lesson, you learned about security technologies designed to authenticate and authorize network users and devices and provide defense in depth by hardening systems against attack.

- Make sure you understand the basic AAA principles of an access control system and the importance of role design and privilege management.
- Social engineering refers to using human or social weaknesses to circumvent access controls.
- Authentication credentials can use different factors (password, token, biometric) together for better security.
- NTLM and Kerberos are used for authentication on Windows networks.
- RADIUS and TACACS+ provide enterprises with user credential management, allowing authentication decisions to be centralized, rather than completed by access devices.
- Port authentication and NAC can be used to control the attachment of devices to a network.
- Devices and services should be hardened to reduce the network attack surface.
- Understand the use of vulnerability scanners and the importance of patch management procedures, covering network infrastructure devices as well as host servers and clients.

How does your organization manage patches and updates? Have you ever found the need to rollback updates? Why and how?

A: Answers will vary. Ideally, students will describe a situation in which their organization likely has policies in place to evaluate and test updates before they are rolled out to production systems. Students should note that if backups then even if you make an update that affects the system, you can restore from backups.

Do you believe there's value in conducting a penetration test in your organization? Why or why not?

A: Answers will vary. Penetration tests are often used to demonstrate vulnerabilities with the support of management. A penetration test can help personnel understand how attacks occur and how they can help to secure systems and data. A penetration test can help an organization understand weaknesses in its security posture.

 Practice Questions: *Additional practice questions are available on the course website.*

Lesson 12

Deploying and Troubleshooting Cabling Solutions

LESSON INTRODUCTION

Bounded network media comes in different types that you can select to best suit the needs of your network. You are likely to work with bounded media daily as part of your duties as a network professional. Understanding the characteristics of bounded media will enable you to properly install and service your networks.

LESSON OBJECTIVES

In this lesson, you will:

- Deploy structured cabling systems.
- Deploy twisted-pair cabling solutions.
- Test and troubleshoot twisted-pair cabling solutions.
- Deploy fiber optic cabling solutions.

Topic A
Deploy Structured Cabling Systems

EXAM OBJECTIVES COVERED
2.1 Given a scenario, deploy the appropriate cabling solution.

The networking industry has developed a standard model for deploying a structured cabling system. The model is adaptable to both small and large networks. In this topic, you will learn about the termination points defined for cabling solutions.

COMMERCIAL BUILDING TELECOMMUNICATIONS WIRING STANDARDS

Cabled networking for client access in an office building will use a structured cabling scheme. In 1991, the Electronic Industries Association introduced the EIA 568 specification. The standard is called the **Commercial Building Telecommunications Wiring Standard** and was the first non-proprietary networking scheme for network designers. The document has been subjected to a variety of revisions and updates, culminating in the latest version ANSI/TIA/EIA 568-D (*tiaonline.org*).

The purpose of wiring standards is to enable businesses to apply best practices and to plan their infrastructure requirements and ensure **return on investment (ROI)**. A standard is generally designed to be valid for about 10 years; that is, a particular category of network installation will support applications using that class for 10 to 15 years following publication of the standard. An **application**, in this sense, is a Data Link protocol, such as Ethernet. Applications tend to develop faster than infrastructure can be replaced. For example, Ethernet has moved from 100 Mbps operation defined in 1995 standards to a 10 Gbps standard, first drafted in 2002. Consequently, it is important that the infrastructure installed now be capable of meeting the requirements of applications 10 years in the future.

Wiring work is also likely to be subject to legal regulations governing safety in commercial and residential property (building codes). The main requirements are **electrical safety** (including proper insulation, grounding, and bonding of electrical wire to reduce the risk of electric shock) and **fire safety**. In the US, these regulations are typically based on the **National Electrical Code (NEC)** but can vary from state to state, county to county, or city to city. The international standard is **IEC 60634**, which also forms the basis of the UK's **BS 7671**.

Note: *Ensure any non-trivial wiring work is supervised by a qualified electrician who knows the local building codes.*

Furthermore, communications cabling and broadcasting equipment may be subject to regulation depending on the frequency in which it operates and power output. In the US, these regulations are formulated by the **Federal Communications Commission (FCC)**.

STRUCTURED CABLING SYSTEM

TIA 568 identifies the following subsystems within a structured cabling system:

- **Horizontal Cabling**—Connects user **work areas** to the nearest horizontal cross-connect. A **cross-connect** can also be referred to as a **distribution frame**. This is wired in a star topology. Horizontal cabling is so-called because it typically consists of the cabling for a single floor and so is made up of cables run horizontally through wall ducts or ceiling spaces.

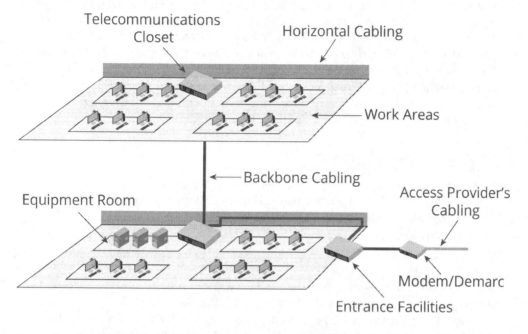

Wiring distribution components. (Image © 123RF.com.)

- **Backbone Cabling**—Connects **horizontal cross-connects (HCCs)** to the main cross-connect (optionally via intermediate cross-connects). These can also be described as vertical cross-connects, because backbone cabling is more likely to run up and down between floors. This is also wired in a star topology.
- **Work Area**—The space where user equipment is located and connected to the network, usually via a wall port.

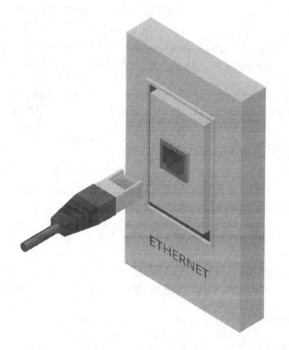

Modular wall plate. (Image by Nikolai Lebedev © 123RF.com.)

- **Telecommunications room**—Houses horizontal cross-connects. Essentially, this is a termination point for the horizontal cabling along with a connection to backbone cabling. An **equipment room** is similar to a telecommunications room but contains the main or intermediate cross-connects. Equipment rooms are also likely to house "complex" equipment, such as switches, routers, and modems.
- **Entrance Facilities/Demarc**—Special types of equipment rooms marking the point at which external cabling (outside plant) is joined to internal (premises) cabling. These are required to join the access provider's network and for inter-building communications. The **demarcation point** is where the access provider's network terminates and the organization's network begins.
- **Administration**—The TIA 606 standard defines a system of identifiers used to describe the elements of the network and manage configuration changes. These are often referred to as MACs (Moves, Adds, Changes).

DISTRIBUTION FRAMES

A **distribution frame** is another way of describing a cross-connect. It is a passive device working at the Physical layer (layer 1), allowing the termination and cross-connection of cabling. These can be installed in a hierarchy:

- **Main Distribution Frame (MDF)**—A signal distribution frame that terminates external cabling and distributes backbone cabling to intermediate or horizontal cross-connects. It is the main point of interconnection for managing telecommunications wiring and distributing signals and supplying services to end users. It is the modern-day version of a telephone switchboard.
- **Intermediate Distribution Frame (IDF)**—An optional level of hierarchy for distributing backbone cabling. Note that the TIA 568 standard allows for only one such intermediate level. IDFs would typically be used in a multi-building (campus) network. An MDF in the main building would connect to IDFs in outer buildings, which would in turn connect to horizontal cross-connects on each floor.

66 BLOCKS AND 110 BLOCKS

Copper wiring is terminated using a **punch-down block**. Several different punch-down block formats have been used for telecommunications and data cabling.

- A **66 block** is an older-style distribution frame used to terminate telephone cabling and legacy data applications (pre-Cat 5). A 66 block comprises 50 rows of 4 insulation-displacement connection (IDC) terminals. The 25-pair cable from the access provider is terminated on one side of the block. On the other side of the block, the terminals terminate the wiring from the PBX. A jumper (bridging clip) is installed over the middle two terminals to complete the connection.

 Note: A private branch exchange (PBX) is a telephone system serving the local extensions of an office.

- The **110 block** is an updated type of IDC supporting 100 MHz operation (Cat 5) and better. "110 block" can describe both a punch-down format and a distribution frame (or wiring block). In the case of distribution frames, these are available in a variety of configurations, supporting between 25 and 300 pairs. A 110 wiring block is arranged horizontally rather than vertically, offering better density than a 66 block. There is also more space for labeling the connectors and each column of connectors is color-coded, making management simpler. The incoming wire pairs are fed into channels on the wiring block, then a connector block is installed to terminate the incoming wiring. Outgoing wire pairs are then punched into the terminals on the connector blocks to complete the circuit.

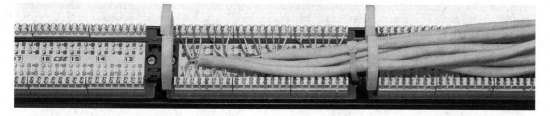

110 block IDCs at the rear of a patch panel. (Image by plus69 © 123RF.com.)

PATCH PANELS AND FIBER DISTRIBUTION PANELS

A **patch panel** is a type of cross-connect that utilizes modular jacks and connectors. A patch panel has 110 block IDCs on one side and pre-wired RJ-45 jacks on the other side. The structured cabling (running from the work area or forming a backbone) is terminated at the back of the patch panel on the IDCs. An RJ-45 patch cord is used to connect the port to another network port, typically a switch port housed in the same rack. This greatly simplifies wiring connections and is the most commonly installed type of wiring distribution where connections need to be changed often.

Patch panel with prewired RJ-45 ports. (Image by Svetlana Kurochkina © 123RF.com.)

A modern build or refurbishment might replace copper wiring with fiber optic cabling. The architecture of the cabling solution is quite similar, however, because continually reconnecting fiber optic cables risks wear and tear damage, and you do not want to have to replace cable runs through conduit. Consequently, the structured links are installed in the same way as copper cabling. Permanent cables are run through conduit to wall ports at the client access end and a fiber distribution panel at the switch end. Fiber patch cables are used to complete the link from the wall port to the NIC and from the patch panel to the switch port.

Fiber distribution panel. (Image by Aleh Datskevich © 123RF.com.)

 *Note: To learn more, watch the related **Video** on the course website.*

COAXIAL CABLE AND CONNECTORS

Structured cabling systems are usually deployed to support a type of copper wire cabling called **twisted pair**. Twisted pair and fiber optic cabling predominate in terms of modern networking applications, and they will be covered in detail later in this lesson, but there are a couple of other copper wire cable and connector types that you should be aware of.

Coaxial (or **coax**) cable is made of two conductors that share the same axis, hence the name ("co" and "ax"). The core conductor of the cable is made of copper wire (solid or stranded) and is enclosed by plastic insulation (dielectric). A wire mesh (the second conductor), which serves both as **shielding** from EMI and as a ground, surrounds the insulating material. A tough plastic sheath protects the cable.

Coax cable. (Image by destinacigdem © 123RF.com.)

Coax cables are categorized using the **Radio Grade (RG)** standard. The Radio Grade (or Radio Guide) classifications were developed by the US military, but are no longer actively maintained by any sort of standards body. They do not prescribe the quality of coax cabling but categorize it by the thickness of the core conductor and the cable's characteristic impedance. Coax cabling is also available with tri- or quad-shielding for better resistance to EMI and eavesdropping.

RG	Core	Impedance	Applications
RG-6	18 AWG	75 ohms	Drop cable for modern Cable Access TV (CATV) and broadband cable modems
RG-59	20 AWG	75 ohms	Drop cable for older CATV/cable modem installs and CCTV network cabling

Coax cable is usually terminated by using **BNC** (alternately **Bayonet Neill-Concelman**, **British Naval Connector**, or **Barrel Nut Connector**) connectors crimped to the ends of the cable. A **BNC coupler** (a connector with female BNC ports at either end) allows two cables terminated with BNCs to be connected to one another. The impedance of the connector must match the cable type (50 or 75 ohm).

BNC connector on the left. (Image created by Krzysztof Burghardt and reproduced under the Creative Commons Attribution ShareAlike 3.0 license.) F-type connector on the right. (Image created by Colin and reproduced under the Creative Commons Attribution ShareAlike 3.0 license.)

Some coax installations use **F-type connectors**. For example, a broadband cable Internet access service is likely to use this connector. F-connectors come in a secure screw-on form or as a non-threaded slip-on connector.

Coax is considered obsolete in terms of LAN applications but is still widely used for CCTV networks and as drop cables for cable TV (CATV) and Internet access, where it can support higher bandwidths but at reduced range. In a **hybrid fiber coax (HFC)** network, coax cable links the fiber optic trunk serving the whole street to the cable modem installed in the customer's premises. Coax suffers less from attenuation than twisted pair but is generally bulkier and more difficult to install.

SERIAL CABLE AND CONNECTORS

All network technologies transfer data in serial, but the term **serial cable** generally refers to the original asynchronous serial transmission standard; one of the oldest and simplest in computing. Asynchronous means there are no timing signals or frames. Each byte of data is identified by start and stop signals. It was used on PCs to connect peripheral devices, and the same technique is used by analog dial-up modems. It can also be deployed as a rudimentary type of network connecting two hosts. Devices with serial ports are defined in two categories:

- **DTE (Data Terminal Equipment)**—A PC is classed as DTE equipment, as are most data terminals and other devices that interact with users.

- **DCE (Data Circuit-terminating Equipment)**—DCE equipment is defined as those items that provide an interface between DTE equipment and other communications systems or networks (for example, modems).

DTE equipment is connected to DCE equipment with a straight-through wired cable (pin 1 on one end of a cable joins to pin 1 on the other end, pin 2 to pin 2, and so on). This cabling works because DTE equipment uses pin 2 (TD) to transmit data and DCE equipment uses pin 2 (RD) to receive data. Where two pieces of DTE equipment (such as two PCs) are to be linked together, a special cable or adapter is needed to compensate for both ends having identical serial port connections. An adapter or cable that is cross-wired to allow two DTE devices to communicate is called a **null modem** cable.

The serial port on the original IBM PC was a 25-pin male D connector (DB25), which followed the **RS-232** standard defined by TIA/EIA. In practice, most PCs used a male DB9 9-pin connector. The 9-pin connector supports the major data and handshake (data flow control) lines needed for peripherals, such as modems or mice, but does not include the advanced signals required for some more specialist devices.

You may also need to configure the link speed, parity, and flow control settings. Usually these are 9,600 bps (baud), 8 data bits/1 stop bit, and no parity or flow control. Serial interfaces are also used for legacy WAN links, such as leased lines. These serial interfaces are typically synchronous and can use a variety of different cabling and connectors.

Activity 12-1
Discussing Structured Cabling Systems

SCENARIO
Answer the following questions to test your understanding of the content covered in this topic.

1. **What would be a typical use of an IDF?**

2. **What is a 110 block?**

3. **At what layer of the OSI model does a fiber distribution panel work?**

4. **Which cable type consists of a core made of solid copper surrounded by insulation, a braided metal shielding, and an outer cover?**

Topic B

Deploy Twisted Pair Cabling Solutions

EXAM OBJECTIVES COVERED
2.1 Given a scenario, deploy the appropriate cabling solution.
5.2 Given a scenario, use the appropriate tool.

Copper wire twisted pair cabling is the most basic networking media type. You are likely to work with this network media daily as part of your duties as a network professional. Understanding the characteristics of twisted pair will enable you to properly install and service your networks.

UNSHIELDED TWISTED PAIR (UTP) CABLE

Twisted pair is a type of copper cable that has been extensively used for telephone systems and data networks. One pair of insulated wires twisted together forms a **balanced pair**. The pair carry the same signal but with different polarity; one wire is positive, and the other is negative. This allows the receiver to identify any noise affecting the line and detect the signal more strongly. Two or four twisted pairs are themselves twisted around one another to form a **twisted pair cable**. The pairs are twisted to reduce external interference and crosstalk. **Crosstalk** is a phenomenon whereby one wire causes interference in another as a result of their proximity. Twisting the wires ensures the emitted signals from one wire are cancelled out by the emitted signals from the other. Each pair is twisted at a different rate to ensure the pairs do not interfere with one another.

Twisted pair cable—Each color-coded pair is twisted at a different rate to reduce interference. (Image by Thuansak Srilao © 123RF.com.)

There is a distinction between solid and stranded cabling. Solid cabling uses a single thick wire per conductor and is used for cables that run behind walls or through ducts. Stranded cabling uses thin filament wires wrapped around one another and is used to make flexible patch cords for connecting computers to wall ports and switch ports to patch panel ports. Copper wire thickness is measured using **American Wire Gauge (AWG)**. Increasing AWG numbers represent thinner wire. Solid cable uses thicker 22 to 24 AWG, while the stranded cable used for patch cords is often 26 AWG.

Most twisted pair cable currently used in networks is unshielded. A major reason for UTP's popularity is because this form of cabling is used in many telephone systems. Modern buildings are often flood-wired using UTP cabling. This involves cables being laid to every location in the building that may need to support a telephone or computer. These cables can then be used for either the telephone system or the data network.

SHIELDED AND SCREENED TWISTED PAIR CABLE

When twisted pair cabling was first used in networks based on IBM's Token Ring product, it was usually **shielded** to make it less susceptible to interference and crosstalk. *Each pair* was surrounded by a braided shield and was referred to as **shielded twisted pair (STP)**. This type of cabling is no longer widespread, but some modern twisted pair cabling installations use screened cables. A **screened cable** has one thin outer foil shield around all pairs. Screened cable is usually designated as **screened twisted pair (ScTP)** or **foiled/unshielded twisted pair (F/UTP)**, or sometimes just **foiled twisted pair (FTP)**. Modern fully shielded cabling, with both a braided outer screen and foil-shielded pairs, is referred to as **shielded/foiled twisted pair (S/FTP)**. Legacy STP cable could be complex to install, as it required bonding each element to ground manually, but modern F/UTP and S/FTP solutions (using appropriate cable, connectors, jacks, and patch panels) reduce this complexity by incorporating grounding within the design of each element.

 Note: *Using screened cable means that you must also use screened connectors and jacks. Screened cable elements should not be mixed with unscreened elements.*

CAT CABLE STANDARDS

The **American National Standards Institute (ANSI)** and the **Telecommunications Industry Association (TIA)/Electronic Industries Alliance (EIA)** have created categories for twisted pair to simplify selection of a suitable quality cable. These **categories**, along with other aspects of telecommunications wiring best practices, are defined in the **ANSI/TIA/EIA 568 Commercial Building Telecommunications Cabling Standards** (*tiaonline.org*).

Cat	Frequency	Capacity	Max. Distance	Network Application
3	16 MHz	10 Mbps	100 m (328 ft)	10BASE-T
5	100 MHz	100 Mbps	100 m (328 ft)	100BASE-TX
5e	100 MHz	1 Gbps	100 m (328 ft)	1000BASE-T
6	250 MHz	1 Gbps	100 m (328 ft)	1000BASE-T
		10 Gbps	55 m (180 ft)	10GBASE-T
6A	500 MHz	10 Gbps	100 m (328 ft)	10GBASE-T
7	600 MHz	10 Gbps	100 m (328 ft)	10GBASE-T

Here are some details about the categories used for network media:

- Cat 5 cable is no longer available. Cat 5e is tested at 100 MHz (like Cat 5 was) but to higher overall specifications for attenuation and crosstalk, meaning that the cable is rated to handle Gigabit Ethernet throughput. With Gigabit Ethernet, all four pairs are used for bidirectional data transfer. Cat 5e would still be an acceptable choice for providing network links for workstations.

- Cat 6 can support 10 Gbps but over shorter distances—nominally 55 m, but often less if cables are closely bundled together.
- Cat 6A is an improved specification cable that can support 10 Gbps over 100 m. It is mostly deployed in data centers or as backbone cabling (links between servers, switches, and routers). Cat 6A cable is bulkier than Cat 5e, and the installation requirements more stringent, so fitting it within pathways designed for older cable can be problematic.

  With Cat 6A, there are UTP and F/UTP variants. Both types are bulkier than Cat 5e or Cat 6, though in fact, the diameter of Cat 6A UTP is slightly larger than 6A F/UTP. The components of F/UTP are more expensive, but UTP requires more testing to ensure proper performance. Also, F/UTP can be bundled more tightly together than UTP.

- Cat 7 cable is fully screened and shielded (S/FTP) and rated for 10GbE applications up to 100 m (328 feet). The cable supports transmission frequencies up to 600 MHz. Cat 7 is not recognized by TIA/EIA but appears in the cabling standards created by the ISO (ISO/IEC 11801).

 Note: Cabling is not the only part of the wiring system that must be rated to the appropriate category. For faster network applications (Gigabit Ethernet and better), the performance of connectors becomes increasingly critical. For example, if you are installing Cat 6A wiring, you must also install Cat 6A patch panels, wall plates, and connectors.

TWISTED PAIR CONNECTOR TYPES

Twisted pair copper cabling uses **Registered Jack (RJ)** connectors. There are many different types of RJ connector, identified by numbers (and sometimes letters). Some are physically different, while others are identical but wired differently for different applications.

RJ-45 CONNECTORS

RJ-45 connectors are used with 4-pair (8-wire) cables. The connectors are also referred to as 8P8C, standing for 8-position/8-contact. This means that all eight "potential" wire positions are supplied with contacts, so that they can all carry signals if needed. RJ-45 is used for Ethernet twisted pair cabling.

RJ-45 port and connector. (Image © 123RF.com.)

RJ-11 CONNECTORS

The smaller **RJ-11** connectors are used with 2- or 3-pair UTP. There is room for six wires, but the four center wires are most commonly used. Typically, the innermost pair, wired to pins 3 and 4, carries the dial tone and voice circuit. These are also called the Tip and Ring wires after the way older phone plugs were wired. The other pair is usually unused but can be deployed for a secondary circuit. RJ-11 connectors are used for telephone systems—for example, to connect a modem to a phone jack.

RJ-11 port and connector. (Image © 123RF.com.)

Note: *Telephone cabling and RJ-11 connectors carry only a small electrical charge, enough to power old analog telephone handsets but not a device such as a modern digital handset or a modem, which will require a separate power source.*

Note: *In the UK, BT 631A connectors are used to connect equipment to analog telephone points. Modems designed for UK use come with a cable with an RJ-11 connector at one end and a BT connector at the other.*

An RJ-11 connector has only two contacts (6P2C). To use more pairs, the jack can be wired as RJ-14 (6P4C) or RJ-25 (6P6C).

COPPER TERMINATION STANDARDS (T568A/T568B)

Each conductor in a 4-pair data cable is color-coded. Each pair is assigned a color (Blue, Orange, Green, or Brown). The first conductor in each pair has a predominantly white insulator with strips of the color; the second conductor has an insulator with the solid color. The ANSI/TIA/EIA 568 standard defines two methods for terminating Ethernet connectors: **T568A** and **T568B**. The wiring for both standards is shown in the following figure.

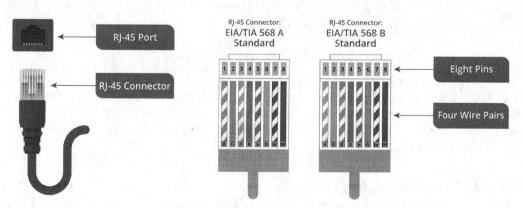

T568A and T568B wiring diagrams. (Image © 123RF.com.)

In T568A, pin 1 is wired to Green/White, pin 2 is wired to Green, pin 3 is wired to Orange/White, and pin 6 is wired to Orange or, put another way, the Orange and Green pairs are swapped over. Organizations should try to avoid using a mixture of the two standards. T568A is mandated by the US government and by the residential cabling standard (TIA 570), but T568B is probably the more widely deployed of the two.

Pin	Wire Color (T568A)	Wire Color (T568B)	10/100 Mbps	1/10 Gbps
1	Green/White	Orange/White	Tx+	BixA+
2	Green	Orange	Tx-	BixA-
3	Orange/White	Green/White	Rx+	BixB+
4	Blue	Blue		BixC+
5	Blue/White	Blue/White		BixC-
6	Orange	Green	Rx-	BixB-
7	Brown/White	Brown/White		BixD+
8	Brown	Brown		BixD-

Ethernet and Fast Ethernet use only two pairs in the cable; one to transmit (Tx) and the other to receive (Rx). Gigabit and 10GbE Ethernet use all four pairs, transmitting and receiving simultaneously (Bix) through the use of improved signal encoding methods.

 Note: *A patch panel may be wired either to T568A or T568B. Make sure you use the same wiring scheme for all the other connectors on your network.*

STRAIGHT THROUGH AND CROSSOVER CABLE

Ethernet and Fast Ethernet cables and connectors carry data over Transmit (Tx) and Receive (Rx) pairs. Normally, an end system would be linked to an intermediate system, such as a hub or a switch, using **straight-through** (or **standard**) cabling and connectors. The hub receives a signal from a host over the Tx pair, performs a crossover, and repeats it over the other ports, for receipt by connected interfaces over their Rx pairs.

A **crossover cable** is created by wiring the connectors at each end differently, so that Tx on one connector goes directly to Rx on the other connector and vice versa (**TX/RX reverse**). The cable itself is ordinary UTP. A crossover cable can therefore be used to connect the same type of network device together directly. This could mean either to connect two end systems (sometimes useful for troubleshooting) or to connect two hubs or switches. Using T568A wiring on one end of a patch cable and T568B on the other creates a crossover cable, connecting pins 1 and 2 on one end of the cable with pins 3 and 6 on the other end, and vice versa.

 Note: *Make sure crossover patch cords are clearly labeled. It's not easy to distinguish a crossover cable from a straight-through one just by inspecting the termination. If you accidentally use a crossover patch cord where a straight-through one is required (or vice versa) and the network ports do not support auto-MDI/MDI-X, the link will not work.*

In fact, crossover cable is no longer required for this type of application, as many switches either have an uplink port for this purpose or can autodetect and select between an uplink and straight-through connection. This is referred to as auto-MDI/MDI-X; MDI means Medium Dependent Interface and MDI-X means a crossover interface. All Gigabit Ethernet ports support auto-MDI/MDI-X.

PLENUM VS. PVC CABLE

A **plenum** space is a void in a building designed to carry **heating, ventilation, and air conditioning (HVAC)** systems. Plenum space is typically a false ceiling, though it could also be constructed as a raised floor. As it makes installation simpler, this space has also been used for communications wiring in some building designs. Plenum space is an effective conduit for fire, as there is plenty of airflow and no fire breaks (such as walls or doors). If the plenum space is used for heating, there may also be higher temperatures. Therefore, building regulations require the use of fire-retardant **plenum**

cable in such spaces. Plenum cable must not emit large amounts of smoke when burned, be self-extinguishing, and meet other strict fire safety standards.

General purpose (non-plenum) cabling uses PVC (polyvinyl chloride) jackets and insulation. Plenum-rated cable uses treated PVC or Fluorinated Ethylene Polymer (FEP). This can make the cable less flexible, but the different materials used have no effect on bandwidth. Data cable rated for plenum use under the US National Electrical Code (NEC) is marked CMP/MMP. General purpose cables are marked CMG/MMG or CM/MP.

Cabling that passes between two floors is referred to as **riser**. Conduit for riser cabling must be fire-stopped. This means that fire cannot spread through the opening created by the conduit. Riser cabling (in conduit or in spaces such as lift shafts) should also conform to the appropriate fire safety standards. These are similar to the requirements for plenum spaces but not quite as strict. Data cable rated for riser use under the NEC is marked CMR/MPR.

WIRING TOOLS AND TECHNIQUES

Installing fixed cable from a bulk spool is referred to as **pulling cable** because the cable must be pulled, carefully, from the telecommunications closet to the work area. Cable is normally routed through conduits or wall spaces, avoiding excessive bends and proximity to electrical power cables and fittings, such as fluorescent lights, as these could cause interference. The main fixed cable run can be up to 90 m (295 feet); stranded-wire patch cords (between the PC and wall port) and jumpers (a stranded-wire cable without connectors used on cross-connects) can be up to 5 m each (16 feet) and no more than 10 m (33 feet) in overall length. This is because the attenuation of stranded cable is higher than solid cable.

Starting at the patch panel, label the end of the cable with the appropriate jack ID, then run it through to the work area. This is also referred to as a **drop**, as in most cases you will be dropping the cable from the ceiling space through a wall cavity. If several cables are going to roughly the same place, you can bundle them and pull them together. There are various tools and techniques for pulling cable through difficult to reach areas, such as ceiling spaces. Leave enough slack at both ends (a service loop) to make the connection, cut the cable, and label the other end with the appropriate ID. Electrician's scissors (**snips**) are designed for cutting copper wire and stripping insulation and cable jackets. Alternatively, there are dedicated **wire stripper** tools that have replaceable blades for different data cable types. Cable cutting blades should be rounded to preserve the wire geometry. Stripping tools should have the correct diameter to score a cable jacket without damaging the insulation wires. Heavy duty cutters are required for armored cable.

TERMINATION TOOLS

Fixed cable is terminated using a **punch down tool**. These tools fix conductors into an **Insulation Displacement Connector (IDC)**. There are different IDC formats (66 Block, 110 Block, and Krone), and these require different blades. Many punch-down tools have replaceable blades, though. Blades are double-sided; one side pushes the wire into the terminal while the other side cuts the excess. Make sure the blade marked "cut" is oriented correctly to cut the excess wire.

A patch cable is created using a **wire** or cable **crimper**. This tool fixes a jack to a cable. The tools are specific to the type of connector and cable, though some may have modular dies to support a range of RJ-type jacks.

Note: *You must untwist the ends of the wire pairs and place them into the connector die in the correct order for the wiring configuration you want to use. You must not untwist the wires too much, however. Cat 6 is demanding in this respect and requires no more than 0.375" (1 cm) of untwisting. Also, ensure that the clip presses down on the plastic outer sheath and not the wire pairs to ensure a secure connection. It is best to use prefabricated patch cords where possible. These are far less likely to create problems.*

Note: *To learn more, watch the related* **Video** *on the course website.*

GUIDELINES FOR INSTALLING BOUNDED NETWORK MEDIA

INSTALL BOUNDED NETWORK MEDIA

Consider these best practices and guidelines when you are installing bounded network media:

- Follow the 568 Commercial Building Telecommunication Cabling Wiring Standard when you are dealing with structured cabling. Make proper use of premise wiring components.
- Create a list of requirements for your network so that you can work toward meeting them. These requirements may include how many users will need to connect, the physical area it will need to cover, external connections, etc.
- Consider the factors that can affect the performance of network media, such as electromagnetic interference and attenuation.
- Consider the environment's limitations, such as the amount of ventilation for the network closet, access to power, or space to run cables that can affect your network.
- Use plenum cables in designated plenum spaces of a building to comply with fire codes and use PVC in non-plenum spaces.
- Use rack systems to maximize the use of space for equipment in a wiring closet.
- Employ good cable management techniques, such as cable trays/baskets, to properly support cables and to keep them organized.
- Make cables the right length: too short cables can pull on connectors and too long cables can make cable management difficult.
- Label cables to help you in tracing a cable to its endpoint. Patch panel ports should be labeled above the port.
- Keep patch panels and patch cables orderly so that you can more easily add, remove, or replace a cable.
- Remove unused cables from the patch panel not only to make it neater, but also to prevent unauthorized network access.

Activity 12-2

Discussing Twisted Pair Cabling Solutions

SCENARIO

Answer the following questions to test your understanding of the content covered in this topic.

1. **What is the measurement standard for wire thickness?**

2. **What is crosstalk?**

3. **Which categories of UTP cables are certified to carry data transmission faster than 100 Mbps?**

4. **True or False? Cat standards apply only to wiring.**

5. **Why is plenum-rated cable used when cable is run in an area where building air is circulated?**

6. **100BASE-T transmit pins are 1 and 2. What color code are the wires terminated to these pins under T568A and T568B?**

7. **Which pins are used for the receive pair under 100BASE-T?**

Topic C

Test and Troubleshoot Twisted Pair Cabling Solutions

EXAM OBJECTIVES COVERED
5.2 Given a scenario, use the appropriate tool.
5.3 Given a scenario, troubleshoot common wired connectivity and performance issues.

A network can be simple or complex—but even at the simplest level, numerous connectivity issues occur regularly. Each time a problem with network connectivity surfaces, you will be faced with many unhappy users. To restore connectivity as quickly as possible, you will need to be aware of the possible physical connectivity issues you may face and the appropriate fixes.

CABLE ISSUES

When you suspect a problem with bad wiring or bad connectors in cabled links, the first step is to isolate the issue with several tests. How can you prove that there is a cable problem? Attempt to ping a known working system on the local subnet (such as the router). If you can ping another local system, the problem is not in the cabling (at least, not this cable).

If you can't ping anything then, assuming you've physically checked the back of the machine for the cable's presence, verify that the patch cord is good. The easiest thing to do is swap the cable to the wall socket with another—known working—cable.

Can you ping anything now? If not, verify the patch cable between the patch panel and the switch. Swap with another known good cable and test again. If you still haven't isolated the problem, try plugging the problem computer into a different network socket (if there is another computer local, just switch their cables over). If there is a cable problem somewhere, then the problem should manifest itself on the other system.

Problems with patch cords are simple to resolve as you can just throw the broken one away and plug in a new one. If the problem is in the structured cabling, however, you will want to use cable testing tools to determine its cause. The solution may involve installing a new permanent link, but there could also be a termination or external interference problem.

Verifying patch cord connections. (Image by Kjetil Kolbjornsrud © 123RF.com.)

Note: *To learn more, watch the related* **Video** *on the course website.*

LOOPBACK ADAPTERS AND CABLE TESTERS

The best time to verify wiring installation and termination is just after you have made all the connections. This means you should still have access to the cable runs. Identifying and correcting errors at this point will be much simpler than when you are trying to set up end user devices. Several tools are available to perform tests on the physical characteristics of a cable link.

Note: *TIA 568 distinguishes between permanent and channel links. A permanent link runs between the ports on the patch panel and wall outlet; a channel link runs between the patch cord used to connect to a port on a hub or switch and the patch cord used to connect to a port on a PC (but does not include the end user devices themselves).*

A network **loopback adapter** (or loopback plug) is a specially wired RJ-45 plug with a 6" stub of cable. The wiring pinout is pin 1 (Tx) to pin 3 (Rx) and pin 2 (Tx) to pin 6 (Rx). This means that the packet sent by the NIC is received by itself. This is used to test for faulty ports and network cards.

More advanced **cable testers** provide detailed information on the physical and electrical properties of the cable. For example, they test and report on cable conditions, crosstalk, attenuation, noise, resistance, and other characteristics of a cable run. Devices classed as **certifiers** can be used to test and certify cable installations to a performance category—for example, that a network is TIA/EIA 568B Category 6A compliant. They use defined transport performance specifications to ensure an installation exceeds the required performance characteristics for parameters such as attenuation and crosstalk.

Technician using a cable certifier. (Image by Wavebreak Media © 123RF.com.)

 Note: *The price of network test equipment can be prohibitive, especially given the limited use the equipment may receive. In this case, leasing the equipment may be an alternative.*

MULTIMETERS AND WIRE MAP TESTERS

If a dedicated cable tester or certifier device is not available, a **multimeter** can be used to check physical connectivity. The primary purpose of a multimeter is for testing electrical circuits, but they can test for the continuity of any sort of copper wire, the existence of a short, and the integrity of a terminator. To perform useful tests, you need to know the readings that are expected from a particular test. For example, if the resistance measured across UTP Ethernet cable is found to be 100 ohms, then the cable is OK, but if the resistance between the two ends of a cable is infinity, the cable has a break. Many multimeters designed for ICT use incorporate the function of a **wire map tester**. These are also available as dedicated devices. Wire map testers can identify the following problems:

- **Continuity (open)**—A conductor does not form a circuit because of cable damage or the connector is not properly wired.
- **Short**—Two conductors are joined at some point, usually because the insulating wire is damaged, or a connector is poorly wired.
- **Incorrect pin-out/incorrect termination/mismatched standards**—The conductors are incorrectly wired into the terminals at one or both ends of the cable. The following transpositions are common:
  - **Reversed pair**—The conductors in a pair have been wired to different terminals (for example, from pin 3 to pin 6 and pin 6 to pin 3 rather than pin 3 to pin 3 and pin 6 to pin 6).
  - **Crossed pair (TX/RX reverse)**—The conductors from one pair have been connected to pins belonging to a different pair (for example, from pins 3 and 6 to

pins 1 and 2). This may be done deliberately to create a crossover cable, but such a cable would not be used to link a host to a switch.

> **Note:** *If you have problems with a patch cord, check that it has not been wired for crossover, rather than straight-through use. Always keep in mind the "known good" technique for troubleshooting easily replaceable parts.*

Another potential cable wiring fault is a **split pair**. This is where both ends of a single wire in one pair are wired to terminals belonging to a different pair. This type of fault can only be detected by a wire map tester that also tests for excessive crosstalk. This is generally the kind of functionality associated with a cable tester or certifier.

TONE GENERATORS AND TDRs

A network **tone generator and probe** are used to trace a cable from one end to the other. This may be necessary when the cables are bundled and have not been labeled properly. This device is also known as a **Fox and Hound** or **toner probe**. The tone generator is used to apply a signal on the cable to be traced where it is used to follow the cable over ceilings and through ducts.

Time domain reflectometers (TDRs) are used to measure the length of a cable run and can locate open and short circuits, kinks/sharp bends, and other imperfections in cables that could affect performance. A TDR transmits a short signal pulse of known amplitude and duration down a cable and measures the corresponding amplitude and time delay associated with resultant signal reflections. A TDR analyzes these reflections and can display any problems found and their location. Problems can be identified because they bounce the signal back at different amplitudes depending on the type of problem. The TDR measures the amount of time taken for the signal to bounce back and can therefore calculate the distance to the cable fault to within a meter, which makes isolating the problem simpler.

WIRED CONNECTIVITY AND PERFORMANCE ISSUES

When you are troubleshooting a suspected cable problem, check the link lights or network connection **LED status indicators** on the NIC at one end and the switch/router port at the other. You will also need the vendor documentation to interpret the LEDs. There may be two LEDs for status and for link. On a switch port, the following LED link states are typical:

- Solid green—The link is connected but there is no traffic.
- Flickering green—The link is operating normally (with traffic).
- No light—The link is not working or is disconnected at the other end.
- Blinking amber—A fault has been detected (duplex mismatch or spanning tree blocking, for instance).
- Solid amber—The port is disabled.

> **Note:** *Use the `ping` utility to test host links, both while troubleshooting an LED status indicator issue and after applying a solution, to demonstrate that the issue has been resolved. If you get a 100% reply, then you are connected. If some, or all, packets fail to deliver, then you need to continue troubleshooting a variety of cable and port issues.*

If a link is not up, use the cable and connector testing tools described in this topic to rule out a physical problem, such as an open or short, Tx/Rx reverse, or incorrect pin out. Inspect the cable and connector for damage, such as kinks in the cable or **bent pins** in the connector or the port. If you suspect a problem with a **damaged patch cable**, substitute with a known good replacement. A TDR can be used to identify the location of cable running in conduit that is difficult to inspect visually.

Also verify that the cable type is appropriate to the application. For example, you cannot expect 10GbE Ethernet to run over an 80 m Cat 5e link. You may also need to verify that unshielded cable has not been installed where shielded or screened cable would be more suitable. Using an **incorrect cable type** might result in lower than expected speed and/or numerous checksum errors and link resets. Check the identifier printed on the cable jacket to verify the type that has been used.

If you suspect a problem with a **bad port**, use a loopback plug or test with a known good host. If the port and NIC are good, the link should be reported as Up by a tool such as `ipconfig` or `ifconfig` when the loopback plug is connected.

ATTENUATION AND INTERFERENCE ISSUES

If a cable link is too long, **attenuation** (or **insertion loss**) may mean that the link experiences problems with high error rates and retransmissions (frame or packet loss) resulting in reduced speeds and possibly loss of connectivity. Insertion loss is measured in **decibels (dB)** and represents the ratio of the received voltage to the original voltage on a logarithmic scale. A detailed explanation of logarithms is beyond the scope of this course, but the essential point is that a logarithmic scale is non-linear, so a small change in value represents a large change in the performance measured.

 Note: *The typical rule of thumb is that -3 dB loss represents a 50% loss of power.*

The maximum value allowed for insertion loss depends on the link category. For example, Cat 5e at 100 MHz allows up to -24 dB, while Cat 6 allows up to -21.3 dB. When you are measuring insertion loss itself, smaller values are better (-20 dB insertion loss is better than -22 dB, for instance). A cable certifier is likely to report the **margin**, which is the difference between the actual loss and the maximum value allowed for the cable standard. Consequently, higher margin values are better. For example, if the insertion loss measured over a Cat 5e cable is -22 dB, the margin is 2 dB; if another cable measures -23 dB, the margin is only 1 dB, and you are that much closer to not meeting acceptable link standards. Higher grade or shielded cable may alleviate the problem; otherwise, you will need to find a shorter cable run or install a repeater or additional switch.

Careful **cable placement** is necessary during installation to ensure that the wiring is not subject to interference from sources such as electrical power cables, fluorescent lights, motors, electrical fans, radio transmitters, and so on. **Electromagnetic interference (EMI)** is something that should be detected when the cable is installed, so you should suspect either some new source that has been installed recently or some source that was not taken into account during testing (machinery or power circuits that weren't activated when the installation testing took place, for instance). Interference from nearby data cables is also referred to as **alien crosstalk**.

 Note: *Radio frequency interference (RFI) is EMI that occurs in the frequencies used for radio transmissions.*

CROSSTALK ISSUES

Crosstalk usually indicates a problem with **bad wiring** (poor quality or damaged or the improper type for the application), a **bad connector**, or **improper termination**. Check the cable for excessive untwisting at the ends and for kinks or crush points along its run. Crosstalk is also measured in dB, but unlike insertion loss, higher values represent less noise. Again, the expected measurements vary according to the cable category and application. There are various types of crosstalk that can be measured:

- **Near End (NEXT)**—This occurs close to the transmitter and is usually caused by excessive untwisting of pairs.
- **Attenuation to Crosstalk Ratio (ACR)**—This is the difference between insertion loss and NEXT. ACR is equivalent to a signal-to-noise ratio (SNR). A high value means that the signal is stronger than any noise present; a result closer to 0 means the link is likely to be subject to high error rates.
- **Attenuation-to-Crosstalk Ratio, Far End (ACRF)**—**Far End Crosstalk (FEXT)** is measured at the recipient end. The difference between insertion loss and FEXT gives ACRF, which measures cable performance regardless of the actual link length.
- **Power sum**—Gigabit and 10GbE Ethernet use all four pairs. Power sum crosstalk calculations (PSNEXT, PSACR, and PSACRF) confirm that a cable is suitable for this type of application. They are measured by energizing three of the four pairs in turn.

Note: *Complete loss of connectivity indicates a break in the cable (or a completely faulty installation), while intermittent loss of connectivity is more likely to be caused by attenuation, crosstalk, or noise.*

Activity 12-3
Discussing Twisted Pair Cabling Issues

SCENARIO

Answer the following questions to test your understanding of the content covered in this topic.

---

1. **When you are troubleshooting a cable link, which should you investigate first—the patch cord, permanent link, or network adapter?**

2. **Patch cables are vulnerable to failure since they often trail from the PC to the wall socket. What could you use to check that a cable is physically intact?**

3. **If you detect a significant increase in noise affecting a cable link, how would you go about determining the cause?**

4. **What cabling faults would a wire map tester detect?**

5. **How would you test for excessive attenuation in a network link?**

6. **Your network uses UTP cable throughout the building. There are a few users who complain of intermittent network connectivity problems, but there is no pattern for these problems that relates to network usage. You visit the users' workstations and find that they are all located close to an elevator shaft. What is a likely cause of the intermittent connectivity problems? How might you correct the problem?**

7. **What is the reason for making power sum crosstalk measurements when testing a link?**

Topic D

Deploy Fiber Optic Cabling Solutions

EXAM OBJECTIVES COVERED
2.1 Given a scenario, deploy the appropriate cabling solution.
2.2 Given a scenario, determine the appropriate placement of networking devices on a network and install/configure them.
5.2 Given a scenario, use the appropriate tool.
5.3 Given a scenario, troubleshoot common wired connectivity and performance issues.

In this topic, you will identify the different types of bounded fiber optic media. Fiber optic media is used by many telecommunications companies to transmit telephone signals, Internet communication, and cable television signals. Even if you don't work with it daily, you will still encounter fiber optic media as a network professional. Understanding the characteristics of fiber optic media and the equipment used will enable you to properly work with it in your networks.

FIBER OPTIC CABLE

Copper wire carries electrical signals, which are subject to interference and attenuation (the reduction of signal quality over distance). Fiber optic cable uses pulses of infrared light for signaling, which are not susceptible to interference, cannot easily be intercepted (eavesdropped), and suffer less from attenuation. Consequently, fiber optic cabling supports much higher bandwidth (multiple gigabits per second) and longer cable runs (measured in kilometers, rather than meters). A single optical fiber is constructed from three elements:

- **Core** provides the transmission path for the light signals (waveguide).
- **Cladding** reflects signals back into the waveguide as efficiently as possible so that the light signal travels along the waveguide by multiple internal reflections. The core and cladding can be made from glass or plastic. The cladding is applied as a thin layer surrounding the core. While made of the same material, the cladding has a different refractive index to the core. The effect of this is to create a boundary that causes the light to bounce back into the core, facilitating the process of total internal reflection that guides the light signal through the core.
- **Buffer** is a protective plastic coating. It may be of a tight or loose configuration, with the loose format using some form of lubricant between the strand and the sheath.

In basic operation modes, each fiber optic strand can only transfer light in a single direction at a time. Therefore, multiple fibers are often bundled within a cable to allow simultaneous transmission and reception of signals or to provide links for multiple applications. There are many different outer jacket designs and materials suited for different installations (indoor/plenum, outdoor, underground, undersea, and so on). Kevlar (Aramid) strands and sometimes fiberglass rods (strength members) are often used to protect the fibers from excessive bending or kinking when "pulling" the cable to install it. For exposed outdoor applications, a steel shield (armor) may be added to deter rodents from gnawing the cable.

SINGLE MODE FIBER (SMF) AND MULTIMODE FIBER (MMF)

Fiber optic cables are specified using the mode, composition (glass/plastic), and core/cladding size; for example, 8.3 micron core/125 microcladding single mode glass or

62.5 micron core/125 microcladding multimode plastic. Fiber optic cables fall into two broad categories: single mode and multimode. **Single Mode Fiber (SMF)** has a small core (8 to 10 microns) and a long wavelength, near infrared (1310 nm or 1550 nm) light signal, generated by a laser. Single mode cables support data rates up to 10 Gbps or better and cable runs of many kilometers, depending on the quality of the cable and optics.

Multimode Fiber (MMF) has a larger core (62.5 or 50 microns) and shorter wavelength light (850 nm or 1300 nm) transmitted in multiple waves of varying length. MMF uses less expensive optics and consequently is less expensive to deploy than SMF. However, it does not support such high signaling speeds or long distances as single mode and so is more suitable for LANs than WANs.

> *Note: Optical transceivers for SMF are now only slightly more expensive than ones for MMF. Consequently, SMF is often used for short range applications in data centers, as well as for long distance links. SMF still comes at a slight price premium, but it provides better support for the next generation of 40 Gbps and 100 Gbps Ethernet standards.*

MMF is graded by **Optical Multimode (OM)** categories, defined in the ISO/IEC 11801 standard. 62.5-micron cable is OM1, while early 50-micron cable is OM2. OM1 and OM2 are mainly rated for applications up to 1 Gbps and use LED transmitters. OM1 and OM2 can run 10GBASE-SR, but only over distances of 33 m and 82 m, respectively. OM3 is also 50-micron cable, but it is manufactured differently, designed for use with 850 nm Vertical-Cavity Surface-Emitting Lasers (VCSEL). It supports 10 Gbps at up to 300 m range. OM4 supports 10GbE at 400 m range or 100 Gbps at up to 150 m. A higher optical mode designation defines a higher bandwidth capability. It is important to determine your needs as OM1 and OM2 are more affordable options compared to OM3 and OM4. However, OM3 and OM4 have the data capabilities to deliver higher performance for enterprise networks and data centers.

FIBER OPTIC CABLE INSTALLATION

Fiber optic can be installed in a star topology with the use of a switch. Long distance cables are typically laid as trunks or rings with **repeaters** or **amplifiers** between cable segments to strengthen the signal. Where there are multiple strands within a single cable for a LAN installation, the strands are usually color-coded (TIA/EIA 598) to differentiate them. Also, by convention, MMF jackets are color-coded orange (OM1 and OM2), aqua (OM3 and sometimes OM4), or violet (OM4), while SMF jackets are yellow. Normally, strands are installed in pairs (duplex) at each device, with one strand for transmit (Tx) and one strand for receive (Rx).

The core of a fiber optic connector is a ceramic or plastic **ferrule** that holds the glass strand and ensures continuous reception of the light signals. The tip of the ferrule can be finished in one of three formats:

- **Physical Contact (PC)**—The faces of the connector and fiber tip are polished so that they curve slightly and fit together better.
- **Ultra Physical Contact (UPC)**—This means the cable and connector are polished to a higher standard than with PC.
- **Angled Physical Contact (APC)**—The faces are angled for an even tighter connection. APC cannot be mixed with PC or UPC. These connectors are usually deployed when the fiber is being used to carry analog signaling, as in Cable Access TV (CATV) networks. They are also increasingly used for long distance transmissions and for **Passive Optical Networks (PON)**, such as those used to implement Fiber to the x (FTTx) multiple subscriber networks.

It is important to match the finishing type when you are selecting a connector type. APC finishing is often not supported by the patch panels, transceivers, and switch ports designed for Ethernet.

FIBER OPTIC CONNECTOR TYPES

Fiber optic connectors are available in many different form factors. Some types are more popular for multimode and some for single mode.

ST (STRAIGHT TIP)

Straight Tip (ST) is an early bayonet-style connector that uses a push-and-twist locking mechanism. ST was used mostly for multimode networks, but it is not widely used for Ethernet installations anymore.

Two ST connectors. (Image by Aleh Datskevich © 123RF.com.)

SC (SUBSCRIBER CONNECTOR)

The **Subscriber Connector (SC)** is a push/pull design, allowing for simple insertion and removal. It can be used for single- or multimode. It is commonly used for Gigabit Ethernet.

LC (LUCENT OR LOCAL CONNECTOR)

The **Lucent Connector (LC)** is a small-form-factor connector with a tabbed push/pull design. LC is similar to SC, but the smaller size allows for higher port density. LC is a widely adopted form factor for Gigabit Ethernet and 10GbE.

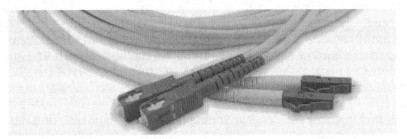

Patch cord with duplex SC format connectors (left) and LC connectors (right). (Image by YANAWUT SUNTORNKIJ © 123RF.com.)

MECHANICAL TRANSFER REGISTERED JACK (MTRJ)

Mechanical Transfer Registered Jack (MTRJ) is a small-form-factor duplex connector with a snap-in design used for multimode networks.

MTRJ connector. (Image by Aleh Datskevich © 123RF.com.)

FIBER OPTIC PATCH CORDS

Connectors for MMF are usually color-coded beige (OM1), black (OM2), aqua (OM3 and some OM4), or violet (OM4), while those for SMF are blue. Connectors with APC finishing are green. Patch cables for fiber optic can come with the same connector on each end (LC-LC, for instance) or a mix of connectors (LC-SC, for instance).

 Note: The patch cord must match the permanent link (SMF or MMF). It is possible to use higher grade MMF patch cord (OM3 or OM4) with a lower grade link (OM1 or OM2), but using an OM1 or OM2 patch cord with an OM3 or OM4 link could cause problems.

Duplex patch cords must maintain the correct polarity, so that the Tx port on the transmitter is linked to the Rx port on the receiver and vice versa. The TIA/EIA cabling standard sets out A to B patch cord to port orientations. Each element in the link must perform a crossover, and there must be an odd number of elements, such as two patch cords and a permanent link (three elements).

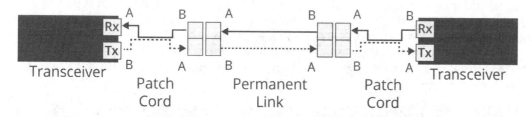

Fiber patch cord polarity.

Most connectors are keyed to prevent incorrect insertion, but if in doubt, an optical power meter can be used to determine whether an optical signal is being received from a particular fiber.

 Note: Transmitted optical signals are visible as bright white spots when viewed through a smartphone camera. This can be used to identify which adapter on an optical interface is transmitting and which fiber patch cord is receiving a signal from the other end of the cable.

 Caution: Never look directly into an optical transceiver or optical fiber with the naked eye. Although infrared light is invisible, it can cause damage to the retina.

 *Note: To learn more, watch the related **Video** on the course website.*

FIBER OPTIC CABLE TESTING TOOLS

Although fiber optic cable does not suffer from attenuation in the same way as copper cable or to the same extent, there will still be some loss of signal strength from one end of the connection to the other. This is due to microscopic imperfections in the structure of the glass fiber and in the smoothness of the edge of the core, leading to some small fraction of the light within the core being scattered or absorbed. As with attenuation in copper cables, the signal loss is increased with increasing cable length. The EIA/TIA 568 specification for fiber allows for a signal loss of between 0.5 dB/km and 3.5 dB/km, depending on the type of fiber used and the wavelength of the light.

Attenuation can be tested using an optical source and optical power meter (or **light meter**), which may be purchased together as a fiber testing kit. If a break is identified in an installed cable, the location of the break can be found using an **optical time domain reflectometer (OTDR)**. This sends light pulses down the cable and times how long it takes for any reflections to bounce back from the break. A broken cable will need to be repaired (spliced) or replaced.

When you are working with fiber optic cabling, it is important to understand that any mismatch between the cables coupled together will result in data loss. This can occur if the fiber cables are not properly aligned, are different sizes, or may have suffered damage (broken/misshaped fiber strands) during transport.

TRANSCEIVERS

A network might involve the use of multiple types of cabling. When this occurs, switch and router equipment must be able to terminate different cable and connector types, and devices must convert from one type to another. Enterprise switches and routers are available with modular, hot-swappable **transceivers** for different types of fiber optic patch cord connections. Historically, these were based on the **Gigabit Interface Converter (GBIC)** form factor, which used SC ports and was designed (as the name suggests) for Gigabit Ethernet. GBIC was very bulky and has largely been replaced by **Small Form Factor Pluggable (SFP)**, also known as mini-GBIC. SFP uses LC connectors and is also designed for Gigabit Ethernet. **SFP+** is an updated specification to support 10GbE but still uses the LC form factor. XFP represents another standard for small form factor, hot-swappable transceivers capable of supporting 10GbE. XFP also uses the LC form factor.

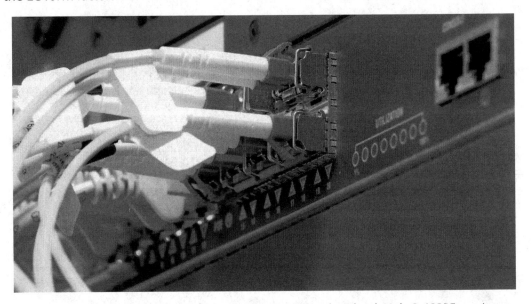

Switch with hot-pluggable SFP fiber transceivers. (Image by Zdenek Maly © 123RF.com.)

GBIC, SFP, and SFP+ are all duplex interfaces, with one transmit port and one receive port. **Bidirectional (BiDi) SFP** and BiDi SFP+ are newer types of transceiver supporting transmit and receive signals over the same strand of fiber (simplex port). This uses a technology called Wavelength Division Multiplexing (WDM) to transmit the Tx and Rx signals over slightly shifted wavelengths. For example, 1270 nm for TX and 1330 nm for RX. BiDi transceivers must be installed in matched pairs tuned to the wavelengths used for the link. Bidirectional links are documented in Ethernet standards (1000BASE-BX and 10GBASE-BX).

Quad SFP (QSFP and QSFP+) is a transceiver form factor designed to support 40GbE plus other high bandwidth applications (including InfiniBand and SONET). Essentially it combines 4 SFP or SFP+ links to support either 4 x 1 Gbps or 4 x 10 Gbps, which can be aggregated into a single 4 Gbps or 40 Gbps channel. QSFP uses a few copper and fiber optic cable and connector types.

The transceivers used in each optical interface (whether SFP, GBIC, or other media converter) are designed to be used with a specific type of optical fiber. For example, transceivers designed for single mode fiber use lasers while multimode fiber transceivers typically use LEDs. Different transceivers are designed to work at different optical wavelengths (typically 850 nm, 1300 nm, or 1550 nm). This means it is important to check the manufacturer's documentation for the interface to ensure the correct fiber type is used, not only for the fiber optic cable, but also for the fiber patch cords used to connect to it at each end. Mismatches between cable, patch cords, and interfaces may lead to significant signal loss.

MEDIA CONVERTERS

Standalone **media converters** are used to convert one cable type to another. These components alter the characteristics of one type of cable to match those of another (that is, make one cable type look like another). Media converters work at the Physical layer of the OSI model. They are usually transparent with regard to the rest of the network infrastructure (the link is treated as one length of cable). They may be supplied as standalone appliances or rack-mounted appliances. The following media conversions are typical:

- Single mode fiber to Ethernet—These powered converters change light signals from SMF cabling into electrical signals carried over a copper wire Ethernet network (and vice versa).
- Multimode fiber to Ethernet—A different media converter model is required to convert the light signals carried over MMF media.

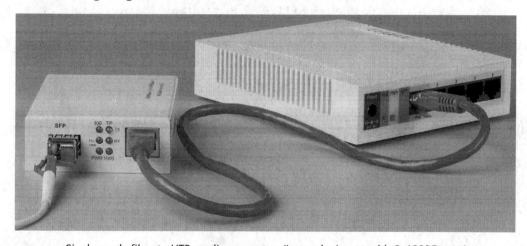

Single mode fiber to UTP media converter. (Image by ironstealth © 123RF.com.)

- Fiber to Coaxial—This type of converter is often used in Hybrid Fiber Coax (HFC) networks to deliver broadband Internet to offices and homes. As with Ethernet, models for SMF and MMF are not interchangeable.
- Single mode to multimode fiber—These passive (unpowered) devices convert between the two fiber cabling types.

Activity 12-4

Discussing Fiber Optic Cabling Solutions

SCENARIO

Answer the following questions to test your understanding of the content covered in this topic.

1.   **What surrounds the core of optical fibers in fiber optic cable?**

2.   **What type of fiber optic cable is suited for long distance links?**

3.   **You are connecting a server to a switch. The server NIC has an LC/UPC port. You have a patch cord marked LC/APC. Is it suitable for use?**

4.   **What device enables termination of different patch cord types in an appliance such as a switch or router?**

Summary

In this lesson, you learned about best practices and technologies underpinning installation of cabled networks.

- Wiring standards provide a framework for installing network infrastructure that will provide ROI over 10-15 years.
- Structured cabling uses main and horizontal cross-connects with backbone and work area cabling wired in a hierarchical star. Cross-connects (distribution frames) come in various formats with 110 block patch panels being the most popular for LANs.
- Twisted pair with RJ connectors is widely deployed on LANs and is defined by various performance categories. Screened (or shielded) twisted pair gives better noise immunity but is more costly and complex to install.
- Devices used to install and test copper cable installations include termination tools, multimeters, toner and probe, TDR, cable certifiers, and protocol analyzers. Learn the symptoms and causes of common cabling issues.
- Coax and serial cabling are no longer mainstream networking products but still have specific applications in some circumstances.
- Fiber optic cabling supports higher bandwidths and distances but is more costly and complex to install. SMF grade cable is used for long-distance links while MMF is used for LANs. Various types of transceiver are used to interface high bandwidth cabling with switch and router ports.
- Media converters work at layer 1 to connect different network media (fiber optic and copper wire, for instance).

What types of cables do you have experience working with?

What challenges have you experienced when trying to deploy cabling systems?

 Practice Questions: *Additional practice questions are available on the course website.*

Lesson 13

Implementing and Troubleshooting Wireless Technologies

LESSON INTRODUCTION

In the previous lesson, you identified bounded network media. With more and more wireless network implementations, you will need different types of media to meet the needs of users with wireless devices. In this lesson, you will identify unbounded network media. Unbounded media technologies have two distinct advantages for businesses over bounded media: first, they are generally easier to install and configure; and second, they afford clients a lot of mobility. They are usually not as secure as bounded media, as the signals are subject to interception. Wireless technology implementations offer various advantages, but you need to understand their limitations to compensate for their disadvantages in your network environments.

LESSON OBJECTIVES

In this lesson, you will:

- Install and configure wireless technologies.

- Troubleshoot wireless performance issues.

- Secure and troubleshoot wireless connectivity.

Topic A

Install and Configure Wireless Technologies

EXAM OBJECTIVES COVERED
1.5 Compare and contrast the characteristics of network topologies, types and technologies.
1.6 Given a scenario, implement the appropriate wireless technologies and configurations.
2.2 Given a scenario, determine the appropriate placement of networking devices on a network and install/configure them.
2.3 Explain the purposes and use cases for advanced networking devices.

In this topic, you will implement wireless technology. Wireless networks are the network of choice in most environments today because they are relatively easy to install and they are flexible. Even more importantly, with users increasingly needing to connect on the move by using different devices, roaming users in both business and leisure environments want the freedom to use their computing devices for work or recreation wherever they are, without a wired connection to the network. With its increasing popularity and widespread appeal, you will undoubtedly be faced with installing and managing a wireless network.

IEEE 802.11 WIRELESS STANDARDS

The wireless LAN (WLAN) standard that dominates business networking is **IEEE 802.11 (Wi-Fi)** (*grouper.ieee.org/groups/802/11*). 802.11 uses radio-based networking, where data is encoded into a radio carrier signal by using a **modulation** scheme. The properties of radio waves include amplitude (the height of peaks and troughs), frequency (the number of peaks per units of time), and phase (the angle of a wave at a point in time). Modulation changes one or more of those properties to encode a signal. Wi-Fi uses several modulation schemes, most of which are variations on **Quadrature Amplitude Modulation (QAM)** and **Phase Shift Keying (PSK)**. As well as modulation schemes, Wi-Fi standards use different **carrier methods** to provide sufficient resistance to interference from noise and other radio sources. Wi-Fi networking standards and products operate in the radio frequency bands **2.4 GHz** and **5 GHz**.

The original 802.11 Wi-Fi standard worked only at 1 Mbps, but like the 802.3 Ethernet standard, it has been revised many times, with each iteration specifying different signaling and transmission mechanisms. Products conforming to the various standards can be certified by the **Wi-Fi Alliance** (*wi-fi.org*).

CSMA/CA (COLLISION AVOIDANCE)

Wireless radio is a shared access medium (a physical bus). The 802.11 Wi-Fi standard uses **Carrier Sense Multiple Access with Collision Avoidance (CSMA/CA)** to cope with contention. **Carrier Sense Multiple Access with Collision Detection (CSMA/CD)** is unsuitable because wireless stations cannot detect whether a collision has occurred. Under CSMA/CA, when a station receives a frame, it performs error checking. If the frame is intact, the station responds with an acknowledgement (**ACK**). If the ACK is not received, the transmitting station resends the frame until timing out. 802.11 also defines a **Virtual Carrier Sense** flow control mechanism to further reduce the incidence of collisions. A station broadcasts a **Request to Send (RTS)** with the source and destination and the time required to transmit. The receiving station responds with a **Clear To Send (CTS)** and all other stations in range do not attempt to transmit within that period.

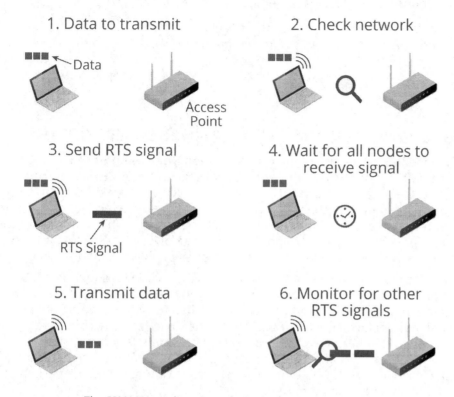

The CSMA/CA media access method. (Image © 123RF.com.)

FREQUENCIES (2.4 GHz AND 5 GHz)

Every wireless device operates on a specific radio frequency within an overall frequency band. It is important to understand the difference between the two frequency bands used by the IEEE 802.11 standards:

- **2.4 GHz** is better at propagating through solid surfaces, making it ideal for providing the longest signal range. However, the 2.4 GHz band does not support a high number of individual channels and is often congested, both with other Wi-Fi networks and other types of wireless technology, such as Bluetooth®. Consequently, with the 2.4 GHz band, there is increased risk of interference, and the maximum achievable data rates are typically lower than with 5 GHz.
- **5 GHz** is less effective at penetrating solid surfaces and so does not support the maximum ranges achieved with 2.4 GHz standards, but the band supports more individual channels and suffers less from congestion and interference, meaning it supports higher data rates at shorter ranges.

 *Note: The use of the relatively inefficient collision avoidance mechanisms means that actual useful data transferred (called **goodput**) is much less than the rated transfer speeds. The rate is also affected by range and interference.*

IEEE 802.11a AND 5 GHz CHANNEL BANDWIDTH

The **IEEE 802.11a** specification was released in 1999 and operated in parallel with 802.11b, though the latter proved more commercially successful. 802.11a specified use of the 5 GHz frequency band and a multiplexed carrier scheme called **Orthogonal**

Frequency Division Multiplexing (OFDM). The 5 GHz band is subdivided into 23 non-overlapping **channels**, each of which is 20 MHz wide. OFDM splits these channels into 52 x 312.5 kHz **sub-carriers**. The sub-carriers are used to transmit multiple signals simultaneously. The precise spacing of the different frequency sub-carrier bands minimizes interference. 802.11a has a nominal data rate of 54 Mbps.

 Note: Initially, there were 11 channels, but the subsequent 802.11h standard added another 12. 802.11h also adds the Dynamic Frequency Selection (DFS) method to prevent access points (APs) working in the 5 GHz band from interfering with radar and satellite signals. The exact use of channels can be subject to different regulation in different countries.

IEEE 802.11b/g AND 2.4 GHz CHANNEL BANDWIDTH

802.11b standardized the use of the carrier method **Direct Sequence Spread Spectrum (DSSS)**, along with **Complementary Code Keying (CCK)** signal encoding. DSSS divides the data into chips. Each chip is transmitted using a different frequency. The sequence of frequency changes is predetermined, and the receiver must be aware of this sequence so that it can reassemble the data correctly. While in some ways it was an inferior technology—with a nominal data rate of just 11 Mbps—802.11b products were quicker to market and became better established than 802.11a.

Unlike 802.11a, 802.11b works in the 2.4 GHz band. This band is subdivided into up to 14 channels, spaced at 5 MHz intervals from 2412 MHz up to 2484 MHz. Because the overall frequency range of the 2.4 GHz band is limited to 72 MHz, the channels have substantial overlap. Consequently, 802.11b channels overlap quite considerably, meaning that co-channel interference is a real possibility unless widely spaced channels are chosen (1, 6, and 11, for instance). Also, in the Americas, regulations permit the use of channels 1-11 only, while in Europe channels 1-13 are permitted, and in Japan all 14 channels are permitted.

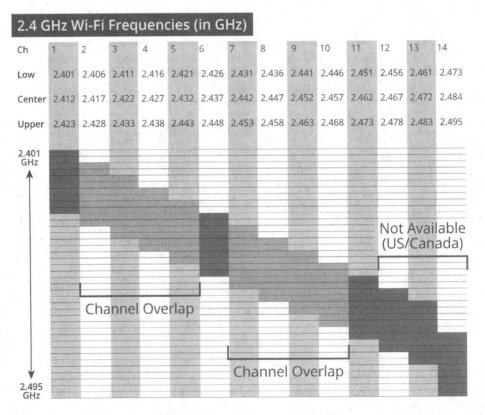

Channel overlap in the 2.4 GHz band.

The introduction of **802.11g** in 2003 offered a relatively straightforward upgrade path from 802.11b. Like 802.11a, 802.11g uses OFDM, but in the 2.4 GHz band used by 802.11b and with the same channel layout. This made it straightforward for vendors to offer 802.11g devices that could offer backwards support for legacy 802.11b clients. 802.11g has a nominal data rate of 54 Mbps. When in 802.11b compatibility mode, it drops back to using DSSS.

IEEE 802.11n, MIMO, AND CHANNEL BONDING

The **802.11n** standard increases bandwidth by multiplexing the signals from 2 to 4 separate antennas in a process called **Multiple Input Multiple Output (MIMO)**. The configuration of 802.11n devices is identified by AxB:C notation, where A is the number of transmit antennas, B is the number of receive antennas, and C is the number of simultaneous transmit and receive streams (spatial streams). The maximum possible is 4x4:4, but common configurations are 2x2:2 or 3x3:2. Having more transmit and receive streams than spatial streams helps to improve signal reliability, rather than boosting bandwidth. Both the transmitter and receiver must support the same number of streams.

802.11n can obtain more bandwidth with the option to use two adjacent 20 MHz channels as a single 40 MHz channel, referred to as **channel bonding**. 802.11n products can also use channels in the 2.4 GHz band or the 5 GHz band, though the 5 GHz band is preferred for optimal bandwidth and to avoid interference with existing 2.4 GHz networks and devices. On a network with multiple APs, channel bonding is a practical option only in the 5 GHz band. The 5 GHz band has a larger frequency range (up to 500 MHz in the USA), so it can provide up to 23 non-overlapping channels. However, those channels are not necessarily contiguous, which slightly reduces the options for bonded channels.

 Note: *Cheaper adapters may support only the 2.4 GHz band. An AP or adapter that can support both is referred to as **dual band**. A dual band AP can support both 2.4 GHz and 5 GHz bands simultaneously. This allows legacy clients to be allocated to the 2.4 GHz band.*

Assuming the maximum number of spatial streams and optimum conditions, the nominal data rates for 802.11n are 288.8 Mbps for a single channel and 600 Mbps for bonded channels. 802.11n can work in **High Throughput (HT)/greenfield mode** for maximum performance or **HT mixed mode** for compatibility with older standards (801.11a-ht, 802.11b-ht, and 802.11g-ht). Mixed mode reduces overall WLAN performance, as it involves the transmission of legacy identification and collision avoidance frames (HT protection) but not to the extent that 802.11n devices are reduced to (say) 802.11g data rates. Operating in greenfield mode is likely to cause substantial interference if there are legacy WLANs operating nearby on the same channel(s). There is also a legacy (non-HT) mode, in which 802.11n's HT mechanisms are disabled completely. You might use this mode if you have an 802.11n-capable access point but don't have any 802.11n client devices.

IEEE 802.11ac AND MU-MIMO

The **802.11ac** standard continues the development of 802.11n technologies. The main distinction is that 802.11ac works only in the 5 GHz band. The 2.4 GHz band can be used for legacy standards (802.11g/n) in mixed mode. The aim for 802.11ac is to get throughput like that of Gigabit Ethernet or better. It supports more channel bonding (up to 80 or 160 MHz channels), up to 8 spatial streams, rather than 4, and denser modulation (at close ranges).

	U-NII-1				U-NII-2				U-NII-2 Extended											U-NII-3			
20 MHz	36	40	44	48	52	56	60	64	100	104	108	112	116	120	124	128	132	136	140	149	153	157	161
40 MHz	38		46		54		62		102		110		118		126		134			151		159	
80 MHz	42				58				106				122							155			
160 MHz	50								114														

```
┌ ─ ─ ─ ─ ─ ─ ─ ─ ─ ─ ─ ─ ─ ─ ─ ─ ─ ─ ─ ─ ─ ─ ─ ─ ┐
        Dynamic Frequency Selection (DFS) Range
└ ─ ─ ─ ─ ─ ─ ─ ─ ─ ─ ─ ─ ─ ─ ─ ─ ─ ─ ─ ─ ─ ─ ─ ─ ┘
```

Bonded channel options in the 5 GHz Unlicensed National Information Infrastructure (U-NII) sub-bands. Channels within the DFS range may be disabled if the site is near a radar transmitter.

As with 802.11n, only high-end equipment will be equipped with enough antennas to make use of up to 8 streams. At the time of writing, no devices support more than 4x4:4 streams. The maximum theoretical data rate with 8 streams and 160 MHz channel bonding is about 6.93 Gbps. Cisco's Aironet 4800 4x4:4 APs support up to 5.2 Gbps with 160 MHz channels.

With the 802.11 standards, bandwidth is shared between all users because of the CSMA/CA contention protocol. An AP can communicate with only one station at a time; multiple station requests go into a queue. Second generation (or wave 2) 802.11ac products address this problem using **beamforming** or **Multiuser MIMO (MU-MIMO)**. MU-MIMO allows the AP to use its multiple antennas to process a **spatial stream** of signals in the direction of a particular station separately to other streams. This means that stations on a different alignment can connect simultaneously and also obtain more bandwidth. For example, if four stations are positioned north, south, east, and west of an AP, the AP should be able to allow each of them to connect at close to the maximum speed. If another station is added to the north, those two northern stations will share the available bandwidth along that beam path. Both stations and AP must support MU-MIMO. Only the AP can initiate beamforming, so it is only available on the downlink from AP to station (not station to AP).

INFRASTRUCTURE TOPOLOGY AND WIRELESS ACCESS POINTS

Most wireless networks are deployed in an **infrastructure topology**. In an infrastructure topology, each station is configured to connect through a **base station** or **access point (AP)**. The AP mediates communications between wireless stations and can also provide a bridge to a cabled network segment. In 802.11 documentation, this is referred to as a **Basic Service Set (BSS)**. The MAC address of the AP is used as the **Basic Service Set Identifier (BSSID)**. More than one BSS can be grouped together in an **Extended Service Set (ESS)**.

Wireless network devices are referred to as stations (STA), similar to a node on a wired network.

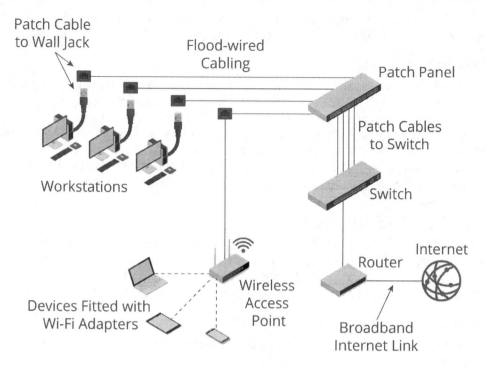

WLAN configuration in infrastructure mode. (Image © 123RF.com.)

The wireless access point (WAP) is normally attached to the LAN by using standard cabling and transmits and receives network traffic to and from wireless devices, acting as a **bridge**. Each client device requires a wireless adapter compatible with the standard(s) supported by the AP.

Cisco Aironet access point. (Image © 123RF.com.)

AD HOC AND MESH TOPOLOGIES

There are also wireless topologies that allow stations to establish peer-to-peer links.

AD HOC TOPOLOGY

In an **ad hoc topology**, the wireless adapter allows connections to and from other devices. In 802.11 documentation, this is referred to as an **Independent Basic Service Set (IBSS)**. This topology does not require an access point. All the stations within an ad hoc network must be within range of one another. An ad hoc network might suit a small workgroup of devices, or connectivity to a single device, such as a shared printer, but it is not scalable to large network implementations.

MESH TOPOLOGY

The **802.11s** standard defines a **Wireless Mesh Network (WMN)**. Unlike an ad hoc network, nodes in a WMN (called **mesh stations**) are capable of discovering one another and peering, forming a **Mesh Basic Service Set (MBSS)**. The mesh stations can perform path discovery and forwarding between peers using a routing protocol, such as the **Hybrid Wireless Mesh Protocol (HWMP)**. A mesh topology is more scalable than an ad hoc topology because the stations do not need to be within direct radio range of one another—a transmission can be relayed by intermediate stations.

WIRELESS SITE DESIGN

Clients join a WLAN through the network name known as the **Service Set Identifier (SSID)**. In infrastructure mode, when multiple APs are grouped into an ESS, this is more properly called the **Extended SSID (ESSID)**. This just means that all the APs are configured with the same SSID. The area served by a single AP is referred to as a **cell**.

SSID BROADCAST AND BEACON FRAME

Most WLANs advertise their presence by **broadcasting the SSID** to any listening clients. This allows a user to connect to a named network. If SSID broadcast is suppressed, the user must configure the connection to the network manually. A **beacon** is a special management frame broadcast by the AP to advertise the WLAN. The beacon frame contains the SSID (unless broadcast is disabled), supported data rates and signaling, plus encryption/authentication requirements. The interval at which the beacon is broadcast (measured in milliseconds) can be modified. The default is usually 100 ms. Increasing the interval reduces the overhead of broadcasting the frame but delays joining the network and can hamper roaming between APs.

 Note: *Even if SSID broadcast is suppressed, it is fairly easy for a network sniffer to detect it as clients still use it when connecting with the AP.*

SPEED AND DISTANCE REQUIREMENTS

A device supporting the Wi-Fi standard should have a maximum indoor range of up to about 30 m (100 feet), though the weaker the signal, the lower the data transfer rate. Each station determines an appropriate data rate based on the quality of the signal using a mechanism called **Dynamic Rate Switching/Selection (DRS)**. If the signal is strong, the station will select the highest available data rate (determined by the 802.11 standard); if the signal is weak, the station will reduce the data rate.

Radio signals pass through solid objects, such as ordinary brick or drywall walls, but can be weakened or blocked by particularly dense or thick material and metal. Other radio-based devices can also cause interference as can devices as various as fluorescent lighting, microwave ovens, cordless phones, and (in an industrial environment), power motors and heavy machinery. Bluetooth uses the 2.4 GHz frequency range but a different modulation technique, so interference is possible but not common.

Consequently, a complex set of factors need to be taken into consideration when you are planning a wireless network. A **site survey** is a critical planning tool to ensure that the WLAN delivers acceptable data rates to the supported number of devices in all the physical locations expected.

SITE SURVEYS AND HEAT MAPS

A **site survey** is performed first by examining the blueprints or floor plan of the premises to understand the layout and to identify features that might produce **radio frequency interference (RFI)**. This can be backed up by a visual inspection that may reveal things that are not shown on the blueprints, such as thick metal shelving surrounding a room that needs to have WLAN access. Each AP mounting point needs a network port and power jack, so it will help to obtain plans that show the locations of available ports.

 Note: *A switch that supports Power over Ethernet (PoE) can be used to power a PoE-compatible AP.*

The next step is to create a new plan on which you will mark the WLAN zones or cells and associated APs and booster antennas. The idea here to is to place APs close enough together to avoid "dead zones"—areas where connectivity is difficult or data transfer rates are below an acceptable tolerance level—but far enough apart that one AP does not interfere with another or that one AP is over-utilized and a nearby one under-utilized.

Position an AP in the first planned location, then use a laptop with a wireless adapter and a **wireless survey tool**, such as Cisco Aironet, Metageek inSSIDer, or Ekahau Site Survey, to record signal strength and supported data rate at various points in the intended WLAN zone. Many tools can show the signal strength obtained in different locations graphically using a **heat map**. The heat map would show areas with a strong signal in greens and yellows with warning oranges and reds where signal strength drops off (or conversely, red may indicate a strong signal, depending on the software). This step is then repeated for each planned location.

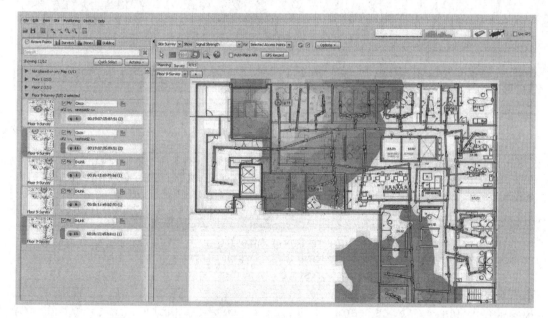

Heat map generated by Ekahau Site Survey. (Image © Ekahau Inc.)

The final step is to install the APs and connect them to the network. Then you should perform a final site survey and write up the baseline signal strength and transfer rates onto your WLAN plan. This gives you resource documentation that will help with the design of any extensions or modifications to the WLAN and assist with troubleshooting. For example, technicians can easily find out whether a user is actually within a zone intended for WLAN access or get them to move to a spot where signal strength is known to be good.

UNIDIRECTIONAL AND OMNIDIRECTIONAL ANTENNA TYPES

Most wireless devices have simple omnidirectional vertical rod-type **antennas**, which receive and send a signal in all directions more-or-less equally. Access points with **omnidirectional antennas** should ideally be ceiling-mounted for best coverage, unless the ceiling is particularly high. The propagation pattern is shaped like a torus (donut), rather than a sphere, and radiates more powerfully in the horizontal plane than it does in the vertical plane. Locating the antenna above head height will minimize interference from obstructing furniture by allowing line-of-sight to most connecting devices, but positioning it too high (above around 25 ft) will reduce signal strength, especially for stations directly below the antenna. You can obtain APs with downtilt omnidirectional antennas for use on high ceilings.

To extend the signal to a dead zone, you can use an antenna focused in a single direction (unidirectional). Both the sender and receiver must use directional antennas, or one will be able to receive signals but not send responses. **Unidirectional antenna** types include the **Yagi** (a bar with fins) and **parabolic** (dish or grid) form factors. Unidirectional antennas are useful for point-to-point connections (a **wireless bridge**). The increase in signal strength obtained by focusing the signal is referred to as the **gain** and is measured in **dBi** (decibel isotropic).

A variety of generic antenna types: from left to right, a vertical rod antenna, a Yagi antenna, a parabolic/dish antenna, and a parabolic grid antenna.

DISTRIBUTION SYSTEM (DS) ROAMING

Clients can **roam** between APs with the same SSID and security configuration when the APs are connected by a wired network, or Distribution System (DS). When the client detects that it is no longer receiving a good signal, it checks for another signal with the same SSID on other channels or on a different frequency band, and if there is a stronger signal, it disassociates from the current AP. The station can then reassociate with the new AP. Depending on the roaming infrastructure and security type, the station may have to reauthenticate, or if 802.11r fast roaming is supported, it may be able to use its existing authentication status to generate security properties for the new association.

Roaming is supposed to be seamless, but in practice re-establishing the connection can often cause time-out problems for applications. To improve mobility, there needs to be a balance between determining what constitutes a "good" signal and the frequency with which a client tries to associate with different APs. Many adapters support a roaming "aggressiveness" setting that can be configured to prevent a Wi-Fi adapter "flapping" between two APs or (conversely) to prevent a client remaining associated with a more distant AP when it could achieve better bandwidth through one closer to it.

WIRELESS DISTRIBUTION SYSTEMS (WDSs) AND WIRELESS RANGE EXTENDERS (WREs)

On a SOHO network, there is likely to be a single **SOHO wireless router** serving a home or small office. Very often, placement of this type of router is limited to the position of the demarc (or the point where the telephone company's wiring enters the property). SOHO networks are typically expanded using devices called **wireless range extenders (WREs)**, which are essentially lightweight APs functioning in repeater mode only. It is important that the extender receives a good signal from the main source. It is not usually possible to daisy chain extenders.

 Note: *For best performance, the range extender needs to match the specification of the source AP. Extenders should normally support both frequency bands (2.4 GHz and 5 GHz) and also support MU-MIMO if the access point does.*

When you are configuring the SSID for the WRE, initiate the setup wizard (if available), and when prompted for the SSID, enter the name identically to the original SSID of the AP or wireless router that is being extended. When you complete the configuration, the extender will then replicate that SSID when broadcasting the signal. The SSID for the extender is typically denoted as the original SSID appended by an additional character (or unique identifier) after the original SSID.

When you are determining the placement of a WAP or WRE, it is important to consider the location, distance from router, number of devices transmitting on the same frequency, and structural barriers (walls, floors, and ceilings). It is also important to understand the material used in the interior or exterior surfaces, and the cabling running through your walls. Best practice is to place the WAP or WRE in a centralized, open area away from other appliances or electronic devices such as TVs. If placing devices on different floors, ensure that they are in similar locations on each floor.

You can also configure multiple access points to cover a larger area. This is referred to as a **wireless distribution system (WDS)**. As with configuring extenders, you must set the APs to use the same channel, SSID, and security parameters. You need to put the APs into WDS/repeater mode. One AP is configured as a base station, while the others are configured as remote stations. The base station can be connected to a cabled segment. The remote stations must not be connected to cabled segments. The remote stations can accept connections from wireless stations and forward all traffic to the base station.

Another use for WDS is to bridge two separate cabled segments. When WDS is configured in bridge mode, the APs will not support wireless clients; they simply forward traffic between the cabled segments. You cannot use WREs for this bridging function.

 Note: *WDSs support and implementation can vary between manufacturers. If you are implementing WDS, it is usually best to use APs from the same vendor.*

WIRELESS CONTROLLERS

An enterprise network might require the use of tens or hundreds of APs, wireless bridges, and antennas. If APs are individually managed, this can lead to configuration errors on specific APs and can make it difficult to gain an overall view of the wireless deployment, including which clients are connected to which APs and which clients or APs are producing the most traffic.

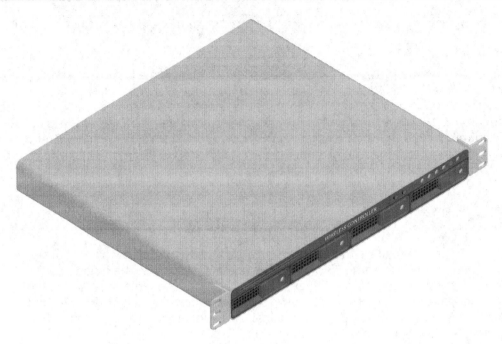

A wireless controller, an enterprise-level appliance capable of supporting up to 1500 APs and 20,000 clients. (Image © 123RF.com.)

Rather than configure each device individually, enterprise wireless solutions such as those manufactured by Cisco, Ruckus, or Ubiquiti allow for centralized management and monitoring of the APs on the network. This may be achieved through use of a dedicated hardware device (a **wireless controller**), which typically implements the required functionality through additional firmware in a network switch. Alternatively, some implementations use a software application to centralize the management function, which can be run on a server or workstation.

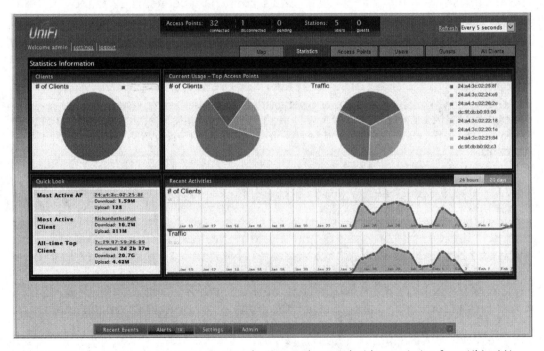

UniFi Wireless Network management console. (Screenshot used with permission from Ubiquiti.)

An AP whose firmware contains enough processing logic to be able to function autonomously and handle clients without the use of a wireless controller is known as a

fat AP, while one that requires a wireless controller in order to function is known as a **thin AP**. Cisco wireless controllers usually communicate with the APs by using the **Lightweight Access Point Protocol (LWAPP)**. LWAPP allows an AP configured to work in lightweight mode to download an appropriate SSID, standards mode, channel, and security configuration. Alternatives to LWAPP include the derivative **Control And Provisioning of Wireless Access Points (CAPWAP)** protocol or a proprietary protocol.

As well as autoconfiguring the appliances, a wireless controller can aggregate client traffic and provide a central switching and routing point between the WLAN and wired LAN. It can also assign clients to separate VLANs. Automated **VLAN pooling** ensures that the total number of stations per VLAN is kept within specified limits, reducing excessive broadcast traffic. Another function is to supply power to wired access points, using Power over Ethernet (PoE).

*Note: To learn more, watch the related **Video** on the course website.*

GUIDELINES FOR IMPLEMENTING A BASIC WIRELESS NETWORK

IMPLEMENT A BASIC WIRELESS NETWORK

By considering several key factors of wireless network installation, along with the cost of implementing and maintaining a secure wireless network, a network professional both demonstrates the proper installation methods and ensures maximum network functionality. To implement a basic wireless network, follow these guidelines:

- Create a list of requirements for your network so that you can work toward meeting them. These requirements may include how many users need to connect, the physical area it will need to cover, external connections, and more.
- Consider the devices you will need and any compatibility requirements they have, in terms of Wi-Fi standards support. Consider the environmental limitations such as the amount of ventilation for a network closet or access to power that can affect your network.
- Choose the appropriate 802.11 technology for your needs, such as 802.11a, b, g, n, and ac and whether to configure compatibility modes to support legacy clients.
- Choose the appropriate AP placement locations for your network.

  - Obtain a scale drawing of the building. This will assist you in all areas of AP placement.
  - Determine the range of the AP for the wireless technology you have chosen. This will help you to better determine how many APs you will need to ensure adequate coverage for the space.
  - Balance the number of users who will have access to the AP, and ensure that the AP can cover all employees in the range of the AP. More employees in a given area means more APs.
  - Tour the area in the range of the AP, and check to see if there are any devices that will interfere with the wireless network. This can include devices such as microwave ovens, Bluetooth-enabled devices, or an existing wireless network—whether from a community network, a neighboring building, or another floor of your company's building. These devices or networks can possibly interfere with your new implementation.

- Ensure that there are no obstacles in the path of the AP, such as doors, closed windows, walls, and furniture, that the wireless signal will need to pass through on its way to a client. If there are too many obstacles in the path, adjust the placement of your AP accordingly.
- Consider bringing in a consultant to help with the site survey, especially if you do not have access to someone who has good knowledge of wireless networks. The survey may include a heat map.
- Install the APs. The specific steps for installing the AP will vary by vendor, but the common steps may include:
  - Connecting the AP to the cabled network (distribution system) via a switch.
  - Configuring the DHCP service as appropriate. A standalone AP could act as the DHCP server for the wireless network. Alternatively, clients could obtain a lease from a DHCP server on the cabled network.
  - Configuring the appropriate encryption schemes.
  - Configuring frequency bands and channel layout within each frequency band.
  - Setting the SSID/ESSID and an 802.11 beacon.
  - If necessary, creating a MAC filtering ACL. The ACL contains a list of users who have access to the wireless network.
  - Configuring the network adapters of the devices that will connect to the AP.
- Test to ensure that the installation is appropriately sized, secure, and operational. Make sure these tests are done under real world conditions so that you have an accurate test.
- Perform period site surveys to check current performance and compare it to previous performance levels from previous site surveys.
- Document the steps and establish a baseline for future installations.

Activity 13-1
Discussing Wireless Technologies

SCENARIO
Answer the following questions to test your understanding of the content covered in this topic.

1. **What mechanism does RTS/CTS support?**

2. **Which IEEE WLAN standards specify a data transfer rate of up to 54 Mbps?**

3. **What options may be available for an 802.11n network that are not supported under 802.11g?**

4. **True or False? Stations with 802.11ac capable adapters must be assigned to the 5 GHz frequency band.**

5. **What is MU-MIMO?**

6. **Which frequency band is less likely to suffer from co-channel interference?**

7. **What is a BSSID?**

8. **What are the advantages of deploying a wireless mesh topology over an ad hoc one?**

9. **True or False? Suppressing transmission of the WLAN beacon improves security.**

10. **What constraints should you consider when planning the placement of an AP?**

11. **What is a heat map?**

12. **You are planning WLAN for an office building with an attached warehouse. Where would you recommend placing Wi-Fi antennas for the best coverage in an office full of cubicles as well as in the warehouse?**

13. **What type of AP requires a wireless controller?**

Topic B

Troubleshoot Wireless Performance Issues

EXAM OBJECTIVES COVERED
5.2 Given a scenario, use the appropriate tool.
5.4 Given a scenario, troubleshoot common wireless connectivity and performance issues.

Users have multiple devices that typically connect to the network through wireless connections. This can include smartphones, tablets, and laptop computers. Often, the wireless connection is used not only by internal employees, but also by vendors and visitors to the organization who need to access online information. In this topic, you will examine some of the wireless connectivity and performance issues that may occur on your network. Knowing how to resolve connectivity and performance issues for your wireless users will keep those users satisfied and connected.

WIRELESS CONNECTIVITY AND PERFORMANCE ISSUES

Wireless issues can be broadly divided into issues with signal strength or interference (like cabling issues in a wired LAN) and configuration issues. You will look at configuration issues later, but always check that the security and authentication parameters are correctly configured before assuming you have a Physical layer connectivity problem.

The signal from radio-based devices weakens considerably as the distance between the devices increases (**attenuation**). In case of signal loss, or if the data rate is low, try moving the devices closer together. As the distance from the antenna increases, the strength of the signal decreases in accordance with the inverse-square rule. For example, doubling the distance decreases the signal strength by a factor of four. Meanwhile, interference sources collectively overlay a competing background signal, referred to as noise. These factors impose **distance limitations** on the position of a client and AP.

On a WLAN adapter, the **Received Signal Strength Indicator (RSSI)** shows how strong the signal from the transmitter is. RSSI is a relative indicator, usually expressed as a percentage of a nominal "perfect" signal. RSSI can be calculated differently as it is implemented by the chipset vendor. Survey tools measure signal strength in dBm, which is the ratio of the measured signal to 1 milliwatt. When you are measuring signal strength, dBm will be a negative value with values closer to zero representing better performance. A value around -65 dBm represents a good signal, while anything over -80 dBm is likely to suffer packet loss or be dropped.

The received signal strength must also exceed the noise level by a decent margin. The comparative strength of the data signal to the background noise is called the **Signal-To-Noise Ratio (SNR)**. This figure should be at least 25 dB or higher. Noise is also measured in dBm, but here values closer to 0 are less welcome as they represent higher noise levels. For example, if signal is -65 dBm and noise is -90 dBm, the SNR is 25 dB; if noise is -80 dBm, the SNR is 15 dB and the connection will be much, much worse.

RSSI and SNR can be measured by using a **Wi-Fi analyzer**. This type of software can be installed to a laptop or smartphone. It will record statistics for the AP that the client is currently associated with and detect any other access points in the vicinity.

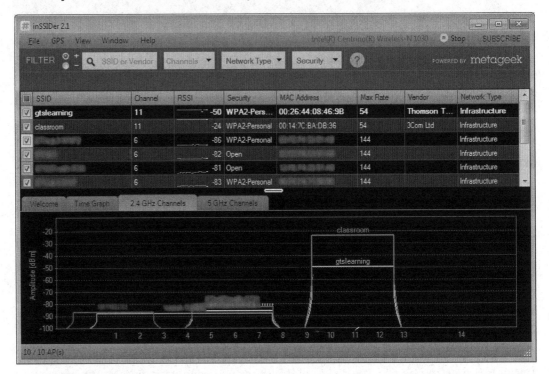

Surveying Wi-Fi networks using inSSIDer. The chart shows which channels are active and the signal strength of different networks in each channel. (Screenshot used with permission from MetaGeek.)

If a sufficient signal strength cannot be obtained and sources of interference cannot be mitigated, the only solution to a distance limitation issue is to install an additional device to cover the dead zone. If you cannot extend the distribution system (cabled network) to support an additional access point, you will need to configure a wireless bridge or use a range extender.

 Note: *If a device has removable antennas, check that these are screwed in firmly. A loose or disconnected antenna may reduce the range of the device or prevent connectivity altogether.*

CHANNEL OVERLAP AND POWER LEVEL ISSUES

One of the design goals for a multi-AP site is to create clean cells so that clients can select an AP with the strongest signal easily and the WLAN operates with a minimum of **Co-Channel Interference (CCI)**. At least 25 MHz spacing should be allowed to avoid **channel overlap**. In practice, therefore, no more than three nearby 802.11b/g APs can have non-overlapping channels. This could be implemented, for example, by selecting channel 1 for AP1, channel 6 for AP2, and channel 11 for AP3. When you are using the 5 GHz band for 802.11a or 802.11n/ac, more non-overlapping channels are available.

In a complex environment, it may be necessary to adjust the **power level** used by an AP on a given channel. Using the maximum available power on an AP can result in it interfering with other "cells" and in situations where a client can "hear" the AP but cannot "talk" to it because it lacks sufficient power.

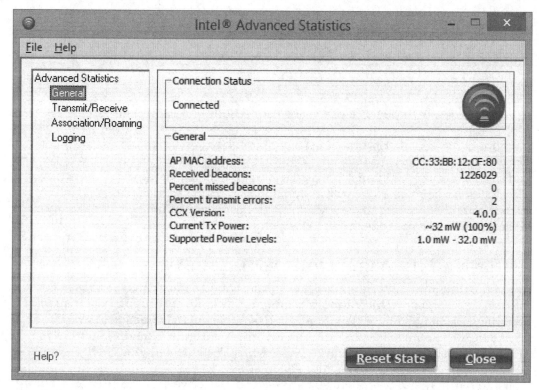

Checking power levels on a wireless station using Intel's PROSet Wi-Fi configuration utility. (Screenshot courtesy of Intel Corp.)

You should also be aware of legal restrictions on power output. These can vary from country to country.

INTERFERENCE, LATENCY, AND JITTER ISSUES

If a device is within the supported range but the signal is very weak or you cannot get a connection, there is likely to be **interference**. Apart from co-channel interference described earlier, there are several other sources of interference to consider:

- **Reflection/bounce** (multipath interference)—Mirrors or shiny surfaces cause signals to reflect, meaning that a variable delay is introduced. This causes packets to be lost and consequently the data rate to drop.

     Note: 802.11n/ac actually uses bounce (multipath) as a means of optimizing throughput via MIMO.

- **Refraction**—Glass or water can cause radio waves to bend and take a different path to the receiver. This can also cause the data rate to drop.
- **Absorption**—This refers to the degree to which walls and windows will reduce signal strength (some of the radio wave's energy is lost as heat when passing through construction materials). An internal wall might "cost" 3 to 15 dB, depending on the material used (concrete being the most effective absorber). The 2.4 GHz frequency has better penetration than the 5 GHz one, given the same power output. To minimize absorption from office furniture (and people), use ceiling-mounted APs.
- **Electromagnetic interference (EMI)**—Interference from a powerful radio or electromagnetic source working in the same frequency band, such as a Bluetooth device, cordless phone, or microwave oven. EMI can be detected by using a **spectrum analyzer**. Unlike a Wi-Fi analyzer, a spectrum analyzer must use a special radio receiver—Wi-Fi adapters filter out anything that isn't a Wi-Fi signal. They are

usually supplied as handheld units with a directional antenna, so that the exact location of the interference can be pinpointed.

> *Note: Also consider that signal problems could be a result of someone trying to attack the network by jamming the legitimate AP and making clients connect to a rogue AP.*

As well as reducing throughput or making connections unreliable, interference problems might cause performance problems, such as latency and jitter. **Latency** is a measure of the Round-Trip Time (RTT) of individual packets while **jitter** is a variable delay in the RTT of packets. Real-time applications such as VoIP are sensitive to latency and jitter, as they result in poor call quality or lags in media streaming. The nature of the wireless radio medium, as well as additional layers of security, makes it high latency compared to a wired network. Interference factors or long distances between AP and station will make the problems worse.

ANTENNA TYPE AND PLACEMENT ISSUES

Any of the distance or interference problems described earlier could be caused by or exacerbated by **incorrect antenna placement**. Use a site survey and heat map to determine the optimum position for APs and (if available) the direction in which to point adjustable antennas. Also, using an **incorrect antenna type** may adversely affect the signal strength at any given point. A unidirectional antenna is only suitable for point-to-point connections, not for general client access. The internal antennas built into APs may also be optimized to transmit and receive in some directions more than others. For example, an AP designed for ceiling mounting may produce a stronger signal in a cone directed downwards from its central axis, whereas the signal from a similar AP designed for wall installation is more likely to be angled outwards. Consult the documentation for your specific model of AP, or use site survey software to produce a heat map.

FREQUENCY MISMATCH ISSUES

To connect to an AP, a station must be able to match the standards compatibility and frequency selection configured on the AP. The most likely cause of a frequency mismatch is where the AP is configured for 5 GHz operation, but a station does not have a 5 GHz radio, as is the case with some of the cheaper 802.11n adapters. Ideally, this problem would be solved by upgrading client adapters. If this is not possible, configure APs working in the 2.4 GHz band and (if necessary) enable support for legacy 802.11b/g/n standards.

> *Note: With 802.11n dual-band APs operating in mixed mode, it is typical to assign the 2.4 GHz frequency band to support legacy clients. The 5 GHz band can be reserved for 802.11n clients, and bonded channels can be configured. With 802.11ac deployed, all legacy clients (including 802.11n) should be assigned to the 2.4 GHz band.*

With compatibility mode enabled, when an older device joins the network, the **throughput** of the whole WLAN can be affected. To support 802.11b clients, an 802.11b/n access point must transmit legacy frame preamble and collision avoidance frames, adding overhead. If possible, upgrade 802.11b devices, rather than letting them join the WLAN. 802.11g and 802.11n are more compatible in terms of negotiating collision avoidance. In a mixed 802.11g/n WLAN, performance of the 802.11n devices operating in the 2.4 GHz band is likely to be severely impacted only when 802.11g devices perform large file transfers. As these take longer to complete, there is less "airtime" available for the 802.11n clients.

Check that the client is configured to use the correct channel. Normally, this is auto-detected by the client, but verify that the configured channel/frequency is available for the chosen Wi-Fi standard. Remember that not all channels are available in all countries. For 802.11n/ac, if a client device is not achieving the expected throughput or distance, check that the client and APs support the same MIMO configuration. On the AP, check that the antennas are properly screwed down, as loose or disconnected antennas will affect the connection. You might be able to obtain a better signal by reorienting the antennas, but check that this does not weaken the signal too much in other areas.

It could also be the case that an AP is using a channel that is not supported by the station. As mentioned earlier, licensing and regulation of the radio spectrum means that channel support can vary from country to country. Some client adapters may not have the ability to use channels on the edge of the frequency band.

OVERCAPACITY ISSUES

Overcapacity (or **device saturation**) occurs when too many client devices connect to the same AP. The maximum number of clients that an AP can support varies, depending on the Wi-Fi standard used and the type of network traffic generated. For example, web browsing will typically place a lighter load on the network than local client-server traffic or is likely at least to move any bottleneck further upstream to the WAN, rather than the wireless network. While individual circumstances must be considered, a maximum of 30 clients per AP is generally accepted as a rule of thumb. In designing the network, enough APs should be provided in appropriate locations to support the expected client density at this ratio. APs can usually be configured to enforce a maximum number of connections, so that additional clients will connect to the next nearest AP. Even with a relatively low number of clients, the wireless network can suffer from **bandwidth saturation**. Since wireless is a broadcast medium, the available bandwidth is shared between all clients. Thus, if one client is a bandwidth hog, others may find it difficult to maintain a reliable connection.

In an enterprise Wi-Fi solution, a controller will normally provide reporting tools to diagnose bandwidth issues and to report on which clients are consuming the most bandwidth. It could also report on **wireless channel utilization** and configure APs and clients to reassign channels dynamically to reduce overutilization. If a traffic shaper is deployed, it may work automatically to throttle bandwidth to overactive nodes.

 Note: *To learn more, watch the related* **Video** *on the course website.*

Activity 13-2
Discussing Wireless Performance Issues

SCENARIO
Answer the following questions to test your understanding of the content covered in this topic.

1. **The lobby area of your office building has undergone a renovation, the centerpiece of which is a large aquarium in the middle of the room, separating a visitor seating and greeting area from the reception desks, where the AP facilitating guest Internet access is located. Since the renovation, many guests have been unable to connect to Wi-Fi from the seating area. Could the aquarium really be the cause, and what solution could you recommend?**

2. **Widget Corporation has provided wireless access for its employees using several APs located in different parts of the building. Employees connect to the network using 802.11g-compatible network cards. On Thursday afternoon, several users report that they cannot log on to the network. What troubleshooting step would you take first?**

3. **Your office block is hosting a conference event. During the morning coffee break, several guests report that they cannot access their webmail. What is the likely cause?**

4. **What is the difference between a Wi-Fi analyzer and a spectrum analyzer?**

5. **Users in the corner of an office building cannot get good Wi-Fi reception. Your office manager doesn't want to use his budget to purchase a new AP. He's noticed that the power level control on the AP is set to 3 out of 5 and wants to know why turning up the power isn't the best solution?**

6. **Users in a warehouse facility report intermittent connectivity problems with the network inventory software as they move in and out of the tall metal storage shelving. The warehouse is served by a single, centrally located AP, positioned on the ceiling. What problem do you suspect? Document your answer.**

Topic C

Secure and Troubleshoot Wireless Connectivity

 EXAM OBJECTIVES COVERED
4.3 Given a scenario, secure a basic wireless network.
4.4 Summarize common networking attacks.
5.4 Given a scenario, troubleshoot common wireless connectivity and performance issues.

In this topic, you will examine ways to secure a wireless network. With the rise in popularity of mobile devices that connect to wireless networks, it has become paramount that the wireless network remains secure, as anyone who is nearby might try to connect to the network if they see it.

WIRELESS SECURITY AND WAR DRIVING

As unguided or **unbounded media**, WLANs are subject to **data emanation**, or signal leakage. On a WLAN, there is no simple way to limit the signal within defined boundaries. It will propagate to the extent of the antenna's transmission range, unless blocked by some sort of shielding or natural barrier. Data emanation means that packet sniffing a WLAN is trivially easy if you can get within range.

War driving is the practice of driving around with a wireless-enabled laptop scanning for unsecure WLANs. It is straightforward to eavesdrop on WLAN communications that have not been secured by encryption. Therefore, the crucial step in enforcing wireless security is to enable encryption. There are three encryption schemes: WEP, WPA, and WPA2.

WIRED EQUIVALENT PRIVACY (WEP)

Wired Equivalent Privacy (WEP) is Wi-Fi's original security mechanism. While it is supported on both old and new devices, the encryption system (based on the RC4 encryption cipher) is flawed. The flaws in WEP allow attackers using **WEP cracking** tools, such as Aircrack-NG (*aircrack-ng.org*) or AirSnort (*airsnort.soft112.com*), to decrypt and eavesdrop traffic.

WEP is not safe to use. If devices support only WEP, the best alternative is to enhance the connection security with another security application, such as IPSec.

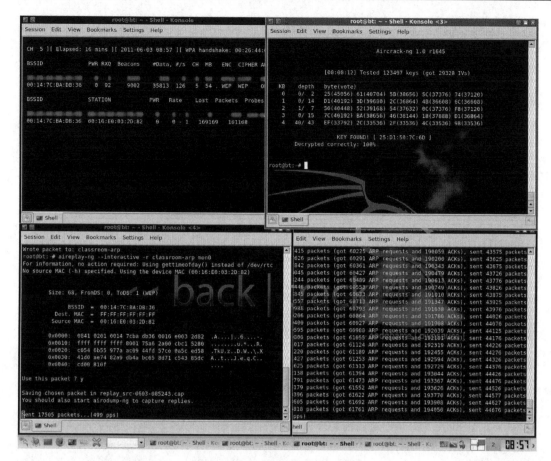

Aireplay sniffs ARP packets to harvest IVs while Airodump saves them to a capture, which Aircrack can analyze to identify the correct encryption key.

WI-FI PROTECTED ACCESS (WPA)

The first version of **Wi-Fi Protected Access (WPA)** was designed to fix the security problems with WEP. Version 1 of WPA still uses the RC4 cipher, but it adds a mechanism called the **Temporal Key Integrity Protocol (TKIP)** to make it stronger.

WPA2 is fully compliant with the 802.11i WLAN security standard. The main difference to the original iteration of WPA is the use of **Advanced Encryption Standard (AES)** for encryption. AES is stronger than RC4/TKIP. AES is deployed within the **Counter Mode with Cipher Block Chaining Message Authentication Code Protocol (CCMP)**. AES replaces RC4, and CCMP replaces TKIP. The only reason not to use WPA2 is if it is not supported by adapters, APs, or operating systems on the network. In many cases, devices will be compatible with a firmware or driver upgrade.

WPA and WPA2 are both much more secure than WEP, though a serious vulnerability was discovered in 2017 (*krackattacks.com*), so you should continue to ensure that device firmware is patched against exploits such as this.

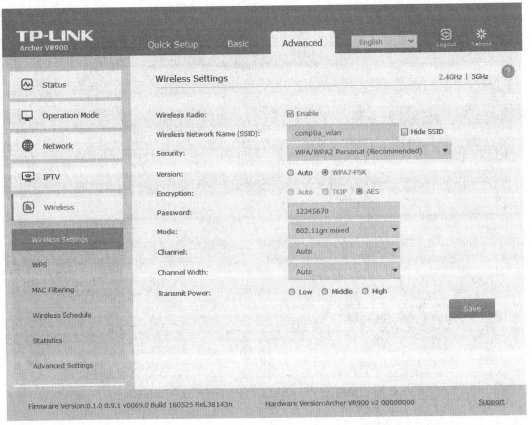

Configuring a TP-LINK SOHO access point with encryption and authentication settings. (Screenshot used with permission from TP-Link.)

Note: *To learn more, watch the related* **Video** *on the course website.*

PRE-SHARED KEY AUTHENTICATION

To secure a network, you need to be able to confirm that only valid users are connecting to it. WLAN authentication comes in three types: pre-shared key, enterprise, and open.

Implementing authentication with a **pre-shared key (PSK)** means using a passphrase to generate the key that is used to encrypt communications. It is also referred to as **group authentication** because a group of users share the same secret. A PSK is generated from a passphrase, which is like a long password. In WPA-PSK, the user enters a passphrase of between 8 and 63 ASCII characters. This is converted to a 256-bit hash (expressed as a 64-character hex value).

Note: *It is critical that PSK passphrases be long (12 characters or more) and complex (contain a mixture of upper- and lowercase letters and digits, and no dictionary words or common names). The passphrase generates a 256-bit master key (MK), which is used to generate the 128-bit temporal key (TK) used for RC4/TKIP or AES/CCMP packet encryption.*

The main problem is that distribution of the key or passphrase cannot be secured properly, and users may choose unsecure phrases. It also fails to provide accounting, as all users share the same key. The advantage is that it is simple to set up. Conversely, changing the key periodically, as would be good security practice, is difficult.

PSK is the only type of authentication available for WEP and is suitable for SOHO networks and workgroups that use WPA or WPA2.

IEEE 802.1X ENTERPRISE AUTHENTICATION

WPA and WPA2 can also implement 802.1X, which uses **Extensible Authentication Protocol (EAP)** authentication. The AP passes authentication information to a RADIUS server on the wired network for validation. The authentication information could be a username and password or could employ smart cards or tokens. This allows WLAN authentication to be integrated with the wired LAN authentication scheme. This type of authentication is suitable for enterprise networks.

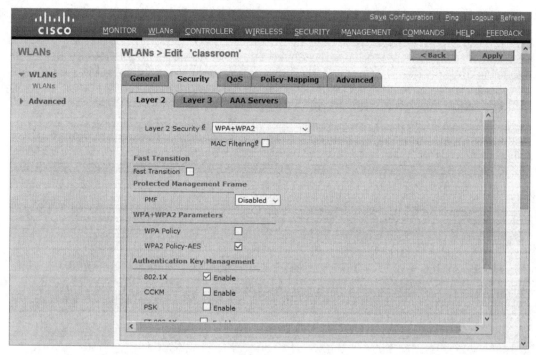

Using Cisco's Virtual Wireless LAN Controller to set security policies for a WLAN—This policy enforces use of WPA2 and the use of 802.1X (Enterprise) authentication. (Image © and Courtesy of Cisco Systems, Inc. Unauthorized use not permitted.)

The EAP framework involves three components:

- **Supplicant**—The client requesting authentication.
- **Authenticator**—The device that receives the authentication request. In this context, the authenticator is the wireless AP. The authenticator establishes a channel for the supplicant and authentication server to exchange credentials using the EAP over LAN (EAPoL) protocol. It blocks any other traffic.
- **Authentication Server**—The server that performs the authentication (typically a RADIUS or TACACS+ server).

EAP can be configured in different modes:

- **EAP-TLS** is currently considered the strongest type of authentication and is very widely supported. An encrypted Transport Layer Security (TLS) tunnel is established between the supplicant and authentication server using public key certificates on the authentication server and supplicant. As both supplicant and server are configured with certificates, this provides **mutual authentication**.
- **Protected Extensible Authentication Protocol (PEAP)** also uses an encrypted tunnel, but PEAP requires only a server-side public key certificate. The supplicant does not require a certificate. With the server authenticated to the supplicant, user authentication can then take place through the secure tunnel with protection against sniffing, password-guessing/dictionary, and MitM attacks.

- **Flexible Authentication via Secure Tunneling (EAP-FAST)** is similar to PEAP, but instead of using a certificate to set up the tunnel, it uses a Protected Access Credential (PAC), which is generated for each user from the authentication server's master key. The problem with EAP-FAST is in distributing (provisioning) the PAC securely to each user requiring access. The PAC can either be distributed via an out-of-band method or via a server with a digital certificate, but in the latter case, EAP-FAST does not offer much advantage over using PEAP. EAP-FAST does offer advantages in terms of seamless roaming between APs.

OPEN AUTHENTICATION AND CAPTIVE PORTALS

Selecting **open authentication** means that the client is not required to authenticate. Put another way, the network is shared with anyone who wants to join it without requiring any sort of key or password. This mode would be used on a public AP (or **hotspot**). This also means that data sent over the link is unencrypted. Open authentication may be combined with a secondary authentication mechanism managed via a browser. When the client associates with the open hotspot and launches the browser, the client is redirected to a **captive portal** or **splash page**. This will allow the client to authenticate to the hotspot provider's network (over HTTPS so the login is secure). The portal may also be designed to enforce terms and conditions and/or take payment to access the Wi-Fi service.

 Note: *Enterprise networks can also use captive portals to ensure clients meet a security health policy.*

When they are using open wireless, users must ensure they send confidential web data only over HTTPS connections and use email, VoIP, IM, and file transfer services only with SSL/TLS enabled. Another option is for the user to join a **virtual private network (VPN)**. The user would associate with the open hotspot then start the VPN connection. This creates an encrypted tunnel between the user's computer and the VPN server. This allows the user to browse the web or connect to email services without anyone eavesdropping on the open Wi-Fi network being able to intercept those communications. The VPN could be provided by the user's company, or they could use a third-party VPN service provider. Of course, if a third-party VPN is used, the user needs to be able to trust them implicitly. The VPN must use certificate-based tunneling to set up the inner authentication method.

MAC FILTERING AND GEOFENCING WLAN ACCESS

MAC filtering is an additional authorization mechanism that involves specifying which MAC addresses are permitted to connect to the AP. This can be done by configuring a list of valid MAC addresses, but this static method is difficult to keep current and is relatively error prone. It is also easy for a wireless sniffer to discover valid MAC addresses and spoof them. Enterprise-class APs (or wireless controllers) allow you to specify a limit to the number of permitted addresses and automatically learn a set number of valid MAC addresses.

Another option is to put a firewall behind the AP in order to filter traffic passing between the wired LAN and WLAN.

Geofencing means using the location services built into mobile devices to configure policies that are specific to the user's precise physical location. Location services can use a mix of methods to determine the device's physical location, including using the Global Positioning System (GPS) receiver and triangulating signal strength from known APs, or detecting Bluetooth beacons. One typical use of geofencing is to disable a device's passcode lock when the device is in range of its "home" AP.

In theory, geofencing could be used as an access control mechanism to block anyone using a device outside the site perimeter from connecting to the wireless network. In practice, this approach is fraught with difficulties, not least because many client devices do not support GPS-based location services and would have to be excluded from the policy. It's also the case that GPS is not completely reliable when used indoors, so any GPS-based access policy is likely to produce numerous support queries.

 Note: The other thing to remember about making your WLAN difficult to connect to is that it makes it easier for an adversary to set up an evil twin.

Another approach is for geolocation to be leveraged by **mobile device management (MDM)** and data loss prevention (DLP) systems so that corporate data on a mobile device is locked down when the device moves out of range of the enterprise network boundaries.

WRONG SSID OR PASSPHRASE ISSUES

While signal loss and interference are factors on larger networks, if there is a basic connectivity problem, then you will probably want to investigate the configuration of the client and/or AP first. If SSID broadcast is suppressed, a station can still connect to it by entering the network name manually. If this is the case, check that the clients are configured with the correct SSID/ESSID. Remember that this value is case sensitive. Technically, an SSID can contain spaces, but this can cause problems so is best avoided. Check that the authentication settings are the same on all devices. If a PSK is used, make sure it is entered correctly. On the AP, ensure the authentication type is not set to open, unless the intention is to provide unrestricted public access.

 Note: It is possible that two APs are operating with the same SSID. If authentication is required, the connection with the wrong SSID will fail. If there is no authentication (open network), then the host will connect but take care, as this may be an attempt to snoop on the host's traffic using a rogue AP. Also, if a user is joining a WLAN for the first time, it may be the case that there are SSIDs from overlapping WLANs with very similar default names and the user may be confused about which name to choose.

If the user is definitely supplying the correct key or credentials, check that the client can support the encryption and authentication standards configured on the AP—a driver update or OS patch may be required. A **security type mismatch** will cause the connection to fail, even if the correct credentials are supplied.

EVIL TWINS AND ROGUE APs

If scans or network logs show that unauthorized devices are connecting, determine whether the problem is an AP with misconfigured or weak security or whether there is some sort of rogue AP. A **rogue AP** is one that has been installed on the network without authorization, whether with malicious intent or not. A malicious user can set up such an AP with something as basic as a smartphone with tethering capabilities, and a non-malicious user could enable such an AP by accident. If connected to a LAN without security, an unauthorized AP creates a very welcoming backdoor through which to attack the network. A rogue AP could also be used to capture user logon attempts, allow MitM attacks, and allow access to private information.

A rogue AP masquerading as a legitimate one is called an **evil twin** or sometimes **Wiphishing**. An evil twin might have a similar name (SSID) to the legitimate one. For example, an evil twin might be configured with the network name "compeny" where the legitimate network name is "company." Alternatively, the evil twin might match the SSID, channel ID, and other properties of the valid network and then the attacker might use some DoS technique to overcome the legitimate AP. After a successful DoS attack, the users will be forced to disconnect from the network and then manually attempt to re-connect. At that point, with many users busy and trying to get back to work, some or all may associate with the evil twin AP and submit the network passphrase or their credentials for authentication.

However it is configured, when a user connects to an evil twin, it might be able to harvest authentication information and, if it is able to provide wider network or Internet access, snoop on connections established with servers or websites.

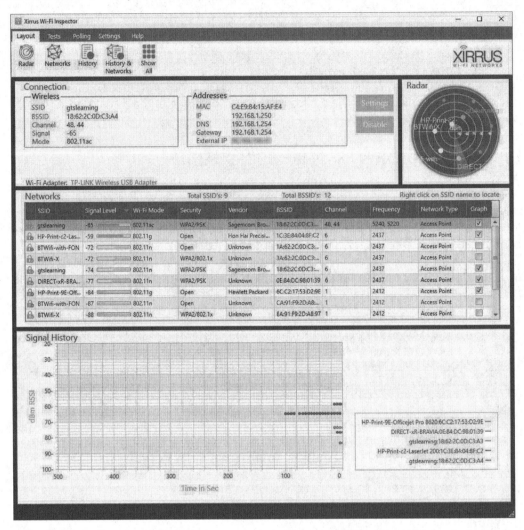

Surveying Wi-Fi networks using Xirrus Wi-Fi Inspector (xirrus.com)—Note the presence of print devices configured with open authentication (no security) and a smart TV appliance (requiring authentication). (Screenshot used with permission from Xirrus.)

One solution is to use EAP-TLS security so that the authentication server and clients perform mutual authentication. There are also various scanners and monitoring systems that can detect rogue APs, including AirMagnet (*enterprise.netscout.com/ products/airmagnet-survey*), inSSIDer (*metageek.com/products/inssider*), Kismet (*kismetwireless.net*), and Xirrus Wi-Fi Inspector (*xirrus.com*). Another option is a **wireless intrusion detection system (WIDS)** or **wireless intrusion prevention system (WIPS)**. As well as rogue access points, WIPSs can detect and prevent attacks against WLAN security, such as **MAC spoofing** and DoS.

DEAUTHENTICATION/DISASSOCIATION ATTACKS

The use of a rogue AP may be coupled with a **deauthentication** attack. This sends a stream of spoofed deauth frames to cause a client to deauthenticate from an AP. This might allow the attacker to interpose the rogue AP or to sniff information about the authentication process (such as a non-broadcast ESSID).

A similar attack hits the target with **disassociation** packets, rather than fully deauthenticating the station. A disassociated station is not completely disconnected, but neither can it communicate on the network until it reassociates. Both attacks may also be used to perform a DoS attack against the wireless infrastructure. These attacks work against both WEP and WPA. The attacks can be mitigated if the wireless infrastructure supports Management Frame Protection (MFP/802.11w). Both the AP and clients must be configured to support MFP.

 Note: *To learn more, watch the related **Video** on the course website.*

Activity 13-3
Discussing Wireless Security

SCENARIO
Answer the following questions to test your understanding of the content covered in this topic.

---

1. **What is the main difference between WPA and WPA2?**

2. **Why might an attacker launch a DoS attack against a WAP?**

3. **What type of enterprise authentication scheme uses server-side certificates to protect the user authentication credential?**

4. **John is given a laptop for official use and is on a business trip. When he arrives at his hotel, he turns on his laptop and finds a WAP with the name of the hotel, which he connects to for sending official communications. He may become a victim of which wireless threat?**

   ○ Interference

   ○ War driving

   ○ Bluesnarfing

   ○ Rogue access point

5. **Your company has a lobby area where guest access is provided so that visitors can get Internet access. The open guest WLAN is currently connected to the production network. The only protection against visitors and hackers getting into the organization's data is file and directory rights. What steps should be taken to provide guest access and better protect the organization's data?**

_____

Activity 13-4

Configuring a Wireless Router

BEFORE YOU BEGIN
Complete this activity on the **HOST** PC. You will need an Internet connection to access the emulator.

SCENARIO
The network administrator informs you that the wireless network is not as secure as it should be. Many of the employees in the branch office are mobile users, and they need to connect to the company network and the Internet through devices such as laptops and smartphones. The network administrator is concerned that attackers may try to steal client information. He says that employees often run applications and transfer customer data and sales information across the network. It is your responsibility to make sure that the routers employees must connect to are configured to prevent unauthorized access.

---

1. Connect to the wireless router's configuration interface.
   a) Open a web browser.
   b) In the **Address** bar, enter *http://ui.linksys.com*
   c) From the list of routers, select the **E1200** link.
   d) Select the **2.0.04** link.
   e) In the **Warning** message box, check the **Do not show me this again** check box and select **OK**.

    *Note: This website emulates a common router configuration interface. When you are working with a real device, you will typically connect to **http:// 192.168.1.1** and be prompted to enter a username and password. For a list of default user names and passwords by router, navigate to **http:// www.routerpasswords.com**.*

2. Set an SSID for your wireless network.
   a) On the menu bar at the top of the page, select the **Wireless** tab.
   b) If necessary, select **Manual**.
   c) In the **Network Name (SSID)** text box, double-click and type *headquarters*
   d) Select **Save Settings** and, in the **Message from webpage** message box, select **OK**.
   e) Select **Continue**.

3. Set WPA2 encryption with a passphrase.
   a) Under the **Wireless** tab on the menu bar, select the **Wireless Security** link.
   b) From the **Security Mode** drop-down list, select **WPA2 Personal**.
   c) In the **Passphrase** text box, type *!Pass1234*
   d) Select **Save Settings**, and then select **Continue**.

4. Configure the router's administration settings.
   a) On the menu bar, select the **Administration** tab.

---

b) In the **Router Password** text box, double-click the existing password (represented by asterisks) and type *Pa$$w0rd*

c) In the **Re-Enter to Confirm** text box, type the same password.

d) In the **Local Management Access** section, uncheck the **HTTP** check box and check the **HTTPS** check box.

e) In the **Local Management Access** section, for the **Access via Wireless** option, select **Disabled**.

f) In the **Remote Management Access** section, verify that **Remote Management** is disabled.

g) At the bottom of the web page, select **Save Settings**.

h) On the **Your settings have been successfully saved** page, select **Continue**.

i) Close the web browser.

Summary

In this lesson, you learned about best practices and technologies underpinning installation of wireless networks.

- Wi-Fi includes specifications for transmission using various radio modulation techniques and frequencies, supporting different speeds and ranges.
- WLANs can be configured in point-to-point (ad hoc), infrastructure (AP), or mesh topologies.
- A site survey determines the optimum positioning and tuning of APs and antennas.
- You learned about the symptoms and causes of common wireless connectivity and configuration issues.
- Wireless security should be enforced by enabling WPA. WEP should be used only if there is no other choice.
- EAP/802.1X can be used to authenticate users over remote and wireless networks.

In your opinion, what are the primary considerations for implementing a wireless network?

What problems have you encountered when setting up a wireless network?

 Practice Questions: *Additional practice questions are available on the course website.*

Lesson 14

Comparing and Contrasting WAN Technologies

LESSON INTRODUCTION

In previous lessons, you identified common components of a local area network (LAN) implementation. There are other technologies that can be implemented on a wide area network (WAN). In this lesson, you will identify the components of a WAN implementation. Many local networks have a wide area connection to a distant network. Moreover, virtually every network connects in one way or another to the biggest WAN of them all, the Internet. As a networking professional, you will need to understand the infrastructure of these WAN connections so that you can ensure connectivity in the networks that you support.

LESSON OBJECTIVES

In this lesson, you will:

- Compare and contrast WAN core service types.

- Compare and contrast WAN subscriber service types.

- Compare and contrast WAN framing service types.

- Compare and contrast wireless and IoT WAN technologies.

Topic A

Compare and Contrast WAN Core Service Types

 EXAM OBJECTIVES COVERED
2.5 Compare and contrast WAN technologies.

Both LANs and WANs allow for interconnectivity between devices. LANs are used for localized networking, whereas WANs cover larger areas, such as cities, and even allow devices in different nations to connect. Even if you don't administer a WAN, your network will most likely connect to one, and understanding some basic components will allow you to do that successfully. In this topic, you will identify the transmission technologies used by service providers in the core of their networks.

WIDE AREA NETWORK (WAN) TECHNOLOGIES

Wide area network (WAN) technologies support data communications over greater distances than LANs. The term **enterprise WAN** is used to describe a WAN that is used and controlled by a single organization. However, even though an enterprise may control its WAN, it rarely owns all the infrastructure that supports it. Long distance communications usually involve the use of public networks. **Public networks** are owned by **telecommunications (telco) companies** and provide WAN services to businesses and households. Organizations often choose to use public networks, as the cost is far less than implementing a private solution. Service providers often have rights of access to locations that are not available to other organizations, such as under roads.

The development of telecommunications and data networks varies from region-to-region but is typically promoted by a mixture of state and market-driven initiatives. Interoperability between international telcos is often guided by standards set by the **International Telecommunication Union (ITU)** (*itu.int*). The **Internet Engineering Task Force (IETF)** (*ietf.org*) develops standards for communications over the Internet but is mostly focused on Network, Transport, and Application layer protocols.

Just like on a LAN, switching is the process used to connect source and destination nodes and the process by which the data is forwarded at intermediary points. WANs have historically made more use of **circuit switched networks**, however. Circuit switched networks provide guaranteed bandwidth. The overall level of network utilization has no effect on performance because the connection is dedicated. Predictable levels of bandwidth are important for time-sensitive data, such as voice and video. On the downside, circuit switched networks make inefficient use of the media as, by definition, a dedicated channel cannot be shared even when it is not being used. The technology is also impractical for some applications because they time-out before a circuit is established.

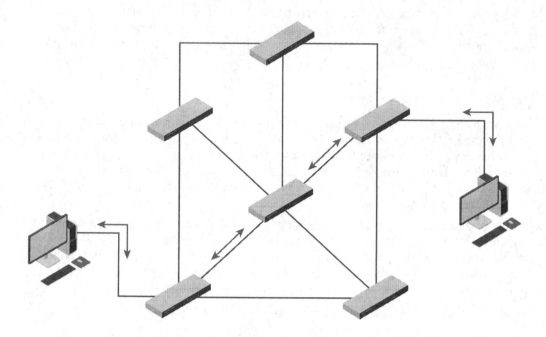

Circuit switched networks provide a dedicated path between nodes. (Image © 123RF.com.)

Packet switching technology was developed on the basis that subscribers share the network infrastructure and pay only for the bandwidth they consume. It is a cost-effective alternative to dedicated lines and provides more efficient use of the network infrastructure than circuit switched technology.

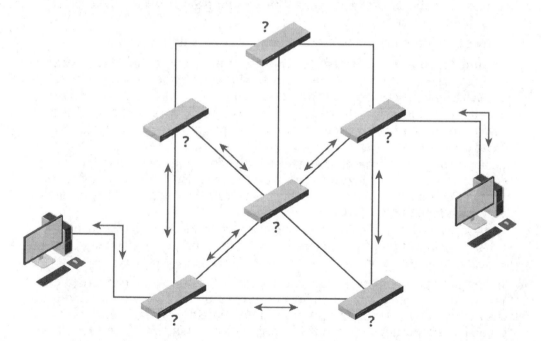

Packet switching networks allow data to take multiple paths. (Image © 123RF.com.)

With the connectionless packet switching typical of IP networks, the individual packets are routed to their destination using media shared with other data so there is normally no guarantee of bandwidth. Modern WANs make use of technology to combine the advantages of circuit and packet switching. Connection-oriented—or **virtual circuit packet switching**—establishes a specific path for all packets to follow. This is known as a **logical connection** or **virtual circuit**. The connection is established once the source and destination machines agree on communications parameters. This allows more control over the link properties, such as minimum bandwidth and maximum latency/jitter.

WAN TOPOLOGIES

Many WAN links are **point-to-point**; that is, a single link to connect two sites. There may be circumstances in which an organization needs links between more than two sites. This can be implemented by creating a **full mesh** (each site has a link to every other site) or a **partial mesh** (each site has a link to some of the other sites). This arrangement offers redundancy but is likely to be costly in terms of the number of links that must be provisioned.

A cheaper alternative is a **hub and spoke** topology. This can function like a star topology, where all communications are channeled via the hub network (so each site has one link to the hub). In this scenario, the hub represents a single point of failure, however; if the hub becomes inoperable, no site can communicate with any other site.

PUBLIC SWITCHED TELEPHONE NETWORK (PSTN)

National telecommunications systems have evolved and combined over the years to create a global (and indeed extra-terrestrial) communications network. This is referred to as the **public switched telephone network (PSTN)**, but it can carry more than voice call services. The basis of PSTN is a circuit switched network, but the infrastructure can also carry packet switched data services. PSTN was designed for transferring voice information. It works by establishing a temporary dedicated circuit between two locations when the conversation commences and then tears down the connection when the conversation ends. The **Signaling System # 7 (SS7)** protocol suite provides these functions.

The PSTN can be described as being composed of several different zones:

*   **Customer premises equipment (CPE)**—Termination and routing equipment placed at the customer site. Some of this equipment may be owned or leased from the telco; some may be owned by the customer.
*   **Local loop**—Cabling from the customer premises to the local exchange. The point at which the telco's cabling enters the customer premises is referred to as the **demarcation point** (often shortened to demarc).
*   **Local exchange**—Switches links between local access subscribers and provides transports to trunk exchanges. The local exchange is also referred to as a Class 5 office or Central Office (CO), while in the US a local telephone company is called a **Local Exchange Carrier (LEC).**
*   **Trunk offices**—These provide switching and interconnections between local exchanges within a metropolitan area or nationally and to international gateway services. Trunk offices are also referred to as Class 4 or toll offices.

While the trunks between the infrastructure parts of the telephone network (the core or the cloud) have been upgraded to fiber optic links, the local loop between the local telephone office and a customer's premises often remains voice-grade copper wire, not capable of supporting high bandwidth applications. This part of the network is referred to as the **plain old telephone service (POTS)**.

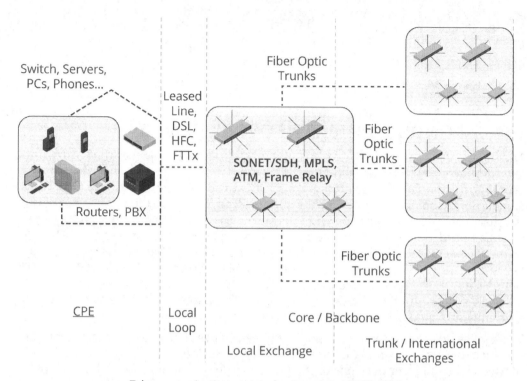

Telecommunications networks. (Image © 123RF.com.)

T-CARRIER AND LEASED LINES

The first generation of **digital signaling (DS)** to be implemented on telecommunications networks was the **Plesiochronous Digital Hierarchy (PDH)** or **T-carrier** system. It was developed by Bell Labs to allow multiple calls to be placed on a single cable. PDH enabled voice traffic to be digitized for transport around the core network. It also enabled other types of digital data to be transported.

PDH is based on **Time Division Multiplexing (TDM)**. TDM enables multiple circuits to be carried over the same media. The protocol assigns each circuit (or channel) a time slot. PDH is an asynchronous version of TDM, meaning that timing signals from the various components are not accurately synchronized (plesiochronous or small timing differences).

Each channel provides enough bandwidth for a voice communications session, digitized using Pulse Code Modulation (PCM). A single 64 Kbps channel is known as a **DS0** or **narrowband** link. For leased line data services, however, the foundation level of T-carrier is the **DS1** or **T1** digital signal circuit. This service comprises 24 channels of 64 Kbps time multiplexed into a single digital connection that can be used for voice, video, and data signals. The devices performing the multiplexing are referred to as **muxes**.

The T1 lines themselves can be multiplexed to provide even more bandwidth.

DSx	Bandwidth	Channels	T1 Units
DS0	64 Kbps	1	-
DS1 (T1)	1,544 Mbps	24	1
DS3 (T3)	44,736 Mbps	672	28

T-carrier is a US designation. In Europe, the system is based around the CEPT/E-carrier equivalent. The E-carrier standards specify 32 channels per unit, rather than 24.

CEPTx	Bandwidth	Channels	E1 Units
CEPT0	64 Kbps	1	-
CEPT1 (E1)	2,048 Mbps	32	1
CEPT3 (E3)	34,368 Mbps	512	16

SYNCHRONOUS OPTICAL NETWORK (SONET)

The second generation of digital transmission standards is known as the **Synchronous Digital Hierarchy (SDH)** as standardized by the ITU or **Synchronous Optical Network (SONET)**, as standardized by ANSI. SDH/SONET was developed principally to provide a standard transport mechanism for the various proprietary PDH fiber optic networks that had been installed over the years. As such, SDH/SONET is principally a Physical layer standard, defining infrastructure, line speeds, and so on. There is an SDH/SONET frame format, but this is designed to transport frames from higher level protocols, rather than provide any sort of addressing capability. Like PDH, SDH/SONET uses TDM, but unlike PDH it is synchronous, meaning that all elements in the network are precisely synchronized to the same time signal. This allows data to be transported very efficiently with little control information required.

The service offers a hierarchy of bandwidth levels based on a basic transmission rate of **Synchronous Transport Signals (STS-1s)** that provides 51.48 Mbps of bandwidth, of which 50.84 Mbps is available to the payload (the remainder is used for control information). The SONET standard refers to STS, while SDH calls the frames **Synchronous Transport Modules (STMs)**. Higher rates are multiples of the basic rate, achieved by multiplexing. **Optical Carrier X (OCx)** is another way of designating this speed. That is, OC-3 is the equivalent of STS-3, and OC-192 is the equivalent of STS-192.

SONET	SDH	Data Rate
STS-1/OC-1	STM-0	51.84 Mbps
STS-3/OC-3	STM-1	155.52 Mbps
STS-12/OC-12	STM-4	622.08 Mbps
STS-48/OC-48	STM-16	2.488 Gbps
STS-96/OC-96	STM-32	4.876 Gbps
STS-192/OC-192	STM-64	9.953 Gbps

 Note: STS is a logical standard that defines the framing and synchronization of data transmission. At the Physical layer, STS frames can be transmitted using the Optical Carrier (OC) standard (fiber optic) or (much more rarely) the Electrical Carrier (EC) standard (copper wire). In practice, the data rates for STS and OC/EC are identical.

SDH/SONET supports the mesh architecture but is more typically installed as point-to-point links or in a dual counter-rotating ring topology. In the ring topology, each node is connected by a fiber optic pair with data travelling around the network in a clockwise direction. A second, redundant ring transports data in a counter-clockwise direction and can be "cut-in" in the event that the main cable between two nodes suffers a failure. The sets of cables could be installed separately from one another to provide redundancy in the event of some physical catastrophe (construction workers cutting the cable, earthquake, and so on).

The nodes in the SDH/SONET infrastructure are usually **add-drop multiplexers (ADM)**. These devices allow inputs from lower bit rate streams to be added and removed (for example, adding or dropping T1 or T3 traffic from an OC-192 trunk).

SDH/SONET is now the mainstream standard for telecommunications trunk lines. However, the future may well see converged voice and data networks based entirely on 10GbE Ethernet (and better) and IP standards.

METROPOLITAN ETHERNET

A **Metropolitan Ethernet** (or simply Metro Ethernet) network is a metropolitan area network (MAN) based on Ethernet standards. These types of services are also more widely described as **Carrier Ethernet**. Standards for Metro Ethernet are developed by the MEF (*mef.net*). Metro Ethernet can use different types of physical connectivity. Some examples include:

- Ethernet over Fiber—Uses the 802.3 10GBASE-LR and 10GBASE-ER specifications.
- Ethernet over SONET/SDH—Uses the SONET OC-192 service and encapsulates Ethernet packets in its frames. The 10GbE WAN PHY protocol uses the same wavelength and interface types (10GBASE-SW, 10GBASE-LW, and 10GBASE-EW) as the LAN PHY equivalents. Because of the different framing, it operates at a slightly slower data rate (9.95328 Gbps) than the LAN PHY version.
- Ethernet over Copper—Uses digital subscriber line (DSL) variants such as SHDSL and VDSL to overcome the usual distance limitations of copper Ethernet. This does not support anything like the same speeds as LAN Ethernet (more typically 2-10 Mbps), but multiple pairs can be aggregated for higher bandwidth.

On top of the physical connectivity method, there are multiple service categories for Metro Ethernet. Two of these are E-line and E-LAN:

- E-line—Establishes a point-to-point link between two sites. Multiple E-lines can be configured on a single Metro Ethernet interface, with each E-line representing a separate VLAN.
- E-LAN—Establishes a mesh topology between multiple sites.

These services can be used by the customer to join multiple sites together or as a way of connecting their enterprise network to the Internet. Metro Ethernet typically provides speeds from a minimum of 4 Mbps up to multi-Gigabit. From the customer's perspective, Metro Ethernet has many advantages. The fact that Metro Ethernet is easily scalable affords businesses the flexibility to match the service to their changing demands. Also, the fact that the same protocol (Ethernet) is used on the LAN and connectivity into the public network space can make the configuration of routers, layer 3 switches, and firewalls simpler, with fewer protocol conversions required.

Activity 14-1

Discussing WAN Core Service Types

SCENARIO

Answer the following questions to test your understanding of the content covered in this topic.

---

1. **What is the main advantage of circuit-switched networks?**

2. **What bandwidth are T1 and E1 links, and why are they different?**

3. **Which 10GbE Ethernet and SONET standards are interoperable?**

4. **What media types can be used to connect to a Metro Ethernet?**

Topic B

Compare and Contrast WAN Subscriber Service Types

EXAM OBJECTIVES COVERED
2.2 Given a scenario, determine the appropriate placement of networking devices on a network and install/configure them.
2.5 Compare and contrast WAN technologies.
5.2 Given a scenario, use the appropriate tool.

To gain access to a WAN, your LAN will have to connect to one. How do you connect your self-contained LAN to a WAN that uses completely different technologies? Understanding the various WAN connectivity devices and methods will help you implement your WAN connections appropriately. From the slowest dial-up to the fastest fiber optic service, you will need to understand the capabilities of and limitations to your network's transmission method to choose the one best suited for your network.

LOCAL LOOP AND INTERNET ACCESS SERVICES

While technologies such as T-carrier and SONET enable traffic to be carried over telecommunications trunks, the trickiest part of providing services to subscribers tends to be the connection over the **local loop**. For a traditional telco, the local loop is likely to be a voice-grade twisted pair network. Cable TV companies have more widespread fiber optic networks, but even these are traditionally connected to customer premises by coax cabling. Both sets of companies are investing in infrastructure to provide fiber optic connections directly (or at least more directly) to customer premises. In the meantime, various technologies have been developed to provide fast "broadband" connections over the local loop.

The major infrastructure of the Internet, also referred to as the Internet backbone, consists of very high bandwidth trunks connecting **Internet eXchange Points (IXPs)**. These trunks and IXPs are mostly created by telecommunications companies and academic institutions. They are typically organized on national and international levels. Within the data center supporting any given IXP, ISPs establish high-speed links between their networks, using transit and peering arrangements to carry traffic to and from parts of the Internet they do not physically own. There is a tiered hierarchy of ISPs that reflects to what extent they depend on transit arrangements with other ISPs. Customers connect to an ISP's network via a local **Point of Presence (PoP)**. The ISP uses a backhaul link (or a transit arrangement with another ISP) to connect each PoP to their core network infrastructure and one or more IXPs.

DEMARCATION POINT

Establishing a WAN or remote access link means terminating the access provider's cabling at some point in your premises, then attaching modem and/or routing equipment to that line. The location at which the access provider's network terminates is called the **demarcation point** (or **demarc** for short). Access equipment that is provided or leased by the customer and installed at their site is referred to as **customer premises equipment (CPE)**. The demarc point represents the end of the telco's responsibility for maintaining that part of the network. Any problems arising from the other side of the demarc point are the responsibility of the customer. The WAN Physical layer describes the interface between the Data Termination Equipment (DTE) and the Data Communications Equipment (DCE). In most cases, the DCE belongs to the service provider, and the DTE is the customer's device. The DCE will almost always be a modem or Channel Service Unit/Data Service Unit (CSU/DSU—used with digital lines) that is installed on the customer's premises.

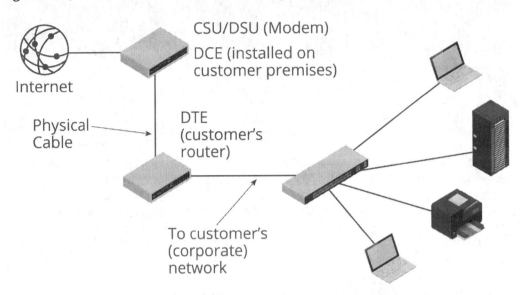

WAN termination equipment. (Image © 123RF.com.)

 Note: *The demarc need not end at cabling. Some companies provide the connectivity equipment and retain ownership of it, meaning that the demarc would be positioned at the CSU/DSU or managed router.*

A **demarc extension** refers to cabling that must be run through the customer premises. A telco will run cabling to the **Minimum Point of Entry (MPOE)**, which is the most convenient place for the cabling to enter the building.

In its original form, a **modem**, meaning **modulator/demodulator**, is a device that converts between analog and digital signal transmissions. The term modem is now widely used to refer to any type of SOHO remote connectivity appliance, even when such appliances do no actual modulation. These include ISDN, DSL, cable, and satellite modems.

DIGITAL SUBSCRIBER LINE (DSL)

Digital subscriber line (DSL) is a technology for transferring data over voice-grade telephone lines. DSL uses the higher frequencies available in a copper telephone line as a communications channel. The use of a filter prevents this from contaminating voice traffic with noise. The use of advanced modulation and echo cancelling techniques enable high bandwidth, full-duplex transmissions.

A DSL modem is installed as CPE, typically as some sort of multifunction router, Ethernet hub/switch, and wireless AP. This provides network ports for connection to computers and switches on the LAN and a WAN port for connection to the phone line. The phone line then makes the connection to a bank of DSL modems in the exchange, called a **DSL access multiplexer (DSLAM)**. The DSLAM channels voice and data traffic to the appropriate network. Depending on the equipment used by the ISP, the Data Link protocol used for DSL may be PPP over ATM (PPPoA) or PPP over Ethernet

(PPPoE). The connection is always on, meaning that there is no need to dial to initiate access, and no call charges are incurred.

The main drawback of DSL is that, as a copper-wire technology, it suffers from attenuation. The maximum range of a DSL modem is typically about 3 miles (5 km), but the longer the connection, the greater the deterioration in data rate. Domestic cabling may also be relatively poor quality and pass through "noisy" environments.

There are various *flavors* of DSL, notably SDSL, G.SHDSL, ADSL, and VDSL. These are standardized by the ITU in a series of G. recommendations.

SYMMETRICAL DSL (SDSL)

Symmetrical DSL (SDSL) is so-called because it provides the same downlink and uplink bandwidth. There are various types of symmetric DSL service. SDSL services tend to be provided as business packages, rather than to residential customers.

ASYMMETRICAL DSL (ADSL)

Asymmetrical DSL (ADSL) (G.992) is a consumer version of DSL that provides a fast downlink but a slow uplink. There are various iterations of ADSL, with the latest (ADSL2+) offering downlink rates up to about 24 Mbps and uplink rates up to 1 Mbps. Service providers may impose usage restrictions to limit the amount of data downloaded per month. Actual speed may be affected by the quality of the cabling in the consumer's premises and between the premises and the exchange, and by the number of users connected to the same DSLAM (contention).

VERY HIGH BITRATE DSL (VDSL) AND FIBER TO THE X (FTTx)

The major obstacle to providing WAN access that can approach LAN performance is bandwidth in the last mile, where the copper wiring infrastructure is generally not good. The projects to update this wiring to use fiber optic links are referred to by the umbrella term **Fiber to the X (FTTx)**.

The most expensive solution is **Fiber to the Premises (FTTP)** or its residential variant **Fiber to the Home (FTTH)**. The essential point about both these implementations is that the fiber link is terminated on CPE. Other solutions can variously be described as **Fiber to the Node (FTTN)** or **Fiber to the Curb (FTTC)**. These retain some sort of copper wiring (twisted pair or coax) while extending the fiber link to a communications cabinet servicing multiple subscribers. The service providers with their roots in telephone networks use VDSL to support FTTC. **Very High Bitrate DSL (VDSL)** (G.993) achieves higher bit rates than other DSL types at the expense of range. It allows for both symmetric and asymmetric modes. Over 300 m (1000 feet), an asymmetric link supports 52 Mbps downstream and 6 Mbps upstream, while a symmetric link supports 26 Mbps in both directions. VDSL2 also specifies a very short range (100 m/300 feet) rate of 100 Mbps (bi-directional).

FTTC enables the telcos to develop "triple play" networks that can compete with the cable and satellite TV operators. "Triple play" means delivering TV (specifically High Definition TV), broadband Internet, and voice simultaneously over the same link.

DSL MODEMS

A standalone DSL modem is installed as CPE. The DSL modem is connected to the phone line via an RJ-11 port and to the local network's router (or a single computer on the local network) via an RJ-45 Ethernet port.

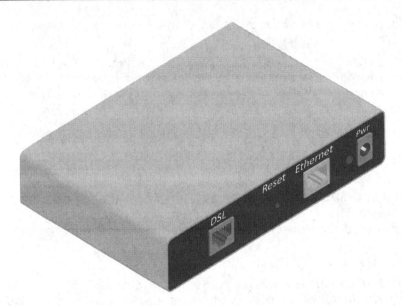

RJ-11 DSL (left) and RJ-45 LAN (right) ports on a DSL modem. (Image © 123RF.com.)

More typically, DSL modems are incorporated in **multifunction network devices**, combining the function of DSL modem, router, hub/switch, and WAP. An enterprise router could be fitted with a DSL WAN interface card. The modem type must match the service. An ADSL modem cannot be used to access a VDSL service, for instance.

A filter (splitter) must be installed to separate voice and data signals. These can either be installed at the demarc point by the telco engineer or self-installed on each phone point by the customer.

Self-installed DSL splitter.

CABLE BROADBAND

A cable Internet connection is usually available along with **Cable Access TV (CATV)**. These networks are sometimes described as hybrid fiber coax (HFC) because they combine a fiber optic core network with coax links to CPE, but are more simply just described as **cable broadband**. The cable operators and telcos are competing with one another to provide "triple play" networks, and the investment in fiber optic links has given the cable operators something of an advantage.

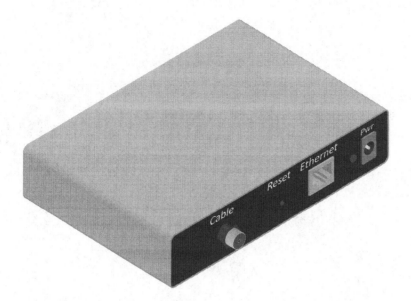

A cable modem—The RJ-45 port connects to the local network, while the coax port connects to the service provider network. (Image © 123RF.com.)

Installation of a cable modem follows the same general principles as for a DSL modem. The cable modem is interfaced to a computer or router through an Ethernet or USB adapter and with the access provider's network by a short segment of coax. More coax then links all the premises in a street with a **Cable Modem Termination System (CMTS)**, which routes data traffic via the fiber backbone (typically a SONET ring) to the ISP's Point of Presence (PoP) and from there to the Internet. Cable based on the **Data Over Cable Service Interface Specification (DOCSIS)** supports downlink speeds of up to 38 Mbps (North America) or 50 Mbps (Europe) and uplinks of up to 27 Mbps. DOCSIS version 3 allows the use of multiplexed channels to achieve higher bandwidth.

DIAL-UP SERVICES

The **dial-up modem** is one of the earliest means of establishing a data network connection over a telephone line. While dial-up offers only very low bandwidth, it remains a fallback option when no other means of making a connection is available. To be transferred over the phone line, data must be converted from digital to analog by using a modem at each end of the connection. Modem is short for modulator/demodulator; modulation is the process of converting digital signals to analog, and demodulation is the reverse process (analog to digital).

Analog modems are now available only either as PCI cards for PCs, or external devices, connected via a serial or USB port. The modem is connected to an analog phone point by 2-pair cable (typically a flat "silver satin" cable) with RJ-11 connectors. In the UK, the phone jack uses a BT connector (BS 6312), rather than RJ-11.

Regardless of the physical interface, the modem must be installed to one of the computer's software COM ports. The modem must also be configured with the local dialing properties, such as tone or pulse dial, access prefix for an outside line, area code, and so on. Connections to remote modems can then be configured by entering the remote modem's telephone number and other connection properties, such as protocol and authentication information. To initiate a connection, the modem dials the telephone number of the ISP's access concentrator, which is a server installed with a modem pool. The connection is typically established using the **Point-to-Point Protocol (PPP)**, which allows for the user to be authenticated and TCP/IP packets to be tunneled over the connection and routed over the wider Internet.

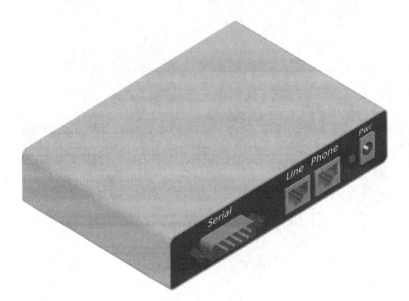

Analog dial-up modem with a serial port PC connection (left) and an RJ-11 port (right). (Image © 123RF.com.)

The main disadvantages of dial-up are low data transfer rates and error-prone links. A low-quality connection can result in high errors, and consequently reduced speed and throughput. This means that the fastest modems can work at only 33.6 Kbps (V.34+), and this speed is reaching the limitations of analog lines. Using the V.90 or V.92 protocol, where the ISP's modem pool has a digital connection to the PSTN (as it usually will), downlink speeds of up 56 Kbps are possible in theory, though rarely achieved in practice. The uplink speed cannot exceed 33.6 Kbps. The slow establishment of the circuit can also cause problems with some applications.

INTEGRATED SERVICES DIGITAL NETWORK (ISDN/PRI)

The **Integrated Services Digital Network (ISDN)** is a fully digital version of the local loop, standardized by the ITU. It has been provided by telecommunications companies since the 1980s. ISDN is a digital circuit switched technology for voice, video, and data (hence "integrated services"). ISDN makes use of existing copper telephone wiring (if the wiring is of sufficient quality). ISDN is a dial-up service billed for by line rental and usage. There are two classes of ISDN:

- **Basic Rate Interface (BRI)** provides two 64 Kbps B channels for data and one 16 Kbps D channel for link management control signals. It is sometimes called 2B+D. It is common to use one B channel for data and leave the other for voice or fax, but you can also provide a 128 Kbps connection by concatenating the two B channels. This form of ISDN is intended for SOHO use.
- **Primary Rate Interface (PRI)** provides either T1 or E1 capacity levels (23xB or 30xB channels, depending on location in the world) and one 64 Kbps D channel. This form of ISDN is intended for larger companies.

Although ISDN is a dial-up technology, it can establish a circuit connection in less than 1 second. This means that many of the applications that time-out when using the analog modems can be used with ISDN. As a WAN access method, it has been superseded by DSL and cable broadband, but it may still be offered by some service providers where those access methods are not available.

An ISDN connection would typically be facilitated through a **terminal adapter (TA)**. The TA may be an external appliance or a plug-in card for a PC or compatible router. The TA is connected to the ISDN network via a **network terminator (NT1)** device. The NT1 would either be incorporated into the TA or provided as an external device (in which case the TA and NT1 are connected via the "S/T" port). The "U" port on the NT1 is connected to the ISDN wall jack. The ISDN-enabled router may then either be connected to a hub or switch to support connections to the WAN link from the LAN.

LEASED LINES

Both dial-up and ISDN lines provide a temporary, circuit switched connection using the telephone network. Each transmission using a dial-up line must establish a circuit between the source and destination machines. Technologies such as DSL and cable broadband provide "always on" connections, but the link is shared between multiple subscribers and can be affected by contention. A **dedicated (or leased) line**, on the other hand, provides a permanent circuit switched connection with guaranteed service levels, such as available bandwidth. Typically, a T1 (or E1) link is used to establish point-to-point links between enterprise sites. The figure shows two LANs connected using a dedicated digital line. The router or bridge on the LAN connects to the leased line through a CSU/DSU device.

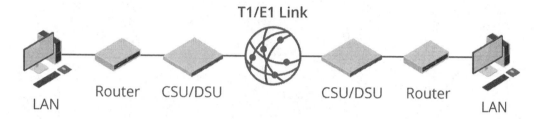

Leased lines connecting two sites.

Often a customer may not require a full T1 or T3 service. The service provider can provide a cheaper fractional T1 (FT1) or fractional T3 (FT3) service, which provides a portion of the total bandwidth. For example, a T1 line can be divided into increments of 64 Kbps.

Digital leased lines use a device called a **Channel Service Unit/Data Service Unit (CSU/DSU)** instead of the modems used for analog systems. The DSU encodes the signal from **Data Terminal Equipment (DTE)**—that is, a PBX or router—to a serial digital signal transmitted over 2-pair copper wiring. The link is full duplex, with one pair used for transmitting and the other for receiving. The CSU is used to perform diagnostic tests on the line. The devices can be supplied separately, but more typically they are combined as a single WAN interface card that can be plugged into a compatible router or PBX.

A T1 line from the telco is usually terminated at a **smart jack** or **Network Interface Unit (NIU)**, which contains line testing facilities (loopback) for the telco to use. The smart jack has an RJ-48C or RJ-48X interface on the customer side that is used to connect to a CSU/DSU. The RJ-48X jack has a shorting bar to provide loopback on the connection if the equipment on the customer side is unplugged. This allows the service provider to test the line remotely. The connection from the smart jack to the CSU/DSU can use an ordinary Cat 5e/RJ-45 patch cord (up to 3 meters/10 feet in length), but a shielded 2-pair 22 AWG cable with connectors wired for RJ-48 is required for any distance longer than that.

A T3 leased line requires coax cabling or a fiber optic link. T3 and higher bandwidth services are now more likely to be provided via Metro Ethernet, however.

BANDWIDTH SPEED TESTERS

A bandwidth or broadband speed tester is a website that measures the time taken to download and upload a randomized stream of data to a web host (selected on the basis of the subscriber's geographic location). Examples include *https://www.speedtest.net* from Ookla and Google's tester, which will appear under any search for "speed test." ISPs may provide their own tools for line and speed testing, and you may also be able to initiate these tests from the DSL/cable router.

Ideally, the test should be run in isolation so that the link is not congested by traffic from other devices on the home network (other computers, smartphones, smart TVs, games consoles, and so on).

If the bandwidth obtained is lower than expected, you could check the router's logs for line condition statistics, but as residential services are fully managed, it is best to contact the ISP.

 Note: *To learn more, watch the related* **Video** *on the course website.*

Activity 14-2

Discussing WAN Subscriber Service Types

SCENARIO

Answer the following questions to test your understanding of the content covered in this topic.

1. **What is an IXP?**

2. **What place does VDSL have in terms of access to public networks?**

3. **What is the upper limit of a dial-up modem's connection speed?**

4. **You are connecting a SOHO network to a VDSL service using a separate VDSL modem. What cables do you require and how should they be connected?**

5. **What is PRI?**

6. **What function does a smart jack serve?**

Topic C

Compare and Contrast WAN Framing Service Types

EXAM OBJECTIVES COVERED
2.5 Compare and contrast WAN technologies.

As you have seen, there are many ways to connect a local network to an access provider's network. DSL and cable broadband provide options for small businesses and residential subscribers, while leased lines and Metro Ethernet provide high bandwidth links for enterprise networks. A WAN implementation must also consider the Data Link and Network protocols that govern transmission of data over these links.

HDLC AND POINT-TO-POINT PROTOCOL (PPP)

The **High-Level Data Link Control (HDLC)** protocol is widely used to transfer data over a serial digital line, such as T1 or ISDN. It performs the same framing and error detection functions as Ethernet but on a point-to-point link between two routers, rather than a shared access medium.

The **Point-to-Point Protocol (PPP)** is an adaptation of HDLC and forms the cornerstone of subscriber dial-up and broadband Internet access methods. It is defined by *RFC 1661*. PPP was developed for dial-up networking, but is still used over a variety of communications links, including DSL, SONET, and cellular. The process of establishing a PPP connection is as follows:

1. After the physical connection is made, the **Link Control Protocol (LCP)** negotiates link parameters, such as frame size and whether to use authentication.
2. If specified, the client and server negotiate use of an authentication protocol and exchange authentication messages.
3. The appropriate **Network Control Protocols (NCP)** are then selected to configure the layer 3 protocol(s) to be used on the local network.
4. At this point, the link is open and PPP frames are exchanged.
5. When the link is to be closed, LCP exchanges terminate packets. The connection could also be closed because the line is dropped or because it times-out.

PPP provides encapsulation for IP traffic (amongst others) plus IP address assignment, authentication, and a means for an ISP to monitor a connection and bill for time used. When used with a broadband service such as DSL to connect to an ISP, the service will often use Ethernet as the Data Link protocol. **PPP over Ethernet (PPPoE)** is simply a means of creating PPP connections over an Ethernet link. The major benefit of PPPoE is that the end-user can just as easily establish these network connections without needing to know more than how to establish a dial-up connection, so neither the telephone company nor the ISP needs to provide any special support. Some ISPs use **Point-to-Point Protocol over ATM (PPPoA)** instead of PPPoE.

FRAME RELAY

Frame Relay evolved from the earlier packet switching protocol X.25 in the 1990s. It provides data packet forwarding for services running over T-carrier lines, ISDN, or even dial-up. The advantage when used with T-carrier is that the customer can select an appropriate bandwidth level—the Committed Information Rate (CIR)—rather than having to incur the full cost of a T1 leased line.

Frame Relay uses variable-length packets of up to 4096 bytes. It can encapsulate data from higher-level protocols, including TCP/IP.

X.25 was based on the use of analog equipment and therefore required error checking and correction information to be transmitted and calculated at each node, creating a substantial overhead. Frame Relay takes advantage of reliable digital lines and terminal equipment and leaves error detection to the communications endpoints. It also makes use of connection-oriented virtual circuits that avoid fragmentation or reassembling of packets. Virtual circuits are either permanent (PVC) or switched (SVC). In a PVC, the connection information (call setup) is permanently available; in an SVC it is established dynamically when needed (analogous to dial-up connections). The actual path through the network is not fixed (hence "virtual circuit") but can be managed by the telecom's provider using its switches. This process is transparent to the end user. All these factors mean that the overhead on the network is reduced (compared to X.25), resulting in a more efficient network with far higher throughput.

Frame Relay provides mechanisms for the service provider to perform congestion control and maintain available bandwidth to an agreed service level, providing Quality of Service (QoS) for latency-sensitive applications, such as Voice over IP (VoIP).

Frame Relay is now considered a legacy protocol in many parts of the world and is not often offered as a service by telecom providers. MPLS and Ethernet WANs have replaced it, but it may still be in use on some networks.

ASYNCHRONOUS TRANSFER MODE (ATM)

Asynchronous Transfer Mode (ATM) is a transport mechanism for all types of data, including voice and video. It is standardized as part of the ITU's Broadband ISDN standard and was maintained by a consortium called the ATM Forum. The ATM Forum has now been merged, along with the Frame Relay Alliance, into the **Broadband Forum** (*broadband-forum.org*). ATM uses a **cell switching** (or cell relay) technology. An ATM cell is a small (53 byte), fixed-length packet that contains 48 bytes of data and 5 bytes of header information. By contrast, variable frame payloads can be up to 1500 bytes. The combination of a consistent cell size, which reduces processing overhead during switching, and the use of faster hardware-based switches (working at up to OC-192) means high levels of capacity can be achieved. The small size of the cells and their fixed length mean traffic flows are more predictable, so time-sensitive data is readily accommodated.

ATM is designed to make highly efficient use of the available bandwidth, with switches used to multiplex data simultaneously from multiple sources onto the network. An ATM switch makes virtual connections with other switches to provide a data path from endpoint to endpoint. Individual connections are called **virtual channels (VCs)**. VCs support the connection-oriented transport between endpoints and are identified by a virtual channel identifier (VCI). VCs with a common path are tied together into virtual paths (VPs) and are identified by a virtual path identifier (VPI). You can form a transmission path (TP) by combining multiple VPs. The header information identifies the transmission path required for the cell to reach its destination and allows bandwidth to be dedicated to particular data. This infrastructure means the packets arrive in order and can be quickly processed.

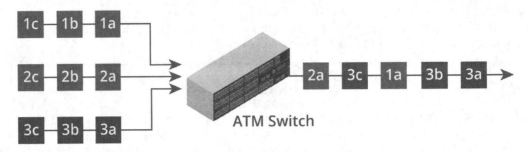

ATM multiplexes transmissions from multiple circuits onto a single channel. (Image © 123RF.com.)

This figure shows an example of a switch allocating additional bandwidth to data source 3 while continuing to provide some bandwidth to the other data sources (1 and 2). ATM combines the bandwidth guarantee of circuit switching with the efficient use of bandwidth provided by packet switching.

ATM has been widely implemented by telecommunications companies and ISPs because it provides mechanisms for traffic shaping and policing, Quality of Service (QoS), and the ability to aggregate different types of traffic. However, as the use of fiber optic cabling makes more bandwidth available, ATM becomes less efficient when transporting protocols with large frame sizes or PDUs, such as Ethernet/IP, as the small cell size means that a substantial overhead is introduced in disassembling and reassembling packets. Consequently, the market developed towards the use of native IP solutions with MPLS providing traffic shaping and QoS.

ATM can make use of a variety of physical media, but in most implementations it runs over either T1/T3 links or SDH/SONET. For end customers in many parts of the world, ATM is not widely offered as a service by telecom providers anymore. It does remain supported for the organizations that have installed it already.

MULTIPROTOCOL LABEL SWITCHING (MPLS)

IP is almost universally deployed on LANs and is the basis for the Internet. IP has not been deployed on telecommunications networks because it has no real means of providing traffic shaping or QoS. These functions have been provided by ATM, but the use of small cell sizes that makes ATM highly suitable for carrying voice traffic also makes it inefficient when carrying packet data such as IP. **Multiprotocol Label Switching (MPLS)** was developed by Cisco from ATM as a means of providing traffic engineering (congestion control), Class of Service (CoS), and QoS within a packet switched, rather than circuit switched, network. MPLS has subsequently been standardized by the IETF (*RFC 3031*).

In effect, MPLS achieves a marriage of layer 3-based routing with layer 2-based switching. Where Frame Relay and ATM provide connection-oriented transfer by establishing a virtual circuit/channel, MPLS establishes connections via **Label Switched Paths (LSPs)** enabled by a mesh network of **Label Switched Routers (LSRs)**. One of the benefits of MPLS is that ATM switches can usually be re-engineered to act as LSRs, reducing initial deployment costs by retaining existing hardware.

For example, in the following diagram, the CPE router at site 1 wants to communicate with site 4. The router is attached to the service provider's MPLS cloud via a Label Edge Router (LER). This router inserts or "pushes" a label or "shim" header into each packet sent from CPE1, and then forwards it to an LSR. Each LSR examines the shim and determines the Label Switched Path (LSP) for the packet, based on the type of data, network congestion, and any other traffic engineering parameters determined by the service provider. It uses the label, rather than the layer 3 header, to forward the packet to its neighbor. In this way, costly routing table lookups are avoided. The shim is removed (or "popped") by the egress LER and delivered to CPE4.

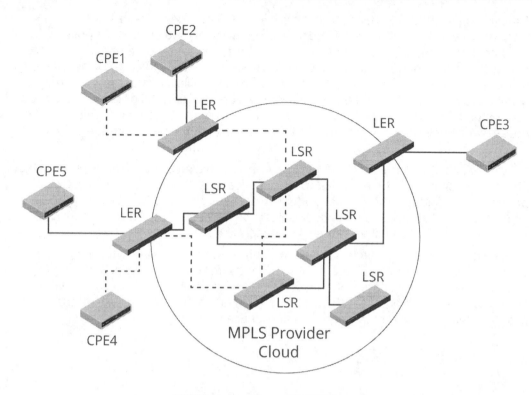

MPLS topology. (Image © 123RF.com.)

Where an IP router uses best-effort delivery to find the shortest available path to a given destination, the MPLS signaling protocols allow constraint-based routing, which enables the network manager to add congestion, CoS, application type, and QoS to the criteria used for path selection. MPLS labels contain a special designation called the **Forward Equivalence Class (FEC)**. The FEC is applied to a stream of packets. It may correspond with a prefix (destination network) or may be based on a class of service (such as IP precedence). A downstream router sends FECs to its upstream neighbor. The upstream neighbor in turn places the correct FEC in the label of a packet and passes the packet to the appropriate downstream neighbor. In this way, the path for a traffic stream in MPLS is pre-determined. Traffic always follows the same path, with the packets being quickly switched from one router to the next.

MPLS allows service providers to offer various solutions for enterprise networking requirements. A basic use of MPLS is to create site-to-site VPNs to interconnect LANs. The traffic passing over an MPLS VPN is isolated from any other customer or public traffic. Different sites can use any access method available (DSL, cellular, leased line, or Ethernet), and the sites can use point-to-point or multipoint topologies as required. MPLS can also be used to provide voice and video networks with minimum service level guarantees. Another use is to provide fast and reliable connectivity to the data centers hosting whatever cloud services are used by the enterprise. The MPLS provider can apply traffic shaping policies to communications between enterprise LANs and the data center to guarantee a service level and provide link redundancy, making the connection much more reliable than one over the open Internet would be.

SIP TRUNKS

With the increasing popularity of Voice over IP (and voice/video/multimedia services generally), a huge number of providers are now offering dedicated services specifically designed to allow enterprise networks to route **Session Initiation Protocol (SIP)** based telephony sessions to other organizations and the public telephone network, both nationally and internationally. A SIP trunk is a service implemented on an underlying access technology, such as MPLS or Metro Ethernet.

Establishing a **SIP trunk** means that the service provider identifies the use of the Internet access channel for voice and video conferencing and uses traffic policing mechanisms to ensure that call quality is not affected by other data passing over the link. A SIP trunk replaces traditional voice lines, such as ISDN PRI or a T1 leased line. As well as being more cost-effective, SIP makes it easier to allow a larger number of simultaneous calls to be made. Voice lines provisioned over ISDN or even leased lines are limited to a fixed number of channels based on TDM. A SIP trunk is limited only by the available network bandwidth and the service level purchased from the provider, which can much more easily be changed than with traditional links.

SIP trunks use a customer's telephony PBX or server-based call control system (such as Skype for Business) as the endpoint for the service. The IP address of the customer's phone system and the SIP trunk provider's IP address are used to set up a pathway which allows individual phone or video calls to be passed. These links are normally encrypted and secured using standard protocols like TLS.

As SIP trunks are used to allow a private organization to make calls onto the public telephone network (or POTS), there is the potential for hackers to exploit unsecure links to make expensive international or premium rate calls. The SIP trunk provider then charges the customer for these calls. To mitigate against this, most SIP trunk providers will provide multiple layers of authentication.

Activity 14-3

Discussing WAN Framing Service Types

SCENARIO

Answer the following questions to test your understanding of the content covered in this topic.

1. **How does PPP work to allow a computer with a dial-up modem to connect to the Internet?**

2. **What distinguishes ATM from Ethernet?**

3. **What is the difference between IP and MPLS routing?**

4. **What type of transmission media is required for a SIP trunk?**

Topic D

Compare and Contrast Wireless and IoT WAN Technologies

EXAM OBJECTIVES COVERED
1.5 Compare and contrast the characteristics of network topologies, types and technologies.
1.6 Given a scenario, implement the appropriate wireless technologies and configurations.
2.5 Compare and contrast WAN technologies.

As more services move to the cloud, cellular access is becoming an increasingly important component of enterprise networks. There are also opportunities to use wireless to link sites. A third component of wireless WANs (WWANs) is the Internet of Things (IoT). Many people and businesses are deploying IoT devices in their homes and offices, and some businesses depend on this technology for manufacturing and inventory control. In this topic, you will examine the technologies used to implement different WWAN environments.

CELLULAR RADIO (GSM/TDMA AND CDMA)

Wireless technologies are now well established in terms of local and personal area networking. There are two main technologies involved in providing **wireless WANs (WWANs)**: cellular radio and microwave satellite.

A cellular phone makes a connection using the nearest available transmitter (cell or base station). Each base station has an effective range of up to 5 miles (8 km). The transmitter connects the phone to the mobile and PSTN networks. Transmitter coverage in many countries is now very good, except for remote rural areas. Cellular radio works in the 850 and 1900 MHz frequency bands (mostly in the Americas) and the 900 and 1800 MHz bands (rest of the world).

Cellular digital communications standards are described as belonging to a generation. For 2G, there were two competing formats, established in different markets:

- **Global System for Mobile Communication (GSM)**-based phones using **Time Division Multiple Access (TDMA)**. With TDMA, each subscriber gets access to the radio channel by being allocated a time slot. GSM allows subscribers to use a **subscriber identity module (SIM)** card to use an unlocked handset with their chosen network provider. GSM is adopted internationally and by AT&T and T-Mobile in the US.
- **TIA/EIA IS-95 (cdmaOne)**-based handsets, using **Code Division Multiple Access (CDMA)**. CDMA means that each subscriber uses a code to key the modulation of their signal and this "key" is used by the receiver to extract the subscriber's traffic from the radio channel. With CDMA, the handset is managed by the provider, not the SIM. CDMA adoption is largely restricted to the telecom providers Sprint and Verizon.

In both cases, the cell network was built primarily to support voice calls, so 2G data access was provided on top, using **Circuit Switched Data (CSD)**. CSD is somewhat similar to a dial-up modem, though no analog transmissions are involved. CSD requires a data connection to be established to the base station (incurring call charges) and is only capable of around 14.4 Kbps at best.

3G

The transition from 2G to 3G saw various packet-switched technologies deployed to mobiles:

- **General Packet Radio Services/Enhanced Data Rates for GSM Evolution (GPRS/ EDGE)** is a precursor to 3G (2.5G), with GPRS offering up to about 48 Kbps and EDGE about 3-4 times that. Unlike CSD, GPRS and EDGE allow "always on" data connections, with usage billed by bandwidth consumption rather than connection time.
- **Evolved High Speed Packet Access (HSPA+)** is a 3G standard developed via several iterations from the Universal Mobile Telecommunications System (UMTS) used on GSM networks. HSPA+ nominally supports download speeds up to 168 Mbps and upload speeds up to 34 Mbps. HSPA+-based services are often marketed as 4G if the nominal data rate is better than about 20 Mbps.

 Note: *Note that with HSPA, the TDMA channel access technology has been abandoned and a type of CDMA used.*

- **CDMA2000/Evolution Data Optimized (EV-DO)** are the main 3G standards deployed by CDMA network providers. EV-DO can support a 3.1 Mbps downlink and 1.8 Mbps uplink.

4G/LTE

Long Term Evolution (LTE) is a converged 4G standard supported by both the GSM and CDMA network providers. LTE has a maximum downlink of 150 Mbps in theory, but no provider networks can deliver that sort of speed at the time of writing, with around 20 Mbps far more typical of real-word performance.

 Note: *LTE uses neither TDMA nor CDMA but Orthogonal Frequency Division Multiple Access (OFDMA), which is like the technology used in Wi-Fi (and DSL).*

LTE Advanced (LTE-A) is intended to provide a 300 Mbps downlink, but again this aspiration is not matched by real-world performance. Current typical performance for LTE-A is around 40 Mbps.

5G

According to the original specification, a 4G service was supposed to deliver 1 Gbps for stationary or slow-moving users (including pedestrians) and 100 Mbps for access from a fast-moving vehicle. Those data rates are now the minimum hoped-for standards for 5G. 5G is expected to be standardized in 2020. Rollout of 5G services will be relatively complex. Rather than a single large antenna serving a large **wireless cell**, 5G involves installing hundreds of smaller antennas, ideally with a fiber optic backhaul to the provider's access network. As well as faster mobile speeds, 5G is expected to provide fixed-wireless broadband solutions for homes and businesses, and to support IoT networks.

 Note: *To learn more, watch the related **Video** on the course website.*

MICROWAVE SATELLITE

Satellite systems provide far bigger areas of coverage than can be achieved by using other technologies. The microwave dishes are aligned to orbital satellites that can either relay signals between sites directly or via another satellite. The widespread use of satellite television receivers allows for domestic Internet connectivity services over satellite connections. Satellite services for business are also expanding, especially in rural areas where DSL or cable services are unlikely to be available.

Satellite connections experience quite severe latency problems as the signal must travel over thousands of miles more than terrestrial connections, introducing a delay of 4 to 5 times what might be expected over a land link. For example, if you know that accessing a site in the US from Europe takes 200 ms over a land (undersea) link, accessing the same site over a satellite link could involve a 900 ms delay. This is an issue for real-time applications, such as videoconferencing, VoIP, and multi-player gaming.

To create a satellite Internet connection, the ISP installs a satellite dish, referred to as a **very small aperture terminal (VSAT)**, at the customer's premises and aligns it with the orbital satellite. The size of a VSAT ranges from 1.2 to 2.4 meters in diameter. The satellites are in geostationary orbit over the equator, so in the northern hemisphere the dish will be pointing south. The antenna is connected via coaxial cabling to a Digital Video Broadcast Satellite (DVB-S) modem. This can be installed in the PC as a PCI card or as an external box connected via a USB or Ethernet port. Modem modules are also available as plug-in cards for enterprise routers.

As well as a home/office broadband solution, a network of VSATs provides a cost-effective solution to users who need to connect several sites or offices that are dispersed geographically. While there can be latency issues, VSATs do support transmission of voice and video. VSAT networks can be connected in a point-to-point, star, or mesh network. There are also transportable terminals that are portable, but remain stationary during transmission, and mobile terminals can communicate with satellites even when they are in motion.

INTERNET OF THINGS (IoT)

The term **Internet of Things (IoT)** is used to describe the global network of personal devices (such as phones, tablets, and fitness trackers), home appliances, home control systems, vehicles, and other items that have been equipped with sensors, software, and network connectivity. These features allow these types of objects to communicate and pass data between themselves and other traditional systems like computer servers; in other words, **Machine to Machine (M2M)** communication.

Each *thing* is identified with some form of unique serial number or code embedded within its own operating or control system and can interoperate within the existing Internet infrastructure, either directly or via an intermediary. As these devices tend to be small and often either unpowered or dependent on battery power, the cellular and Wi-Fi networking products that connect computers are often not suitable for use. Other wireless networking standards and products have been developed to facilitate IoT networks. Some of the connectivity technologies used by IoT devices are covered in the following sections.

IEEE 802.11 WI-FI DIRECT AND TETHERING

Wi-Fi remains an important technology for high-bandwidth IoT applications. Its only drawbacks are power consumption and antenna size. Peer-to-peer Wi-Fi connections can also be established using 802.11 radio standards through a mechanism such as **Wi-Fi Direct**, though in this case one of the devices functions as a **soft access point**. Wi-Fi Direct has the advantage over standard Wi-Fi ad hoc networks, as the latter support only the weak WEP security standard while Wi-Fi Direct can use the much more secure WPA2. There are also various means for a mobile device to share its cellular data or Wi-Fi connection with other devices (**tethering**).

Newer Wi-Fi standards are being developed to address the low power, long-distance transmission requirements of IoT devices:

- **IEEE 802.11ah**—This standard, marketed as **HaLow**, uses the sub 1 GHz band to achieve long-distance transmissions. The standard optimizes low power consumption by making use of sleep states, shortened contention negotiation, and small packet sizes. This suits devices that have to transmit small amounts of information sporadically to a controller application.
- **IEEE 802.11af**—This standard, marketed as **White-Fi**, uses white space in the broadcast TV portion of the spectrum (up to about 700 MHz) to achieve long-distance (potentially several kilometers), non-line-of-sight transmissions. There are mechanisms to prevent interference with local TV stations.

BLUETOOTH LE, ANT+, Z-WAVE, AND ZIGBEE

Bluetooth radio communication supports speeds of up to 3 Mbps. Adapters supporting version 3 or 4 of the standard can achieve faster rates (up to 24 Mbps) through the ability to negotiate an 802.11 radio link for large file transfers (BT + HS [High Speed]). Bluetooth does not require line-of-sight and supports a maximum range of 10 m (30 feet), though signal strength will be weak at this distance. Bluetooth devices can use a pairing procedure to authenticate and exchange data securely.

Version 4 also introduced a **Bluetooth Low Energy (BLE)** version of the standard. BLE is designed for small battery-powered devices that transmit small amounts of data infrequently. A BLE device remains in a low power state until a monitor application initiates a connection. BLE is not backwards compatible with "classic" Bluetooth, though a device can support both standards simultaneously. The data rate for BLE is 1 Mbps, and the range is 50m. Bluetooth version 5 improves the BLE specification to provide a 2 Mbps transfer rate. Version 5 also allows the use of lower transfer rates (1 Mbps, 500 Kbps, and 250 Kbps) to achieve longer ranges (up to 200m).

ANT+

The **ANT** protocol was developed by Garmin and its associated product standard **ANT+** has seen widespread use in communicating health and fitness sensor data between devices. However, it can also be found in applications such as bicycle/car tire pressure monitors and smartphones. It uses a similar radio frequency range to Bluetooth but has a very low power consumption and is therefore popular in applications which require long battery life.

Z-WAVE

Z-Wave is a wireless communications protocol used primarily for home automation. It was developed in 2001 by Zensys, a Danish company, but with interest and investment from other technology and engineering companies such as Cisco, Intel, Panasonic, and Danfoss, the Z-Wave Alliance was formed. Z-Wave operates a certification program for devices and software.

Z-Wave creates a mesh network topology, using low-energy radio waves to communicate from one appliance to another. Devices can be configured to work as repeaters to extend the network but there is a limit of four "hops" between a controller device and an endpoint. This allows for wireless control of residential appliances and other devices, such as lighting control, security systems, thermostats, windows, locks, swimming pools, and garage door openers. Z-Wave has been registered in most countries worldwide and uses radio frequencies in the high 800 to low 900 MHz range. It is designed to run for long periods (years) on battery power.

ZIGBEE

Zigbee has similar uses to Z-Wave and is an open source competitor technology to it. The Zigbee Alliance operates certification programs for its various technologies and standards. Zigbee uses the 2.4 GHz frequency band. This higher frequency allows more data bandwidth at the expense of range compared to Z-Wave and the greater risk of interference from other 2.4 GHz radio communications. Zigbee supports more overall devices within a single network (65,000 compared to 232 for Z-Wave), and there is no hop limit for communication between devices.

RFID, NFC, AND INFRARED

Radio frequency ID (RFID) is a means of tagging and tracking objects by using specially encoded tags. When an RFID reader scans a tag, the tag responds with the information programmed into it. A tag can either be an unpowered, passive device that only responds when scanned at close range (up to about 25 m) or a powered, active device with a range of 100 m. Passive RFID tags can be embedded in stickers and labels to track parcels and equipment and are used in passive proximity smart cards.

Near Field Communications (NFC) is a peer-to-peer version of RFID; that is, an NFC device can work as both tag and reader to exchange information with other NFC devices. NFC normally works at up to 2 inches (6 cm) at data rates of 106, 212, and 424 Kbps. NFC sensors and functionality are starting to be incorporated into smartphones. NFC is mostly used for contactless payment readers, security ID tags, and shop shelf edge labels for stock control. It can also be used to configure other types of connection (pairing Bluetooth devices, for instance).

As standardized by the **Infrared Data Association (IrDA)**, **infrared** links typically support speeds up to about 4 Mbps and ranges up to about 1 meter (or 3 feet). There are coding schemes specifying 16, 96, and 512 Mbps transmissions, but products supporting these standards have not been widely developed. Infrared communication requires line-of-sight and can be easily interrupted by someone walking between the communicating devices or even by bright sunlight. IrDA has become less common on modern peripherals and computer systems thanks to the growth of radio-based systems, such as Wi-Fi and Bluetooth. The use of infrared in smartphones, wearable technology, and IoT peripherals focuses on two other uses:

- IR blaster—This allows the device to interact with an IR receiver and operate a device such as a TV or HVAC monitor as though it were the remote-control handset.
- IR sensor—These are used as proximity sensors (to detect when a smartphone is being held to the ear, for instance) and to measure health information (such as heart rate and blood oxygen levels).

Activity 14-4

Discussing Wireless and IoT WAN Technologies

SCENARIO

Answer the following questions to test your understanding of the content covered in this topic.

---

1. **What standard(s) are intended to support 4G mobile wireless services?**

2. **Assuming that sufficient bandwidth can be provided, what factor limits the usefulness of a microwave satellite Internet link?**

3. **What type of network topology is used by IoT technologies such as Z-Wave and Zigbee?**

4. **What is a principal requirement of IoT technologies, as demonstrated by the latest version of Bluetooth?**

Summary

In this lesson, you learned about best practices and technologies underpinning installation of cabled, wireless, and remote access networks.

- Public WANs make more use of circuit switching technologies than LANs.
- The core infrastructure of telecommunication networks and the Internet is supported by fiber optic trunk links, mostly using SDH/SONET or Carrier Ethernet.
- T-carrier and E-carrier describe service levels for providing leased or dedicated access lines to subscribers. Other subscriber access technologies include ISDN, DSL, and broadband cable.
- WAN links can be used to run several packet switched data services, including Frame Relay, ATM, MPLS, and PPP.
- The demarc represents the end of an access provider's cabling. WAN links can be implemented using several devices, from CSU/DSUs for leased lines, though dial-up modems, to DSL/cable/satellite adapters and router/modems.
- Wireless WANs are implemented by using cellular radio and satellite links.
- Internet of Things (IoT) networks can be supported by low power wireless standards, including Z-Wave, Zigbee, and RFID.

What methods have you used in your environments to connect to WANs?

Has your organization implemented any IoT devices? If so, what standard(s) are they based on?

 Practice Questions: *Additional practice questions are available on the course website.*

Lesson 15

Using Remote Access Methods

LESSON INTRODUCTION

So far in this course, you have described technologies for implementing local networks where users have a device with a direct connection to the network. You have also seen that WAN technologies allow remote networks to be interconnected. This allows enterprise networks to communicate across multiple sites and for employees to access an enterprise LAN from their home network or while travelling. A further use case for remote networking is for technicians to access the management interfaces of switches, routers, and other hosts over a network rather than via a local console. In this lesson, you will identify the components of remote access network implementations.

LESSON OBJECTIVES

In this lesson, you will:

- Use remote access VPNs.

- Use remote access management methods.

Topic A

Use Remote Access VPNs

EXAM OBJECTIVES COVERED
2.3 Explain the purposes and use cases for advanced networking devices.
2.5 Compare and contrast WAN technologies.
3.4 Given a scenario, use remote access methods.

With today's mobile workforce, most networks have to support connections by remote employees, contractors, and customers to their network resources. These remote connections often make use of untrusted public networks, such as the Internet. When organizations opt to take advantage of public networks such as the Internet, the issue of securing data transmissions becomes critical. To counter the security risks associated with public networks, organizations implement a VPN within the public network to ensure secure communications. Consequently, understanding how to implement secure remote access VPN protocols will be a major part of your job as an information security professional.

REMOTE ACCESS SERVICES (RAS)

Remote access means that the user's device does not make a direct cabled or wireless connection to the network. The connection occurs over or through an intermediate network, usually a public WAN. Historically, remote access might have used analog modems connecting over the telephone system or possibly a private link (a leased line). These days, most remote access is implemented as a **virtual private network (VPN)**, running over the Internet. Given that, administering remote access involves essentially the same tasks as administering the local network. Only authorized users should be allowed access to local network resources and communication channels. Additional complexity comes about because it can be more difficult to ensure the security of remote workstations and servers and there is greater opportunity for remote logins to be exploited.

TUNNELING/ENCAPSULATION

Remote access depends on tunneling protocols. **Tunneling** is used when the source and destination computers are on the same logical network but connected via different physical networks. To illustrate the way tunneling works, look at this example of a legacy dial-up remote access connection.

1. Computer A is located at a user's home and requires remote access to information on Server C using TCP/IP networking.
2. Computer A uses its modem to dial the modem of Server B, which is a **Remote Access Service (RAS)** server and establishes a physical connection.
3. The local protocol request (TCP/IP packets) generated by Computer A is encapsulated into **Point-to-Point Protocol (PPP)** frames for transfer across the dial-up serial connection.
4. Server B receives the PPP frames and extracts the local protocol request.
5. The TCP/IP packets are placed onto the network in Ethernet frames for Server C to recognize and respond to.

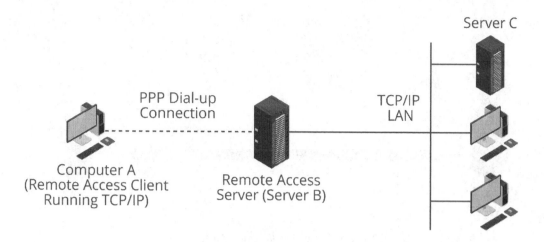

TCP/IP data is tunneled via PPP. (Image © 123RF.com.)

The Point-to-Point Protocol (PPP) is an **encapsulation** protocol. This means that the protocol sits around other protocol data. This allows a virtual **tunnel** to be created. PPP works at the Data Link layer of the OSI model (layer 2) and is designed to support layer 3 protocols, notably IP. Recall that PPP is used for many types of broadband Internet access, including DSL and cable broadband. In this scenario, however, PPP provides no security for data transmissions. Other protocols have been developed to provide connection security.

When the client initiates the connection, this can be referred to as a **demand dial** or **voluntary** tunnel. It is also possible for tunneling to use **compulsory** tunnels. A compulsory tunnel is established by routers across the Internet with no involvement on the part of their clients. From the client's perspective, it is simply sending data to its default gateway for delivery to the remote network. The router then establishes a VPN tunnel with its peer at the remote location, and all data is sent through the tunnel without affecting the client. Compulsory tunnels can be in place permanently (static), or they can be put in place based on the data or client type (dynamic).

VIRTUAL PRIVATE NETWORK (VPN) TOPOLOGIES

Historical remote access methods such as secure leased lines or dial-up connections are slow and expensive. A more practical solution is to use Internet access infrastructure and setup a secure tunnel for private communications through the Internet. This is referred to as a **virtual private network (VPN)**. Most business and residential sites have Internet connectivity, so this solution is very efficient in terms of cost. The main concerns are providing security for the transmissions that pass through the public network and preventing unauthorized users from making use of the VPN connection.

A VPN can be implemented in several topologies.

CLIENT-TO-SITE VPN

In a **client-to-site** or **remote access** topology, the VPN client connects over the public network to a VPN gateway (a VPN-enabled router) positioned on the edge of the local network (typically the VPN access server will be in a DMZ). Client-to-site is the "telecommuter" model, allowing home-workers and employees working in the field to connect to the corporate network. This often uses voluntary tunneling, but if the remote connections are established by fully managed hosts, network policies might be deployed to use compulsory tunneling, also referred to in this context as an always on VPN.

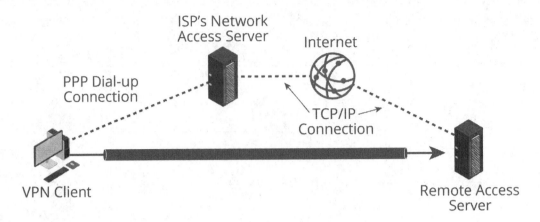

Remote access VPN. (Image © 123RF.com.)

SITE-TO-SITE VPN

VPNs can also be deployed in other topologies to suit the type of network access required. The **site-to-site** model connects two or more local networks, each of which runs a VPN gateway (or router). Historically, this type of connection might have been made by ISDN or a leased line. Using a VPN brings significant cost-savings, especially over long distances. Site-to-site VPNs are more likely to use compulsory tunneling. They can be established using point-to-point links (as shown) or they may use point-to-multipoint or multipoint-to-multipoint (mesh) links to route between more than two sites.

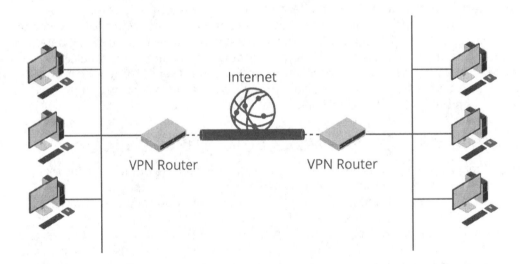

Site-to-site VPN. (Image © 123rf.com.)

Note: *VPNs are not always established over the public Internet. As you saw earlier, a WAN provider can implement MPLS VPNs via its network. The provider can use VLAN-like technology to isolate a customer's data from other traffic. This is a common model for site-to-site VPNs.*

HOST-TO-HOST VPN

A **host-to-host** VPN is similar to a site-to-site VPN, but rather than connecting two or more subnets, the link is between two hosts only, or between a server and its client. There might be special security reasons for configuring a secure tunnel between two hosts. It may also be the case that a single host on each network acts as a proxy for other network client computers.

Note: *While VPNs are being covered here as part of remote access, they can be just as usefully deployed on local networks. For example, the department for product development might need to provide secure communications with the marketing department.*

SSL/TLS/DTLS VPNs

Several VPN protocols have been used over the years. Legacy protocols such as the **Point-to-Point Tunneling Protocol (PPTP)** have been deprecated because they do not offer adequate security. Transport Layer Security (TLS) and IPSec are now the preferred options for configuring VPN access.

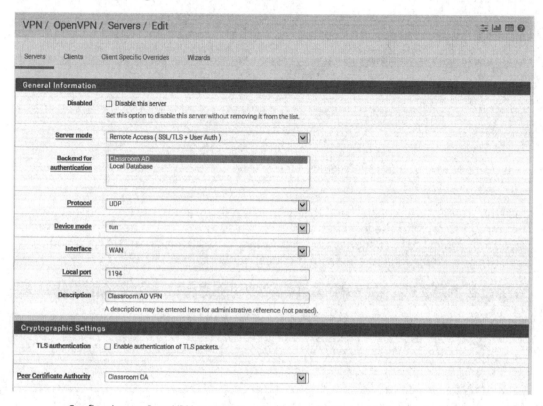

Configuring an OpenVPN server. (Screenshot used with permission from pfSense.)

A **TLS VPN** (still more commonly referred to as an SSL VPN) requires a remote access server listening on port 443 (or any arbitrary port number). The client makes a connection to the server using TLS (the same technology used to secure website access) so that the server is authenticated to the client (and optionally the client's certificate must be authenticated by the server). This creates an encrypted tunnel for the user to submit authentication credentials, which would normally be processed by a RADIUS server.

Note: *The port can be either TCP or UDP. UDP might be chosen for marginally superior performance, especially when tunneling latency-sensitive traffic, such as voice or video. TCP might be easier to use with a default firewall policy. TLS over UDP is also referred to as* **Datagram TLS (DTLS)**.

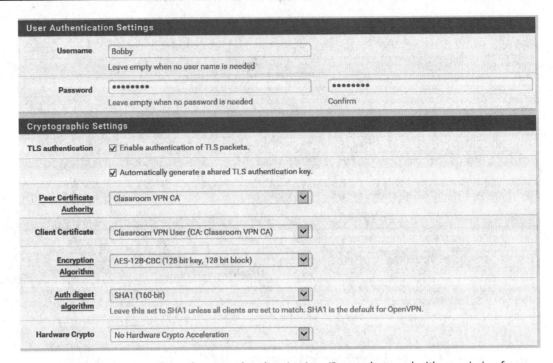

Configuring a client certificate for mutual authentication. (Screenshot used with permission from pfSense.)

Once the user is authenticated and the connection fully set up, the RAS server tunnels all communications for the local network over the secure socket. The client is normally placed in a dedicated VPN subnet and Network Address Translation (NAT) is used to forward communications to and from the local network.

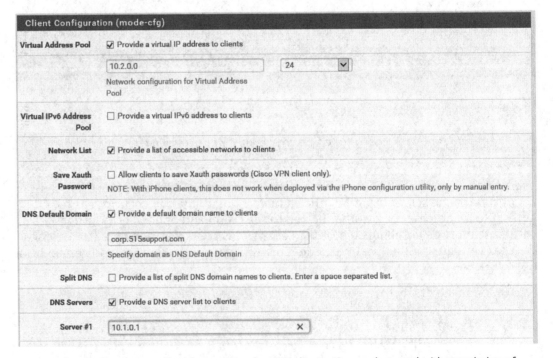

Configuring local network address setting for VPN clients. (Screenshot used with permission of pfSense.)

OpenVPN is an open source example of a TLS VPN (*openvpn.net*). OpenVPN can work in TAP (bridged) mode to tunnel layer 2 frames or in TUN (routed) mode to forward IP packets.

Another option is Microsoft's **Secure Socket Tunneling Protocol (SSTP),** which works by tunneling Point-to-Point Protocol (PPP) layer 2 frames over a TLS session (*docs.microsoft.com/en-us/openspecs/windows_protocols/ms-sstp/70adc1df-c4fe-4b02-8872-f1d8b9ad806a*). Microsoft developed SSTP to replace PPTP.

INTERNET PROTOCOL SECURITY (IPSec)

Internet Protocol Security (IPSec) is a set of open, non-proprietary standards that you can use to secure data as it travels across the network or the Internet. A connection security protocol such as Transport Layer Security is designed to protect application data. Unlike SSL/TLS, IPSec operates at the Network layer (layer 3) of the OSI model, so the protocol is not application-dependent. IPSec can provide both confidentiality (by encrypting data packets) and integrity/anti-replay (by signing each packet). The main drawback is that it is quite processor intensive, adding an overhead to data communications. IPSec can be used to secure communications on local networks and as a remote access protocol.

 Note: When IPv6 was being drafted, IPSec was considered a mandatory component as it was felt that all traffic over the new protocol should be secure. In recent years, RFCs have been revised so that now, IPSec is recommended for IPv6 but no longer mandatory (section 11 of RFC 6434).

IPSec can be used with several cryptographic algorithms. Algorithms that an implementation must support to be standards-compliant are defined in *RFC 8221*. There are also some obsolete ciphers that the RFC deprecates. Vendors can support additional, perhaps proprietary, ciphers as they see fit.

An IPSec policy is a set of security configuration settings that define how an IPSec-enabled system will respond to IP network traffic. The policy determines the security level and other characteristics for an IPSec connection. Each host that uses IPSec must have an assigned policy. Policies work in pairs; each of the endpoints in a network communication must have an IPSec policy with at least one matching security method for the communication to succeed. In Windows, a host-to-host IPSec policy is configured via the **Connection Security Rules** node of the **Windows Advanced Firewall** console. On a network, a **group policy object (GPO)** can be used to push the configuration to multiple computers. In Linux, a package such as StrongSwan (*https://www.strongswan.org*) can be used.

There are two core protocols in IPSec, which can be applied singly or together, depending on the policy.

AUTHENTICATION HEADER (AH)

The **Authentication Header (AH)** protocol performs a cryptographic hash on the packet plus a shared secret key (known only to the communicating hosts) and adds this **HMAC** in its header as an Integrity Check Value (ICV). The recipient performs the same function on the packet and key and should derive the same value to confirm that the packet has not been modified. The payload is not encrypted so this protocol does not provide confidentiality and is consequently not often used.

IPSec datagram using AH—The integrity of the payload and IP header is ensured by the Integrity Check Value (ICV), but the payload is not encrypted.

ENCAPSULATION SECURITY PAYLOAD (ESP)

This provides confidentiality and authentication by encrypting the packet, rather than simply calculating an HMAC. ESP attaches three fields to the packet (a header, a trailer that provides padding for the cryptographic function, and an Integrity Check Value).

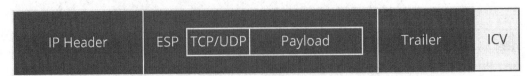

IPSec datagram using ESP—The TCP header and payload from the original packet is encapsulated within ESP and encrypted to provide confidentiality.

 Note: *The principles underlying IPSec are the same for IPv4 and IPv6, but the header formats are different. IPSec makes use of extension headers in IPv6 while in IPv4, ESP and AH are allocated new IP protocol numbers (50 and 51), and either modify the original IP header or encapsulate the original packet.*

IPSec TRANSPORT AND TUNNEL MODES

IPSec can be used in two modes:

- Transport mode—The IP header for each packet is not encrypted, just the data (or payload). This mode would be used to secure communications on a private network (an end-to-end implementation).

IPSec datagram using AH and ESP in transport mode.

- Tunnel mode—The whole IP packet (header and payload) is encrypted and a new IP header added. This mode is used for communications across an unsecure network (creating a VPN). This is also referred to as a router implementation.

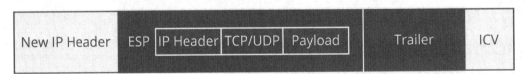

IPSec datagram using ESP in tunnel mode.

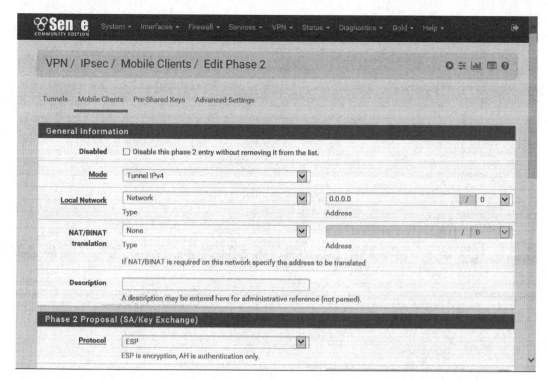

Configuring an IPSec tunnel in the pfSense security appliance. (Screenshot used with permission from pfSense.)

INTERNET KEY EXCHANGE (IKE) AND L2TP

AH and ESP both depend on the idea of a **shared secret**; that is, a **key** known only to the two hosts that want to communicate. For this to happen securely, the secret must be communicated to both hosts and the hosts must confirm one another's identity (mutual authentication). Otherwise, the connection is vulnerable to MitM and spoofing attacks.

The **Internet Key Exchange (IKE)** protocol is the part of the IPSec protocol suite that handles authentication and **key exchange**, referred to as **Security Associations (SA)**. IKE is also referred to as **Internet Security Association and Key Management Protocol (ISAKMP)**. IKE negotiations use UDP port 500. The negotiations take place over two phases:

- Phase I establishes the identity of the two hosts and performs key agreement using an algorithm called Diffie-Hellman to create a secure channel. Phase 1 is usually initiated in Main Mode, which involves six messages. The alternative is Aggressive Mode, which packs the information in these six messages into three messages. This is quicker but means that identifiers are exchanged in the clear. This may allow a snooper to perform a dictionary or brute-force password-guessing attack on the authentication information.

Diffie-Hellman key agreement establishes the shared secret used to sign the packets for message integrity. Diffie-Hellman does not authenticate the endpoints, however. Two methods of authenticating hosts are commonly used:

- PKI—The hosts use certificates issued by a mutually trusted CA to identify one another. This is the most secure mechanism but requires PKI architecture.
- Pre-shared key—The same passphrase is configured on both hosts. A pre-shared key (PSK) is also referred to as group authentication, as a single password or passphrase is shared between all hosts. Obviously, this is not very secure, as it is difficult to keep the pre-shared key a secret known only to valid hosts. It can also be difficult to change the key.

- Phase II uses the secure channel created in Phase 1 to establish which ciphers and key sizes will be used with AH and/or ESP in the IPSec session.

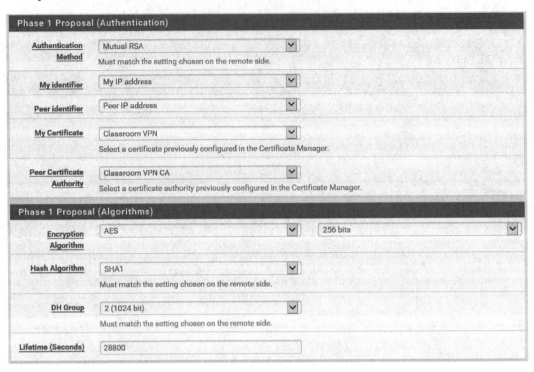

Configuring IKE in the pfSense security appliance. (Screenshot used with permission from pfSense.)

This first version of IKE is set up to ensure the mutual authentication of two peer hosts. On its own, it does not provide a simple means for a client user account to authenticate to a remote network. Consequently, for remote access VPNs, a combination of IPSec with the **Layer 2 Tunneling Protocol (L2TP)** VPN protocol is most often used. With L2TP/IPSec, the client and server hosts can authenticate using digital certificates or a PSK. The user can then authenticate to the remote access server using whatever method is supported (**MS-CHAP** or EAP, for instance). L2TP uses UDP port 1701 for data and connection control.

IKE v2

The drawbacks of the original version of IKE were addressed by an updated protocol. IKE v2 has some additional features that have made the protocol popular for use as a standalone remote access VPN solution. The main changes are:

- Support for EAP authentication methods, allowing, for example, user authentication against a RADIUS server.
- Simplified connection set up—IKE v2 specifies a single 4-message setup mode, reducing bandwidth without compromising security.
- Reliability—IKE v2 allows NAT traversal and MOBIKE multihoming. **Multihoming** means that a client such as a smartphone with multiple interfaces (such as Wi-Fi and cellular) can keep the IPSec connection alive when switching between them.

Compared to L2TP/IPSec, using IKE v2 is more efficient. This solution is becoming much better supported, with native support in Windows® 10, for instance.

DYNAMIC MULTIPOINT VPN (DMVPN)

A **dynamic multipoint VPN (DMVPN)** allows IPSec-based VPNs to be set up dynamically according to traffic requirements and demand. The original concept was developed by Cisco (*cisco.com/c/en/us/products/security/dynamic-multipoint-vpn-dmvpn/*

index.html) but has been adopted by other vendors and now runs on diverse router platforms.

A standard site-to-site VPN that involves more than two sites connects the remote sites (or spokes) to a headquarters site (hub) by using static tunnels configured between the hub and each spoke. This is referred to as a **hub and spoke** topology. DMVPN allows for the use of a dynamic mesh topology between multiple remote sites, effectively setting up direct VPNs, rather than the remote sites having to route traffic via the hub. Each site can communicate with all other spokes directly no matter where they are located.

To configure a DMVPN, each remote site's router is still connected to the hub router using an IPSec tunnel. As a large percentage of a remote site's traffic is likely to be with the main HQ, this ensures this normal traffic is dealt with efficiently. If two remote sites (spokes) wish to communicate with one another, the spoke instigating the link informs the hub. The hub will provide the connection details for the other spoke facilitating a dynamic IPSec tunnel to be created directly between the two spokes. This process invokes the use of the **Next Hop Router Protocol (NHRP)** to identify destination addresses and the **Generic Routing Encapsulation (GRE)** protocol. GRE is a tunneling protocol like PPP, but supports a wider range of features, including the ability to establish multipoint links. GRE encapsulates the encrypted IPSec packets. The two remote sites use the physical communications links between the two locations but all traffic flows over the temporary, encrypted VPN tunnel setup between them. DMVPN will then decide how long this temporary VPN remains in place based on timers and traffic flows.

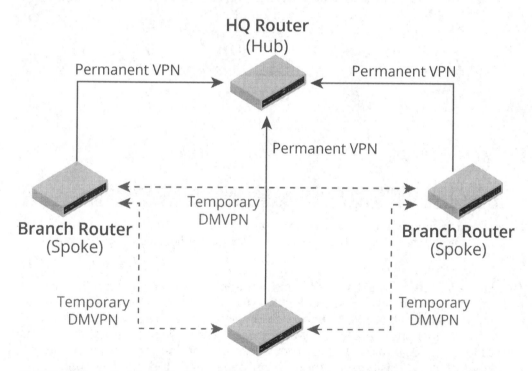

DMVPN topology. Each branch office establishes a permanent VPN with the HQ (hub) but can also create spoke-to-spoke VPNs dynamically. (Image © 123RF.com.)

In this way, DMVPN allows remote sites to connect with each other over the public WAN or Internet, such as when using video conferencing, but doesn't require a static VPN connection between sites. This on-demand deployment of IPSec VPNs is more efficient. Routing policies can be used to select the most reliable path between the remote sites, which potentially reduces the chance of latency and jitter affecting any voice/video services running over the VPN.

VPN CONCENTRATORS

All the major NOSs are bundled with software supporting VPNs. A server configured in this role is usually called a **Network Access Server (NAS)** or **Remote Access Server (RAS)**. Where the functionality is part of a router or dedicated security appliance, it may be called a **VPN concentrator**. In either case, the server would be placed on the network edge, protected by a firewall configuration in a demilitarized zone (DMZ).

The drawbacks of using a software solution for VPN are security (the server is exposed to the Internet) and performance (if the server is performing other tasks). A hardware or appliance-based solution overcomes these problems and a range of devices is available to meet different performance requirements at different price points. Many SOHO routers support IPSec and/or SSL VPNs with tens of simultaneous connections. These are all-in-one boxes combining the functions of VPN, Internet router, firewall, and DSL modem.

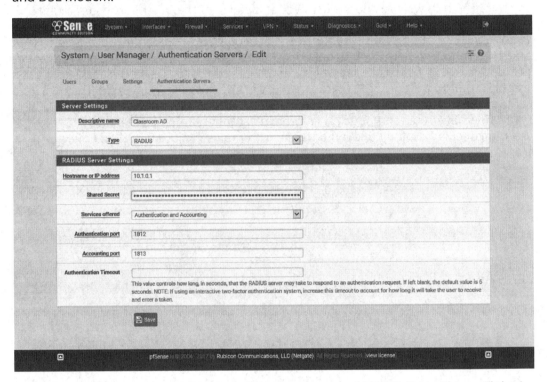

Configuring a pfSense security appliance as a VPN concentrator and RADIUS client—This avoids having to host the authentication server on the network edge. (Screenshot used with permission from pfSense.)

There are also dedicated SSL VPN concentrator appliances, such as those from Netgear, again aimed at the SME market. These are intended to be installed alongside a router, firewall, or IPSec VPN to enable secure access to web applications on the corporate intranet or extranet. Heavyweight, dedicated VPN concentrator appliances, such as Cisco's 3000 and 5000 series, provide scalable performance for hundreds or thousands of users. This type of product is no longer marketed, however (both the 3000 and 5000 series have been discontinued), as the same functionality is more economically incorporated into enterprise-class routers.

The creation of a RAS should be accompanied by documentation describing the uses of the service, security risks and countermeasures, and authorized users of the service. There should also be authorization to run the service from the network manager. The remote access policy should then implement the measures identified through compiling the documentation. Typical policy restrictions would be:

- Restricting access to defined users or groups.

- Restricting access to defined times of day or particular days of the week.
- Restricting privileges on the local network (ideally, remote users would only be permitted access to a clearly defined part of the network).
- Logging and auditing access logons and attempted logons.

In addition to this, a management plan should ensure that RASs and other hardware are kept up to date with the latest software or firmware updates. Administrative access to the devices should also be secured, using strong authentication.

 *Note: To learn more, watch the related **Video** on the course website.*

GUIDELINES FOR CONFIGURING SECURE REMOTE ACCESS PROTOCOLS

CONFIGURE A SECURE REMOTE ACCESS VPN

Follow these guidelines for configuring a secure remote access VPN:

- Implement VPN technology to support access to your networks by remote clients over the Internet and secure communications between sites across public networks.
- Select a VPN protocol that gives the most effective security while also being supported by your servers and client devices.
- Install the VPN concentrator to the network edge by using a secure firewall configuration to prevent compromise.
- Develop a remote access policy to ensure only authorized users can connect and ensure that the network is not compromised by remote clients with weak security configurations.

Activity 15-1

Discussing Remote Access VPNs

SCENARIO

Answer the following questions to test your understanding of the content covered in this topic.

---

1. **What are the three main topologies for implementing a VPN?**

2. **How does TLS improve the security of a VPN connection compared to PPTP?**

3. **What IPSec mode would you use for data confidentiality on a private network?**

4. **What difference does DMVPN make to a hub and spoke VPN topology?**

5. **What step can you take to prevent unauthorized use of a remote access server?**

Topic B

Use Remote Access Management Methods

EXAM OBJECTIVES COVERED
1.1 Explain the purposes and uses of ports and protocols.
3.4 Given a scenario, use remote access methods.

A remote access VPN provides a secure means for remote users to access network services. There are also many cases where a user needs to remotely access an individual host. This is most commonly implemented to allow administrators to perform remote management of workstations, servers, and network appliances, but it can also be used to provide ordinary users access to a desktop as well.

TELNET

Remote administration tools allow administrators to manage and configure a host over a network. They can work over a local network, over a VPN, or even across the Internet, if the appropriate ports are opened on the firewall. Remote administration tools are enormously useful, but they also represent a significant security exploit if their use is not secured.

Telnet is terminal emulation software to support a remote connection to another computer. It does not support file transfer directly; however, when connected, you can use the same commands as a local user on the remote computer via your computer's keyboard. In order to support Telnet access, the remote computer must run a service known as the Telnet Daemon. Telnet uses TCP port 23 by default.

```
mail.classroom.local - PuTTY
220 mail.classroom.local ESMTP
helo localhost
250 Hello.
mail from:<administrator@web.local>
250 OK
rcpt to:<administrator@classroom.local>
250 OK
data
354 OK, send.
from: Tech Support <administratator@web.local>
to: Hostmaster <administrator@classroom.local>
subject: Virus infection
mime-version: 1.0;
content-type: text/html;

<html>
<body>
<p>Viruses have been detected on your hosted server. Visit the <a href="http://w
www.notagoodidea.net">Hosting Services Portal</a> and enter your password to sca
n and remove them.</p>
</body>
</html>
.
250 Queued (199.078 seconds)
```

PuTTY Telnet client. (Screenshot courtesy of PuTTY.)

A Telnet interface can be password protected but the password and other communications are not encrypted and therefore could be vulnerable to packet sniffing, replay, MitM, and so on. Historically, Telnet has provided a simple means to configure switch and router equipment, but only secure access methods should be used for these tasks now. Ensure that the Telnet service is uninstalled or disabled, and block access to port 23.

SECURE SHELL (SSH)

Secure Shell (SSH) is the principal means of obtaining secure remote access to a UNIX or Linux server. The main uses of SSH are for remote administration and secure file transfer (SFTP). There are numerous commercial and open source SSH products available for all the major NOS platforms (UNIX®, Linux®, Windows®, and macOS®). The most widely used is OpenSSH (*openssh.com*). An SSH server listens on TCP port 22 by default.

SSH servers are identified by a public/private key pair (the **host key**). A mapping of host names to public keys can be kept manually by each SSH client, or there are various enterprise software products designed for SSH **key management**.

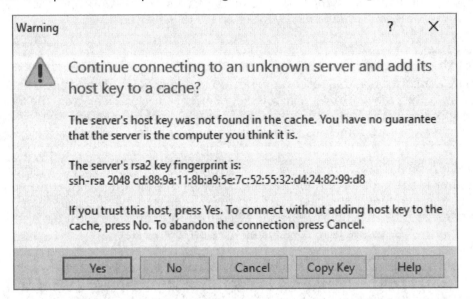

Confirming the SSH server's host key using the PuTTY SSH client. (Screenshot courtesy of PuTTY.)

 Note: *The host key must be changed if any compromise of the host is suspected. If an attacker has obtained the private key of a server or appliance, they can masquerade as that server or appliance and perform a MitM attack, usually with a view to obtaining other network credentials. You might also change the key to use a longer bit strength.*

SSH CLIENT AUTHENTICATION

The server's host key is used to set up a secure channel to use for the client to submit authentication credentials. SSH allows various methods for the client to authenticate to the SSH server. Each of these methods can be enabled or disabled as required on the server:

- **Username/password**—The client submits credentials that are verified by the SSH server either against a local user database or using an AAA server, such as RADIUS or TACACS+.
- **Kerberos**—The client submits the Kerberos credentials (a Ticket Granting Ticket) obtained when the user logged onto the workstation to the server using the Generic Security Services Application Program Interface (GSSAPI). The SSH server contacts

the Ticket Granting Service (in a Windows environment, this will be a domain controller) to validate the credential.

- **Host-based authentication**—The server is configured with a list of authorized client public keys. The client requests authentication using one of these keys, and the server generates a challenge with the public key. The client must use the matching private key it holds to decrypt the challenge and complete the authentication process. This provides non-interactive login but there is considerable risk from intrusion if a client host's private key is compromised.

- **Public key authentication**—Host-based authentication cannot be used with fine-grained access controls as the access is granted to a single user account. The same sort of public key authentication method can be used for each user account. Each remote user's public key is added to a list of keys authorized for each local account on the SSH server. The user's private key can be configured with a passphrase that must be input to access the key, providing an additional measure of protection compared to host-based authentication.

 Note: *Managing valid client public keys is a critical security task. Many recent attacks on web servers have exploited poor key management. If a user's private key is compromised, delete the public key from the appliance then regenerate the key pair on the user's (remediated) client device and copy the public key to the SSH server. Always delete public keys if the user's access permissions have been revoked.*

SSH COMMANDS

SSH features a rich command set, fully documented at the OpenSSH website (*openssh.com/manual.html*). Some of the most important commands are:

- `sshd`—Start the SSH Daemon (server). Parameters such as the host's certificate file, port to listen on, and logging options can be set via switches or in a configuration file.

- `ssh-keygen`—Create a key pair to use to access servers. The private key must be protected with a passphrase and stored securely on your local computer. The public key must be copied to the server. You can use the `ssh-copy-id` command to do this, or you can copy the file manually.

- `ssh-agent`—Configure a service to use to store the keys used to access multiple hosts. The agent stores the private key for each public key securely and reduces the number of times use of a private key has to be confirmed with a passphrase. This provides a single sign-on (SSO) mechanism for multiple SSH servers. The `ssh-add` command is used to add a key to the agent.

- `ssh `*`Host`*—Use the SSH client to connect to the server running at *Host*. *Host* can be an FQDN or IP address. You can also create a client configuration file.

- `ssh `*`Username@Host`*—Use the SSH client to connect to the server running at *Host* with a different username.

- `ssh `*`Host`*` "Command or Script"`—Use the SSH client to execute a command or script on the remote server running at *Host* without starting a shell.

- `scp `*`Username@Host:RemoteFile /Local/Destination`*—A file transfer client with remote copy/`rcp`-like command interface

- `sftp`—A file transfer client with FTP-like command interface.

REMOTE DESKTOP PROTOCOL (RDP) AND VIRTUAL NETWORK COMPUTING (VNC)

Telnet and SSH provide access to command-line prompts. This is sufficient for most administrative tasks, but where users want to connect to a desktop, they usually prefer to work with a graphical interface. A GUI remote administration tool sends screen and audio data from the remote host to the client and transfers mouse and keyboard input from the client to the remote host. **Remote Desktop Protocol (RDP)** is Microsoft's protocol for operating remote GUI connections to a Windows machine. RDP uses TCP port 3389. The administrator can specify permissions to connect to the server via RDP and can configure encryption on the connection. RDP has acquired several security enhancements as the product has developed. Two of the most important are NLA and Remote Credential Guard:

- **Network level authentication (NLA)** requires the client to authenticate before a full remote session is started. An RDP server that does not enforce NLA can be subject to DoS attacks, as the server uses resources to prepare for each requested session. It also sends information about the server to an attacker (such as the computer and domain names), regardless of whether they have valid authentication credentials.

- **RDP Restricted Admin (RDPRA) mode/Remote Credential Guard**—Making an RDP connection to a compromised workstation means an adversary could obtain the password hash for the account used to connect and then use it in a **pass-the-hash (PtH)** or ticket-forging attack. RDPRA was unsuccessful in mitigating this (it was itself vulnerable to PtH). Remote Credential Guard means that any access requests are processed by the RDP client machine, not on the server.

RDP is mainly used for the remote administration of a Windows server or client, but another function is to publish software applications on a server, rather than installing them locally on each client (application virtualization).

 Note: While RDP can be used to manage only Windows machines, RDP clients are available for other operating systems, including Linux, macOS, iOS, and Android so you can connect to a Windows desktop remotely using a non-Windows device.

There are several popular alternatives to RPD. Most support remote access to platforms other than Windows (macOS and iOS, Linux, Chrome OS™, and Android™, for instance). Examples include TeamViewer (*teamviewer.us*) and **Virtual Network Computing (VNC)**. VNC is a freeware product with similar functionality to RDP. There are versions, such as TightVNC (*https://www.tightvnc.com*), for Windows, Linux, and macOS. It works over TCP port 5900. Freeware versions of VNC provide no connection security and so should only be used over a secure connection, such as a VPN. However, there are commercial products packaged with encryption solutions, notably *realvnc.com*.

OUT-OF-BAND MANAGEMENT METHODS

Some network appliances, such as **unmanaged switches**, do not offer any configuration options or interface. You just have to plug them in, and they operate automatically. These switches are usually inexpensive and are intended only for home or small office use. **Managed switches** and appliances, such as routers, firewall/UTM devices, and WAPs, support more complex functions and can be configured and monitored over several interfaces. The functions of a managed appliance can be accessed via one of the device's management interfaces. An appliance may support the following interfaces:

- **Console port**—This requires connecting a terminal (a laptop, for instance) to the device via a separate physical interface using a special console (or rollover) cable. The terminal can then be used to start a command line interface (CLI).

- **AUX port**—This port is designed to connect to a modem and provide remote access over a dial-up link. Once the AUX port is enabled and configured, the modem can be connected to it by using an RS-232 serial cable, a specially wired RJ-45 rollover cable and terminal adapter (RJ-45 to DB9), or a management cable (RJ-45 to DB9). Configure the modem with appropriate serial link settings (refer to the vendor guide), connect it to an appropriate telephone line, and allocate an extension number. A remote host can connect to the appliance CLI by using a terminal emulation program such as HyperTerminal or PuTTY.

- **Management port**—This means configuring a virtual network interface and IP address on the device to use for management functions and connecting to it via one of the normal Ethernet ports. The port must be enabled for this function (some appliances come with a dedicated management port). Using Telnet (unsecure) or Secure Shell (SSH) to connect to a CLI remotely over the management interface in this way is referred to as a **virtual terminal**.

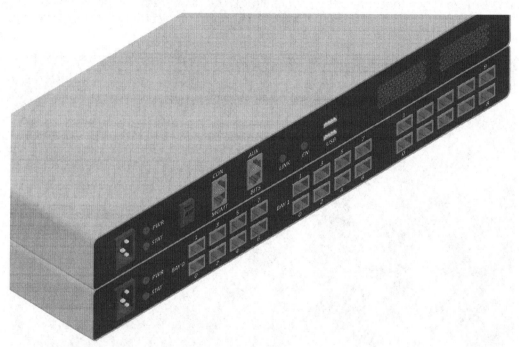

USB and RJ-45 type console ports plus AUX and other management interfaces on a router. (Image © 123RF.com.)

Management methods can be described as either **In-Band** or **Out-Of-Band (OOB)**. An in-band management link is one that shares traffic with other communications on the "production" network. The console port is a physically out-of-band management method; the link is limited to the attached device. When you are using a browser-based management interface or a virtual terminal, the link can be made out-of-band by connecting the port used for management access to physically separate network infrastructure. Obviously, this is costly to implement, but out-of-band management is more secure and means that access to the device is preserved when there are problems affecting the production network.

With an in-band connection, better security can be implemented by using a VLAN to isolate management traffic. This makes it harder for potential eavesdroppers to view or modify traffic passing over the management interface. This sort of virtual OOB does still mean that access could be compromised by a system-wide network failure, however.

 Note: Use a secure connection protocol (HTTPS rather than HTTP, or SSH rather than Telnet) for the management interface. This applies to OOB too, but it is critical for in-band management.

Lights-Out Management (LOM) is a good example of OOB management. LOM uses a dedicated management channel to access servers and network devices. The servers and network devices can be managed remotely, whether or not they are turned on. It works even if the operating system is not working or has yet to be installed. One example of LOM is Hewlett-Packard's Integrated Lights-Out (ILO). It is embedded on some HP servers, or it can be added as a card to HP servers. Another example of a network-based hardware OOB management tool is Dell's Integrated Dell Remote Access Controller (iDRAC).

CONSOLE CABLE AND CONSOLE ROUTERS

A console port connection on the appliance can use either a DB9/DB25 port or a standard RJ-45 jack (but wired in a different way to Ethernet). A **rollover** or **console cable** is used for connection to the terminal (PC). The HyperTerminal program on the PC is used to establish the connection using the appropriate settings for the serial link. On some newer appliances, a USB cable can be used.

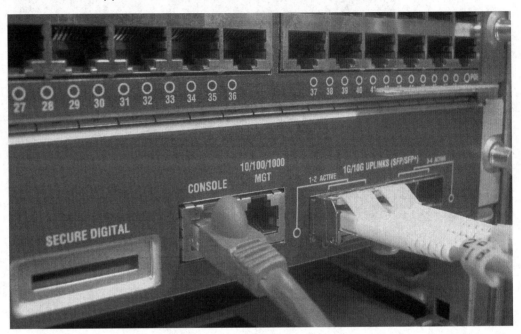

RJ-45 console port with cable connected. The Secure Digital slot for firmware updates and the MGT port next to the console port. (Image by Sorapop Udomsri © 123RF.com.)

A **console router** or **console server** is a device that hosts connections to the serial management ports of multiple switch, router, and security appliances. Typically, a single console router would facilitate connections to appliances in the same rack. This means that rather than attach a console cable from the management station to each appliance, the management station can connect to the management IP and port configured on the console router to open a terminal on the target appliance.

MANAGEMENT URL

Some enterprise appliances and most consumer or SOHO market devices can be managed via a browser by using the IP address of the management interface and either the HTTP or HTTPS (HTTP Secure) protocol. You need to connect the management station (the PC or laptop you are using to access the device) to the same subnet as the management interface or set up an appropriate route to it.

For example, the following **management URLs** would allow you to manage a Netgear SOHO router via a web browser on a PC with an IP address of 192.168.0.100 (or similar).

```
http://192.168.0.1
```

```
http://www.routerlogin.com
```

When you log on for the first time, you must change the default password to a secure passphrase (14 characters or longer). If possible, also change the default username.

FILE TRANSFER PROTOCOL (FTP)

As well as obtaining terminal or shell access, it is often necessary to transfer files to and from appliances or servers from a remote host. Most methods of **remote file access** use some form of the File Transfer Protocol (FTP).

The **File Transfer Protocol (FTP)** was one of the earliest protocols used on TCP/IP networks and the Internet. It is a connection-oriented protocol running over TCP that is especially useful for transferring files between hosts, especially when the hosts run different operating systems. While HTTPS-based web services and web applications can now offer simpler file transfer services to end users, FTP is still often used to perform administrative upload/download of files to and from servers and appliances. For these uses, it is important to secure the FTP session.

ACTIVE VS. PASSIVE FTP

An FTP client connects to TCP port 21 on an FTP server and opens a chosen dynamic client port number (N). The TCP port 21 **control port** is used to transfer commands and status information, but not for data transfer. Data transfer can operate in one of two modes: active or passive. In active mode, the client sends a PORT command specifying its chosen **data connection** port number (typically N+1), and the server opens the data connection between the chosen client port and TCP port 20 on the server.

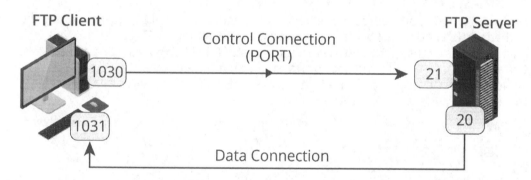

FTP in active mode. (Image © 123RF.com.)

In passive mode, the client opens a data port (again, typically N+1) and sends the PASV command to the server's control port. The server then opens a random high port number and sends it to the client using the PORT command. The client then initiates the connection between the two ports.

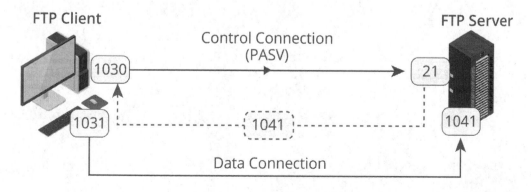

FTP in passive mode. (Image © 123RF.com.)

Active FTP poses a configuration problem for some firewalls, as the server is initiating the inbound connection, but there is no way of predicting which port number will be utilized. However, not all FTP servers and clients can operate in passive mode. If this is the case, check that firewalls installed between the client and server can support active FTP (stateful inspection firewalls).

 Note: *If you are unable to send/receive data via FTP, your network may have port filtering enabled for FTP traffic, therefore blocking communication traffic on those ports. Another problem is that the control connection can remain idle when the data connection is in use, meaning that the connection can be "timed out" by the firewall (or other routing device).*

 Note: *You should check that users do not install unauthorized servers on their PCs (**rogue servers**). For example, a version of IIS that includes HTTP, FTP, and SMTP servers is shipped with client versions of Windows, though it is not installed by default.*

TRIVIAL FILE TRANSFER PROTOCOL (TFTP)

The **Trivial File Transfer Protocol (TFTP)** is another file transfer service, but unlike FTP it is a **connectionless** protocol running over UDP port 69. Consequently, TFTP does not provide the guaranteed delivery offered by FTP and is only suitable for transferring small files. Also, it only supports reading (GET) and writing (PUT) files, not directory browsing, file deletion, or any of the other features of FTP. TFTP is not often deployed but could be used by a switch or router to download configuration files.

SSH FTP (SFTP) AND FTP OVER SSL (FTPS)

Secure FTP (SFTP) addresses the privacy and integrity issues of FTP by encrypting the authentication and data transfer between client and server. In SFTP, a secure link is created between the client and server using Secure Shell (SSH) over TCP port 22. Ordinary FTP commands and data transfer can then be sent over the secure link without risk of eavesdropping or MitM attacks. This solution requires an SSH server that supports SFTP and SFTP client software.

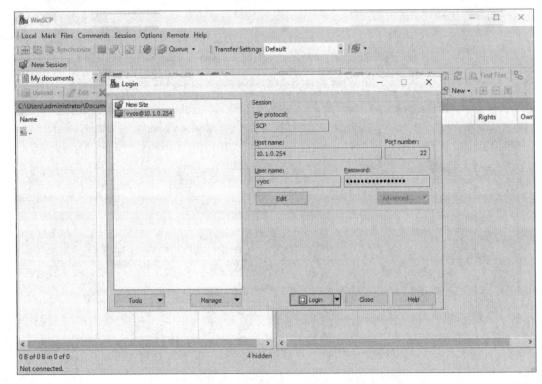

WinSCP SFTP client. (Screenshot courtesy of WinSCP.)

Another means of securing FTP is to use the connection security protocol SSL/TLS. As with SMTP, there are two means of doing this:

- **Explicit TLS (FTPES)**—Use the AUTH TLS command to upgrade an unsecure connection established over port 21 to a secure one. This protects authentication credentials. The data connection for the actual file transfers can also be encrypted (using the PROT command).
- **Implicit TLS (FTPS)**—Negotiate an SSL/TLS tunnel before the exchange of any FTP commands. This mode uses the secure port 990 for the control connection.

FTPS is tricky to configure when there are firewalls between the client and server. Consequently, FTPES is usually the preferred method.

 *Note: To learn more, watch the related **Video** on the course website.*

Activity 15-2

Discussing Remote Access Management Methods

SCENARIO

Answer the following questions to test your understanding of the content covered in this topic.

---

1. **What TCP/IP application protocol is associated with TCP port 23?**

2. **What are the main uses of SSH?**

3. **What type of attack is RDP Remote Credential Guard designed to protect against?**

4. **What is a virtual terminal?**

5. **What distinguishes TFTP from FTP?**

Activity 15-3
Configuring Secure Access Channels

BEFORE YOU BEGIN

Start the VMs used in this activity in the following order, adjusting the memory allocation first if necessary, and waiting at the ellipsis for the previous VMs to finish booting before starting the next group. You do not need to connect to a VM until prompted to do so in the activity steps.

1. **RT1-LOCAL** (256 MB)
2. **RT2-ISP** (256 MB)
3. **RT3-INT** (256 MB)
4. **DC1** (1024—2048 MB)
5. ...
6. **MS1** (1024—2048 MB)
7. ...
8. **PC1** (1024—2048 MB)
9. **PC2** (512—1024 MB)

 *Note: If you can allocate more than the minimum amounts of RAM, prioritize **DC1** and **PC1**.*

SCENARIO

One of the policies used to ensure defense in depth is to secure communications passing over a local network from snooping. In this activity, you will investigate some different ways to apply encryption to a communications channel. This activity is designed to test your understanding of and ability to apply content examples in the following CompTIA Network+ objectives:

*   1.1 Explain the purposes and uses of ports and protocols.
*   3.4 Given a scenario, use remote access methods.
*   4.5 Given a scenario, implement network device hardening.

---

1. To use the **PC2** VM to test connectivity from the Internet, attach the **PC2** VM to the **vINT02** switch and log on as the local Admin user.

    a) Open a connection window for the **PC2** VM. On the **PC2** VM console window, select **File→Settings**.

    b) Select the **Network Adapter** node. From the **Virtual switch** box, select **vINT02**. Select **OK**.

    c) From the logon screen, select **Switch User** then **Other User**. Log on as **.\Admin** with the password **Pa$$w0rd**

         *Note: Remember, instead of **Ctrl+Alt+Delete**, press **Ctrl+Alt+End** or use the button on the toolbar to access the logon screen.*

d) In the **Set Network Location** dialog box, select **Home network**. When configuration is complete (you don't need to wait to continue with the activity), select **Close**. Make sure you are familiar with the activity topology, summarized here. Note that you won't be using the **LAMP** VM in this activity.

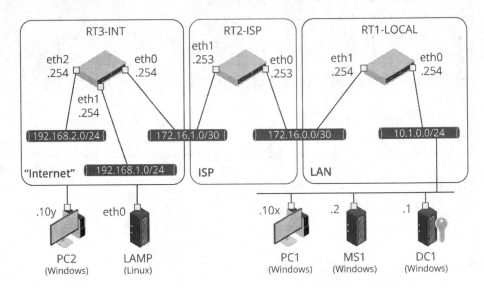

Lab topology—PC2 has been moved onto the Internet. (Image © 123RF.com.)

2. Use WinSCP (*winscp.net*) to access the SSH server running on the VyOS appliance. Connect to the file system using SCP and modify the /config/config.boot file.

a) Open a connection window for the **PC1** VM and log on as **515support\Administrator** with the password **Pa$$w0rd**

b) Double-click the **WinSCP** icon on the desktop.

c) From the **File protocol** box, select **SCP**.

d) In the **Host name** box, type **10.1.0.254**

e) In the **User name** box, type **vyos**

f) In the **Password** box, type **Pa$$w0rd**

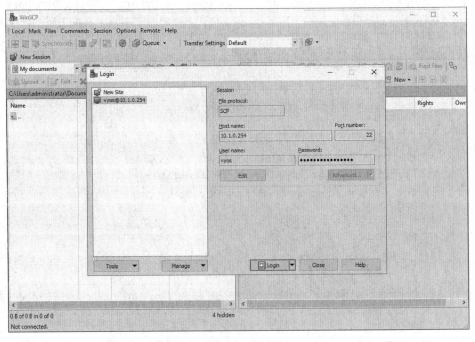

Configuring an SSH connection using WinSCP. (Screenshot courtesy of WinSCP.)

g) Select the **Save** button. In the **Save session as site** dialog box, check the **Save password** box then select **OK**.

h) Select the **Login** button. Observe the **Warning** dialog box.

The dialog box is displaying the public fingerprint part of the SSH server's host key pair. The public key is used to establish a secure session. The problem here is in authenticating the public key. You might keep a separate record of SSH keys configured on appliances.

 Note: *The public key does not need to be kept a secret.*

i) Select **Yes** to trust the host, and then select **Continue**.

j) In the directory explorer for the remote host (on the right) double-click the **Up One Directory** icon to go to home directory and again to open the root directory. Double-click the **config** directory to open it.

k) Drag **config.boot** to the left pane (to the local file system). Select **OK** to the confirmation.

l) In the left pane, right-click **config.boot** and select **Rename**. Change the name to **config2.boot** and press **Enter**.

m) Double-click the file to open it. Make a minor change, such as adding a description to the interfaces. For example:

```
interfaces {

ethernet eth0 {

description      PRIVATE

address         10.1.0.254/24

...
```

n) Save and close the file, and then copy it from the local system to the remote host by dragging it to the pane on the right.

o) Leave the WinSCP window open.

3. WinSCP lets you use scp or sftp for file transfer, but doesn't give you a shell on the remote host. For that you can use a terminal emulation program such as PuTTY (*chiark.greenend.org.uk/~sgtatham/putty*).

a) On the **PC1** VM desktop, double-click **PuTTY**.

b) In the **Host name** box, type **10.1.0.254**

c) From the **Connection type** options, leave **SSH** selected.

d) In the **Saved Sessions** box, type **10.1.0.254**

e) Select the **Save** button then click the **Open** button. Read the information in the **Warning** dialog box.

f) Select **Yes** to trust the host.

g) At the **login as** prompt, type **vyos** and press **Enter** then enter **Pa$$w0rd** when prompted.

h) Run the following commands:

```
conf

load config2.boot

commit

save

exit

show conf
```

Note: *Note that tab completion is not available with the SSH terminal.*

The descriptions you added should be present.

    i)   Press **q** to exit the configuration report. Leave PuTTY open.

4. Connect to the **VyOS** appliance from **PC2**.

    a)   Switch to the **PC2** VM. Double-click the **WinSCP** icon on the desktop.

    b)   From the **File protocol** box, select **SCP**.

    c)   In the **Host name** box, type *172.16.0.254*

    d)   In the **User name** box, type *vyos*

    e)   In the **Password** box, type *Pa$$w0rd*

    f)   Select the **Save** button. In the **Save session as site** dialog box, check the **Save** password box, and then select **OK**.

    g)   Select the **Login** button. Select **Yes** to trust the host then select **Continue**.

    h)   From the **Session** menu, select **Disconnect**.

5. In some circumstances, it might be appropriate to allow SSH access from the external interface, but it is a significant risk. Re-configure the **SSH server** to listen on its vLOCAL-connected interface only.

    a)   Switch to the **PC1** VM. In **PuTTY**, run the following commands:

```
conf

set service ssh listen-address 10.1.0.254

commit

save

exit
```

    b)   Close the terminal window and select **OK** to confirm.

    c)   On **PC2**, in WinSCP, select the **Login** button to test the connection to **172.16.0.254**. It should be refused. Leave the WinSCP window open.

Note: *Of course, this is only half the story. With the router configured as it is, there is nothing to stop an external host accessing the internal interface anyway. (You would need to configure a firewall on **RT1-LOCAL** to prevent this, but that's a job for another day.)*

6. As you can see, SSH is a good option for secure terminal access and secure file upload/download, but it is not always supported. Regular FTP is an alternative option for file transfer, but it must be secured by using SSL/TLS. To start the process of adding secure FTP publishing to the default website on the **MS1** server, first configure a digital certificate.

    a)   Open a connection window for the **MS1** VM, and sign in as *515support\Administrator* with the password *Pa$$w0rd*

    b)   In **Server Manager**, select **Tools→Internet Information Services (IIS) Manager**.

    c)   In the **Connections** pane, select the **MS1** server icon. In the **MS1 Home** pane, in the **IIS** section, open the **Server Certificates** applet.

    d)   In the **Actions** pane, select **Create Domain Certificate**.

    e)   In the **Common Name** field, type *updates.corp.515support.com*

f) In the other fields, enter **515support** for the Organization, **MIS** for the Organizational Unit, and any city or state as appropriate.

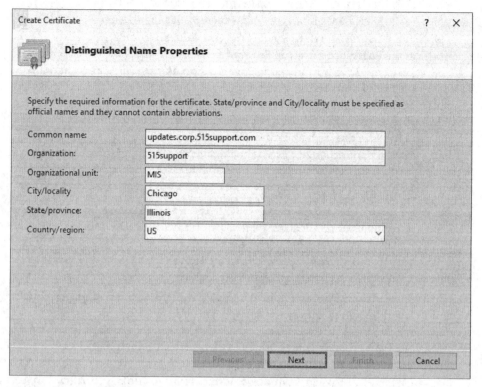

Completing a certificate signing request. (Screenshot used with permission from Microsoft.)

g) Select **Next**.

h) On the **Online Certification Authority** page, select the **Select** button, then select **515support-CA** and select **OK**.

i) In the **Friendly name** box, type **updates.corp.515support.com Domain-issued Certificate**. Select **Finish**.

 Note: The Common Name must match the FQDN clients will use to access the server. The Friendly Name is a way of identifying and selecting the certificate through the configuration dialog boxes.

7. After a few seconds, the certificate request will be granted. Bind the certificate to a secure FTP port.

a) Expand **Sites→Default Web Site**. Right-click **Default Web Site** and select **Add FTP Publishing**.

b) Select **Require SSL** and from the **SSL Certificate** box, select **updates.corp. 515support.com Domain-issued Certificate**.

 *Note: You are not changing the options under Binding, but note that the IP address is **All unassigned**, meaning the server will listen on any configured interface, and that you are using the default FTP connection port (21).*

c) Select **Next**.

d) Check the **Basic** box under **Authentication**. From the **Allow access to** box, select **Specified roles or user groups**. In the box below, type **Domain Admins**

e) Check both **Permissions** boxes then select **Finish**.

f) Select **OK** to the confirmation.

8. Test the new FTP service from the **PC2** VM.

a) Switch to the **PC2** VM. In **WinSCP**, select **New Site** from the box on the left.

b) From the **File protocol** box, select **FTP**.

c) From the **Encryption** list box, select **TLS/SSL Explicit encryption**.
Recall that you configured FTP SSL on the server using the default connection port (21). This is referred to as explicit mode.

d) In the **Host name** box, type *updates.corp.515support.com*

e) In the **User name** box, type *515support\Administrator*

f) In the **Password** box, type *Pa$$w0rd*

g) Select the **Save** button. In the **Save session as site** dialog box, check the **Save password** box then select **OK**.

h) Select the **Login** button. Select **Yes** to trust the host.

i) Drag **index.htm** to the left pane. Select **OK** to the confirmation.

j) In the left pane, right-click **index.htm** and select **Edit**.

k) Make a minor change, such as adding an update paragraph on a new line just after the opening <body> tag line. For example:

```
<p class="auto-style2">Secure FTP publishing is now
available</p>
```

l) Save and close the file, and then copy it from the local system to the remote host by dragging it to the pane on the right. Select **Yes** to confirm overwriting the existing file.

m) Use the **Run** dialog box to open the following URL to check the update you made:

```
http://updates.corp.515support.com
```

n) Close the browser, and then in WinSCP, from the **Session** menu, select **Disconnect**.

o) Select the **Close** button to exit WinSCP.

9. Configure an IPSec connection security policy. To start, use Group Policy to configure a domain-joined computer to obtain a digital certificate automatically.

a) On the **PC1** VM, select **Windows Administrative Tools→Certification Authority**. Select **OK** at the error.

b) In the **certsrv** console, right-click **Certification Authority (Local)** and select **Retarget Certification Authority**.

c) In the dialog box, select **Another computer** and type *dc1* in the box. Select **Finish**.

d) In the **Certification Authority** window, expand the **515support-CA** server icon and select the **Certificate Templates** folder.

e) Right-click the **Certificate Templates** folder and select **Manage**.
To issue a certificate with autoenroll permissions, you need to create a new template, using a suitable existing certificate as a model. Different certificate templates reflect different usages; a certificate used to authenticate a web server has different properties from one used to sign email, for instance.

f) In the **Certificate Templates Console** window, right-click the **Workstation Authentication** template and select **Duplicate Template**.

g) In the **Properties of New Template** dialog box, select the **General** tab.

h) In the **Template display name** box, adjust the text to *Workstation Authentication— 515support*.

i) Check the **Publish certificate in Active Directory** check box. Select the **Apply** button.

j) Select the **Security** tab. This defines the accounts able to access the certificate.

k) Select the **Domain Computers** account, then in the **Permissions for Domain Computers** section, check the **Autoenroll** check box in the **Allow** column.

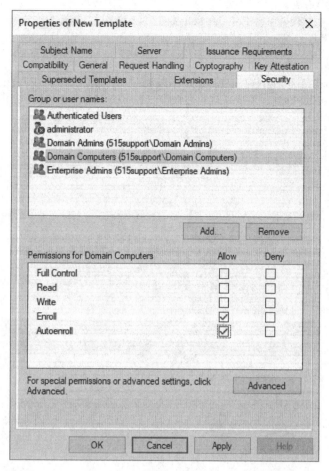

Configuring certificate template security settings. (Screenshot used with permission from Microsoft.)

This gives machines that have joined the domain (that is, that have a valid computer account in **Active Directory Users and Computers**) the right to autoenroll with the certificate. You can autoenroll user certificates to user accounts too, but that is not the purpose here.

l) Select **OK**, and then close the Certificate Templates Console window.

m) In the **Certification Authority** console, right-click the **Certificate Templates** folder and select **New→Certificate Template to Issue**.

n) Select **Workstation Authentication—515support** and select **OK**.

o) Close the certsrv console window.

10. Configure a **GPO (Group Policy Object)** to autoenroll computers with the certificate.

a) On the **PC1** VM, select **Windows Administrative Tools→Group Policy Management**.

b) In the **Group Policy Management** console, expand **Forest→ Domains→corp. 515support.com→ComputersOU**. Right-click **ComputersOU** and select **Create a GPO in this domain, and Link it here**.
The ComputersOU is a container for all domain-joined computers, other than the domain controller.

c) In the **Name** box, type *Workstation Certificate Autoenrollment Policy* and select **OK**.

d) Right-click the new policy and select **Edit**.

e) In the **Group Policy Management Editor** console, expand **Computer Configuration→Policies→Windows Settings→Security Settings→ Public Key Policies**.

f) With **Public Key Policies** selected, in the right pane, double-click **Certificate Services Client—Auto-Enrollment**.

g) In the **Certificate Services Client—Auto-Enrollment Properties** dialog box, from the **Configuration Model** list box, select **Enabled**.

h) Select the **Renew expired certificates, update pending certificates, and remove revoked certificates** and **Update certificates that use certificate templates** check boxes.

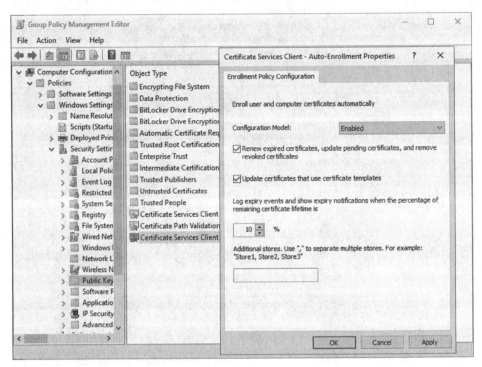

Configuring certificate autoenrollment. (Screenshot used with permission from Microsoft.)

i) Select **OK**.

j) Close the Group Policy Management Editor window, but leave the **Group Policy Management** console open.

11. Configure a domain isolation IPSec policy.

This means that domain-joined computers require authentication for inbound connections, so only computers with valid domain-issued certificates can connect. This type of policy cannot be applied to the domain controller (or to DHCP and DNS services).

a) In the **Group Policy Management** console, right-click **ComputersOU** and select **Create a GPO in this domain, and Link it here**.

b) In the **Name** box, type *515support Domain Connection Security Rules* and select **OK**.

c) Right-click the new policy and select **Edit**.

d) In the **Group Policy Management Editor** console, expand **Computer Configuration→Policies→Windows Settings→Security Settings→Windows Firewall with Advanced Security→Windows Firewall with Advanced Security→Connection Security Rules**.

e) Right-click **Connection Security Rules** and select **New Rule**. With the **Isolation** radio button selected, select **Next**.

f) Select the option **Require authentication for inbound connections and request authentication for outbound connections** and select **Next**.
Requiring connection security for outbound connections would be a highly restrictive policy.

g) On the **Authentication Method** page, select **Computer and user (Kerberos V5)**. Select **Next**.

h) Check only the **Domain** profile and select **Next**.

i) In the **Name** box, type *515support Domain Isolation Policy* and then select **Finish**.

12. Run **gpupdate** to apply the new policy, and then test it by accessing the web server on **MS** from **PC1**.

   a) On both the **PC1** and **MS1** VMs, open a command prompt and run the following commands:

   ```
   gpupdate

   certlm.msc
   ```

   b) Select **Yes** at the **UAC** prompt, then use the **Certificates** manager opened by the second command to verify that the new computer certificates are present in **Certificates—Local Computer→Personal→Certificates**. If the certificate is not shown yet, wait a few more seconds and then refresh the console.

   c) On the **MS1** VM, select the **Start** button and type *firewall*. Select the **Windows Firewall with Advanced Security** link that appears.

   d) In the **Windows Firewall with Advanced Security** console, expand **Monitoring→Connection Security Rules**. Verify that the **515support Domain Isolation Policy** is present.

   e) Start **Wireshark** and begin a packet capture.

   f) Switch to the **PC1** VM and connect to the following URL:

   ```
   http://updates.corp.515support.com
   ```

   g) Switch back to the **MS1** VM.

   h) In the **Windows Firewall with Advanced Security** console, expand **Monitoring→Security Associations→Main Mode**. The connection made by **PC1** (10.1.0.10x) is listed.

   i) Select the **Quick Mode** node. Note the protocols enabled:

   - AH Integrity (Authentication Header)—Not enabled (listed as None).
   - ESP Integrity (Encapsulating Security Payload)—Using the Secure Hash Algorithm version 1.
   - ESP Encryption—Not enabled (listed as None).

   The effect of this policy is to authenticate and prove the integrity of communications, but not to encrypt the payload contents.

   j) Select the **Wireshark** window, and stop the capture.

   k) Enter the following filter, where x completes the DHCP-assigned octet for the **PC1** VM:

   ```
   ip.src == 10.1.0.10x or ip.dst == 10.1.0.10x
   ```

l) Observe the sequence of the IPSec connection setup:

- The hosts exchange information about ciphers supported and then exchange credentials securely to form a security association.
- This negotiation uses the ISAKMP protocol over UDP port 500.
- The actual data is exchanged in ESP packets (IP protocol number 50). The original IP addresses are transmitted in the clear (transport mode), and you can read the cleartext HTTP transmissions (encryption is not enabled).

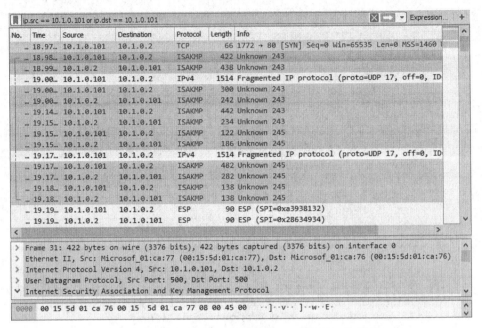

Observing IPSec. (Screenshot courtesy of Wireshark.)

m) Switch to the **PC2** VM and connect to the following URL:

`http://updates.corp.515support.com`

The connection is refused because **PC2** has not connected to the domain since the new policies were applied and, therefore, does not have a valid certificate to use to establish the IPSec security association.

13. Change the IPSec policy to enable confidentiality.

a) On **PC1**, edit the **515support Domain Connection Security Rules** GPO.

b) Expand **Computer Configuration→Policies→Windows Settings→Security Settings→Windows Firewall with Advanced Security→Windows Firewall with Advanced Security** then right-click **Windows Firewall with Advanced Security** and select **Properties**.

c) On the **IPSec Settings** tab, under **IPSec defaults**, select **Customize**.

d) Under **Data protection (Quick Mode)**, select **Advanced** then select the **Customize** button.

e) Check the **Require encryption for all connection security rules that use these settings** check box and select **OK**.

f) Select **OK** to close all the dialog boxes.

g) Run `gpupdate` on the **MS1** and **PC1** VMs, and then repeat the connection test, monitoring in Wireshark on **MS1**.
The ESP payload should be undecipherable.

14. Discard changes made to the VMs in this activity.

a) Switch to the **Hyper-V Manager** window.

b) Select one of the running VMs. From the **Action** menu, select **Revert** then select the **Revert** button (or use the right-click menu in the **Hyper-V Manager** console). Repeat on each VM to revert all the VMs to their saved checkpoints.

Summary

In this lesson, you learned about best practices and technologies underpinning installation of remote access networks.

- SSL/TLS and IPSec enable the creation of secure VPNs by encrypting traffic (secure tunneling). VPNs can be used in different topologies, such as host-to-site or site-to-site.

- Remote access protocols can be used for administration and file transfer, but care must be taken to distinguish secure and unsecure protocols.

What remote administration tools are used in your workplace? Would you suggest others based on what you just learned?

Share your experiences with using VPNs. What protocols did you use? Can you think of any reasons why you would not update the protocols?

Practice Questions: *Additional practice questions are available on the course website.*

Lesson 16

Identifying Site Policies and Best Practices

LESSON INTRODUCTION

The cabling, switches, routers, security appliances, servers, and clients that make up a local network must all be located within a site. Managing a site so that the network is robust and efficient involves drafting and following policies and best practices, supported by documentation. This might seem less immediately rewarding than getting a new application or server up-and-running, but these kinds of operational procedures are just as important to well-managed networks.

LESSON OBJECTIVES

In this lesson, you will:

- Manage networks with documentation and diagrams.

- Summarize the purposes of physical security devices.

- Compare and contrast business continuity and disaster recovery concepts.

- Identify policies and best practices.

Topic A

Manage Networks with Documentation and Diagrams

 EXAM OBJECTIVES COVERED
3.1 Given a scenario, use appropriate documentation and diagrams to manage the network.

In this topic, you will identify how configuration management documentation and diagrams are used to manage networks. In case of a disaster, it is imperative that you already have critical documentation in place that will help you rebuild as quickly as possible. Without detailed documentation, you would have to rely on memory to determine your network layout, which would likely be very time consuming, costly, and ultimately inaccurate. A complete set of configuration documentation will give you a solid base from which to recover from incidents or plan upgrades.

CHANGE AND CONFIGURATION MANAGEMENT

Configuration management means identifying all components of ICT infrastructure (hardware, software, and procedures) and their properties. **Change management** means putting policies in place to reduce the risk that changes to these components could cause service disruption (network downtime). **ITIL®** is a popular documentation of good and best practice activities and processes for delivering IT services. Under ITIL, configuration management is implemented using the following elements:

- **Service assets** are things, processes, or people that contribute to the delivery of an IT service.
- A **Configuration Item (CI)** is an asset that requires specific management procedures for it to be used to deliver the service. Each CI must be identified by some sort of label. CIs are defined by their **attributes**, which are stored in a **Configuration Management Database (CMDB)**.
- **Baseline**—A fundamental concept in configuration management is the baseline. The baseline represents the way it was. A baseline can be a **configuration baseline** (the ACL applied to a firewall, for instance) or a **performance baseline** (such as the throughput achieved by a server).
- A **Configuration Management System (CMS)** is the tools and databases that collect, store, manage, update, and present information about CIs. A small network might capture this information in spreadsheets and diagrams; there are dedicated applications for enterprise CMS.

One of the goals of the CMS is to understand the relationships between CIs. Another is to track changes to CI attributes (and, therefore, variance from the baseline) over time. The purpose of documentation in terms of change and configuration management is:

- Identify each component (CI) and label it.
- Capture each CI and its (relevant) attributes in a CMDB.
- Capture relationships between CIs—This is best done using diagrams.
- Capture changes to a CI as a job log and update the CMDB.

CHANGE MANAGEMENT DOCUMENTATION

Each individual network component should have a separate document or database record that describes its initial state and all subsequent changes. This document should include configuration information, a list of patches applied, backup records, and even details about suspected breaches. Printouts of hash results, last modification dates of critical system files, and contents of log files may be pasted into this book. System maintenance can be made much smoother with a comprehensive change document. For instance, when a patch is available for an OS, it typically applies in only certain situations. Manually investigating the applicability of a patch on every possible target system can be very time consuming; however, if logs are available for reference, the process is much faster and more accurate.

 Note: *An example of change management documentation that you can use as a starting point when creating this document for your organization can be found at sans.org/cyber-security-summit/archives/file/summit-archive-1493830822.pdf.*

To reduce the risk that changes to configuration items will cause service disruption, a documented management process can be used to implement changes in a planned and controlled way. Change requests are usually generated when something needs to be corrected, something changes, or there is room for improvement in a process or system currently in place. The need to change is often described either as **reactive**, where the change is forced on the organization, or as **proactive**, where the need for change is initiated internally. Changes can also be categorized according to their **potential impact** and level of risk (major, significant, minor, or normal, for instance).

In a formal change management process, the need or reasons for change and the procedure for implementing the change is captured in a **Request for Change (RFC)** document and submitted for approval. The RFC will then be considered at the appropriate level and affected stakeholders will be notified. This might be a supervisor or department manager if the change is normal or minor. Major or significant changes might be managed as a separate project and require approval through a **Change Advisory Board (CAB)**.

Regardless of whether an organization is large enough to require formal change management procedures and staff, the implementation of changes should be carefully planned, with consideration for how the change will affect dependent components. For most significant or major changes, organizations should attempt to trial the change first. Every change should be accompanied by a **rollback** (or remediation) plan, so that the change can be reversed if it has harmful or unforeseen consequences. Changes should also be scheduled sensitively if they are likely to cause system downtime or other negative impact on the workflow of the business units that depend on the IT system being modified. Most networks have a scheduled **maintenance window** period for **authorized downtime**.

When the change has been implemented, its impact should be assessed, and the process reviewed and documented to identify any outcomes that could help future change management projects.

STANDARD OPERATING PROCEDURE (SOP) AND WORK INSTRUCTIONS

The main difficulty in implementing a workable configuration management system is in determining the level of detail that must be preserved. This is not only evident in capturing the asset database and configuration baseline in the first place, but also in managing **moves, adds, and changes (MACs)** within the network infrastructure. In terms of network tasks, a CMS will require that configuration changes be made only when there is a valid job ticket authorizing the change. This means that the activity of all network personnel, whether it be installing new devices or troubleshooting, is recorded in **job logs**. In a fully documented environment, each task will be governed by some sort of procedure. Formal configuration management models often distinguish between two types of procedural documentation:

- **Standard Operating Procedure (SOP)**—Sets out the principal goals and considerations (such as budget, security, or customer contact standards) for performing a task and identifies lines of responsibility and authorization for performing it.
- **Work instruction**—Step-by-step instructions for performing an installation or configuration task using a specific product or technology and credentials.

INVENTORY MANAGEMENT AND VENDOR DOCUMENTATION

It is crucial for an organization to have a well-documented inventory of its tangible and intangible assets and resources. In terms of network management, these include network appliances (routers, switches, threat management devices, access points), servers, workstations, and passive network infrastructure (cabling and cross-connects).

There are many software suites and associated hardware solutions available for tracking and managing assets (or **inventory**). An asset management database can be configured to store as much or as little information as is deemed necessary, though typical data would be type, model, serial number, asset ID, location, user(s), value, and service information. Tangible assets can be identified using a barcode label or RFID tag attached to the device (or more simply using an identification number). An RFID tag is a chip programmed with asset data. When in range of a scanner, the chip powers up and signals the scanner. The scanner alerts management software to update the device's location. As well as asset tracking, this allows the management software to track the location of the device, making theft more difficult.

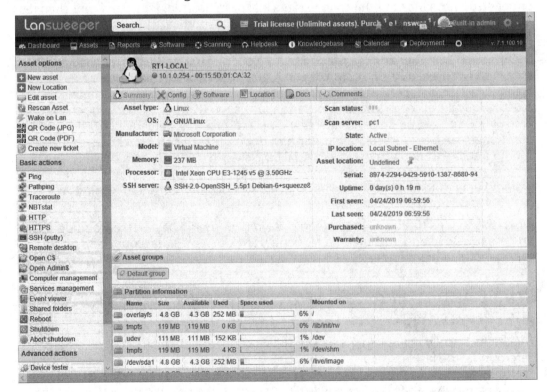

A product such as Lansweeper assists inventory management by scanning network hosts and compiling an asset information database automatically. (Screenshot used with permission from Lansweeper.)

For each asset record, there should also be a copy of or link to the appropriate **vendor documentation**. This includes both an invoice and warranty/support contract and support and troubleshooting guidance.

> *Note: To learn more, watch the related **Video** on the course website.*

BLUEPRINTS AND WIRING DIAGRAMS

A **diagram** is the best way to capture the complex relationships between network elements. It is also the most effective means of locating a host or node within the network. Network documentation is likely to make use of various types of diagrams. A **blueprint** is a detailed diagram of wiring and port locations. For example, you might use blueprints to document wall port locations and cable runs in an office. Physically accurate blueprints are hard to design and are likely to require the help of an architect or graphics professional.

A **wiring diagram** (or pin-out) shows detailed information about the termination of twisted pairs in an RJ-45 or RJ-48C jack or Insulation Displacement Connector (IDC). You might also use a wiring diagram to document how fiber-optic strands are terminated.

> *Note: You should document the wiring diagrams used to terminate twisted pairs. Ethernet is wired by T568A or T568B, and the same standard should be used consistently throughout the network.*

A **port location diagram** identifies how wall ports located in work areas are connected back to ports in a distribution frame or patch panel and then from the patch panel ports to the switch ports. Remember that there are two types of distribution frame:

- **Main Distribution Frame (MDF)**—The location for distribution/core level internal switching. The MDF will terminate trunk links from multiple Intermediate Distribution Frames (IDFs). The MDF also serves as the location for termination of external (WAN) circuits. You should ensure that WAN links to the Internet or to remote offices from the MDF are clearly labeled and that key information such as IP addresses and bandwidth is documented. The WAN provider will assign a circuit ID, and you will need to quote this if raising any sort of support issue.

- **Intermediate Distribution Frame (IDF)**—In a large network, one or more IDFs provides termination for access layer switches that serve a given area, such as a single office floor. Each IDF has a trunk link to the MDF. Make sure that these are clearly labeled and distinct from access ports.

> *Note: In a small network, IDFs may not be necessary, in which case the MDF will terminate access layer switch ports directly.*

> *Note: In addition to having a diagram, it can be very useful to take a photo of the current configuration by using a digital camera or smartphone. This provides an additional visual reference for troubleshooting and identifying unauthorized changes.*

LABELING

In order for a physical diagram of cabling and assets to make any sense, there must be a system of labeling in place for identifying these assets. The **ANSI/TIA/EIA 606 Administration Standard for Commercial Telecommunications Infrastructure** sets out a basic scheme for documenting a typical office network installation. It includes suggested identifiers for different subsystems and elements of the installation, including cables, distribution frames/patch panels, ports, circuits, and systems (appliances or computers).

A typical type of **port naming convention** is for alphanumeric identifiers for the campus (for multi-campus networks), building (for campus networks), telecommunications space, and port. For example, CB01-01A-D01 could refer to a cable terminating at Main Campus Building (CB01), telecommunications space A on floor 1 (01A), data port 1 (D01). Structured cable and patch cords should be labeled at both ends to fully identify the circuit.

A similar convention can be adopted for infrastructure and systems, such as distribution frames, patch panels, switches, routers, APs, and servers. It can be more complex to use location-based identifiers, though, as hardware may get moved around during its service life, requiring the tag to be changed.

The naming convention might also try to encode other information, such as the type and function of a device or its service/warranty support code.

It is also helpful to use color-coding for cable types. One suggested scheme is as follows.

Color	Usage
Orange	Demarc/access provider
Green	Demarc/CPE
Purple	Router/PBX links
Red	Work area telephone links
White	MDF/1st level backbone
Gray	IDF/2nd level backbone
Brown	Campus backbone
Blue	Work area data links
Yellow	Other (alarm systems)

LOGICAL VS. PHYSICAL NETWORK DIAGRAMS

Diagrams can be used to model **physical** and **logical** relationships at different levels of scale and detail. A **schematic** is a simplified representation of a system. In terms of the physical network topology, a schematic diagram can show the general placement of equipment and telecommunications rooms, plus device and port IDs without trying to capture the exact position or relative size of any one element. Schematics can also be used to represent the logical structure of the network in terms of zones and subnets.

When you make network schematics, resist the urge to represent too much in a single diagram. For example, create separate diagrams for the PHY, Data Link, and Logical (IP) layers. Some of the information appropriate to show at each layer includes:

- PHY (Physical layer)—Asset IDs and cable links. You can use color-coding to represent the cable type (make sure the diagram has an accompanying legend to explain your color scheme).
- Data Link (layer 2)—Shows interconnections between switches and routers, with asset IDs (or the management IP of the appliance), interface IDs, and link-layer protocol and bandwidth. You could use line thickness to represent bandwidth, but for clarity it is a good idea to use labels as well.
- Logical (IP/layer 3)—IP addresses of router interfaces (plus any other static IP assignments) and firewalls, plus links showing the IP network ID and netmask, VLAN ID (if used), and DHCP scopes.
- Application—Server instances and TCP/UDP ports in use. You might also include configuration information and performance baselines (CPU, memory, storage, and network utilization) at this level.

Schematics can either be drawn manually using a tool such as Microsoft® Visio® or compiled automatically from **network mapping** software.

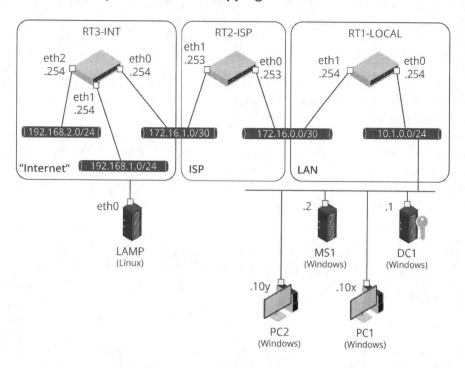

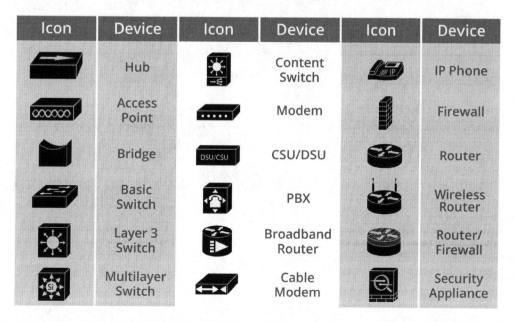

Use a tool such as Visio to create network diagrams. (Image © 123RF.com.)

NETWORK DIAGRAM SYMBOLS

Schematics can use either representative icons or pictures or drawings of actual product models. As far as icons go, the ones created by Cisco are recognized as standards. These are freely available (without alteration) from Cisco's website (*cisco.com/c/en/us/about/brand-center/network-topology-icons.html*).

Icon	Device	Icon	Device	Icon	Device
	Hub		Content Switch		IP Phone
	Access Point		Modem		Firewall
	Bridge		CSU/DSU		Router
	Basic Switch		PBX		Wireless Router
	Layer 3 Switch		Broadband Router		Router/ Firewall
	Multilayer Switch		Cable Modem		Security Appliance

Icons for some of the more commonly used network devices. (Images © and Courtesy of Cisco Systems, Inc. Unauthorized use not permitted.)

RACK DIAGRAMS

A **rack system** is a specially configured steel shelving system for server and network equipment. Racks are standard widths and can fit appliances using standard height multiples of 1.75" called **units (U)**. For example, a basic switch might be 1U while a server might be 4U (7") in height. The standard height for a full-size rack is 42U. Therefore, it is just over six feet tall. Smaller half-racks are available, however. Specs such as the 19" width format and rail spacing are defined by standards documented by the EIA. Using a rack allows equipment to be stored more securely and compactly than ordinary desks or shelving would allow.

A rack diagram records the position of each appliance in the rack. You can obtain stencils that represent vendor equipment from their websites or a collection such as *visiocafe.com*. You can record key configuration information for each item using labels. As well as service tags and port IDs and links, you should identify which power outlets on the uninterruptible power supply (UPS) connect to which appliance power supply units (PSU)s.

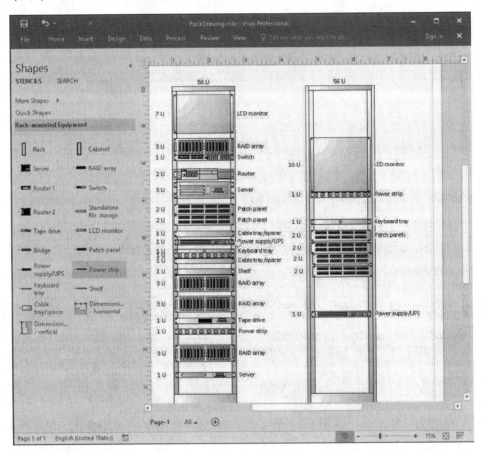

Designing rack layout in Microsoft Visio. (Screenshot used with permission from Microsoft.)

Activity 16-1

Discussing Network Documentation and Diagrams

SCENARIO

Answer the following questions to test your understanding of the content covered in this topic.

1. **What types of baselines are useful when you are performing configuration management?**

2. **In terms of day-to-day tasks, what demonstrates that effective configuration management procedures are in place?**

3. **What is the difference between physical and logical schematics?**

4. **You are analyzing a network schematic and notice the icon shown here. What does it represent?**

5. **True or False? Rack units are sold in models of varying width.**

6. You are working at a telecommunications point and notice that the cables in one patch panel are all red while the ones in another are all blue. What, if anything, does this represent?

Topic B
Summarize the Purposes of Physical Security Devices

EXAM OBJECTIVES COVERED
4.1 Summarize the purposes of physical security devices.

In this topic, you will examine ways to enhance the physical security of your facilities and network. Part of securing a network is to ensure that it is physically secure from threats, which includes access to the building and certain areas. An understanding of procedures and hardware that increase the physical security of your network will help reduce the potential for intrusion.

BADGES AND SECURE ENTRY SYSTEMS

Physical site security can be thought of in terms of **zones**. Each zone should be separated by its own barrier(s). **Access points** through the barriers need to be controlled by one or more security mechanisms. Progression through each zone should be progressively more restricted. **Preventive** controls are ones that stop an intruder from gaining unauthorized access, if they work effectively. Most preventive controls involve mechanisms that only allow authorized persons through access points. A **barricade** is something that prevents access. As with any security system, no barricade is completely effective; a wall may be climbed or a lock may be picked, for instance. The purpose of barricades is to channel people through defined access points. Each access point should have an **authentication** mechanism (or **door access control**) so that only authorized persons are allowed through.

A photographic **ID badge** showing name and (perhaps) access details is one of the cornerstones of building security. Color-coding could be used to make it obvious which zones a badge grants access to. Anyone moving through secure areas of a building should be wearing an ID badge or visitor pass. Anyone without an ID should be challenged.

Most door access controls depend on some type of **lock mechanism**. A lock mechanism is used to physically secure the access point until an authorized person provides authentication at the access point. A secure gateway will normally be self-closing and self-locking, rather than depending on the user to close and lock it. Locks can use a variety of mechanisms. A conventional lock prevents the door handle from being operated without the use of a key. More expensive types offer greater resistance against lock picking. A deadbolt is a bolt on the frame of the door, separate from the handle mechanism, that serves as a secondary locking mechanism other than the doorknob lock on a standard door frame.

Rather than a key, the lock is operated by entering a PIN on an electronic keypad. This type of lock is also referred to as cipher, combination, or keyless.

KEY FOB AND SMART CARD LOCKS

An electronic smart lock may be opened using a magnetic swipe card or feature a proximity reader to detect the presence of a wireless key fob, one-time password generator (physical token), or smart card. A **smart card** ID badge can be combined with authentication credentials, such as a digital certificate or a biometric sensor, such as a fingerprint reader, giving the ability to authenticate with electronic door access controls.

A smart card is a credit card-sized device with an integrated chip and data interface. A smart card is either **contact based**, meaning that it must be physically inserted into a reader, or **contactless**, meaning that data is transferred using a tiny antenna embedded in the card. Most door access controls will use contactless readers to avoid wear-and-tear. A contactless smart card can also be described as a **proximity card**. Older proximity cards requiring contact use 125 kHz proximity, while the newer "contactless" smart cards use 13.56 MHz proximity. The ISO has published various ID card standards to promote interoperability, including ones for smart cards (ISO 7816 for contact and ISO 14443 for contactless types).

 Note: *Near field communications (NFC) allows a smartphone to emulate proximity card standards and be used with standard proximity card readers.*

Electronic **key fobs** are small devices which can be used for activating things such as remote keyless entry systems on motor vehicles, and in buildings for access to certain areas. The fob operates in much the same manner as a proximity card to communicate with a central server for the building, which can be programmed to allow access only to certain areas, or only within certain time frames. Some fobs may generate a token that can be used only once. The code displayed by the token must be entered by using the lock's PIN pad.

Using a contactless smart card entry system (left) and a key fob token generator (right). (Image © 123RF.com.)

BIOMETRIC LOCKS

An electronic lock may also be integrated with a biometric scanner. A **biometric** device is activated by human physical features, such as a fingerprint, voice, retina, or signature. Biometric access makes it more difficult for someone to gain access to the locked room, hardware, or protected data. An example of a biometric lock is an optical or thermal scanner that reads and stores the fingerprints of authorized users. The user then places his or her hand on the scanner to gain access to a door.

Using a biometric entry system with fingerprint reader. (Image © 123RF.com.)

DETECTION-BASED DEVICES

Detection-based controls provide an important additional layer of defense in the event that prevention-based controls fail to work. For example, **surveillance** is another layer of security designed to improve the resilience of perimeter gateways. Effective surveillance mechanisms ensure that attempts to penetrate a barricade are detected. Surveillance may be focused on perimeter areas or within security zones themselves. Surveillance can be performed by security guards. **Video surveillance** is a cheaper means of monitoring than maintaining separate guards at each gateway or zone, though still not cheap to set up if the infrastructure is not already in place on the premises. It is also quite an effective deterrent.

The other big advantage is that movement and access can be recorded. The main drawback is that response times are longer, and security may be compromised if not enough staff are in place to monitor the camera feeds.

A camera is either fixed or can be operated using Pan-Tilt-Zoom (PTZ) controls. Different cameras suit different purposes. If you want to record the image of every person entering through a door, a fixed, narrow focal length camera positioned on the doorway will be perfectly adequate. If you want to survey a large room and pick out individual faces, a camera with PTZ is required.

The cameras in a **Closed Circuit Television (CCTV)** network are typically connected to a multiplexer using coaxial cabling. The multiplexer can then display images from the cameras on one or more screens, allow the operator to control camera functions, and record the images to tape or hard drive. Newer camera systems may be linked in an IP network, using regular data cabling. Small **IP cameras** can use Power over Ethernet (PoE), avoiding the need to provision a separate power circuit.

Pan-tilt-zoom CCTV installed to monitor a server room. (Image by Dario Lo Presti © 123RF.com.)

RFID asset tracking tags allow electronic surveillance of managed assets. The tags can be detected at entry/exit points to prevent theft. A battery-powered component might be in the tag, or the tag might be passive and read and scanned by a powered device. The tags are entered into a tracking database, which also usually has a map of the coverage area so that a particular asset can be located. The asset tags can also be used to maintain a history of purchase, repairs, location, users, and other information about the device.

ALARMS AND TAMPER DETECTION

Alarms are another standard type of security control. Alarms provide a detection-based security mechanism, though an audible alarm can also be an effective deterrent by causing the attacker to abandon the intrusion attempt. There are three main types:

- **Circuit**—A circuit-based alarm sounds when the circuit is opened or closed, depending on the type of alarm. This could be caused by a door or window opening or by a fence being cut. A closed-circuit alarm is more secure because an open circuit alarm can be defeated by cutting the circuit. This type of system can be used for tamper detection.
- **Motion detection**—A motion-based alarm is linked to a detector triggered by any movement within a relatively large area, such as a room. The sensors in these detectors are either microwave radio reflection (similar to radar) or passive infrared (PIR), which detect moving heat sources.
- **Duress**—This type of alarm is triggered manually by staff if they come under threat. There are many ways of implementing this type of alarm, including wireless pendants, concealed sensors or triggers, and DECT handsets. Some electronic entry locks can also be programmed with a duress code that is different from the ordinary access code. This will open the gateway but also alert security personnel that the lock has been operated under duress.

As well as protecting building areas, alarms can be installed on rack systems and appliance chassis. For example, a chassis intrusion alarm can alert an administrator if a server case is opened. **Tamper detection** is an additional layer of security that can be found in computers, alarm systems, surveillance systems, and even a security fence. Tampering is detected when a circuit is broken or when a switch is tripped on a device. On a security system, as a result, an alarm is set off and emergency personnel are contacted. Tamper devices can also be seen when you open configured models of computer hardware or if you open the casing of a home security system. It immediately notifies you that the system has been tampered with. Even security fences sometimes have tamper systems installed to detect and alert authorities when the fence wire has been cut.

Another possibility is that an attacker could splice a tap into network data cable. A physically secure cabled network is referred to as a **Protected Distribution System (PDS)**. A hardened PDS is one where all cabling is routed through sealed metal conduit and subject to periodic visual inspection. Lower grade options are to use different materials for the conduit (plastic, for instance). Another option is to install an alarm system within the cable conduit, so that intrusions can be detected automatically.

Activity 16-2

Discussing the Purposes of Physical Security Devices

SCENARIO

Answer the following questions to test your understanding of the content covered in this topic.

---

1. **Some of the businesses near Greene City Interiors have recently had break-ins where some equipment was stolen. As news of these events spread, it generated some concern within the organization that their physical security measures should be reviewed and possibly enhanced. There is currently a security guard on duty during business hours, video monitoring of the front and back doors, and employees use plastic badges with their name and photo to enter the building. Access beyond the lobby area requires swiping a badge to enter the rest of the building. What, if anything, would you recommend adding or improving for their physical security?**

    While they have a good start on physical security, they should consider installing motion sensors or cameras for after hours. There should also have doors to install video monitoring on those doors, to update to using smart cards or key fobs for entrance.

2. **What type of door access control would allow entry based on the possession of a cryptographic smart card?**

3. **What technology could be used to provision security cameras without having to provide a separate circuit for electrical power?**

4. **What is a PDS, and what type of security control does it provide?**

Topic C

Compare and Contrast Business Continuity and Disaster Recovery Concepts

EXAM OBJECTIVES COVERED
3.2 Compare and contrast business continuity and disaster recovery concepts.

While you have considered troubleshooting scenarios in which a single host loses network connectivity or where a fault in a switch, router, or DHCP/DNS service creates problems for a network segment, you also need to consider problems with network availability across an entire site. The plans used to minimize the risk of these site-wide problems are referred to as business continuity, while the plans used to mitigate these issues if they do occur are called disaster recovery. At this stage in your career, it is important that you understand the concepts underpinning these plans, so that you can assist with business continuity and disaster recovery operations.

RESILIENCY STRATEGIES

A **business continuity plan (BCP)** or **continuity of operations plan (COOP)** is a collection of processes that enable an organization to maintain normal business operations in the face of some adverse event. There are numerous types of events, both natural and man-made, that could disrupt the business and require a continuity effort to be put in place. They may be instigated by a malicious party, or they may come about due to careless or negligence on the part of non-malicious personnel. The organization may suffer loss or leakage of data; damage to or destruction of hardware and other physical property; impairment of communications infrastructure; loss of or harm done to personnel; and more. When these negative events become a reality, the organization will need to rely on resiliency and automation strategies to mitigate their effect on day-to-day operations.

When you are implementing a network, the goal should be to minimize the **single points of failure** and to allow ongoing service provision despite a disaster. To perform **IT contingency planning (ITCP)**, think of all the things that could fail, determine whether the result would be a critical loss of service, and whether this is unacceptable. Then identify strategies to make the system resilient. The resilience of a system can be determined by measuring or evaluating several properties.

AVAILABILITY CONCEPTS

One of the key properties of a resilient system is **high availability**. **Availability** is the percentage of time that the system is online, measured over the defined period (typically one year). The corollary of availability is downtime; that is, the percentage or amount of time during which the system is unavailable. The **Maximum Tolerable Downtime (MTD)** metric states the requirement for a business function. Downtime is calculated from the sum of scheduled service intervals (Agreed Service Time) plus unplanned outages over the period. High availability is usually loosely described as 24x7 (24 hours per day, 7 days per week) or 24x365 (24 hours per day, 365 days per year). For a critical system, availability will be described as two-nines (99%) up to five- or six-nines (99.9999%).

Availability	Annual MTD (hh:mm:ss)
99.9999%	00:00:32
99.999%	00:05:15
99.99%	00:52:34
99.9%	08:45:36
99.0%	87:36:00

A system where there is almost no scheduled downtime and outages are extremely rare is also referred to as **continuous availability**. This sort of availability is required when there is not just a commercial imperative, but a danger of injury or loss of life associated with systems failure. Examples include networks supporting medical devices, air traffic control systems and communications satellites, as well as emerging technologies such as networked autonomous vehicles and new smart-city applications, from smart law enforcement systems to smart traffic signaling systems.

Each IT system will be supported by assets, such as servers, disk arrays, switches, routers, and so on. **Key Performance Indicators (KPIs)** can be used to determine the reliability of each asset. Some of the main KPIs relating to service availability are as follows:

- **Mean Time to Failure (MTTF)** and **Mean Time Between Failures (MTBF)** represent the expected lifetime of a product. MTTF should be used for non-repairable assets. For example, a hard drive may be described with an MTTF, while a server, which could be repaired by replacing the hard drive, would be described with an MTBF. You will often see MTBF used indiscriminately, however. For most devices, failure is more likely early and late in life, producing the so-called bathtub curve.
  - The calculation for MTBF is the total time divided by the number of failures. For example, if you have 10 devices that run for 50 hours and two of them fail, the MTBF is 250 hours/failure (10*50)/2.
  - The calculation for MTTF for the same test is the total time divided by the number of devices, so (10*50)/10, with the result being 50 hours/failure.

  MTTF/MTBF can be used to determine the amount of asset redundancy a system should have. A redundant system can failover to another asset if there is a fault and continue to operate normally. It can also be used to work out how likely failures are to occur.

- **Mean Time to Repair (MTTR)** is a measure of the time taken to correct a fault so that the system is restored to full operation. This can also be described as mean time to replace or recover.

SERVICE LEVEL AGREEMENT (SLA) REQUIREMENTS

A **service level agreement (SLA)** is a contractual agreement setting out the detailed terms under which an ongoing service is provided. This can be a legally binding formal contract between supplier and customer businesses or a less formal agreement, such as an SLA agreed between internal departments. SLA requirements define aspects of the service, such as scope, quality, and responsibilities that are agreed upon between the service provider(s) and the customer. A common feature of an SLA is a contracted delivery time of the service or performance. In this case, the SLA will typically have a technical definition in terms of MTD, MTBF, and MTTR. An SLA may also define performance metrics for network data rates, such as throughput, latency, jitter, and packet loss. An SLA will also identify which party is responsible for reporting faults. This document specifies the service levels for support and documents any penalties for the service level not being met by the provider. Depending on the nature of your organization's business, you may be responsible for maintaining SLA requirements agreed with your customers, use SLAs to guarantee service standards from your suppliers, or both.

Unless there are specific exceptions, service standards need to be preserved during a disaster, or the service provider will become liable for penalties or losses imposed on the customer. Any downtime that an organization's staff spends in the workplace without access to the computer system is likely to be time wasted and therefore a significant cost. Similarly, time that customers cannot access a sales site or make inquiries because a system is down, represents costs in terms of lost sales opportunities and reputation. If you can quantify these costs, you can provide a cost-based justification for upgrading the network infrastructure to improve reliability.

FAULT TOLERANCE AND REDUNDANCY

A system that can experience failures and continue to provide the same (or nearly the same) level of service is said to be fault tolerant. **Fault tolerance** is often achieved by provisioning **redundancy** for critical components and single points of failure. A redundant component is one that is not essential to the normal function of a system but that allows the system to recover from the failure of another component. Examples of devices and solutions that provide fault tolerance include the following:

- **Redundant spares**—Components such as power supplies, network cards, drives (**RAID**), and cooling fans provide protection against hardware failures. A fully redundant server configuration is configured with multiple components for each function (power, networking, and storage). A faulty component will then automatically failover to the working one.
- **Network links**—If there are multiple paths between switches and routers, these devices can automatically failover to a working path if a cable or network port is damaged.
- **Uninterruptible power supplies (UPSs)** and **standby power supplies**—Provide power protection in the event of complete power failure (blackout) and other types of building power issues.
- **Backup strategies**—Provide protection for data.
- **Cluster services**—A means of ensuring that the total failure of a server does not disrupt services generally.

While these computer systems are important, thought also needs to be given about how to make a business fault tolerant in terms of staffing, utilities (such as heat, power, communications, and transport), customers, and suppliers.

 Note: The emphasis is on resiliency and fault tolerance, rather than reliability. The system design should expect faults and disasters and compensate for them instead of trying to design them out of existence.

PORT AGGREGATION AND LOAD BALANCING

A network link is very often a critical single point of failure. Routers and switches can provide multiple paths through a network to prevent over-dependence on **single critical nodes**. Ideally, network cabling should be designed to allow for **multiple paths** between the various servers, so that during a failure of one part of the network, the rest remains operational. Routers are great fault tolerant devices, because they can communicate system failures and IP packets can be routed via an alternate device. Provisioning redundant links can be expensive, however.

Note: Switches and routers can be fault tolerant only if there are multiple routes to choose from.

NIC TEAMING AND PORT AGGREGATION

Link aggregation means combining two or more separate cabled links into a single logical channel, referred to as an **EtherChannel**. From the host end, this can also be called **NIC teaming**; at the switch end, it can be called **port aggregation**. The term **bonding** is also widely substituted for aggregation. For example, a single network adapter and cable segment might support 1 Gbps; bonding this with another adapter and cable segment gives a link of 2 Gbps.

Link aggregation can also provide **redundancy**; if one link is broken, the connection is still maintained by the other (**failover**). It is also often cost-effective; a 4-port Gigabit Ethernet card might not match the bandwidth of a 10GbE port (4 Gbps compared to 10 Gbps) but will cost less. There are proprietary port bonding mechanisms, such as Cisco's Port Aggregation Protocol (PAgP), but it has been standardized as **IEEE 802.3ad/ 802.1ax**. 802.3ad bonded interfaces are described as a **Link Aggregation Group (LAG)**. 802.3ad also defines the **Link Aggregation Control Protocol (LACP)**, which can be used to detect configuration errors and recover from the failure of one of the physical links.

Note: This configuration is fully redundant only if the business function does not depend on the full speed of the bonded link. If one port fails, and the link drops to 1 Gbps, but that bandwidth is insufficient, there is not full redundancy.

LOAD BALANCING

A load balancer can switch client traffic to alternative processing nodes, reducing bottlenecks and allowing for failover services in the event of a host or network route going down.

CLUSTERING

Cluster services are a means of ensuring that the total failure of a server does not disrupt services generally. A cluster is a group of servers, each of which is referred to as a node. A cluster provides fault tolerance for critical applications. They do this by being able to take over the processing of a failed node in the cluster should a problem occur. **Clustering** is generally used to provide fault tolerance for back-end applications where the servers share data in common. For example, if you wanted to provide a resilient online purchasing system based around a web application using SQL Server for storage, you would install a clustering solution to support the SQL database servers. Fault tolerant client connections to the online purchasing system front-end (the web servers) would be provisioned by load balancing.

Most implementations of clustering work on the principle of linking the nodes together using a private network, which does not support end-user client connections. A heartbeat message is sent periodically between the nodes to demonstrate that a node is healthy and available. Absence of this message from a node would cause a failover.

There are essentially two types of clustering: Active/Active and Active/Passive.

- **Active/Active** configurations have all nodes processing concurrently. This means that performance will be reduced during failover, as there are fewer nodes than before.
- **Active/Passive** configurations use a redundant node to failover, preserving performance during failover at the cost of provisioning the redundant resource.

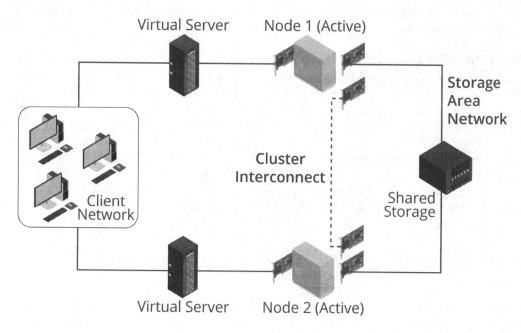

Server cluster. (Image © 123RF.com.)

POWER MANAGEMENT

All types of network nodes require a stable power supply to operate. Electrical events, such as voltage spikes or surges, can crash computers and network appliances, while loss of power from brownouts or blackouts will cause equipment to fail. **Power management** means deploying systems to ensure that equipment is protected against these events and that network operations can either continue uninterrupted or be recovered quickly.

DUAL POWER SUPPLIES

An enterprise-class server or appliance enclosure is likely to feature two or more power supply units (PSUs) for redundancy. A hot plug PSU can be replaced (in the event of failure) without powering down the system. Hot plug PSUs do not have their own ATX and SATA/SAS connectors. They plug into a distribution board (backplane), which houses the connectors. System software will allow you to disable the PSU prior to removing it. A power supply LED should indicate when the PSU is safe to remove. The PSU will have a lever to use to remove it. Installing the replacement is simply a case of sliding the unit into the bay until it clicks into place. The PSUs must all be rated for the same power output—you could not mix one 400 W and one 700 W PSU, for instance.

POWER DISTRIBUTION UNITS

The **power circuits** supplying grid power to a rack, network closet, or server room must be enough to meet the load capacity of all the installed equipment (plus room for growth). Consequently, circuits to a server room will typically be higher capacity than domestic or office circuits (30 or 60 amps as opposed to 13 amps, for instance). These circuits may be run through a **power distribution unit (PDU)**. These come with circuitry to "clean" the power signal, provide protection against spikes, surges, and brownouts, and can integrate with uninterruptible power supplies (UPSs).

On a smaller scale, PDUs are also available as "strip" sockets that can take a higher load than a typical 13 amp rated strip. Such sockets are rack mounted and can be oriented horizontally or vertically to allow for different cabling and layout options. PDUs also often support remote power monitoring functions, such as reporting load and status, switching power to a socket on and off, or switching sockets on in a particular sequence.

REDUNDANT CIRCUITS

As well as dual power supplies in critical servers and appliances, redundancy is an important consideration in designing power circuits. A PDU can be connected to multiple circuits so that if one fails, there will be no interruption to the power supply. You could also connect multiple circuits to multiple PDUs and then connect the PSUs to different PDUs within the same rack. A redundant circuit is two separate power supply lines from electricity suppliers. This is sometimes referred to as A+B power. An automatic transfer switch (ATS) is connected to each power supply line. The ATS continuously monitors power from the utility provider, and if service interruption is detected, the ATS automatically switches to backup power provided by generators, UPS, and PDUs.

BATTERY BACKUPS AND UNINTERRUPTIBLE POWER SUPPLIES (UPSs)

If there is loss of power, system operation can be sustained for a few minutes or hours (depending on load) using battery backup. Battery backup can be provisioned at the component level for disk drives and RAID arrays. The battery protects any read or write operations cached at the time of power loss.

At the system level, an **uninterruptible power supply (UPS)** will provide a temporary power source in the event of a blackout (complete power loss). This may range from a few minutes for a desktop-rated model to hours for an enterprise system. In its simplest form, a UPS comprises a bank of **batteries** and their **charging circuit** plus an **inverter** to generate AC voltage from the DC voltage supplied by the batteries. Factors to consider when purchasing an UPS include reliability, cost, uptime, maintenance, and system performance and features. Different UPS models support different power outputs and form factors—from desktop to rack mounted depending on your needs.

The time allowed by a UPS should be sufficient to failover to an alternative power source, such as a standby generator. If there is no secondary power source, UPS will at least allow the administrator to shut down the server or appliance properly—users can save files, and the OS can complete the proper shut down routines.

A **backup power generator** can provide power to the whole building, often for several days. Most generators use diesel, propane, or natural gas as a fuel source. With diesel and propane, the main drawback is safe storage (diesel also has a shelf-life of between 18 months and 2 years); with natural gas, the issue is the reliability of the gas supply in the event of a natural disaster. A UPS is always required to protect against any interruption to computer services. A backup generator cannot be brought online fast enough to respond to a power failure.

Data centers are also investing in renewable power sources, such as solar, wind, geothermal, hydrogen fuel cells, and hydro. The ability to use renewable power is a strong factor in determining the best site for new data centers. Large-scale battery solutions, such as Tesla's Powerpack (*https://www.tesla.com/powerpack*), may be able to provide an alternative to backup power generators. There are also emerging technologies to use all the battery resources of a data center as a microgrid for power storage (*https://www.scientificamerican.com/article/how-big-batteries-at-data-centers-could-replace-power-plants/*).

BACKUP MANAGEMENT

All business continuity and disaster recovery planning procedures make use of **backups**. The execution and frequency of backups must be carefully planned and guided by policies. **Data retention** needs to be considered in the short and long term:

- In the short term, files that change frequently might need retaining for version control. Short term retention is also important in recovering from malware infection. Consider the scenario where a backup is made on Monday, a file is infected with a virus on Tuesday, and when that file is backed up later on Tuesday, the copy made on Monday is overwritten. This means that there is no good means of restoring the uninfected file.
- In the long term, data may need to be stored to meet legal requirements or to comply with company policies or industry standards.

For these reasons, backups are kept back to certain points in time. Backups take up a lot of space, and there is never limitless storage capacity. This introduces the need for storage management routines and techniques to reduce the amount of data occupying backup storage media while supporting the recovery objectives defined in a retention policy. A retention policy can either be based on redundancy (the number of copies of each file that should be retained) or on a recovery window (the number of days into the past that should be retained). Advanced backup software can prevent media sets from being overwritten in line with the specified retention policy.

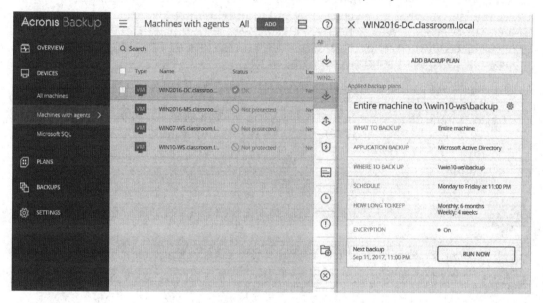

Backing up a domain controller using Acronis backup—The How Long to Keep field specifies the retention period. (Screenshot used with permission from Acronis.)

BACKUP TYPES

Utilities that support enterprise backup operations come with features to support retention policies. They also support concepts such as media rotation. When considering a backup made against an original copy of data, the backup can usually be performed using one of three main types: full, incremental, and differential. In Windows, a **full backup** includes all selected files and directories, while **incremental** and **differential backups** check the status of the **archive attribute** before including a file. The archive attribute is set whenever a file is modified. This allows backup software to determine which files have been changed and therefore need to be copied.

 Note: *Linux doesn't support a file archive attribute. Instead, a date stamp is used to determine whether the file has changed.*

The following table summarizes the three different backup types.

Type	Data Selection	Backup/Restore Time	Attribute
Full	All selected data, regardless of when it was previously backed up.	High/low (one tape set)	Cleared
Incremental	New files and files modified since the last backup.	Low/high (multiple tape sets)	Cleared
Differential	All data modified since the last full backup.	Moderate/moderate (no more than two sets)	Not Cleared

The criteria for determining which method to use is based on the time it takes to **restore** versus the time it takes to **back up**. Assuming a backup is performed every working day, an incremental backup includes only the files changed during that day, while a differential backup includes all files changed since the last full backup. Incremental backups save backup time, but they can be more time-consuming when the system must be restored. The system must be restored from the last full backup set and then from each incremental backup that has subsequently occurred. A differential backup system involves only two tape sets when restoration is required. Doing a full backup on a large network every day takes a long time. A typical strategy for a complex network would be a full weekly backup followed by an incremental or differential backup at the end of each day.

- The advantage of using a full daily backup is that only one tape set is required to restore the system.
- The advantage of an incremental backup is that it takes less time to back up, but several tape sets may need to be restored before the system is operational.
- The advantage of a differential backup is the balance of time for both restoring and backing up.

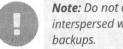 **Note:** *Do not combine differential and incremental backups. Use full backups interspersed with differential backups or full backups interspersed with incremental backups.*

 Note: *Most software also has the capability to do copy backups. These are made outside the tape rotation system (ad hoc) and do not affect the archive attribute.*

 Note: *To learn more, watch the related **Video** on the course website.*

SNAPSHOTS

Snapshots are a means of getting around the problem of open files. If the data that you're considering backing up is part of a database, such as SQL data or a messaging system, such as Microsoft Exchange, then the data is probably being used all the time. Often copy-based mechanisms will be unable to back up open files. Short of closing the files, and so too the database, a copy-based system will not work. A snapshot is a point-in-time copy of data maintained by the file system. A backup program can use the snapshot, rather than the live data, to perform the backup. In Windows, snapshots are provided for on NTFS volumes by the **Volume Shadow Copy Service (VSS)**. They are also supported on Sun's ZFS file system, and under some enterprise distributions of Linux.

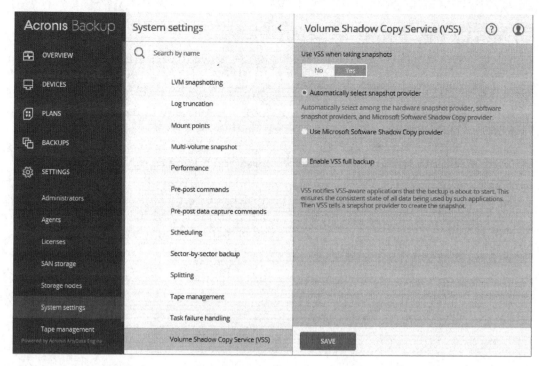

Configuring VSS settings in Acronis Backup. (Screenshot used with permission from Acronis.)

Virtualization hypervisors can usually take snapshot or cloned copies of the VM guests. A snapshot remains linked to the original VM, while a clone becomes a separate VM from the point that the cloned image was made.

RECOVERY SITES

Within the scope of business continuity planning, **disaster recovery plans (DRPs)** describe the specific procedures to follow to recover a system or site to a working state. A disaster could be anything from a loss of power or failure of a minor component to man-made or natural disasters, such as fires, earthquakes, or acts of terrorism.

Providing redundant devices and spares or network links allows the spare devices to be swapped in if existing systems fail. Enterprise-level networks often also provide for spare sites. A spare site is another location that can provide the same (or similar) level of service. A disaster or systems failure at one site will cause services to failover to the alternate processing site. Disaster recovery planning must demonstrate how this will happen, what checks need to be made to ensure that failover has occurred successfully (without loss of transactional data or service availability), and how to revert to the primary site once functionality is restored there.

Recovery sites are referred to as being hot, warm, or cold. A **hot site** can failover almost immediately. It generally means that the site is already within the organization's ownership and is ready to deploy. A **cold site** takes longer to set up (up to a week), and a **warm site** is something between the two. For example, a hot site could consist of a building with operational computer equipment that is kept updated with a live data set. A warm site could be similar, but with the requirement that the latest data set will need to be loaded. A cold site may be an empty building with a lease agreement in place to install whatever equipment is required when necessary.

Clearly, providing redundancy on this scale can be very expensive. Sites are often leased from service providers, such as Comdisco or IBM. However, in the event of a nationwide emergency, demand for the services is likely to exceed supply! Another option is for businesses to enter into **reciprocal arrangements** to provide mutual support. This is cost effective but complex to plan and set up.

DISASTER RECOVERY PLANNING

Disasters can take many forms. An organization sensitive to these risks will develop an effective, documented **disaster recovery plan (DRP)**. This should accomplish the following:

- Identify scenarios for natural and non-natural disasters and options for protecting systems.
- Identify tasks, resources, and responsibilities for responding to a disaster.
- Train staff in the disaster planning procedures and how to react well to change.

When a disaster occurs, the recovery plan will endeavor to get the failed part of the network operational as soon as possible. If a disk has failed, swap it out. If a node in a cluster has failed, remove and replace or repair the node to provide for high reliability as soon as possible. If data becomes corrupted or lost, use your restoration plan to recover the data.

Activity 16-3

Discussing Business Continuity and Disaster Recovery Concepts

SCENARIO

Answer the following questions to test your understanding of the content covered in this topic.

1. **What is MTBF, and why is it associated with a bathtub curve?**

2. **A server is equipped with 4 Ethernet interfaces, and you want to aggregate them to a single interface using a non-proprietary protocol. What feature must the switch support?**

3. **What technologies can be used to make network infrastructure fault tolerant?**

4. **What rack-mountable device can provide line filtering and power monitoring features?**

5. **What type of security control provisions resources and procedures to cope with major incidents?**

Topic D

Identify Policies and Best Practices

 EXAM OBJECTIVES COVERED
3.5 Identify policies and best practices.

All network operations and users should be guided by written policies and best practices. These policies cover everything from what is acceptable to do on the network, to password requirements, to dealing with security breaches, and more. In this topic, you will identify network security policies you should consider implementing and how to enforce those policies.

POLICIES AND BEST PRACTICES

Running an efficient network is not just about installing cabling and network devices. The administration, documentation, and management of the network is a critical task. As well as procedures for technical staff to follow to perform updates, maintenance, and troubleshooting, network administration requires policies to guide end users of the network services. As a vital component of a company's IT infrastructure, employees must understand how to use computer and network systems securely and safely and be aware of their responsibilities. To support this, an organization needs to create proper documentation, to help staff to understand and fulfill their responsibilities and follow proper procedures.

Policy is an overall statement of intent. In order to establish the correct working practices, three different mechanisms can be put in place:

- **Standard**—A standard is a measure by which to evaluate compliance with the policy.
- **Procedure**—A procedure is an inflexible, step-by-step listing of the actions that must be completed for a given task. A written procedure is often referred to as a standard operating procedure (SOP) or an internal operating procedure (IOP). Most critical tasks should be governed by SOPs.
- **Best practice**—Guidelines can be written for areas of policy where there are no procedures, either because the situation has not been fully assessed or because the decision-making process is too complex and subject to variables to be able to capture it in an SOP. Best practice guidance may also describe circumstances where it is appropriate to deviate from a specified procedure.

SAFETY PROCEDURES

As a network technician, you must comply with local health and safety codes and regulations. This affects both the way you work and the way you manage equipment in the workplace, whether that is an office or data center. Safety policies should be clearly set out for you in an employee handbook or work orders, but you can consider the following general advice.

TOOL SAFETY

When handling tools, you must be aware of risks that could arise from carelessness or improper use.

- Do not work on electrical systems (especially an energized circuit) unless you have a good understanding of the risks and appropriate safety procedures.
- Disconnect the power to a circuit if you must handle it, and always test live parts with a multimeter to ensure that no voltage is present.
- Always use properly insulated tools and never grip a tool by its metal parts.
- Take care not to touch any part of a circuit with both hands to reduce the risk of a serious shock. (The "hand in pocket" rule reduces the chance that the current will pass through your chest and cause a heart attack.)
- Be aware that the tools used to prepare cables and connectors can have sharp edges or could crush your fingers if used carelessly.
- Use proper tools and safety equipment when you are working with lasers, such as installing fiber optic cabling.

ELECTRICAL SAFETY

A connection to **ground** (or **earth**) provides a return path for electrical current. This is a safety feature; if an electrical connection short circuits into the metal chassis, a ground wire ensures that the current flows to earth, rather than electrocuting someone handling the faulty device. Some power circuits contain a ground wire. If the circuit does not contain a ground wire, any electrical devices with metal cases (or any metal objects that could come into contact with electrical wires) must be bonded to the building's earth system. This particularly includes rack systems and cable trays. Do not disconnect the ground wire. If it must be removed, make sure it is replaced by a competent electrician.

FIRE SAFETY

All public and commercial buildings should comply with local fire codes. This will mean having fire/smoke alarms, emergency escape routes and procedures, and possibly fire extinguisher systems. It is vital that any network installation work you do does not compromise fire safety:

- Do not block fire exits or escape routes with boxes or equipment.
- Do not run cables where they could be trip or fire hazards.

LIFTING EQUIPMENT

Lifting a heavy object in the wrong way can damage your back, but lifting and manual handling risks are not limited to particularly heavy objects. An object that is large or awkward to carry could cause you to trip over or walk into something else. An object that has sharp or rough edges or contains a hot or corrosive liquid could cause you to cut or hurt yourself. If necessary, you should obtain protective clothing (gloves and possibly goggles).

To lift a heavy object safely, plant your feet around the object with one foot slightly toward the direction in which you are going to move. Bend your knees to reach the object while keeping your back as straight as is possible and comfortable and your chin up. Find a firm grip on the object then lift smoothly by straightening your legs—do not jerk the object up. Carry the object while keeping your back straight. To lower an object, reverse the lifting process; keep your chin up and bend at the knees. Take care not to trap your fingers or to lower the object onto your feet.

If you cannot lift an object because it is too awkward or heavy, get help. If you need to carry an object for some distance, make sure that the route is unobstructed and that the pathway (including stairs or doorways) is wide and tall enough.

MATERIAL SAFETY DATA SHEET (MSDS)

Suppliers of chemicals or materials treated with chemicals are required to identify the hazards (or dangers) of the substances they supply. If a chemical is dangerous, the supplier must provide information about the hazards that it presents; some hazard information will be provided on labels, but the supplier must also provide more detailed hazard information on a **Material Safety Data Sheet (MSDS)**. An MSDS will contain information about ingredients or composition, health hazards, precautions, fire-fighting measures, and first aid information, and how to recycle any waste product or dispose of it safely. You may need to refer to an MSDS in the course of installing cabling.

ELECTROSTATIC DISCHARGE (ESD)

An **electrostatic discharge (ESD)** occurs when a surface with low potential difference is brought near a surface with high potential difference. This can cause a spark to leap between the two surfaces. The spark is not dangerous to human health (it is high voltage but low current), but it can cause serious damage to electronic circuits, such as CPUs and system memory modules.

Where possible, handle vulnerable components by holding the edges of the plastic mounting card and avoid touching the surfaces of the chips themselves. Using an **anti-ESD wrist strap** can dissipate static charges more effectively. The wrist band should fit snugly around your wrist to maximize contact with the skin. Do not wear it over clothing. The wrist strap ground is made either using a grounding plug that plugs into a wall socket or a crocodile clip that attaches to a grounded point or an unpainted part of the computer's metal chassis. An anti-ESD service mat is also useful. Sensitive components can be placed on the mat safely.

INCIDENT RESPONSE POLICIES

Incident management or **incident response policy** are the actions and guidelines for dealing with security incidents. An incident is where security is breached or there is an attempted breach; NIST describes an incident as the act of violating an explicit or implied security policy. Incident management is vital to mitigating risk. As well as controlling the immediate or specific threat to security, effective incident management preserves an organization's reputation.

However, incident response is also one of the most difficult areas of security to plan for and implement because its aims are often incompatible:

- Re-establish a secure working system.
- Preserve evidence of the incident with the aim of prosecuting the perpetrators.
- Prevent reoccurrence of the incident.

The actions of staff immediately following detection of an incident can have a critical impact on these aims, so an effective policy and well-trained employees are crucial. They help to calm nerves in the aftermath of an incident. Incident response is also likely to require coordinated action and authorization from several different departments or managers, which adds further levels of complexity.

COMPUTER SECURITY INCIDENT RESPONSE TEAM (CSIRT)

Larger organizations will provide a dedicated **Computer Security Incident Response Team (CSIRT)** as a single point of contact for the notification of security incidents. The members of this team should be able to provide the range of decision making and technical skills required to deal with different types of incidents.

FIRST RESPONDER

When a suspicious event is detected, it is critical that the appropriate person on the CSIRT be notified so that they can take charge of the situation and formulate the appropriate response. This means that employees at all levels of the organization must be trained to recognize and respond appropriately to actual or suspected security incidents. A good level of security awareness across the whole organization will reduce the incidence of false positives and negatives. The person dealing with an incident once it has been reported is referred to as the **first responder**. For the most serious incidents, the entire CSIRT may be involved in formulating an effective response.

PRIVILEGED USER AGREEMENT (PUA)

Policies and standard procedures are also vital tools in ensuring data security. Part of the task lies in creating effective privilege management policies and procedures, and part in ensuring that information assets are classified and handled correctly by staff members at all levels of the company hierarchy.

A **privileged user** is one who is given rights to administer a resource. There might be different levels of privilege, ranging from responsibility for managing a data set, through departmental IT services administrators, and up to company-wide service administrators. The rules of behavior for these employees may be set out in the contract terms or in a separate **privileged user agreement (PUA)**. Rules of behavior will include things like:

- Only use privileges to perform authorized job functions.
- Protect the confidentiality and integrity of personal account credentials, plus any shared accounts that the privileged user has access to.
- Be aware of and in compliance with any legal and regulatory issues that affect data processing.
- Respect the privacy of other network users.

Additional polices are likely to be enforced to prevent abuse of privileged accounts. **Separation of duties** is a means of establishing checks and balances against the possibility that critical systems or procedures can be compromised by rogue use of access permissions. Several different policies can be applied to enforce separation of duties:

- The principle of least privilege means that a user is granted sufficient rights to perform their job and no more.
- Provisioning dual accounts means that administrators have separate accounts for management and general use. The administrator must use the privileged account only to perform specific job tasks.
- The existence of relevant SOPs mean that an employee has no excuse for not following protocol in terms of performing this type of critical operation.
- Shared authority means that no one user is able to take action or enable changes on his or her own authority. At least two people must authorize the change.
- Effective auditing means that decisions and changes are recorded and can be scrutinized independently of the person that made the decision.
- **Mandatory vacations** mean that employees are forced to take their vacation time, during which someone else fulfills their duties.
- **Job rotation** (or rotation of duties) means that no one person is permitted to remain in the same job for an extended period. For example, managers may be moved to different departments periodically, or employees may perform more than one job role, switching between them throughout the year. Job rotation is also seen as beneficial in terms of developing skills and experience.

 Note: *You can view examples of PUAs at https://security.berkeley.edu/model-privileged-access-agreement and https://www.unfpa.org/sites/default/files/admin-resource/ICT_MIS_Privileged_User_Account_Access_Policy.pdf*

DATA SECURITY POLICIES

Data breach exposes an organization to huge reputational and financial costs. Consequently, data processing is an area of activity that should be tightly managed by both policies and technical controls.

NON-DISCLOSURE AGREEMENT (NDA)

A **non-disclosure agreement (NDA)** is the legal basis for protecting information assets. It defines what uses of sensitive data are permitted, what storage and distribution restrictions must be enforced, and what penalties breaches of the agreement will incur. A contract of employment is highly likely to contain NDA clauses. NDAs are also used between companies and contractors and between two companies.

PERSONALLY IDENTIFIABLE INFORMATION (PII)

The rise in consciousness of identity theft as a serious crime and growing threat means that there is an increasing impetus on government, educational, and commercial organizations to take steps to obtain, store, and process **personally identifiable information (PII)** more sensitively and securely. PII is data that can be used to identify, contact, or locate an individual (or in the case of identity theft, to impersonate them). A Social Security Number (SSN) is a good example of PII. Others include name, date of birth, email address, telephone number, street address, biometric data, occupation, and so on. Some types of information may be PII depending on the context. For example, when someone browses the web using a static IP address, the IP address is PII. An address that is dynamically assigned by the ISP may not be considered PII. These are the sort of complexities that must be considered when laws are introduced to control the collection and storage of personal data.

Staff should be trained to identify PII and to handle personal or sensitive data appropriately. This means not making unauthorized copies or allowing the data to be seen or captured by any unauthorized persons. Examples of treating sensitive data carelessly include leaving order forms with customers' credit card details in view on a desk, putting a credit card number in an unencrypted notes field in a customer database, and revealing email addresses by failing to use blind copy (BCC) where appropriate.

DATA LOSS PREVENTION (DLP)

In a workplace where mobile devices with huge storage capacity proliferate and high bandwidth network links are readily available, attempting to prevent the loss of data by controlling the types of storage devices allowed to connect to PCs and networks can be impractical. Users must of course be trained about document confidentiality and make sure that they are aware that unencrypted communications are not secure. This should also be backed up by HR and auditing policies that ensure staff are trustworthy. Soft measures such as these do not protect against user error or insider threats.

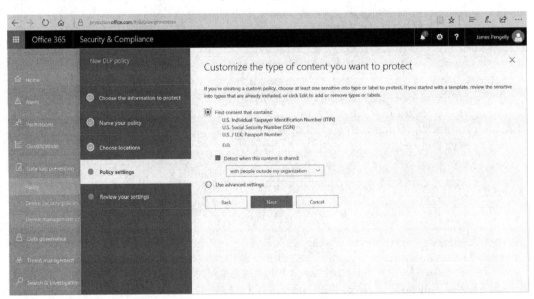

Creating a data loss prevention policy in Office 365. (Screenshot used with permission from Microsoft.)

Data loss prevention (DLP) products scan content in structured formats (such as a database with a formal access control model) or unstructured formats, such as email or word processing documents. These products use some sort of dictionary database or algorithm (regular expression matching) to identify confidential data, including PII. The transfer of content to removable media (or by email or IM or even social media) can then be blocked if it does not conform to a predefined policy.

INTERNATIONAL EXPORT CONTROLS

The laws that a country enforces to control imports and exports can have an impact on network and security management. This is especially the case where the organization has offices in multiple countries.

One area in export control relevant to ICT is the concept of **dual use**. Dual use is technology that can have both civilian and military/secret service applications. The most obvious example of dual use is exports that could be used in the manufacturing of nuclear or chemical weapons. In ICT, dual use principally means scanning tools, hacking tools, and malware. Governments are increasingly monitoring and regulating the transfer of this kind of software. If a class of product appears on a control list, a company must gain authorization to export (or import) it. In the US, the principal office responsible for this is the **Bureau of Industry and Security** (*bis.doc.gov*), who administer the **Export Administration Regulations (EAR)**. Technologies identified as having a specific military application can be governed by the **Bureau of Political Military Affairs' Directorate of Defense Trade Controls** (DDTC *pmddtc.state.gov*), who manage the **International Traffic in Arms Regulations (ITAR)**.

The other major impact of export controls lies in the collection and processing of PII. Most countries have introduced **data protection** legislation to allow citizens to control the use that is made of information they give to companies and charities. A common feature of this type of legislation is to prevent personal data from being transferred to a different legal jurisdiction, where the controls on its proper use may not be strongly enforced. This can be a problem for companies that use cloud services, as the hosts processing the data may not be in the same country as the organization itself or the subject. Organizations handling personal information must put safeguards in place to ensure that it is stored, processed, and transmitted in accordance with the appropriate legislation.

The US has complex data protection and privacy regulations, deriving from different federal and state laws. In terms of international exports and transfers, the main area of interest is between the US and European Union (EU). The EU has introduced a **General Data Protection Regulation (GDPR)** framework, covering all aspects of data and privacy for all member states. Previously EU-US data transfers were covered by compliance with the **Safe Harbor** scheme, but that was ruled invalid and is being replaced by a new framework called **Privacy Shield**.

LICENSING RESTRICTIONS

Software licensing agreements can be complex and keeping track of usage requires investment in license management and auditing software. Some of the activities involved in ensuring compliance with license agreements include:

- Identifying unlicensed and unauthorized software installed on clients, servers, and virtual machines. Ideally privilege management and change controlled instances would prevent this from happening. Best intentions are not enough, however, so periodic inspections are required to ensure continued compliance. It is particularly important to audit field devices (laptops and mobiles).

- Identifying per-seat or per-user compliance with licensed software. The complex nature of client access type licensing means that many companies over-allocate seats compared to what their license agreement allows. There is also the complexity of managing software over multiple sites (and possibly also different countries) and remote devices.

- Preparing for vendor audits—Most license agreements specify that the vendor may undertake a **software license compliance (SLC)** audit. This means that the vendor or their nominated third party may access the customer's systems to audit license usage.

- Ensuring compliance with the terms of open source licensing. If open source code is reused (whether in commercial or in-house software), the product must be distributed in compliance with the terms of the original open source license.

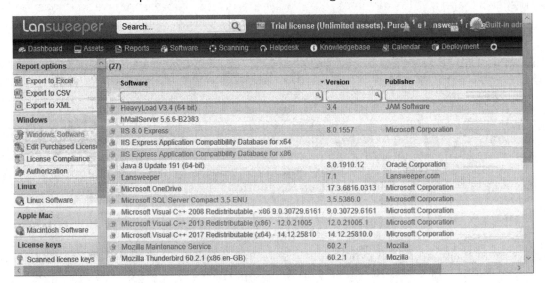

Use tools such as Lansweeper network inventory management to keep track of software license usage. (Screenshot used with permission from Lansweeper.)

SYSTEM LIFECYCLE AND ASSET DISPOSAL

Data security is an important consideration when it comes to disposing of assets such as servers and workstations at the end of their system lifecycles, when they are no longer useful to the organization. The problem has become particularly prominent as organizations recycle their old workstations or servers, either by donating them to charities or by sending them to a recycling company, who may recover and sell certain parts. The problem also applies to network printers, which often have installable hard disks to use to cache print jobs. **Hard drive sanitation** refers to fully erasing hard disks. More generally, **remnant removal** refers to decommissioning various media, including flash drives, tape media, CD and DVD ROMs, and so on.

There are at least three reasons that make remnant removal critical:

- An organization's own confidential data could be compromised.
- Third-party data that the organization processes could be compromised, leaving it liable under Data Protection legislation (in addition to any contracts or SLAs signed).
- Software licensing could be compromised.

The main issue is understanding the degree to which data on different media types may be recoverable. Data deleted from a magnetic-type disk (such as a hard disk) is not erased. Rather, the sectors are marked as available for writing and the data they contain will only be removed as new files are added. Similarly, using the standard Windows format tool will only remove references to files and mark all sectors as useable. In the right circumstances and with the proper tools, any deleted information from a drive could be recoverable.

Data remnants can be dealt with either by destroying the media or by purging it (removing the confidential information but leaving the media intact for reuse). There are several different ways of either purging or destroying media:

- **Overwriting/disk wiping**—Disk wiping software ensures that old data is destroyed by writing to each location on the media. A simple means of doing this is zero filling, which sets each bit to zero. Zero filling can leave patterns that can be read with specialist tools. A more secure method is to overwrite the content with ones and zeros using pseudorandom input. Overwriting might also be performed in multiple passes.
- **Pulverizing/degaussing**—A magnetic disk can be mechanically shredded or degaussed (exposing the disk to a powerful electromagnet disrupts the magnetic pattern that stores the data on the disk surface) in specialist machinery.
- **Disk encryption**—This method encrypts all the information in a volume, so that any remnants could not be read without possession of the decryption key.

Optical media cannot be reformatted. Discs should be destroyed before discarding them. Shredders are available for destroying CD and DVD media. All paper documents should be shredded before disposal. Apart from ensuring personal data is not leaked, this is because even quite innocuous information (such as employee telephone lists, calendar appointments, and so on) can help an attacker with impersonation attacks.

PASSWORD POLICY

A **password policy** instructs users on best practice in choosing and maintaining passwords. More generally, a **credential management policy** should instruct users on how to keep their authentication method secure, whether this be a password, smart card, or biometric ID. Password protection policies mitigate against the risk of attackers being able to compromise an account and use it to launch other attacks on the network. The credential management policy also needs to alert users to different types of social engineering attacks.

The soft approach to training users can also be backed up by hard policies defined on the network. System-enforced policies can help to enforce credential management principles by stipulating requirements for user-selected passwords. The following rules enforce password complexity and make them difficult to guess or compromise:

- **Length**—The longer a password, the stronger it is.
  - A typical strong network password should be 12 to 16 characters.
  - A longer password or passphrase might be used for mission critical systems or devices where logon is infrequent.
- **Complexity**—Varying the characters in the password makes it more resistant to dictionary-based attacks.
  - No single words—It is better to use word and number/punctuation combinations.
  - No obvious phrases in a simple form—Avoid birthdays, usernames, job titles, and so on.
  - Mix upper- and lowercase (assuming the software uses case-sensitive passwords).
  - Use an easily memorized phrase—Underscore characters or hyphens can be used to represent spaces if the OS does not support these in passwords.
- Do not write down a password or share it with other users.

 Note: If users must make a note of passwords, at the very least they must keep the note physically secure. They should also encode the password in some way. If the note is lost or stolen, it is imperative that the password be changed immediately, and the user account closely monitored for suspicious activity.

- **History and aging**—Change the password periodically (password aging), and do not reuse passwords.
  - User passwords should be changed every 60 to 90 days.
  - Administrative passwords should be changed every 30 days.
  - Passwords for mission critical systems should be changed every 15 days.

You should also note that the most recent guidance issued by NIST (*nvlpubs.nist.gov/nistpubs/SpecialPublications/NIST.SP.800-63b.pdf*) deprecates some of the "traditional" elements of password policy:

- Complexity rules should not be enforced. The user should be allowed to choose a password of between 8 and 64 ASCII or Unicode characters, including spaces. The only restriction should be to block common passwords such as dictionary words, repetitive strings (like 12345678), strings identified from breach databases, and strings that repeat contextual information, such as username or company name.
- Aging policies should not be enforced. Users should be able to select if and when a password should be changed, though the system should be able to force a password change if compromise is detected.
- Password hints should not be used. A password hint allows account recovery by submitting responses to personal information, such as first school or pet name.

 Note: *One approach to a password hint is to treat it as a secondary password and submit a random but memorable phrase, rather than an "honest" answer.*

Another concern is personal password management. A typical user might be faced with having to remember dozens of logons for different services and resort to using the same password for each. This is unsecure, as your security becomes dependent on the security of these other (unknown) organizations. Users must be trained to practice good password management (at the least, not to re-use work passwords). One technical solution is to use a **password manager**. Password manager software generates a pseudorandom passphrase for each logon. The passphrase generation rules can be configured to match the requirements of the authentication system. The password manager can then submit the credential on behalf of the user. These account credentials are protected by a master passphrase. Password managers have been associated with weaknesses and vulnerabilities, and may not be compatible with local authentication systems. Your password policy might include provisions for allowing or prohibiting use of password managers on the corporate network, and identifying approved and supported vendors.

EMPLOYEE POLICIES

Human Resources (HR) is the department given the task of recruiting and managing the organization's most valuable and critical resource: people. Personnel management policies can be conceived as applying in three phases:

- **Recruitment** (hiring)—Locating and selecting people to work in particular job roles. Security issues here include screening candidates and performing background checks.
- **Operation** (working)—It is often the HR department that manages the communication of policy and training to employees (though there may be a separate training and personal development department within larger organizations). As such, it is critical that HR managers devise training programs that communicate the importance of security to employees.
- **Termination** or **separation** (firing or retiring)—Whether an employee leaves voluntarily or involuntarily, termination is a difficult process, with numerous security implications.

Operational policies include privilege management, data handling, and incident response, as discussed earlier. One function of HR is to communicate these policies to employees, including any updates to the policies. Another function is to enforce disciplinary measures (perhaps in conjunction with departmental managers).

ONBOARDING AND BACKGROUND CHECKS

Onboarding at the HR level is the process of welcoming a new employee to the organization. Similar principles apply to taking on new suppliers or contractors. Some of the tasks that most affect security during the onboarding process are as follows:

- **Background check**—This process essentially determines that a person is who they say they are and are not concealing criminal activity, bankruptcy, or connections that would make them unsuitable or risky. Employees working in high confidentiality environments or with access to high value transactions will obviously need to be subjected to a greater degree of scrutiny.
- **Identity and access management (IAM)**—Create an account for the user to access the computer system, assign the appropriate privileges, and ensure the account credentials are known only to the valid user.
- **Asset allocation**—Provision computers or mobile devices for the user or agree on the use of BYOD devices.
- **Training/policies**—Schedule appropriate security awareness and role-relevant training and certification.

OFFBOARDING / EXIT INTERVIEWS

An **exit interview** (or **offboarding**) is the process of ensuring that an employee leaves a company gracefully. In terms of security, there are several processes that must be completed:

- **IAM**—Disable the user account and privileges. Ensure that any information assets created or managed by the employee but owned by the company are accessible (in terms of encryption keys or password-protected files).
- **Retrieving company assets**—Secure mobile devices, keys, smart cards, USB media, and so on. The employee will need to confirm (and in some cases prove) that they have not retained copies of any information assets.
- **Returning personal assets**—Employee-owned devices need to be wiped of corporate data and applications. The employee may also be allowed to retain some information assets (such as personal emails or contact information), depending on the policies in force.

The departure of some types of employees should trigger additional processes to re-secure network systems. Examples include employees with detailed knowledge of security systems and procedures and access to shared or generic account credentials. These credentials must be changed immediately.

ACCEPTABLE USE POLICIES

As the name suggests, an **acceptable use policy (AUP)** (or **fair use policy**) sets out the permitted uses of a product or service. It might also state explicitly prohibited uses. Such a policy might be used in different contexts. For example, an AUP could be enforced by a business to govern how employees use equipment and services, such as telephone or Internet access, provided to them at work. Another example might be an ISP enforcing a fair use policy governing usage of its Internet access services.

Enforcing an AUP is important to protect the organization from the security and legal implications of employees (or customers) misusing its equipment. Typically, the policy will forbid the use of equipment to defraud, defame, or to obtain illegal material. It is also likely to prohibit the installation of unauthorized hardware or software and to explicitly forbid actual or attempted intrusion (snooping). An organization's AUP may forbid use of Internet tools outside of work-related duties or restrict such use to break times.

The equipment used to access the Internet in the workplace is owned by the employer. Many employees expect relatively unrestricted access to Internet facilities for personal use. In fact, employees' use of the social networking and file sharing poses substantial risks to the organization, including data breach, threat of virus infection or systems intrusion, lost work time, copyright infringement, and defamation. If an employee breaks copyright laws or libels someone using an organization's equipment, the organization itself could be held liable. To avoid confusion, an employee's handbook should set out the terms under which use of web browser, email, social networking, and P2P software is permitted for personal use, and what penalties infringements could incur. Employers are within their rights to prohibit all private use of Internet tools.

Users should be aware that any data communications, such as email, made through an organization's computer system are liable to be stored within the system, on servers, backup devices, and so on. Consequently, users should not use computers at work to send personal information (for their own security if nothing else).

A mobile deployment model describes the way employees are provided with smartphone or tablet devices and applications. Some companies issue employees with corporate-owned and controlled devices and insist that only these are used to process company data. Other companies might operate a **bring your own device (BYOD)** policy. BYOD means that the mobile is owned by the employee but will have to meet whatever profile is required by the company (in terms of OS version and functionality). The employee will have to agree on the installation of corporate apps and to some level of oversight and auditing. Very often, BYOD devices are registered with enterprise management software and configured with sandboxed corporate workspaces and apps.

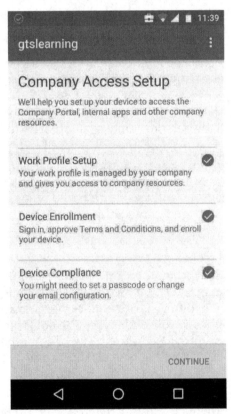

Enterprise management software can be used to segment corporate data from personal data on BYOD devices. (Screenshot used with permission from Google.)

Other portable devices such as unauthorized smartphones/tablets, USB sticks, media players, and so on pose a considerable threat to data security as they make it so easy to copy files. Camera and voice recording functions are other obvious security issues. Network access control/endpoint security and data loss prevention solutions can be of some use in preventing the attachment of such devices to corporate networks. Some companies may try to prevent staff from bringing such devices on site. This is quite difficult to enforce, though.

REMOTE ACCESS POLICIES

Where employees are assigned the right to connect to the corporate network from a remote location using a VPN, their use of remote access privileges must be governed by technical and policy controls. The integrity of the client computer and public network link presents many issues:

- **Malware protection**—The computer may not be accessible to network systems used to update and enforce malware protection. This may have to be left to the end-user. If a worm or Trojan is installed, network security may be compromised.
- **Security information**—Authentication information may be stored on the client (saving a password, for instance), making the network vulnerable if the computer is stolen.
- **Data transfer**—Files copied to the client may no longer be properly secured, raising the potential that confidential information could be stolen along with the device.
- **Local privileges**—The user of a remote computer might be configured with administrative privileges but have no understanding of how such privileges can be exploited or misused. They might install unauthorized software on the machine or make it more vulnerable to malware by browsing the web using their administrative account.
- **Weak authentication**—Relying on a username and password combination is simply not secure enough in a remote access scenario. Two-factor authentication using smart cards or biometric recognition in addition to a PIN or password should be enforced. If this is not an option, a strong password policy must be enforced, and users made aware of the very real risks of writing down or sharing their password.
- **Untrusted networks**—The user might configure weak authentication on a home wireless network or use a public access point, raising the risk of sniffing and MitM attacks.

The principal solution to remote access security problems is to educate remote users about security risks and their responsibilities. Enforcement can be provided by having remote devices audited periodically to ensure that anti-virus, firewall, and OS/browser/application patches are being kept up to date and to check that unlicensed software has not been installed. It is also wise to limit what remote users can access on the local network and to severely restrict the rights of remote computer accounts. The principle of least privilege should be applied. Technologies such as Remote Desktop provide an opportunity to lock down the user's privileges more than they would have been in the past. Technicians can provide support and assistance without having to go offsite or conversely without the machine having to be brought onsite.

GUIDELINES FOR CREATING POLICIES AND BEST PRACTICES

CREATE NETWORK OPERATIONS POLICIES

Policies and best practices supporting network operations are living documents and need to be updated as needed. For example, you might need to add a social media policy or update an existing social media policy. Make sure all employees are fully trained to follow the security policies you have created. Follow these guidelines for creating network operations policies:

- Decide on the overall goal the policies need to achieve. This goal should focus on business functions, rather than the network assets that support those functions.
- Create a root policy to state the overall goal, and identify persons responsible for determining and enforcing policies in different departments.
- Determine the number and type of sub-policies that must be created, such as privileged user, AUPs, onboarding/offboarding, remote access, and so on.
- For each policy, determine the objective, the owner (the person enforcing the policy), the objects (assets to which the policy applies), subjects (users to which the policy applies), the policy statements, and the penalties for non-compliance. Try to make each policy as concise as possible.
- When you are drafting policies, remember to account for any legal or regulatory compliance issues.
- For each policy, determine which tasks must be supported by SOPs and/or best practice statements.
- Create and test the SOPs and best practice statements.
- Establish a system for detecting and reporting policy violations. You might use configuration and performance baselines to identify deviations, for instance.
- Establish a change management system for revising and expanding policies and procedures when necessary.

Activity 16-4
Discussing Policies and Best Practices

SCENARIO
Answer the following questions to test your understanding of the content covered in this topic.

1. **What is the difference between a policy and a best practice?**

2. **What are the main elements of fire safety procedures?**

3. **True or False? An ESD wrist strap is designed to provide a personal ground to protect a technician from electrocution when they are working on energized electrical devices.**

4. **How is the person who first receives notification of a potential security incident designated?**

5. **How does the principle of least privilege apply to privileged users?**

6. **True or False? DLP technology can assist with managing PII.**

7. **What technology provides data security assurance during the asset disposal phase of system lifecycle?**

   Hard drive/media sanitation, such as encryption or disk overwriting.

8. **What are the main elements of a password policy?**

   Ensuring strong password selection and preventing sharing of passwords. You might also mention password aging (changing passwords regularly).

9. **What configuration request would be implemented by IT services during employee onboarding?**

   Account creation, issuance of user credentials, and allocation of permissions/roles.

10. **What type of policy governs use of a VPN?**

    Remote access policy.

11. Review the following excerpt from a password policy. Locate the information on how often administrators and users need to change their passwords.

    4.0 Policy Specifications
    4.1 General
    - All system-level passwords (e.g., root, enable, administrator, application administration accounts, etc.) must be changed on at least a monthly basis.
    - All user-level passwords (e.g., email, web, desktop computer, etc.) must be changed at least once every three months.
    - User accounts that have system-level privileges granted through group memberships must have a unique password from all other accounts held by that user.
    - Passwords must not be inserted into email messages or other forms of electronic communication.
    - All user-level and system-level passwords must conform to the guidelines described in the following section.

    4.2 Guidelines
    A. General Password Construction Guidelines
    Passwords are used for various purposes at Greene City Interiors. Some of the more common uses include: user-level accounts, web accounts, email accounts, screensaver protection, voice mail, and local router logins. Everyone should select strong passwords for all systems.

    Strong passwords have the following characteristics:

    - Contain both upper and lowercase characters (e.g., a-z, A-Z).
    - Have digits and punctuation characters as well as letters (e.g., 0-9, !@#$%^&*()_+|~-=\`{}[]:";'<>?,./).
    - Are at least eight alphanumeric characters long.
    - Are not a word in any language, slang, dialect, jargon, etc.
    - Are not based on personal information, names of family, etc.
    - Are easily remembered by the password holder. Create your password based on a known phrase. For example, the phrase might be: "This May Be One Way To Remember" and the password could be: *TmB1w2R!* or *Tmb1W>r~* or some other variation.

    NOTE: Do not use either of these examples as passwords!

    DO NOT USE ANY OF THE FOLLOWING AS PASSWORDS:

    - A word found in a dictionary (English or foreign).
    - A common usage string such as:
      o Names of family, pets, friends, coworkers, fantasy characters, etc.
      o Computer terms and names, commands, sites, companies, hardware, or software.
      o The words "Greene," "City," "Interiors," or any derivation.
      o Birthdays and other personal information such as addresses and phone numbers.
      o Word or number patterns like aaabbb, qwerty, zyxwvuts, 123321, etc.
      o Any of the above spelled backwards.
      o Any of the above preceded or followed by a digit (e.g., secret1, 1secret).

12. **Do you agree with the time listed? Why or why not?**

13. **One of the users tried to create a password by entering gooddog. According to the policy, does this meet the requirements? Why or why not?**

Summary

In this lesson, you learned about operational procedures that effect the smooth running of network sites, including documentation, physical security, business continuity, and policies/best practices.

- Configuration and change management ensures that network installation and maintenance is well-planned and documented. Up-to-date schematics and logical network diagrams are essential parts of a well-administered network.
- Physical security means controlling access to premises and ensuring a safe and stable operating environment for computer and network systems. Sites can be protected through gateways, locks, and alarms and through surveillance methods, such as CCTV.
- Business continuity planning, disaster recovery planning, and IT contingency planning reduce risk by making systems fault tolerant and resilient.
- Effective backup procedures are essential for protecting business data.
- Policies, procedures, and agreements provide clarity and set expectations for employees and contractors.
- Be aware of the safety considerations when performing network maintenance and installation.
- Make sure you understand the use of policies to govern privilege and data management and employee use of IT systems.

What security policies and physical security measures has your organization implemented? Are they cumbersome to use? Are they effective in protecting the network and its data?

What types of protections and measures does your company include in your business continuity plan?

 Practice Questions: *Additional practice questions are available on the course website.*

Course Follow-Up

Congratulations! You have completed *The Official CompTIA®Network+® (Exam N10-007): 2019 Update* course. You have gained fundamental knowledge about and experience with installing, configuring, and troubleshooting network technologies.

You also covered the objectives that you need to prepare for the CompTIA Network+ (Exam N10-007) certification examination. If you combine this class experience with review, private study, and hands-on experience, you will be well prepared to demonstrate your networking expertise both through professional certification and with solid technical competence on the job.

What's Next?

Become a CompTIA Network+ Certified Professional!

CompTIA Network+ is a global certification that validates the baseline skills you need to perform core network administration functions and pursue an IT career.

In order to become a CompTIA Network+ Certified Professional, you must successfully pass the Network+ exam (Exam Code N10-007).

In order to help you prepare for the exam, you may want to invest in CompTIA's exam prep product, *CertMaster Practice for Network+*.

CertMaster Practice is an online knowledge assessment and certification training companion tool specifically designed for those who have completed *The Official CompTIA Network+* course. It helps reinforce and test what you know and close knowledge gaps prior to taking the exam.

CertMaster Practice features:

- Adaptive knowledge assessments with feedback, covering all domains of the Network+ exam.
- Practice tests with performance-based questions.
- Question-first design and smart refreshers to get feedback on the questions you get wrong.
- Learning analytics that track real-time knowledge gain and topic difficulty to help you learn intelligently.

Taking the Exam

When you think you have learned and practiced the material sufficiently, you can book a time to take the test.

Preparing for the Exam

We've tried to balance this course to reflect the percentages in the exam so that you have learned the appropriate level of detail about each topic to comfortably answer the exam questions.

Questions in the exam are weighted by domain area as follows:

CompTIA Network+ (Exam N10-007) Certification Domain Areas	Weighting
1.0 Networking Concepts	23%
2.0 Infrastructure	18%
3.0 Network Operations	17%
4.0 Network Security	20%
5.0 Network Troubleshooting and Tools	22%

For more information about how to register for and take your exam, please visit the CompTIA website: *https://certification.comptia.org/testing*.

Achieving CompTIA Network+ certification requires candidates to pass Exam N10-007. This table describes where the exam objectives for Exam N10-007 are covered in this course.

Domain and Objective	Covered In
Domain 1.0 Networking Concepts	
1.1 Explain the purposes and uses of ports and protocols.	
• Protocols and ports	4F, 6D, 7A, 7B, 8A, 11B, 15B
• SSH 22	15B
• DNS 53	6D
• SMTP 25	7A
• SFTP 22	15B
• FTP 20, 21	15B
• TFTP 69	15B
• TELNET 23	15B
• DHCP 67, 68	4F
• HTTP 80	7A
• HTTPS 443	7A
• SNMP 161	8A
• RDP 3389	15B
• NTP 123	7A
• SIP 5060, 5061	7B
• SMB 445	7A
• POP 110	7A
• IMAP 143	7A
• LDAP 389	11B
• LDAPS 636	11B
• H.323 1720	7B
• Protocol types	4A, 4B, 6A
• ICMP	4B
• UDP	6A
• TCP	6A
• IP	4A
• Connection-oriented vs. connectionless	6A
1.2 Explain devices, applications, protocols, and services at their appropriate OSI layers.	
• Layer 1 – Physical	1A
• Layer 2 – Data link	1A
• Layer 3 – Network	1A
• Layer 4 – Transport	1A
• Layer 5 – Session	1A
• Layer 6 – Presentation	1A

Domain and Objective	Covered In
• Layer 7 – Application	1A
1.3 Explain the concepts and characteristics of routing and switching.	
• Properties of network traffic	1A, 2A, 2B, 2C, 4E
• Broadcast domains	2A
• CSMA/CD	2A
• CSMA/CA	2A
• Collision domains	2A
• Protocol data units	1A
• MTU	2B
• Broadcast	2C
• Multicast	4E
• Unicast	2C
• Segmentation and interface properties	2C, 3B, 9B, 9C
• VLANs	9B
• Trunking (802.1q)	9B
• Tagging and untagging ports	9B
• Port mirroring	3B
• Switching loops/spanning tree	3B
• PoE and PoE+ (802.3af, 802.3at)	3B
• DMZ	9C
• MAC address table	3B
• ARP table	2C
• Routing	5A
• Routing protocols (IPv4 and IPv6)	5A
• Distance-vector routing protocols	5A
• RIP	5A
• EIGRP	5A
• Link-state routing protocols	5A
• OSPF	5A
• Hybrid	5A
• BGP	5A
• Routing types	5A
• Static	5A
• Dynamic	5A
• Default	5A
• IPv6 concepts	4E
• Addressing	4E
• Tunneling	4E
• Dual stack	4E
• Router advertisement	4E
• Neighbor discovery	4E
• Performance concepts	7B
• Traffic shaping	7B

Domain and Objective	Covered In
• QoS	7B
• Diffserv	7B
• CoS	7B
• NAT/PAT	9C
• Port forwarding	9C
• Access control list	9C
• Distributed switching	3D
• Packet-switched vs. circuit-switched network	1B
• Software-defined networking	3D

1.4 Given a scenario, configure the appropriate IP addressing components.

• Private vs. public	4D
• Loopback and reserved	4D
• Default gateway	4A
• Virtual IP	5B
• Subnet mask	4A
• Subnetting	4C, 4D
• Classful	4C
• Classes A, B, C, D, and E	4C
• Classless	4C, 4D, 4E
• VLSM	4D
• CIDR notation (IPv4 vs. IPv6)	4C, 4D
• Address assignments	4E, 4F
• DHCP	4F
• DHCPv6	4F
• Static	4F
• APIPA	4F
• EUI-64	4E
• IP reservations	4F

1.5 Compare and contrast the characteristics of network topologies, types, and technologies.

• Wired topologies	3C
• Logical vs. physical	3C
• Star	3C
• Ring	3C
• Mesh	3C
• Bus	3C
• Wireless topologies	13A
• Mesh	13A
• Ad hoc	13A
• Infrastructure	13A
• Types	3D
• LAN	3D
• WLAN	3D

Domain and Objective	Covered In
• MAN	3D
• WAN	3D
• CAN	3D
• SAN	3D
• PAN	3D
• Technologies that facilitate the Internet of Things (IoT)	14D
• Z-Wave	14D
• Ant+	14D
• Bluetooth	14D
• NFC	14D
• IR	14D
• RFID	14D
• 802.11	14D

1.6 Given a scenario, implement the appropriate wireless technologies and configurations.

Domain and Objective	Covered In
• 802.11 standards	13A
• a	13A
• b	13A
• g	13A
• n	13A
• ac	13A
• Cellular	14D
• GSM	14D
• TDMA	14D
• CDMA	14D
• Frequencies	13A
• 2.4 GHz	13A
• 5.0 GHz	13A
• Speed and distance requirements	13A
• Channel bandwidth	13A
• Channel bonding	13A
• MIMO/MU-MIMO	13A
• Unidirectional/omnidirectional	13A
• Site surveys	13A

1.7 Summarize cloud concepts and their purposes.

Domain and Objective	Covered In
• Types of services	7D
• SaaS	7D
• PaaS	7D
• IaaS	7D
• Cloud delivery models	7D
• Private	7D
• Public	7D
• Hybrid	7D
• Connectivity methods	7D

Domain and Objective	Covered In
• Security implications/considerations	7D
• Relationship between local and cloud resources	7D
1.8 Explain the functions of network services.	
• DNS service	6C, 6D
• Record types	6D
• A, AAAA	6D
• TXT (SPF, DKIM)	6D
• SRV	6D
• MX	6D
• CNAME	6D
• NS	6D
• PTR	6D
• Internal vs. external DNS	6D
• Third-party/cloud-hosted DNS	6D
• Hierarchy	6C
• Forward vs. reverse zones	6D
• DHCP service	4F
• MAC reservations	4F
• Pools	4F
• IP exclusions	4F
• Scope options	4F
• Lease time	4F
• TTL	4F
• DHCP relay/IP helper	4F
• NTP	7A
• IPAM	6D
Domain 2.0 Infrastructure	
2.1 Given a scenario, deploy the appropriate cabling solution.	
• Media types	12A, 12D
• Copper	12A, 12B
• UTP	12B
• STP	12B
• Coaxial	12A
• Fiber	12D
• Single-mode	12D
• Multimode	12D
• Plenum vs. PVC	12B
• Connector types	12A, 12B, 12D
• Copper	12A, 12B
• RJ-45	12B
• RJ-11	12B
• BNC	12A
• DB-9	12A

Domain and Objective	Covered In
• DB-25	12A
• F-type	12A
• Fiber	12D
• LC	12D
• ST	12D
• SC	12D
• APC	12D
• UPC	12D
• MTRJ	12D
• Transceivers	12D
• SFP	12D
• GBIC	12D
• SFP+	12D
• QSFP	12D
• Characteristics of fiber transceivers	12D
• Bidirectional	12D
• Duplex	12D
• Termination points	12A
• 66 block	12A
• 110 block	12A
• Patch panel	12A
• Fiber distribution panel	12A
• Copper cable standards	12A, 12B
• Cat 3	12B
• Cat 5	12B
• Cat 5e	12B
• Cat 6	12B
• Cat 6a	12B
• Cat 7	12B
• RG-6	12A
• RG-59	12A
• Copper termination standards	12B
• TIA/EIA 568a	12B
• TIA/EIA 568b	12B
• Crossover	12B
• Straight-through	12B
• Ethernet deployment standards	2B
• 100BaseT	2B
• 1000BaseT	2B
• 1000BaseLX	2B
• 1000BaseSX	2B
• 10GBaseT	2B

Domain and Objective	Covered In

2.2 Given a scenario, determine the appropriate placement of networking devices on a network, and install/configure them.

• Firewall	10A
• Router	5B
• Switch	3B
• Hub	3A
• Bridge	3A
• Modems	14B
• Wireless access point	13A
• Media converter	12D
• Wireless range extender	13A
• VoIP endpoint	7B

2.3 Explain the purposes and use cases for advanced networking devices.

• Multilayer switch	7B
• Wireless controller	13A
• Load balancer	7B
• IDS/IPS	10B
• Proxy server	10A
• VPN concentrator	15A
• AAA/RADIUS server	11B
• UTM appliance	10B
• NGFW/Layer 7 firewall	10A
• VoIP PBX	7B
• VoIP gateway	7B
• Content filter	10A

2.4 Explain the purposes of virtualization and network storage technologies.

• Virtual networking components	7C
• Virtual switch	7C
• Virtual firewall	7C
• Virtual NIC	7C
• Virtual router	7C
• Hypervisor	7C
• Network storage types	7C
• NAS	7C
• SAN	7C
• Connection type	7C
• FCoE	7C
• Fibre Channel	7C
• iSCSI	7C
• InfiniBand	7C
• Jumbo frame	7C

2.5 Compare and contrast WAN technologies.

Domain and Objective	Covered In
• Service type	14A, 14B
• ISDN	14B
• T1/T3	14A
• E1/E3	14A
• OC-3 – OC-192	14A
• DSL	14B
• Metropolitan Ethernet	14A
• Cable broadband	14B
• Dial-up	14B
• PRI	14B
• Transmission mediums	14A, 14B, 14D
• Satellite	14D
• Copper	14A, 14B
• Fiber	14A, 14B
• Wireless	14D
• Characteristics of service	14C, 15A
• MPLS	14C
• ATM	14C
• Frame relay	14C
• PPPoE	14C
• PPP	14C
• DMVPN	15A
• SIP trunk	14C
• Termination	14B
• Demarcation point	14B
• CSU/DSU	14B
• Smart Jack	14B

Domain 3.0 Network Operations

3.1 Given a scenario, use appropriate documentation and diagrams to manage the network.

• Diagram symbols	16A
• Standard operating procedures/work instructions	16A
• Logical vs. physical diagrams	16A
• Rack diagrams	16A
• Change management documentation	16A
• Wiring and port locations	16A
• IDF/MDF documentation	16A
• Labeling	16A
• Network configuration and performance baselines	16A
• Inventory management	16A

3.2 Compare and contrast business continuity and disaster recovery concepts.

• Availability concepts	16C
• Fault tolerance	16C

Domain and Objective	Covered In
• High availability	16C
• Load balancing	16C
• NIC teaming	16C
• Port aggregation	16C
• Clustering	16C
• Power management	16C
• Battery backups/UPS	16C
• Power generators	16C
• Dual power supplies	16C
• Redundant circuits	16C
• Recovery	16C
• Cold sites	16C
• Warm sites	16C
• Hot sites	16C
• Backups	16C
• Full	16C
• Differential	16C
• Incremental	16C
• Snapshots	16C
• MTTR	16C
• MTBF	16C
• SLA requirements	16C

3.3 Explain common scanning, monitoring, and patching processes and summarize their expected outputs.

Domain and Objective	Covered In
• Processes	6B, 8A, 11E
• Log reviewing	8A
• Port scanning	6B
• Vulnerability scanning	11E
• Patch management	11E
• Rollback	11E
• Reviewing baselines	8A
• Packet/traffic analysis	6B, 8A
• Event management	8A
• Notifications	8A
• Alerts	8A
• SIEM	8A
• SNMP monitors	8A
• MIB	8A
• Metrics	8A
• Error rate	8A
• Utilization	8A
• Packet drops	8A
• Bandwidth/throughput	8A

Domain and Objective	Covered In
3.4 Given a scenario, use remote access methods.	
• VPN	15A
• IPSec	15A
• SSL/TLS/DTLS	15A
• Site-to-site	15A
• Client-to-site	15A
• RDP	15B
• SSH	15B
• VNC	15B
• Telnet	15B
• HTTPS/management URL	15B
• Remote file access	15B
• FTP/FTPS	15B
• SFTP	15B
• TFTP	15B
• Out-of-band management	15B
• Modem	15B
• Console router	15B
3.5 Identify policies and best practices.	
• Privileged user agreement	16D
• Password policy	16D
• On-boarding/off-boarding procedures	16D
• Licensing restrictions	16D
• International export controls	16D
• Data loss prevention	16D
• Remote access policies	16D
• Incident response policies	16D
• BYOD	16D
• AUP	16D
• NDA	16D
• System life cycle	16D
• Asset disposal	16D
• Safety procedures and policies	16D
Domain 4.0 Network Security	
4.1 Summarize the purposes of physical security devices.	
• Detection	16B
• Motion detection	16B
• Video surveillance	16B
• Asset tracking tags	16B
• Tamper detection	16B
• Prevention	16B
• Badges	16B
• Biometrics	16B

Domain and Objective	Covered In
• Smart cards	16B
• Key fob	16B
• Locks	16B

4.2 Explain authentication and access controls.

Domain and Objective	Covered In
• Authorization, authentication, and accounting	11A, 11B
• RADIUS	11B
• TACACS+	11B
• Kerberos	11B
• Single sign-on	11A
• Local authentication	11B
• LDAP	11B
• Certificates	11B
• Auditing and logging	11B
• Multifactor authentication	11A
• Something you know	11A
• Something you have	11A
• Something you are	11A
• Somewhere you are	11A
• Something you do	11A
• Access control	11B, 11C
• 802.1X	11C, 13C
• NAC	11C
• Port security	11C
• MAC filtering	11C
• Captive portal	11C
• Access control lists	11B

4.3 Given a scenario, secure a basic wireless network.

Domain and Objective	Covered In
• WPA	13C
• WPA2	13C
• TKIP-RC4	13C
• CCMP-AES	13C
• Authentication and authorization	13C
• EAP	13C
• PEAP	13C
• EAP-FAST	13C
• EAP-TLS	13C
• Shared or open	13C
• Preshared key	13C
• MAC filtering	13C
• Geofencing	13C

4.4 Summarize common networking attacks.

Domain and Objective	Covered In
• DoS	9A
• Reflective	9A
• Amplified	9A

Domain and Objective	Covered In
• Distributed	9A
• Social engineering	11A
• Insider threat	11A
• Logic bomb	11A
• Rogue access point	13C
• Evil twin	13C
• War driving	13C
• Phishing	11A
• Ransomware	11A
• DNS poisoning	9A
• ARP poisoning	9A
• Spoofing	9A
• Deauthentication	13C
• Brute force	11A
• VLAN hopping	9B
• Man-in-the-middle	9A
• Exploits vs. vulnerabilities	9A
4.5 Given a scenario, implement network device hardening.	
• Changing default credentials	11D
• Avoiding common passwords	11D
• Upgrading firmware	11E
• Patches and updates	11E
• File hashing	11D
• Disabling unnecessary services	11D
• Using secure protocols	11D
• Generating new keys	11D
• Disabling unused ports	11D
• IP ports	11D
• Device ports (physical and virtual)	11D
4.6 Explain common mitigation techniques and their purposes.	
• Signature management	10B
• Device hardening	11D
• Change native VLAN	9B
• Switch port protection	3B, 11C
• Spanning tree	3B
• Flood guard	11C
• BPDU guard	3B
• Root guard	3B
• DHCP snooping	11C
• Network segmentation	9B, 9C
• DMZ	9C
• VLAN	9B

Domain and Objective	Covered In
• Privileged user account	11A
• File integrity monitoring	10B
• Role separation	11A
• Restricting access via ACLs	10A
• Honeypot/honeynet	11E
• Penetration testing	11E

Domain 5.0 Network Troubleshooting and Tools

5.1 Explain the network troubleshooting methodology.

• Identify the problem	8B
• Gather information	8B
• Duplicate the problem, if possible	8B
• Question users	8B
• Identify symptoms	8B
• Determine if anything has changed	8B
• Approach multiple problems individually	8B
• Establish a theory of probable cause	8B
• Question the obvious	8B
• Consider multiple approaches	8B
• Top-to-bottom/bottom-to-top OSI model	8B
• Divide and conquer	8B
• Test the theory to determine the cause	8B
• Once the theory is confirmed, determine the next steps to resolve the problem	8B
• If the theory is not confirmed, reestablish a new theory or escalate	8B
• Establish a plan of action to resolve the problem and identify potential effects	8B
• Implement the solution or escalate as necessary	8B
• Verify full system functionality and, if applicable, implement preventive measures	8B
• Document findings, actions, and outcomes	8B

5.2 Given a scenario, use the appropriate tool.

• Hardware tools	12B, 12C, 12D, 13B
• Crimper	12B
• Cable tester	12C
• Punch down tool	12B
• OTDR	12D
• Light meter	12D
• Tone generator	12C
• Loopback adapter	12C
• Multimeter	12C
• Spectrum analyzer	13B
• Software tools	2C, 4B, 5B, 6B, 6D, 10A, 14B
• Packet sniffer	2C

Domain and Objective	Covered In
• Port scanner	6B
• Protocol analyzer	6B
• Wi-Fi analyzer	13B
• Bandwidth speed tester	14B
• Command line	2C, 4B, 5B, 6B, 6D, 10A
• ping	4B
• tracert, traceroute	5B
• nslookup	6D
• ipconfig	4B
• ifconfig	4B
• iptables	10A
• netstat	6B
• tcpdump	2C
• pathping	5B
• nmap	6B
• route	5B
• arp	2C
• dig	6D

5.3 Given a scenario, troubleshoot common wired connectivity and performance issues.

• Attenuation	12C
• Latency	7B
• Jitter	7B
• Crosstalk	12C
• EMI	12C
• Open/short	12C
• Incorrect pin-out	12C
• Incorrect cable type	12C
• Bad port	12C
• Transceiver mismatch	12D
• TX/RX reverse	12C
• Duplex/speed mismatch	8C
• Damaged cables	12C
• Bent pins	12C
• Bottlenecks	7B, 8A
• VLAN mismatch	9B
• Network connection LED status indicators	12C

5.4 Given a scenario, troubleshoot common wireless connectivity and performance issues.

• Reflection	13B
• Refraction	13B
• Absorption	13B
• Latency	13B
• Jitter	13B

Domain and Objective	Covered In
• Attenuation	13B
• Incorrect antenna type	13B
• Interference	13B
• Incorrect antenna placement	13B
• Channel overlap	13B
• Overcapacity	13B
• Distance limitations	13B
• Frequency mismatch	13B
• Wrong SSID	13C
• Wrong passphrase	13C
• Security type mismatch	13C
• Power levels	13B
• Signal-to-noise ratio	13B

5.5 Given a scenario, troubleshoot common network service issues.

• Names not resolving	8C
• Incorrect gateway	8C
• Incorrect netmask	8C
• Duplicate IP addresses	8C
• Duplicate MAC addresses	8C
• Expired IP address	8C
• Rogue DHCP server	8C
• Untrusted SSL certificate	7A
• Incorrect time	7A
• Exhausted DHCP scope	8C
• Blocked TCP/UDP ports	10A
• Incorrect host-based firewall settings	10A
• Incorrect ACL settings	10A
• Unresponsive service	8C
• Hardware failure	8C

Solutions

Activity 1-1: Discussing OSI Model Layers

1. **What OSI model layer transmits bits from one device to another and modulates the transmission stream over a medium?**

    ● Physical

    ○ Transport

    ○ Data Link

    ○ Network

2. **At which OSI layer do programs on a network node access network services?**

    ○ Data Link

    ○ Physical

    ● Application

    ○ Presentation

3. **Which OSI layer is responsible for establishing reliable connections between two devices?**

    ● Transport

    ○ Presentation

    ○ Application

    ○ Data Link

4. **Which OSI layer packages bits of data from the Physical layer into frames?**

    ○ Presentation

    ○ Transport

    ○ Session

    ● Data Link

5. **At which sublayer of the OSI model do network adapter cards operate?**
    The Media Access Control (MAC) sublayer of the Data Link layer.

6. **What component is responsible for translating the computer's digital signals into electrical or optical signals that travel on network cable?**

   A transceiver.

7. **True or False? The Session layer is responsible for passing data to the Network layer at the lower bound and the Presentation layer at the upper bound.**

   False. The Session layer is between the Transport and Presentation layers.

8. **Which OSI layer handles the concept of logical addressing?**

   The Network layer.

9. **At which OSI layer is the concept of a port number introduced?**

   The Transport layer.

Activity 1-2: Discussing the TCP/IP Suite

1. **To which layer of the OSI model does the TCP/IP model Internet layer correspond?**

   The Network layer (layer 3).

2. **Which TCP/IP model layer might also be described as the Host-to-Host layer?**

   The Transport layer.

3. **What is fragmentation?**

   Dividing the contents of large messages into smaller packets for delivery over an internetwork.

4. **Which organization is responsible for the development of Internet standards?**

   The Internet Engineering Task Force (IETF).

Activity 2-1: Discussing Media Types and Access Methods

1. **What is attenuation?**

   The loss of signal strength that occurs as the signal travels through the media.

2. **Why might the baud rate be different from the bit rate?**

   Baud is the number of symbols measured in Hertz; bit rate is the amount of information, measured in bits per second. A signaling technique might encode more than one bit per symbol.

3. **True or False? All the nodes shown in the following figure are in the same collision domain.**

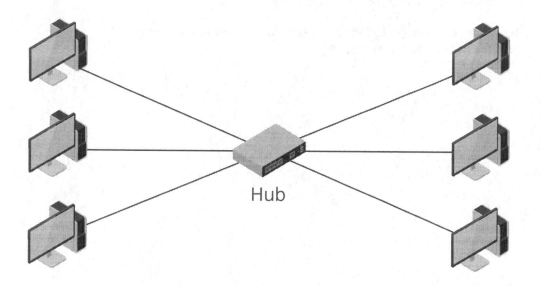

True. Hubs work at the Physical layer (layer 1) and just repeat the same signal out of each port.

4. **Identify the transmission method depicted in the following graphic.**

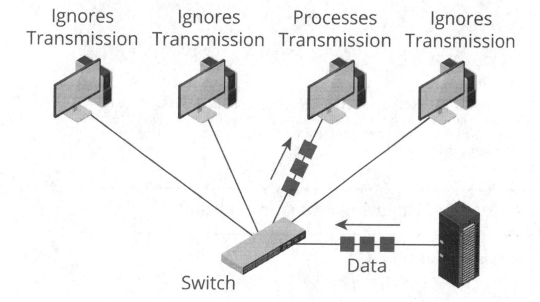

○ Broadcast

○ CSMA/CD

○ CSMA/CA

● Unicast

○ Switched

5. **With CSMA/CD, what will happen if a host has data to transmit and there is already data on the cable?**

   The host will wait until the cable is clear to transmit the data.

6. **Assuming unmanaged switches, how many broadcast domains are present in the following figure?**

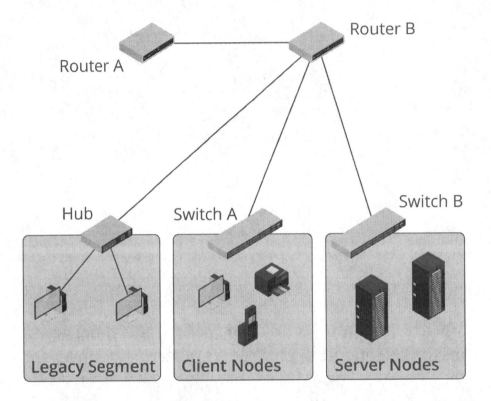

Four. Each router interface is a separate broadcast domain. One collision domain contains Router A and Router B, another contains the nodes on the legacy segment, and the last two are the client nodes Switch A broadcast domain and the server nodes Switch B broadcast domain.

Activity 2-2: Discussing Ethernet Standards

1. **What is an MTU?**

   Maximum transmission unit—the maximum amount of data that a frame can carry as payload.

2. **True or False? The CRC mechanism in Ethernet allows for the retransmission of damaged frames.**

   False. The CRC indicates only that a frame may be corrupt.

3. **True or False? A computer with a 10BASE-T Ethernet adapter cannot be joined to a 100BASE-T network.**

   False. Fast Ethernet is backwards-compatible with 10BASE-T (and Gigabit Ethernet is backwards-compatible with Fast Ethernet).

4. **What maximum distance is defined in standards documentation for 1000BASE-LX running over MMF?**

   550 m (1804 feet). Note that 1000BASE-LX can run over MMF or SMF. SMF has much higher range.

Activity 2-3: Discussing Network Interface Configuration and Monitoring

1. **What is an I/G bit?**

   The part of a MAC address that determines whether a frame is addressed to an individual node (0) or group (1). The latter is used for multicast and broadcast.

2. **If a mapping for a local destination host is not found in a source host ARP cache, how does the source host send an ARP request?**

   As a broadcast to all local hosts.

3. **If a packet is addressed to a remote network, what destination MAC address will the sending node use?**

   The MAC address of the default gateway.

4. **True or False? The arp utility allows you to discover another host's MAC address.**

   Partially False—while that is the function of the Address Resolution Protocol, the arp *utility* is used to inspect the ARP table cache, which may or may not contain the other host's address. Note that a standard means to ensure the MAC address is cached is to ping the destination address first. This is the basis of a utility called arping.

5. **On a switched network, what configuration changes must be made to allow a host to sniff unicast traffic from all hosts connected to a switch?**

   The network adapter must be put in p-mode (promiscuous mode) and the switch must be configured to mirror traffic to the sniffer's port.

6. **Write the command to use tcpdump to capture traffic from the IP address 172.16.16.254 on the interface eth0 and output the results to the file router.pcap.**

   ```
   tcpdump -i eth0 -w 'router.pcap' src host 172.16.16.254
   ```

Activity 3-1: Discussing Hubs and Bridges

1. **True or False? Devices can only transmit on an Ethernet network when the media is clear, and the opportunity to transmit becomes less frequent as more devices are added. Also, the probability of collisions increases. These problems can be overcome by installing a hub.**

   False. The description of the problem is true, but the solution is not. This issue is resolved by using a bridge or (more likely these days) a switch.

2. **If you connect two hubs with a crossover cable, are nodes connected to either hub in the same collision domain?**

   Yes.

3. **True or False? A bridge does not forward broadcast or multicast traffic.**

   False. Segments on different bridge ports are in separate collision domains but the same broadcast domain.

Activity 3-2: Discussing Switch Configuration

1. **What is microsegmentation?**

   Each switch port creates a separate collision domain for each attached host, essentially eliminating the effect of collisions on network performance and allowing each host exclusive use of the full media bandwidth.

2. **How does a switch keep track of the hardware addresses of hosts connected to its ports?**

   It uses a MAC address table stored in content addressable memory (CAM).

3. **What is happening if a switch is flooding?**

   It is sending frames out on all ports (other than the source port). This typically happens when it is learning MAC addresses or forwarding broadcast traffic.

4. **True or False? Switch ports should normally be set to autonegotiate speed and duplex settings.**

   True; the speed/duplex setting rarely needs to be manually configured on modern networks.

5. **What is the function of STP?**

   Spanning Tree Protocol (STP) prevents switching loops. A switching loop is where flooded traffic is continually looped around a network with redundant links between switches.

6. **Under STP, if a host port is working as normal, what state is it in?**

   Forwarding.

7. **What mechanisms protect the switching infrastructure from malicious STP traffic?**

   Configuration settings such as BPDU Guard and BPDU Filter prevent hosts from injecting bridge protocol data units (BPDUs) into the network. Root guard prevents devices from attempting to become root.

8. **What is PoE?**

   Power over Ethernet is an IEEE specification for delivering power to devices from switch ports over network cabling.

Activity 3-3: Discussing Network Topologies

1. **What term is used to describe a topology in which two nodes share a single link?**

   Point-to-point.

2. What is characteristic of the bandwidth of a bus topology?

The bandwidth is shared between all nodes connected to the bus.

3. Identify the physical network topology depicted in the following graphic.

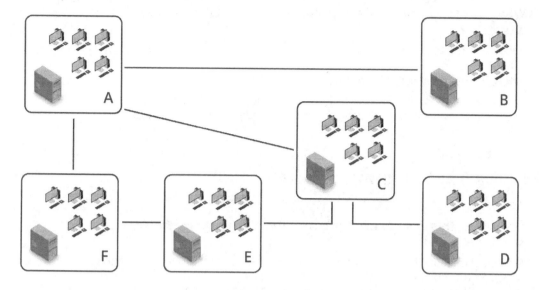

○ Star.

○ Bus.

● Mesh.

○ Ring.

4. What type of device is used to implement a physical star topology?

Any type of node that connects multiple devices over multiple ports, including hubs, bridges, switches, and routers.

5. You need operations to continue if one link fails. How many links does it take to connect three sites?

Three.

Activity 3-4: Discussing Network Types

1. What is a WLAN?

Wireless local area network.

2. What network infrastructure implementation is larger than a LAN but smaller than a WAN?

Metropolitan area network (MAN). You could also mention campus area network (CAN).

3. What is the purpose of a SAN?

A storage area network (SAN) links together different kinds of storage devices (RAID array, hard disks, SSDs, tape drives, and so on) and makes "pools" of storage capacity available to servers.

4. **What types of devices are connected in a PAN?**

   A personal area network (PAN) links devices such as laptops and smartphones and provides connectivity with peripheral devices (printers, input devices, headsets, and so on) plus wearable technology, such as fitness trackers and smart watches.

5. **What four layers can be used to conceptualize distributed switching hierarchy?**

   Access, distribution, core, and data center.

6. **What is the function of a network controller?**

   Implements the policies defined by software defined networking (SDN) control applications by interfacing with the configuration interfaces of network appliances.

Activity 3-5: Designing a Switch Topology

1. **Looking at this design, what are its potential weaknesses and strengths?**

   Strengths: multiple links to the router for resilience, and switch link speeds increase as you go towards the core switch. Weaknesses: no resilience in the case of link failure, and a whole floor could be isolated with a single cable disconnect.

3. **What would Janice need to ensure about the configuration of the switches, given the revised network layout?**

   They would need to support the Spanning Tree Protocol; otherwise broadcast storms will occur and the switch's MAC address tables will be constantly updating.

4. **Assuming the switches are configured with suitable protocols, what would determine which switch became the root bridge? How could this be changed to ensure that the main switch was root?**

   By default, the switch with the lowest MAC address would become the root, unless a priority has been set on one or several switches, then the switch with the lowest priority number would win the election.

5. **Given this design and assuming all switch connections were in place, how many links would be placed in a blocking state by the STP algorithm?**

   Three—That would be the minimum number of links that would need to be blocking to ensure loops were not formed. The blocks could be positioned between the floor 1 and floor 2 switch, between the floor 2 and floor 3 switch, and the floor 2 extension switch and floor 3 extension switch, for example.

Activity 4-1: Discussing IPv4 Addressing Components

1. **What is the function of the Protocol field in an IPv4 header?**

   It indicates the protocol type of the payload. This would typically be TCP or UDP, but it could also be something else (ICMP or GRE, for instance).

2. **Convert the decimal value 72 into binary.**

   01001000.

3. **Convert the binary value 11110010 to decimal.**

   242.

4. **What is the dotted decimal representation of an 8-bit netmask?**

   255.0.0.0.

5. **What is the dotted decimal representation of an 18-bit netmask?**

   255.255.192.0.

6. **Given an 18-bit netmask, are the IP addresses 172.16.1.10 and 172.16.54.10 on the same network?**

   Yes. Convert the IP addresses to binary, and you will see that the first 18 binary digits in each address are the same (10101100 00011110 00).

7. **Given the subnet mask 255.255.255.128, are the IP addresses 192.168.0.1 and 192.168.1.1 on the same network?**

   No. You can see from the decimal mask and dotted decimal IP addresses that an octet within the network portion is different. If you do convert to binary to check, remember that the subnet mask contains 25 bits. You can see that the 24th bit is different in each address. As that bit occurs within the netmask, the hosts are on different IP networks.

8. **Given the subnet mask 255.255.255.128, are the IP addresses 192.168.0.1 and 192.168.0.65 on the same network?**

   No. This subnet mask contains 25 bits. If you convert the IP addresses to binary, you can see that the 25th bit is different in each address. As that bit occurs within the netmask, the hosts are on different IP networks.

9. **True or False? A router will not forward a packet when the TTL field is 0.**

   True.

10. **Which TCP/IP parameters must be defined for a host to be able to communicate with hosts on a remote network?**

    IP Address, Subnet Mask, and Default Gateway (address of the router).

Activity 4-2: Discussing IP Interface Testing Tools

1. **Once it is installed, how would you check the TCP/IP configuration at the command line?**

   Run ipconfig on a Windows host or ifconfig or ip on Linux/UNIX.

2. **Which of the protocols included with TCP/IP reports messages and errors regarding packet delivery?**

   Internet Control Message Protocol (ICMP).

3. **True or False? Receiving an echo reply message indicates that the link between two hosts is operational.**

   True.

4. **True or False? The ipconfig utility can be used to empty the DNS cache.**

   True (though this functionality is not available in ifconfig).

5. **If you have a workstation that cannot connect to a server, what is the first test you could perform to establish whether the cabling is OK?**

Ping another local system.

Activity 4-4: Discussing IPv4 Subnetting

1. **What technology or technologies can you use to isolate broadcast domains?**

Routers and virtual LANs (VLANs).

2. **What is a Class D address?**

One used for multicasting.

3. **Which of the following are Class C IP addresses? (Choose four.)**

☑ 195.243.67.51

☐ 165.247.220.100

☐ 190.234.24.6

☑ 11001101 01110100 00000100 00101110

☑ 11001111 10000001 01111110 10010010

☑ 213.54.53.52

☐ 233.168.24.6

4. **Which of the following IP addressing rules is true? (Choose two.)**

☑ The host ID must be unique on the network.

☑ Network and host IDs cannot be all zeroes.

☐ A network ID can be any number.

☐ A network ID can be 255.

5. **If a host is configured with the IP address 10.0.10.22 and mask 255.255.255.192, what is the broadcast address of the subnet?**

10.0.10.63. Convert the IP address to binary (00001010 00000000 00001010 00010110), then work out the number of bits in the mask (26). Change the remaining host bits (6) to 1s and convert back to dotted decimal.

6. **A host is configured with the IP address 10.0.10.22 and subnet mask 255.255.255.192. How many hosts per subnet would this addressing scheme support?**

62. Either subtract the least significant octet from 256, then subtract 2 for the network and broadcast addresses, or having worked out that there are 6 host bits, calculate (2^6)-2.

7. **A technician is troubleshooting a network and has asked your advice. He is trying to ping 192.168.16.192. The network has been subnetted with the custom mask 255.255.255.224. Why might this return a "Destination host unreachable" message?**

   The IP address resolves to the subnet network address, not a host address. Windows does not normally allow pinging the network address. Other OSs treat it as an alternative broadcast address, but most systems are configured to disallow such directed broadcasts for security reasons.

8. **If the IP address 10.0.10.22 were used with an /18 mask, how many subnets and hosts per subnet would be available?**

   1024 subnets each with 16,382 hosts. From the default mask, 10 bits are allocated to the subnet ID and 14 remain as host bits.

Activity 4-5: Designing an IP Subnet

1. **To divide the network in half, what subnet mask do you need to use?**

   Adding a single bit to the mask creates two subnets. The mask and network prefix will be 255.255.255.128 (/25).

2. **What are the subnet IDs for each network?**

   192.168.1.0 /25 and 192.168.1.128 /25. An easy way to find the first subnet ID is to deduct the least significant octet in the mask (128 in the example) from 256, giving the answer 128.

3. **What is the broadcast address for each subnet?**

   192.168.1.127 and 192.168.1.255. You can work these out quite simply from the subnet ID that you calculated. The broadcast address for the first subnet is 1 less than the next subnet ID. The second subnet's broadcast address is the last possible address.

4. **What is the range of assignable IP addresses for each subnet?**

   192.168.1.1 to 126 and 192.168.1.129 to 254. If you have each subnet ID and the broadcast ID, the host ranges are simply the values in between.

5. **Your manager has considered his original plan and realized that it does not accommodate the need for a WAN link to the head office or a separate segment for a team that works with sensitive data. What mask will you need to accommodate this new requirement, and how many hosts per subnet will it allow?**

   You now need four subnets: a /28 prefix or 255.255.255.240 mask. There are only 4 bits left to work with for host addressing, though, so there are just 14 host addresses per subnet.

6. **Your manager is not satisfied with the new scheme and wants to reduce the number of subnets to make more host addresses available in each subnet. Is there a way to use the same subnet for the two floors of the office?**

   Yes. You can configure virtual LANs (VLANs) by using the switches. You would need to do this anyway to support the security requirement. One VLAN can support ordinary users, while the other can be used for the secure subnet. The switches can be configured with the same VLAN information, so whether a host is on the first or second floor does not impede the design.

Activity 4-7: Discussing Private and Public IPv4 Addressing Schemes

1. **True or False? The IP address 172.24.0.1 is routable over the Internet.**

   False. 172.16.0.0—172.31.255.255 is the Class B private address range.

2. **What two methods can an organization use to facilitate Internet access for hosts configured with private addresses?**

   One method is to use Network Address Translation (NAT) and a router configured with one or more public addresses. NAT allows the router to translate between the two schemes. The second option is to use a proxy server with a public IP address. The proxy fulfils requests on behalf of the LAN clients and forwards responses back to them.

3. **What is the significance of the address 127.0.0.1?**

   This is the default loopback address for most hosts. The loopback address facilitates testing the TCP/IP implementation on a host.

4. **A company has four networks, using the addresses 192.168.0.0/24, 192.168.1.0/24, 192.168.2.0/24, and 192.168.3.0/24. What network prefix and subnet mask can be used to summarize a supernet route to these networks?**

   The network prefix is /22 and the mask is 255.255.252.0.

5. **True or False? VLSM means using more than one mask to subnet an IP network.**

   True. By using different mask sizes, variable length subnet masking (VLSM) allows designers to match subnet sizes to requirements more precisely.

Activity 4-8: Designing VLSM Subnets

1. **How large will each of the subnets that join the three routers together need to be?**

   Large enough for just 2 IP addresses. Just 2 host bits, so /30 mask.

2. **Which is the largest subnet in the topology? What is the minimum number of bits that will be needed for that number of hosts? How many IP addresses will that subnet provide? What would be the VLSM and address range for the largest subnet?**

   Branch A is the largest subnet with 16,000 hosts. 14 bits are needed, providing 16,382 addresses (16384-2). /18 will be the VLSM mask, giving an IP address range of 172.30.0.1—172.30.63.254.

3. **What is the next largest subnet in the design? How many host bits will be needed for that subnet? How many IP addresses will that subnet provide and what is the VLSM?**

   Branch B is the next largest subnet with 8,000 hosts. 13 bits are needed, providing 8,190 addresses (8,192-2). /19 will be the VLSM mask, giving an IP address range of 172.30.64.1—172.30.95.254.

4. **Work out the remaining subnets, remembering to ensure that subnet ranges do not overlap, but equally that you do not waste IP addresses. Complete the table.**

Subnet Name	Number of Hosts	VLSM Subnet ID	Number of IP Addresses
Branch A			
Branch B			
Branch C			
Branch D			
Branch E			
Branch F			
Router 1 to 2			
Router 2 to 3			
Router 1 to 3			

Your completed table should have the following information. You can also compare your completed table with what is shown on the solution slide. **Branch A:** 16,000 hosts; VLSM subnet ID: 172.30.0.0/18; 16,382 IP addresses. **Branch B:** 8,000 hosts; VLSM subnet ID 172.30.64.0/19; 8,190 hosts. **Branch C:** 4,000 hosts; VLSM mask 172.30.96.0/20; 4,094 IP addresses. **Branch D:** 4,000 hosts; VLSM mask 172.30.112.0/20; 4,094 IP addresses. **Branch E:** 2,000 hosts; VLSM mask 1172.30.128.0/21; 2,046 IP addresses. **Branch F:** 1,000 hosts, VLSM mask 172.30.136.0/22; 1,022 IP addresses. **Router 1 to 2:** 2 hosts; VLSM mask 172.30.140.0/30; 2 IP addresses. **Router 2 to 3:** 2 hosts; VLSM mask 172.30.140.4/30; 2 IP addresses. **Router 1 to 3:** 2 hosts; VLSM mask 172.30.140.8/30; 2 IP addresses.

Activity 4-9: Discussing IPv6 Addressing Components

1. **Convert the binary value 1010 0001 1000 1100 to hex.**

   A18C.

2. **Which of the following IPv6 addresses is a valid unicast host address?**

   ● fe80::218:8bff:fea7:bd37

   ○ fe80::219:d2ff::7850

   ○ ff02::219:d2ff:fea7:7850

   ○ ::/128

3. **What is an EUI-64, and how might it be used by IPv6?**

   Extended unique identifier (EUI) is IEEE's preferred term for a MAC address. EUI-64 is a 64-bit hardware interface ID. A 48-bit MAC address can be converted to an EUI-64 by using a simple mechanism. The EUI-64 can be used as the IPv6 interface ID, though a randomly generated token is often preferred.

4. **In IPv6, how is the loopback address best expressed?**

   ::1

5. **In IPv6, how could you distinguish a unicast address with global scope from other addresses?**

   It starts with binary 001 or hex 2 or 3.

6. **With a single global IPv6 address prefix, how many bits are available for subnetting?**

   16 bits.

7. **What type of IPv6 unicast addresses are not routable over the Internet?**

   Link-local addresses and unique local addresses (ULA).

8. **In IPv6, how can a client obtain a routable IPv6 address without requiring manual configuration?**

   Stateless address autoconfiguration (SLAAC) allows a host to autoconfigure an interface by listening for Router Advertisements to obtain a network prefix.

9. **What is 6to4?**

   A method of tunneling IPv6 packets over an IPv4 network.

Activity 4-11: Discussing DHCP Services

1. **What is the advantage of having a DHCP server in a TCP/IP network?**

   It simplifies the administrative task of configuring hosts and reduces the chance of configuration errors.

2. **What port should be open on the client for it to negotiate with a DHCP server?**

   UDP port 68.

3. **True or False? If a client accepts a DHCPOFFER, the DHCPREQUEST packet is broadcast on the network.**

   True.

4. **If a network adapter is using the address 169.254.1.10 on a host connected to the LAN, what would you suspect?**

   That a DHCP server is offline. The system is configured to obtain an address automatically but cannot contact a DHCP server and is using APIPA.

5. **On the DHCP server, what is a range of IP addresses that are available to be leased or assigned to clients called?**

   Address pool.

6. **When configuring multiple DHCP servers for redundancy, what should you take care to do?**

   Configure the servers with non-overlapping address pools.

7. **True or False? DHCP options can be configured on a per-scope basis.**

   True.

8. **What is an RFC 1542 compliant router?**

   One that can forward DHCP traffic to and from remote networks (using IP helper, for instance).

9. **What address is used to contact a DHCPv6 server?**

   IPv6 does not support broadcasts, so clients use the multicast address ff:02::1:2 to discover a DHCP server.

10. **In a stateless environment, what sort of information does DHCPv6 provide?**

    In a stateless environment, the host autoconfigures an address using a network prefix provided by the router (typically). DHCPv6 is then used to provide the IPv6 addresses used to access network services, such as DNS or SIP gateways.

Activity 5-1: Discussing Characteristics of Routing

1. **What is a directly connected route?**

   A host or subnet connected to one of the router's interfaces.

2. **An entry in a routing table will list the destination network address and netmask plus a gateway and metrics. What other piece of information is required?**

   Interface—the local port used to route to the destination.

3. **If a routing protocol carries a subnet mask field for route updates, what feature of IP routing does the routing protocol support?**

   Classless addressing (subnetting and supernetting).

4. **True or False? A router would normally have more than one network interface.**

   True. You might also say that routers with a single interface (a router on a stick) might be used to route between VLANs, though.

5. **Referring to the routing table in the previous question, to which IP address would packets be sent if they were going to the Internet or another network?**

   The packets would be sent to the gateway IP address 192.168.1.200.

6. **What does it mean if a routing protocol converges to a steady state quickly?**

   Changes to the network topology are propagated between routers quickly. This makes the network quicker and more reliable.

7. **Which general class of dynamic routing protocol provides the best convergence performance?**

   Link-state.

8. **If forced to pick just one, which routing metric might you prioritize for a VoIP application?**

   Latency (minimizing delay) is important.

9. **Refer to the following routing table to answer the question. Which route determines the destination for packets to the 172.16.0.0 network? What adapter will they be delivered to?**

```
IPv4 Route Table
===========================================================================
Active Routes:
Network Destination        Netmask          Gateway       Interface  Metric
        0.0.0.0          0.0.0.0     192.168.1.200   192.168.1.11     276
      127.0.0.0        255.0.0.0         On-link         127.0.0.1     306
      127.0.0.1  255.255.255.255         On-link         127.0.0.1     306
127.255.255.255  255.255.255.255         On-link         127.0.0.1     306
     172.16.0.0      255.255.0.0         On-link        172.16.0.1     286
     172.16.0.1  255.255.255.255         On-link        172.16.0.1     286
 172.16.255.255  255.255.255.255         On-link        172.16.0.1     286
    192.168.1.0    255.255.255.0         On-link      192.168.1.11     276
   192.168.1.11  255.255.255.255         On-link      192.168.1.11     276
  192.168.1.255  255.255.255.255         On-link      192.168.1.11     276
      224.0.0.0        240.0.0.0         On-link         127.0.0.1     306
      224.0.0.0        240.0.0.0         On-link        172.16.0.1     286
      224.0.0.0        240.0.0.0         On-link      192.168.1.11     276
255.255.255.255  255.255.255.255         On-link         127.0.0.1     306
255.255.255.255  255.255.255.255         On-link        172.16.0.1     286
255.255.255.255  255.255.255.255         On-link      192.168.1.11     276
===========================================================================
```

The fifth route in the table with a network destination of 172.16.0.0. These packets will be delivered to the 172.16.0.1 network adapter.

10. **What is an ASN and how does it assist route aggregation?**

An Autonomous System Number (ASN) identifies a group of network prefixes under the administrative control of a single entity (such as an ISP). The AS can be advertised to other ASs through a single prefix (route aggregation), hiding the complexity of the internal network from other autonomous systems.

Activity 5-2: Designing a Branch Office Internetwork

1. **Given the current scenario of the charity, how would the routers at each local office be configured?**

As the link is only used for web browsing and online email, the local office routers would just be configured with a static route/default gateway/gateway of last resort to forward all traffic to the main site, which would forward the web traffic on.

3. **With this new infrastructure in place, what changes would need to be made to the router's configuration?**

Due to the need for offices and therefore routers to be able contact each other, additional routing table entries will be needed. This could be through more static routes, but a dynamic routing protocol would be better able to cope with any future changes to the topology.

4. **Which protocol would be best here?**

There are several choices. The network is relatively simple with only a few network hops, so RIPv2 could be used as it is easier to configure.

6. **Considering the potential changes a successful pilot in the East region might bring about in the whole organization, would your router configuration options change?**

Due to the potential increase in the number of routers and subnets, OSPF may be the better choice of dynamic routing protocol. This is especially true due to potential IP subnet numbering differences, including VLSM.

7. What might you do to manage the much larger number of IP subnets?

It may be worth considering different OSPF areas to manage the size of the OSPF topology tables and use route summarization to reduce the router's CPU load.

Activity 5-3: Discussing Router Configuration

1. How would you view the routing table on a Linux PC?

Just enter `route` without any other parameters. You can also use the `ip route show` command.

2. If you receive a Request timed out error message when using ping, what would you attempt next?

Use `tracert` to try to identify the routing problem.

3. What tool(s) could you use to measure link statistics over time?

`pathping` or `mtr`.

4. What is a looking glass site?

A server allowing third parties to inspect the routing infrastructure of remote network, such as routing within an ISP's autonomous system, assisting troubleshooting.

5. What is the purpose of HSRP and VRRP?

Hot Standby Router Protocol (HSRP) and Virtual Router Redundancy Protocol (VRRP) allow multiple physical router appliances to act as the same logical router, providing redundancy, load balancing, and failover.

Activity 6-1: Discussing the Uses of Ports and Protocols

1. Why would a developer choose to use unreliable delivery over reliable, connection-oriented delivery?

When speed is more important than reliability.

2. What is the purpose of the window field in a TCP segment?

It is used for flow control. The window indicates the amount of data that the host can receive before sending another acknowledgement.

3. If the client is in the TIME-WAIT state, is the connection with the server still open?

Not normally—The server closes the connection when it receives the ACK from the client; if this packet is lost, the server connection may still be open.

4. What are the sizes of TCP and UDP headers?

TCP is 20 bytes (or more) while UDP is 8 bytes.

5. A function of TCP is to handle flow control. What is the purpose of the flow control function?

Flow control makes sure the sender does not inundate the receiver with data packets.

6. **True or False? User Datagram Protocol (UDP), like TCP, uses flow control in the sending of data packets.**

   False.

7. **Which port is used by the Network Time Protocol (NTP)?**

   UDP port 123.

Activity 6-2: Discussing Port Scanners and Protocol Analyzers

1. **If you wanted to investigate connections on your machine, which built-in utility could you use?**

   `netstat`

2. **What is CPE?**

   Common platform enumeration (CPE) is a standard naming system for OS and applications software. A fingerprinting tool such as nmap will try to match the software running on a host to a CPE identifier by analyzing responses to network probes.

3. **You need to audit services made publicly available on a web server. What command-line tool could you use?**

   Nmap is an ideal tool for scanning remote hosts to discover which ports they have open and the applications or services running them.

4. **You need to analyze the information saved in a .pcap file. What type of command-line tool or other utility is best suited to this task?**

   This type of file will contain a network packet capture. You could use a command-line tool such as `tcpdump` to display the contents, but a graphical tool such as Wireshark will make analysis easier.

Activity 6-4: Discussing Name Resolution Services

1. **What is a generic top-level domain?**

   FQDNs are arranged in a hierarchy from the root. Top-level domains are those farthest to the right. Generic TLDs are those maintained by ICANN (.com, .org, .net, .info, .biz), while the other main sets of TLDs are country codes and sponsored.

2. **What characters are allowed in a DNS host name?**

   Up to 63 alphanumeric characters and the hyphen, although the hyphen cannot be used at the beginning or end of the name.

3. **What is the location of the HOSTS file?**

   In Windows, it is %SystemRoot%\system32\drivers\etc\, while in Linux, it is usually placed in the /etc directory.

4. **Why would the following HOSTS file entry not affect name resolution?**

   `#198.134.5.6 www.comptia.org`

   Everything after the # character on the same line is treated as a comment.

5. **When you configure name server addresses as part of a host's IP settings, do you need to specify servers perform iterative queries only or ones that accept recursive queries?**

   Recursive queries. These DNS servers are designed to assist clients with queries and are usually separate to the DNS server infrastructure designed to host authoritative name records.

Activity 6-5: Discussing DNS and IPAM Services

1. **What type of DNS record resolves IPv6 addresses?**

   AAAA.

2. **What use is a PTR DNS record?**

   A pointer maps an IP address to a host name, enabling a reverse lookup. Reverse lookups are used (for example) in spam filtering to confirm that a host name is associated with a given IP address.

3. **What types of DNS records have priority or preference values?**

   Typically, mail (MX) and service (SRV) records.

4. **What type of DNS record is used to prove the valid origin of email?**

   Sender Policy Framework (SPF) and DomainKeys Identified Mail (DKIM) records can be used to validate the origin of email and reject spam. These are configured in DNS as text (TXT) records.

5. **What type of DNS enables clients to report a change of IP address to a DNS server?**

   Dynamic DNS.

6. **What is the function of the command** `nslookup - 8.8.8.8`**?**

   To start nslookup in interactive mode with the DNS server set to 8.8.8.8 (Google's public DNS server).

7. **What is the function of a** `dig` **subcommand such as** `+nostats`**?**

   Control what is shown by the tool. You can use these commands to suppress certain kinds of output, such as sections of the response from the DNS server.

8. **What type of server infrastructure is IPAM designed to monitor?**

   IP address management (IPAM) is used to monitor and manage DHCP and DNS services (as well as domain controllers in a Windows network environment).

Activity 7-1: Discussing the Uses of Network Applications

1. **What is SNTP?**

   Simple Network Time Protocol—A simpler protocol derived from NTP that enables workstations to obtain the correct time from time servers.

2. **What must be installed on a server to use secure (HTTPS) connections?**

   A digital certificate and the corresponding private key.

3. **What happens if a message sent via SMTP cannot be delivered?**

   The server generates a non-delivery report (NDR) with an appropriate error code.

4. **What protocol would enable a client to manage mail subfolders on a remote mail server?**

   Internet Message Access Protocol (IMAP) or IMAP Secure (IMAPS). Post Office Protocol (POP3) allows download of mail messages, but not management of the remote inbox.

Activity 7-3: Discussing the Uses of Voice Services and Advanced Networking Devices

1. **True or False? SIP enables the location of user agents via a specially formatted URI.**

   True.

2. **Which component in a VoIP network allows calls to be placed to and from the voice telephone or public switched telephone network (PSTN)?**

   This function is performed by a VoIP gateway.

3. **How is jitter mitigated by a VoIP application?**

   By buffering packets.

4. **How many different traffic classes can be defined by 802.1Q/p?**

   The field is 3-bit, allowing up to 8 values. 7 is reserved for network infrastructure (routing table updates), 6-5 for 2-way communications, 4-1 for streaming multimedia, and 0 for "ordinary" Best Effort delivery.

5. **How does a traffic shaper benefit real-time data applications?**

   A traffic shaper can reserve bandwidth so that QoS parameters, such as maximum latency and jitter, for a real-time data application can be guaranteed.

6. **What would be a typical scenario for implementing a content switch?**

   Using the switch as an interface for a web server farm. The switch performs load balancing by connecting clients to different servers depending on traffic conditions and policies.

Activity 7-4: Discussing the Uses of Virtualization and Network Storage Services

1. **What is a hypervisor?**

   The software that hosts, configures, and manages multiple guest operating systems or virtual machines (VMs). A hypervisor can be implemented as an OS itself ("bare metal") or as an application running on the host OS.

2. **If a VM is connected to a bridged virtual switch, what sort of network access does it have?**

   A bridged switch connects the VM via the host's NIC. In Hyper-V, there are two types of bridged connection. An external switch allows access to the wider physical network. An internal switch allows just the VMs and the host to communicate on the same network.

3. **What are the main differences between NAS and SAN?**

   Network attached storage (NAS) is typically a single appliance providing file-level access to clients. Storage area networks (SANs) provide block-level access to multiple storage devices to file and database servers, rather than to all network hosts indiscriminately.

4. **What protocol can be used to implement a SAN without provisioning dedicated storage networking adapters and switches?**

   iSCSI.

5. **Is InfiniBand a competitor technology to Fibre Channel or an upgrade path allowing integration with legacy infrastructure?**

   InfiniBand is a competitor technology to Fibre Channel.

6. **What is the MTU of a jumbo frame compared to a regular Ethernet frame?**

   A regular Ethernet frame carries a 1500-byte payload, while a jumbo frame can carry about 9000 bytes.

Activity 7-5: Discussing the Concepts of Cloud Services

1. **What is the key difference between purchasing cloud web server instances and a virtual hosted server?**

   The cloud instances should offer better elasticity—being able to provision and pay for peak resources as needed, rather than trying to anticipate demand and provision for peak resources at the outset.

2. **What is meant by a public cloud?**

   A solution hosted by a third party and shared between subscribers (multi-tenant). This sort of cloud solution has the greatest security concerns.

3. **What type of cloud solution would be used to implement a SAN?**

   This would usually be described as Infrastructure as a Service (IaaS).

4. **What are the main options for implementing connections to a cloud service provider?**

   You can use the Internet and the provider's web services (possibly over a VPN) or establish a direct connection for better security and performance. A direct connection could be established by co-locating resources in the same data center or provisioning a direct link to the data center.

5. **What is a Cloud Access Security Broker?**

   Enterprise management software mediating access to cloud services by users to enforce information and access policies and audit usage.

Activity 8-1: Discussing Network Interface and Log Monitoring

1. **Gathering systems' statistics regularly allows system administrators to identify bottlenecks. Why do they want to do this?**

   To identify resource usage problems before they critically affect performance.

2. **What is a top listener in terms of network monitoring?**

   An interface that receives the most incoming traffic.

3. **You suspect that a network application is generating faulty packets. What interface metric(s) might help you to diagnose the problem?**

   Monitoring errors and discards/drops would help to prove the cause of the problem.

4. **What sort of log would you inspect if you wanted to track web server access attempts?**

   History/security/audit log.

5. **What is the function of a SIEM?**

   A Security Information and Event Management (SIEM) is designed to consolidate security alerts from firewalls, anti-malware, intrusion detection, audit logs, and so on.

6. **How does an SNMP agent report an event to the management system?**

   Via a trap.

7. **What would be the purpose of configuring thresholds in network monitoring software?**

   The software could produce an alert if network performance did not meet any given metric.

Activity 8-3: Discussing Network Troubleshooting Methodology

1. Gather information Duplicate the problem, if possible Question users Identify symptoms Determine if anything has changed

   Which step has been omitted from the list of activities related to identifying the problem?

   Approach multiple problems individually.

2. **After asking the three basic questions of anyone reporting a problem, what should you have determined? (Choose three.)**

   ☑ Whether to look for recent change or an oversight in configuration.

   ☑ Where to look for the problem.

   ☑ The severity of the problem.

   ☐ If the problem should be escalated.

3. **Which three means of establishing a theory of probable cause refer to the OSI model?**

   Top-to-bottom, bottom-to-top, and divide and conquer.

4. **When should you escalate a problem?**

   If you cannot solve it yourself (though it won't be good for your career if you give up too easily). You might also escalate if you do not have authorization to perform the necessary changes or if the system is under some sort of warranty.

5. **Which step follows "Implement the solution or escalate as necessary" in the troubleshooting methodology?**

   Verify full system functionality and (if applicable) implement preventive measures.

6. **True or False? Documentation should be created only at the end of the troubleshooting process.**

   False—The last step of the methodology is to ensure that findings, actions, and outcomes are documented, but you cannot do this effectively without existing notes. Most troubleshooting takes place within a ticket system. Ideally, a documented job ticket would be opened at the start of recording the incident.

Activity 8-4: Discussing Common Network Services Issues

1. **You have connected a new computer to a network port and cannot get a link. You have tested the adapter and cable and can confirm that there are no problems. No other users are experiencing problems. The old computer also experienced no problems. What cause would you suspect, and what is a possible next step?**

   Speed mismatch—Check the autonegotiate settings on the adapter and port.

2. **Users on a floor served by a single switch cannot get a network connection. What is the best first step?**

   Reset the switch—If that works, also investigate possible underlying causes, such as a malicious spoofing attack on the switch or a poorly seated plug-in module.

3. **You have pinged the router for the local subnet and confirmed that there is a valid link. The local host cannot access remote hosts, however. No other users are experiencing problems. What do you think is the cause?**

   The router is not configured as the default gateway for the local host. You can ping it, but the host is not using it for routing.

4. **Following maintenance on network switches, users in one department cannot access the company's internal web and email servers. You can demonstrate basic connectivity between the hosts and the servers by IP address. What might the problem be?**

   It is likely that there is a problem with name resolution. Perhaps the network maintenance left the hosts unable to access a DNS server, possibly due to some VLAN assignment issue.

5. **Users on a network segment have been experiencing poor performance. The cause has been identified as a broadcast storm. What is often the cause of broadcast storms?**

   Defective network card or switch, misconfiguration of Spanning Tree Protocol (STP), or the unauthorized or unplanned attachment of bridging devices that create a loop.

6. **You are planning to reconfigure static and DHCP-assigned IP addresses across the network during scheduled downtime. What preliminary step should you take to minimize connectivity issues when the network is re-opened?**

   Ensure that clients obtain a new DHCP lease, either by shortening the lease period in advance or by using a script to force clients to renew the lease at startup.

Activity 8-5: Troubleshooting Network Issues

1. **You receive a call from the user of host A who has always been able to connect to the LoB application servers, but today she is unable to connect. You verbally check with other users and discover that none of the hosts on subnet 20 can connect, but that users in subnet 10 report no problems. What tests should you perform to narrow down the cause of the problem?**

   You should *not* assume from the information gathered so far that the user can connect to the servers in subnet 10. There are two likely causes—either the link to the router from subnet 20 has failed, perhaps because of a faulty switch, or hosts in subnet 20 are no longer receiving a correct IP configuration from the network servers. To test methodically, from any host in subnet 20, ping the loopback address and then ping that host's IP address. If either of these tests fail or if the host is using APIPA, investigate communications with the network servers. If the local IP configuration on each host is good, ping the router. If this fails, suspect a problem with the switch or cabling.

2. **You send a junior technician to the equipment room to fix the problem. Some time later, another user from subnet 20 calls complaining that he cannot connect to the Internet. What questions should you ask to begin troubleshooting?**

   Again, do not assume that Internet connectivity is the only issue. The user might not have any sort of network link, but has only complained about accessing the Internet because that's the particular application he was trying to use. Ask if the user can connect to one of the LoB server applications. If this fails, check whether other users are experiencing the problem and establish the scope—just the one user? All users on subnet 20? All users on both subnets?

3. **You asked a junior technician to step in because your manager had asked you to deploy a wireless access point on the network to support a sales event due to start the next day. There will be lots of guests, and your manager wants them all to have Internet access. You did not have much time, so you simply added the access point to the switch supporting subnet 10. The next day arrives, and some time after the sales event starts, multiple employees in subnet 10 report that when they attempt to connect to the network, they get a message that the Windows network has limited connectivity. What might be the cause and what test should you use to confirm the issue?**

The most likely cause is that guest devices have exhausted the DHCP address pool for that scope. You can confirm by identifying that the hosts have autoconfigured APIPA addresses, perhaps by using `ipconfig`.

Activity 9-1: Discussing Common Networking Attacks

1. **Response time on the website that hosts the online version of your product catalog is getting slower and slower. Customers are complaining that they cannot browse the catalog items or search for products. What type of attack do you suspect?**

   ○ Trojan horse attack.

   ○ Spoofing attack.

   ○ Social engineering attack.

   ● DoS attack.

2. **The network administrator at your organization analyzes a network trace capture file and discovers that packets have been intercepted and retransmitted to both a sender and a receiver during an active session. This could be a(n):**

   ○ IP spoofing attack.

   ○ Session hijacking attack.

   ○ Replay attack.

   ● Man-in-the-middle attack.

3. **What type of activity is often a prelude to a full-scale network attack?**

   Footprinting—Obtaining information about the network and security system. This might be done by port scanning, eavesdropping, or social engineering.

4. **What is the usual goal of an ARP spoofing attack?**

   To redirect traffic to the attacker's machine by masquerading as the subnet's default gateway. This allows the attacker to eavesdrop on traffic or perform a MitM attack.

5. **Why are most network DoS attacks distributed?**

   Most attacks depend on overwhelming the victim. This typically requires a large number of hosts.

6. **What means might an attacker use to redirect traffic to a fake site by abusing DNS name resolution?**

   By injecting false mappings into the client cache or into the server cache or by getting the client to use a rogue DNS resolver.

7. **What type of DoS is a DNS amplification attack, and how is it perpetrated?**

   This is classed as a distributed reflection DoS (DRDoS). The attacker leverages a botnet to make multiple DNS queries to Internet DNS servers using the spoofed IP address of the target server. The DNS queries use small request packets but use a technique to make the response packet as large as possible. The multiple queried servers direct the responses to the victim IP address, which can overwhelm the victim network.

8. **Greene City Interiors IT staff discovered an entry when reviewing their audit logs showing that a junior employee from the R&D department had logged into the network at 3:00 a.m. Further review of the audit logs show that he had changed his timecard on the HR server. Which security factor was breached, and did the attack exploit a software vulnerability or a configuration vulnerability?**

   The attack compromised the integrity of data stored in the network. It exploited a configuration weakness. The employee should not have had permission to alter the timecard.

Activity 9-2: Discussing the Characteristics of VLANs

---

1. **Why should VLANs be carefully planned before implementing them?**

   Because the switch will not forward frames between VLANs. If a node in one VLAN needs to communicate with a node in another VLAN, some other mechanism (like a router) must be used to allow that communication.

2. **What methods can you use to allocate a host to a VLAN?**

   The simplest is by connection port (static VLAN membership), but it can also be configured by MAC address or user authentication (dynamic VLAN membership).

3. **When you are connecting an ordinary client workstation to a switch and assigning it to a VLAN, should the switch port be tagged or untagged?**

   Untagged—This means the switch strips any tag used to transport the frame over a trunk link and forwards an ordinary Ethernet frame to the host. When the switch receives a frame from the host, it determines whether or not to tag the frame for forwarding over a trunk link.

4. **What distinguishes a layer 3 switch from a router?**

   An L3 switch performs "hardware routing" using Application-Specific Integrated Circuits (ASICs). This performs very well at routing traffic around Ethernet networks with VLANs configured, but it is less flexible than dedicated router appliances. A layer 3 switch is unlikely to support the interfaces for WAN routing.

5. **What is a trunk port?**

   A port used to connect switches. This allows hosts connected to different switches to communicate and to configure VLANs across multiple switches.

6. How do you correct a VLAN mismatch error?

Ensure the same native VID is configured on the ports on both switches participating in a trunk link.

Activity 9-3: Discussing the Characteristics of NAT and Port Forwarding

1. What is the purpose of a DMZ?

To provide services such as web and email that require Internet connectivity without allowing direct access to the private network from the Internet.

2. How can an enterprise DMZ be implemented?

Either using two firewalls (external and internal) as a screened subnet, or using a triple-homed firewall (one with three network interfaces).

3. What distinguishes PAT from static NAT?

Static NAT establishes a 1:1 mapping between a public and private address. PAT uses port numbers to share one or more public addresses between many privately addressed hosts.

4. What is the difference between port forwarding and other types of NAT?

NAT can be configured to work on any IP address translation, regardless of the port number. Port forwarding is a type of destination NAT configured for a specific port or protocol. The router takes incoming requests for that port and changes the destination IP address (and optionally also the destination port number) to forward the packet to a server on the DMZ or LAN.

Activity 10-1: Discussing Firewall and Proxy Configuration

1. What parameters can a layer 3 firewall ruleset use?

IP source and destination address, protocol type, and port number.

2. What OSI layer does an NGFW work at and why?

OSI layer 7 (Application) because the next generation firewall (NGFW) is configured with application-specific filters that can parse the contents of protocols such as HTTP, SMTP, or FTP.

3. Other than attempting to block access to sites based on content, what security options might be offered by Internet content filters?

Blocking access based on time of day or total usage.

4. Why would you deploy a reverse proxy?

To publish a web application without directly exposing the servers on the internal network to the Internet.

5. What is the default rule on a firewall?

Deny anything not permitted by the preceding rules.

6. Using iptables, in which chain would you create rules to block all outgoing traffic not meeting certain exceptions?

OUTPUT chain.

7. **You are troubleshooting a connectivity problem with a network application server. Certain clients cannot connect to the service port. How could you rule out a network or remote client host firewall as the cause of the problem?**

   Connect to or scan the service port from the same segment with no host firewall running.

Activity 10-3: Discussing the Uses of IDS/IPS and UTM

1. **What component does a network-based IDS use to scan traffic?**

   A sniffer or sensor.

2. **A company has suffered a data breach. Investigators are able to establish exactly when the data breach occurred, but on checking the IDS logs, no evidence of the breach is present. What type of intrusion detection error condition is this?**

   A false negative.

3. **What is shunning?**

   Configuring an IPS to set a temporary firewall rule to block the suspect IP address.

4. **What sort of maintenance must be performed on signature-based monitoring software?**

   Definition/signature updates.

5. **What is the main purpose of UTM?**

   Unified Threat Management (UTM) consolidates multiple security functions in a single appliance with a single management console.

Activity 11-1: Discussing Authentication Controls and Attacks

1. **What element is missing from the following list, and what is its purpose? Identification, Authentication, Accounting**

   Authorization—Assigning privileges over the network object to the subject.

2. **Why do malicious insider threats often pose greater risk than malicious users generally?**

   Malicious insiders are trusted users, meaning they have existing privileges to work on the network and access resources.

3. **Why is a logic bomb unlikely to be detected by anti-virus software?**

   Most anti-virus software depends on signatures of known malware to detect threats. A logic bomb is a specially crafted script or program that runs according to specific triggers, usually perpetrated by an insider threat, and so unlikely to be detectable by routine scans.

4. What is the purpose of SSO?

Single Sign-on allows users to authenticate once to gain access to different resources. This reduces the number of login credential sets a user must remember.

5. How do social engineering attacks succeed?

They generally depend on lack of security awareness in users. An attacker can either be intimidating (exploiting users' ignorance of technical subjects or fear of authority) or persuasive (exploiting the "customer service" mindset to be helpful developed in most organizations).

6. How might an attacker recover a password from an encrypted hash?

By using a password cracking tool. This may recover the password if it uses a simple dictionary word or if it is insufficiently long and complex (brute force).

7. What are the two main types of tokens that a user can present as part of an authentication mechanism?

A smart card or fob is normally used for a hardware token. The hardware token could contain a digital certificate issued by a trusted authority to validate the user's identity. Another approach is for a fob to generate a one-time password (OTP). This shows a code that is good for one use only, or that must be used within 30-60 seconds of generation.

8. Which factor is missing from the following list? Something You Know, Something You Are, Something You Have, Somewhere You Are.

Something You Do—This type of factor is related to biometric recognition, but depends on an action, such as writing a signature or typing a phrase in your own distinctive way.

Activity 11-2: Discussing the Uses of Authentication Protocols and Directory Services

1. What are the main features of a digital certificate?

A digital certificate contains the subject's public key, which can be used to cryptographically authenticate the subject and encrypt messages sent to it. The certificate is signed by a certificate authority (CA) that has validated the subject's identity. The certificate contains other information to identify the subject and describe its purpose.

2. What authorization feature makes Kerberos a good choice for a network authentication protocol?

Support for SSO.

3. What is a RADIUS client, and how should it be configured?

A device or server that accepts user connections. In a RADIUS architecture, the client does not need to be able to perform authentication itself; it passes the logon request to an AAA server. The client needs to be configured with the RADIUS server address and shared secret.

4. What is an LDAP distinguished name?

A unique identifier in the LDAP database for any given resource, defined by a series of attribute=value pairs delimited by commas. The most specific attribute is listed first, and successive attributes become progressively broader.

Activity 11-4: Discussing the Uses of Port Security and NAC

1. **What type of attack does a switch port flood guard prevent?**

   A MAC flooding attack, where the attacker tries to overwhelm the switch's CAM table, mapping which MAC addresses are associated with which ports. If this table is overwhelmed, the switch can start flooding frames out of all ports. This facilitates eavesdropping of all traffic passing over the switch.

2. **What is the role of EAPoL in implementing port-based network access control?**

   A switch that supports 802.1X port-based access control can enable a port but allow only the transfer of Extensible Authentication Protocol over LAN (EAPoL) traffic. This allows the client device and/or user to be authenticated before full network access is granted.

3. **What is a dissolvable agent?**

   Some NAC solutions perform host health checks via a local agent, running on the host. A dissolvable agent is one that is executed in the host's memory and CPU but not installed to a local disk.

4. **What is meant by remediation in the context of NAC?**

   The ability to logically park a client that does not meet the health policy in a more restricted area of the network. For example, these areas may only allow basic Internet access, or be given access to required software patches, and so on.

Activity 11-5: Discussing Network Device Hardening

1. **What is a common password?**

   Any password that is easy to guess, especially if a password cracking system is doing the guessing. Apart from ordinary dictionary words, common passwords include names, birthdays, vehicle registrations, sequential number strings, and, of course, the word "password."

2. **Other than completely disabling the protocol, how could you mitigate the risk posed by an open port?**

   Using a firewall to block the port on segments of the network where the protocol should not be in use, or restricting use of the port to authorized hosts.

3. **True or False? Telnet is a secure channel for host administration.**

   False—Telnet has no security mechanisms.

4. **What type of key allows a user to access an SSH server without a password, and where is it stored?**

   The user's public key, stored on the SSH server. The user must have the matching private key, stored on his or her workstation.

Activity 11-6: Discussing Patch Management and Vulnerability Scanning Processes

1. How would a router appliance be patched to protect against a specific vulnerability described in a security advisory?

This type of OS does not support patching of individual files, so the whole OS has to be replaced with a new version. Vendors keep track of which version first addresses a specific security advisory.

2. How does a configuration backup assist rollback?

Some patches cannot be uninstalled, so reverting the update would involve reinstalling the OS or image. In this scenario, a configuration backup allows you to restore settings more quickly and reliably.

3. What type of information is updated when a scanner receives a new set of feeds or plug-ins?

These contain information about newly detected vulnerabilities and scripts used to detect whether a vulnerability is present on a host.

4. What type of security audit performs active testing of security controls?

A penetration test (pen test). A vulnerability assessment is one that uses passive testing techniques.

Activity 12-1: Discussing Structured Cabling Systems

1. What would be a typical use of an IDF?

To cross-connect backbone cabling in a multi-building (campus) network. The Intermediate Distribution Frame introduces a hierarchy of cable organization between the Main Distribution Frame and horizontal cross-connects.

2. What is a 110 block?

A type of Insulation Displacement Connector (IDC) used to terminate copper cabling at the back of a wall port or patch panel.

3. At what layer of the OSI model does a fiber distribution panel work?

All types of distribution frames work at the Physical layer (layer 1).

4. Which cable type consists of a core made of solid copper surrounded by insulation, a braided metal shielding, and an outer cover?

Coax.

Activity 12-2: Discussing Twisted Pair Cabling Solutions

1. What is the measurement standard for wire thickness?

American Wire Gauge (AWG).

2. **What is crosstalk?**

   Signal interference between adjacent conductors within a single cable or between adjacent cables.

3. **Which categories of UTP cables are certified to carry data transmission faster than 100 Mbps?**

   Cat 5e, Cat 6/6A, and Cat 7.

4. **True or False? Cat standards apply only to wiring.**

   False—Connectors and interconnects are also rated to Cat standards.

5. **Why is plenum-rated cable used when cable is run in an area where building air is circulated?**

   Plenum-rated cable produces minimal amounts of smoke if burned, must be self-extinguishing, and must meet other strict fire safety standards.

6. **100BASE-T transmit pins are 1 and 2. What color code are the wires terminated to these pins under T568A and T568B?**

   Green/White (pin 1) and Green (pin 2) for T658A or Orange (pin 1)/White and Orange (pin 2) for T568B.

7. **Which pins are used for the receive pair under 100BASE-T?**

   3 and 6.

Activity 12-3: Discussing Twisted Pair Cabling Issues

1. **When you are troubleshooting a cable link, which should you investigate first—the patch cord, permanent link, or network adapter?**

   Apply the principle of eliminating simple causes first—Check the patch cord by substitution, and check the link lights on the network adapter.

2. **Patch cables are vulnerable to failure since they often trail from the PC to the wall socket. What could you use to check that a cable is physically intact?**

   Cable tester.

3. **If you detect a significant increase in noise affecting a cable link, how would you go about determining the cause?**

   Ask what has changed—It is likely that some equipment or power cabling has been installed near the data cable link.

4. **What cabling faults would a wire map tester detect?**

   Opens, shorts, and transpositions (reversed and crossed pairs).

5. **How would you test for excessive attenuation in a network link?**

   Measure the insertion loss in dB by using a cable tester.

6. **Your network uses UTP cable throughout the building. There are a few users who complain of intermittent network connectivity problems, but there is no pattern for these problems that relates to network usage. You visit the users' workstations and find that they are all located close to an elevator shaft. What is a likely cause of the intermittent connectivity problems? How might you correct the problem?**

   If the cabling is being run too close to the elevator equipment, when the elevator motor activates, it produces interference on the network wire. You can replace the UTP cable with screened/shielded copper wire or reposition the cables away from the elevator shaft.

7. **What is the reason for making power sum crosstalk measurements when testing a link?**

   Power sum crosstalk measures cable performance when all four pairs are used, as Gigabit and 10G Ethernet do.

Activity 12-4: Discussing Fiber Optic Cabling Solutions

1. **What surrounds the core of optical fibers in fiber optic cable?**

   Cladding.

2. **What type of fiber optic cable is suited for long distance links?**

   Single Mode.

3. **You are connecting a server to a switch. The server NIC has an LC/UPC port. You have a patch cord marked LC/APC. Is it suitable for use?**

   No, you should use a patch cord with the matching finishing (LC/UPC).

4. **What device enables termination of different patch cord types in an appliance such as a switch or router?**

   A transceiver or interface converter such as a GBIC, SFP, SFP+, or QSFP.

Activity 13-1: Discussing Wireless Technologies

1. **What mechanism does RTS/CTS support?**

   Carrier sense multiple access with collision avoidance (CSMA/CA). Rather than try to detect collisions, a wireless station indicates its intent to transmit by broadcasting a Request To Send (RTS) and waits to receive a Clear To Send (CTS) before proceeding.

2. **Which IEEE WLAN standards specify a data transfer rate of up to 54 Mbps?**

   802.11a and 802.11g.

3. **What options may be available for an 802.11n network that are not supported under 802.11g?**

   Channel bonding, Multiple-Input-Multiple-Output (MIMO), and use of either 2.4 GHz or 5 GHz frequency bands.

4. **True or False? Stations with 802.11ac capable adapters must be assigned to the 5 GHz frequency band.**

   True—802.11ac is designed to work only in the 5 GHz frequency band, with the 2.4 GHz band used for legacy clients.

5. **What is MU-MIMO?**

   Multiuser MIMO (MU-MIMO) is a means for an AP to allocate higher bandwidth to multiple stations at the same time. An AP equipped with multiple antennas uses beamforming and separate spatial streams to transmit a signal more strongly in the direction of each station. The stations must be in different locations relative to the AP (north and east of it, for example). Stations aligned in the same general direction with the AP share the bandwidth of the spatial stream.

6. **Which frequency band is less likely to suffer from co-channel interference?**

   The 5 GHz band.

7. **What is a BSSID?**

   The MAC address of an AP.

8. **What are the advantages of deploying a wireless mesh topology over an ad hoc one?**

   Stations in a wireless mesh network are capable of discovering one another, forming peering arrangements, and performing path discovery and forwarding between peers (routing). These factors make a mesh-based network more scalable than an ad hoc network.

9. **True or False? Suppressing transmission of the WLAN beacon improves security.**

   False—The beacon cannot be suppressed completely because clients use it when connecting with the AP. Increasing the broadcast interval reduces network overhead, but it increases the time required to find and connect to the network.

10. **What constraints should you consider when planning the placement of an AP?**

    Range, interference, and obstructions, and access to a network port and power supply. On a very large network, you may also need to consider number of clients within small areas (device density and bandwidth requirements).

11. **What is a heat map?**

    A site survey plotting the strength of wireless signals in different parts of a building.

12. **You are planning WLAN for an office building with an attached warehouse. Where would you recommend placing Wi-Fi antennas for the best coverage in an office full of cubicles as well as in the warehouse?**

    Placing omnidirectional antennas on the ceiling would provide the best coverage with good line-of-sight and reduced interference between the APs and stations. Depending on the height of the warehouse ceiling, you may need to obtain APs with downtilt antennas.

13. **What type of AP requires a wireless controller?**

    A lightweight or thin AP (or one working in thin mode).

Activity 13-2: Discussing Wireless Performance Issues

1. **The lobby area of your office building has undergone a renovation, the centerpiece of which is a large aquarium in the middle of the room, separating a visitor seating and greeting area from the reception desks, where the AP facilitating guest Internet access is located. Since the renovation, many guests have been unable to connect to Wi-Fi from the seating area. Could the aquarium really be the cause, and what solution could you recommend?**

   Yes, a dense body of water could cause absorption and refraction of the radio waves, weakening the signal. You could ceiling-mount the AP so that signals are less affected by the body of water. You could also add a second AP at the front of the lobby area to act as a repeater. For optimum performance, both APs should be ceiling-mounted, to preserve line of sight.

2. **Widget Corporation has provided wireless access for its employees using several APs located in different parts of the building. Employees connect to the network using 802.11g-compatible network cards. On Thursday afternoon, several users report that they cannot log on to the network. What troubleshooting step would you take first?**

   Following troubleshooting methodology, establish the scope of the problem early on the in the process. In this case, check whether the problem machines are trying to use the same AP. If the problem is apparent across multiple APs, suspect a wireless controller disabling 802.11g compatibility mode.

3. **Your office block is hosting a conference event. During the morning coffee break, several guests report that they cannot access their webmail. What is the likely cause?**

   Device saturation—The AP is likely to be experiencing greater load than usual and cannot cope with the volume of requests.

4. **What is the difference between a Wi-Fi analyzer and a spectrum analyzer?**

   A Wi-Fi analyzer is a software-based tool that interrogates the wireless adapter to display detailed information, based on what the Wi-Fi radio can receive. A spectrum analyzer uses dedicated radio hardware to report on frequency usage outside of Wi-Fi traffic, and so can be used more reliably to detect interference sources.

5. **Users in the corner of an office building cannot get good Wi-Fi reception. Your office manager doesn't want to use his budget to purchase a new AP. He's noticed that the power level control on the AP is set to 3 out of 5 and wants to know why turning up the power isn't the best solution?**

   This might work, but you should investigate the root cause of the issue and determine whether the solution will have adverse effects. The most obvious issue is that client stations might then be able to *hear* the AP but not be able to *speak* to it. Depending on the rest of the WLAN infrastructure, increasing power on one AP may cause more co-channel interference with other cells.

6. **Users in a warehouse facility report intermittent connectivity problems with the network inventory software as they move in and out of the tall metal storage shelving. The warehouse is served by a single, centrally located AP, positioned on the ceiling. What problem do you suspect? Document your answer.**

   The metal in the shelves is interfering with the omnidirectional radio signals from the transmitter. If you need complete coverage in the warehouse area, you might need to install additional antenna stations in the areas between the shelving units.

Activity 13-3: Discussing Wireless Security

1. **What is the main difference between WPA and WPA2?**

   WPA2 supports a stronger encryption algorithm, based on the Advanced Encryption Standard (AES). AES is deployed within the Counter Mode with Cipher Block Chaining Message Authentication Code Protocol (CCMP). WPA uses the same RC4 cipher as WEP. WPA uses a mechanism called the Temporal Key Integrity Protocol (TKIP) to make it stronger than WEP, but WPA2 offers the best security available.

2. **Why might an attacker launch a DoS attack against a WAP?**

   This could be a simple DoS attack to prevent network access, but the attacker could also be attempting to use an evil twin/rogue AP to intercept network traffic.

3. **What type of enterprise authentication scheme uses server-side certificates to protect the user authentication credential?**

   Protected Extensible Authentication Protocol (PEAP). EAP-TLS requires both server-side and client-side certificates. EAP-FAST uses a Protected Access Credential (PAC), rather than a certificate.

4. **John is given a laptop for official use and is on a business trip. When he arrives at his hotel, he turns on his laptop and finds a WAP with the name of the hotel, which he connects to for sending official communications. He may become a victim of which wireless threat?**

   ○ Interference

   ○ War driving

   ○ Bluesnarfing

   ● Rogue access point

5. **Your company has a lobby area where guest access is provided so that visitors can get Internet access. The open guest WLAN is currently connected to the production network. The only protection against visitors and hackers getting into the organization's data is file and directory rights. What steps should be taken to provide guest access and better protect the organization's data?**

   The guest WLAN should be connected to a separate network segment, isolated from the production network. Typically, this would be accomplished using a virtual LAN (VLAN) and a router/firewall to inspect and filter traffic using the Internet link. You could configure a captive portal so that users must register before accessing the WLAN. You could also change to using PSK authentication, with the password obtained from the receptionists.

Activity 14-1: Discussing WAN Core Service Types

1. **What is the main advantage of circuit-switched networks?**

   They can provide a guaranteed level of bandwidth.

2. **What bandwidth are T1 and E1 links, and why are they different?**

   T1s are 1.544 Mbps and E1s are 2.048 Mbps; E-carrier uses 32 channels compared to T-carrier's 24.

3. **Which 10GbE Ethernet and SONET standards are interoperable?**

   The 10GbE WAN PHY (10GBASE-SW, -LW, and -EW) are interoperable with OC-192.

4. **What media types can be used to connect to a Metro Ethernet?**

   Either copper wire or fiber optic lines.

Activity 14-2: Discussing WAN Subscriber Service Types

1. **What is an IXP?**

   An Internet exchange point (IXP) is a data center and network access point where ISPs establish high-speed links between their networks, using transit and peering arrangements to carry traffic to and from parts of the Internet they do not physically own.

2. **What place does VDSL have in terms of access to public networks?**

   Very High Bitrate DSL (VDSL) supports high data rates over a limited distance. In this respect, it supports Fiber to the Curb (providing the final link from the fiber distribution frame to the customer premises).

3. **What is the upper limit of a dial-up modem's connection speed?**

   56 Kbps for the downlink and 33.3 Kbps for the uplink.

4. **You are connecting a SOHO network to a VDSL service using a separate VDSL modem. What cables do you require and how should they be connected?**

   The WAN/DSL port on the modem is connected to the service provider network via a 2-pair cable with RJ-11 connectors. The LAN/Ethernet port on the modem should be connected to the SOHO router via an Ethernet cable with RJ-45 connectors.

5. **What is PRI?**

   Primary rate interface (PRI) is an Integrated Services Digital Network (ISDN) service type providing T1 or E1 level bandwidth.

6. **What function does a smart jack serve?**

   A smart jack is a means of terminating a T1 serial digital leased line. The smart jack typically provides a loopback facility for the access provider to test the line.

Activity 14-3: Discussing WAN Framing Service Types

1. **How does PPP work to allow a computer with a dial-up modem to connect to the Internet?**

   The Point-to-Point Protocol (PPP) is a layer 2 protocol. IP packets are encapsulated within PPP frames to be transported to the ISP's router via the dial-up link.

2. **What distinguishes ATM from Ethernet?**

   ATM uses fixed size cells compared to Ethernet's variable size frames, and it provides mechanisms for traffic shaping and policing.

3. **What is the difference between IP and MPLS routing?**

   IP routing is "best effort," while MPLS allows for constraint-based routing, enabling traffic shaping.

4. **What type of transmission media is required for a SIP trunk?**

   A SIP trunk does not specify a media type. It can use any available link between the customer and service provider network. A fiber optic link will offer more bandwidth, but for a small site a copper wire link may well be adequate.

Activity 14-4: Discussing Wireless and IoT WAN Technologies

1. **What standard(s) are intended to support 4G mobile wireless services?**

   Long Term Evolution (LTE) and LTE Advanced (LTE-A).

2. **Assuming that sufficient bandwidth can be provided, what factor limits the usefulness of a microwave satellite Internet link?**

   The link will be subject to high latency, which will impact real-time data services.

3. **What type of network topology is used by IoT technologies such as Z-Wave and Zigbee?**

   Mesh topology.

4. **What is a principal requirement of IoT technologies, as demonstrated by the latest version of Bluetooth?**

   Low power consumption.

Activity 15-1: Discussing Remote Access VPNs

1. **What are the three main topologies for implementing a VPN?**

   Many virtual private networks (VPNs) use a client-to-site topology, where one or more hosts connect to a site (a remote access VPN). Other options include site-to-site and host-to-host topologies.

2. **How does TLS improve the security of a VPN connection compared to PPTP?**

   Transport Layer Security (TLS) uses a digital certificate on the VPN gateway to authenticate the remote host and create an encrypted tunnel before the user transmits authentication credentials.

3. **What IPSec mode would you use for data confidentiality on a private network?**

   Transport mode with Encapsulation Security Payload (ESP). Tunnel mode encrypts the IP header information, but this is unnecessary on a private network. Authentication Header only provides authentication and integrity validation, not confidentiality.

4. What difference does DMVPN make to a hub and spoke VPN topology?

It allows the spokes to establish a direct connection, rather than relaying all communications via the hub,

5. What step can you take to prevent unauthorized use of a remote access server?

Define which user accounts have dial-in rights and ensure each user protects their authentication credentials.

Activity 15-2: Discussing Remote Access Management Methods

1. What TCP/IP application protocol is associated with TCP port 23?

Telnet.

2. What are the main uses of SSH?

Typically to provide a secure terminal to a remote Linux or UNIX host (or any other host with an SSH server installed).

3. What type of attack is RDP Remote Credential Guard designed to protect against?

Pass-the-Hash (PtH) attacks. In PtH, the attacker obtains credentials from an RDP session from the RDP server and tries to re-use them. Credential Guard is designed to prevent the RDP server from storing or processing the password hash.

4. What is a virtual terminal?

Configuring a management IP address on a switch to connect to its command line interface over the network (rather than via a serial port).

5. What distinguishes TFTP from FTP?

Trivial FTP only supports GET and PUT commands—not directory browsing, file deletion, and so on.

Activity 16-1: Discussing Network Documentation and Diagrams

1. What types of baselines are useful when you are performing configuration management?

A configuration baseline records the initial setup of software or appliance. A performance baseline records the initial throughput or general performance of a network (or part of a network). These baselines allow changes in the future to be evaluated.

2. In terms of day-to-day tasks, what demonstrates that effective configuration management procedures are in place?

Job logs and standard operating procedures (SOPs) to control and document configuration and troubleshooting work.

3. What is the difference between physical and logical schematics?

A logical schematic shows the topology of the network in abstract (such as IP networks); a physical schematic shows the locations of components and their IDs.

4. **You are analyzing a network schematic and notice the icon shown here. What does it represent?**

A router.

5. **True or False? Rack units are sold in models of varying width.**

False—Width is standard (nominally 19"), while the *height* varies in units of 1.75".

6. **You are working at a telecommunications point and notice that the cables in one patch panel are all red while the ones in another are all blue. What, if anything, does this represent?**

The TIA 606 Administration standard recommends the use of red color-coding for telephone links and blue for data links to the work area (horizontal cabling).

Activity 16-2: Discussing the Purposes of Physical Security Devices

1. **Some of the businesses near Greene City Interiors have recently had break-ins where some equipment was stolen. As news of these events spread, it generated some concern within the organization that their physical security measures should be reviewed and possibly enhanced. There is currently a security guard on duty during business hours, video monitoring of the front and back doors, and employees use plastic badges with their name and photo to enter the building. Access beyond the lobby area requires swiping a badge to enter the rest of the building. What, if anything, would you recommend adding or improving for their physical security?**

While they have a good start on physical security, they should consider installing motion detection systems for after hours; if there are additional doors, to install video monitoring on those doors; to update to using smart cards or key fobs for entrance.

2. **What type of door access control would allow entry based on the possession of a cryptographic smart card?**

Proximity reader.

3. **What technology could be used to provision security cameras without having to provide a separate circuit for electrical power?**

IP cameras could be powered over data cabling using Power over Ethernet (PoE).

4. **What is a PDS, and what type of security control does it provide?**

A Protected Distribution System (PDS) is a system for hardened network cable distribution. It can work as both a preventive and a detective control. The preventive element comes from enclosing the cable in metal conduit. The detective element can be supplied by alarms that detect if the conduit has been opened or damaged.

Activity 16-3: Discussing Business Continuity and Disaster Recovery Concepts

1. **What is MTBF, and why is it associated with a bathtub curve?**

   Mean Time Between Failures (MTBF). The bathtub curve is a plot of instances of failure over time and tends towards a "bathtub" shape because failures are more likely early or late in the service life of an appliance than in the middle.

2. **A server is equipped with 4 Ethernet interfaces, and you want to aggregate them to a single interface using a non-proprietary protocol. What feature must the switch support?**

   Port bonding/Link Aggregation Control Protocol (LACP), IEEE 802.3ad/802.1ax.

3. **What technologies can be used to make network infrastructure fault tolerant?**

   Redundancy and failover need to be provided at all levels: power, cabling/adapter teaming, switching, routing, and name services/addressing. Cluster services and load balancers can be deployed to make application and database servers fault tolerant.

4. **What rack-mountable device can provide line filtering and power monitoring features?**

   A power distribution unit (PDU).

5. **What type of security control provisions resources and procedures to cope with major incidents?**

   A disaster recovery plan (DRP).

Activity 16-4: Discussing Policies and Best Practices

1. **What is the difference between a policy and a best practice?**

   Policy establishes definite rules, while best practice is fuzzier and might be demonstrated through examples or scenarios instead of explicit rules.

2. **What are the main elements of fire safety procedures?**

   Fire/smoke detection and alarms, plus safe escape routes from the building and emergency drills/procedures. Training on the safe use of portable fire extinguisher equipment may be provided to some employees.

3. **True or False? An ESD wrist strap is designed to provide a personal ground to protect a technician from electrocution when they are working on energized electrical devices.**

   False—A safety or utility ground is a pathway for electricity to flow in the event of a short so that it is less likely to electrocute someone touching a "live" bit of metal, but the technician should NEVER be part of this grounding path. An ESD ground equalizes the electrical potential between surfaces to reduce the chance of damage to components. Such wrist straps should have working resistors to prevent any dangerous amount of current from flowing through them, but they are not safety devices.

4. **How is the person who first receives notification of a potential security incident designated?**

   First responder.

5. **How does the principle of least privilege apply to privileged users?**

   Privileges can be allocated by role/domain, rather than by creating all-powerful superusers. Holders should only log on to privileged accounts to perform specific tasks. The accounts should be subject to auditing and oversight.

6. **True or False? DLP technology can assist with managing PII.**

   True—Data loss prevention (DLP) software can be configured to identify personally identifiable information (PII) strings or fields and prevent transfer of such data by unauthorized mechanisms or formats.

7. **What technology provides data security assurance during the asset disposal phase of system lifecycle?**

   Hard drive/media sanitation, such as encryption or disk overwriting.

8. **What are the main elements of a password policy?**

   Ensuring strong password selection and preventing sharing of passwords. You might also mention password aging/changing passwords regularly.

9. **What configuration request would be implemented by IT services during employee onboarding?**

   Account creation, issuance of user credentials, and allocation of permissions/roles.

10. **What type of policy governs use of a VPN?**

    Remote access policy.

12. **Do you agree with the time listed? Why or why not?**

    The password policy states that administrator passwords should be changed every month and regular system users should change their passwords every three months to remain secure. The most recent guidance from NIST deprecates automatic password expiry. This sort of policy is typical for most organizations though, so unless specific needs for different time frames have been identified or the NIST recommendations have been fully adopted, it can stay as it is.

13. **One of the users tried to create a password by entering gooddog. According to the policy, does this meet the requirements? Why or why not?**

    No. Eight characters is the minimum length for security purposes, and the phrase does not meet the complexity requirements that most network policies would enforce.

Glossary

*aas
(*Something* as a Service) An ownership model for cloud services where the *something* can refer to infrastructure, network, platform, or software. See **IaaS**, **SaaS**, and **PaaS**.

10GbE
(10 Gigabit Ethernet) An Ethernet technology that multiplies the nominal speed of Gigabit Ethernet by a factor of 10. 10GbE is not deployed in many access networks, however, as the cost of 10GbE network adapters and switches is high.

110 block
Punch-down cross-connect format offering high density (supporting up to 300 pairs). 110 wiring blocks are used for various applications. The 110 IDC format is used in most patch panels and wall jacks.

4to6
Internet transition mechanism that allows IPv4 packets to be transmitted over an IPv6 network.

66 block
An older-style distribution frame used to terminate telephone cabling and legacy data applications (i.e., pre-Cat 5).

6to4
Transmits IPv6 traffic over IPv4 networks by mapping IPv4 addresses onto a special range of IPv6 prefixes.

802 standards
A family of standards, published by the LAN/MAN Standards Committee of the Institute of Electrical and Electronics Engineers (IEEE), that define technologies working at the Physical and Data Link layers of the OSI model.

802.11 standard
A family of specifications developed by the Institute of Electrical and Electronics Engineers (IEEE) for wireless LAN technology.

802.1X
A standard for encapsulating EAP communications over a LAN or wireless LAN and that provides port-based authentication. Also known as EAP (Extensible Authentication Protocol).

A record
Used to resolve a host name to an IPv4 address.

AAA
(authentication, authorization, and accounting) A security concept where a centralized platform verifies object identification, ensures the object is assigned relevant permissions, and then logs these actions to create an audit trail.

AAAA record
Used to resolve a host name to an IPv6 address.

access control
The process of determining and assigning privileges to resources, objects, and data. Each resource has an access control list (ACL) specifying what users can do.

accounting
Tracking authorized usage of a resource or use of rights by a subject and alerting when unauthorized use is detected or attempted.

ACK
(Acknowledgement) An acknowledgement signal sent between hosts to signify receipt of the data as part of the **connection-oriented**

communications protocol to indicate that data is received in the expected condition.

ACL
(access control list) Specifies which subjects (user accounts, host IP addresses, and so on) are allowed or denied access and the privileges given over the object (read only, read/write, and so on).

Active Directory
The standards-based directory service from Microsoft that runs on Microsoft Windows servers.

ad hoc network
A type of wireless network where connected devices communicate directly with each other instead of via a centralized access point.

adaptability
The ability to accommodate new or changed services and applications with minimum disruption to the existing physical and logical topology.

address pool
The valid IP addresses within the DHCP scope that are available or in use on your network.

addressing (network)
In order to communicate on a network, each host must have an address. Different protocols use different methods of addressing. For example, IPv4 uses a 32-bit binary number, typically expressed as a 4-part decimal number (dotted decimal notation), while IPv6 uses a 128-bit binary number expressed in hexadecimal. A routable addressing scheme such as IP also provides identification for distinct networks as well as hosts.

admission control
The point at which client devices are granted or denied access based on their compliance with a health policy.

adware
Software that records information about a PC and its user. Adware is used to describe software that the user has

acknowledged can record information about their habits.

AES
(Advanced Encryption Standard) A symmetric 128-, 192-, or 256-bit block cipher based on the Rijndael algorithm developed by Belgian cryptographers Joan Daemen and Vincent Rijmen and adopted by the US government as its encryption standard to replace DES.

AH
(Authentication Header) An IPSec protocol that provides authentication for the origin of transmitted data as well as integrity and protection against replay attacks.

air gap
A type of network isolation that physically separates a network from all other networks.

algorithm
Any defined method of performing a process. In encryption, the term specifically refers to the technique used to encrypt a message.

amplification attack
A network-based attack where the attacker dramatically increases the bandwidth sent to a victim during a DDoS attack by implementing an amplification factor.

analog signal
A signal that carries information as continuous waves of electromagnetic or optical energy.

anomaly-based monitoring
A network monitoring system that uses a baseline of acceptable outcomes or event patterns to identify events that fall outside the acceptable range.

ANT+
Low-power connectivity standard working in the 2.4 GHz range closely associated with fitness monitors and sensor equipment.

antenna
Specially arranged metal wires that can send and receive radio signals. These

are used for radio-based wireless networking.

anti-virus
Software capable of detecting and removing virus infections and (in most cases) other types of malware, such as worms, Trojans, rootkits, adware, spyware, password crackers, network mappers, DoS tools, and so on.

AP
(access point) A device that provides a connection between wireless devices and can connect to wired networks.

API
(application programming interface) A library of programming utilities used, for example, to enable software developers to access functions of the TCP/IP network stack under a particular operating system.

APIPA
(Automatic Private Internet Protocol Addressing) An addressing scheme that was developed so that Windows clients that were configured to obtain an address automatically but could not contact a DHCP server could still communicate on the local subnet. The host randomly selects an address from the range 169.254.x.y. This is also called a link-local address.

appliance firewall
A standalone hardware device that performs only the function of a firewall which is embedded into the appliance's firmware.

application aware firewall
A layer 7 firewall technology that inspects packets at the Application layer of the OSI model.

application firewall
Software designed to run on a server to protect a particular application such as a web server or SQL server.

Application layer
OSI model layer providing support to applications requiring network services (file transfer, printing, email, databases, and so on).

ARP
(Address Resolution Protocol) The mechanism by which individual hardware MAC addresses are matched to an IP address on a network.

ARP inspection
(Address Resolution Protocol inspection) An optional security feature that prevents excessive ARP replies from flooding a network segment.

ARP poisoning
A network-based attack where an attacker with access to the target network redirects an IP address to the MAC address of a computer that is not the intended recipient. This can be used to perform a variety of attacks, including DoS, spoofing, and MitM.

ARP table
(Address Resolution Protocol table) A table used to maintain a correlation between each MAC address and its corresponding IP address.

AS
(Autonomous System) A self-contained network on the Internet that deploys a single protocol and has a single administration. Also called a routing domain.

asymmetric encryption
See **public key cryptography**.

ATM
(Asynchronous Transfer Mode) A cellswitching network technology designed for the high-speed transfer of voice, video, and data in LANs, WANs, and telephone networks.

attack surface
The portion of a system or application that is exposed and available to attackers.

attenuation
Degradation of a signal as it travels over media. This determines the maximum distance for a particular media type at a given bit rate.

auditing
The portion of accounting that entails security professionals examining logs of what was recorded.

AUP
(acceptable use policy) A policy that governs employees' use of company equipment and Internet services. ISPs may also apply AUPs to their customers.

authentication
A method of validating a particular entity's or individual's unique credentials.

authenticator
A PNAC switch or router that activates EAPoL and passes a supplicant's authentication data to an authenticating server, such as a RADIUS server.

authoritative name server
A name server that holds complete records for a domain.

authorization
The process of determining what rights and privileges a particular entity has.

automatic allocation
An address that is leased permanently to a client. Unlike static address assignment, the administrator does not determine which IP address will be leased.

autonegotiation
A Fast Ethernet protocol that allows devices to choose the highest supported connection parameters (10 or 100 Mbps and half- or full-duplex).

availability
The fundamental security goal of ensuring that computer systems operate continuously and that authorized persons can access data that they need.

AWG
(American Wire Gauge) The measurement standard for wire thickness. A higher AWG number represents thinner wire. Solid cable uses thicker 22-24 AWG, while the stranded cable used for patch cords is often 26 AWG.

backbone
A fast link that connects the various segments of a network.

backdoor
A mechanism for gaining access to a computer that bypasses or subverts the normal method of authentication.

backup
A system-maintenance task that enables you to store copies of critical files and folders on another medium for safekeeping.

bandwidth
The number of bits of data that can be transmitted from a source to a destination over the network in one second.

bare-metal hypervisor
A virtualization environment installed directly on the server hardware (an OS is not installed first). Also known as a Type I hypervisor.

base
A numbering system in which the number following the word *base* indicates how many different values any given digit can have and the factor by which the value of a digit increases as you move from right to left in a number.

base 10 numbering system
See **decimal numbering system**.

base 16 numbering system
See **hexadecimal numbering system**.

base 2 numbering system
See **binary values**.

baseband
Transmission that uses the complete bandwidth of the media as a single transmission path. LAN signaling normally uses this transmission method.

baseline
The point from which something varies. A configuration baseline is the original or recommended settings for a device while a performance baseline is the originally measured throughput.

bastion host
A computer typically found in a DMZ that is configured to provide a single service to reduce the possibility of compromise.

baud
The number of symbols per second transmitted in a signal (a symbol being some characteristic of the signal, such as a change in frequency or amplitude). Modern signaling methods can encode more than one bit per symbol (between 6 and 10 bits), which derives the data rate or transmission speed. However, "baud" is frequently used loosely to mean data rate.

baud rate
The number of symbols that can be transmitted per second that is measured in hertz (or MHz or GHz).

BCP
(business continuity plan) A policy that describes and ratifies the organization's overall business continuity strategy.

beacon
A special management frame broadcast by the AP to advertise the WLAN.

behavior-based detection
In IDSs and IPSs, an operation mode where the analysis engine recognizes baseline normal traffic and events, and generates an incident when an anomaly is detected.

BGP
(Border Gateway Protocol) A path vector routing protocol used by ISPs to establish routing between one another.

binary values
The numbering system used by electronic machines to store and manipulate data. Each place position consists of only two values, 0 and 1. Each position, starting from the rightmost, signifies a higher power of 2. Also called base 2 numbering system.

biometric
Authentication schemes based on individuals' physical characteristics.

bit rate
The amount of information that can be transmitted, measured in bits per second (bps), or some multiple thereof.

black hole
A means of mitigating DoS or intrusion attacks by dropping (discarding) traffic. Or, in routing, a term describing the loss of a packet without notification being sent back to the sender.

BLE
(Bluetooth Low Energy) See **Bluetooth LE**.

Bluetooth
A short-range wireless radio network transmission medium normally used to connect two personal devices, such as a mobile phone and a wireless headset.

Bluetooth LE
(Bluetooth Low Energy) A Bluetooth variant designed for use in Internet of Things (IoT) networks by battery-powered devices.

BNC
(Bayonet Neill-Concelman) Twist and lock connector for coaxial cable.

BNC coupler
(Bayonet Neill-Concelman coupler) A connector with female BNC ports at either end that allows two cables terminated with BNCs to be connected to one another.

BOOTP
(Bootstrap Protocol) TCP/IP protocol enabling a host to acquire IP configuration information from a server or download a configuration program using TFTP. BOOTP is an earlier, simpler form of DHCP and also works over UDP port 67. Unlike DHCP, the configuration settings for each host must be manually configured on the server.

border router
A router situated on the edge of a network that connects that network to one or more remote networks. Also called an edge router.

botnet
A set of hosts that has been infected by a control program called a bot that enables

attackers to exploit the hosts to mount attacks.

bottleneck
Generally, a component of a device that performs poorly when compared to other components and reduces the overall performance of a device. It can also be defined as a link or forwarding/processing node that becomes overwhelmed by the volume of traffic.

bounded media
A network medium that uses a physical conductor typically made of metal or glass. (See also **cabled transmission medium**.)

BPDU
(Bridge Protocol Data Unit) The frames package exchanged by switches to prevent switching loops.

bps
(bits per second) A unit used to describe data transfer speed - the higher the number, the higher the transmission speed.

BRI
(Basic Rate Interface) An **ISDN** class that provides two 64 Kbps (B channels) for data and one 16 Kbps (D channel) for link management control signals.

bridge
A device that joins two network segments at the Data Link layer. Each bridge port is a separate collision domain, but the segments joined to each bridge port are in a single broadcast domain.

broadband
A transmission technique in which a single medium carries multiple channels of data, usually through modulation.

broadcast
A transmission method in which data is sent from a source node to all other nodes on a network.

broadcast domain
All hosts, within the boundaries established by routers at the OSI Network layer, receive the same broadcast packets.

broadcast storm
The flooding of a network with frames caused by a **switching loop**.

brute force attack
A type of password attack where an attacker uses an application to exhaustively try every possible alphanumeric combination to crack encrypted passwords.

buffer overflow
An application attack that exploits fixed data buffer sizes in a target piece of software by sending data that is too large for the buffer.

BYOD
(bring your own device) Mobile deployment model that describes how employees can use their own personal mobile devices to get work done, if they so choose.

CA
(certificate authority) A server that can issue digital certificates and the associated public/private key pairs.

CAB
(Change Advisory Board) In change management, the team responsible for approving or denying RFCs.

cable certifier
A type of networking tool that enables you to perform tests, such as cable testing and validity testing.

cable tester
An electrical instrument that verifies if a signal is transmitted by a cable. Also called a media tester or line tester.

cabled transmission medium
A physical signal conductor is provided between two nodes. Examples include cable types such as copper or fiber optic.

cache-only servers
DNS servers that don't maintain a primary or secondary zone.

caching engine
A feature of many proxy servers that enables the servers to retain a copy of frequently requested web pages.

CAM
(content addressable memory) A special type of memory optimized for searching rather than random access that is used for MAC address tables.

CAN
(campus area network) A LAN that spreads over several buildings within the same overall area.

captive portal
A web page that a client is automatically directed to when connecting to a network, usually through public Wi-Fi.

CARP
(Common Address Redundancy Protocol) A redundancy protocol that allows a number of devices to be grouped together to use a single virtual network interface among them.

CASB
(Cloud Access Security Broker) Enterprise management software designed to mediate access to cloud services by users across all types of devices.

Cat cable standards
Twisted pair cabling is rated by the ANSI/TIA/EIA Cat (category) standards for different Ethernet applications. Cat3 is rated for 10 Mbps applications at up to 100 m, Cat5 for 100 Mbps and Cat5e and Cat6 for 1 Gbps. Cat6 and Cat6a are also rated for 10 Gbps at 55 m and 100 m, respectively.

CCMP
(Counter Mode with Cipher Block Chaining Message Authentication Code Protocol) An encryption protocol used for wireless LANs supporting the WPA2 standard that addresses the vulnerabilities of the WEP protocol.

CDMA
(Code Division Multiple Access) Method of multiplexing a communications channel using a code to key the modulation of a particular signal. CDMA is associated with Sprint and Verizon cellular phone networks.

cell switching network
A type of network, similar to a packet switching network, in which data is transmitted as fixed-length packets called cells.

CERT
(Computer Emergency Response Team) A group of experts that handles computer security incidents.

certificate
An X.509 digital certificate is issued by a certificate authority (CA) as a guarantee that a public key it has issued to an organization to encrypt messages sent to it genuinely belongs to that organization.

change management
The process of approving and executing change in order to assure maximum security, stability, and availability of IT services.

channel
Wi-Fi frequency bands are divided into smaller channels to allow multiple networks to operate at the same location without interfering with one another.

channel bonding
The practice of combining wireless channels for increased data capacity.

CI
(Configuration Item) In change management, an asset that requires specific management procedures for it to be used to deliver the service. Each CI is identified with a label and defined by its attributes and stored in a **CMDB**.

CIA triad
(confidentiality, integrity, availability) The three basic principles of security control and management: confidentiality, integrity, and availability. Also known as the information security triad or triple.

CIDR
(Classless Inter-Domain Routing) Using network prefixes to aggregate routes to multiple network blocks ("supernetting"). This replaced the old method of assigning class-based IP addresses based on the network size.

circuit switching
Form of switching that establishes a temporary dedicated path between nodes. The telephone network (PSTN) uses circuit switching.

circuit-level stateful inspection firewall
A layer 5 firewall technology that tracks the active state of a connection, and can make decisions based on the contents of network traffic as it relates to the state of the connection.

CIRT
(cyber incident response team) A group that handles events involving computer security breaches.

classful addressing
The addressing method of dividing the IP address space for IPv4 into five address classes based on the first octet of the IP address.

classless addressing
The addressing method of using an appropriately sized network prefix instead of address classes and default masks.

cleartext
Unencrypted, readable data that is not meant to be encrypted.

client
A network device or process that initiates a connection to a server.

client-server
A network or relationship in which servers provide resources to clients.

cloud computing
A method of computing that involves real-time communication over large distributed networks to provide the resources, software, data, and media needs of a user, business, or organization.

cloud storage
A type of Software as a Service where the vendor provides reliable data storage and backup.

clustering
A load balancing technique where a group of servers are configured as a unit and work together to provide network services.

CMDB
(Configuration Management Database) In change management, the database in which **configuration items** are stored, identified using a label, and defined by their attributes.

CMS
(Configuration Management System) The tools and databases that collect, store, manage, update, and present information about **CIs**.

CNAME
(Canonical Name) A DNS record used to represent an alias for a host.

coaxial cable
(coax) A type of copper cable that features a central conductor surrounded by an insulator and braided or foil shielding.

code signing
A form of digital signature that guarantees that source code and application binaries are authentic and have not been tampered with.

cold site
A predetermined alternate location where a network can be rebuilt after a disaster.

collision
In early Ethernet implementations, using a physical bus or hub, media access is shared between nodes. If two nodes attempt to transmit at the same time, a collision is detected and the nodes must backoff before attempting to retransmit. This area of shared access is also called a collision domain.

conditional forwarder
A DNS server that performs the **forwarder** function only for certain domains.

confidentiality
The fundamental security goal of keeping information and communications private and protected from unauthorized access.

configuration baseline
Settings for services and policy configuration for a server operating in a particular application role (web server, mail server, file/print server, and so on).

configuration management
The process of setting up and changing the configuration of a network and its components.

connection
The data link between network addresses or nodes.

connection-oriented protocol
A data transmission method where a connection is established before any data can be sent, and where a stream of data is delivered in the same order as it was sent.

connectionless protocol
A data transmission method that does not establish a connection between devices and where data may be delivered out of order and may be delivered over different paths.

console cable
See **rollover cable**.

console router
A device used to provide remote access to the command-line interface of multiple switch and/or router appliances.

content filter
A software application or gateway that filters client requests for various types of Internet content (web, FTP, IM, and so on).

contention
A media access method in which nodes compete or cooperate among themselves for media access time. Also called competitive media access.

control
See **security control**.

cookie
Text file used to store information about a user when they visit a website. Some sites still use cookies to support user sessions.

COOP
(continuity of operations plan) See **BCP**.

copper cable
A type of bounded media that uses one or more copper conductors surrounded by an insulated coating.

CoS
(Class of Service) Similar types of traffic are grouped together and each type or class is given separate service priorities.

CPE
(common platform enumeration) A naming standard used to identify an organization's hardware, software, and operating systems.

CRC
(Cyclical Redundancy Check) An error detection method used in Ethernet as the Frame Check Sequence (FCS). Sending and receiving hosts apply the same CRC algorithm to the contents of the frame and should expect to derive the same value.

crimper
A tool used to join a network jack to the ends of network patch cable.

cross-connect
See **distribution frame**.

crossover cable
A twisted pair cable wired as T568A on one end and as T568B on the other end.

crosstalk
A phenomenon whereby one wire causes interference in another as a result of their close proximity.

crypto-malware
A class of ransomware that attempts to encrypt data files on the victims' drives, making the user unable to access the files without paying to obtain the private encryption key.

cryptography
The science of hiding information, most commonly by encoding and decoding a secret code used to send messages.

CSIRT
(Computer Security Incident Response Team) See **CIRT**.

CSMA/CA
(Carrier Sense Multiple Access/Collision Avoidance) A contention-based media access method where nodes try to avoid data collisions by transmitting when they deem the channel to be idle.

CSMA/CD
(Carrier Sense Multiple Access/Collision Detection) A contention-based media access method where nodes send data when they deem the channel to be idle, but take steps to retransmit when collisions occur.

CSU/DSU
(Channel Service Unit/Data Service Unit) A combination of two WAN connectivity devices on a frame relay network that work together to connect a digital WAN line with a customer's LAN.

data emanation
A concern for wireless media, as the signals can be received for a considerable distance and shielding/containment is not a realistic option in most environments.

data exfiltration
The process by which an attacker takes data that is stored inside of a private network and moves it to an external network.

Data Link layer
The OSI model layer responsible for transferring data between nodes. This layer is split into two sublayers: Media Access Control (MAC) and Logical Link.

data retention
The process an organization uses to maintain the existence of and control over certain data in order to comply with business policies and/or applicable laws and regulations.

datagram
See **packet**.

dB
(decibel) The unit of measurement to express the loss of signal strength from the point of origin to the destination.

DDoS attack
(distributed denial of service attack) An attack uses multiple compromised computers (a botnet of zombies) to launch the attack.

decimal numbering system
A numbering system based on 10 digits. Each position, starting from the rightmost,

signifies a higher power of 10. Also called base 10 numbering system.

deduplication
A technique for removing duplicate copies of repeated data. In SIEM, the removal of redundant information provided by several monitored systems.

default account
Default administrative and guest accounts configured on servers and network devices that can be possible points of unauthorized access.

default gateway
An IP configuration parameter that identifies the location of a router on the local subnet that the host can use to contact other networks.

default route
A special type of static route that identifies the next hop router for an unknown destination.

defense in depth
See **layered security**.

demarcation point
The physical location where a building's wiring ends and the telephone company's wiring begins. Also referred to as a demarc.

designated port
A switch port that can forward traffic down through the network with the least cost.

desktop switch
A simple unmanaged switch, typically with 5 or 8 ports, that can be placed on a desktop.

DHCP
(Dynamic Host Configuration Protocol) A protocol used to automatically assign IP addressing information to IP network computers.

DHCP relay agent
A service that captures a BOOTP broadcast and forwards it through the router as a unicast transmission to a DHCP server on a remote subnet.

DHCP scope
In DHCP, the IP addresses that a DHCP server is configured with and can assign to clients.

DHCP server
(Dynamic Host Configuration Protocol server) A networking service that allows a client to request an appropriate IP configuration from a server.

DHCP snooping
A configuration option that enables a switch to inspect DHCP traffic to prevent MAC spoofing.

diagram
A drawing that captures the relationships between network elements and identifying the location of items on the network.

dial-up
A remote network access method that utilizes the local telephone line, or plain old telephone service (POTS), to establish a connection between two computers fitted with modems.

dictionary attack
A type of password attack that compares encrypted passwords against a predetermined list of possible password values.

differential backup
A backup type in which all selected files that have changed since the last full backup are backed up.

DiffServ
(Differentiated Services) A layer 3 identifier used to manage traffic.

dig
(Domain Information Groper) Utility to query a DNS and return information about a particular domain name.

digital certificate
An electronic document that associates credentials with a public key.

digital signal
A signal modulation and encoding method that transmits discrete values (1 and 0).

direct-attached storage
Server hosted data that is stored on its internal hard drives or on a USB or eSATA external device connected only to that server.

directory
A database that stores information about users, data, and other entities in a hierarchical format.

directory services
A network service that stores identity information about all the objects in a particular network, including users, groups, servers, client computers, and printers.

distance vector routing
A dynamic routing method used on packet-switched networks to calculate route costs and routing table entries.

distributed switching
An enterprise network will feature multiple switch appliances arranged in a fault-tolerant hierarchy and often centrally managed and automated using Software Defined Networking (SDN).

distribution frame
A device working at the Physical layer that terminates cables and enables connections with other devices.

DKIM
(DomainKeys Identified Mail) An email authentication method that decides whether you should allow received email from a given source, preventing spam and mail spoofing.

DLP
(data loss/leak prevention) A software solution that detects and prevents sensitive information in a system or network from being stolen or otherwise falling into the wrong hands.

DMVPN
(dynamic multiport VPN) A software-based mechanism that allows VPNs to be built and deleted dynamically.

DMZ
(demilitarized zone) A small section of a private network that is located behind one

firewall or between two firewalls and made available for public access.

DNAT
(Destination Network Address Translation) See **port forwarding**.

DNS
(Domain Name System) The service that maps names to IP addresses on most TCP/IP networks, including the Internet.

DNS server cache poisoning
A network-based attack where an attacker exploits the traditionally open nature of the DNS system to redirect a domain name to an IP address of the attacker's choosing.

DNSSEC
(Domain Name System Security Extensions) A security protocol that provides authentication of DNS data and upholds DNS data integrity.

document management
The process of managing information over its lifecycle (from creation to destruction).

domain
In Windows networking, a group of computers that share a common accounts database, referred to as the directory.

domain controller
Any Windows-based server that provides domain authentication services (logon services). Domain controllers (DCs) maintain a master copy of the database of network resources.

domain suffix
The top-level domain used as the last portion of a domain name. See **TLD**.

DoS attack
(denial of service attack) A network-based attack where the attacker disables systems that provide network services by consuming a network link's available bandwidth, consuming a single system's available resources, or exploiting programming flaws in an application or operating system.

dotted decimal notation
In IP addresses, each binary octet is converted to its decimal equivalent value with each octet being separated by a period (or dot).

downgrade
Reverting to a previous version of software or firmware.

DRDoS attack
(distributed reflection denial of service) See **amplification attack**.

DRP
(disaster recovery plan) A documented and resourced plan showing actions and responsibilities to be used in response to critical incidents.

DSCP
(Differentiated Services Code Point) The IP header field used to indicate a priority value for the packet.

DSL
(digital subscriber line) A technology for transferring data over voice-grade telephone lines using higher frequencies available in a copper telephone line as a communications channel.

DSLAM
(digital subscriber line access multiplexer) A concentrator at the telephone company central office that receives signals from DSL customers, then uses multiplexing protocols to move the signals on to their high-speed backbone.

DSSS
(Direct Sequence Spread Spectrum) A type of radio transmission in which a single data signal is converted into multiple digital data signals called chips that are sent across a wide band of adjacent frequencies.

DTLS
(Datagram Transport Layer Security) A communications protocol that is usually used with TCP-based protocol. DTLS refers to UDP secured with TLS. This is often used for VPNs.

dual stack
A host operating multiple protocols simultaneously on the same interface. Most hosts are capable of dual stack IPv4 and IPv6 operation, for instance.

dynamic allocation
A method of assigning IP addresses to networked devices that does not guarantee that any given client will retain the same IP address over time.

Dynamic DNS
A DNS (domain name system) server that allows clients to update their records automatically when their IP addresses change.

dynamic NAT
(dynamic Network Address Translation) The type of NAT service that builds a table of public to private address mappings to map devices to multiple public IP addresses in order to support inbound and outbound connections between the private network and the Internet.

dynamic port number
Another name for **private port number**.

dynamic routing protocol
Routing protocols that automatically create routing entries for the router to connect all devices on the network.

EAP
(Extensible Authentication Protocol) An authentication framework that allows network access devices (switches and wireless APs) to relay user credentials between a supplicant (wired or wireless host) and an authentication server.

EAP-FAST
(EAP Flexible Authentication via Secure Tunneling) An EAP method where supplicants and authenticating servers are identified using a Protected Access Credential (PAC).

EAP-TLS
(EAP Transport Layer Security) An EAP method that requires a client-side certificate for authentication using SSL/TLS.

EAPoL
(Extensible Authentication Protocol over LAN) EAP client devices such as switches use EAPoL to allow the supplicant to submit credentials for processing by the authenticating server. Any other type of network access is blocked until the supplicant is authenticated.

eavesdropping
Some transmission media are susceptible to eavesdropping (listening in to communications sent over the media). To secure transmissions, they must be encrypted.

edge router
See **border router**.

EGP
(Exterior Gateway Protocol) The protocol responsible for exchanging routing information between two neighboring gateways.

EIGRP
(Enhanced Interior Gateway Routing Protocol) An improvement over IGRP that includes features that support VLSM and classful and classless subnet masks.

embedded system
A computer system that is designed to perform a specific, dedicated function, such as a microcontroller in a medical drip or components in a control system managing a water treatment plant.

EMI
(electromagnetic interference) A disruption of electrical current that occurs when a magnetic field around one electrical circuit interferes with the signal being carried on an adjacent circuit.

encapsulation
The process of adding delivery information to the actual data in each layer of the OSI or TCP/IP model.

encryption
A security technique that converts data from plain, or cleartext form, into coded, or ciphertext form, so that only authorized parties with the necessary decryption information can decode and read the data.

endpoint security
A set of security procedures and technologies designed to restrict network access at a device level.

enterprise WAN
A wide area network that is used and controlled by a single organization.

ephemeral ports
A client application or process that is dynamically assigned a port number greater than 1024 by the operating system when there is a request for service.

escalation
In terms of privilege management, escalation (or elevation) is where a user gains additional privileges without authorization. With regard to troubleshooting and incident response, escalation is the process of involving additional senior staff to assist in incident management.

ESD
(electrostatic discharge) The phenomenon that occurs when electrons rush from one body with a static electrical charge to another with an unequal charge, following the path of least resistance.

Ethernet
A set of networking technologies and media access methods, originally specified for LANs but now widely used on MANs and WANs too.

EUI
(extended unique identifier) IEEE's preferred term for a network interface's unique identifier.

evil twin
A wireless access point that deceives users into believing that it is a legitimate network access point.

exit interview
See **offboarding**.

exploit
A specific means of using a vulnerability to gain control of a system or damage it in some way.

external DNS zones
Records that Internet clients must be able to access.

extranet
A private network that provides some access to outside parties, particularly vendors, partners, and select customers.

failover
A technique that ensures a redundant component, device, or application can quickly and efficiently take over the functionality of an asset that has failed.

fair use policy
See **AUP**.

false negative
Something that is identified by a scanner or other assessment tool as not being a vulnerability, when in fact it is.

false positive
Something that is identified by a scanner or other assessment tool as being a vulnerability, when in fact it is not.

Fast Ethernet
An Ethernet technology that can transmit data at speeds of 100 Mbps.

fat AP
(fat access point) An access point whose firmware contains enough processing logic to be able to function autonomously and handle clients without the use of a wireless controller.

fault tolerance
Protection against system failure by providing extra (redundant) capacity. Generally, fault tolerant systems identify and eliminate single points of failure.

FC
(Fibre Channel) High speed network communications protocol used to implement SANs.

FC-SW
(Fibre Channel Switched Fabric) All devices or loops of devices are connected to Fibre Channel switches, similar to Ethernet implementations.

FCoE
(Fibre Channel over Ethernet) Standard allowing for a mixed use Ethernet network with both ordinary data and storage network traffic.

FCS
(Frame Check Sequence) The value derived from performing a CRC on an Ethernet frame used to detect errors.

fiber optic cable
A network cable composed of one or more bundled glass threads (fibers or filaments) that are coated in plastic and are used to transmit data by pulses of light.

File and Print Sharing Service
A Windows-based system service, based on the Server Message Block (SMB) protocol, that allows users on the same network to access and copy files and use printers that have been configured as shared.

FIM
(file integrity monitoring) A type of software that reviews system files to ensure that they have not been tampered with.

fingerprinting
Identifying the type and version of an operating system (or server application) by analyzing its responses to network scans.

firewall
A device that protects a system or network by blocking unwanted network traffic. A firewall can be implemented as software running on a general computing host or as a dedicated network appliance.

firmware
Software instructions stored semi-permanently (embedded) on a hardware device. Modern types of firmware are stored in flash memory and can be updated more easily than legacy programmable Read Only Memory (ROM) types.

first responder
The first experienced person or team to arrive at the scene of an incident.

fixed switch
A switch that comes with a set number of ports that cannot be changed or upgraded.

flood guard
Switch port protection features that prevent an attached host from using spoofed MAC addresses and ARP traffic to try to engineer a situation where the switch starts flooding all unicast traffic. See also **MAC flooding**.

flow control
In TCP transmissions, the adjustment between nodes to let the other node know that the data stream needs to be slowed down so that the receiving node can be sure that all incoming data is received and is received undamaged.

footprinting
A process of information gathering in which the attacker attempts to learn about the configuration of the network and security systems.

forward lookup zones
Store resource records that contain information needed to resolve host names to IP addresses including **A records** and **SOA records**.

forwarder
In DNS, the server that transmits a client query to another DNS server and routes the replies it gets back to the client.

Fox and Hound
Another term for **tone generator and probe**.

FQDN
(Fully Qualified Domain Name) A name in DNS specifying a particular host within a subdomain within a top-level domain.

fragmentation
An IP process that divides packets into small pieces (fragments) for transmission over a communication medium.

frame
The basic unit of data transmitted at layer 2. Frames contain the source and target MAC (hardware) addresses and also the data and error checking regions.

Frame Relay
Packet switched WAN protocol running over T-carrier or ISDN. Frame Relay is no longer widely deployed.

FTP
(File Transfer Protocol) A communications protocol that enables the transfer of files between a user's workstation and a remote host.

full backup
A backup type in which all selected files, regardless of prior state, are backed up.

full duplex
Network link that allows simultaneously sending and receiving. Most network links are full duplex.

gain
The reliable connection range and power of a wireless signal, measured in decibels.

gateway
In physical security, a wall with a door or a fence with a gate, that allows movement from one area to another. In networking, a host that provides a translation service between different types of systems and protocols, such as a VoIP to PSTN gateway.

GBIC
(Gigabit Interface Converter) A transceiver used to convert electrical signals into optical signals and vice versa.

geofencing
The practice of creating a virtual boundary based on real-world geography.

geolocation
The identification or estimation of the physical location of an object, such as a radar source, mobile phone, or Internet-connected computing device.

Gigabit Ethernet
An Ethernet technology that can transmit data at speeds of 1,000 Mbps. Gigabit Ethernet is implemented using switches and can use copper and fiber optic cabling.

goodput
Typically used to refer to the actual useful data rate at the Application layer (less overhead from headers and lost packets).

GPO
(group policy object) On a Windows domain, a way to deploy per-user and per-computer settings such as password policy, account restrictions, firewall status, and so on.

GPS
(Global Positioning System) Means of determining a receiver's position on the Earth based on information received from GPS satellites. The receiver must have line-of-sight to the GPS satellites.

GRE
(Generic Routing Encapsulation) Tunneling protocol allowing the transmission of encapsulated frames or packets from different types of network protocol over an IP network.

GSM
(Global System for Mobile Communications) Standard for cellular radio communications and data transfer. GSM phones use a SIM card to identify the subscriber and network provider. 4G and later data standards are developed for GSM.

guaranteed delivery
See **connection-oriented protocol**.

guest OS
The operating system installed in a Type II hypervisor.

H.323
Session control protocol for VoIP and messaging networks running over TCP port 1720.

half duplex
Network link where simultaneously sending and receiving is not possible.

handshake
In networking, the process used to verify the speed, connection, and authorization between nodes attempting to make a connection.

hardening
Making a system more secure.

hash
The value that results from hashing encryption. Also known as hash value or message digest.

HCC
(horizontal cross-connect) A wiring closet where the horizontal cabling connects to a patch panel that is attached to the main facility by a backbone cable.

header
A unit of information that precedes a data object, but is considered to be part of the data packet, and contains information about the file or the transmission.

health policy
A minimum security configuration that devices must meet to obtain network access.

heat map
In a Wi-Fi site survey, a diagram showing signal strength at different locations.

hexadecimal numbering system
A numbering system where each digit is the equivalent of four binary digits. Each position, starting from the rightmost, signifies a higher power of 16. Also called base 16 numbering system.

HFC
(hybrid fiber coax) Commonly used by cable television suppliers, this type of broadband network combines coax cable and fiber optic trunk to serve the cable modem installed in the customer's premises.

HIDS
(host-based intrusion detection system) A type of IDS that monitors a computer system for unexpected behavior or drastic changes to the system's state.

high availability
The property that defines how closely systems approach the goal of providing data availability 100 percent of the time while maintaining a high level of system performance.

HIPS
(host-based intrusion prevention system) A means of preventing system files from being modified or deleted, prevents system services from being stopped, logs off unauthorized users, and filters network traffic.

HMAC
(Hash-based Message Authentication Code) A method (described in RFC-2104) used to verify both the integrity and authenticity of a message by combining cryptographic hash functions, such as MD5 or SHA-1, with a secret key.

hoax
An email-based, IM-based, or web-based attack that is intended to trick the user into performing unnecessary or undesired actions, such as deleting important system files in an attempt to remove a virus, or sending money or important information via email or online forms.

honeynet
An entire dummy network used to lure attackers.

honeypot
A security tool used to lure attackers away from the actual network components. Also called a decoy or sacrificial lamb.

hop
One link in the path from a host to a router or from router to router. Each time a packet passes through a router, its hop count (or TTL) is decreased by one.

host
In TCP/IP networking terminology, a device that can directly communicate on a network. In this sense, it is similar to a node.

host ID
The unique portion of an IP address that identifies individual network nodes and devices.

host name
The unique name given to a network node on a TCP/IP network.

host operating system
The OS installed on a computer before installing the hypervisor software and the guest OS in a Type II hypervisor.

host-based firewall
A software application running on a single host and designed to protect only that host. (See also **personal firewall**.)

host-based hypervisor
A virtualization environment that runs within an operating system—you install the OS first and then install the hypervisor. This is also known as a Type II hypervisor.

HOSTS file
A file, now primarily used for troubleshooting, that maps network addresses to names.

hot site
A fully configured alternate network that can be online quickly after a disaster.

hotfix
A patch that is often issued on an emergency basis to address a specific security flaw.

hotspot
A public, open WLAN.

HSPA
(High Speed Packet Access) A family of technologies based on the 3GPP Release 5 specification, offering high data-rate services in mobile networks.

HTTP
(HyperText Transfer Protocol) The protocol used to provide web content to browsers. HTTP uses port 80. HTTPS(ecure) provides for encrypted transfers, using SSL/TLS and port 443.

HTTPS
(HTTP Secure) A subset of HTTP that allows for secure communication, using SSL/TLS, between the client and server.

hub
A networking device working at the Physical layer that is used to connect the drops in a physical star topology network into a logical bus topology. Also called a multiport repeater.

hub and spoke
A star network. Also used to describe networks composed of WANs with remote sites.

HVAC
(heating, ventilation, air conditioning) Building control systems maintain an optimum heating, cooling, and humidity level working environment for different parts of the building.

hybrid topology
A network that uses a combination of physical or logical topologies. In practice most networks use hybrid topologies. For example, modern types of Ethernet are physically wired as stars but logically operate as buses.

hypervisor
In virtualization technology, the component that manages the virtual machine environment and facilitates interaction with the computer hardware and network.

Hz
(hertz) A measure of the number of cycles per second in an analog signal. One cycle per second equals one hertz.

IaaS
(Infrastructure as a Service) A computing method that uses the cloud to provide any or all infrastructure needs.

IAB
(Internet Architecture Board) A committee of ISOC that provides long-range technical direction for Internet development, ensuring the Internet continues to grow and evolve as a platform for global communication and innovation.

IAM
(identity and access management) A security process that provides identification, authentication, and authorization mechanisms for users, computers, and other entities to work with organizational assets like networks, operating systems, and applications.

IANA
(Internet Assigned Numbers Authority) An international organization established in 1993 to govern the use of IP addresses.

ICANN
(Internet Corporation for Assigned Names and Numbers) The organization that is

currently responsible for leasing IP addresses worldwide.

ICMP
(Internet Control Message Protocol) IP-level protocol for reporting errors and status information supporting the function of troubleshooting utilities such as ping.

IDC
(Insulation Displacement Connector) Block used to terminate twisted pair cabling at a wall plate or patch panel. The main formats are 110 and Krone.

identification
The process by which a user account (and its credentials) is issued to the correct person. Sometimes referred to as enrollment.

IDF
(Intermediate Distribution Frame) A cable rack that interconnects the telecommunications wiring between an MDF and any end-user devices.

IDS
(intrusion detection system) A software and/or hardware system that scans, audits, and monitors the security infrastructure for signs of attacks in progress.

IEEE
(Institute of Electrical and Electronics Engineers) Formed as a professional body to oversee the development and registration of electronic standards. Examples of IEEE standards include the 802 protocols that describe the function and architecture of different network technologies.

IETF
(Internet Engineering Task Force) An international community of network designers, operators, vendors, and researchers concerned with the evolution of the Internet architecture and the smooth operation of the Internet.

ifconfig command
A UNIX/Linux-based utility used to gather information about the IP configuration of the network adapter or to configure the network adapter. It has been replaced with

the ip command in most Linux distributions.

IGMP
(Internet Group Management Protocol) A protocol in the TCP/IP suite that supports multicasting in a routed environment.

IGP
(Interior Gateway Protocol) The protocol responsible for exchanging routing information between gateways within an AS.

IGRP
(Interior Gateway Routing Protocol) A distance-vector routing protocol developed by Cisco as an improvement over RIP and RIP v2.

IIS
(Internet Information Services) The web server product shipped with Windows.

IMAP
(Internet Message Access Protocol) TCP/IP application protocol providing a means for a client to access email messages stored in a mailbox on a remote server. IMAP4 utilizes TCP port number 143.

implicit deny
A basic principle of security stating that unless something has explicitly been granted access, it should be denied access.

incident management
Practices and procedures that govern how an organization will respond to an incident in progress.

incident response policy
Procedures and guidelines covering appropriate priorities, actions, and responsibilities in the event of security incidents.

incremental backup
A backup type in which all selected files that have changed since the last full or incremental backup (whichever was most recent) are backed up.

InfiniBand
A high-speed switching fabric used in SANs and data center networks.

infrastructure topology
A wireless network configuration that uses one or more WAPs to connect wireless workstations to the base station, or cable backbone.

insider threat
Attacks launched by the organization's own trusted users.

integrity
The fundamental security goal of keeping organizational information accurate, free of errors, and without unauthorized modifications.

interface
A means of connection that enables network nodes to communicate.

internal DNS zones
Domains used on the private network only.

Internet
A worldwide network of networks based on the TCP/IP protocol.

intranet
A private network that is only accessible by the organization's own personnel.

inventory
A list of things, usually stored in a database. Inventories are usually compiled for assets.

IoT
(Internet of Things) A group of objects (electronic or not) that are connected to the wider Internet by using embedded electronic components.

IP
(Internet Protocol) A connectionless Network-layer protocol that is responsible for sending data packets across a network.

IP address
(Internet Protocol address) A unique identifier assigned to every node connected to a TCP/IP network. An IPv4 address is 32 bits and must be used with a subnet mask or network prefix. An IPv6 address is 128 bits and used with a network prefix.

ip command
A Linux-based utility used to gather information about the IP configuration of the network adapter or to configure the network adapter. Replaces the older ifconfig command.

IP spoofing
An attack in which an attacker sends IP packets from a false (or spoofed) source address to communicate with targets.

IPAM
(Internet Protocol address management) Software consolidating management of multiple DHCP and DNS services to provide oversight into IP address allocation across an enterprise network.

ipconfig command
A Windows-based utility used to gather information about the IP configuration of a workstation.

IPS
(intrusion prevention system) An inline security device that monitors suspicious network and/or system traffic and reacts in real time to block it.

IPSec
(Internet Protocol Security) A set of open, non-proprietary standards that are used to secure data through authentication and encryption as the data travels across the network or the Internet.

IPv4 mapped addresses
An address used by IPv4/IPv6 routers to forward traffic between IPv4 and IPv6 networks.

IPv6
An addressing scheme that uses a 128-bit binary address space.

IR
(infrared) Infrared Data Association (IrDA) was a wireless networking standard supporting speeds up to about 4 Mbps. Infrared (IR) sensors are used in mobile devices and with IR blasters to control appliances.

ISAKMP
(Internet Security Association and Key Management Protocol) A framework for

creating a Security Association (SA) which establishes trust between two hosts and agree upon secure protocols and cipher suites to exchange data. Commonly referred to as part of the Internet Key Exchange (IKE) protocol used in IPSec.

ISATAP
(Intra-Site Automatic Tunnel Addressing Protocol) A protocol used by a dual-stack router to rewrite an IPv6 packet as an IPv4 packet.

iSCSI
(Internet Small Computer System Interface) An IP tunneling protocol that enables the transfer of SCSI data over an IP-based network to create a SAN.

ISDN
(Integrated Services Digital Network) A digital phone/fax/data service used to provide Internet connectivity. See also the two classes of ISDN: **BRI** and **PRI**.

ISO
(International Organization for Standardization) Develops many standards and frameworks governing the use of computers, networks, and telecommunications, including ones for information security (27000 series).

ISOC
(Internet Society) An American nonprofit organization founded in 1992 to provide leadership in Internet-related standards, education, access, and policy.

ISP
(Internet Service Provider) An organization that provides a connection to the Internet and other web- and email-related services.

iterative query
A name server responds to a query with whatever information it has, passing the address of an authoritative name server to the requester.

ITIL
An IT best practice framework, emphasizing the alignment of IT Service Management (ITSM) with business needs. ITIL was first developed in 1989 by the UK government and originally stood for IT Infrastructure Library. Now marketed by AXELOS, ITIL is no longer an acronym and ITIL 4 was released in 2019.

ITU
(International Telecommunication Union) An international organization within the United Nations that defines global technical standards for telecommunications.

Java
Programming language used to create web server applications (J2EE) and client-side applications (running in the Java VM).

jitter
The variability of latency over time across a network.

job rotation
The policy of preventing any one individual performing the same role or tasks for too long. Personnel should rotate between job roles to prevent abuses of power, reduce boredom, and improve professional skills.

jumbo frame
An Ethernet frame with a payload larger than 1500 bytes (up to about 9000 bytes).

Kerberos
An authentication service that is based on a time-sensitive ticket-granting system.

key
A specific piece of information that is used in conjunction with an algorithm to perform encryption and decryption.

key management
In cryptography, the process of administering cryptographic keys, often performed by a CA, and including the management of usage, storage, expiration, renewal, revocation, recovery, and escrow. In physical security. a scheme for identifying who has copies of a physical key or key card.

L2TP
(Layer 2 Tunneling Protocol) A VPN protocol for tunneling PPP sessions across a variety of network protocols such as IP, Frame Relay, or ATM.

LACP
(Link Aggregation Control Protocol [IEEE 802.3ad/802.1ax]) IEEE protocol governing the use of bonded Ethernet ports. Also referred to as NIC teaming.

LAN
(local area network) A type of network covering various sizes but generally considered to be restricted to a single geographic location and owned/managed by a single organization.

latency
The time it takes for a signal to reach the recipient. A video application can support a latency of about 80 ms, while typical latency on the Internet can reach 1000 ms at peak times.

Layer 7 firewall
See **NGFW**.

layered security
Configuring security controls on hosts (endpoints) as well as providing network (perimeter) security, physical security, and administrative controls. Also known as defense in depth.

LC
(Lucent Connector) Small form factor version of the SC push-pull fiber optic connector; available in simplex and duplex versions.

LDAP
(Lightweight Directory Access Protocol) A network protocol used to access network directory databases, which store information about authorized users and their privileges, as well as other organizational information.

LDAP injection
An application attack that targets web-based applications by fabricating LDAP statements that are typically created by user input.

LDAPS
(Lightweight Directory Access Protocol Secure) A method of implementing LDAP using SSL/TLS encryption.

least privilege
A basic principle of security stating that something should be allocated the minimum necessary rights, privileges, or information to perform its role.

LED status indicator
(light emitting diode status indicator) Colored lights on a device that provide information about whether or not the device is connected, working normally, blocked, or the port is disabled.

legacy
A system where the vendor no longer provides support or fixes for problems.

link
Communication pathways between network nodes.

link state routing
A dynamic routing method that floods routing information to all routers within a network to build and maintain a more complex network route database.

LLC sublayer
(Logical Link Control sublayer) A division of the Data Link layer described by the IEEE. It is responsible for establishing and maintaining a link between communicating devices for the transmission of frames.

load balancer
A type of switch or router that distributes client requests between different resources, such as communications links or similarly configured servers. This provides fault tolerance and improves throughput.

local address
Any interface address that resides on the same network as a given node.

local exchange
Switches that link between local access subscribers and provide transports to trunk exchanges.

local loop
Cabling from the customer premises to the local exchange.

logic bomb
A malicious program or script that is set to run under particular circumstances or in response to a defined event.

logical bus
A network topology in which all nodes receive a data transmission at the same time, regardless of the physical wiring layout of the network.

logical topology
A topology that describes the data-flow patterns in a network.

logs
OS and applications software can be configured to record data about activity on a computer. Logs can record information about events automatically.

looking glass site
A web server that enables external users to view routing and network behavior as it originates from a remote network.

loop
A situation where a packet is continually forwarded around a network until its TTL expires.

loopback interface
A virtual network interface that network applications can communicate with when executing on the local device.

LTE
(Long Term Evolution) A packet data communications specification providing an upgrade path for both GSM and CDMA2000 cellular networks. LTE Advanced is designed to provide 4G standard network access.

MAC address
(Media Access Control address) A unique hardware address hard-coded into a network adapter. This provides local addressing on Ethernet and Wi-Fi networks. A MAC address is 48 bits long with the first half representing the manufacturer's organizationally unique identifier (OUI).

MAC address table
(Media Access Control address table) On a switch, the table that keeps track of the MAC addresses associated with each port. As the switch uses a type of memory called Content Addressable Memory (CAM), this is sometimes called the CAM table.

MAC filtering
(Media Access Control filtering) Applying an access control list to a switch or access point so that only clients with approved MAC addresses can connect to it.

MAC flooding
(Media Access Control flooding) A variation of an ARP poisoning attack where a switch's cache table is inundated with frames from random source MAC addresses.

MAC reservation
A type of static address assignment where a MAC address is mapped to a specific IP address within the DHCP server's address pool. Also referred to as IP reservation.

MAC spoofing
(Media Access Control spoofing) An attack in which an attacker falsifies the factory-assigned MAC address of a device's network interface.

MAC sublayer
(Media Access Control sublayer) A division of the Data Link layer described by the IEEE. It is responsible for defining how multiple network interfaces share a common transmission medium.

MACs
(moves, adds, changes) A record of any requested moves, adds, or changes to computers, devices, users, or related policies.

mailbox
Part of a message store designed to receive emails for a particular recipient. A mailbox may be associated with more than one email address by creating aliases for the recipient.

MAN
(metropolitan area network) A network that covers an area equivalent to a city or a municipality.

man-in-the-middle attack
See **MITM attack**.

managed switch
A switch that enables you to monitor and configure its operation. Also called an intelligent switch.

management URL
An IP address or FQDN used to access the management interface of a network appliance. Ideally, the management URL should use HTTPS to ensure a secure connection and prevent snooping of any administrative credentials used to gain access to the device.

mandatory vacations
A requirement that employees are forced to take their vacation time, during which someone else fulfills their duties.

MDA/MD5
(Message Digest Algorithm v5) The Message Digest Algorithm was designed in 1990 by Ronald Rivest, one of the founders of modern cryptography. The most widely used version is MD5, released in 1991, which uses a 128-bit hash value. It is used in IPSec policies for data authentication.

MDF
(Main Distribution Frame) A cable rack that interconnects external communication cables and the cables that comprise the internal network.

MDM
(mobile device management) Software suites designed to manage use of smartphones and tablets within an enterprise.

measured service
A cloud model where the customer pays for the CPU, memory, disk, and network bandwidth resources they are actually consuming rather than paying a monthly fee for a particular service level.

media converter
A network device that enables networks running on different bounded media to interconnect and exchange signals

media sanitization
The process of decommissioning storage media, including hard drives, flash drives/ SSDs, tape media, CD and DVD ROMs, and so on.

mesh topology
A topology often used in WANs where each device has (in theory) a point-to-point connection with every other device (fully connected); in practice, only the more important devices are directly interconnected (partial mesh).

message digest
See **hash**.

Metro Ethernet
A metropolitan area network (MAN) using Ethernet standards and switching fabric.

MIB
(Management Information Base) A database that holds statistics relating to the activity of the SNMP-compatible network devices, such as the number of frames per second handled by a switch.

microsegmentation
The means by which an Ethernet switch establishes per-port collision domains, allowing full duplex communication and eliminating the effect of contention across all of the switch ports.

MIMO
(Multiple Input Multiple Output) Wireless technology used in 802.11n/ac and 4G standards. MIMO is the use of multiple reception and transmission antennas to boost bandwidth. See also **MU-MIMO**.

Miredo
Client encapsulates the IPv6 packets into IPv4 on Linux-based and Mac OS systems. The IPv4 encapsulation is removed at the corporate network end.

MITM attack
(man-in-the-middle attack) A form of eavesdropping where the attacker makes an independent connection between two victims and steals information to use fraudulently.

MLD protocol
(Multicast Listener Discovery protocol) An IPv6 protocol that allows nodes to join a multicast group and discover whether members of a group are present on a local subnet.

MMF
(Multimode Fiber) Category of fiber optic cable. Compared to SMF, MMF is cheaper (using LED optics rather than lasers) but supports shorter distances (up to about 500m).

mobile device
Portable phones and smartphones can be used to interface with workstations using technologies such as Bluetooth or USB.

modem
A device that enables digital data to be sent over an analog medium, such as a telephone line.

modular switch
A switch that uses plug-in cards to configure the switch with different numbers and types of ports.

MPLS
(Multiprotocol Label Switching) Developed by Cisco from ATM as a means of providing traffic engineering (congestion control), Class of Service, and Quality of Service within a packet switched, rather than circuit switched, network.

MPOE
(minimum point of entry) The most convent location for telecommunications cabling to enter a building.

MS-CHAP
(Microsoft Challenge Handshake Authentication Protocol) A protocol that strengthens the password authentication provided by **Protected Extensible Authentication Protocol (PEAP)**.

MSDS
(Material Safety Data Sheet) Information sheet accompanying hazardous products or substances explaining the proper procedures for handling and disposal.

MTBF
(Mean Time Between Failures) The rating on a device or component that predicts the expected time between failures.

MTD
(Maximum Tolerable Downtime) The longest period of time a business can be inoperable without causing irrevocable business failure.

mtr command
(my traceroute) Utility combining the ping and traceroute commands.

MTRJ
(Mechanical Transfer Registered Jack) Small form factor duplex fiber optic connector with a snap-in design; used for multimode networks.

MTTF
(Mean Time to Failure) The average time a device or component is expected to be in operation.

MTTR
(Mean Time to Repair/Replace/Recover) The average time taken for a device or component to be repaired, replaced, or otherwise recover from a failure.

MTU
(maximum transmission unit) The maximum size in bytes of a packet's payload. For example, the MTU of most types of Ethernet frame is 1500. If the payload cannot be encapsulated within a single packet of the transporting layer, it must be fragmented.

MU-MIMO
(Multi-user MIMO) An access point that can use separate streams to connect multiple MU-MIMO-capable stations at full speed simultaneously, providing the stations are not on the same directional path.

multicast
A packet sent to a selection of hosts (in IP, those belonging to a multicast group). IPv4 multicast uses special routers and IP/MAC address ranges. In IPv6, multicast support is mandatory and link-local multicast addresses replace functions handled by broadcasts in IPv4.

multicast address
Identifies multiple network interfaces and always starts with ff. Functions that required broadcast addresses in IPv4 can be performed more efficiently in IPv6 by using multicast addresses.

multifactor authentication
An authentication scheme that combines the requirements of something you know, something you have, and something you are.

multilayer switch
A switch that can route based on the contents of packets at layers 3 and up. A layer 3 switch is used to route more effectively in a VLAN environment.

multimeter
An electrical meter capable of measuring voltage, resistance, and current. Voltage readings can be used to determine whether, for example, a power supply unit is functioning correctly. Resistance readings can be used to determine whether a fuse or network cable is functioning correctly.

multiport repeater
Another name for a **hub**.

multipurpose proxy
A proxy that is configured to filter and service several protocol types, as opposed to an application-specific proxy, which services only one application.

mutual authentication
A security mechanism that requires that each party in a communication verifies the identity of every other party in the communication.

MX
(Mail Exchanger) A DNS record used to identify an email server for the domain.

NAC
(network access control) A means of ensuring endpoint security—ensuring that all devices connecting to the network conform to a health policy (patch level, anti-virus/firewall configuration, and so on).

NACK
(Negative Acknowledgement) See **NAK**.

NAK
(Negative Acknowledgement) In a connection-oriented protocol, a signal sent to the sender to indicate that the data was not received or was corrupted. Sometimes abbreviated as NACK.

name resolution
The process for resolving a host name or FQDN to an IP address using either the HOSTS file or DNS.

NAPT
(Network Address Port Translation) Similar to NAT, NAPT (or PAT or NAT overloading) maps private host IP addresses onto a single public IP address.

NAS
(network attached storage) A storage device with an embedded OS that supports typical network file access protocols.

NAT
(Network Address Translation) A simple form of Internet security that conceals internal addressing schemes from the public Internet by translating between a single public address on the external side of a router and private, non-routable addresses internally.

NAT overloading
See **NAPT**.

native VLAN
(native virtual local area network) A VLAN into which any untagged traffic is put when receiving frames over a trunk port.

ND
(Neighbor Discovery protocol) The IPv6 protocol that replaces the IPv4 ARP protocol.

NDA
(non-disclosure agreement) This legal document between two parties (individuals and/or organizations) specifies restrictions on sharing any confidential or proprietary information with outside parties.

NDR
(non-delivery report) Message sent to the sender after the SMTP server has retried sending at regular intervals and each time timing out.

nearline storage
Technology such as tape loaders or "slow" hard disk media that can operate in low-power states.

neighbors
Nodes on the same network.

Nessus
One of the best-known commercial vulnerability scanners, produced by Tenable Network Security.

NetBIOS
A session management protocol used to provide name registration and resolution services on legacy Microsoft networks. WINS provides NetBIOS name resolution.

netmask
An IPv4 address contains both a network ID and host ID. A netmask is applied to the IP address to distinguish the network ID; where there is a 1 in the mask, the corresponding bit in the IP address is part of the network ID.

netstat
Utility to show network information on a machine running TCP/IP, notably active connections and the routing table.

network
Two or more computer systems linked together by some form of transmission medium that enables them to share information.

network adapter
The physical connection between the host and the transmission media, it can address other cards and can recognize data that is destined for it, using a unique address known as the **Media Access Control (MAC) address**.

network ID
The portion of an IP address that identifies a network within an internetwork or a subnetwork (subnet) within a network.

Network layer
OSI model layer responsible for moving data across disparate networks.

network mapping
Software that can scan a network and identify hosts, addresses, protocols, network interconnections, and so on.

network monitoring
Auditing software that collects status and configuration information from network devices. Many products are based on the Simple Network Management Protocol (SNMP).

network prefix
The portion of an IP address that identifies the IP network.

network segmentation
A network segment can be established at the Physical layer, where all nodes connect to the same shared media (collision domain), or logical segments can be established by isolating traffic within broadcast domains.

NFC
(Near Field Communications) A standard for peer-to-peer (2-way) radio communications over very short (around 4") distances, facilitating contactless payment and similar technologies. NFC is based on **RFID**.

NGFW
(next generation firewall) A firewall capable of parsing Application layer protocol headers and data (such as HTTP or SMTP) so that sophisticated, content-sensitive ACLs can be developed.

NIC
(network interface card) See **network adapter**.

NIDS
(network intrusion detection system) A system that uses passive hardware sensors to monitor traffic on a specific segment of the network.

Nmap
Versatile port scanner used for topology, host, service, and OS discovery and enumeration.

node
Any device that can connect to the network through one or more network interfaces.

noise
In electronics, random changes and disturbances in an electrical signal, such as EMI or RFI.

non-authoritative answer
Result from a DNS server that derives from a cached record rather than directly from the zone records.

non-designated port
A port that would create a switching loop and is therefore blocked from sending data.

non-guaranteed delivery
See **connectionless protocol**.

non-persistence
The property by which a computing environment is discarded once it has finished its assigned task.

non-repudiation
The security goal of ensuring that the party that sent a transmission or created data remains associated with that data and cannot deny sending or creating that data.

non-transparent proxy server
A proxy server in which the client must be configured with the proxy server address and port number to use it.

NOS firewall
(Network Operating System) A software-based firewall running on a network server OS, such as Windows or Linux, so that the server can function as a gateway or proxy for a network segment.

NS record
(Name Server record) A DNS record that identifies an authoritative DNS name server for the zone.

nslookup
Software tool for querying DNS server records.

NTLM
(NT LAN Manager) A challenge-response authentication protocol created by Microsoft for use in its products.

NTP
(Network Time Protocol) TCP/IP application protocol allowing machines to synchronize to the same time clock that runs over UDP port 123.

octet
1 byte, which is 8 bits, and can be represented in decimal as the values 0—255.

OCx
(Optical Carrier) Alternative designation for SONET bandwidth service levels.

OFDM
(Orthogonal Frequency Division Multiplexing) A data-encoding method used on multiple carrier frequencies.

offboarding
The process of ensuring that all HR and other requirements are covered when an employee leaves an organization.

offline storage
Requires physical interaction to access the stored data.

omnidirectional antenna
A type of antenna that radiates the signal beam out in all directions and has lower gain but a wider coverage area than a directional antenna.

on-demand
A cloud service in which the customer can initiate service requests where the cloud provider responds to the customer immediately.

onboarding
The process of bringing in a new employee, contractor, or supplier.

OOB management
(out of band) Accessing the administrative interface of a network appliance using a separate network from the usual data network. This could use a separate VLAN or a different kind of link, such as a dial-up modem.

open relay
A type of mail server that is configured so that anyone can use the server to send mail.

OSI Model
(Open Systems Interconnection model) A functional reference for network communication that defines a series of seven layers, each with specific inputs and outputs.

OSPF
(Open Shortest Path First) A link-state routing protocol used on IP networks.

OTDR
(optical time domain reflectometer) A variation of TDR that transmits light-based signals of different wavelengths over fiber optic cabling to determine cabling issues.

OTP
(one-time password) A password that is generated for use in one specific session and becomes invalid after the session ends.

OUI
(Organizationally Unique Identifier) The first three bytes of a MAC address that uniquely identify a network device manufacturer.

P2P
(peer-to-peer) File sharing networks where data is distributed around the clients that use the network. Apart from consuming bandwidth and disk space, P2P sites are associated with hosting malware and illegal material.

PaaS
(Platform as a Service) A computing method that uses the cloud to provide any platform-type services.

packet
A unit of data transfer between devices that communicate on a network.

packet analyzer
Software that decodes a network traffic capture (obtained via a packet sniffer) and displays the captured packets for analysis, allowing inspection of the packet headers and payload unless the communications are encrypted.

packet drop
When a switch or router does not forward a packet due to congestion or because the packet does not match the requirements of an ACL.

packet filtering
A Layer 3 firewall technology that compares packet headers against ACLs to determine which network traffic to accept.

packet loss
The number of packets that are lost or damaged during transmission due to transmission errors, congestion, or security policies.

packet sniffer
Software that records data from frames as they pass over network media, using methods such as a mirror port or tap device.

packet switching
A method used to make more efficient use of the available bandwidth by splitting data into small packets and routing them via any available path.

PAN
(personal area network) A network that connects two to three devices with cables and is most often seen in small or home offices.

password attack
Any attack where the attacker tries to gain unauthorized access to and use of passwords.

password cracker
Software used to determine a password, often through brute force or dictionary searches.

password policy
A policy document that promotes strong passwords by specifying a minimum password length, requiring complex passwords, requiring periodic password changes, and placing limits on reuse of passwords.

PAT
(Port Address Translation) A subset of dynamic NAT functionality that maps either one or multiple unregistered addresses to a single registered address using multiple ports. Also called overloading.

patch
A small unit of supplemental code meant to address either a security problem or a functionality flaw in a software package or operating system.

patch management
Identifying, testing, and deploying OS and application updates. Patches are often classified as critical, security-critical, recommended, and optional.

patch panel
A type of wiring cross-connect with IDCs to terminate fixed cabling on one side and modular jacks to make cross-connections to other equipment on the other. Patch panels simplify Moves, Adds, and Changes (MACs) in network administration.

pay-per-use
See **measured service**.

payload
The portion of a data packet that contains the actual message to be transferred, without the headers attached for transport and without any metadata.

PBX
(private branch exchange) A device used to route incoming calls to direct dial numbers and provide facilities such as voice mail, Automatic Call Distribution (ACD), and Interactive Voice Response (IVR).

PDU
(protocol data unit) An umbrella term that refers to the data packets, frames, packets, segments, and datagrams that carry information across a network.

PDU
(power distribution unit) A device designed to provide power to devices that require power, and may or may not support remote monitoring and access.

PEAP
(Protected Extensible Authentication Protocol) Similar to EAP-TLS, PEAP is an open standard developed by a coalition made up of Cisco Systems, Microsoft, and RSA Security.

peer
A self-sufficient device that acts as both a server and a client.

penetration testing
White hat hacking to try to discover and exploit any weaknesses in network security. Also referred to as pen testing.

performance monitor
A software tool that monitors the state of services or daemons, processes, and resources on a device.

permissions
Security settings that control access to objects including file system items and network resources.

persistence
In load balancing, the configuration option that enables a client to maintain a connection with a load-balanced server over the duration of the session. Also referred to as sticky sessions.

personal firewall
A firewall implemented as applications software running on the host, and can provide sophisticated filtering of network traffic as well as block processes at the application level. (See also **host-based firewall**.)

pharming
An attack in which a request for a website, typically an e-commerce site, is redirected to a similar-looking, but fake, website.

phishing
A type of email-based social engineering attack, in which the attacker sends email from a supposedly reputable source, such as a bank, to try to elicit private information from the victim.

physical bus
A physical topology in which network nodes share access to the same network medium.

Physical layer

Lowest layer of the OSI model providing for the transmission and receipt of data bits from node to node. This includes the network medium and mechanical and electrical specifications for using the media.

physical medium

See **transmission medium**.

physical ring

A network topology in which all network nodes are connected in a circle.

physical security

Controlling access to specific physical areas or assets through measures such as physical barriers, physical tokens, or biometric access controls.

physical topology

A topology that describes how nodes are connected to the network media.

PII

(personally identifiable information) Data that can be used to identify or contact an individual or in the case of identity theft, to impersonate them.

PKI

(public key infrastructure) A system that is composed of a CA, certificates, software, services, and other cryptographic components, for the purpose of enabling authenticity and validation of data and/or entities.

plaintext

Unencrypted data that is meant to be encrypted before it is transmitted, or the result of decryption of encrypted data.

plenum

The space above false ceilings in an office used by HVAC systems.

PNAC

(Port-based Network Access Control) A switch (or router) that performs some sort of authentication of the attached device before activating the port.

PoE

(Power over Ethernet) A standard that specifies a method for supplying electrical power over Ethernet connections. Devices can draw about 13 W (or 25 W for PoE+).

point-to-point connection

A topology that provides a one-to-one connection between two nodes.

policy violation

Any act that bypasses or goes against an organizational security policy.

PON

(passive optical network) A point-to-multipoint optical network, most widely deployed in Fiber to the X (FTTx) broadband solutions.

POP

(Post Office Protocol) TCP port 110 protocol that enables a client to access email messages stored in a mailbox on a remote server. The server usually deletes messages once the client has downloaded them.

port

A network port is the value assigned in a Transport layer header to identify a communication stream. Server ports often use well-known port numbers, while client ports are assigned dynamically. *Port* can also refer to a hardware interface on a NIC or switch.

port aggregation

Using multiple network adapters for a single link for fault tolerance and load balancing. For Ethernet, this type of adapter teaming is defined in 802.3ad. 802.11n/ac Wi-Fi channels can also be bonded to improve bandwidth.

port forwarding

A process in which a router takes requests from the Internet for a particular application (such as HTTP) and sends them to a designated host on the LAN.

port location diagram

A diagram that identifies how wall ports located in work areas are connected back to ports in a distribution frame or patch panel and then from the patch panel ports to the switch ports.

port mirroring
Copying ingress and/or egress communications from one or more switch ports to another port. This is used to monitor communications passing over the switch.

port scanner
Software that enumerates the status of TCP and UDP ports on a target system. Port scanning can be blocked by some firewalls and IDS.

port scanning
A process that enumerates the TCP or UDP application ports that are open on a host.

port security
Preventing a device attached to a switch port from communicating on the network unless it matches a given MAC address or other protection profile.

PortFast
A configuration on a switch port that designates it as an access port (used by end systems only) and excludes it from Spanning Tree Topology change notifications.

post-admission control
A type of admission control that polls devices already on the network to ensure that they still meet a health policy.

posture assessment
The process for verifying compliance with a health policy by using host health checks.

POTS
(plain old telephone service) The standard telephone network that uses voice-grade cabling.

power level controls
Enterprise-class wireless access points and adapters support configurable power level controls. In some circumstances, increasing power can increase range and overcome local interference.

power management
The practice of ensuring sufficient electrical power to electronic and other devices.

PowerShell
A Windows-based command interpreter designed as an administrative management and configuration environment, to create automated scripts and run cmdlets.

PPP
(Point-to-Point Protocol) Dial-up protocol working at layer 2 (Data Link) used to connect devices remotely to networks.

PPTP
(Point-to-Point Tunneling Protocol) Protocol developed by Cisco and Microsoft to support VPNs over PPP and TCP/IP. PPTP uses TCP port 1723. Encryption can be provided by Microsoft Point-to-Point Encryption.

preadmission control
A type of admission control that requires a device meet a health policy before logging in to a network.

Presentation layer
OSI model layer that transforms data between the formats used by the network and applications. Examples include character set transformation, compression, and encryption.

PRI
(Primary Rate Interface) An **ISDN** class that provides either T1 or E1 capacity levels (23B or 30B) channels, depending on location in the world and one 64 Kbps D channel.

primary zone
A DNS name server in which the zone can be edited.

privacy filter
A security control that allows only the computer user to see the screen contents, thus preventing shoulder surfing.

private IP address
An address used for nodes that require IP connectivity within an enterprise network, but do not require direct connections to the global Internet.

private key
In asymmetric encryption, the private key is known only to the holder and is linked

to, but not derivable from, a public key distributed to those with which the holder wants to communicate securely.

private port number
Port numbers in the 49,152 through 65,535 range that are available for use by any program to communicate with any other program communicating through TCP or UDP.

privilege management
The use of authentication and authorization mechanisms to provide an administrator with centralized or decentralized control of user and group role-based privilege management.

privileged user account
One who is given rights to administer a resource that can range from managing a data set to handling company-wide service administration.

proprietary information
Information created by an organization, typically about the products or services that it makes or provides. Also known as intellectual property.

protocol
Rules and formats enabling systems to exchange data. In general terms, a protocol defines header fields to describe each packet, a maximum length for the payload, and methods of processing information from the headers.

protocol analyzer
A type of diagnostic software that can examine and display data packets that are being transmitted over a network. Also called a network analyzer.

provisioning
The process of deploying an application to the target environment, such as enterprise desktops, mobile devices, or cloud infrastructure.

proximity card
A smart card with contactless capability that can simply be touched to a card reader.

proxy
A device that acts on behalf of one end of a network connection when communicating with the other end of the connection.

proxy server
A server that mediates the communications between a client and another server. It can filter and often modify communications, as well as provide caching services to improve performance.

pruning
Removing transmissions related to designated VLANs from a trunk to preserve bandwidth.

PSE
(power sourcing equipment) Devices that provide power over an Ethernet cable to devices connected to the Ethernet cable.

PSK
(pre-shared key) A secret that was shared between two parties via a secure channel prior to its use in encrypted communications.

PSTN
(public switched telephone network) An international telephone system that carries analog voice data.

PtH attack
(pass the hash) A network-based attack where the attacker steals hashed user credentials and uses them as-is to try to authenticate to the same network the hashed credentials originated on.

PTR record
(Pointer) A DNS record that creates an IP address to host name mapping that corresponds to the host (A) record stored in the forward lookup zone.

PUA
(privileged user agreement) Rules of Behavior that govern the responsibilities of the privileged users and the specific actions that they are expected to perform, such as only using privileges to perform authorized job functions, protecting the confidentiality and integrity of accounts, maintaining compliance of legal and

regulatory data processing issues, and respecting the privacy of network users.

public IP address
An IP address that is routable across the Internet.

public key
The component of asymmetric encryption that can be accessed by anyone.

public key cryptography
A two-way encryption algorithm where encryption and decryption are performed by a pair of linked but different keys. Also referred to as asymmetric encryption.

punch down tool
A tool used to connect cable wires permanently to a patch panel or wall port.

QoS
(Quality of Service) Systems that differentiate data passing over the network that can reserve bandwidth for particular applications. A system that cannot guarantee a level of available bandwidth is often described as Class of Service (CoS).

quarantine
The process of isolating a file, computer system, or computer network to prevent the spread of a virus or another cybersecurity incident.

RA
(router advertisement) Messages periodically sent by a router on an IPv6 network and used by clients to determine the network prefix for the local network.

rack system
A standardized frame or enclosure for mounting multiple electronic equipment and devices.

rack-mounted switch
Large switches designed to fit the standard-size racks that are used to hold networking equipment.

RADIUS
(Remote Authentication Dial-in User Service) A standard protocol used to manage remote and wireless authentication infrastructures.

RAID
(redundant array of independent/inexpensive disks) A set of vendor-independent specifications that support redundancy and fault tolerance for configurations on multiple-device storage systems.

ransomware
A type of malware that tries to extort money from the victim; for instance, by appearing to lock the victim's computer or by encrypting their files.

rapid elasticity
The cloud can scale up or down quickly to meet peak demand.

RARP
(Reverse Address Resolution Protocol) An autoconfiguration mechanism that enables a host to obtain an IP address from a server configured with a list of MAC:IP address mappings.

RAS
(Remote Access Service) A server configured to process remote connections.

RDP
(Remote Desktop Protocol) Microsoft's protocol for operating remote connections to a Windows machine (Terminal Services), allowing specified users to log onto the Windows computer over the network and work remotely. The protocol sends screen data from the remote host to the client and transfers mouse and keyboard input from the client to the remote host. It uses TCP port 3389.

real-time services
Services that require response times measured in milliseconds because delayed responses will result in poor call or video quality.

recursive query
If a server in a name query is not authoritative, it takes on the task of referring to other name servers until an authoritative server is located and used to resolve the name.

redundancy
See **fault tolerance**.

remediation
The result of a device not meeting a security profile or health policy, including gaining access to a guest or quarantine network.

remnant removal
See **media sanitization**.

repeater
A layer 1 device that takes a signal and repeats it to the devices that are connected to it. Repeaters can be used to maintain signal integrity and amplitude to overcome distance limitations imposed by a particular media type.

resilience
A network's quality of service (QoS), or a control system's ability to compartmentalize its various components to prevent a compromise from spreading to other components.

resource pooling
The hardware making up the cloud provider's data center is not dedicated or reserved for a single customer account.

resource records
The records that allow the DNS server to resolve queries for names and services hosted in the domain into IP addresses.

reverse lookup zones
Resolve IP addresses to host names using **PTR records**.

reverse proxy server
A type of proxy server that protects servers from direct contact with client requests.

RF
(radio frequency) Radio waves propagate at different frequencies and wavelengths. Wi-Fi network products work at 2.4 GHz or 5 GHz.

RFC
(Request for Comments) A document drafted by the Internet Engineering Task Force (IETF) that describes the specifications for a particular technology or that documents informational data related to networking.

RFC
(Request for Change) In change management, the formal document submitted to the **CAB** that has the details of the proposed alteration.

RFID
(radio frequency identification) A means of encoding information into passive tags, which can be easily attached to devices, structures, clothing, or almost anything else.

RG
(Radio Grade) A standard that is used to categorize coaxial cables.

ring topology
All of the computers are connected in a circle. The ring comprises a series of point-to-point links between each device. Signals pass from device to device in a single direction with the signal regenerated at each device.

RIP
(Routing Information Protocol) A routing protocol that configures routers to periodically broadcast their entire routing tables. RIP routers broadcast their tables, regardless of whether or not any changes have occurred on the network.

risk
The likelihood and impact (or consequence) of a threat actor exercising a vulnerability.

risk assessment
The process of assessing threats and vulnerabilities to an organization's assets and processes.

RJ
(registered jack) Connector used for twisted pair cabling. 4-pair network cabling uses the larger RJ-45 connector. Modem/telephone 2-pair cabling uses the RJ-11 connector.

rogue AP
See **rogue device**.

rogue device
An unauthorized device or service, such as a wireless access point DHCP server, or DNS server, on a corporate or private

network that allows unauthorized individuals to connect to the network.

rollback
See **downgrade**.

rollover cable
Rollover cable is used to connect the serial port on a host or modem to the console port on a network appliance.

root bridge
The bridge at the top of a spanning tree hierarchy.

root certificate
A self-signed certificate that identifies the root CA.

root port
A port that forwards data up to the root bridge.

route command
Command utility to configure and manage the routing table on a Windows or Linux host.

route convergence
The period of time between a network change and when the routers update to reach a steady state once again.

router
A network device that links dissimilar networks and can support multiple alternate paths between location-based parameters such as speed, traffic loads, and cost.

router firewall
A hardware device that has the primary function of a router, but also has firewall functionality embedded into the router firmware.

routing
The process of selecting the best route for moving a packet from its source to its destination on a network.

routing loop
A routing process in which two routers discover different routes to the same location that include each other but never reach the endpoint.

routing protocols
Rules that govern how routers communicate and forward traffic between networks.

routing table
A database created manually or by a route discovery protocol that contains network addresses as perceived by a specific router. A router uses its route table to forward packets to another network or router.

RS
(router solicitation) A request sent by a host on a network to a local router requesting the router to send router advertisement messages.

RTCP
(RTP Control Protocol) Used with each RTP stream to monitor the quality of the connection and to provide reports to the endpoints.

RTP
(Real-Time Transport Protocol) Opens a data stream for video and voice applications over UDP. The data is packetized and tagged with control information (sequence numbering and time-stamping).

rule-based management
An administration technique that relies on the principle of least privilege and implicit deny to restrict access to resources.

SaaS
(Software as a Service) A computing method that uses the cloud to provide application services to users.

SAN
(storage area network) A network dedicated to data storage, typically consisting of storage devices and servers connected to switches via host bus adapters.

satellite
A transmission medium in which orbital satellites relay signals between terrestrial receivers or other orbital satellites.

SC
(Subscriber Connector) A push/pull connector used with fiber optic cabling.

scalability
The property by which a computing environment is able to gracefully fulfill its ever-increasing resource needs.

schema
A set of rules in a directory service for how objects are created and what their characteristics can be.

schematic
A simplified representation of a system.

scope
A region of a network.

scope id
Another term for **zone index**.

screened cable
A type of twisted pair cable that has one thin outer foil wrapped around all the pairs in the cable. Referred to as screened twisted pair (ScTP), foiled/unshielded twisted pair (F/UTP), or foiled twisted pair (FTP).

screened host
A dual-homed proxy/gateway server used to provide Internet access to other network nodes, while protecting them from external attack.

SDN
(software defined networking) A software application for defining policy decision on the control plane.

secondary zone
A DNS name server which contains a read-only copy of the zone.

security control
A technology or procedure put in place to mitigate vulnerabilities and risk and to ensure the confidentiality, integrity, and availability (CIA) of information.

security policy
A document or series of documents that are backed by senior management and that detail requirements for protecting technology and information assets from threats and misuse.

segment
In TCP transmissions, the breaking up of the data stream into smaller increments.

segmentation
See **network segmentation**.

self-signed certificate
A type of digital certificate that is owned by the entity that signs it.

separation of duties
A concept that states that duties and responsibilities should be divided among individuals to prevent ethical conflicts or abuse of powers.

serial cable
A type of bounded network media that transfers information between two devices using serial transmission.

service discovery
The practice of using network scans to discover open TCP and UDP ports, plus information about the servers operating them.

session affinity
A scheduling approach used by load balancers to route traffic to devices that have already established connections with the client in question.

session hijacking
A type of spoofing attack where the attacker disconnects a host then replaces it with his or her own machine, spoofing the original host's IP address or session cookie.

Session layer
OSI model layer that provides services for applications that need to exchange multiple messages (dialog control).

SFP
(Small Form Factor Pluggable) A transceiver used to convert electrical signals to optical signals.

SFTP
(Secure File Transfer Protocol) A secure version of the File Transfer Protocol that

uses a Secure Shell (SSH) tunnel as an encryption method to transfer, access, and manage files.

SHA
(Secure Hash Algorithm) A cryptographic hashing algorithm created to address possible weaknesses in MDA. The current version is SHA-2.

shielding
A method of counteracting signal leakage from network media (and thus eavesdropping); it can be applied to a variety of items, from a twisted-pair cable up to an entire room or building.

shunning
Configuring an intrusion prevention system to set a temporary firewall rule to block the suspect IP address.

SIEM
(Security Information and Event Management) A solution that provides real-time or near-realtime analysis of security alerts generated by network hardware and applications.

signal strength
The amount of power used by the radio in an access point or station.

signature-based detection
The analysis engine is loaded with a database of attack patterns or signatures and if traffic or host activity matches one of the patterns, an incident is generated.

SIM
(subscriber identity module) A small chip card that identifies the user and phone number of a mobile device via an International Mobile Subscriber Identity (IMSI).

SIP
(Session Initiation Protocol) A protocol used to establish, disestablish, and manage VoIP and conferencing communications sessions. It handles user discovery (locating a user on the network), availability advertising (whether a user is prepared to receive calls), negotiating session parameters (such as use of audio/video), and session management and termination.

site survey
Information about a location for the purposes of building an ideal infrastructure; it often contains optimum locations for wireless antenna and access point placement to provide the required coverage for clients and identifying sources of interference.

SLA
(service level agreement) Operating procedures and standards for a service contract.

SLAAC
(stateless address autoconfiguration) An IPv6 process in which clients determine their own address based on the advertised prefix.

slash notation
In IP addresses, the value after the slash, which represents the number of bits available for the **network prefix**.

SLE
(single loss expectancy) The amount that would be lost in a single occurrence of a particular risk factor.

sliding window
A method used in TCP connections in which a single acknowledgement can be used to indicate multiple packets were successfully received.

SLIP
(Serial Line IP) Prior to the emergence of PPP, this protocol provided dial-up TCP/IP support.

smart card
A device similar to a credit card that can store authentication information, such as a user's private key, on an embedded microchip.

smart jack
The termination point for a telecoms access provider's cabling. Also referred to as the Network Interface Unit (NIU).

smartphone
A mobile device that provides both phone and SMS text messaging functionality and general purpose computing functionality,

such as web browsing and email plus running software apps.

SMB
(Server Message Block) A protocol that works on the Application layer and is used to share files, serial ports, printers, and communications devices—including mail slots and named pipes—between devices.

SME
(small and medium sized enterprise) A network supporting tens of users.

SMF
(Single Mode Fiber) A category of fiber optic cable. SMF is more expensive than MMF (using high quality cable and optics) and supports much longer distances (up to about 70 km).

SMS
(Short Message Service) A system for sending text messages between cell phones.

SMTP
(Simple Mail Transfer Protocol) The protocol used to send mail between hosts on the Internet. Messages are sent over TCP port 25.

Smurf attack
An attack in which the adversary spoofs the victim's IP address and pings the broadcast address of a third-party network with each host directing its echo responses to the victim server.

SNAT
(source Network Address Translation) See **port forwarding**.

sniffing
See **eavesdropping**.

SNMP
(Simple Network Management Protocol) A protocol for monitoring and managing network devices.

SNMP agent
(Simple Network Management Protocol agent) A process (software or firmware) running on a switch, router, server, or other SNMP-compatible network device.

SNMP monitor
(Simple Network Management Protocol monitor) Management software that provides a location from which network activity can be overseen. The monitor polls agents at regular intervals for information from their MIBs and displays the information for review.

SOA
(Start of Authority) A DNS record that specifies authoritative information about a DNS zone.

social engineering
An activity where the goal is to use deception and trickery to convince unsuspecting users to provide sensitive data or to violate security guidelines.

socket
An identifier for an application process on a TCP/IP network.

soft access point
A device configured to allow wireless clients to connect and share its Internet access. Also referred to as personal hotspot.

SOHO network
(small office home office) A small network that provides connectivity and resource sharing for a small office or home office.

SONET
(Synchronous Optical Network) A standard for synchronous data transmission on optical media.

source NAT
An address translation type where source addresses and ports in a private IP address range are replaced with public addresses.

spam
Junk messages sent over email (or instant messaging, which is called spim).

SPAN
(Switched Port Analyzer) The CISCO implementation of **port mirroring**.

spear phishing
A phishing campaign that uses a high degree of customization and

personalization to target a specific individual or company.

spectrum analyzer
A device that can detect the source of interference on a wireless network.

SPF
(Sender Policy Framework) A DNS record used to list the IP addresses or names of servers permitted to send email from a particular domain and is used to combat the sending of spam.

SPoF
(single point of failure) A component or system that would cause a complete interruption of a service if it failed.

spoofing
An attack technique where the attacker disguises their identity.

SRV record
(Service record) A DNS record used to identify a record that is providing a network service or protocol.

SSH
(Secure Shell) A remote administration and file-copy program that supports VPNs by using port forwarding, and that runs on TCP port 22.

SSID
(Service Set Identifier) A character string that identifies a particular wireless LAN (WLAN).

SSL
(Secure Sockets Layer) Security protocol that uses certificates for authentication and encryption to protect web communication.

SSO
(single sign-on) An authentication technology that enables a user to authenticate once and receive authorizations for multiple services.

SSTP
(Secure Socket Tunneling Protocol) A protocol that uses the HTTP over SSL protocol and encapsulates an IP packet with a PPP header and then with an SSTP header.

ST connector
(Straight Tip connector) A Bayonet-style twist-and-lock connector for fiber optic cabling.

stackable switch
Switches that can be connected together and operate as a group, and managed as a single unit.

star topology
A network design in which each node is connected to a central point, typically a switch or a router. The central point mediates communications between the attached nodes.

state table
Information about sessions between hosts that is gathered by a stateful firewall.

stateless protocol
A protocol where the server is not required to preserve information about the client during a session.

static address assignment
The practice of using IP addresses outside a DHCP server's address pool or MAC reservations to ensure that certain systems retain the same IP address indefinitely.

static routing
A type of routing used by a network administrator to manually specify the entries in the routing table.

station
A node on a wireless network.

storage virtualization
A software layer is inserted between client operating systems and applications and the physical storage medium.

STP
(Spanning Tree Protocol) A switching protocol that prevents network loops by dynamically disabling links as needed.

STP
(shielded twisted pair) A type of twisted pair cable that is less susceptible to interference and crosstalk because each pair is surrounded by a braided shield.

Current offerings are both shielded and screened (S/FTP).

straight-through cable
A network cable that connects unlike devices. Also called a patch cable.

stress testing
A software testing method that evaluates how software performs under extreme load.

STS
(synchronous transport signals) A logical standard that defines the framing and synchronization of data transmission.

subnet mask
The dotted decimal representation of a network prefix. See also **netmask**.

subnetting
The process of logically dividing a network into smaller subnetworks with each subnet having a unique address.

supernetting
See **CIDR**.

supplicant
A device requesting access via an AAA or EAP mechanism.

switch
A networking device that receives incoming data, reviews the destination MAC address against an internal address table, and sends the data out through the port that contains the destination MAC address.

switching loop
A problem that occurs when two Layer 2 switches are connected over redundant paths with either two switches being connected using two different links or a ring of switches connected to each other. This causes flooded frames to circulate the network perpetually.

symmetric encryption
A two-way encryption scheme in which encryption and decryption are both performed by the same key. Also known as shared-key encryption.

SYN flood
A DoS attack where the attacker sends numerous SYN requests to a target server, hoping to consume enough resources to prevent the transfer of legitimate traffic.

SYSLOG
Used in UNIX and Linux, log files that allow for centralized collection of events from multiple sources.

T-carrier
A digital and packet switched system that makes communication more scalable than analog, circuit-switched systems.

T568A
A legacy twisted pair standard that was used in commercial buildings and cabling systems that support data networks, voice, and video. It further defines cable performance and technical requirements.

T568B
A twisted pair standard that defines the standards for preferred cable types that provide the minimum acceptable performance levels for home-based networks.

TACACS+
(Terminal Access Controller Access Control System Plus) An alternative to RADIUS developed by Cisco. The version in current use is TACACS+; TACACS and XTACACS are legacy protocols.

tagged port
A switch port that is expected to forward frames with a VLAN ID header (IEEE 802.1Q). Tagged ports usually form trunk links between switches.

tail drop
Typical traffic policing devices will simply fail to deliver packets once the configured traffic threshold has been reached.

tap
A device used to eavesdrop on communications at the Physical layer. An Ethernet tap can be inserted between a switch and a node, while a passive tap can intercept emanations from unshielded cable.

TCP
(Transmission Control Protocol) Protocol in the TCP/IP suite operating at the Transport layer to provide connection-oriented, guaranteed delivery of packets. Hosts establish a session to exchange data and confirm delivery of packets using acknowledgements. This overhead means the system is relatively slow.

TCP/IP
(Transmission Control Protocol/Internet Protocol) The network protocol suite used by most operating systems and the Internet. It is widely adopted, industry standard, vendor independent, and open.

tcpdump
A command-line packet sniffing utility.

TDM
(Time Division Multiplexing) A multiplexing method in which the communication channel is divided into discrete time slots that are assigned to each node on a network.

TDMA
(Time Division Multiple Access) Method of multiplexing a communications channel using time slots. TDMA is associated with early GSM cellular phone networks.

TDR
(time domain reflectometer) A measuring tool that transmits an electrical pulse on a cable and measures the way the signal reflects back on the TDR to determine network issues.

Telnet
A TCP/IP application protocol supporting remote command-line administration of a host (terminal emulation).

Teredo
Client encapsulates the IPv6 packets into IPv4 on Windows-based systems. The IPv4 encapsulation is removed at the corporate network end.

TFTP
(Trivial File Transfer Protocol) A simplified form of FTP supporting only file copying.

thin AP
(thin access point) An access point that requires a wireless controller in order to function.

third-party DNS
Another organization is responsible for hosting your DNS records.

threat
The potential for an entity to exercise a vulnerability (that is, to breach security).

three-way handshake
A method of establishing a TCP connection between nodes through the exchange of SYN and ACK packets prior to sending data.

threshold
When monitoring network performance, the value that signals that an object or component is functioning outside acceptable performance limits.

throughput
The amount of data that the network can transfer in typical conditions. This can be measured in various ways with different software applications. See also **goodput**.

TKIP
(Temporal Key Integrity Protocol) A mechanism used in the first version of WPA to improve the security of wireless encryption mechanisms, compared to the flawed WEP standard.

TLD
(top-level domain). The last portion of a domain name, such as .com, .gov, .net, or .org. Two-letter country specific codes are also used such as .us for United States of America or .jp for Japan.

TLS
(Transport Layer Security) A security protocol that uses certificates and public key cryptography for mutual authentication and data encryption over a TCP/IP connection.

token
A physical or virtual item that contains authentication data, commonly used in multifactor authentication.

tone generator and probe
A network connectivity tool that is used to trace a cable from one end to the other. This may be necessary when the cables are bundled and have not been labeled properly.

top listener
A network host that receives an above-average amount of network data.

top talker
A network host that generates an above-average amount of network traffic by sending data.

topology
A network specification that determines the network's overall layout, signaling, and dataflow patterns.

traceroute
A Linux/UNIX IP diagnostic utility used to trace the route taken by a packet as it hops to the destination host on a remote network.

tracert
A Windows IP diagnostic utility used to trace the route taken by a packet as it hops to the destination host on a remote network.

traffic analysis
Monitoring statistics related to communications flows.

traffic filtering
The basic function of a firewall, comparing network traffic to established rules, and preventing access to messages that do not conform to the rules.

traffic shaping
A QoS mechanism that introduces some amount of delay in traffic that exceeds an administratively defined rate. Also called bandwidth shaping.

transceiver
A device that has a transmitter and a receiver integrated into it to send and receive data.

transfer rate
A measure of how fast data can be transferred. Transfer rate is also described variously as data rate, bit rate, connection speed, transmission speed, or (sometimes inaccurately) bandwidth or baud.

transmission medium
The bounded or unbounded conduit through which signals flow from one network node to another.

transparent proxy server
A proxy server that must be implemented on a switch or router or other inline network appliance.

Transport layer
OSI model layer responsible for ensuring reliable data delivery. In TCP/IP, this service is provided by the TCP protocol.

troubleshooting
A methodical approach to identifying a problem, establishing a theory, testing the theory, establishing a plan, verifying the issue was resolved, and documenting the findings, actions, and outcomes.

trunk
A communication link between switches and routers designed to carry signals that provide network access between two points.

trunk offices
In the telephone network, provide switching and interconnections between local exchanges within a metropolitan area or nationally and to international gateway services.

TTL
(Time to Live) A value for the ping command that determines how many hops an IP packet can travel before being discarded.

tunneling
The practice of encapsulating data from one protocol for transfer over another network such as the Internet.

tuples
In a firewall rule, a related set of parameters that describe the rule and the traffic it is designed to allow or block.

twisted pair cable
A type of cable in which two insulated copper wires are twisted around each other and bundled together; often combined with other pairs (usually four in data networking).

TXT record
(Text) A DNS record used to store any free-form text that may be needed to support other network services, often used with **SPF** and **DKIM**.

Type I hypervisor
See **bare-metal hypervisor**.

Type II hypervisor
See **host-based hypervisor**.

UDP
(User Datagram Protocol) A protocol in the TCP/IP suite operating at the Transport layer to provide connectionless, non-guaranteed communication with no sequencing or flow control. Faster than TCP, but does not provide reliability.

ULA
(unique local addressing) On an IPv6 network, an addressing scheme that assigns addresses that are only routable within a site or a collection of sites.

unbounded media
A network medium that does not use a physical connection between devices and can transmit electromagnetic signals through the air using radio waves, microwaves, or infrared radiation. (See also **wireless transmission medium**.)

unicast
Data transfer from one source address to one destination address.

unicast address
The destination address for a packet addressed to a single host. If the host is not on the local subnet, the packet must be sent via one or more routers.

unidirectional antenna
A type of antenna that concentrates the signal beam in a single direction. Also called a directional antenna.

unmanaged switch
A switch that does not need configuration.

unpatched
A system that has not been updated with OS and application patches.

untagged port
In a VLAN, any port that connects a switch to a host, as opposed to an intermediate system, such as another switch or router. The switch will strip any VLAN ID header before forwarding to the host or add an appropriate header when receiving frames from the host.

updates
Software revisions that are made freely available by the software manufacturer to fix problems in a particular software version, including any security vulnerabilities.

UPS
(uninterruptible power supply) An alternative AC power supply that a computer can use in the event of power failure.

URL
(Uniform Resource Locator) An application-level addressing scheme for TCP/IP, allowing for human-readable resource addressing.

URL hijacking
An attack in which an attacker registers a domain name with a common misspelling of an existing domain, so that a user who misspells a URL they enter into a browser is taken to the attacker's website.

user account
The logon ID required for any user who wants to access a Windows computer.

UTM
(Unified Threat Management) All-in-one security appliances and technologies that combine the functions of a firewall, malware scanner, intrusion detection, vulnerability scanner, Data Loss Prevention, content filtering, and so on.

VDI
(virtual desktop infrastructure) A virtualization implementation that

separates the personal computing environment from a user's physical computer.

version control
The practice of ensuring that the assets that make up a project are closely managed when it comes time to make changes.

video surveillance
A physical security control that uses cameras and recording devices to visually monitor the activity in a certain area.

VIP address
(virtual Internet Protocol address) An IP address that is assigned to multiple hosts or routers, rather than to a single interface. VIPs are often used for loopback or management interfaces on switches and routers and to configure load-balanced services.

virtual circuit packet switching
A switching technique over a WAN that makes use of technology to combine advantages of circuit and packet switching and establishes a specific path for all packets to follow.

virtual NIC
In a virtual machine, a software-based representation of a network adapter that functions and is configurable in the same way as a physical network adapter.

virtual switch
In a hypervisor environment, a software-based switch that functions as a Layer 2 physical switch.

virtualization
The process of creating a simulation of a computing environment, where the virtualized system can simulate the hardware, operating system, and applications of a typical computer without being a separate physical computer.

virus
Code designed to infect computer files (or disks) when it is activated.

VLAN
(virtual local area network) A logically separate network created by using switching technology. Even though hosts on two VLANs may be physically connected to the same cabling, local traffic is isolated to each VLAN so they must use a router to communicate.

VLAN hopping
(virtual local area network hopping) An attack designed to send traffic to a VLAN other than the one the host system is in.

VLAN pooling
A mechanism that enables WAPs to choose from among available VLANs when they are accepting incoming client connection requests.

VLSM
(variable length subnet masking) A scheme to maximize IP address space capacity through use of different size subnet masks within the same IP network.

VM
(virtual machine) A guest operating system installed on a host computer using virtualization software (a hypervisor), such as Microsoft Hyper-V or VMware.

VNC
(Virtual Network Computing) Remote access tool and protocol. VNC is the basis of macOS screen sharing.

VoIP
(Voice over Internet Protocol) A protocol that enables carrying voice traffic over data networks.

VoIP gateway
A means of connecting VoIP systems with the telephone network and with analog modems and handsets.

VoIP/SIP endpoint
End user devices (or user agents) which can be physical IP handsets or software running on a computer or smartphone.

VPN
(virtual private network) A secure tunnel created between two endpoints connected via an unsecure network (typically the Internet).

VPN concentrator
A single device that incorporates advanced encryption and authentication methods in order to handle a large number of VPN tunnels.

VSAT
(very small aperture terminal) A small telecommunications Earth station that consists of a small antenna that transmits and receives signals from satellites.

VT
(virtualization technology) Software allowing a single host computer to run multiple guest operating systems or virtual machines (VMs).

VTC
(video teleconferencing) A service that enables multiple users from multiple locations to participate in a live session over the Internet for meetings, training sessions, or other group activities.

VTP
(VLAN Trunking Protocol) A protocol for distributing VLAN information across multiple switches.

vulnerability
A weakness that could be triggered accidentally or exploited intentionally to cause a security breach.

vulnerability assessment
Scanning a network and analyzing its configuration, user behavior, policies, and documentation to identify any weaknesses and/or poor practice.

vulnerability scanner
Software configured with a list of known weaknesses and exploits and can scan for their presence in a host OS or particular application.

WAF
(web application firewall) A firewall designed specifically to protect software running on web servers and their backend databases from code injection and DoS attacks.

WAN
(wide area network) A network that spans multiple geographic locations.

war driving
The practice of using a Wi-Fi sniffer to detect WLANs and then either making use of them (if they are open/unsecured) or trying to break into them (using WEP and WPA cracking tools).

warm site
A location that is dormant or performs noncritical functions under normal conditions, but which can be rapidly converted to a key operations site if needed.

weak password
A fruitful exploit for attackers, whether used to access web services, networks, or the administration interface of network devices such as switches and access points; it is a password that is not sufficiently complex enough to escape discovery by guessing or other means.

web conferencing
See **VTC**.

web security gateway
An appliance or proxy server that mediates client connections with the Internet by filtering spam and malware and enforcing access restrictions on types of sites visited, time spent, and bandwidth consumed.

WEP
(Wired Equivalent Privacy) A protocol that provides 64-bit, 128-bit, and 256-bit encryption using the Rivest Cipher 4 (RC4) algorithm for wireless communication that uses the 802.11a and 802.11b protocols.

whaling
A form of phishing that targets individuals who are known to be upper-level executives or other high-profile employees, with the goal of obtaining sensitive information.

Wi-Fi
IEEE standard for wireless networking based on spread spectrum radio transmission in the 2.4 GHz and 5 GHz bands. The standard has five main iterations (a, b, g, n, and ac), describing different modulation techniques, supported distances, and data rates.

WIDS

(wireless intrusion detection system) A type of NIDS that scans the radio frequency spectrum for possible threats to the wireless network, primarily rogue access points.

WIPS

(wireless intrusion prevention system) An active, inline security device that monitors suspicious network and/or system traffic on a wireless network and reacts in real time to block it.

wire crimper

A tool used to join cables to connectors.

wireless

A transmission medium that uses the electromagnetic broadcast spectrum. Most wireless transport takes place using spread-spectrum radio, but microwave transmitters and infrared are also used.

wireless cell

A component of a network of transmitters (or base stations), arranged in a cell-like structure, that provides cell phone coverage.

wireless controller

A device that provides wireless LAN management for multiple APs.

wireless transmission medium

Uses free space between nodes (no signal conductor), such as microwave radio.

Wireshark

A widely used packet analyzer.

wiring schematic

A combination of a floor plan and a physical network topology. Similar to physical network diagrams, you can see the nodes on the network and how they are physically connected. Also called a wiring diagram.

WLAN

(wireless local area network) A network using wireless radio communications based on some variant of the 802.11 standard series.

worm

A type of virus that spreads through memory and network connections rather than infecting files.

WPA

(Wi-Fi Protected Access) An improved encryption scheme for protecting Wi-Fi communications, designed to replace WEP.

WPA2

(Wi-Fi Protected Access version 2) A security protocol that provides WPA with AES cipher-based CCMP encryption for even greater security and to replace TKIP.

WRE

(wireless range extender) A device that is designed to repeat the signal from an access point to extend the range of a WLAN.

WWAN

(wireless wide area network) A large wireless network, such as a cellular data network or line-of-sight microwave transmission.

xBASE-y

The IEEE 802.3 (Ethernet) standard uses the following notation to indicate Ethernet type: xBASE-y, where x indicates the data rate (in Mbps), BASE denotes that baseband transmission is used, and y either describes the maximum media distance or the cable type. More recent standards define gigabit (1000BASE-y) and 10 Gigabit (10GBASE-y) speeds.

XML

(eXtensible Markup Language) A widely adopted markup language used in many documents, websites, and web applications.

Z-Wave

Low-power wireless communications protocol used primarily for home automation. Z-Wave uses radio frequencies in the high 800 to low 900 MHz range and a mesh topology.

zero-day exploit

An attack that exploits a vulnerability in software that is unknown to the software vendor and users.

zone
In networking, an area of a network where the security configuration is the same for all hosts within it. In physical security, an area separated by barriers that control entry and exit points.

zone index
The portion of a link-local address that defines the source of the address and makes it unique to a particular link.

zone transfer
In DNS, the replication process from the zone master (usually a primary zone) to a secondary zone.

Index

ISBN-13 978-1-6427-4185-8
ISBN-10 1-6427-4185-X